Color Plate 3
An example of the Ishihara test for color deficiency

Reprint authorized by Graham-Field Surgical Co., Inc.,
415 Second Avenue, New Hyde Park, N.Y. 11040.
Sole Distributors.

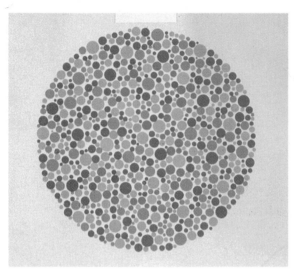

Color Plate 4
Atmospheric perspective

Photo by Ron Pretzer.

Sensation
and
Perception

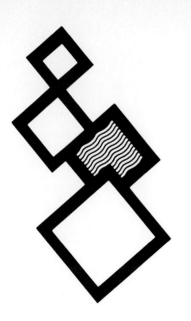

Sensation
and
Perception

SECOND EDITION

Margaret W. Matlin

State University of New York
at Geneseo

Allyn and Bacon, Inc.

Boston ◊ London ◊ Sydney ◊ Toronto

for Arnie

Series Editor: John-Paul Lenney
Senior Editorial Assistant: Leslie B. Galton
Production Administrator: Annette Joseph
Production Coordinator: Susan Freese
Editorial-Production Service: CRACOM Corporation
Cover Administrator: Linda K. Dickinson
Cover Designer: Lynda Fishbourne

Library of Congress Cataloging-in-Publication Data

Matlin, Margaret W.
  Sensation and perception.

  Rev. ed. of: Perception. c1983.
  Includes bibliographies and index.
  1. Perception. 2. Senses and sensation. I. Matlin,
Margaret W. Perception. II. Title.
  BF311.M4263   1987   152.1   87-17562   65118
  ISBN 0-205-11125-4
  ISBN 0-205-11594-2 (International Edition)

Printed in the United States of America
10 9 8 7 6 5 4 3 2 1   92 91 90 89 88 87

Contents

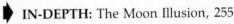

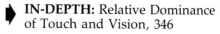

Preface

The purpose of this textbook is to provide an introduction to sensation and perception. I have written it for students who have no specialized background in physiology, mathematics, or experimental psychology. It is intended for use in courses in perception or in sensation and perception. *Sensation and Perception* is primarily a textbook for undergraduates, although graduate students who want an overview of the subject will also find it useful.

Sensation and Perception is organized in terms of four major parts. The first part contains an introductory chapter and a chapter on psychophysics, and the second part includes six chapters on vision. Nonvisual perception (hearing, touch and related senses, smell, and taste) is examined in the third part. Finally, the fourth part covers additional topics in sensation and perception, specifically, attention and perceptual development.

Sensation and perception are fascinating topics, yet there is often a major gap between the richness of our perceptual experiences and the pallid, academic discussion of these experiences in most textbooks. Furthermore, students typically.regard the material in sen-

sation and perception textbooks as difficult—perhaps only slightly more approachable than statistics or physiological psychology. To overcome these problems, I've tried to write a textbook that is interesting and student oriented yet comprehensive. Here are some of the features included in this edition:

1. The writing style is clear and straightforward.

2. There are numerous examples of how the sensory systems and perception operate in everyday experiences.

3. Throughout the text are applications in areas such as education, art, traffic safety, advertising, and industry.

4. The text includes many small-scale demonstrations that students can try by themselves, using minimal equipment and time.

5. There are 14 In-Depth sections in the book, focusing on recent research on selected topics and providing details on research methods.

6. New terms are introduced in boldface print, with their definition in the same sentence.

7. Each chapter begins with an outline and preview.

8. There is a summary at the end of each of the major sections in the chapter, rather than a long summary at the end of the entire chapter.

9. Each chapter includes review questions and a list of new terms.

10. Each chapter ends with a list of rec-

ommended readings, including a brief summary of each resource.

11. Four major themes are introduced in
the first chapter and traced throughout the
book to provide students with a sense of continuity across many diverse topics. The four
themes are (a) the senses share clear similarities with one another; (b) the stimuli themselves are rich with information; (c) the
human sensory systems perform well in gathering information about stimuli; and (d) prior
knowledge, context, and expectations help
shape our perceptions.

12. At the end of the book a glossary contains a definition for each of the new terms
introduced in the book; a phonetic pronunciation is included for terms with potentially
ambiguous pronunciations.

Professors and students who used the first
edition of this textbook, *Perception*, responded
enthusiastically to the clarity of writing, the
interest level, and the student-oriented features of that book; these features have all been
included in the second edition. When I asked
reviewers what areas merited additional coverage in the second edition, they requested
detailed coverage of certain topics; this request was incorporated in the In-Depth section. They also suggested additional information on sensory processes. The coverage
of sensation was extensively expanded, and
this expansion is reflected in the new title,
Sensation and Perception.

Here are some of the major additions and
changes:

1. The chapter on psychophysics was
moved to the beginning of the book. Additional coverage and examples of signal detection theory were added, as well as information on multidimensional scaling.

2. In response to the request for more details on sensory processes the chapter on the
visual system (Chapter 3) was expanded to
include more specific information on the

anatomy of the eye and on cortical processing.

3. Chapter 4 contains additional coverage
on types of acuity and on eye movements in
reading.

4. Chapter 5 covers sensory aspects of
color in more detail and also discusses additional color phenomena and categorical
perception.

5. The chapter on shape now includes details on lateral inhibition, Fourier analysis,
and top-down processing.

6. Chapter 7 has been expanded to include event perception and biological motion,
as well as time perception.

7. The chapter on constancy and illusion
includes more information on size constancy
and a detailed discussion of current theories
about the moon illusion.

8. There are now two chapters on hearing.
Chapter 9 is an introduction to hearing, containing more information on sensory processes and on sound localization.

9. The perception of music and speech
merits a full chapter in this second edition,
including topics such as organization, constancy, and illusion in music and categorical
speech perception, top-down speech processing, and theories of speech perception.

10. Chapter 11, on touch and related
senses, contains more information on the
skin receptors, a discussion of the relative
dominance of touch and vision, updated information on theories of pain perception and
pain control, and coverage of the kinesthetic
and vestibular senses.

11. Chapter 12 now includes an In-Depth
discussion of odor recognition, as well as information on odor constancy and odor illusions.

12. Chapter 13 has been expanded to include coverage of the interaction between
taste and smell, as well as the hedonics of
food.

13. Chapter 14 now contains a discussion
of the attention-shift and eye-movement

issue, a new section on vigilance, and In-Depth coverage of the two levels of processing in search tasks.

14. Because of the recent extensive research on perceptual development, Chapter 15 has been almost completely rewritten; topics that were greatly expanded include visual abilities in infancy, infant speech perception, and hearing in adulthood and old age.

In preparing this new edition I made every possible effort to include recent research. I examined every entry on sensation and perception in *Psychological Abstracts* between 1980 and 1986 and pursued every relevant book reviewed in *Contemporary Psychology*. In addition, I wrote to more than 200 researchers in the discipline, requesting reprints and preprints. Most of the references contained in this second edition have been written since 1980. The research on sensation and perception is progressing at a fast pace, and I want this textbook to capture the excitement of these recent findings!

ACKNOWLEDGMENTS

Many people deserve credit for their contributions to the second edition of *Sensation and Perception*. The people with whom I've worked at Allyn and Bacon deserve the same high praise they earned on the first edition. John-Paul Lenney, psychology editor, provided many excellent suggestions and strategies. Bill Barke, editor-in-chief, who suggested that I write the first edition, supplied additional guidance during the revision process. The team in charge of editing the manuscript was superb; I'd like to thank Annette Joseph, Susan Freese, Lois Benson Rosenfeld, and Mary Espenschied (CRACOM Corporation); all are exceptional!

I would like to acknowledge several professors who inspired my interest in perception. These include Leonard Horowitz, Douglas Lawrence, and Eleanor Maccoby of Stanford University and Daniel Weintraub, Richard Pew, Irving Pollack, and W. P. Tanner at the University of Michigan.

Other people helped in diverse ways. Three members of Milne Library, SUNY, Geneseo, deserve special thanks: Paula Henry ordered numerous books for me and kept her eye out for relevant material; Judith Bushnell tracked down wayward references and conducted computer searches for the In-Depth sections; Harriet Sleggs ordered dozens of references for me from interlibrary loan.

In addition, Victoria Beitz, Stacy Rogers, Lois Rogers, and Christine Teoli worked diligently in tracking down references and preparing the name index. Beth Matlin and Sally Matlin helped assemble the bibliography. Eileen Stepien read the page proofs. Ron Pretzer supplied most of the photographs for the book and willingly took photographs of waffles, feet, and other more ordinary objects. Jean Amidon typed the bibliography and the Instructor's Manual; her intelligence, speed, and accuracy are much appreciated. Mary Lou Perry and Connie Ellis kept other aspects of my life running smoothly, allowing me more time to work on the project.

Many people supplied useful information and reviewed portions of the book in which they are experts. I would particularly like to thank Nila Aguilar-Markulis, A. K. Das, John Foley, Morton Heller, Peter Lennie, Daniel Levin, Arnold H. Matlin, Ray Mayo, Sally Wendkos Olds, George Rebok, Lanna Ruddy, David Van Dyke, Susan K. Whitbourne, and Melvyn Yessenow.

In addition, I wish to thank the reviewers who provided useful suggestions for improving both factual and stylistic aspects of the manuscript. The reviewers who helped on the first edition included Douglas Bloomquist (Framingham State College), Tom Bourbon (Steven F. Austin State University), Lester Lefton (University of South Carolina), and William Tedford (Southern Methodist University). The reviewers who gave assistance on the second edition included Douglas Bloomquist (Framingham State College), Susan E. Dutch (Westfield State College), Phyllis Freeman (State University of New York, New Paltz), Larry Hochhaus (Oklahoma State University), Mary Peterson (State University of New York, Stonybrook), Alan Searleman (St. Lawrence University), and Dejan Todorovic (Boston University and University of Beogradu, Belgrade, Yugoslavia). Their advice and guidance were extremely valuable.

Finally, I want to thank my husband, Arnie, and my children, Beth and Sally, for their encouragement, optimism, appreciation, and helpful suggestions. Their enthusiasm and support are inspiring!

M. W. M.

*Sensation
and
Perception*

chapter *1*
Introduction

This very moment your sensory and perceptual processes are demonstrating their extraordinary skills. Your eyes move along this page at a steady pace, identifying letters and words so fast as to defy explanation. You glance away and perceive a world rich with color, depth, and motion. From the moment you awoke you have been continuously sensing and perceiving: you heard, you touched, you smelled, and you tasted.

Sensation refers to immediate and basic experiences generated by isolated, simple stimuli. **Perception** involves the interpretation of those sensations, giving them meaning and organization. When a musician strikes a note on the piano, such qualities as its loudness and pitch are sensations. If you hear the first four notes and recognize that they form a tune, you have experienced a perception. In practice, no clear-cut distinction exists between these two terms. How complex can stimuli become before they involve perception rather than sensation? How much interpretation is necessary before sensation becomes perception? Psychologists acknowledge a fuzzy boundary between these two terms.

Furthermore, there is a fuzzy boundary between perception and a term referring to a still more complex and interpretive process, cognition. **Cognition** involves the acquisition, storage, retrieval, and use of knowledge. If you identified those first four notes on the piano as the beginning of "The Star Spangled Banner," recalled that it was the U.S. national anthem, and realized that you must rise to your feet, you were using cognition. Still, when *exactly* did that perception become a cognition? This textbook will examine the two more immediate, less interpretive processes—sensation and perception. Information on cognition can be found elsewhere (e.g., Anderson, 1985; Bourne, Dominowski, Loftus, & Healy, 1986; Matlin, 1983).

We tend to take sensation and perception for granted because it seems so natural and automatic to see, hear, touch, smell, and taste. We open our eyes and see people, ferns, and parrots. We open our mouths, insert a morsel of food, and taste tomatoes, cheesecake, curried goat. Perception, however, is really a puzzle that has mystified philosophers and psychologists for centuries. Basically, it is challenging to explain how the qualities of objects in the world can be recreated in our heads.

Consider an example. Figure 1.1 shows an ordinary scene. Each structured segment is broken up by sensory receptors and nervous system into a series of impulses. As Gregory (1974) notes, "All of the rich information about perceptual structure which we take for granted has somehow dissolved into a series of yes or no electrical blips moving along some tiny, poorly insulated fibers" (p. 76). Nonetheless, our nervous system manages to reconstruct the real world of steps, pillars, and doors from this series of electrical blips. Our perceptions are neatly organized, and they are a reasonably accurate mirror of the real world.

Why should you study sensation and perception? There are four basic reasons, although others may occur to you as you explore the topic more thoroughly. The first concerns philosophy. We mentioned the dilemma of recreating the qualities of objects, of bringing the outside world to the inside mind. A branch of philosophy called **epistemology** concerns how we acquire knowledge, including knowledge of the properties of objects. One intriguing concern of epistemology is whether we require experience with the world before we can perceive it accurately. Can your 2-month-old niece have accurate knowledge, for instance, about how far away the side of the crib is from her nose, or must she learn about distance through repeated experiences of reaching, grasping, and bumping?

Exploring sensation and perception also provides a background for other areas of psychology. These two areas are closely associated with cognition, clearly a vital topic in psychology in the last half of the twentieth century. Knowledge of sensation and perception would be helpful in some other representative areas:

- Motivation—An important topic is eating and weight control, and an essential background area for this topic is taste perception.
- Psychology of language—Any attempt to explain comprehension of spoken language must begin with sound perception.
- Nonverbal behavior depends on sending and receiving information about body position, facial expression, and intonation—all perceptual attributes.
- Gerontology—Understanding the isolation that elderly people may experience is easier if we know about the hearing impairment that may accompany aging.
- Abnormal psychology—People with schizophrenia and infantile autism can be better understood with information about attentional processes.

In fact, if you have an introductory psychology textbook handy, turn to the table of contents and note how each of the major topics is related to sensation and perception.

Sensation and perception also have numerous practical applications in schools, occupations, and industries. Reading teachers can apply what psychologists have learned about eye movements (Chapter 4) and letter identification (Chapter 6). Physicians can use information about reducing pain (Chapter 11) and examining X rays (Chapter 14). Environmental scientists should be aware of research on odor pollution (Chapter 12) and excessive noise levels (Chapter 9).

A final reason for continuing to read this book is more personal. You own some exceptional equipment. Your eyes, ears, skin, nose, tongue, and nervous system are extremely

Figure 1.1 Organization in perception (Photo by Ron Pretzer.)

skilled and efficient. Nonetheless, you may know more about how a vacuum cleaner, an automobile, or a typewriter works. You'll be living the remainder of your life with your sensory systems, so it should be both interesting and useful to know them more intimately.

PREVIEW OF THE BOOK

This book examines how we take in information about the outside world and how the world appears. It will consider the anatomy and physiology of the sensory systems, how energy from stimuli in the outside world is conveyed to the brain, and how sensory information is interpreted to form perceptions. Chapter 1 outlines the scope of the book, summarizes the major theoretical approaches to sensation and perception, presents several themes that will be traced throughout the text, and offers hints on how to use it.

Chapter 2 discusses psychophysics, the study of the relationship between physical stimuli and our psychological reaction to them. Two questions considered are: Why are you more likely to '"hear'' a subway coming (even if it hasn't left the previous station) when you've been waiting a long time? Why can you notice a 5-pound weight loss more easily for Pat, who weighs 100 pounds, than for Chris, who weighs 200 pounds?

Chapter 3 provides an overview of the visual system, since we need to know the structure of the visual equipment before proceeding to other topics. It will examine the anatomy of the eye and discuss how visual information travels to the brain. The topics considered in this chapter may answer some questions about the visual system. Why can you see clearly objects in your direct line of sight, whereas objects ''in the corner of your eye'' look fuzzy? What causes diseases of the eye such as conjunctivitis and cataracts? Why are diabetics likely to have visual disorders?

Chapter 4 discusses several basic skills of the visual system: the ability to see fine detail, the change in sensitivity that occurs when moving from light to dark settings or from dark to light settings, several distinct kinds of eye movements, and focusing. The chapter will also address questions such as: What does 20/20 vision mean? If you are driving at night and you look at the headlights of the oncoming car, why do you have trouble seeing afterwards? Why are eye movements important in reading?

Chapter 5 examines color vision, including color vision deficiencies and theories about color perception. It will also discuss how we can perceive colors even in simple black-and-white designs. Some questions answered include: Why do we get green if we mix yellow and blue paints, but we get gray if we mix yellow and blue lights? Why is the term *color-blind* incorrect? Why should someone stranded on a desert island wear red or green rather than yellow or blue?

Chapter 6 considers shape. Shapes have contours, or sudden changes in brightness; our visual system enhances them. Our perception of shape also shows impressive organization; a door seems to have a shape that sets it apart from the surrounding building. We also recognize patterns; we identify a curved line as part of a tree, not a cat's tail. Two issues discussed are: How do advertisements and paintings make effective use of similar shapes? Do we recognize a letter more quickly if it is part of an English word than if it appears by itself?

Chapter 7 is concerned with distance, motion, and time. Our visual world is neither flat nor stationary, and time passes. Somehow, we manage to perceive objects as three-dimensional, even though our eyes appear to represent only two dimensions. We also perceive a wide variety of movements, even when objects are immobile. Time perception depends upon the situation and the characteristics of the observer. Three questions answered in this chapter are: Why is your depth perception poor if you use only one eye? When you see a distant person walking, why is it possible to decide almost instantly whether the person is female or male? Does a watched pot really seem to take longer to boil?

Chapter 8 examines two closely related areas, constancy and illusion. Constancy means that objects seem to stay the same, even when the way we view the object changes; our perceptions match reality accurately. In illusions, such as the one in Figure 1.2, perceptions do not match reality. For example, the two central circles are really of equal size, although the one on the left looks larger. Here are some issues considered in Chapter 8: Why does your friend seem to stay the same size as she walks away from you, even though the image registered in your eye clearly shrinks? Why does vanilla ice cream look white in the moonlight, even though it reflects less light than a lump of coal in the sunlight? How did an illusion cause a plane crash that left four people dead and forty-nine injured?

Chapters 3 through 8 concern vision. The next five chapters discuss the nonvisual perceptual systems.

Chapter 9 examines basic aspects of hearing. After discussing sound waves and the auditory system, it considers pitch, loudness, timbre, tone combinations, and localizations. Two additional topics represent applications of hearing research, noise pollution, and hearing impairments. Some issues addressed clude: How does the ear manage to record the pitch of a train squeaking to a halt, Placido Domingo singing a Verdi aria, and your grandfather snoring? Why do some tone combinations sound pleasant, whereas others are unbearable? How can you decide that a sound is coming from the left side rather than from another direction?

Chapter 10 discusses more complex aspects of hearing in music and speech perception. It first addresses pitch, loudness, timbre, and tone combinations as they relate to music. Examples are provided of organization and pattern in music and musical constancy and illusions. The speech perception section begins with a description of the sounds in speech; other topics include how thought processes influence speech perception and theories of speech perception. The following questions are answered: How can you recognize a tune, even if it is played in an unfamiliar key? How do we manage to hear speech accurately when so much of it is fuzzy or distorted?

Chapter 11 examines the senses related to the skin. Objects and people in the world touch us, and we touch them back. We also perceive pain and warm and cold, and we know the positions of our body parts and whether we are standing upright or tilted. Here are some of the topics covered: Why were you aware of your wristwatch's pressing against your skin when you put it on this morning, although you hadn't noticed it again until now? Why do people have to feel pain to survive? Why do you sometimes have difficulty deciding whether water is warm or cold?

Chapter 12 deals with smell. It is difficult to describe and to classify various smells, so it is a challenge to examine this perceptual system. We will discuss sensitivity to smells, how smells become less noticeable as we are exposed to them, recognition for smells, and constancy and illusions related to smell. Several applications of research on smell will also be considered, including odor pollution control, medicine, perfume, and communication. Some issues we will examine include: Why don't you smell the perfume or shaving lotion you applied this morning, although a friend who joins you for lunch notices it immediately? Can parents recognize their children on the basis of smell alone?

Chapter 13, on taste, is closely related to the chapter on smell. Tastes are easier to categorize than smells. This chapter begins with a discussion of taste categories and then ex-

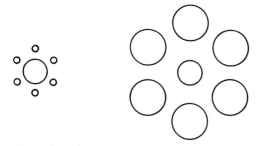

Figure 1.2 Example of an illusion.

amines taste receptors and the taste system. Other topics include sensitivity to taste, how tastes become less noticeable as we are exposed to them, how smell interacts with taste, the pleasantness of various foods, and applications of taste research. Some questions answered include, What characteristics of food do we notice in addition to taste and odor? Why was the information incorrect that your junior-high science teacher told you about the regions of the tongue? Why does water taste vaguely sweet after your morning grapefruit? How might smokers' reactions to sweet foods explain why they often gain weight once they stop smoking?

The last chapters cover two additional topics in perception. The emphasis is on vision and hearing, primarily because the other perceptual systems have not been so completely investigated.

Chapter 14 discusses attention. One aspect of attention is vigilance, which occurs when you watch for something over a long time. A related topic is search, which occurs when you scan a scene for a particular object. A final topic is selective attention, which occurs when you pay attention to one activity and therefore notice little about anything else. Some issues raised include: Whom would you be more likely to trust to listen for a particular story on the news, the life-of-the-party or the shy wallflower? Can you search just as fast for three objects as for one? Why can't you pay attention to three simultaneous conversations in a crowded restaurant?

Chapter 15 is concerned with the development of perception. You will learn that the perceptual skills are rather well developed in infancy. However, these skills become more sophisticated during childhood. Elderly people sometimes have impaired vision or hearing, but most people do not experience major perceptual disabilities as they grow older. Three of the questions to be discussed are: Can babies hear the difference between some sounds that adults think are identical? Why do young children reverse their letters so often? Do elderly people and young adults differ in their ability to identify various foods?

OVERVIEW OF THEORETICAL APPROACHES TO SENSATION AND PERCEPTION

This section will outline some major approaches to provide a background for several theoretical topics that will be discussed more completely in other chapters.

A thorough review of theories of sensation and perception would probably begin with theories of perception proposed by Greek philosophers more than 2000 years ago; it would continue to early explorations of the physiology of the eye and the physics of light. This survey will be limited to the more recent past and will examine five approaches: empiricist, Gestalt, behaviorist, Gibsonian, and information processing. Other sources can be consulted for details on the early history of perception (for example, Boring, 1942; Wertheimer, 1974).

The Empiricist Approach

In the early 1700s George Berkeley struggled with a basic problem: How can we perceive objects as having a third dimension, depth, if our eyes register only height and width? We will consider this important question again in Chapter 7 when we discuss the perception of distance and depth. Berkeley (1709/ 1957) was influential in developing **empiricism**, which states that basic sensory experiences are combined through learning to produce perception. We do not know how to perceive depth when we are born; instead, we must acquire this perceptual ability by learning (Hochberg, 1979; Uttal, 1981).

A relatively modern empiricist, William James, has often been called America's greatest psychologist. James created the phrase "blooming, buzzing confusion" to describe the perceptual world of the newborn infant. He proposed that babies live in a confusing world that, through learning, becomes relatively orderly.

The empiricist explanations for topics such as distance perception and size constancy are still popular today, as we will see in later chapters. Developmental psychologists, however, have discovered that babies have more perceptual capacities than James described. Their perceptual worlds are not so orderly as they will become in adulthood, but they are far from random.

The Gestalt Approach

A number of German Gestalt psychologists in the first part of this century objected to the empiricist approach to perception. They argued that the empiricists' approach was too artificial and that it did not pay enough attention to the relationship among the various parts of a stimulus (Hochberg, 1979; Köhler, 1947). **Gestalt** can be translated as "configuration" or "pattern" (Uttal, 1981), and the **Gestalt approach** emphasizes that we perceive objects as well-organized, whole structures rather than as separated, isolated parts. Thus, the shape that we see is more than an accumulation of its individual elements. For example, the design that you see in Figure 1.3 is more than the simple combination of eight separate lines; it is a well-organized configuration that suggests a table.

The Gestalt approach developed many principles to account for the organization of

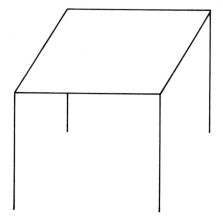

Figure 1.3 Well-organized configuration; the whole is more than the accumulation of isolated parts.

shapes. Whereas the empiricists emphasized the contribution of learning and experience to perception, Gestalt theorists discussed but did not stress these factors. Instead, they emphasized humans' inborn ability to perceive form. In Chapter 6 we will see that the Gestalt principles are still considered to be an important part of shape perception.

The Behaviorist Approach

Behaviorism stresses the objective description of an organism's behavior. Strict behaviorists are uncomfortable with the area of perception, which examines how the world *appears* rather than how people behave. Since behaviorism was the dominant psychological theory in the United States from the 1930s to the 1960s, research in the more complex areas of perception declined significantly during those years (Hochberg, 1979; Uttal, 1981).

The area least influenced by the behaviorists' bias against perception was psychophysics. Psychophysics uses clearly defined methods to assess people's reactions to physical stimuli. This objective, quantitative approach was compatible with behaviorism and therefore survived its reign well.

The Gibsonian Approach

James J. Gibson, a Cornell University psychologist who died in 1979, approached perception differently from the empiricists or Gestaltists. The **Gibsonian approach** emphasized that our perceptions are rich and elaborate because the stimuli in our environment are rich with information, rather than because our thought processes or experiences provide that richness (Michaels & Carello, 1981). For example, Gibson proposed that we perceive objects as having a third dimension because of information about qualities such as their surface texture. Whereas the empiricists argued that we need to learn to perceive depth, Gibson stressed that all the information we need is in the stimulus itself. As Neisser (1981) remarked in an obituary about Gibson: "Gibson begins not with the sense organs or even with organisms but with the environment that is to be perceived" (p. 215). We will consider the Gibsonian approach to perception in some detail in Chapters 6 and 7.

Indirect perception theories assume that the senses receive an impoverished description of the world; the stimuli do not provide accurate, complete information about objects or events (Michaels & Carello, 1981). In contrast, Gibson describes a **direct perception theory** in which we can directly perceive our environment from the information in the stimulus; we do not need memories or reasoning processes.

Gibson also emphasized that our investigation of perception should concentrate on real-world perception (Gibson, 1979). He saw little value in perceptual experiences found only in laboratories, such as looking at a white bar on a black screen in a darkened room, while your head movements are minimized because you have been strapped into a head vice.

A chapter by Mace (1977) provides an excellent overview of Gibson's theory, and its title summarizes the Gibsonian approach: "James J. Gibson's strategy for perceiving: Ask not what's inside your head, but what your head's inside of." Gibson believed that when we can adequately describe the features of environmental stimuli, we do not need to devise elaborate theories to explain the psychological processes that might underlie perception.

The Information-Processing Approach

Information processing was developed by people who were interested in computers and communication science, and it is a dominant area in psychology today. In the **information-processing approach**, researchers identify psychological processes and connect these processes together by proposing specific patterns of information flow (Uttal, 1981). For example, one influential model proposed that information from our sensory receptors passes through a series of stages: brief sensory storage, short-term memory, and long-term memory (Atkinson & Shiffrin, 1968). After one stage performs its specified operations, the information passes on to the next stage for another kind of processing.

As Uttal points out, it is a mistake to refer to the information-processing approach as a theory: "In fact, in its current form, it is far from a theory at all, but instead should be considered to be a particular language and orientation toward psychological processes" (p. 117). For example, the information-processing approach usually provides a description of the phases of psychological processes but does not specify whether these phases were acquired by learning or inborn ability. In contrast, the other four theories are more likely to focus on explanations for psychological processes, such as the origin of perceptual ability.

Information-processing models typically stress that humans have limited capacities. Thus we cannot perceive too many items at one time. If we are paying close attention to one message, we must ignore another message. (We will discuss the limited capacity of human information processing in detail in Chapter 14, "Attention.")

The information-processing approach points out that there is a continuity in the way we handle information. Earlier psychologists, such as those who favored the empiricist approach, often made distinctions among several areas of experimental psychology. For example, *sensation* referred to the immediate contact between stimuli and the sensory receptors. The term *perception* referred to adding meaning and interpretation to these basic sensations. Thus these psychologists believed that sensations were pure and were not influenced by previous learning and experience. Perceptions, they believed, were very different from sensations because they were influenced by learning and experience. Information-processing psychologists, however, stress that sensation, perception, and higher mental processes—such as memory—must all be treated within a single system (Haber, 1974). Thus we may use strategies that involve memory when we perceive. Information-processing psychologists urge us not to divide sensation, perception, memory, and other processes into isolated compartments. Instead, we must realize that each process depends upon others.

We have reviewed five approaches. Each has had a substantial impact on the discipline. This textbook is eclectic; it will borrow elements of all five frameworks.

Summary: Overview of Theoretical Approaches to Sensation and Perception

1. Empiricism, which was primarily developed by Berkeley, proposes that all information is derived from sensory perceptions and experience. Similarly, William James argued that babies' perceptual experiences are random and disorganized.
2. Empiricists believe that perception involves sensory information and interpretation of sensory information.
3. The Gestalt approach emphasizes that we perceive objects as well-organized wholes instead of separate parts.
4. The Gestalt approach proposes that shape perception is inborn and that learning is relatively unimportant.
5. The behaviorist approach stresses the objective description of behavior. Consequently, behaviorists have not been very interested in perception, an area concerned with less observable psychological processes.
6. The Gibsonian approach stresses that stimuli in the environment are rich with information.
7. The Gibsonian approach argues that perception is direct; we do not need to perform calculations and interpretations to perceive.
8. The information-processing approach maintains that information is handled by a series of stages.
9. The information-processing approach stresses that sensation, perception, and other higher mental processes are interconnected rather than isolated; this approach should be considered an orienta-

tion to, rather than a theory of, psychology.

THEMES OF THE BOOK

Four themes traced throughout this textbook are intended to provide some additional structure for the material and to encourage you to find patterns and relationships among areas that may initially seem unrelated. You will note, incidentally that the themes reflect the eclectic theoretical orientation of the textbook; for example, the second theme is based on Gibson's theories, whereas the fourth theme is consistent with the empiricist approach.

1. *The senses share some clear similarities with one another.* Naturally, tasting is not identical to seeing or hearing, but they have important commonalities. Sensation begins with a form of physical energy that stimulates the sensory receptors, this energy is converted into a form that can be transmitted along the neurons, and the stimulation ultimately reaches the brain. Another similarity is adaptation; when a stimulus is presented repeatedly, its perceived intensity tends to decrease. For instance, the odor in a fragrant locker room—fortunately—seems less overpowering after several minutes. Similarly, you feel the pressure of your watch on your wrist when you first put it on in the morning, but moments later you no longer notice it.

2. *The stimuli themselves are rich with information.* Clearly, this second theme is based on the Gibsonian approach to sensation and perception. For example, compare the surface texture of the rug or flooring surrounding your feet with the surface texture several yards away. The texture becomes denser as the distance increases, and this information about the stimulus is useful when you want to judge distance. Now take your book and move it from left to right. Notice that it systematically covers up part of the background and uncovers another part as you move it. Try several different patterns of movement

and notice how much information about direction and speed of motion is available from the stimulus, that is, the pattern of covering and uncovering.

3. *The human sensory systems perform well in gathering information about stimuli.* Stimuli in the outside world may be rich with information, yet all of it would be wasted if our sensory systems weren't so well adapted to picking it up. A bat, for example, would be unlikely to appreciate a Rembrandt painting, and the subtleties of a fine burgundy would be lost on a chicken. The more subtle, cognitive aspects of appreciation aside, these organisms do not have adequate sensory systems to encode stimulus attributes. Consider, for instance, how our visual system can encode the attributes of an apple. Obviously, it can register information about the apple's color, shape, size, and distance. However, it can also detect more subtle qualities, such as whether it has been polished, whether it has a bruise on one side, and how much the stem area is indented. The sheer number of attributes is impressive.

The sensory systems are also impressive because of the range of environments in which they can operate. You can see in extremely bright sunlight and also in a darkened room, for instance. Furthermore, your sensory apparatus can be exquisitely sensitive. For example, a certain chemical with a musky smell can be detected when less than 0.0000001 milligram (mg) of it is spread through 1 liter (L) of air (Wenger, Jones, & Jones, 1956). If a peanut, which weighs about 1 gram (g), were divided into 10 billion parts, one of those parts would weigh more than the amount of the musky chemical that could be detected in a liter of air!

Our sensory systems seem to be particularly well adapted to humans' specific needs. For instance, our visual system is especially competent in detecting motion by other humans (see Chapter 7). Our hearing apparatus is particularly sensitive to the frequency range of the human voice. Newborns arrive with their senses in reasonably good order: they can follow movement, hear distinctions

between sounds, and recognize the odors of familiar people.

Our sensory systems are sensitive and flexible enough to provide very good "bottom-up" processing, which we will discuss in more detail in Chapter 6. In brief, **bottom-up processing** (or **data-driven processing**) explains how the sensory receptors register the stimuli. The information flows from this "bottom" level upward to the higher, more cognitive levels. We begin with the data and transform and combine them until we have perceptions and cognitions.

4. *Prior knowledge, context, and expectations help shape our perceptions.* Perception involves more than the combination of data from the sensory receptors. As emphasized by the empiricists, sensory information is supplemented and transformed by higher, more cognitive processes. The bottom-up or data-driven approach can be contrasted with **top-down processing** (or **conceptually driven processing**), which emphasizes the importance of observers' concepts in shaping perception. According to this view, observers have accumulated ideas about how the world is organized. On a Nevada ranch, for example, that four-legged creature on the horizon is more likely to be a horse than a zebra. We will perceive that creature as a horse unless the "data" provide us with very clear information about stripes. You may *hear* your friend mutter as you leave a test, "How did you like the exam?" although the data in that stimulus were really, "Howja like thuzamm?" Once again, your knowledge and expectations, combined with the context, allowed you to interpret some potentially ambiguous data.

Our knowledge and expectations also lead us to try to "make sense" of ambiguous stimuli by exploring them further until our perceptions are clearer. Humans are active and inquiring organisms who are typically not satisfied with uncertainties. If you are groping for your bathrobe in a dark room and you're not certain whether you grabbed a sock by mistake, you actively explore the fabric until you find a button, a familiar feel to the material, or a belt. If you can't read the bumper sticker on the car in front of you, you creep forward until you can. If you can't hear the operator on the telephone, you ask for the message to be repeated. Thus, our concepts about the world help to clarify many ambiguities, and they guide us in active efforts to clarify many other ambiguities.

It is pointless to argue, incidentally, about which approach is correct, the bottom-up or the top-down; clearly both processes are necessary to explain how we manage to perceive so quickly and so accurately. These two approaches, representing the third and fourth themes of this book, combine with the second theme—about the wealth of information available in the stimulus—in order to help answer the mystery of perception. Our perceptions are a reasonably accurate mirror of the real world for three reasons: (1) stimuli are rich with information; (2) human sensory systems are effective in gathering information; and (3) concepts help shape our perceptions.

HOW TO USE THIS BOOK

Several different features in this book have been included to help you understand, learn, and remember the material. This section tells you how to use these features most effectively.

Each chapter begins with an outline. Inspect the outline before you read a new chapter and pay particular attention to the structure of the topic. For example, notice the two major sections in Chapter 2 ("Psychophysics"): (1) Measuring Responses to Low-Intensity Stimuli and (2) Measuring Responses to More Intense Stimuli.

Each of the remaining chapters includes a chapter preview, a brief summary of the material to be covered. This preview supplements the outline and explains important terms in the outline that might be unfamiliar.

This textbook stresses applications. One is the application of perception research to such professions as medicine, food technology,

and consumer psychology. This feature has been included because it is useful to know how theoretical research can be applied to solve real-life problems. This material may also help you learn, since concrete material is typically more memorable than abstract material.

A second application involves recalling phenomena from your own experience. Psychologists concerned with human memory have demonstrated that we recall material better if we ask ourselves whether it applies to us (e.g., Rogers, Kuiper, & Kirker, 1977). Therefore take advantage of your experience!

The third application consists of informal experiments labeled "Demonstrations." Each requires only a short time commitment and no equipment more exotic than flashlights, paper and pencils, and glasses of sugar water. You can perform most of these demonstrations by yourself. These demonstrations should also help to make the material more concrete and easy to relate to your own experiences.

Chapters 2 to 15 have an "In-Depth" section, which examines recent research on a selected topic relevant to the chapter. These sections focus on experimental methodology and the outcome of experiments.

Throughout each chapter new terms are introduced in boldface print (for example, **empiricism**), and their definition appears in the same sentence. Each of these new terms also appears in the glossary, which includes a phonetic pronunciation for potentially ambiguous terms. These pronunciations are not intended to insult your intelligence but to aid you in learning. Furthermore, it will be easier to ask a question in class when you know that the superior colliculus is a "kole-*lick*-you-luss" and not a "kole-like-*you*-loos."

You will notice that an unusual feature of this textbook is a summary at the end of each of the major sections in a chapter, rather than at the end of the entire chapter. I chose to include frequent, small summaries rather than a single lengthy summary for two reasons: (1) you can review the material more frequently, and (2) you can master small segments before you move on to unfamiliar material. You can take advantage of this feature by testing yourself when you reach the end of a section. Read the summary and notice which items you omitted. Test yourself once more, rechecking your accuracy. Some students report that they prefer to read only one section at a time rather than the whole chapter. Then when they begin a study session in the middle of a chapter, they reread the previous section summaries before reading the new material.

Each chapter ends with review questions and a list of new terms. The review questions may ask you to apply your knowledge to a practical problem or to integrate material from several parts of the chapter. The new terms are listed in their order of occurrence. You may wish to test yourself on these terms, checking the glossary if you are uncertain.

The final feature of each chapter is a list of recommended readings intended to supply you with resources if you want to write a paper on a particular topic or if the area is personally interesting. In general, I tried to locate books, chapters, and articles that provide more than an overview of the subject yet are not overly technical.

Review

1. What are sensation and perception, and why have they been particularly mystifying topics? Describe this puzzle with respect to your perception of a letter of the alphabet on this page.
2. How do sensation and perception differ from cognition? The book provided an example to clarify the distinctions among these three concepts. That example concerned hearing a melody. Select two or more additional sensory systems and provide examples of the distinctions among the three terms. Point out how the boundaries among the concepts must be fuzzy rather than precise.
3. This introduction stressed that sensation and perception have applications to numerous professions. Contemplate the profession that you would like to enter and inspect the preview of the book, noting how some of the topics might be relevant to it.
4. Imagine yourself eating a piece of pizza. Review the preview of the book and illustrate how some aspect of the mundane act of eating a piece of pizza can be related to each chapter.
5. Describe in one or two sentences each of the major approaches to perception. Explain briefly how each of these approaches would account for your perception of the picture in Figure 1.1.
6. How much would each of the theoretical approaches emphasize learning in connection with perception? (In at least one approach it may be difficult to determine.)
7. Which of the theoretical approaches most closely fits your current ideas about sensation and perception? Which of them seems the least likely to you?
8. Review the first theme of the book, similarities among the sensory processes. Think about different kinds of adaptation you have noticed. Can you suggest any other kinds of similarities among the processes that you have noticed?
9. Review the last three themes of the book. Now describe how each explains how you are able to read this question at a fairly rapid rate.

New Terms

sensation	Gestalt approach	information-processing approach
perception	behaviorism	bottom-up processing
cognition	Gibsonian approach	data-driven processing
epistemology	indirect perception theories	top-down processing
empiricism		conceptually driven processing
Gestalt	direct perception theory	

Recommended Readings

Boring, E. G. (1942). *Sensation and perception in the history of experimental psychology.* New York: Appleton-Century-Crofts. *This classic book will provide a good introduction to empiricism and Gestalt psychology, as well as to earlier approaches to the area.*

Gibson, J. J. (1979). *The ecological approach to visual perception.* Boston: Houghton Mifflin. *This book gives an overview of Gibson's theory, emphasizing his idea of ambient vision.*

Hochberg, J. (1979). Sensation and perception. In E. Hearst (Ed.), *The first century of experimental psychology* (pp. 89–142). Hillsdale, NJ: Erlbaum. *Hochberg, a well-known researcher in the area of perception, wrote this chapter as part of a volume commemorating the 100-year birthday of Wundt's experimental psychology laboratory. The chapter offers a concise introduction, including a summary of several theories not considered in this book.*

Uttal, W. R. (1981). *A taxonomy of visual processes.* Hillsdale, NJ: Erlbaum. *Chapter 2 of this book, "Theories of Perception," is particularly useful because it attempts to classify the major theories of perception according to dimensions such as wholistic-elementalistic and nativistic-empiricistic.*

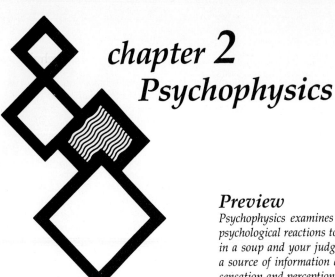

chapter 2
Psychophysics

Preview

Psychophysics examines the relationship between physical stimuli and psychological reactions to them, for example, between the amount of salt in a soup and your judgment of its saltiness. The topic is important as a source of information about humans. It is also useful in the study of sensation and perception, in its application to other areas of psychology, and in solutions to some everyday problems. This chapter is divided into two parts: (1) measuring responses to low-intensity stimuli and (2) measuring responses to more intense stimuli.

Suppose that we are interested in people's responses to a low-intensity stimulus such as a faint noise. One way to investigate this would be to measure a detection threshold, which is the intensity required for the stimulus to be reported half the time. The threshold could be measured by three classical psychophysical methods: the method of limits, the method of adjustment, and the method of constant stimuli. A more recent approach to studying low-intensity stimuli is signal detection theory. This approach emphasizes that people's decision-making strategies and their sensitivity determine whether they report the perception of a stimulus. Signal detection theory is particularly useful in studying pain perception. One person may be less likely than others to report pain because he or she is not sensitive to it or because he or she actually feels pain but is reluctant to report it. Either of these explanations can apply, depending upon the particular people participating in the study.

Suppose, instead, that we are interested in people's responses to more intense stimuli, such as a noise that is clearly audible. One way to investigate would be to use classical psychophysics methods to determine whether people can tell the difference between two similar stimuli or to discover how big that difference should be before it is noticeable half the time. An important topic of research with more intense stimuli concerns the relationship between the intensity of the physical stimuli and the magnitude of the psychological response. For example, does a solution taste twice as sweet if the amount of sugar it contains is doubled?

The next part of the chapter examines the nature of the relationship between physical intensity and psychological response. The final topic is multidimensional scaling, which is useful in determining the relationships among objects that vary along more than a single dimension. For example, multidimensional scaling might be useful if you wanted to figure out what dimensions people think are important in making decisions about facial similarity.

It's early in the morning, and you think you've just heard the ring of your alarm clock. However, it's difficult to be certain, since you buried the clock in a dresser drawer so that you couldn't hear that bothersome ticking last night. You turn on the lamp next to the bed and wonder whether a 60-watt bulb would be noticeably less bright—and less annoying—than the 75-watt bulb that you customarily use. At breakfast you add a tablet of artificial sweetener to your coffee and contemplate whether you can detect a hint of bitterness. You sample the bacon and suspect that it is slightly saltier and substantially crisper than your usual brand.

Psychophysics figures prominently in many of the decisions we make each day. These decisions may be relatively trivial speculations about alarm clocks, lightbulbs, sweeteners, and bacon, or they may be of major significiance, for example, when you are driving on a rainy night and trying to decide whether a pedestrian is in your path. **Psychophysics** is the study of the relationship between physical stimuli and psychological reactions to them. For example, one brand of bacon may have a trace more salt than another; these two *physical* stimuli are slightly different. But will a bacon taster be able to discriminate between them, thereby indicating that the two samples are *psychologically* different?

A typical psychophysics study might investigate people's perception of the intensity of a tiny spot of light. The intensity of the physical stimulus—that spot of light—can be precisely measured and described using techniques devised by physicists. The challenge, however, is to measure human perception. After all, perception is a private activity. If you are watching a friend who is busy watching a spot of light, you won't notice anything dramatic. For more than a hundred years, psychologists have been devising methods of measuring these private perceptions and converting them into numbers. The purpose of this chapter is to explore these measurement techniques and the nature of the relationship

between physical stimuli and psychological responses.

Why are psychologists so interested in psychophysics? One answer is that psychophysics is important as a self-sufficient area of inquiry. If we are concerned about how the mind works, then we should be curious about how the mind processes physical stimuli from the environment.

Psychophysics is also an essential tool for studying sensation and perception. For example, as you will see in Chapter 13, psychophysical techniques have been used to show that you are better able to taste sweetness when food is served at 30° C than when it is too hot or too cold. Some areas of sensation and perception may initially seem to be unrelated to psychophysics, until someone points out a connection. For instance, in Chapter 4 we will discuss acuity, the ability to see fine details. As Benzschawel and Cohn (1985) argue, acuity is really like a detection task from psychophysics. To tell the difference between a P and an R on an eye chart on your doctor's wall, you need to decide whether you detect an extra little bar in the lower-right corner of the letter.

In addition, psychophysical techniques have been used in other areas of psychology. In the field of personality psychology, stress and anxiety have been studied via a technique called magnitude estimation, a topic we'll consider at the end of this chapter (Dawson, 1982). Another popular psychophysical method, signal detection theory, is useful when psychologists examine why older people are less accurate than younger people on certain memory tasks (Grossberg & Grant, 1978). Finally, social attitudes, such as opinions about the prestige of various professions, have been examined with psychophysical tools (Wegener, 1982).

Applied psychologists also use psychophysics. An environmental psychologist may want to determine whether people who live along a busy highway detect less traffic noise when the highway is bordered by huge concrete blocks. A drug company may hire a psychophysicist to see whether its new analgesic increases tolerance for pain. A syrup company may conduct psychophysics tests to see whether consumers think that their new, low-calorie syrup is substantially thinner than the sugar-laden version.

In summary, then, psychophysics is an important topic because it allows us to know more about psychological processes, because it can be applied to other areas of psychology both within and beyond sensation and perception, and because it can be applied to practical problems in everyday life. Let's now turn our attention to these psychophysical techniques.

The discussion is divided into two sections. In the first section we will describe how people respond to low-intensity stimuli that are difficult to detect. We will discuss both the classical psychophysical methods and the newer signal detection theory in this first section. In the second section, on responding to more intense stimuli, we will examine how people respond to stimuli that are easy to detect. We will now look at the classical psychophysical methods for measuring discrimination and at the nature of the relationship between physical intensity and psychological response.

MEASURING RESPONSES TO LOW-INTENSITY STIMULI

You are standing on the subway platform, gazing down the dark tunnel to your right. Is that a faint light that you see, signaling the arrival of your train? Do you hear a distant rumble, assuring you that the Lexington Avenue Express is on its way? These are questions involving detection. In detection studies we provide low-intensity stimuli and notice whether people report them. Let's examine two approaches to the detection problem.

Classical Psychophysical Measurement of Detection

The classical psychophysics approach to detection centers upon the measurement of de-

tection thresholds. A **detection threshold** is the smallest amount of energy required for the stimulus to be reported 50% (.50) of the time. For example, we might want to measure a detection threshold for sound to determine how intense a sound must be for people to say "I hear it" half the time and "I don't hear it" half the time.

One way to envision a threshold—actually an *incorrect* way—is to think of a threshold as an abrupt change. Thus a person might say "I *can't* see it" whenever the stimulus intensity is 1, 2, 3, or 4. However, at a stimulus intensity of 5 and above, the person consistently says, "I *can* see it." Figure 2.1 illustrates the proposed relationship between stimulus intensity and the observer's responses. In reality, however, we rarely find abrupt changes from "I can't see it" to "I can see it." Figure 2.2 shows the relationship between stimulus intensity and the observer's response that is typically obtained. Notice that the observer shows a gradual increase in the proportion of "I can see it" responses. In real life, then, our perceptual systems show a gradual transition as stimulus intensity increases in the region of the threshold.

Let's discuss the relationship between threshold and sensitivity, because people often find this relationship confusing. When you have a low threshold for a stimulus, that means that only a low intensity of that stimulus is required for you to say, "I perceive it." In other words, you are sensitive to that stimulus. Thus the *lower* the threshold, the

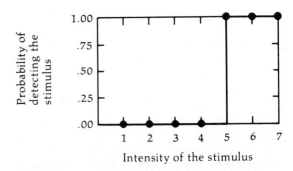

Figure 2.1 Incorrect conception of a threshold, showing abrupt change.

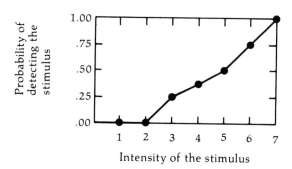

Figure 2.2 Results of typical threshold study, showing gradual change.

Table 2.1 Some Approximate Detection Threshold Values

Sense Modality	Detection Threshold
Light	A candle flame seen at 30 miles on a dark clear night
Sound	The tick of a watch under quiet conditions at 20 feet
Taste	One teaspoon of sugar in 2 gallons of water
Smell	One drop of perfume diffused into the entire volume of a three-room apartment
Touch	The wing of a bee falling on your cheek from a distance of 1 cm

Source: Adapted from Galanter, 1962. Used with permission.

higher the sensitivity. Conversely, the *higher* the threshold, the *lower* the sensitivity. For example, when you have been out in the bright sunshine and first enter a dark room, you have a high threshold for perceiving a dim light; your sensitivity is low. After you have been in the dark room for 20 minutes, however, you have a low threshold for perceiving a dim light; your sensitivity is high. Since the terms *threshold* and *sensitivity* are potentially confusing, it is important to inspect psychophysics graphs carefully to see whether large numbers reflect a high threshold or a high sensitivity.

Table 2.1 shows some approximate detection thresholds. These thresholds are intriguing, but they shouldn't be taken too seriously. I don't know many psychophysicists who spend their work hours dropping bee wings on people's cheeks.

Three classical methods of measuring detection thresholds exist. They were developed by Gustav Fechner, a nineteenth-century German physicist and mathematician who became intrigued by psychophysics in the last thirty-five years of his life (Gescheider, 1985).

Method of Limits

Try Demonstration 2.1, which is an example of how the method of limits can be used to measure a detection threshold. In the **method of limits** you begin with a stimulus that is clearly noticeable, and then you present increasingly weaker stimuli until the observer reports, "No, I *can't* detect it." On other occasions you begin with a stimulus that is clearly too weak, and then you present increasingly stronger stimuli until the observer reports, "Yes, I *can* detect it." Thus the observer is presented with a series of descending and ascending trials in which a stimulus is systematically decreased (**descending series**) or increased (**ascending series**) in intensity.

The method of limits needs to use both ascending and descending series because observers typically have different thresholds, depending on which series is used. This difference in thresholds has some practical applications. For example, suppose that someone is playing a radio in the room in which you are studying. You could turn down the volume, using descending series. However, you may discover that the final sound intensity is less if you turn down the volume until it cannot be heard and gradually make it louder, using ascending series.

Psychophysicists use both ascending and descending series to correct for the human tendency to perceive different thresholds, depending on which stimuli have been presented previously. These two sets of series also correct for two other kinds of tendencies.

Demonstration 2.1

*Using the Method of
Limits to Measure
Detection Threshold*

In this demonstration you will use the method of limits to measure an observer's ability to detect sweetness. First, take 1 teaspoon of table sugar and dissolve it in one 8 oz. glass of cool tap water; stir to dissolve. Line up five empty glasses and fill them as indicated:

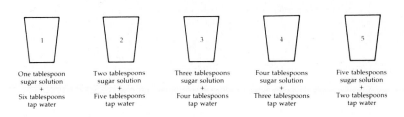

| One tablespoon sugar solution + Six tablespoons tap water | Two tablespoons sugar solution + Five tablespoons tap water | Three tablespoons sugar solution + Four tablespoons tap water | Four tablespoons sugar solution + Three tablespoons tap water | Five tablespoons sugar solution + Two tablespoons tap water |

Now you may begin the trials. Blindfold your observer and present a solution (as specified below). The observer tastes a small sip and says "yes" if sweetness is detected and "no" if sweetness is not detected. Then the observer spits out the solution, rinses with tap water for about 20 seconds, and repeats the procedure with the next trial in the series. Continue a series until your observer shifts responses from "yes" to "no" or from "no" to "yes." When the shift occurs, begin the next series.

Below is a table indicating the order in which you should present the solutions. For example, begin the first series with Solution 1 because this has an asterisk. Begin the second series with Solution 4, follow with Solution 3, etc. I have recorded my observer's responses; record your observer's responses next to mine. (Incidentally, save any remaining solution for Demonstrations 2.2 and 2.4)

		SERIES NUMBER					
		1	2	3	4	5	6
not very sweet	1	*No *				*No *	
	2	No	No	*No *	No	No	No
	3	No	Yes	No	Yes	Yes	Yes
	4	Yes	*Yes *	Yes	Yes		Yes
very sweet	5				*Yes *		*Yes *
Threshold for each series		3.5 ___	2.5 ___	3.5 ___	2.5 ___	2.5 ___	2.5 ___

The overall threshold equals the average of the midpoints (thresholds) calculated for the individual series. The overall threshold for my observer was 2.8. What is the overall threshold for your observer?

Some people make **errors of habituation**; they operate on the principle that "the stimulus is likely to be the same as last time, so I'll keep giving the same answer." Thus, they tend to keep saying no on ascending series and to keep saying yes on descending series for some time after it is appropriate to change their response pattern. Other people make **errors of anticipation**; they operate on the opposite principle, that "the stimulus is likely to be different from last time, so I'll change my answer." As a result, they "jump the gun." On ascending series they claim that they can detect the stimulus, when in fact they can't quite. On descending series, they claim that they can no longer detect the stimulus when in fact they still can.

How can we correct for errors of habituation and errors of anticipation? If we assume that a person who makes errors of habituation is just as likely to make them on ascending series as on descending series, the errors will cancel each other out. The threshold we obtain will be too high on ascending series, but it will be too low on descending series. If the two are averaged, therefore, we should end up with an accurate threshold. The same kind of cancellation of errors will work for errors of anticipation.

One other human factor can contaminate the method of limits and produce an inaccurate threshold, unless it is controlled. Suppose, in Demonstration 2.1, that every ascending series started with Cup 1. Tasters might notice on the first series that the sugar is detectable by the third cup. If every series began with that same stimulus, when tasters reach the third cup again, they might simply shout "I taste it" without even paying attention to the taste. If we are inconsistent about the starting point for each series, however, participants in a psychophysics study cannot get away with simply counting trials. Thus, the ascending series sometimes begins with Cup 1 and sometimes with Cup 2, and the descending series begins with either Cup 4 or Cup 5.

In Demonstration 2.1 we include only six series of trials. A formal psychophysics experiment would be more likely to have 100 series, however. Notice that the method of limits is an appropriate name because a series of trials stops when the observer reaches a limit and changes the responses either from yes to no or from no to yes.

The method of limits can be modified to meet the needs of the experiment. For example, if you want to measure the threshold for perceiving a spot of light when a person has been adapted to darkness, it would be a mistake to include series of trials that begin with an intense light. Instead, you would use series of trials that begin with a low-intensity light and present increasingly more intense lights; this method is called the **ascending method of limits**.

Another variation of the method of limits asks observers to identify a stimulus, not merely to detect it. Using the ascending method of limits, the experimenter presents increasing amounts of the stimulus until the observers can supply a label. For example, in a study on taste an observer would be required to tell whether a substance was salty, bitter, sweet, or sour. In a study on vision an observer might be instructed to indicate whether the orientation of a line is vertical, horizontal, or diagonal. In the "pure" method of limits the observer must simply tell us whether a stimulus is present or absent. When the method of limits is used in conjunction with **identification**, the observer must be able to classisfy the stimulus as being one of two or more alternatives (Thomas, 1985). The familiar Snellen eye chart (Figure 4.1) is an application of variations of the method of limits. The tester begins with a row of large letters and presents smaller letters until the letters are too small to be recognized. Thus, the descending method of limits is used. In addition, the task requires identification of letters, rather than simple "yes" or "no" responses.

We have discussed the method of limits in some detail. Now let's move on to the second classical method of measuring detection thresholds, which is called the method of adjustment.

Method of Adjustment

In the **method of adjustment** the observer—rather than the experimenter—adjusts the intensity of the stimulus. Typically, the observer makes adjustments that are continuous—for example, by adjusting a knob—rather than discrete—for example, by tasting separate solutions containing different amounts of a substance.

This method can be used to obtain a threshold very quickly, and so it may be used to locate an approximate threshold. However, many observers tend to be sloppy when they use this method, and there is great variation from one observer to the next. Consequently, psychophysicists use it less than other methods. Notice, though, that the method of adjustment is what you use most often in everyday life, for example, when you adjust the knob on your radio so that the sound is barely audible.

Usually, in the method of adjustment the experimenter begins half the trials with a stimulus level far above threshold (descending series) and half the trials with a stimulus level far below threshold (ascending series). However, this precaution is not quite so necessary as in the method of limits; in the method of adjustment, observers spontaneously go both above and below the threshold as they approach their final decision on the threshold.

Similarly, the other problems discussed in connection with the method of limits are less important for the method of adjustment. People will be less likely to show errors of habituation and errors of anticipation, and they will be less likely to change the response on a predetermined trial. After all, they can adjust the stimulus themselves, at their own preferred rate, and they can make fine adjustments as they fluctuate on either side of the threshold.

Method of Constant Stimuli

In the **method of constant stimuli** the stimuli are presented in random order, as in Demonstration 2.2. The experimenter usually selects between five and nine stimuli, such that the weakest stimulus is clearly below threshold and the strongest stimulus is clearly above threshold. (As you can imagine, these values must be chosen after pretesting with a speedy

method such as the method of adjustment.) Notice that the name *constant stimuli* is appropriate because the researchers select a constant set of stimuli before the testing begins, and they present these stimuli a constant number of times during testing.

In Demonstration 2.2 each of the five solutions is presented four times. In contrast, in a formal psychophysics experiment each stimulus might be presented 100 times (Gescheider, 1985). The method of constant stimuli is extremely time consuming, particularly because the stimuli must be pretested. However, this method is preferred when psychophysicists want to obtain a careful measurement of a threshold, since it eliminates some biases in the other two methods. For example, when the stimuli are presented in random order, the observer does not know what kind of stimulus to expect on the next trial, unlike in the method of limits or the method of adjustment. Consequently, the method of constant stimuli does not need to take special precautions to correct for problems such as errors of habituation and errors of anticipation.

Let's review these three methods by describing how each method would be used to measure the threshold for perceiving a low-intensity tone. To use the *method of limits*, the experimenter begins by presenting the tone at an intensity high enough that the observer is certain to say, "Yes, I hear it." Then the experimenter presents weaker and weaker tones until the observer reports, "No, I can't hear it." On alternate trials the experimenter begins with a low-intensity tone and increases the intensity until the observer says, "Yes, I hear it."

To use the *method of adjustment*, the observer makes adjustments in the intensity of the tone by perhaps turning a knob. On half the trials the observer begins with a high-intensity tone and turns the knob until it is inaudible. On the other half of the trials the observer begins with a low-intensity tone and turns the knob until it is audible.

To use the *method of constant stimuli*, the experimenter presents in random order a variety of tones having differing intensities.

Demonstration 2.2

Using the Method of Constant Stimuli to Measure Detection Threshold

In this demonstration you will use the method of constant stimuli to measure the ability to detect sweetness. Use the solutions from Demonstration 2.1 or mix up more according to those instructions. Blindfold an observer. The observer will sip, report, spit, and rinse as in the previous demonstration. However, you will present the solutions in random order, as indicated below. Again record your observer's responses next to my observer's responses.

TRIAL	SOLUTION NUMBER	RESPONSE	TRIAL	(TRIALS, CONTINUED) SOLUTION NUMBER	RESPONSE
1	2	No	11	5	Yes
2	5	Yes	12	4	Yes
3	4	Yes	13	1	No
4	1	No	14	2	No
5	3	Yes	15	3	Yes
6	2	No	16	2	Yes
7	4	Yes	17	5	Yes
8	1	No	18	1	No
9	5	Yes	19	4	Yes
10	3	No	20	3	Yes

SUMMARY TABLE

SOLUTION NUMBER	NUMBER OF "YES" RESPONSES	PROPORTION OF "YES" RESPONSES
1	0	.00
2	1	.25
3	3	.75
4	4	1.00
5	4	1.00

Now plot the proportion of "Yes" responses below, as I have done. Notice where the horizontal line corresponding to .50 "Yes" responses crosses the line you make to connect the plotted proportion. This is the threshold.

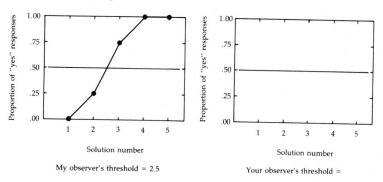

My observer's threshold = 2.5   Your observer's threshold =

Each time a tone is presented, the observer reports either "No, I can't hear it" or "Yes, I can hear it."

How do experimenters decide which method to use? The method of constant stimuli provides the most reliable data, and it is relatively free of biases. However, a disadvantage is that the experimenter needs to pretest the stimuli to locate stimuli at near-threshold levels. The method of adjustment produces errors and is typically used only for stimuli that are continuously adjustable; however, it may be useful for pretesting the stimuli that will be used with the method of constant stimuli. The method of limits requires less preplanning than the method of constant stimuli and may be the choice of an experimenter who wants fairly reliable thresholds without too much investment of time.

Signal Detection Theory

The three classical psychophysics methods that we have examined have a common goal: locating a threshold. The implication is that a certain stimulus intensity can be determined that constitutes a borderline between stimuli that can be detected and those that cannot. More recent signal detection theory criticizes the notion of a fixed threshold, since thresholds vary with the situation.

A student provided an example of situational factors that can determine how an observer responds (Edington, 1979). He had applied for a job, and the manager had said that he would call between 3:30 and 4:00 on a particular afternoon. Within that half-hour period the student thought that he heard the phone ring two or three times. In other words, the response "I can hear it" was much more likely than it would have been in other circumstances. The "I can hear it" response was more frequent for two reasons: (1) the high probability that the phone would actually ring during that period and (2) the important benefits of answering the phone if it did actually ring, as opposed to the substantial harm in not answering if it did ring. In other words, the probability of saying "I de-

tect a stimulus" is influenced by people's decision-making strategies.

Classical theories about thresholds would not predict that factors such as expectation and motivation would influence observers' responses. However, consistent with one of the themes of this book, signal detection theory stresses the importance of top-down processing. Concepts are critical determinants of perceptions.

Signal detection theory, or **SDT**, argues that the thresholds obtained by classical psychophysics methods measure not only the observer's sensitivity but also his or her decision-making strategy or criterion (Baird & Noma, 1978; Gescheider, 1985; Green & Swets, 1966). The **sensitivity measure** depends upon two factors, the intensity of the stimulus and the sensitivity of the observer. The sensitivity measure would be high in a study on hearing when the stimulus is a very loud tone and when the observer has excellent hearing. The sensitivity measure would be low if the stimulus were a weak tone or the observer had impaired hearing.

The **criterion** measures the observer's willingness to say "I detect the stimulus" when he or she is uncertain about whether the stimulus has been presented. For example, suppose that you are waiting for the subway and you know that another train left one minute ago. Your criterion would be different than if you know that the last train had left 20 minutes earlier. In signal detection theory the criterion is symbolized by the Greek letter β (beta).

The criterion that an observer selects depends upon several factors. An important one is the probability that the stimulus will occur. For example, the stimulus "light from an approaching subway train" is more likely or probable if the last train left 20 minutes earlier than if it left one minute earlier.

Another important determinant of the criterion is the **payoff**, the rewards and punishments associated with a particular response. From the beginning of SDT, theorists assumed that observers can be persuaded to adjust their criterion to earn more money (von Winterfeldt & Edwards, 1982). For example, suppose I say that I will pay you 50¢ every time you correctly report seeing a light and that you will pay me 10¢ every time you report seeing a light that was never presented. You would calculate the payoff and say "I see it" if there is any chance that the light had been presented.

Contrast this pattern of responding with your behavior if I tell you that I will pay you 50¢ every time you correctly report that you *didn't* see a light that was not presented and you will pay me 10¢ every time you fail to report seeing a light that was presented. Wouldn't you shift your criterion dramatically so that you would say "I see it" only if you were convinced that the light had been presented? Notice that the criterion is determined by our strategies in making decisions rather than our perceptual sensitivity. The criterion and the sensitivity combine to determine how we respond in a psychophysics study.

We should mention, incidentally, that SDT is not an alternate procedure for determining thresholds. In fact, we *cannot* calculate thresholds with this method. SDT has, however, contributed to understanding some problems in measuring thresholds with classical methods. For example, experimenters sometimes modify the classical methods by introducing so-called catch trials in which no stimulus is presented. Nonetheless, observers often report that they detect the stimulus on these trials. SDT explains that these errors occur because the observer is very willing to say, "I detect the stimulus."

Let us examine SDT in more detail by discussing situations involving an observer who must listen for a weak tone, although SDT can be applied equally well to vision, the skin senses, smell, and taste. The topics include (1) outcomes of a signal detection trial, (2) receiver operating characteristic curves, and (3) probability distributions.

Outcomes of a Signal Detection Trial

In a signal detection experiment the experimenter presents a stimulus or **signal** that is weak and difficult to detect. Thus the signal has an intensity close to the observer's threshold. Usually, the intensity of the signal remains constant throughout a single testing session, unlike the situation in the classical psychophysics methods. Furthermore, the experimenter presents the signal on some trials and does not present the signal on other trials. For example, the experimenter might decide to present the signal on 50% of the trials in a given session.

Examine Table 2.2. Notice that the signal can be either present or absent. In the best of all possible worlds the observer says "Yes, I hear it" whenever the signal is present and "No, I don't hear it" whenever the signal is absent.

In reality, however, observers make mistakes. As Table 2.2 shows, there can be two different kinds of mistakes. Observers sometimes think that they hear a signal when the signal is absent, and they sometimes think that they do not hear a signal when the signal is present. Notice that each of the four pos-

Table 2.2 Four Possible Outcomes of a Signal Detection Trial

		What Did the Observer Respond?	
		"Yes, I hear it"	*"No, I don't hear it"*
Was the signal present or absent?	Present	hit (correct)	miss (mistake)
	Absent	false alarm (mistake)	correct rejection (correct)

sible outcomes of a signal detection trial has a descriptive name. Spend some time memorizing these names, because we will use them in our discussion of SDT. Imagine yourself trying to decide whether your doorbell just rang. Notice that your decision could represent a **hit** or a **correct rejection** (two kinds of correct decisions) or a **false alarm** or a **miss** (two kinds of mistakes).

In a typical signal detection experiment an observer listens for a tone that has a constant intensity and frequency. The experimenter presents the tone on 50% of the trials and presents no tone on the other 50% of the trials. Table 2.3 shows how often each of the four possible outcomes might occur in a hypothetical experiment. Notice that when the signal is really present, the observer reports it 70% of the time. However, when the signal is absent, the observer reports it (incorrectly) 32% of the time.

Remember that one factor influencing the criterion is the probability that the stimulus will occur. Table 2.3 presented a situation in which the probability of the stimulus was .50. If the probability of the stimulus changes, then the observer's criterion can also change. As a consequence, the observer will change the frequency of reporting the stimulus. Table 2.4 shows some representative frequencies as a function of stimulus probability.

It is traditional in signal detection tables to list only the hit and false alarm rates. The miss rate can readily be calculated by subtracting the hit rate from 1.00. For example, when the probability of a signal is .10, the probability of a hit is .32; therefore the probability of a miss is 1.00 − .32, or .68. Similarly, the correct rejection rate can be calculated by subtracting the false alarm rate from 1.00. When the probability of a signal is .10, the correct rejection rate is 1.00 − .08, or .92.

Receiver Operating Characteristic Curves

The data from signal detection experiments are often depicted in a **receiver operating characteristic curve** (**ROC curve**), which shows the relationship between the probability of a hit and the probability of a false alarm. Figure 2.3 shows a typical ROC curve. The data in an ROC curve are obtained from many sessions in which the experimenter has manipulated the observer's criterion.

For any given ROC curve, the sensitivity is constant; that is, the tone does not increase or decrease in intensity and the observer does not change in perceptual ability. The observer's *criterion* changes within an ROC curve, however, either because the experimenter manipulates the probability of the tone's occurrence (as in Table 2.4) or because the experimenter manipulates the payoffs (for example, by varying the amount of money paid for each hit or subtracted for each false alarm). Each point along a given ROC curve represents a different criterion. For example, Figure 2.3 shows an ROC curve plotted for the data from Table 2.4. The left-hand portion of any ROC curve represents a strict criterion in which the observer is very likely to say "No, I don't hear it" and is very unlikely to say "Yes, I hear it." In contrast, the right-hand portion of any ROC curve represents a liberal

---

Table 2.3   Percentages of Hits and Misses When Signal Was Present and False Alarms and Correct Rejections When Signal Was Absent (Hypothetical Experiment)

		What Did the Observer Respond?	
		"Yes, I hear it"	*"No, I don't hear it"*
Was the signal	Present	hit = .70	miss = .30
present or absent?	Absent	false alarm = .32	correct rejection = .68

Table 2.4 Probability of a Hit or a False Alarm, as Signal Probability Increases from .10 to .90 (Hypothetical Experiment)

	Probability	
	Hit	*False Alarm*
.10	.32	.08
.20	.42	.12
.30	.52	.17
.40	.62	.25
.50	.70	.32
.60	.78	.41
.70	.84	.50
.80	.90	.61
.90	.93	.73

Probability of a Signal

moves from left to right (just the opposite of the situation in politics).

Suppose the signal detection experiment is repeated with a more intense tone (or a more sensitive observer). Again the experimenter manipulates the probability of the tone's occurrence so that the observer changes his or her criterion. In this case the resulting ROC curve might resemble Curve A in Figure 2.4. For comparison's sake, Curve B is taken from Figure 2.3. Curve C represents either a weaker tone or a less sensitive observer. Compare the three curves. Notice that for any given false alarm rate, the three curves differ enormously with respect to the probability of a hit. For example, when the probability of a false alarm is .20, Curve A has a very high hit rate (.88), Curve B has a medium hit rate (.53), and Curve C has a low hit rate (.32).

Notice that Curves A, B, and C in Figure 2.4 are labeled $d' = 2.0$, $d' = 1.0$, and $d' = .5$, respectively. The measure d' (or d-prime) is an index of sensitivity; this measure tells

criterion in which the observer is very unlikely to say "No, I don't hear it" and is very likely to say "Yes, I hear it." The criterion becomes increasingly liberal as the curve

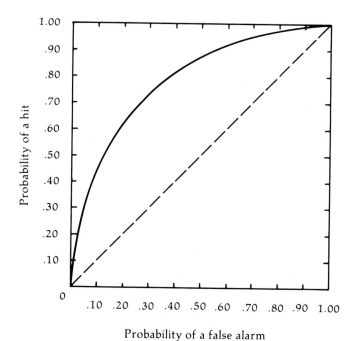

Figure 2.3 A receiver operating characteristic (ROC) curve.

about the loudness of the tone or the sensitivity of the observer. When d' is 0, the observer is guessing; hits and false alarms occur equally often. A large d' (Curve A in Figure 2.4) means that the tone is loud or the observer is sensitive; with a large d' the observer has a high hit rate and a low false alarm rate.

Psychologists calculate the number of hits and false alarms obtained in an experiment and plot them on a graph. Then they calculate d' from formulas or by comparing their ROC curves with published curves (for example, Baird & Noma, 1978; Gescheider, 1985). Try Demonstration 2.3 to make certain that you know how to plot and interpret an ROC curve.

Probability Distributions

So far, we have discussed two major points: (1) how a signal detection trial can produce a hit, a miss, a false alarm, or a correct rejection and (2) how the proportion of hits and false alarms can be plotted in a ROC curve. Now we will look at detection from a more theoretical perspective. Specifically, we need to

examine the probability distributions for noise and signal plus noise situations.

Imagine that you are sitting in a room, trying to decide whether you heard a car drive up. We refer to situations in which no signal occurs as **noise** trials. Thus if a car did *not* drive up, you experienced a noise trial in which the only sounds were the irrelevant background noises from the environment and the internal noises that your body makes. (Notice that we can have noise in the other perceptual systems as well; irrelevant visual stimuli, for example, constitute visual noise.) Noise refers to irrelevant stimuli that might be mistaken for the signal.

On the other hand, it is possible that the car really did drive up. We would refer to this situation as a **signal + noise** trial (pronounce the + as "plus"), because the appropriate signal (the car sound) really did occur, in addition to all the irrelevant noise.

Figure 2.5 shows a hypothetical graph of the two possible situations, *noise* and *signal + noise*. Notice that each curve is in the shape of a **probability distribution**, which shows

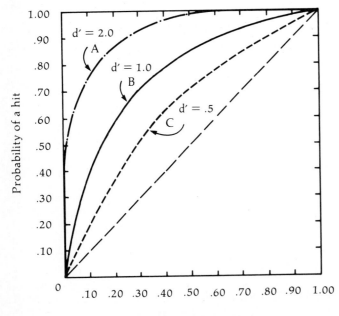

Figure 2.4 Three receiver operating characteristic curves.

Demonstration 2.3

Understanding ROC Curves

The purpose of this demonstration is to make certain that you know how to plot and interpret ROC curves. Suppose that you have gathered the data shown below at left from an observer by varying the probability of a signal's occurrence. Plot the data in the figure, and then answer the questions.

PROBABILITY OF A HIT	PROBABILITY OF A FALSE ALARM
.52	.05
.71	.15
.82	.30
.90	.42
.92	.58

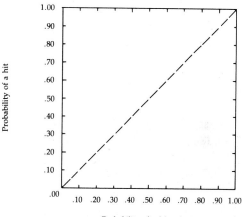

Questions about the ROC curve (answers at bottom of the demonstration):

1. Comparing your curve with the curves in Figure 2.4, what would you estimate is your d'?

2. What method, other than changing the probability of the signal, could also have been used to get your observer to change his or her criterion?

3. Notice the diagonal line in the figure. If an observer had that kind of performance, would this person be more or less sensitive than your observer?

4. Is there any point along the curve at which the false alarm rate is higher than the hit rate?

5. Does your observer's sensitivity vary from one situation to the next for the points you have plotted in the figure? If not, what does vary?

6. As the probability of a hit increases, does the probability of a false alarm increase, decrease, or stay the same?

Answers: 1. The d' is approximately 1.5. 2. You could pay money for hits and/or subtract money for false alarms. 3. Less sensitive; in fact, this person would be responding at a chance level. 4. No, the hit rate is always higher. 5. No, the sensitivity does not vary; the criterion varies. 6. The probability of a false alarm increases.

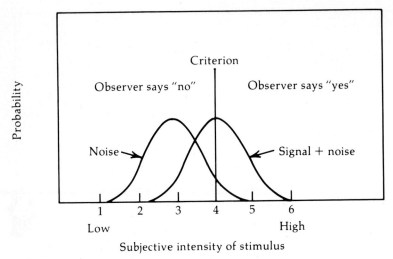

Figure 2.5 Hypothetical graph of noise and signal + noise distributions in signal detection (fairly high criterion).

the probability of various sound intensities. As these distributions indicate, we cannot list just a single value for the loudness of the noise or the signal + noise situations. After all, loudness varies from one moment to the next. (For example, you may hear your roommate's ticking wristwatch one moment, but it may be inaudible the next moment.) However, notice that the intensity of the noise fluctuates around a particular average level. Similarly, the intensity of the signal + noise fluctuates around another, higher average level.

Notice that if the subjective intensity of the stimulus is fairly low, say around 2 or 3, the stimulus is most likely to represent just noise; there is only a negligible portion of the signal + noise distribution in this region. When the subjective intensity of the stimulus is somewhat higher, perhaps 3.5, the stimulus is equally likely to represent either noise or signal + noise. However, as the subjective intensity of the stimulus increases further to 5 and beyond, the stimulus is likely to represent signal + noise.

In Figure 2.5 the noise curve and the signal + noise curve overlap so that it is difficult to tell the difference between the situations with only noise and those with signal +

noise. The size of this overlap corresponds to d', the measure of sensitivity discussed earlier. Figure 2.5 shows a d' of 2.0. For comparison's sake, Figure 2.6 illustrates d's ranging between .5 and 2.0. With the lower d's it is even more difficult to tell the difference between the situations with only noise and those with signal + noise. Use Figure 2.4 to compare these noise and signal + noise distributions with the corresponding ROC curves.

Figure 2.5 tells about d', sensitivity. Figure 2.5 also shows a vertical line labeled *criterion*, and the figure's title indicates that this graph shows a situation in which the criterion is fairly high, or strict. The observer says "Yes, I hear it" when the subjective intensity of the stimulus is loud enough to exceed his or her personal criterion. In the situation represented in Figure 2.5, the observer will usually say, "No, I don't hear it." Whenever the intensity is below that criterion line, the observer says, "No, I don't hear it." Notice in Figure 2.5 that when the observer says "I hear it," he or she can be either correct (a hit because there was signal + noise) or incorrect (a false alarm because there was only noise). Similarly, an observer who says "I don't hear it" may be either correct (a correct rejection)

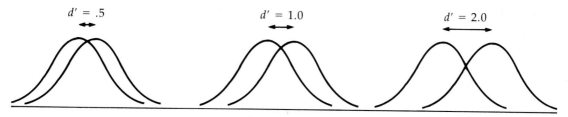

Figure 2.6 Noise and signal + noise distributions for three different *d*'s.

or incorrect (a miss). Thus the four regions of the two curves correspond to the four terms in Table 2.2.

Figure 2.5 shows a situation in which a person has set a fairly high criterion; this person says "I hear it" only if he or she is fairly certain that the signal has occurred. Notice in this case that hits occur on only half the trials in which the signal is presented. Furthermore, false alarms rarely occur.

Figure 2.7 shows a situation in which the *d'* is the same as in Figure 2.5, but the person has set a fairly low criterion; this person says "I hear it" if there is even the slightest chance that the signal has occurred. In this case both hits and false alarms occur often. Think about situations in which you set the criterion fairly

low. For example, suppose that you know that a friend should be driving by to pick you up in the next few minutes. Do you leap up at the slightest rustle of leaves or the faintest hint of anything with four wheels? Similarly, the student described earlier in his agonizing wait for the phone call about the job had also set a low or liberal criterion for saying, "Yes, I hear it."

What kind of observer is best with respect to sensitivity and criterion? Clearly, it is best to have a large *d'*—that is, noise and signal + noise curves as separate as possible. With a large *d'* the ratio between the hit rate and the false alarm rate is large. However, is it better to set your criterion high or low? This question has no easy answer because you

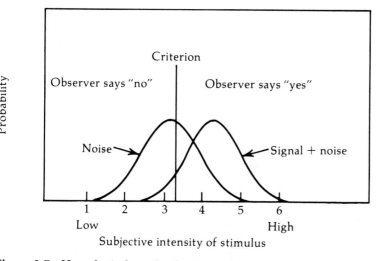

Figure 2.7 Hypothetical graph of noise and signal + noise distributions in signal detection (fairly low criterion).

must consider the payoff, the relative advantages and disadvantages, of each outcome. The advantage of a low or liberal criterion is a high hit rate, which is good, but a high false alarm rate, which is bad. You can lower that false alarm rate by setting a higher or stricter criterion. That low false alarm rate is good, but you now have a low hit rate, which is bad. Notice that the same trade-off between hit rate and false alarm rate can be demonstrated on the ROC curve in Figure 2.3. It may be helpful to think of situations in which you would want a low criterion for detecting a stimulus and to identify how you would feel about a hit, false alarm, correct rejection, and miss. Repeat this process with situations in which you would want a high criterion.

▶ IN-DEPTH:
USING SIGNAL DETECTION THEORY TO ASSESS PAIN PERCEPTION

We have stressed that an advantage of signal detection theory is that it allows us to measure not only the observer's sensitivity but also decision-making strategy. In many psychophysical studies, decision-making strategies may not be crucial. In pain perception research, however, investigators must consider two possibilities when a person seems to be able to tolerate pain. One possibility is that the person is not very sensitive to pain; you could run over this person's foot with a Greyhound bus, and he or she might simply wince. Another possibility, however, is that this person *feels* the pain but for any of a variety of reasons does not want to say, "It hurts." If standard psychophysical techniques are used to explore pain, we cannot know whether pain tolerance is due to low sensitivity or a high criterion, requiring intense pain before complaining.

SDT has been used in pain research for about two decades. One early application of SDT was in the study of placebos. A placebo is an inactive substance, such as a sugar pill, that a patient believes is a medication. If the patient believes that the pill should relieve pain, then he or she is likely to report less

pain after swallowing it. Several researchers wondered whether placebos influence β, the criterion for reporting pain, or whether they influence d', the sensitivity to pain (Clark, 1969; Feather, Chapman, & Fisher, 1972). In general, research showed that the placebo does not influence d'; people actually experience the same amount of pain after they have swallowed the sugar pill. Instead, the placebo appears to influence β. That is, people who have swallowed the sugar pill are somehow inhibited about reporting pain, even though they feel it.

Other research has examined whether the effects of individual differences and experimental instructions can be traced to d' or β. Dougher (1979), for example, was interested in the pain perceptions of high- and low-anxiety people. He asked 500 students in an introductory psychology class to take the Taylor Manifest Anxiety Scale, a standardized test that assesses a person's characteristic level of anxiety. From those 500 students, he selected 48 of the most anxious people and 48 of the least anxious people. Dougher also gave half of each group different sets of instructions. Half were told that people who have emotional problems tend to report pain too quickly; the other half were told that people who have emotional problems are reluctant to report pain.

Dougher's painful stimulus was a dull Lucite knife edge, which was adjusted to apply continuous pressure on the finger. Participants were asked to rate their pain experiences; the top two categories ("slight pain" and "definite pain") were considered reports of pain. Furthermore, 10 seconds of the lightest pressure was considered "noise" (no pain), whereas 30 seconds of the heaviest pressure was considered "signal" (pain). By using standard formulas, measures of d' and β were calculated for each of the four groups (two anxiety groups, each receiving one of two kinds of instructions).

The results showed that the four groups were nearly identical in their sensitivity. In other words, high-anxiety people did not differ from low-anxiety people in their sensory experience of pain. Similarly, people who received instructions encouraging them to report pain quickly did not differ in sensitivity from those whose instructions encouraged them to hold back in reporting pain. The four groups were remarkably different, however, in their criteria for reporting pain. In Figure 2.8, low numbers indicate that the criterion for saying "I feel pain" is very low; these people frequently report pain. Notice that the people who are most likely to report pain are the high-anxiety people who have been told, essentially, that it's fine to complain. The people who are least likely to report pain are the low-anxiety people who have been told to be brave. In this case, then, both anxiety and instructions influenced criterion, but not sensitivity.

By now you might have the impression that medication, individual differences, and

instructions may influence only criterion. Malow, Grimm, and Olson (1980) located a group of people who differed from a control group in terms of both sensitivity and criterion. These people have a disorder called myofascial pain dysfunction (MPD), which involves pain in the joints surrounding the jaw; the disorder is often associated with emotional stress and anxiety. Previous research had demonstrated that MPD patients show a greater pain reaction than nonpatients. Malow and his coauthors wondered whether this abnormal reaction could be traced to criterion or sensitivity. They used SDT methods to contrast MPD patients with nonpatients.

Malow and his colleagues used the same kind of dull-knife technique for inducing pain that Dougher had employed. The "noise"

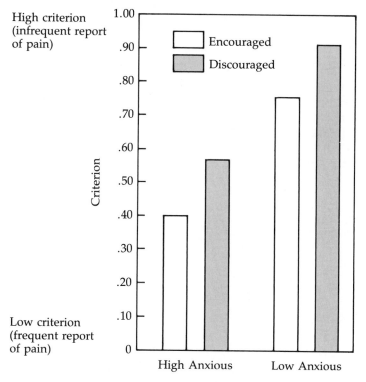

Figure 2.8 Response criteria for reporting pain, as a function of anxiety level and whether the participant was encouraged about or discouraged from reporting pain. Low numbers indicate frequent report of pain. (Based on Dougher, 1979.)

stimulus was defined as the least painful, and the "signal" stimulus was defined as the most painful stimulus. The results demonstrated that MPD patients were more sensitive to pain than were nonpatients, and they also differed in criterion; that is, they were likely to report a stimulus as painful that a nonpatient would consider painless. People who have MPD, then, have two reasons to be more likely than other people to say, "It hurts." ■

We have seen that signal detection theory provides two kinds of information about the perceptual responses of individuals. For example, criteria, but not sensitivity, differ for (1) placebo takers and people who have not taken placebos, (2) high- and low-anxiety people, and (3) people who have been encouraged to report pain and people who have been encouraged not to report it. However, both criteria and sensitivity differ for people with MPD versus nonpatients.

This discussion should alert you to the value of the signal detection method in sorting out the causes of differences between two groups. You may, for example, read about a study that uses classical psychophysical techniques in a situation where SDT would provide more information. For example, consider an interesting study by Jaremko, Crusco, and Lau (1983). These researchers found that participants who had publicly described a painful experience had lower pain thresholds than did those participants who did not describe the pain. It's intriguing to speculate whether those who had described the pain were likely to report "It's painful" because talking about pain had made them (1) more sensitive to pain or (2) more willing to *report* that they detected pain.

Summary: Measuring Responses to Low-Intensity Stimuli

1. Psychophysics is the study of the relationship between physical stimuli and the psychological reactions to them.
2. Psychologists are interested in psychophysics because it is an important area of inquiry in itself, because it is a useful tool for studying sensation and perception,

because these techniques can be applied to other areas of psychology, and because it can be applied in solving everyday environmental and commercial problems.
3. The classical psychophysics methods measure detection thresholds, the smallest amount of energy required for the stimulus to be reported 50% of the time. The transition between nondetection and detection is gradual rather than abrupt.
4. The method of limits involves presenting systematically increasing or decreasing amounts of a stimulus. It provides a fairly reliable threshold without too much time investment.
5. The method of limits can use both ascending and descending series to correct for errors of habituation and errors of anticipation. The series do not begin with the same starting point every time; this precaution guards against observers' merely counting trials before reporting detection.
6. The method of limits can be modified by using only the ascending method of limits or by using the identification method.
7. The method of adjustment involves the observer's adjusting the intensity of the stimulus until it is barely detectable. It provides a threshold very rapidly, but errors are more likely than with the other two methods.
8. The method of constant stimuli involves presenting near-threshold stimuli in random order. It provides a highly accurate threshold, but it is time consuming.
9. Signal detection theory measures both sensitivity and criterion.
10. Sensitivity depends upon stimulus intensity and the sensitivity of the observer.
11. The criterion, which measures willingness to report the stimulus, depends upon factors such as probability of stimulus occurrence and payoff (rewards and punishments).
12. The outcome of a signal detection trial can be a hit, a correct rejection, a false alarm, or a miss.
13. The probability of each of these four outcomes depends upon the sensitivity measure, d', and the criterion measure, β.

14. ROC curves can be used to plot the proportion of hits and false alarms. Each separate ROC curve represents a different d'.

15. Signal detection theory can also be represented in terms of probability distributions for trials in which signal + noise occurred and for trials in which only noise occurred.

16. As an observer, it is best to have a large d', but whether the criterion is high or low should be decided on the basis of the payoff.

17. Signal detection theory is particularly useful in research on pain perception to determine whether differences in reports of pain can be attributed to criteria or to sensitivity.

18. Results of this research show that criteria, not sensitivity, differ for (1) placebo takers versus people who haven't taken placebos, (2) high- versus low-anxiety people, and (3) people who have been encouraged to report pain versus people who have been encouraged not to report it.

19. Both criteria and sensitivity differ for people with myofascial pain dysfunction versus nonpatients.

MEASURING RESPONSES TO MORE INTENSE STIMULI

So far the discussion of psychophysics has focused on how people respond to low-intensity stimuli such as dim lights and weak tones. In this section, attention shifts to the measurement of stimuli that can be easily detected. These more intense stimuli figure prominently in everyday experience. We usually have no trouble detecting the vinegar in the hot-and-sour soup at the Chinese restaurant. Instead, the question is whether the Pink Pearl Restaurant uses more vinegar than the Golden Dragon Restaurant and, if so, is that difference just barely noticeable or very clearly noticeable. This section will examine (1) the classical psychophysical measurement of discrimination, (2) the relationship between the physical intensity of the stimulus and the psychological reaction of the observer, and (3) multidimensional scaling.

Classical Psychophysical Measurement of Discrimination

In **discrimination** studies researchers try to determine the smallest amount that a stimulus must be changed to be perceived as just noticeably different. Observers' discrimination ability is measured by a **difference threshold**, defined as the smallest change in a stimulus that is required to produce a difference noticeable 50% of the time. For example, suppose you manufacture candy bars and you want to produce a new version of a popular favorite that is noticeably larger, but you don't want it too big because of the expense. You could ask people to make judgments about a range of sizes to determine what size is perceived to be larger 50% of the time. You would then know that your new candy bar would have to be at least that big.

In a discrimination experiment the **standard stimulus** remains constant, whereas the **comparison stimulus** varies. In general the comparison stimulus changes according to a specified schedule, and the experimenter records how much change is necessary before the observer notices that the comparison stimulus is different from the standard stimulus. The term *difference threshold* was introduced earlier, and it can be used in defining another important term. A difference threshold is the amount of change in a physical stimulus required to produce a **just noticeable difference** (jnd) in the psychological sensation. For example, if the intensity of the physical stimulus is 10 units, and the stimulus has to be increased to 12 units to produce a just barely noticeable change in the sensation, the difference threshold of 2 units would correspond to one jnd (Gescheider, 1985). Notice that the term *difference threshold* refers to the physical stimulus, whereas the term *jnd* refers to the psychological reaction.

The phrase *just noticeable difference* or its abbreviation, jnd, can be useful in everyday life. If your college installs new lights on campus but the change in apparent brightness is only minimal, you could describe the situation as being one jnd brighter. You might notice that when you use super gas rather than regular gas your car runs about one jnd more smoothly.

One additional term should be mentioned before discussing the measurement of discrimination. The **point of subjective equality** is the value of the comparison stimulus the observer considers equal to the value of the standard stimulus; as the name implies, it is the point where the two stimuli are subjectively equal (Baird & Noma, 1978).

Remember the three classical methods for measuring detection thresholds: the method of limits, the method of adjustment, and the method of constant stimuli. Each of these methods can also be adapted to measure discrimination. We will describe these methods briefly; details can be found elsewhere (Baird & Noma, 1978; Engen, 1971; Matlin, 1979).

In the **method of limits for measuring discrimination** the standard stimulus remains the same, and the comparison stimulus varies from low to high on some series of trials and from high to low on others. For example, suppose that you want to examine the discrimination of pitch. Specifically, you want to determine how much change you can make in the comparison stimulus before the observer notices that it is different from a 1000 Hz standard stimulus. On some series of trials you present comparison stimuli that increase in frequency from, say, 950 to 1050 Hz. On other series of trials you present comparison stimuli that decrease in frequency from 1050 Hz to 950 Hz. Your observer must reply whether the comparison stimulus is higher pitched, lower pitched, or the same as the standard stimulus. The calculation of the just noticeable difference involves noticing the frequency of the comparison stimulus at which the judgments change from "higher than" to "same as" and the frequency at which they change from "same as" to "lower than."

In the **method of adjustment for measuring discrimination** the observer adjusts the comparison stimulus until the comparison stimulus seems to match the standard stimulus. The observer repeats this adjustment many times. Consequently, we have a large number of selections of comparison stimuli

that the observer believes are equivalent to the standard stimulus. For example, suppose you want to examine discrimination for tones of different frequencies and the standard stimulus is a 1000 Hz tone. An observer might select a 995 Hz stimulus the first time, a 1003 Hz stimulus the second time, and so forth. The method of adjustment yields several measures of discrimination, but a common measure is a statistical calculation, the standard deviation.

In the **method of constant stimuli for measuring discrimination** the experimenter presents the comparison stimuli in random order and asks the observer to judge whether each comparison stimulus is greater than or less than the standard stimulus. (In some variations the observer can also say that the two stimuli are the same.) In a study on tone discrimination, for example, comparison tones of 1010, 1005, 1000, 995, and 990 Hz might each be presented 100 times for comparison with the 1000 Hz standard stimulus. Demonstration 2.4 shows how the method of constant stimuli for measuring discrimination could be used for tasting sweet solutions. Notice that the just noticeable difference is the size of the difference between the standard stimulus and the comparison stimulus that can be discriminated half the time.

Also, the point of subjective equality is the value of the stimulus on the x-axis that corresponds to .50 on the y-axis. In the example in Demonstration 2.4, that value is exactly 3.0 because the observer made a perfect match between the standard stimulus and the comparison stimulus. The three classical psychophysical techniques can be used to measure discrimination and detection. The advantages and disadvantages of each method were discussed earlier, and the three methods may yield somewhat different results (McKelvie, 1984).

Relationship between Physical Stimuli and Psychological Reactions

Suppose you add 1 ml of vinegar to one glass of water and 2 ml of vinegar to a second glass of water. Does the second solution taste twice

Demonstration 2.4

Using the Method of Constant Stimuli to Measure Discrimination

In this demonstration you will use the method of constant stimuli to measure an observer's ability to judge differences in sweetness. First, take 2 teaspoons of table sugar and dissolve in one 8 oz. glass of cool tap water; stir to dissolve. Line up five empty glasses and fill them as indicated:

Two tablespoons sugar solution + Two tablespoons tap water	2½ tablespoons sugar solution + 1½ tablespoons tap water	3 tablespoons sugar solution + 1 tablespoon tap water	3½ tablespoons sugar solution + ½ tablespoon tap water	4 tablespoons sugar solution + 0 tablespoon tap water

In addition, mix up a "standard stimulus" glass that has the same concentration as Solution 3 by mixing 6 tablespoons sugar solution + 2 tablespoons tap water.

Now you may begin the trials. Blindfold your observer and present a solution (as specified below). The observer tastes a small sip, spits it out, rinses with tap water briefly, then tastes a small sip from a second solution, spits it out, rinses with tap water, and selects one of these two responses: (1) the first was sweeter than the second, or (2) the first was less sweet than the second. (Notice that "same as" responses are not permitted in this particular version.) You sometimes presented the standard stimulus first and sometimes presented the comparison stimulus first, so some of the responses must be "translated" prior to recording. Record whether the comparison stimulus is sweeter or less sweet than the standard stimulus.

Below is a table indicating the order in which you should present the solutions and whether the standard stimulus or the comparison stimulus should be presented first. For example, on Trial 1 you present the standard stimulus first and the comparison stimulus, Solution 4, second. I have recorded my observer's responses; record your observer's responses next to mine.

TRIAL	WHICH STIMULUS IS FIRST?	SOLUTION NUMBER OF COMPARISON STIMULUS	RESPONSE: "THE COMPARISON STIMULUS IS _____ "	
1	standard	4	sweeter	
2	comparison	1	less sweet	
3	standard	3	sweeter	
4	comparison	2	sweeter	
5	standard	5	sweeter	

(continued)

6	comparison	1	less sweet
7	standard	4	sweeter
8	comparison	2	less sweet
9	standard	5	sweeter
10	comparison	3	less sweet
11	standard	1	less sweet
12	comparison	4	sweeter
13	standard	2	less sweet
14	comparison	5	sweeter
15	standard	3	less sweet
16	comparison	4	less sweet
17	standard	1	less sweet
18	comparison	5	sweeter
19	standard	2	less sweet
20	comparison	3	sweeter

Tabulate the number and proportion of the "sweeter" responses supplied for each of the five solutions. Record your observer's responses next to mine.

SOLUTION NUMBER	NUMBER OF TIMES OBSERVER SAID "SWEETER" FOR COMPARISON	PROPORTION OF THE TIME OBSERVER SAID "SWEETER" FOR COMPARISON
1	0	.00
2	1	.25
3	2	.50
4	3	.75
5	4	1.00

Now plot your values in the space on the right; mine are on the left. Record where the horizontal lines corresponding to .25 "sweeter" and .75 "sweeter" cross the curve you make to connect the points. Notice that for my values, the lines cross at 2 and at 4. The just noticeable difference is calculated below; calculate that value for your observer as well.

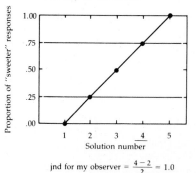

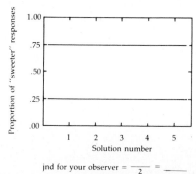

jnd for my observer = $\frac{4-2}{2} = 1.0$

jnd for your observer = $\frac{\quad}{2} = \underline{\quad}$

as sour? Similarly, does a room that has four candles seem four times as bright as a room with only one candle? In this section we will discuss the relationship between the intensity of the physical stimulus and the magnitude of the observer's reaction. For example, what is the relationship between the amount of vinegar in a solution and how sour the solution seems? Also, what is the relationship between the intensity of the light in a room and how bright the light seems? Three prominent researchers have attacked this problem, and we will briefly examine their conclusions.

Weber's Law

In the early 1800s, Ernst Weber examined the relationship between physical stimuli and psychological reactions by focusing on the just noticeable difference. Consider the following problem. Suppose that you can discriminate between a room in which 60 candles are lit and a room in which 61 candles are lit (surprisingly, most people can). Now suppose that 120 candles are lit in a room. Can you discriminate between that room and a room in which 121 candles are lit? After all, we have added the same one candle to make the room brighter. In fact, Weber found that the important determinant of observers' psychological reaction was not the *absolute* size of the change (for example, one candle). Instead, the important determinant was the *relative* size of the change. Specifically, we require one additional candle for *each* 60 candles if we want to notice a difference. If the standard stimulus is 60 candles, we notice the difference when one candle is added. If the standard stimulus is 120 candles, we require 122 candles in the comparison stimulus to notice a difference.

Weber's law states that when I represents stimulus intensity,

$$\frac{\Delta I}{I} = k$$

Verbally, Weber's law says that if we take the change in intensity (Δ or delta is the Greek letter used to symbolize change) and divide

it by the original intensity, we obtain a constant number (k). The constant, k, is called **Weber's fraction**. With candlelit rooms, k equals $\frac{1}{60}$. Notice how you can obtain a k of $\frac{1}{60}$ by dividing the jnd of 1 by an I of 60 or by dividing the jnd of 2 by an I of 120. Notice also that the jnd for 300 candles would be 5.

We have seen that Weber's fraction is $\frac{1}{60}$ when people judge the brightness of a room. However, this fraction varies widely from one judgment task to another. For example, Weber's fraction for judging the pitch of pure tones is $\frac{1}{333}$ (Engen, 1971). That means that we only need to change a tone's pitch by 0.3% ($\frac{1}{333}$) for the difference to be noticeable. However, we are much less competent in noticing changes in taste and smell. For example, Weber's fraction is generally about $\frac{1}{5}$ for judging taste (McBurney, 1978), and it is generally about $\frac{1}{4}$ for judging smells (Engen, 1971). If a particular solution contains 5 ml of vinegar, we would need to add 1 ml to the solution for the change in the taste to be detectable. Notice, incidentally, that smaller fractions indicate better discrimination abilities.

In summary, Weber found *no* one-to-one correspondence between physical stimuli and psychological reactions. The same stimulus that was sufficient to produce a noticeably brighter light in one situation (1 candle added to 60 candles) was not sufficient to produce a noticeably brighter light in another situation (1 candle added to 120 candles).

Weber's law is well over a century old. How well does it predict the results of psychophysical studies? Research has demonstrated that Weber's law holds true for a variety of psychophysical judgments (Laming, 1985). However, it is more successful in the middle ranges than in predicting discrimination ability for high-intensity or low-intensity stimuli.

Fechner's Law

Gustav Fechner used Weber's law to derive a scale that related the size of the physical stimulus to the size of the observer's psychological reaction. The derivation of Fechner's scale is discussed elsewhere (Baird & Noma, 1978; Matlin, 1979). However, **Fechner's law** states that

$$R = k \log I$$

Verbally, Fechner's law says that the magnitude of the psychological reaction (R) is equal to a constant (k) multiplied by the logarithm of the intensity of the physical stimulus (I). In other words, Fechner's law states that psychological magnitude is proportional to the logarithm of stimulus intensity.

As you may recall, the **logarithm** of a number equals the exponent, or power, to which 10 must be raised to equal that number. It is important to know that a logarithmic transformation shrinks large numbers more than it shrinks small numbers. In other words, as I grows larger, R also grows larger; however, R does not grow as rapidly as I. For example, suppose that k has a value of 1. If the intensity of the stimulus is 100 units, then $R = 2$ (because the logarithm of 100 is 2; $10^2 = 100$). Now if we double the intensity of the stimulus to 200 units, then $R = 2.3$ (because the logarithm of 200 is 2.3; $10^{2.3} = 200$).

Notice that a doubling of the intensity of the physical stimulus does *not* lead to a doubling of the psychological response. As I grows from 100 to 200, R grows only from 2 to 2.3. Once again, there is not a one-to-one correspondence between physical stimuli and psychological reactions. Incidentally, it should be mentioned that Fechner's law is reasonably accurate in many situations, but— like Weber's law, on which it is based—it is inaccurate in others.

Stevens's Power Law

More recent research by S. S. Stevens (1962, 1975) provides an alternative view of the relationship between stimulus intensity and psychological reaction. In general, psychophysicists are more impressed with the predictive abilities of Stevens's power law than Fechner's law (Myers, 1982). According to **Stevens's power law**

$$R = kI^n$$

Verbally, Stevens's power law says that the magnitude of the psychological reaction (R) is equal to a constant (k) multiplied by the

intensity (I) of the stimulus, which has been raised to the nth power.[1]

The size of the exponent has a major effect on the nature of the relationship between the intensity of the stimulus and the magnitude of the psychological reaction. If the exponent is exactly one, a linear relationship exists between the intensity of the stimulus and the magnitude of the psychological reaction. The graph of this relationship is a straight line, such that an increase in the intensity of the stimulus is accompanied by a regular and consistent increase in the magnitude of the psychological reaction. When the exponent is greater than one, a small increase in the intensity of the stimulus is accompanied by a huge increase in the magnitude of the psychological reaction; the graph of this relationship curves upward. Finally, if the exponent is less than one, a large increase in the intensity of the stimulus is accompanied by only a small increase in the magnitude of the psychological reaction; the graph of this relationship curves downward.

Figure 2.9 illustrates three curves, one for each kind of relationship. Notice that there is generally a one-to-one correspondence when people are making judgments about the apparent length of a line. When people are supplying their psychological responses to electric shock, a modest change in stimulus intensity literally sends the responses through the ceiling of the graph. For brightness, though, the experimenter must increase the stimulus by tremendous proportions before the observer has a substantial increase in the psychological reaction.

Electric shock has an extremely large exponent, and brightness has an extremely small exponent. Table 2.5 illustrates several other kinds of physical dimensions that Stevens investigated. It's interesting to note, for example, that taste does not have a stable ex-

---

[1] As you may remember, the power to which a number is raised indicates the number of times that a number should be multiplied by itself. For example, 10^3 equals $10 \times 10 \times 10$. Furthermore, powers less than one involve taking the root of a number. For example, $9^{.5}$ or $9^{1/2}$ means that you must take the square root of 9, which is 3.

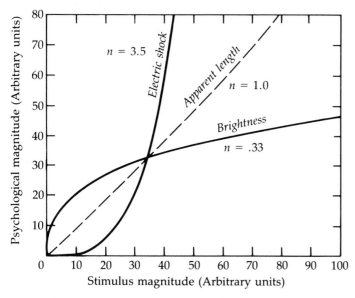

Figure 2.9 Relationship between stimulus intensity and magnitude of psychological response. (Based on Stevens, 1962.)

ponent; it's less than 1 in the case of saccharine and more than 1 in the case of salt. Furthermore, the specific exponent also depends upon how the concentration of these

Table 2.5 Representative Examples of Physical Dimensions, Their Measured Exponents in Power Functions, and How They Were Measured

Physical Dimension	Measured Exponent	How Measured
Brightness	.33	Small target in the dark
Loudness	.67	Sound pressure of a high tone
Taste	.8	Saccharine
Length	1.0	Projected length of line
Taste	1.4	Salt
Heaviness	1.45	Lifted weights
Warmth	1.6	Metal contact on arm
Electric shock	3.5	Electric current through fingers

solutions is measured (Myers, 1982). Nonetheless, Stevens's power law holds true for a wide variety of physical dimensions, not only when people judge physically present stimuli but also when they judge their *memories* of objects (Moyer, Sklarew, & Whiting, 1982; Wiest & Bell, 1985). The power law has also been applied to the measurement of observers' likes and dislikes (Moskowitz, 1982).

A technique that Stevens frequently used to obtain judgments is called magnitude estimation. In the **magnitude estimation** technique the observer is told that one stimulus, called the **standard**, is to be assigned a certain value. The value that is assigned to the standard is called the **modulus**, and this value is to be used as the yardstick in estimating the magnitude of all future stimuli. For example, suppose that we assign a value of 100 to the taste of Solution 3 in Demonstration 2.4. What values would you assign for how sweet Solutions 1, 2, 4, and 5 taste? The magnitude estimation technique allows the observer to provide a direct estimate of the magnitude of stimuli, based on a specified reference value. Usually, only a small number of observations are taken from each observer, and the data of all observers are combined (Falmagne, 1985).

Stevens also used **cross-modality comparisons**. Here the observers are asked to judge stimuli in one mode of perception (such as hearing) by providing responses from another mode of perception (such as sight). At first the method seems somewhat bizarre. How can we draw a line that looks as long as the loudness of a particular tone? However, once observers become accustomed to the idea, they consider it reasonable. Try turning the volume on your radio to its customary position and drawing a line to represent that loudness. Then try turning the volume dial to other positions and drawing new lines to represent these loudnesses.

When the method of cross-modality comparisons uses line drawing, the experimenter measures the length of the line that the observer draws to obtain a measure of the observer's psychological reaction (R) to the intensity of the stimulus (I). The power law, $R = kI^n$ fits data obtained by cross-modality comparisons just as well as data obtained from magnitude estimation. As Gescheider (1976) says, "There is little doubt that the power function represents the best description of the relationship between an observer's judgments and stimulus intensity" (p. 144).

In this section we have examined the relationship between the intensity of physical stimuli and the magnitude of psychological reactions. In some cases there is a one-to-one correspondence between these two factors. More often, however, a change in the physical stimulus is translated into either a magnified or a diminished change in the psychological reaction. Thus each perceptual system transforms physical stimuli in its own systematic fashion.

Multidimensional Scaling

So far we have been concerned with psychophysical scales that involve only a single dimension. For example, lights are judged on the dimension of brightness, and foods are judged on the dimension of sweetness. **Multidimensional scaling** is a mathematical procedure by which observers' judgments about the similarities and dissimilarities of objects can be represented spatially, as on a map (Carroll, 1984; Schiffman, Reynolds, & Young, 1981). A graph of a multidimensional analysis shows similar items near each other on the graph. Multidimensional scaling involves judgments that cannot be represented by a single line, dimension, or quality.

Multidimensional scaling is also important when we do not know the underlying dimensions that are important when people make judgments. For instance, when you say that your friend Pete looks like your friend Steve, are the important dimensions the color of their hair, the height of their foreheads, or the length of their noses? Sometimes multidimensional scaling may reveal that the underlying dimensions are not what the researchers would have predicted. For instance, when Schiffman and her colleagues asked mothers of young children to make judgments about strawberry-flavored beverages, the selected beverages varied in sweetness and intensity of color. These researchers expected, quite reasonably, that these two dimensions would be most important in the observers' judgments. However, the multidimensional analysis showed that one important dimension was sweetness, as anticipated, but the other was the similarity of the stimulus, in terms of both sweetness and color, to a normal strawberry-flavored soft drink. Intensity of color per se was not important.

Multidimensional scaling involves gathering similarity judgments about all pairs of a large number of stimuli. The details of obtaining these judgments and converting them mathematically into a maplike diagram are beyond the scope of this book but are described in a book by Schiffman, Reynolds, & Young (1981) called *Introduction to Multidimensional Scaling*.

This method is particularly useful for studying taste and smell, two perceptual systems that cannot be neatly described in terms of physical dimensions such as wave length (for vision) or pitch (for sound). For example, Schiffman and her colleagues asked elderly people to judge 14 food flavors. Figure 2.10 shows the results of the multidimensional

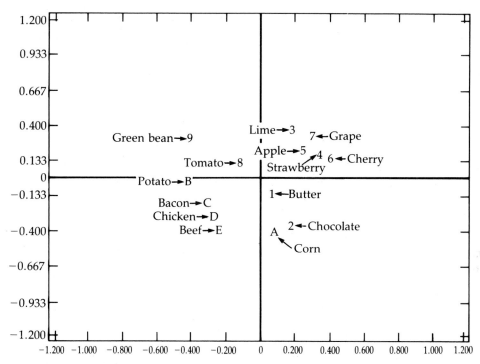

Figure 2.10 Multidimensional scaling analysis for food flavors. (From Schiffman, Reynolds, & Young, 1981. Used with permission.)

scaling analysis. Notice that in this case no clearcut dimensions seem to underlie the similarity judgments. However, foods that seem similar to one another do appear near each other on the diagram. All the fruits are together in the upper-right corner, and all the meats cluster in the lower-left corner. Thus, multidimensional scaling provides a way of representing people's psychological reactions to stimuli that cannot be simplified to a single dimension.

Summary: Measuring Responses to More Intense Stimuli

1. Discrimination studies examine how much a stimulus must be changed to be perceived as just noticeably different.
2. Discrimination studies ask people to compare a standard stimulus with a comparison stimulus. These studies typically calculate the just noticeable difference.
3. In the method of limits for measuring discrimination, the comparison stimulus is systematically increased or decreased.
4. In the method of adjustment for measuring discrimination, the observer adjusts the comparison stimulus.
5. In the method of constant stimuli for measuring discrimination, comparison stimuli are presented in random order.
6. Three researchers—Weber, Fechner, and Stevens—have been primarily responsible for formulating equations to describe the relationship between physical stimuli and psychological reactions.
7. Ernst Weber found that observers require larger changes in a stimulus to notice a difference if they are discriminating between intense, rather than weak, stimuli.
8. Gustav Fechner proposed that as stimulus intensity increases, the magnitude of the psychological response increases, but not as dramatically. For example, as the stim-

ulus intensity increases from 100 to 200 units, the magnitude of the psychological response increases only from 2.0 to 2.3.

9. Fechner's law states that the magnitude of the psychological response is related to the logarithm of the intensity of the physical stimulus.

10. S. S. Stevens proposed that the magnitude of the psychological response is related to the intensity of the stimulus, raised to a certain power, n. The value of n depends upon the nature of the judgments.

11. Stevens frequently used magnitude estimation and cross-modality comparisons to obtain judgments of the magnitude of the psychological response.

12. In general Stevens's predictions are more accurate than Fechner's.

13. Multidimensional scaling is useful when researchers want to obtain judgments about stimuli that differ from each other along more than one dimension; the method involves gathering similarity judgments.

Review

1. Describe how psychophysics might be relevant if you wanted to examine low-intensity stimuli in each of the following areas: vision, hearing, touch, temperature perception, pain, smell, and taste. In each case, briefly describe how you would use the method of limits (or an appropriate modification) to measure a detection threshold.

2. Why do we need both ascending trials and descending trials in the method of limits? Why don't we need to worry about the two kinds of trials in the method of constant stimuli? Similarly, why do we need to vary the stimulus with which we begin when using the method of limits, and why is this precaution unnecessary when using the method of constant stimuli?

3. Return to question 1 and describe how you would use the method of adjustment and the method of constant stimuli to measure detection thresholds in each of the areas listed.

4. Describe the advantages and disadvantages of each of the three classical psychophysics methods, illustrating each method with an example from vision.

5. Suppose you are standing near an electric coffee urn, waiting for the red light to turn on to indicate that the coffee is ready. Apply signal detection theory to this sit-

uation, describing aspects of sensitivity and criterion. Now describe the four possible outcomes in this situation with respect to the occurrence of the signal and your response.

6. The following questions apply to ROC curves:
   a. If d' is large, is the probability of a hit larger or smaller than if d' is small?
   b. What does d' measure?
   c. Suppose that one observer has a d' of .5 and another has a d' of 1.5. If they have the same hit rate, which observer has the higher false alarm rate?
   d. How is a particular point on a ROC curve related to the criterion line in the probability distributions in Figure 2.5?

7. Why is signal detection theory particularly useful for examining the perception of pain? In research on pain perception, what is d' and what is β? Do the research findings suggest that people differ from each other in their sensitivity, their criterion, or both factors?

8. Describe how you could use each of the three classical psychophysics methods to measure color discrimination. Then discuss how psychophysics might be relevant if you wanted to examine high-intensity stimuli in each of the areas mentioned in question 1 (in addition to color discrimination). Mention both dis-

crimination studies and studies concerning the relationship between physical stimuli and psychological responses.

9. The section on the relationship between physical stimuli and psychological reactions ended with a statement that a change in the physical stimulus is typically translated into either a magnified or a diminished change in the psychological reaction. Discuss this statement with reference to Fechner and Stevens. Discuss how the research of Weber, Fechner, and Stevens could be related to people's judgments about how heavy various chocolate bars feel.

10. Briefly describe multidimensional scaling and think of examples from your everyday experience to illustrate it, related to judgments about the following areas: (a) popular music, (b) cola drinks, (c) paintings, and (d) colors.

New Terms

psychophysics

detection threshold

method of limits

descending series

ascending series

errors of habituation

errors of anticipation

ascending method of limits

identification (in method of limits)

method of adjustment

method of constant stimuli

signal detection theory (SDT)

sensitivity measure

criterion

β

payoff

signal

hit

correct rejection

false alarm

miss

receiver operating characteristic curve (ROC curve)

d'

noise

signal + noise

probability distribution

discrimination

difference threshold

standard stimulus

comparison stimulus

just noticeable difference (jnd)

point of subjective equality

method of limits for measuring discrimination

method of adjustment for measuring discrimination

method of constant stimuli for measuring discrimination

Weber's law

Weber's fraction

Fechner's law

logarithm

Stevens's power law

magnitude estimation

standard

modulus

cross-modality comparisons

multidimensional scaling

Recommended Readings

Baird, J. C., & Noma, E. (1978). *Fundamentals of scaling and psychophysics.* New York: Wiley. *This book includes chapters on Fechner's law, Weber's law, and Stevens' law, as well as chapters on signal detection theory, multidimensional scaling, and other topics.*

Gescheider, G. A. (1985). *Psychophysics: Method, theory, and application.* Hillsdale, NJ: Erlbaum. *Although intended for an advanced-level course, this textbook is generally fairly clear. A positive feature is that each chapter is accompanied by psychophysics problems to be solved by the student; the answers are at the back of the book.*

Schiffman, S. S., Reynolds, M. L., & Young, F. W. (1981). *Introduction to multidimensional scaling.* New York: Academic. *Several books are available on multidimensional scaling, but this seems particularly well written, with good examples.*

Stevens, S. S. (1975). *Psychophysics.* New York: Wiley. *Published after Stevens's death, this book is a complete discussion of his theories and research. However, it does not cover additional topics, such as signal detection theory, as do Baird and Noma's and Gescheider's books.*

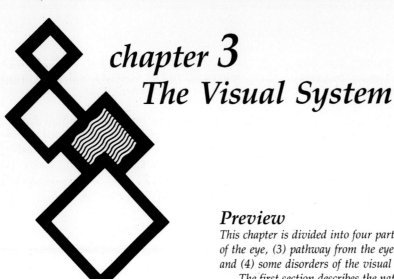

chapter 3
The Visual System

Outline

Visual Stimulus

Anatomy of the Eye
External structures
Internal structures

Pathway from the Eye to the Brain and the Visual Cortex
Optic chiasm
Superior colliculus
Lateral geniculate nucleus
Visual cortex
In-Depth: Cortical columns

Some Disorders of the Visual System
Disorders of external parts of the eye
Disorders involving binocular coordination
Disorders of the lens and retina
Disorders of the optic nerve and visual cortex

Preview

This chapter is divided into four parts: (1) visual stimulus, (2) anatomy of the eye, (3) pathway from the eye to the brain and the visual cortex, and (4) some disorders of the visual system.

The first section describes the nature of light, or the visual stimulus. Light can be represented by wavelengths. The distance between the wave peaks is related to hue, the purity of the mixture of wavelengths is related to perceived saturation, and the amplitude is related to brightness.

The second section explains the visible parts of the eye, including the sclera, the iris, and the pupil and the transparent covering, the cornea. Behind the cornea lie the lens and the retina. The retina is particularly important because it contains the photoreceptors (rods and cones) and the ganglion cells.

The third section follows the visual pathway from the eye to the brain and also discusses the visual cortex in detail. Parts of the optic nerves cross over to the other side of the head, an arrangement useful for two eyes working together. The nerve fibers then proceed to the superior colliculus and the lateral geniculate nucleus. From the lateral geniculate nucleus, nerve fibers continue to the visual cortex. The primary visual cortex is organized according to columns, with all the cells in a particular column especially responsive to lines of the same orientation. Other parts of the visual cortex process depth perception, associations, and other complex visual information.

The final section discusses some common eye problems, including disorders of the external parts of the eye and disorders in which the two eyes do not coordinate properly. Another serious disorder involves a clouding of the lens known as cataracts. Four disorders of the retina will also be discussed. Diseases that can attack the nerve pathway from the retina to the brain and visual cortex damage will be covered. The last section should be particularly useful to students interested in applied psychology.

The human eye is an amazing organ. It is about the size of a jumbo olive, yet it performs impressive tasks. It can handle information about colored and uncolored objects either near or far away and can work when the lighting is dim or glaring. This chapter focuses on the structure of the eye, how it encodes information about the visual stimulus, and how this information is passed on to various areas of the brain.

VISUAL STIMULUS

What are the properties of light? Light is one kind of electromagnetic radiation. **Electromagnetic radiation** refers to all forms of waves produced by electrically charged particles. As Figure 3.1 illustrates, the visible light that humans see occupies only a small portion of the electromagnetic radiation spectrum. Other organisms respond to other portions of the spectrum. For example, pit vipers and boa constrictors have sensory organs that are sensitive to infrared rays, which are to the right of the visible spectrum. These animals can therefore form heat-sensitive images of their potential prey (Sinclair, 1985). The human visual system cannot detect wavelengths as long as those in infrared rays. Our visual system also cannot detect short wavelengths, such as the ultraviolet rays that give you a suntan and the X-rays used by radiologists.

Light is made up of waves. We can describe light in terms of its **wavelength**, which is the distance the light travels during one cycle, that is, the distance between two peaks as illustrated in Figure 3.2. The light wave in Figure 3.2a has a longer wavelength than the one in Figure 3.2b.

Wavelength is typically measured in nanometers. A **nanometer** (nm) equals 1 billionth of a meter. The shortest wavelengths that we can see are represented by violet, which has a wavelength of about 400 nm; the longest, by red, which has a wavelength of

about 700 nm. Color Plate 1, inside the front cover of this book, illustrates the spectrum between red and violet.

In summary, then, **light** is the portion of the electromagnetic radiation spectrum made up of waves that range from about 400 to about 700 nm.

We have talked about the length of light waves. As we will discuss in the chapter on color vision (Chapter 5), the length of light waves is related to the **hue** of a visual stimulus. Light waves have two other characteristics, purity and amplitude. **Purity**, the mixture of wavelengths in the light, is related to the perceived saturation of a visual stimulus. Finally, **amplitude**, the height of the light wave, is related to the brightness of a visual stimulus. Figure 3.3 shows how light waves can differ in the height of their peaks. Notice that Figure 3.3a has greater amplitude than Figure 3.3b; its peaks are higher. Light waves that have greater amplitude are perceived as brighter.

You may have noticed that we mentioned three *pairs* of attributes: (1) wavelength and hue, (2) purity and saturation, and (3) amplitude and brightness. The first member of each pair describes a characteristic of the physical stimulus, whereas the second member describes what we perceive, a psychological reaction. For example, large-amplitude wavelengths in a physical stimulus will usually be perceived by humans as bright. Thus we should say "a light that *looks* bright" rather than "a bright light" because brightness describes our perceptions rather than the physical stimulus.

We said that wavelength is typically measured in nanometers. Boyce (1981) summarizes numerous ways to measure the amplitude of light. A frequent measure used in psychology journals is **candelas per meter square (cd/m^2)**, a measure based on how much light is reflected from the surface of the stimulus. To give you a feeling for this measure, the light reflected from the page you are reading now is approximately 32 cd/m^2. However, under the best conditions, you can detect a light that is only 0.000003 (3 millionth) cd/m^2.

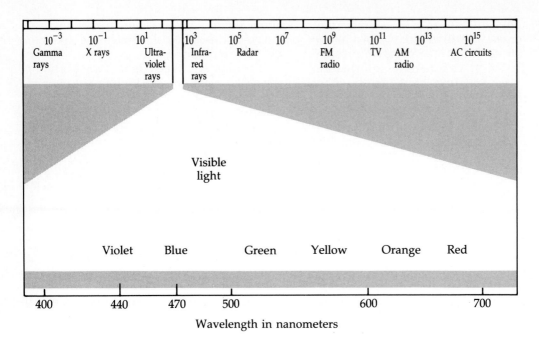

Figure 3.1   Electromagnetic spectrum.

a.   Example of long wavelength

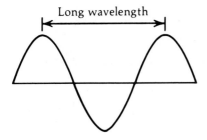

b.   Example of short wavelength

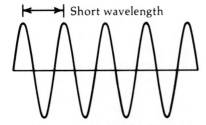

Figure 3.2   Examples of light waves varying in wavelength.

a.   Example of a bright-looking light, with light waves of greater amplitude

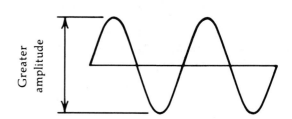

b.   Example of a dim-looking light, with light waves of smaller amplitude

Figure 3.3   Examples of light waves varying in amplitude.

The measurement of purity is more complex than the measurement of wavelength and amplitude. Purity will be discussed in detail in the chapter on color.

Summary: Visual Stimulus

1. Light is part of the electromagnetic spectrum; wavelengths for light range between 400 nm and 700 nm.
2. Wavelength is measured in nanometers; short wavelengths are perceived as violet, and long wavelengths are perceived as red.
3. Other organisms are sensitive to other portions of the electromagnetic spectrum, but these wavelengths are either too long or too short for the human visual system.
4. Light can also be described in terms of its purity and its amplitude; amplitude is measured in many different ways, including candelas per meter square.
5. Wavelength, purity, and amplitude describe physical stimuli, whereas hue, saturation, and brightness describe perceptions.

ANATOMY OF THE EYE

Our discussion of the eye will cover external eye structures and internal eye structures and functions.

External Structures

If you look at your eye in the mirror, you'll notice three conspicuous parts: the sclera, the iris, and the pupil. Figure 3.4 shows these three parts.

The **sclera** is the shiny white part made of relatively thick membrane. The sclera helps to maintain the shape of the eye and to protect it from injury. The floating eyeballs you see in horror movies are accurate in one respect: The sclera does continue around on the back of the eye.

The **iris** is a ring of muscles ranging from light blue to dark brown. We tend to attach great importance to eye color, writing songs, stories, and poetry in which eye color is

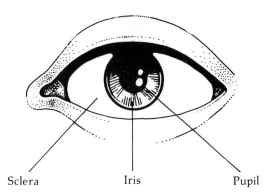

Sclera   Iris   Pupil

Figure 3.4 Three noticeable eye parts.

stressed. It certainly sounds unromantic, then, to describe the iris simply as a ring of muscle!

The iris has two kinds of muscles, one to make the iris **constrict** or close (making the pupil smaller) and one to make it **dilate** or open (making the pupil larger). When the lights are bright, the iris closes up; when the lights are dim, it opens. Try Demonstration 3.1 to illustrate this process. Furthermore, researchers have discovered that the size of the iris changes as you become interested in something.

The **pupil** is the opening in the center of the iris. In humans this opening is round. The next time you look at a cat, however, notice that its pupils are not round. In fact, they become thin vertical slits when the lights are bright. It is important to note that the pupil isn't actually a structure in the eye, as many people think; instead, the pupil is just a hole.

Why does the pupil look black? Why can't you look into the pupil and see the eye's internal structure? There are two reasons. First, most of the light that enters the eye is absorbed by substances inside the eye. However, a small amount of the light is reflected directly out of the pupil. You might think that doesn't make sense because the pupil doesn't look at all lighted; it looks pure black. The second reason is that you ordinarily cannot see the small amount of reflected light from someone's eye. If you stand directly in front of someone, you will be blocking the source

---

Demonstration 3.1

Iris and Pupil Size

Go into a dark room or closet with a door that can be opened to let in a little light. Bring with you a mirror and a flashlight. Open the door just enough so that your left eye (next to the door) can see your right eye (away from the door) in the mirror. Notice the size of your pupil. It should be relatively large because the iris is open. Now quickly turn on the flashlight so that it beams directly upon your right eye. Watch how rapidly the pupil shrinks in size because the iris is closing up. Turn off the flashlight and watch the pupil dilate.

---

of light right in front of that person's pupil. On the other hand, if you stand to the side, you will not block the light source. Unfortunately, however, the light will be reflected from the person's eye to a point straight ahead. You will not see this reflection, since you are standing at the side.

Ophthalmologists—doctors specializing in eye diseases—and other physicians use a special tool called an **ophthalmoscope** to look inside the eye. The ophthalmoscope is equipped with a special mirror and lens so that the light from a person's eye *can* be reflected back to the observer. Instead of the black pupil we ordinarily see, the physician can see structures inside the eye.

One structure exists on the outside that you cannot ordinarily see, because it is transparent. This is the **cornea**, a clear membrane just in front of the iris, which joins with the sclera and bulges out slightly. The cornea is illustrated in Figure 3.5. You may have noticed a cornea if you ever looked sideways at someone wearing "hard" contact lenses. If you look carefully, you will notice that the contact lens seems to be floating some distance away from the iris, but it really is resting on the cornea. The cornea is important because it bends light rays as they enter the eye.

The cornea and sclera are made of the same material, so it is initially puzzling that they should look so different. A major reason that the cornea is transparent is that the fibers are lined up in an organized fashion in the

cornea area, whereas they are arranged in a disorganized fashion in the sclera. The situation is similar to what happens in a hot sugar solution, which can be cooled down carefully to form clear candy, like lollipops, or can be spun to make an opaque "cotton candy" that light could never show through. Fortunately, the eye is well constructed. The tissue is firm where strength is needed in the sclera. (To continue the metaphor, it's as if you squeezed all the air out of the cotton candy to obtain a dense, fibrous material.) This same tissue is transparent at the cornea, where light must pass through on its way to the retina.

If you look once more in the mirror, you will see the **conjunctiva**, the pink mucous membrane that lines the eyelid and attaches the eye to the eyelid. Many people buy contact lenses for the first time and secretly worry that a lens might slip around to the back of

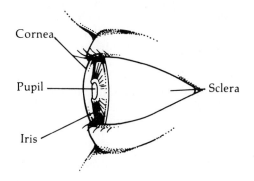

Figure 3.5   Cornea as seen from side.

the eye. Fortunately, the conjunctiva prevents this from happening.

The conjunctiva also covers the **extraocular muscles**, the muscles that allow our eyes to move; notice that these muscles are outside the eye. Figure 3.6 is not designed to induce jargon shock or to disgust you unnecessarily but to impress you with the admirable set of muscles that surround each eye. We typically are not aware of these muscles, but Chapter 4 will expand upon the importance of eye movements.

Before we move on, let's review quickly. Visible parts of the eye include the sclera, the iris, and the pupil. The cornea is in front of the iris, and the conjunctiva is the pink part under the eyelids that covers the muscles.

Internal Structures

In the internal structures illustrated in Figure 3.7, notice that the lens is between the pupil and the iris. The **lens** is important because its shape changes to bring objects into focus. We will discuss this process in detail in the next chapter, and in Chapter 15 we'll examine how the lens changes as people grow older.

We noted earlier that the cornea bends light rays as they enter the eye. The lens completes the task. Since the lens can change its shape, it can focus light rays from both nearby and faraway objects. (The details of this process will be discussed in the next chapter.) As a result, you can see clear, crisp objects rather than blurs. The lens is slightly yellow, but it is almost completely transparent. This transparency is necessary to allow light rays to pass through to the cornea. The lens's structure consists of a series of layers, a bit like the layers of an onion.

Now notice the ciliary muscles in Figure 3.7. These **ciliary muscles** are attached to the lens, and they control its shape. For example, when you are looking at a nearby object, the ciliary muscles contract. These muscles, located inside the eye, should not be confused with the muscles outside the eye that were illustrated in Figure 3.6.

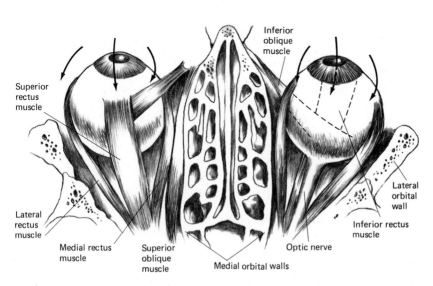

Figure 3.6 Extraocular muscles. (From Carlson, 1986. Used with permission.)

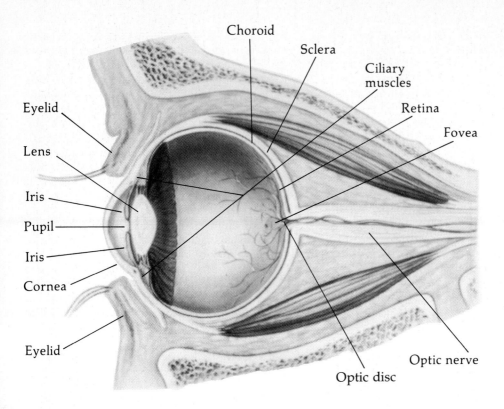

Figure 3.7 Inside human eye.

Notice that the lens divides the eye into two compartments. Both are filled with special material. The small area between the cornea and the lens is filled with **aqueous humor**, a watery liquid that resembles the cerebrospinal fluid surrounding the brain. Aqueous humor supplies oxygen and nutrients for the cornea and the lens. Blood performs this task for other parts of your body, but obviously blood would be a poor choice for an area that must allow light to pass through.

The aqueous humor performs an additional task: It must help maintain the shape of the eyeball. Imagine that there were no liquid in that left-hand portion of the eye shown in Figure 3.7. It could readily deflate and collapse against the iris or the lens. Once again,

as stressed in one of the themes of the book, the human sensory system is remarkably well adapted for the jobs it must perform.

Behind the lens is a second, larger compartment that contains **vitreous humor**, a thick, jelly-like substance that helps maintain the shape of the eyeball. If you press gently on an eyelid covering the sclera, you will notice that your eyeball can be slightly depressed, but you clearly cannot collapse it. The fluids keep it almost round.

The vitreous humor is largely transparent except for floaters. **Floaters** are groups or strings of material formed from the red blood cells that have leaked out of the retina (Walker, 1982). Once these cells have left the retina, they swell and lose their color, clump with other cells, and float around in the vitreous humor. You can see your own floaters by looking at a brightly lit wall of a light, uniform color.

Figure 3.7 also shows the choroid, which is on the back of the eye just inside the sclera. The **choroid** has two functions. It contains many small arteries and veins, which provide nutrients and oxygen for the retina in front of it, and it absorbs extra light scattered in the eye. The choroid is dark brown. This dark color makes it an ideal light absorber, just like the inside of a camera. The choroid is so thin that it is nearly invisible without a microscope, yet it performs functions that make it vital to visual processes in humans.

The Retina

The **retina** absorbs light rays and transforms them into information that can be transmitted by the **neurons**, or nerve cells. Notice that the retina is at the back of the eyeball and covers a large part of the inner surface. This extremely important part of the eye is only about as thick as a page in this book. It contains light receptors called rods and cones and different kinds of nerve cells, which will be discussed shortly.

Look carefully at one area on the retina as shown in Figure 3.7. The **fovea** is a region smaller than the period at the end of this sentence in which vision is the sharpest. In fact, as you are reading this paragraph, your eyes are jumping along the page to register new words on your fovea. As you look at a single word on this page, you will notice that other words more than 3 cm away look somewhat blurry. Those words are reaching areas of the retina outside the fovea where the vision is substantially less clear, and you must move your fovea to read them.

Figure 3.8 shows a sketch of a cross-section of the retina in the area of the fovea. Notice that the upper layer of cells is much thinner in the central, fovea region. As you have probably come to expect about the anatomy of sensory processes, this arrangement is not accidental. Instead, it allows light to pass through the cells much more readily to reach the region of the retina so critical for most of our vision.

Incidentally, ophthalmologists are more likely to use the term **macula lutea** (or simply macula) than fovea. The macula is a slightly larger region in this important part of the ret-

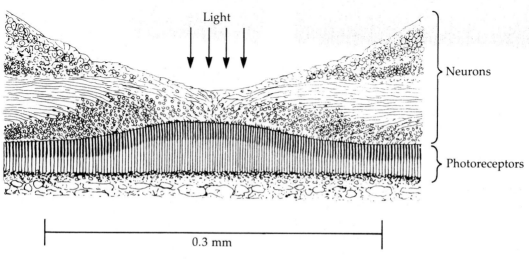

Figure 3.8 Cross-section through fovea.

ina. The fovea is about 0.3 mm wide, whereas the macula is about 2 mm wide, about the size of this letter: O.

Now notice the area of the retina in Figure 3.7 labeled "optic disc." At the **optic disc** the optic nerve leaves the eye. The optic disc has no light receptors, so you cannot see anything that reaches this part of the retina. The optic disc therefore creates a **blind spot**. Try Demonstration 3.2 to illustrate the blind spot.

Since the retina is extremely important in vision, we will consider the kinds of cells in the retina in some detail. Figure 3.9 shows six kinds of cells. Cones and rods are the two kinds of light receptors, or **photoreceptors**. They will be discussed in more detail later, after we've introduced the other cells in the retina. For now, though, you should know that **cones** are used for color vision under well-lit conditions. **Rods**, on the other hand, are used for black-and-white vision under poorly lit conditions.

Since rods and cones receive the light, they begin the visual process. Bipolar cells are next in the chain. **Bipolar cells** receive information from the rods and cones and pass it on to the next level in the chain, the ganglion cells. **Ganglion cells** take the information from the bipolar cells and bring it toward the brain. A later section will provide more information on the ganglion cells.

The chain of cells—from cones and rods to bipolar cells and then to the ganglion cells—carries information vertically from the eye to the brain. However, information also travels horizontally across the retina through horizontal cells and amacrine cells, which allow for communication among adjacent cells. **Horizontal cells** allow the photoreceptors (rods and cones) to communicate, and they also allow communication between bipolar cells. Furthermore, horizontal cells communicate with each other. **Amacrine cells** allow ganglion cells to communicate, and they also allow bipolar cells to communicate. Finally, amacrine cells communicate with each other. Later sections will discuss why these kinds of communications with other cells are important. Specifically, when one photoreceptor is stimulated, the activity of a nearby photoreceptor can be inhibited. This kind of inhibition would be impossible if there were no horizontal cells and amacrine cells to connect cells with their neighbors.

Now that you have a basic knowledge of the cells in the retina, we will pursue the details on the photoreceptors and the ganglion cells.

Demonstration 3.2
———————————
Blind Spot

Close your left eye and use your right eye to look at the X. Gradually move this page toward your eye and then away from it, keeping the distance in the range of 10 to 40 cm. At some point you will reach a distance at which the spot seems to disappear. At this distance the spot is falling upon the blind spot. In the blind spot, the nerve fibers gather together and leave the eye. There are no light receptors at this point, so there is no way to register the spot on the retina here. In Chapter 4 we will discuss how our visual system compensates for the blind spot.

●   X

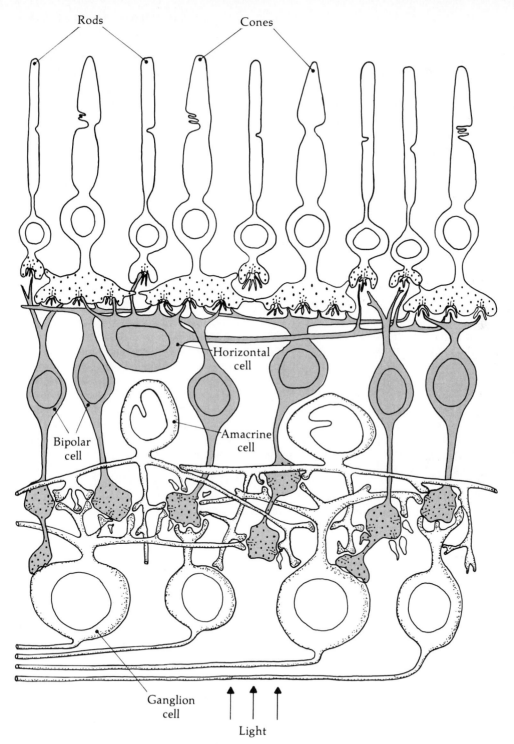

Figure 3.9 Diagram of kinds of cells in retina. (Adapted from Dowling & Boycott, 1966. Used with permission.)

Details about photoreceptors. There are two kinds of photoreceptors. **Duplicity theory**, an approach to vision formulated more than a century ago, proposed two separate kinds of photoreceptors, each with different characteristics. Later research confirmed that duplicity theory was correct. Vision that uses cones is called **photopic vision**, from the Greek stem *phot*, which means "light," and *opia*, which means "eye." Vision that uses rods is called **scotopic vision**, from the Greek stem *skot*, which means "darkness."

Table 3.1 summarizes a number of facts about cones and rods.

As mentioned, cones are used for color vision in well-lit environments, whereas rods are used for black-and-white vision in poorly lit environments. Animals that are awake at night have more rods than cones. Bats, for example, have no cones at all (Riggs, 1971), a fact that should make you very curious about the light receptors in Count Dracula's retinas. Animals that are awake during the day, in contrast, have a good supply of cones. Some of these animals, such as lizards, snakes, birds, and squirrels, have no rods at all (Riggs, 1971). Humans, fortunately, have both rods and cones, so that we can function well in both photopic and scotopic conditions.

In Table 3.1 notice that specific ranges are listed for the two lighting environments.

Cones function well when the lighting is more than about 3 cd/m^2, whereas rods function well when the lighting is less than about 3 cd/m^2. What happens when the lighting is just around 3 cd/m^2? In this situation, it is too dim for the cones and too bright for the rods to work at their peak efficiency. This ambiguous time occurs just before sunset, and you may have noticed that it is difficult to see well at this time.

Cones and rods also differ in their shape and number. As you can see from Figure 3.9, cones are fatter, with pointed ends, a little like the classic ice-cream cone. Rods, like the objects they are named after, are thin and blunt-ended. Each eye has "only" 7 million cones, whereas each eye has 125 million rods.

Cones and rods are concentrated in different parts of the retina. Cones are densely concentrated at the fovea in the center of the retina. In contrast, rods are found nearly everywhere *except* at the fovea. As Figure 3.10 illustrates, the highest concentration for rods is in the region about one third of the way, or about 7 mm, out from the fovea toward either edge of the retina. Notice that the rod density in this region is about the same as the cone density in the fovea.

Let's combine some of the information in Table 3.1. If we know that rods are used in poorly lit conditions and that there are no rods at the fovea, then vision should be poor

Table 3.1 Comparison of Cones and Rods

Characteristic	Cones Photopic (color)	Rods Scotopic (black and white)
Lighting conditions required for best functioning	Well-lit (more than 3 cd/m^2)	Dimly lit (less than 3 cd/m^2)
Shape	Fat, pointed	Thin, blunt
Number	7 million	125 million
Distribution	In the fovea	Not in the fovea
Relative number of receptors for each ganglion cell (convergence)	Few	Many
Acuity	Excellent	Poor
Sensitivity	Poor	Excellent

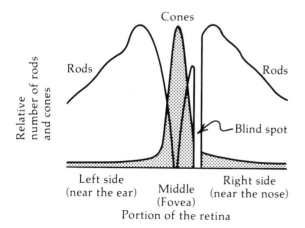

Figure 3.10 Distribution of rods and cones in retina of left eye. Cones are concentrated in fovea and rods in area outside fovea. Notice no rods or cones in blind spot.

for objects registered on the fovea at night. Try Demonstration 3.3 to illustrate foveal vision at night.

Figure 3.9 shows many more receptor cells than ganglion cells. In fact, the entire retina has only about 1 million ganglion cells; this means that many receptor cells have to "share" each ganglion cell. As it turns out, however, the sharing is unequal, because the cones get more than their share. In the fovea, which is rich with cones, a ganglion cell might receive information from only one, two, or three cones. Toward the edge of the retina, which is rich with rods, a ganglion cell might

receive information from as many as 100 rods. In other words, there is greater pooling of information, or convergence, for rods than cones.

The convergence of information from receptor cells for each ganglion cell is related to **acuity**, the precision with which we can see find details.

Why should acuity be greater in the cone region? When you want to see fine details in a picture, for example, you would like each tiny receptor on the retina to keep its information separate from the information that neighboring receptors have. If you pooled all the information, however, acuity would be reduced. Suppose, for example, that a design consisting of narrow black-and-white stripes is falling on an area in which 100 receptor cells share a single ganglion cell. All the information about black and white would be combined at the ganglion, making a blurry gray. If each receptor cell had its own ganglion cell, however, the black-and-white pattern would be preserved. Thus acuity is greater in the cone region because cones have a lower receptor-to-ganglion cell ratio than rods.

It makes sense that acuity would be greater in the cone region because you know already that acuity is best in the fovea area.

Convergence explains why acuity is lower in the rod region than in the cone region; convergence inhibits acuity. Convergence also helps explain why sensitivity is better in the rod region than in the cone region. Sensitivity

---

Demonstration 3.3

Night Vision and the Fovea

Choose a clear night and find a place with no bright lights nearby. Look up at the stars and locate a dim star slightly to the right or left of the point at which you are gazing. If you shift your focus to gaze at this star, however, it seems to disappear. In dim light rods operate but cones do not. If an object is registered on the areas of your retina rich with rods, you can see it; that is, you can see objects best on the areas slightly outside the fovea. If an image of an object falls on the area of your retina rich with cones, you cannot see it. Consequently, at night you will not see an image that falls precisely on the fovea.

involves the ability to detect weak stimuli. Since a single rod needs somewhat less energy than a single cone to be active, rods already have a "head start." They have an additional advantage because convergence allows them to pool information. Each signal may be weak, but when the individual signals are pooled, the cumulative effect may be strong enough to stimulate the ganglion cell. In contrast a weak signal from a cone, which may be the only receptor "assigned" to a ganglion cell, will probably be ignored.

In summary, the duplicity theory describes one system of photoreceptors with excellent acuity but poor sensitivity (cones) and another system with poor acuity but excellent sensitivity (rods).

So far we have contrasted cones with rods. We must now focus on how these photoreceptors perform **transduction**, or converting light into a form that can be transmitted through the visual system.

Notice the portion of the rods and cones at the top of Figure 3.10, specifically the disc-like structures in the photoreceptors. The membranes of these structures contain chemical substances called **photopigments** that accomplish the transduction of light. A single rod, for example, contains about 10 million photopigment molecules (Carlson, 1986).

In humans the photopigments have two components, a large protein called **opsin** and another component called **retinal**, which is related to vitamin A. This retinal component is the same for all photopigments, but the exact form of opsin varies from one photopigment to the next. Like other higher primates, humans have four kinds of photopigments, one for rods and three for cones. Each photopigment absorbs much more light in one portion of the electromagnetic spectrum than in any other portion. For example, Bowmaker and Dartnall (1980) studied material in the retina of a man whose eye had been removed because of a tumor in the choroid layer. They discovered that the photopigment in the rods was particularly responsive to wavelengths at 498 nm, whereas the three photopigments found in the cones were each particularly responsive to one specific wave-

length: one to 420 nm, another to 534 nm, and the last to 564 nm. (The significance of these three photopigments will be discussed more completely in the chapter on color.)

When you are in a completely darkened room, the two components of each photopigment are stable and do not separate. However, when light hits a photopigment molecule, it becomes unstable, and a series of changes takes place. For example, consider **rhodopsin**, which is the photopigment found in rods. When light reaches the rhodopsin molecule, it separates into its two components. (Vitamin A and other substances aid in the later regeneration of rhodopsin from these two components.)

The change in the rhodopsin provides a message that can be transmitted to the bipolar cells, although the details of this process are not well established. According to one explanation, however, the splitting of rhodopsin allows less sodium to flow through the membrane of the rod (Carlson, 1986). Electrochemical information about the electrical imbalance in the rod can then be transmitted to the next level in visual processing.

Part of the rod itself also regenerates periodically. Recall the disc-like structures in the outer portion of the rods illustrated in Figure 3.10. Researchers have discovered that new discs are formed at the bottom of the stack, and the stack moves upward. Early in the morning the oldest discs at the top of the stack are cast off, a process called **disc-shedding**. Additional studies on cone renewal have demonstrated that a similar process occurs for cones, except that cones perform the disc-shedding ceremony at night (O'Day & Young, 1978). In other words, each system renews itself after the period in which it operates best.

Now we'll move on to the next higher level in visual processing. After light has been captured by the photoreceptors, transformed into an electrochemical format, and passed on to the bipolar cells, the next major event happens at the ganglion cells.

Details about the ganglion cells. The purpose of the ganglion cells in the retina is to collect information from the photoreceptors (via the bipolar cells) and to convey it to the optic nerve, which travels toward the brain. The ganglion cells generate **action potentials**, short bursts of electrical activity. When there is no visual stimulus, the ganglion cell fires at a relatively low rate, perhaps 50 action potentials each second (Enroth, Cugell, & Robson, 1984). Some activity occurs, then, even when the cell is resting. When a visual stimulus is presented, the ganglion cell may either be activated and fire more often or be inhibited and fire less often.

To examine ganglion cells more completely, an overview of the research technique **single cell recording** is necessary. In single cell recording, researchers use special electrodes called **microelectrodes**, whose tips are often less than .01 mm in diameter. They operate on the experimental animal, such as a monkey or a cat, to place the microelectrode in an exact location in the visual system. To study ganglion cells, for example, the microelectrode can be carefully placed within the eye so that it can record the action potentials generated by a single ganglion cell; the name "single cell recording" is therefore appropriate. Small spots of light are then shined on the animal's eye, and the ganglion cell's responses to these stimuli can be recorded. The portion of the retina that, when stimulated, produces a change in the activity of the ganglion cell is called the ganglion's **receptive field**. The single cell recording technique can therefore provide information about the nature of a ganglion cell's receptive field.

What does the receptive field of a ganglion cell look like? In mammals these receptive fields are circles or ovals (Thompson, 1985). They generally come in one of two varieties: (1) on-center, off-surround, or (2) off-center, on-surround. For example, if a ganglion cell has an on-center, off-surround receptive field it will produce a burst of electrical activity when light shines in the center; the cell will show activation. However, if light shines in the surrounding, outer portion of its receptive field, the ganglion cell will show inhibition. If no light reaches any portion of the

receptive field, the ganglion cell will fire spontaneously at a low rate, as mentioned earlier. Furthermore, if light shines on the entire receptive field, the activation in the center will be roughly equal to the inhibition in the surround, and the result will be a low rate of spontaneous firing—the same as when there is no light. Figure 3.11 illustrates how an on-center, off-surround ganglion cell would respond in these four situations.

The second variety of ganglion cell, the off-center, on-surround cell, responds in exactly the opposite fashion; it fires more often if the surround receives light and less often if the center receives light. Spend a moment figuring out how this cell would react to the four stimulus situations illustrated in Figure 3.11.

Retinal ganglion cells are fairly complicated. Recent research on cat retinas has revealed three structurally different ganglion cells (Lennie, 1980). Fortunately for students of sensation and perception, they are referred to by letters rather than multisyllable names. Characteristics of the two most important kinds of cells are listed in Table 3.2. X and Y cells appear to have either the on-center, off-surround or the off-center, on-surround receptive field just described. However, W cells seem to respond to more homogeneous, evenly distributed stimulation.

Let's focus on some key characteristics of the three kinds of cells. **X cells** are the most common; they respond in a steady, sustained fashion during stimulation, and they seem to be best at picking up precise details about the stimulus. **Y cells** respond with quick bursts of action potentials when they are stimulated, and then they return to the previous firing rate (Sterling, 1983). They seem to be particularly sensitive to movement. The **W cells**, which Lennie (1980) prefers to call "sluggish cells," respond slowly to stimulation, but—like the Y cells—they respond best to moving stimuli.

Every process discussed so far occurs on the paper-thin retina. Even at this relatively primitive level of visual processing, however, information is registered about color, contrast, and movement. Now we must move

onward to see what happens to the information gathered by the ganglion cells.

Summary: Anatomy of the Eye

1. Three visible parts of the eye are the
   sclera, the iris, and the pupil.

2. The cornea, a clear membrane in front of
   the iris, bends light rays.

3. The conjunctiva is the pink membrane
   that lines the eyelid and attaches the eye
   to the eyelid; it covers muscles that provide eye movements.

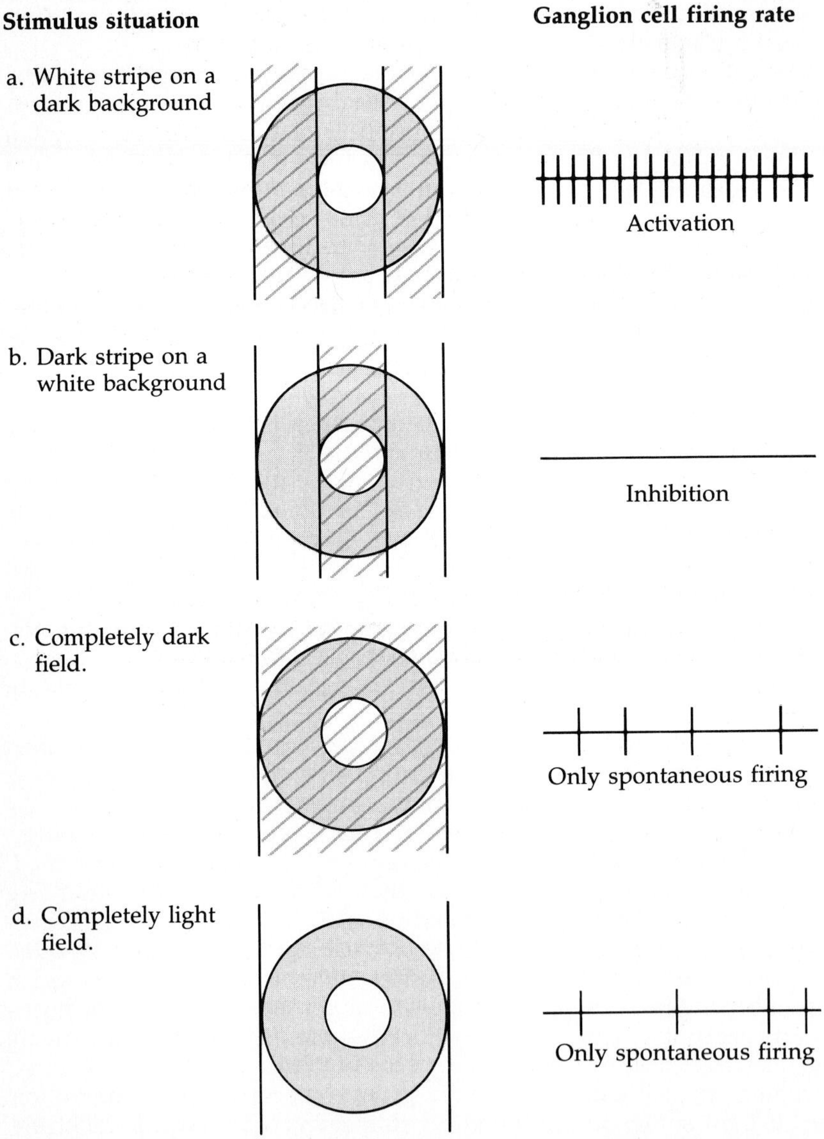

Stimulus situation

Ganglion cell firing rate

a. White stripe on a
   dark background

Activation

b. Dark stripe on a
   white background

Inhibition

c. Completely dark
   field.

Only spontaneous firing

d. Completely light
   field.

Only spontaneous firing

Figure 3.11 Electrical activity produced by on-center, off-surround ganglion cell in
response to four stimulus situations.

4. The shape of the lens changes to bring objects into focus; the shape of the lens is controlled by the ciliary muscles.
5. The eye has two compartments, each filled with special material called aqueous humor and vitreous humor; vitreous humor often holds floaters.
6. The choroid layer contains arteries and veins, and it absorbs extra light.
7. The retina absorbs light rays and changes them into information that can be transmitted by the neurons. The retina contains the fovea, where vision is sharpest, and the optic disk, where a blind spot is created because there are no light receptors.
8. The cells in the retina are the photoreceptors, bipolar cells, ganglion cells, horizontal cells, and amacrine cells.
9. Cones allow color vision in well-lit or photopic conditions. They are in the fovea, and very few cones share each ganglion cell. As a result acuity in the cone region is excellent but sensitivity is poor.
10. Rods, which allow black-and-white vision in dimly lit or scotopic conditions, are in the part of the retina outside the fovea, and many rods share each ganglion cell. As a result acuity in the rod region is poor but sensitivity is excellent.
11. Rods and cones contain photopigments that are transformed by light into a different chemical substance; this process appears to create an electrical imbalance, and this information is transmitted to higher levels in visual processing.
12. Ganglion cell electrical activity is studied by inserting a microelectrode near a ganglion cell, using single cell recording techniques.
13. Ganglion cells usually are either on-center, off-surround or off-center, on-surround.
14. There are three structurally different kinds of ganglion cells found in the cat retina: X cells, which respond in a sustained fashion and pick up precise details about the stimulus; Y cells, which respond with quick bursts and are sensitive to movement; and W cells, which respond slowly and are sensitive to movement.

PATHWAY FROM THE EYE TO THE BRAIN AND THE VISUAL CORTEX

Look again at Figure 3.9 and notice at the bottom how the ends from the ganglion cells are gathered together. The bundle of ends is called the **optic nerve**. This nerve is almost as

Table 3.2 Characteristics of X and Y Ganglion Cells

Characteristic	Type of Ganglion Cell	
	X	Y
Nature of receptive field	Center-surround	Center-surround
Cell size	Small	Large
Size of receptive field	Small	Large
Kind of response	Sustained	Quick bursts
Speed of conduction	Slow	Fast
Kind of stimulus responded to	Precise details	Movement
Area of brain where ganglion terminates	Lateral geniculate nucleus	Lateral geniculate nucleus and superior colliculus

big around as your little finger. Figure 3.12 shows the optic nerve and other structures in the pathway to the brain.

Optic Chiasm

Now look at Figure 3.13 to see the best illustration of the **optic chiasm**, the area in which the two optic nerves come together and cross over. The name *optic chiasm* makes sense because optic means "having to do with the eye" and chiasm is based on the Greek letter χ; the shape in the χ corresponds to the crossover in the optic chiasm. The visual system actually provides two kinds of crossovers; one occurs before the stimulus is registered on the retina.

Suppose that you are looking at a series of numbers from 1 to 8. The lens in the eye reverses the images and turns them upside down. Notice that the numbers are reversed and upside down on the retina in Figure 3.13. As you look at the world, something on the left-hand side (**left visual field**) is registered on the *right*-hand side of each retina. In contrast, something on the right-hand side (**right visual field**) is registered on the *left*-hand side of each retina.

The ganglion cell endings from the optic nerve continue on the other side of the optic chiasm; they do not transfer information to new cells. However, their neat job of splitting and regrouping should instill envy in professional square dancers. Consider the retina on the right-hand side of the diagram. Trace the path of the optic nerve and notice how the paths separate at the optic chiasm. Half the fibers cross over, but half remain on the same side. The same pattern is true for the retina on the left-hand side. Notice that these two sets of complex crossings produce an interesting effect. Everything in the left portion of each eye's visual field (here the numbers 1, 2, 3, and 4) is registered on the right side of each retina. Ultimately, this information ends up on the right side of the brain after crossing the optic chiasm. Notice that the numbers 1, 2, 3, and 4 are shown in the right visual cortex at the bottom of the diagram. Similarly, everything that in the right portion of each eye's visual field (for instance, the numbers 5, 6, 7, and 8) eventually ends up in the left visual cortex. Demonstration 3.4 may help to solidify your understanding of these processes.

Why does this complex crossing pattern exist? Many other species have a complete

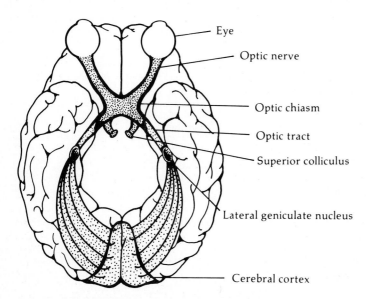

Figure 3.12   Visual pathway from eye to brain.

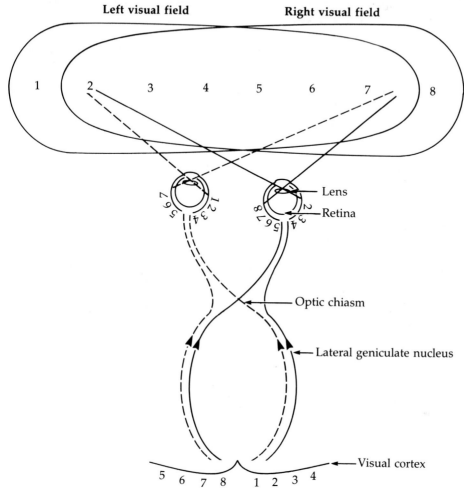

Figure 3.13 Schematic diagram of visual processing, showing two kinds of crossings, one through lens and the other at optic chiasm.

crossover: Everything registered on the right retina crosses to the left, and everything from the left retina crosses to the right. Humans and some other species, however, have binocular vision; their eyes work together and have partially overlapping fields of view. We need some way of coordinating what our eyes see. Look straight ahead and notice some object at the left of each visual field. Although this object is being registered on both the right and the left retinas, information from both sources will end up on the right side of

your head, where the information can be combined. As you'll learn in later chapters, humans use information from their binocular vision to know the distance of a particular object.

Notice in Figure 3.12 that the bundle of fibers is called the **optic tract** after it crosses the optic chiasm. The order of the structures in visual processing, after leaving the retina, is (1) optic nerve, (2) optic chiasm, and (3) optic tract. Each branch of the optic tract carries information from both eyes but does not

Demonstration 3.4
_____

Understanding the
Crossovers at the
Lens and at the
Optic Chiasm

The purpose of this demonstration is to make certain that you have mastered the complex crossovers in the visual system. It often helps if you relate something abstract to your own body and experiences.

First of all, notice some prominent object at the *left* side of your visual field—something that both eyes can see. This object will be registered on the *right* side of your retinas. Point to the right side of both your left and right eyes. Now trace across the top of your head how the information about this object travels to your cerebral cortex. (For a reference point, the optic chiasm is located several centimeters above the point where your tongue is attached in your mouth.) That is, from the right side of the retina of your right eye, trace a path to the optic chiasm and then to right side of the back of your head. From the right side of the retina of your left eye, similarly trace a path to the optic chiasm and then to the right side of the back of your head. Notice then that the objects on the left of the visual field end up on the right side.

Now repeat this exercise with some object on the right side of your visual field, using Figure 3.13 as your guide. Notice that objects on the right side of the visual field end up on the left side.

combine the information. The optic tract fibers travel to two areas. Some of the fibers go to the superior colliculus, but most go to the lateral geniculate nucleus.

Superior Colliculus

The superior colliculus would make a good name for a rock group, but so far nobody has rushed to claim it. The **superior colliculus** is a relatively primitive part of the brain that is important for locating moving objects. There are two superior colliculi, one for each optic tract. The pathway of visual processing continues from the superior colliculus to Areas 18 and 19 of the visual cortex.

In birds and some other vertebrates, most of the optic tract fibers proceed to a structure similar to the superior colliculus (Abramov & Gordon, 1973). Moving targets, such as bugs, are important to these animals, so you can appreciate why the superior colliculus is so critical.

In humans some of the Y ganglion cells and all the W ganglion cells go to the superior colliculus rather than to the lateral geniculate nucleus. Notice from Table 3.2 that the Y ganglion cells detect movement. These ganglion cells do not notice precise details or information about shape. Instead, if something moves and this movement is picked up by a ganglion cell outside the fovea, the information will alert the eye muscles to move the eye so that the ganglion cells in the fovea can analyze the details of the object. Thus, the superior colliculus does serve a function in humans. However, the lateral geniculate nucleus is generally more important.

Lateral Geniculate Nucleus

Jargon shock may have reached an advanced state when you saw the name of this section, but the name "lateral geniculate nucleus" makes sense. Lateral means "on the side," and there is one structure on each side of the brain. Geniculate means "bent like a knee," and this description is also accurate. Nucleus means "little nut." So a lateral geniculate nucleus looks like a little nut that is bent like a knee, located on the side of the brain.

The **lateral geniculate nucleus (LGN)** is a part of the thalamus where 80% of the ganglion cells that began in the retina finally stop, transferring their information to new neurons. (The other 20% stop at the superior colliculus.) Since the distance between the retina and the LGN is substantial, ganglion cells are fairly long in comparison to most other cells in the human body.

Whereas the superior colliculus is particularly responsive to moving stimuli, the LGN is important in shape perception. Furthermore, the LGN is more likely than the superior colliculus to receive stimulation that originated in the fovea. The LGN is also more likely to receive information about color (Lennie, 1984). These two middle-level structures differ substantially in the kind of information they receive and the functions they perform.

Ganglion cells terminate in the LGN. They do not, however, arrive at the LGN in a random fashion. Instead, the arrangement is **retinotopic**; ganglion cells that receive information from neighboring areas of the retina terminate near each other in the visual cortex. The LGN has six layers. Each layer of the LGN represents a rough map that corresponds to the information registered on the retina. The structure therefore resembles six similar maps stacked on top of each other. At any given point similar information is registered on upper and lower layers.

The neurons in the LGN, to which the ganglion cells transfer their information, function much like the ganglion cells. That is, the LGN cells are either on-center, off-surround, or off-center, on-surround. Some also share the characteristics of X cells, and some share the characteristics of Y cells. Incidentally, this information—as well as other characteristics of the LGN—has been obtained by the single cell recording technique, in which a microelectrode is placed near a single cell in the LGN. The technique is similar to the one used in studying the retinal ganglion cell.

Each of the six layers of the LGN receives input from only one eye. If the layers remain distinctly separate, there is no opportunity for information from both eyes to be combined in the LGN. In other words, the coordination of information from both eyes—so necessary for binocular vision—must occur at a higher level. For this coordination to occur, the information must travel to the visual cortex. Notice that the pathway from the LGN to the visual cortex is straightforward with no additional crossovers.

Visual Cortex

The **visual cortex** is the part of the **cerebral cortex**, or outer part of the brain, concerned with vision. Notice in Figure 3.14 that the visual cortex is in the rear part of the brain. If you place your hand at the back of your head, just above your neck, the visual cortex will be immediately in front of your hand.

The cerebral cortex consists of many other parts in addition to the visual cortex and is vital for human functions. In animals other than mammals, the cerebral cortex is either extremely tiny or nonexistent. In some primates such as monkeys and chimpanzees, the cerebral cortex is important, but in humans it is even more essential. As Hubel and Wiesel (1979, p. 150) remark, a human "without a cortex is almost a vegetable, speechless, sightless, senseless."

The entire cerebral cortex is only about 2 mm thick. In other words, the cover on your textbook is thicker than the covering on your brain! This covering is elaborately folded; if we could spread it out, the total area would be about 1400 cm^2, about the size of the screen on a 21-inch (53 cm) television. As Hubel and Wiesel note, the folding probably occurs because this extensive structure has to be packed into a box the size of a human skull.

Notice that the rear portion of the visual cortex in Figure 3.14 has three sections. Neurons from the lateral geniculate nuclei terminate in **Area 17**, which is also referred to as the **primary visual cortex** or the **striate cortex**. Striate means "striped": a microscopic investigation of this area of the cortex reveals pale stripes. By convention, the layers within Area 17 are identified by roman numerals.

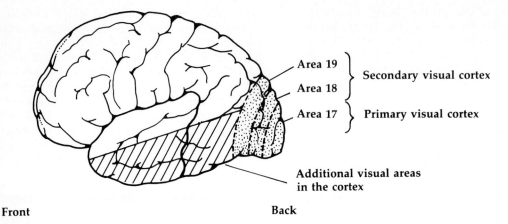

Area 19 } Secondary visual cortex

Area 18

Area 17 } Primary visual cortex

Additional visual areas
in the cortex

Front   Back

Figure 3.14   Visual cortex.

The layer next to the skull is layer I, and the innermost layer is layer VI. (See Figure 3.16.) In this numbering system the cells from the LGN terminate in the region at the bottom of layer IV, which is called layer IVc. All those neuronal messages traced from the photoreceptors in the retina, through the bipolar cells, through the ganglion cells, and through the LGN finally arrive in layer IVc of Area 17 of the visual cortex. (The cells in layer IVc, incidentally, have the same kind of center-surround organization as ganglion cells and LGN cells. Other cells in the cortex have a different kind of organization.)

We have several topics to discuss in connection with the visual cortex. These topics include: the spatial organization in the visual cortex, neurons in the visual cortex, and the regions of the visual cortex beyond Area 17.

Spatial Arrangement in the Visual Cortex

The arrangement of the LGN is not random but retinotopic. In other words, the pattern of information in the LGN has an approximately map-like correspondence to the pattern of information on the retina. Similarly, the spatial arrangement of layer IVc of Area 17 of the visual cortex has a retinotopic arrangement. This retinotopic structure has been demonstrated using both the single cell recording technique and careful anatomical

examinations with special kinds of radioactively labeled chemicals (Tootell, Silverman, Switkes, & DeValois, 1982).

We could make a map showing how each point on the retina is represented on the visual cortex. When you look at a road map, you see that Michigan is closer to Ohio than to California, and this map corresponds to geographic reality. Similarly, when you look at a picture of the Mona Lisa, this visual cortex map would represent her left eye as being closer to her right eye than to her mouth. Thus this visual cortex map corresponds to the patterns registered on your retina.

Do not take this retinotopic arrangement too literally, however. When you look at a picture of the Mona Lisa, there is *not* a perfect representation of her (complete with smile) in your visual cortex. Many factors make the representation less than perfect. For example, about half of the neurons in the visual cortex receive information from the fovea, that small central part of the retina. Thus the part of a picture registered on the fovea will be represented by more than its normal share of space in the visual cortex. The overrepresentation of information from the fovea with respect to the cortex is called **cortical magnification.**

Still, the correspondence between the pattern on the retina and the pattern on the visual cortex is remarkable. Dobelle, Mladejovsky, and Girvin (1974) conducted a study in which electrodes arranged in a particular shape were placed over a person's visual cortex. The person reported "seeing" the geometric shape that corresponded to the pattern of electrode stimulation. It would be wonderful if this kind of system could be used to restore sight to people whose blindness is peripheral and whose visual cortexes could work correctly if they received appropriate stimuli. Unfortunately, however, tissues are damaged when the electrical stimulation is used on a long-term basis. Therefore simple, direct stimulation of the cortex is not a satisfactory solution. The research of Dobelle and his colleagues is, however, important in confirming the retinotopic organization of the cortex.

Neurons in the Visual Cortex

Much of the credit for our understanding of the visual cortex can be awarded to David Hubel and Torsten Wiesel, who presented the first reports of their research in the late 1950s and later received the Nobel Prize. Hubel and Wiesel used the single cell recording technique to determine the characteristics of cells in the visual cortex. Probing with the microelectrode might reveal, for example, that one neuron produces a sudden burst of activity when a horizontal line is presented, whereas another neuron produces activity only when a vertical line is presented. These findings were particularly exciting to psychologists because they suggested a way in which the visual system could analyze the parts of a pattern.

Hubel and Wiesel (1965, 1979) isolated three kinds of neurons, each with response patterns different from the center-surround patterns found at earlier stages in visual processing. Their names are impressively straightforward: simple, complex, and hypercomplex. (The prefix hyper- means "extra.")

1. **Simple cells** are in layer IVb of Area 17, and they receive input from layer IVc neurons directly underneath. Neurons in the earlier

stages of visual processing have roughly circular receptive fields, but the simple cells respond most vigorously to lines and to edges. These cells are fairly selective. Like a picky eater who responds only to vanilla ice cream, not chocolate and certainly not rum raisin, these simple cells respond only when the conditions are just right. The light must fall in a particular part of the visual field. Diffuse illumination of that area will not work, although the cells might give a sputter of activity to small spots of light. They respond *enthusiastically* only to lines with the correct orientation. The most effective line orientation depends upon which cell you are examining. Furthermore, these cells are so picky that a change of about 15° may cause them to stop responding. For example, a cell that would respond optimally to the small (hour) hand of a clock that reads 12:00 would stop responding if that hand advanced a mere 15° to its position at 12:30! Figure 3.15a illustrates the electrical activity that might be generated if this cell were to respond to several different orientations of a line. Notice that the cell produces only a low level of spontaneous firing if the line is horizontal. There is somewhat more firing if the line is close to vertical, but a maximum firing rate occurs only when the line is perfectly vertical. These firing rates can be used to construct a graph illustrating the relationship between the angular orientation of the line and the cell's response rate; this graph is known as an **orientation tuning curve**, and it is illustrated in Figure 3.15b. Similar tuning curves can be constructed for other cells, which might be optimally responsive to other orientations such as diagonal or horizontal lines.

2. **Complex cells** are usually found in layers II, III, V, and VI of the cortex (but not in layer IV, like the simple cells), and they respond most to moving stimuli (Lennie, 1980). Simple cells respond to lines registered in a specific portion of the retina. In contrast, complex cells respond to a larger receptive field. Some complex cells respond with particularly vigorous bursts of electrical activity when a line moves in a particular direction, for example, when a vertical line moves to the

Stimulus ⟶ Response

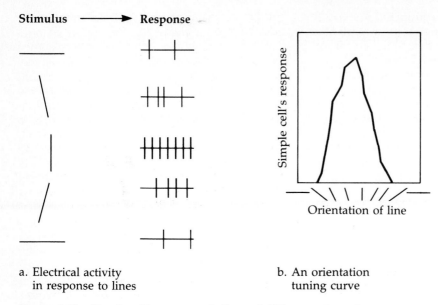

a. Electrical activity
   in response to lines

b. An orientation
   tuning curve

Figure 3.15 Simple cell's response to lines of different orientations.

left (but not to the right). Other complex cells respond to movement in both directions.

3. **Hypercomplex cells** are usually found in Areas 18 and 19 of the visual cortex, and they respond most to moving lines or corners of a specific size (Hubel, 1982). Complex cells would respond to any line of the appropriate orientation moving in the appropriate direction. However, hypercomplex cells are so picky that a typical hypercomplex cell might respond vigorously only if a right angle containing lines of certain sizes moved diagonally upward and toward the left. This cell might not respond at all if the same stimulus moved in the opposite direction, downward and toward the right. Furthermore, hypercomplex cells refuse to respond if the stimulus is appropriately oriented but too long. (Recent research summarized by DeValois, Thorell, and Albrecht [1985] has suggested that some simple and complex cells may also share this characteristic.)

A consistent trend emerges in moving toward higher levels in the visual processing system; cells become more selective. Photoreceptors respond when light reaches them. Ganglion cells and LGN cells respond only if there is a contrast between the center of the receptive field and the surrounding area. Simple cells require lines, complex cells require moving lines, and hypercomplex cells require moving lines of particular dimensions.

Hubel and Wiesel and their coauthors, as well as other research groups, have performed more recent research that provides additional details about the structure of the visual cortex. In particular, their explorations have revealed that the primary visual cortex is arranged in a series of columns.

▶ **IN-DEPTH:**
CORTICAL COLUMNS

When Hubel and Wiesel were exploring the properties of individual cells, they became intrigued with a feature that they refer to as "architecture" (Hubel, 1982). When they lowered an electrode through the layers of the cortex, they discovered that all the cells they encountered had the highest response rate to a line of one orientation; they referred to this vertical series of cells as a **column**. Figure 3.16 illustrates how an electrode inserted perpen-

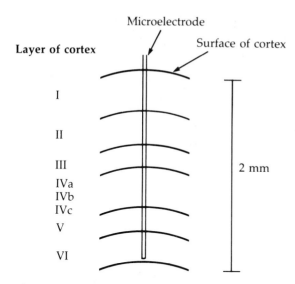

Figure 3.16 Inserting microelectrode down through the visual cortex.

dicular to the surface of the cortex might pass through a large number of cells (including simple, complex, and hypercomplex), all of which produced the highest response rate when a line was presented in the visual field at a 45° angle. Hubel and Wiesel inserted the electrode through the 2 mm thickness of one point in the primary visual cortex, tested the animal, and recorded the orientation the cells in that column preferred. Then they moved on to a new location a fraction of a millimeter away and again tested.

Hubel and Wiesel discovered that by moving the electrode as little as .05 mm—literally a hairbreadth—from its previous location they found a column of cells that no longer responded so enthusiastically to a line of the previously tested orientation. Instead, the preferred orientation had shifted to a line that had rotated by about 10°. For example, if cells in the previously tested column had produced the highest response rate to a line at a 45° angle, the cells in the column .05 mm away would be likely to produce the highest response rate to a line at a 55° angle. Incidentally, Hubel (1982) describes the painstaking nature of this research, spending 5

solid hours at a time to record 53 successive orientations.

From repeated recordings Hubel and Wiesel found that by moving the electrode a distance of 1 mm along the cortex, they encountered a series of columns in which the preferred stimulus had changed from a perfectly horizontal line to a vertical line and completed the cycle by returning to a perfectly horizontal line. Figure 3.17 illustrates these results schematically. (Since layer IVc has cells with center/surround preferences rather than orientation preferences, there is a blank space at that layer.) Since 18 to 20 adjacent columns are required to complete a full cycle of stimulus-orientation preferences, Hubel and Wiesel called this sequence of columns a **hypercolumn**.

Notice that Figure 3.17 is a three-dimensional diagram. The third dimension is labeled "right eye ocular dominance" and "left eye ocular dominance." Cells in the cortex receive information from both eyes, but they usually have a higher response rate to one eye, a tendency called **ocular dominance**. The clump of cells nearest to the viewer would be more responsive to stimuli from the right eye; the cells farthest away, to stimuli from the left eye.

It might be tempting to believe that all the columns are similar as long as they share a given preference for stimulus orientation and a given ocular dominance. Within each set, however, each column corresponds to a particular location in the visual field. Thus, within every tiny patch in Area 17 of your visual cortex—a patch no bigger than 1 mm² and 2 mm deep—your visual system encodes a variety of stimulus orientation preferences, two kinds of ocular dominance (right-eye and left-eye), and a variety of locations.

The research discussed so far involved the single cell recording technique. To verify the column structure of the cortex other researchers used the **2-deoxyglucose (2-DG) technique**, so called because is uses a radioactive chemical similar to glucose to record cell activity.

Hubel, Wiesel, and Stryker (1978) injected an anesthetized monkey with 2-DG, then

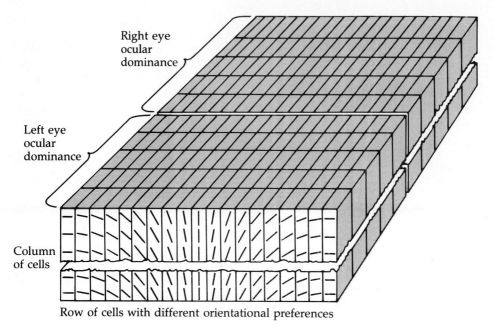

Right eye
ocular
dominance

Left eye
ocular
dominance

Column
of cells

Row of cells with different orientational preferences

Figure 3.17 Schematic diagram of hypercolumn. Note that hypercolumn includes cells from all layers of cortex (I through VI), cells with all orientation preferences, and cells with both right and left eye ocular dominance.

showed the monkey a pattern of vertical stripes that rotated from left to right. This pattern was displayed for 45 min, a period clearly long enough to stimulate every cell that would be responsive to vertical lines.

The 2-DG technique is based on the fact that cells use glucose as a source of energy. The more active a cell is, the more glucose it uses. The 2-DG is a close enough relative of glucose that active cells take it up; however, when cells break down 2-DG, some remaining molecules—unlike the end products of glucose breakdown—cannot pass out of the cell. Fortunately for researchers, a cell's activity can be measured in terms of the quantity of 2-DG that has accumulated.

The radioactivity of 2-DG is important because it permits a technique called **autoradiography**; after the monkey was sacrificed, its brain was sliced into thin sections and each section was placed on a microscope slide. In a darkroom the slides were then coated with the chemical used in photographic film. The slides were allowed to develop, and the areas

of the brain that had absorbed the most radioactive 2-DG appeared as black spots, whereas the parts that had not absorbed the radioactive 2-DG appeared as white spots. As Carlson (1986) points out, autoradiography can be translated approximately as "writing with your own radiation."

Suppose the cycle of stimulus orientation preferences repeats about every millimeter, as had been demonstrated with the single cell recording technique. If so, then a dark band should occur about every millimeter because columns that preferred a perfectly vertical orientation (the one the monkey had seen for 45 minutes) should be at approximately 1 mm intervals. Figure 3.18 shows an autoradiograph of a section of the monkey's cortex. The bar at the lower right is 1 mm long, and the dark bands on the autoradiograph are about 1 mm apart, exactly as predicted by the earlier research. The dark horizontal band shows that the cells in layer IVc were not selective for orientation, as had also been predicted.

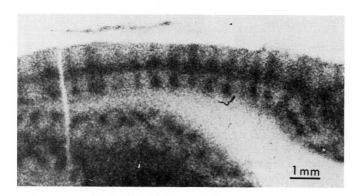

Figure 3.18 Autoradiograph of cross section of visual cortex of monkey injected with 2-DG and exposed to vertical stripes. (From Hubel, Wiesel, & Stryker, 1978. Used with permission.)

Ocular dominance was studied in related research (Hubel & Wiesel, 1977; Hubel, Wiesel, & Stryker, 1978). One eye of a monkey was injected with a radioactive substance, and the other eye was covered with a patch. The autoradiograph for a section of the monkey's cortex showed 1 mm wide dark stripes, representing areas with ocular dominance for the unpatched eye, alternating with 1 mm-wide light stripes, representing areas with ocular dominance for the patched eye. As Figure 3.17 illustrated, regions of right ocular and left ocular dominance alternate in the cortex.

At about the time of this research, Hubel and Wiesel announced to the general public that Area 17 of the visual cortex was fairly well understood. As Hubel (1982, p. 524) recalls, "This was done deliberately: one did not want the well to dry up. When one wants rain the best strategy is to leave raincoat and umbrella at home. So the best way to guarantee future employment was to declare the job finished."

The deception proved an effective stimulant. Later research demonstrated a polka-dot pattern of neurons—referred to by the delightfully straightforward name "blobs"—that appeared at regular intervals throughout the column structure in Area 17 (Humphrey & Hendrickson, 1980; Livingstone & Hubel, 1983). Similar research techniques were then extended to study the structure of Area 18

(Livingstone & Hubel, 1983). More recent research has also demonstrated a columnar structure for the cells in other areas of the visual cortex. In this research Albright, Desimone, and Gross (1984) revealed that columnar structure is not limited to the primary visual cortex or even to the part of the cortex in the rear of the brain. Instead, organization into columns may be a feature characteristic of most of the visual cortex. ■

Beyond Area 17

The clear majority of research on cortical processing in vision has concentrated on Area 17, also called the primary visual cortex, or striate cortex. As Figure 3.14 illustrated, two other regions at the back of the brain are concerned with vision. These are **Area 18** and **Area 19**, often called the **secondary visual cortex** (as opposed to primary visual cortex) or the **extrastriate cortex** (where extra means "beyond," as in "extraterrestrial"). These areas were mentioned in the discussion of the superior colliculus because the superior colliculus sends messages to Areas 18 and 19, rather than 17. Since some information is sent on from Area 17 to the complex and hypercomplex cells in Areas 18 and 19, they receive information that has already been processed and coded for information such as orientation of lines. Many cells in Areas 18 and 19 respond well to input from both eyes; binocular depth information therefore may be handled in this region.

In all, probably at least 15 regions in the brain process visual information (Ornstein & Thompson, 1984). The additional visual areas generally occupy the lower region of the cortex in front of Area 19, as illustrated in Figure 3.13. These additional areas receive information from Areas 18 and 19 and they handle extremely complex visual processing.

So far, this chapter has emphasized a "bottom-up," or data-driven, approach to perception. Data gathered from the receptors are passed up to higher levels in the visual processing system. Consistent with Theme 3, the chapter has emphasized that our visual systems are impressively designed to pass information through increasingly sophisticated kinds of processing. So far, we have not mentioned any form of learning or any role it can play in perception, Theme 4 has not even been mentioned. However, learning does appear to be relevant in these additional visual areas of the cortex. For example, monkeys who have had this area of the brain surgically removed are no longer able to recall which objects are food, and should be eaten, and which objects are metal, and should be rejected. This task depends not merely on vision but on the association between visual qualities and experience. For this reason part of this region of the visual cortex is known as the **association cortex**.

Thompson (1985) provides a particularly vivid account of an exciting episode in the history of research on vision. Using the single cell recording technique, Charles Gross and his colleagues at Harvard University were investigating cells in the association cortex of monkeys. They presented the usual visual stimuli, including spots of light, bars, and other simple stimuli, to one monkey. The neurons responded weakly to these stimuli, but they did not provide any enthusiastic bursts of electrical activity. The researchers had been studying a particular cell for an extended time, but the response had been so minimal that they decided to move on to another cell. One whimsical experimenter bid that cell a symbolic farewell by raising his hand in front of the monkey's eye and waving

goodbye. The cell immediately began to fire rapidly to the moving hand. As you can imagine, the researchers did *not* proceed to the next cell, but instead began cutting out a variety of hand-shaped stimuli and waving them in front of the monkey's eyes. Their inquiry demonstrated that what the cell really responded to most vigorously was the upright hand shaped like the monkey's paw! It seems then that the cells in this part of the visual cortex each have the highest response rate to specific complex shapes.

Outside of Area 17, there are areas of the brain that analyze qualities of the visual stimulus such as motion, size, and specific shape, and researchers are beginning to explore these qualities (for example, Albright, 1984). Unfortunately, however, many mysteries remain about these more sophisticated levels of visual processing. As Riggs (1983, p. 738) remarks, "One gets the impression at this point that a huge gap exists between the body of knowledge obtained from single-cell probing of the visual cortex and the body of knowledge about visual perception. . . . We still have no evidence, for example, of what areas of the cortex may be involved in recognizing letters of the alphabet, faces of people, or foreground objects as distinct from their backgrounds."

Review: Pathway from the Eye to the Brain and the Visual Cortex

1. The bundle of ends from ganglion cells is called the optic nerve.
2. The visual system has two kinds of crossovers: (a) visual material is reversed by the lens onto the retina, and (b) at the optic chiasm, half the fibers in each optic nerve cross over. As a result of these crossovers, everything from the left side of the visual field ends up on the right-hand side of the head, and everything from the right side of the visual field ends up on the left-hand side of the head.
3. The optic tract, as the optic nerve is called after the optic chiasm, travels to the superior colliculus, which is important in the detection of movement, and to the lateral geniculate nucleus.

4. The lateral geniculate nucleus is organized into six layers that have retinotopic arrangements; cells in the LGN function like ganglion cells.
5. The visual cortex is the portion of the outer part of the brain concerned with vision. The cortex is responsible for higher levels of visual processing.
6. The visual cortex at the rear of the brain is divided into three portions known as Areas 17, 18, and 19.
7. Neuronal messages from the lateral geniculate nucleus arrive in layer IVc of Area 17, which has a retinotopic arrangement.
8. The cortex has three kinds of neurons: simple, complex, and hypercomplex.
9. Neurons in Area 17 appear to be arranged in columns; in each column neurons have the highest response rate to a line of one particular orientation. Cells in an adjacent column have the highest response rate to a line whose orientation has shifted by about 10°.
10. A hypercolumn is a series of columns that covers a full cycle of stimulus-orientation preferences.
11. Cells in the cortex are arranged according to ocular dominance and location as well as stimulus orientation preference; research by Hubel, Wiesel, and Stryker has confirmed this point by using a technique called autoradiography.
12. Areas 18 and 19 of the visual cortex receive information from Area 17; and they pass this information on for more complex visual processing.
13. Additional areas of the visual cortex are responsible for complex visual processing, involving learning and associations; the functions of these areas are not well understood.

SOME DISORDERS OF THE VISUAL SYSTEM

The branch of medicine concerned with visual problems is **ophthalmology**. A brief discussion of ophthalmology should be useful because most people know someone who has had eye problems. If you choose a career in education, industrial psychology, or counseling, you will be working with people with visual problems; an overview of these disorders will be helpful.

In the next chapter we will talk about the disorders that you know best, nearsightedness and farsightedness, when we consider the focusing ability of the eye; Chapter 5 will cover color deficiencies. In this current chapter we will look at some other common problems, beginning with the external parts of the eye and then moving on to disorders involving binocular coordination, disorders of the lens and retina, and disorders of the optic nerve and visual cortex.

Disorders of External Parts of Eye

The cornea is the transparent layer at the front of the eye. Even though it is almost invisible, the cornea is a strong barrier against disease germs. If the cornea is injured, however, disease germs can enter easily (Vaughan & Asbury, 1986). Without proper treatment, the cornea could be destroyed within 24 hours. Consequently, corneal problems are considered serious. One of the most common is the presence of a foreign body. A **foreign body** is an object that does not belong in a particular location, such as a small chip of metal from an industrial accident. Anyone with a corneal foreign body should be taken immediately to an ophthalmologist. A foreign body can also scratch the cornea, producing a painful **corneal abrasion**, which also requires medical attention.

The iris is the colored area just underneath the cornea. **Iritis**, or inflammation of the iris, is a reasonably common disorder (Vaughan & Asbury, 1986). Its cause is usually unknown, and it typically affects only one eye. A person with iritis complains of pain and blurred vision and feels more comfortable if the light is not overly bright. Iritis usually produces a red area in the part of the sclera that circles the iris. If iritis is not treated, parts of the iris may become attached to the lens, causing the opening of the pupil to be fixed in size, rather than variable. With medication, the disorder is typically corrected in about 10 days.

Conjuctivitis is an inflammation of the conjuctiva, the pink membranes that line the eyelids and attach to the eye. Sometimes called "pinkeye," it is one of the most common eye diseases in the Western Hemisphere. The conjunctiva is exposed to numerous organisms, irritants, and dangerous materials. This membrane is attacked by smog, smoke, dust, bacteria, viruses, and substances that produce allergies. Fortunately, tears usually help resist these attacks; they dilute the offending substances and wash them away. Conjunctivitis occurs when tears have failed. The major symptoms of conjunctivitis are the bright red of the conjunctiva and an itchy sensation. The treatment for conjunctivitis depends upon the cause of the disease. For example, soothing eyedrops may help some kinds of conjunctivitis, whereas antibiotics may be used when the conjunctivitis has been caused by bacteria.

Disorders Involving Binocular Coordination

The muscles that move the eyeball were illustrated in Figure 3.6. Normally, the muscles move the two eyes so that an image falls upon the same part of both retinas. **Strabismus**, sometimes called "cross-eye," occurs when the muscles for the two eyes do not work together, causing the image to fall upon the fovea in one retina and a different region of the retina in the other eye. Strabismus occurs in about 3% of the population (Sanders, 1986), beginning in childhood. Strabismus must be corrected for three reasons: (1) to allow good vision in each eye, (2) to allow binocular vision, and (3) to improve appearance. Otherwise, the child will favor the strong eye and ignore the image of the weaker eye. If this happens, the child may develop amblyopia. **Amblyopia**, or "lazy eye," involves blurry vision in one eye.

If strabismus is not corrected, a second disorder develops called stereoblindness. **Stereoblindness** refers to the inability to use depth information from binocular vision to see the world in depth. People with stereoblindness *can* use the depth cues involving one eye, but they are deprived of the extremely useful information that comes from each eye presenting the brain with a slightly different view of the world. Stereoblindness seems to have other serious consequences other than a deficit in depth perception. For example, Bedwell, Grant, and McKeown (1980) reported that people with stereoblindness are more likely than people with normal binocular vision to experience reading difficulties.

If the strabismus is noticed early enough, the condition can be corrected by placing a patch over the good eye. "The sooner, the better" is the rule here. If the eye is patched at 1 year of age, treatment may take only a week. If the child is 6 years old, however, it may take a year to make the acuity equal for the two eyes. After the acuity has been restored to the weaker eye, a surgeon can correct the unbalanced muscles.

Disorders of the Lens and Retina

The lens of the eye is usually almost transparent. **Cataracts** occur when injury or disease causes clouding. If the lens is too cloudy, light cannot pass through it, and blindness will result. Although most cataracts are not visible to a casual observer until they become dense enough to cause blindness, even in the early stages they can be detected with an ophthalmoscope (Vaughan & Asbury, 1986). Most cataracts are found in elderly people, and some cataract formation is normal in people over 70. Infants may be born with cataracts, which must be treated early to prevent blindness; von Noorden (1981) recommends that ideal results can be obtained only if cataracts are removed in the first few days after birth.

There is no way to prevent cataracts, unfortunately, and no cure, but there are partial remedies. The lens can be surgically removed and special contact lenses or thick eyeglasses worn. Also, an **intraocular lens**, a substitute lens, can be inserted through the pupil after the defective lens has been removed. If the technology of intraocular lenses can be successfully developed, numerous people will benefit. More than 1 million people develop cataracts each year in the United States, and cataract removal is the sixth most common of all surgical operations performed in this country (Van Heyningen, 1975).

Several disorders can occur in the retina. **Detached retina** occurs when a hole in the retina permits fluid to flow through, separating the retina from the choroid layer. Look back at Figure 3.7 and imagine a small hole in the retina that would permit the vitreous humor to seep through the retina and detach it from the choroid layer. A person who has a detached retina may complain about a sudden loss of vision or perceive lightning flashes. The treatment, which involves surgically reattaching the retina, is usually effective if it is performed soon after the condition is noticed (Vaughan & Asbury, 1986).

Diabetes has become a leading cause of blindness in the Western world (Vaughan & Asbury, 1986). The blindness caused by diabetes, **diabetic retinopathy**, is more likely for people who have had diabetes for a long time and for those whose diabetes has been poorly controlled. Blindness occurs because the blood vessels that supply the retina become thicker. Fluid leaks out, often causing a deposit of substances on the retina and a fluid-filled retina. As a result the light on the retina is scattered. Sometimes vision can improve spontaneously, but two surgical techniques have been developed to aid diabetic retinopathy (Henkind, Priest, & Schiller, 1983). One technique focuses a laser beam on the leaking blood vessels, sealing them and blocking passage of additional liquid. Another technique involves removing the vitreous humor, which has become filled with debris, and replacing it with a clear solution. This technique provides temporary relief, but it does not prevent future leakage.

Many visual disorders increase during old age; **retinopathy of prematurity** is a danger at the other end of the age continuum. Glass and her coauthors (1985) reported on how the standard conditions in a hospital nursery can produce retinal disorders. These researchers discovered that the normal levels of light experienced by premature babies, combined with other sources of light, such as the heat lamp and the phototherapy lamp, can produce severe damage to the retina and even blindness. You've probably heard that looking directly at the sun can cause blindness in adults. In the undeveloped retina of the premature infant, bright lights can have the same effect. If you know of any parents who have a new, premature baby, share this information with them!

Various liquids inside the eyeball maintain the eye's characteristic shape and nourish other parts. In **glaucoma**, however, too much fluid inside the eye causes too much pressure. Pressure that is great enough for a long time creates extensive damage. The ganglion cells in the retina and the optic nerve deteriorate, and the iris and the ciliary muscles are damaged. The lens may become cloudy, resulting in cataracts.

Vaughan and Asbury estimate that about 1.5% of people over age 40 have glaucoma and that about 50,000 people in the United States are blind as a result of it. Because glaucoma is relatively common, a test for this disease is usually included in eye examinations for older people. Most often, ophthalmologists use a technique called tonometry. As Havener (1979) remarks, the description of the technique takes much longer than the procedure itself. **Tonometry** uses a special instrument to measure the pressure inside the eye by pushing directly on the cornea. Although the eye is anesthetized, the procedure is mildly unpleasant. Nonetheless, tonometry is necessary for the early detection of glaucoma. If glaucoma is detected in time, the outlook is usually good because special drugs can be prescribed to reduce the pressure inside the eye.

This section began by discussing a disorder of the lens called cataracts, then looked at four disorders of the retina. The retina can become detached (*detached retina*); the blood vessels can be damaged as a result of diabetes (*diabetic retinopathy*); the retina in premature babies can be damaged by intense lights (*retinopathy of prematurity*); and too much pressure inside the eye can damage the retina and other parts of the visual system (*glaucoma*). Unfortunately, each of these disorders is particularly disabling because the retina is central in visual processes.

Disorders of the Optic Nerve and Visual Cortex

The visual pathway from the eye to the brain is also susceptible to a variety of diseases. For example, some diseases attack the coating of the optic nerve; multiple sclerosis, a disorder of the nervous system, is one. Common symptoms include a blind area in some part of the visual field. Tumors near the optic chiasm can also affect vision. Physicians can often detect the exact anatomical location of a tumor because a mass in a given location has a predictable effect on the visual fields. If the patient cannot see anything in a particular region of the visual fields, the physician can use this information to figure out the problem areas in the visual pathway.

Multiple sclerosis can also attack the visual cortex. A person with multiple sclerosis may have difficulty seeing a stimulus at a particular orientation. As Regan (1982) points out, physicians can trace this particular disorder to the visual cortex because orientation-specific neurons are not found at lower levels in visual processing.

The visual cortex can also be damaged in accidents or in war. For example, a bullet may enter through the back of the head, causing damage to the visual cortex. As a consequence, the person will be blind in a particular part of the visual field. This blind area is called a **scotoma**; the plural is **scotomata**. You will recall that there is a correspondence between the pattern on the retina and the pattern on the visual cortex. Some information about this correspondence has been gathered from patients who have scotomata. The researcher notes the damaged area of the visual cortex and the area of the visual field containing the scotoma.

Migraine headaches affect the blood flow to the visual cortex. Therefore one common symptom of migraines is visual disturbances.

In many cases the disturbance may be simple blurring of vision. Other times, people suffering from migraines report abnormal sensations such as pinwheels or lightning flashes. Some people report even more complex visual phenomena. Objects may appear to shrink or grow, for instance. There is an interesting suggestion for the amazing size changes that Alice experiences in *Alice in Wonderland* (Lippman, 1952; Van Dyke, 1980). Lewis Carroll, the author, suffered from migraines, and the shrinking and growing may simply reflect his own visual experiences!

Summary: Some Disorders of the Visual System

1. Ophthalmology is the branch of medicine concerned with visual problems.
2. The cornea can be damaged by a foreign body, allowing disease germs to enter, or by a corneal abrasion.
3. Iritis is an inflammation of the iris. If untreated, parts of the iris may become attached to the lens.
4. Conjunctivitis is a common disorder that involves an inflammation of the conjunctiva.
5. Strabismus occurs when the muscles for the two eyes do not work together. If uncorrected, this may lead to amblyopia, or suppression of the image in the weaker eye, and stereoblindness, or the inability to use binocular vision cues for depth perception.
6. Cataracts involve a clouding of the lens and are often found in elderly people. They can be partially treated by removing the lens and by using contact lenses or thick eyeglasses; intraocular lenses are currently being tested.
7. Four disorders of the retina are discussed in this chapter: (a) detached retina, (b) diabetic retinopathy, (c) retinopahy of prematurity, and (d) glaucoma.
8. The visual cortex can be damaged in accidents or in war. Migraine headaches may affect the blood flow to the visual cortex, leading to visual disturbances.

Review

1. The beginning of the chapter discussed the visual stimulus. List the three pairs of attributes that are concerned with light, specifying which member of the pair concerns the physical stimulus and which concerns the psychological reaction. What psychological reaction do we have to (a) short wavelengths, (b) long wavelengths, (c) low-amplitude wavelengths, and (d) high-amplitude wavelengths?

2. Discuss the portion of the electromagnetic radiation spectrum that humans can see. Discuss differences among species with respect to (a) the part of the spectrum to which they are sensitive; (b) the nature of the photoreceptors—rods and cones; (c) the crossover pattern at the optic chiasm; and (d) the superior colliculus.

3. Review the location and the function of the following: sclera, iris, pupil, cornea, and conjunctiva. Describe the kinds of diseases that can damage or irritate the iris, the cornea, and the conjunctiva.

4. What is the fovea, and where is it? How is the distribution of rods and cones relevant to a discussion of the fovea? Compare acuity in the fovea and nonfovea regions of the retina; then compare sensitivity in these two regions, noting how the issue of convergence is relevant.

5. Compare photopic and scotopic vision with respect to (a) lighting conditions in which the receptor functions best, (b) shape of photoreceptor, and (c) number of photoreceptors. Briefly describe the transduction process in rods.

6. Ganglion cells in the retina were discussed in some detail. Discuss how the electrical activity of these cells is studied; then describe the two kinds of receptive fields that ganglion cells are likely to have.

7. What are the two areas to which the fibers in the optic tract travel? What is the function of these two areas?

8. The arrangement of the neurons in the lateral geniculate nucleus and in layer IVc of the visual cortex were described as retinotopic. Discuss this term in relation to those two areas.

9. What is the structure of neurons in the remaining layers of Area 17, above and below layer IVc? Describe two research techniques that helped clarify our knowledge of cortical structure.

10. Discuss the function of the lens, the disorder called cataracts, and methods used to treat it. Describe four kinds of disorders that can severely affect the retina.

New Terms

electromagnetic radiation
wavelength
nanometer
light
hue
purity
amplitude
candelas per meter square (cd/ m^2)
sclera
iris
constrict

dilate
pupil
ophthalmologists
ophthalmoscope
cornea
conjunctiva
extraocular muscles
lens
ciliary muscles
aqueous humor
vitreous humor
floaters

choroid
retina
neurons
fovea
macula lutea
optic disk
blind spot
photoreceptors
cones
rods
bipolar cells
ganglion cells

horizontal cells
amacrine cells
duplicity theory
photopic vision
scotopic vision
acuity
transduction
photopigments
opsin
retinal
rhodopsin
disc shedding
action potentials
single cell recording
microelectrodes
receptive field
X cells
Y cells
W cells
optic nerve
optic chiasm
left visual field

right visual field
optic tract
superior colliculus
lateral geniculate nucleus
   (LGN)
retinotopic
visual cortex
cerebral cortex
Area 17
primary visual cortex
striate cortex
cortical magnification
simple cells
orientation tuning curve
complex cells
hypercomplex cells
column
hypercolumn
ocular dominance
2-deoxyglucose technique
autoradiography
Area 18

Area 19
secondary visual cortex
extrastriate cortex
association cortex
ophthalmology
foreign body
corneal abrasion
iritis
conjunctivitis
strabismus
amblyopia
stereoblindness
cataracts
intraocular lens
detached retina
diabetic retinopathy
retinopathy of prematurity
glaucoma
tonometry
scotoma (scotomata)

Recommended Readings

Carlson, N. R. (1986). *Physiology of behavior* (3rd ed.). Newton, MA: Allyn & Bacon. *There are a number of physiological psychology textbooks available, but this is one of the most current and clearly written.*

Henkind, P., Priest, R. S., & Schiller, G. (1983). *Compendium of ophthalmology.* Philadelphia: J. B. Lippincott. *This is an excellent dictionary for pursuing terms related to ophthalmology that would not be listed in standard dictionaries.*

Hubel, D. H. (1982). Exploration of the primary visual cortex, 1955–1978. *Nature, 299,* 515–524. *Readers will probably be intrigued by this first-hand recollection of what it's like to conduct the kind of research that wins the Nobel Prize.*

Thompson, R. F. (1985). *The brain: An introduction to neuroscience.* New York: Freeman. *This relatively short paperback provides information on neuronal functions, brain anatomy, neurotransmitters, and other topics; a chapter on sensory processes is particularly relevant.*

Vaughan, D., & Asbury, T. (1986). *General ophthalmology* (11th ed.). Los Altos, CA: Lange Medical Publications. *I examined many ophthalmology textbooks and discovered that most required an extensive medical background. In contrast, this book is clearly written and well organized. People who are not fascinated by pictures of diseased eyes may want to turn the pages cautiously.*

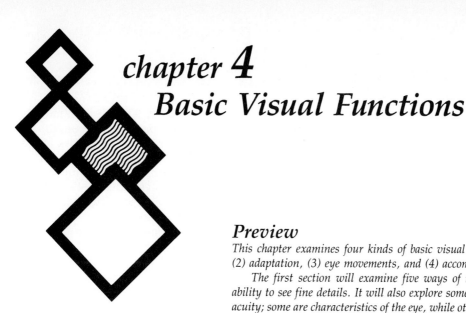

chapter 4
Basic Visual Functions

Preview

This chapter examines four kinds of basic visual functions: (1) acuity, (2) adaptation, (3) eye movements, and (4) accommodation.

The first section will examine five ways of measuring acuity, the ability to see fine details. It will also explore some factors that influence acuity; some are characteristics of the eye, while others are characteristics of the stimulus. The chapter will also note several applications of acuity.

Adaptation involves the change in sensitivity as the observer is exposed to darkness (dark adaptation) or light (light adaptation). During dark adaptation sensitivity increases gradually until the eyes reach their maximum sensitivity after about 30 minutes. During light adaptation the eyes become less sensitive to a light stimulus. This process is much faster and takes about 1 minute.

Eye movements can be divided into two basic groups, depending upon whether the eyes, during movement, keep the same angle between the lines of sight (version movements) or whether the angle changes (vergence movements). The most common version movement is saccadic movement, rapid movement of the eyes from one fixation point to the next; we will examine saccadic movement during reading in some detail. Other version movements include pursuit movements, those made in tracking a moving object, and involuntary eye movements. Vergence movements include convergence and divergence; they are necessary because both eyes must focus upon the same target. For example, you use vergence movements when you move your eyes away from an object in the distance toward a nearby object.

In accommodation the shape of the lens within the eye changes. This change is necessary to keep an image in focus on the retina. In this section we will also discuss focusing abnormalities: nearsightedness, farsightedness, and astigmatism.

The previous chapter discussed the anatomy of the visual system, concentrating on the physical and physiological characteristics. The current chapter discusses the basic visual functions; it will concentrate on what the eye can do.

It seems that we often do not appreciate these basic functions sufficiently. They are so basic that we take them for granted. However, imagine how inadequate we would be without them. Without acuity, for example, we could not read, watch movies, or look at a painting. Clearly, we would be limited without this ability to see details. Without adaptation we would be unable to function in both sunlight and moonlight. Eye movement is also essential; without it we could change our fixation points only by moving our heads. If you doubt the importance of eye movements, try walking to class without moving your eyes, or try reading the next sentence without eye movement. Finally, without accommodation we could see things clearly only if they were a certain, fixed distance from us. How would you operate if you could see clearly only those objects 2 ft (0.6 m) away from you, for example, everything closer or farther away being a big blur?

So let's look at our visual system's basic talents: We can discriminate, we can see in various lighting conditions, we can move our eyes, and we can focus.

ACUITY

Visual acuity is the ability to see fine details in a scene. More formally, "Acuity measures the resolution capabilities of the visual system in terms of the smallest high-contrast detail to be perceived at a given distance" (Olzak & Thomas, 1986, pp. 7–45). With good acuity, for example, we can discriminate two black dots placed close to each other on a white background as two separate objects rather than one blurred object. Good acuity allows us to notice, for example, that a friend has chicken pox—rather than a mild sunburn— before the friend gets too close. It also permits

us to read a road sign announcing the name of the next exit in enough time to move into the right-hand lane.

Acuity is concerned with discriminations between stimuli in space. For example, an acuity task might involve judgments about whether a white area separates two black areas. Several methods of measuring acuity are available. All involve a description of the amount of space occupied by the target, called visual angle. **Visual angle** means the size of the angle formed by extending two lines from your eye to the outside edges of the target. (Consult Demonstration 4.1 as we discuss this term.)

The visual angle is measured in degrees, minutes, and seconds. A circle has 360 degrees (symbolized °), but since your eyes cannot see in back of your head or even straight above your head, visual angles are always much smaller than 360°. Just as an hour is divided into minutes and seconds, a degree in space is divided into minutes and seconds. Each degree has 60 minutes (symbolized '), and each minute has 60 seconds (symbolized ").

The size of the visual angle depends upon the size of the target and the distance of the target from the eye. In Demonstration 4.1, you are looking at a circle 1.2 cm across. Larger circles would occupy larger visual angles. The size of the visual angle also depends upon the distance of the target from the eye. As you move the circle away from you, it occupies an increasingly smaller visual angle. Draw a diagram to convince yourself that a circle 2.4 cm across, viewed from a distance of 70 cm, would occupy the same visual angle as a circle 1.2 cm across viewed from a distance of 35 cm.

Since acuity tests are easy to administer, they have become the standard procedure for assessing visual capability (Olzak & Thomas, 1986). In everyday life we think of "good vision" as equivalent to "good acuity." Other visual abilities, such as rapid dark adaptation, color vision, and the speed of eye movements, are either secondary or irrelevant to our intuitive concept of visual ability.

In this section we need to consider several

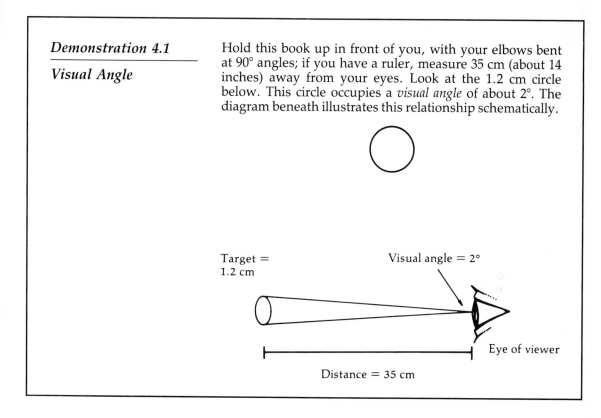

Demonstration 4.1

Visual Angle

Hold this book up in front of you, with your elbows bent at 90° angles; if you have a ruler, measure 35 cm (about 14 inches) away from your eyes. Look at the 1.2 cm circle below. This circle occupies a *visual angle* of about 2°. The diagram beneath illustrates this relationship schematically.

Target = 1.2 cm

Visual angle = 2°

Eye of viewer

Distance = 35 cm

issues. What kinds of acuity exist and how are they measured? What factors influence acuity? What are some applications of acuity?

Types of Acuity

Five basic types of acuity tests are illustrated in Demonstration 4.2. Four involve **static visual acuity,** or the observer's ability to perceive details of an object that is not moving; the fifth involves a moving object. Identification is the most common measure (Cohn & Lasley, 1986), but others may be more reliable. Most acuity tasks involve determining some kind of threshold, a procedure described in Chapter 2.

Identification

Identification, which requires observers to identify a figure, is probably one measure you know well. The Snellen eye chart, devised by Snellen in 1862, is a standard screening test

in many doctors' offices. As Figure 4.1 will remind you, the eye chart has rows of letters ranging from large to small. The task of the observer is to say the names of the letters in each row. The tester notes the row with the smallest letters that the observer can name correctly.

Acuity on the Snellen chart is often measured by comparing performance with the performance of a normal observer. You stand 20 ft (6.1 m) from the chart. If you can read the letters that a person with normal sight can read at 20 ft, then you have 20/20 vision. If your acuity is poor, however, you would have to stand closer to read the letters. If you stood 10 ft (3.0 m) from the chart, then you would have 10/20 vision, which is usually called 20/40 vision. (The figure is doubled, since numbers below 20 are not typically used.) That means that you could see at 20 ft what a person with normal sight could see at 40 ft. In some states a person with 20/400 vi-

Demonstration 4.2

Five Kinds of Acuity Tasks

Try each of these kinds of acuity tasks. Stand across the room from your book (after reading the instructions) and see whether you can identify, detect, resolve, localize, and recognize a moving figure.

A. Identification tasks.
 N   What letter is this?

B. Detection tasks.
 | Can you see this line?
 ·   Can you see this dot?

C. Resolution tasks.
 ··   Is this one dot or two?
 |||||| Is this a grating of black and white bars, or is it a uniform gray patch?

D. Vernier acuity task.
 | Is the upper line to the right or the left of the
 | lower line?

E. Dynamic visual acuity tasks.
 B   Ask a friend to move the book from side to side. Try to identify the letter as it is moving.

sion is declared "legally blind" (Riggs, 1971). This person would need to stand 1 ft from the chart to read the letters that a person with normal vision could read at 20 ft.

Let's relate this method of reporting acuity to the visual angle method used earlier. If you have 20/20 vision, you can make discriminations in letter widths that occupy 1 minute (1') of an arc when you are standing 20 ft from the letters. If you have 20/40 vision, you can recognize letters that occupy 2 minutes (2') of an arc at a distance of 20 ft.

The Snellen eye chart has some problems, though. Some letters, like Y and V, are easily confused with each other. Other letters, like T, are easy to recognize. In most cases too many letter features can help the observer arrive at the correct response. Consider the big E at the top of the chart, for instance. The straight horizontal line on the top tells us that the letter cannot be a C, D, G, H, and so on. The straight vertical line on the left tells us that the letter cannot be an A, C, G, J, and so on. The Snellen chart has another disadvantage that a student pointed out to me.

Young children, eager to avoid having to wear glasses, may memorize the eye chart! A final disadvantage is that the chart does not include enough letters on the top two lines to provide an accurate test for people with severe visual impairment (Sloan, 1980).

Because of these drawbacks the Snellen chart has often been replaced by other acuity measures. In its defense, however, the Snellen chart has practical significance. In real life we need to identify letters at a distance, and the Snellen chart does measure letter identification.

Other Acuity Measures

We have discussed the identification measure of acuity in some detail because it is still the most common. We must also consider four other acuity tasks that assess other aspects of visual precision. **Detection** tasks require the observer to judge whether a target is present or absent. Olzak and Thomas (1986) note that observers can detect a dark line $\frac{1}{2}$ second wide.

Resolution tasks require the observer to

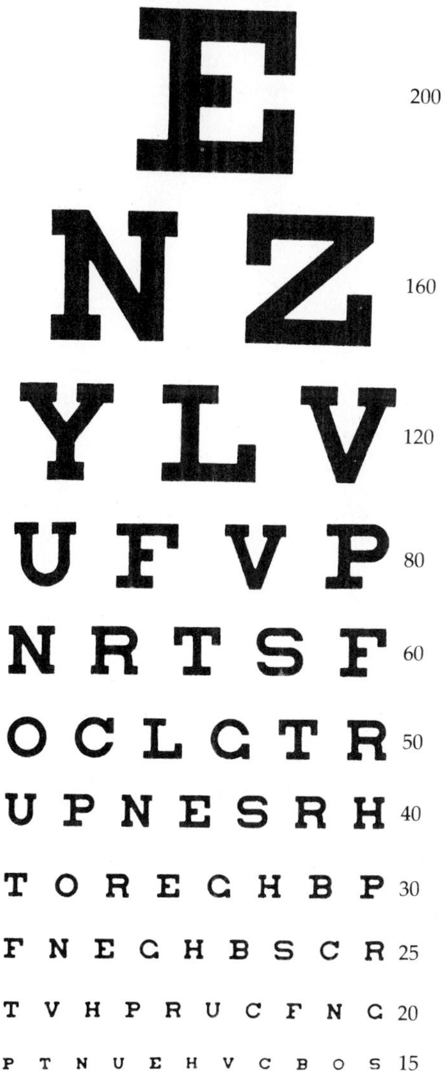

E 200

N Z 160

Y L V 120

U F V P 80

N R T S F 60

O C L G T R 50

U P N E S R H 40

T O R E G H B P 30

F N E G H B S C R 25

T V H P R U C F N G 20

P T N U E H V C B O S 15

Figure 4.1 Snellen chart. Note that size on this chart is reduced. On full-sized chart, someone with 20/20 vision would be able to recognize letters on next-to-last line at distance of 20 ft (6.1 m). On this substantially reduced chart, someone with 20/20 vision should be able to read the last line at about 30 inches (76 cm, arm's length).

discriminate a separation between the parts of a target. Demonstration 4.2 shows a grating pattern used in resolution tasks, with black and white bars of equal width. If you

hold the book close to your eyes, you can see distinct black lines. If you prop the book up and walk across the room, however, this grating will probably look like a uniform gray patch. Under the best conditions, human eyes can **resolve** (detect a separation in) a pattern in which the line widths are about 30 seconds wide (Olzak & Thomas, 1986). Notice that this width is about 60 times as great as for the detection of a single line. Acuity for resolution is therefore much poorer than acuity for detection.

Riggs (1971) points out that the grating pattern is often used to test optical performance of instruments such as cameras and telescopes. Notice why resolution is an appropriate acuity measure for a telescope. Astronomers need equipment that will not only detect a distant star but will also tell whether that spot is one star or two stars close together with just a narrow dark space between.

Vernier acuity tasks, which require the observer to tell whether an upper vertical line (see Demonstration 4.2) is displaced to the right or the left of the lower line, measure relative position. Naturally, if the upper line is a great distance from the lower line, the task is easy. When the two lines are close together, however, the task is difficult. At some point the observer will no longer be able to report reliably on the position of the upper line. Olzak and Thomas (1986) report that this barely discriminable displacement is about 1–2 seconds wide, a distance somewhat greater than for detection of a single line but substantially smaller than for identification or resolution tasks. This outstanding ability to detect a displacement is difficult to explain because the photoreceptors in the fovea are much bigger, about $\frac{1}{2}$ *minute* in diameter (Geisler, 1984). As noted frequently in the previous chapter, our visual system has numerous physiological and anatomical features that provide exceptional visual abilities.

Incidentally, in everyday life we often perform tasks that require vernier acuity. For example, to open childproof aspirin bottles, the points of two arrows must be matched exactly. When you open a combination lock, you must carefully line up the notch above the dial with the appropriate notch on the dial. Take a moment to recall other examples of localization from your daily activities.

The four acuity tests discussed so far have all assessed static visual acuity; neither the test object nor the observer moves during testing. In contrast, **dynamic visual acuity** is tested by measuring acuity when there is relative motion between the observer and the object. For example, a special slide projector may rotate the test pattern from side to side. Typically, dynamic visual acuity is poorer than static visual acuity (Morgan, Watt, & McKee, 1983). One reason for this relatively poor acuity is that the eyes frequently cannot move as fast as the test pattern, so the critical part of the pattern may not be consistently registered on the fovea (Murphy, 1978).

Dynamic visual acuity has numerous applications in everyday life because humans and the objects they look at move frequently. For example, you use dynamic visual acuity in reading bulletin boards as you walk to class and as you walk around a room looking for a lost pen.

Factors Affecting Acuity

Characteristics of the Eye

The focus of the eye is one obvious factor influencing acuity. Some people have spectacular acuity, perhaps as good as 20/10. In contrast, other people have poor acuity; remember that people with vision worse than 20/400 may be classified as legally blind. We will consider eyesight problems and their correction in the section on accommodation in this chapter.

Try Demonstration 4.3 to illustrate another important influence on acuity, position on the retina. We discussed this issue briefly in Chapter 3; now let's consider the details. You can see letters in Demonstration 4.3 clearly only when they are registered on the fovea. The fovea is the central 1° to 2° of the eye, which is not large. In fact, if you are holding your book about 45 cm away from you— a normal reading distance—only about eight

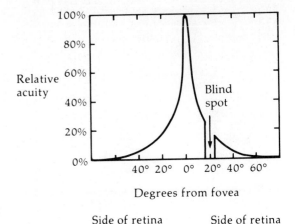

Figure 4.2 Relative visual acuity as function of position on retina. Note that acuity at center of fovea is set at 100%; observe how relative acuity declines on either side of fovea.

letters of the text will fall on the fovea. Just a short distance from the center, acuity drops off rapidly. Look at Figure 4.2, which illustrates the relative acuity at various points on the retina. As the figure illustrates, 10° away from the center, the relative visual activity is only about 20% of the acuity found at the fovea. Notice the relative acuity for different parts of your eye as you look at this sentence in your book. The letters you are looking at right now are clear and sharp, but on either side the letters are blurry. We will discuss this phenomenon in more detail later in a section called "Eye Movements in Reading."

Anstis (1974) created an unusual chart that illustrates the relationship between position on the retina and acuity. He measured identification thresholds for letters at different distances from the fovea. As you have learned, acuity is lower at increasing distances from the fovea; therefore these distant letters had to be proportionately larger to be visible. Figure 4.3 shows the results. If you hold Anstis's chart at roughly arm's length and fixate the center dot, all letters should lie at threshold. (Be certain to fixate the dot, or the letters intended for the outer portions of your retina

---

Demonstration 4.3

Retinal Location and Acuity

Place this book flat on your desk and move your head until it is about 13 cm (about 5 inches) away from the book. Cover your left eye with your left hand. Look directly at the cross on the right-hand side of the figure, just above the 0° mark. Keep your eye on this fixation point. Notice that you can see the letter at 0° quite clearly, and the letter at 5° is also fairly clear. However, the letters at 10°, 20°, and 30° are fuzzy. You will probably be unable to read the letters at 50°.

D	P	N	A	B	Q	W
+	+	+	+	+	+	+
50°	40°	30°	20°	10°	5°	0°

---

may instead be registered on the fovea and consequently will be far above threshold.)

Think about how you may have noticed the relationship between acuity and retinal position in your past experiences. A friend may have accused you of snubbing her, but in fact she may have been in your **peripheral vision** (that is, the image was registered on the side of the retina rather than at the fovea). To use the correct terms for acuity tasks, you may have detected the presence of someone but failed to identify that person. You may have been astounded by the performance of a close-up magician because everything happening in the area registered on your fovea looked honest and legal, and you did not see the cards being exchanged in your peripheral vision. You may have had a near accident while driving because you did not notice the car to your left as you entered the left-hand lane.

Notice that Figure 4.2 includes the blind spot, which we discussed in Chapter 3. Hochberg (1978a) comments on why we are unaware of the blind spot in everyday visual activities. Usually, if we miss something with one eye, we pick it up with the other. Second, we have a tendency to spontaneously complete objects that are interrupted by the blind spot; we will return to this issue in the chapter on shape perception. Third, and perhaps most important, the blind spot is in an area far from the fovea. If we really want to see something, we look at it with our sensitive foveas, rather than keeping the object in our peripheral vision. Our relative acuity would be only about 15% in this region even if there were no blind spot.

You may recall the explanation for the tremendous increase in acuity at the fovea. Look back at Figure 3.11, which shows the distribution of cones across the retina. Clearly, this is similar to Figure 4.2. In the fovea, where cones are abundant, acuity is excellent; in the periphery, where cones are few and far between, acuity is poor.

Another characteristic of the eye has a more modest influence on acuity: pupil size. As Olzak and Thomas (1986) conclude, acuity is best when the pupil is an intermediate diameter, between about 2 and 5 mm. This is the normal range for pupil size, and within this range acuity remains very good. When pupil size has been made artificially large or artificially small, however, acuity decreases. The important point, however, is that for our everyday visual activities, pupil diameter is not very important.

Figure 4.3   Chart created by Anstis (1974). When observer fixates central dot, all letters should lie at threshold. (Reprinted with permission from *Vision Research, 14,* S. M. Anstis, A chart demonstrating variations in acuity with retinal position, Copyright 1974, Pergamon Press, Ltd.)

Characteristics of the Stimulus

If you have ever struggled to read a map in the car at night, you know one stimulus characteristic that influences acuity: **luminance,** or the amount of light that enters the eye. That map would be perfectly legible in the daytime, but you will not find the street you are pursuing if you have to rely on occasional light from dim street lamps. Riggs (1971) notes that in starlight (luminance of about .0003 cd/m^2) we can see the white pages of a book but not the writing on them. In moonlight (luminance of about .03 cd/m^2) we can notice separate letters but cannot read the text. (In other words, if you plan to read poetry by moonlight, bring a flashlight.) We require a luminance of about 30 cd/m² before we feel comfortable about reading. The recommended luminance standard in measuring acuity is 85 cd/m² (Olzak & Thomas, 1986). Acuity continues to increase as luminance increases until it levels off at about 3,000 cd/m². Figure 4.4 illustrates the relationship between luminance and acuity.

Notice that Figure 4.4 actually consists of two curves. With low levels of luminance, only the rods are called into action. Acuity is poor at these low levels because rods are not in the fovea where vision is best. As you know, they are concentrated in the outer portion of the retina.

Notice the second curve now, the one that operates at higher levels of luminance. This curve represents vision with cones. In this brighter region the fovea can now be used. The higher acuity in the foveal region is responsible for the dramatic improvement in acuity as the luminance increases. Now try Demonstration 4.4 to illustrate the relationship between luminance and acuity for yourself.

We have seen that luminance is one stimulus factor that influences acuity. It will not surprise you to learn that a related factor, glare, is also relevant. When there is glare, acuity is substantially reduced (Finlay & Wilkinson, 1984).

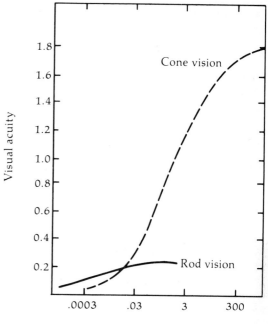

Figure 4.4 Visual acuity as function of luminance.

Let's summarize the discussion of factors influencing acuity. Characteristics of the eye that influence acuity include: (1) focus of the eye (to be examined in more detail later), (2) position on the retina, and (3) pupil size.

Demonstration 4.4

Relationship between Luminance and Acuity

Try to identify five different levels of luminance that you encounter in a typical day, for example: (1) outside in the intense sunlight at noon; (2) your room in the late afternoon, with all lights turned on; (3) your room at night, with one medium light turned on; (4) your room at night with just one small light turned on, far away from you; and (5) your room at night with no lights on, but some light coming in the window. In each of these conditions, turn to the Snellen eye chart in Figure 4.1, prop the book up, and move about 3 m (about 10 feet) away. Try to see which is the smallest print for which you can successfully identify all the letters accurately. Does your acuity decrease as the luminance decreases?

Characteristics of the stimulus that influence acuity include: (1) luminance and (2) glare.

Applications of Acuity

One important application of acuity is in the area of consumer psychology. Have you ever squinted at the list of ingredients and additives on a carton of cereal? Poulton (1969) took lists of ingredients from the containers of 60 different foods and reproduced these lists using different sizes of type. Figure 4.5 shows an example of the largest and the smallest prints he used. There were two levels of illumination in the experiment, corresponding to the level of brightness typically found in supermarkets and the considerably lower level of brightness typically found in home pantries. Women were instructed to look through the lists for certain key words. The women found the words about twice as fast when the large print, rather than the small print, was used. They were also faster with the bright, supermarket-style lights than with the dim, pantry-style lights. As noted earlier, lighting is an important determinant of acuity because cones work best at high luminance levels.

Visual acuity has numerous applications for driving. Forbes (1972) summarized many studies on the visibility of highway signs. A rule of thumb derived from these studies is that a person with 20/20 vision can read familiar signs with letters 10 cm high at a distance of 80 m. For unfamiliar signs you would need to be about 67 m away. However, most states require only 20/40 vision. A driver with 20/40 vision would therefore be only 40 m away when those 10 cm letters are visible.

In many cases, however, time is a limiting factor in looking at a sign. Forbes notes that drivers on a highway often have time for only one short glance, lasting about 1 second. With such a short glance, a driver would need to be 10%–15% closer to read the sign. A driver with 20/20 vision, for example, might need to be 70 m—rather than 80—from a sign with 10 cm letters to read it. Also, only three to four familiar words can be recognized with a short glance. If you have ever been driving and glanced up at a sign that said something like "Kensington Expressway, left lane; Scajaquada Expressway, right lane," you have realized the limits of acuity under time pressure!

On the New York State Thruway, most of the road signs are white letters on a green background—something most drivers seldom contemplate. Forbes cites data to demonstrate that with white letters on a green background, you can read a sign at a distance about 30% farther away than with black letters on a white background.

Driving requires excellent dynamic visual acuity. After all, drivers are moving in relation to the roadway; they are not static. Burg (1971) wanted to determine what factors were most closely related to the number of traffic accidents and traffic citations for automobile drivers. He obtained information on about 18,000 California drivers and compared it with their driving records. As you can imagine, factors such as age, sex, and mileage driven were closely related to accidents and citations.

However, our interest lies in the visual factors related to driving. Static visual acuity was weakly related to the measures of traffic safety. That is, people with good static visual acuity tended to have somewhat fewer traffic accidents and citations. The visual test that was the best predictor of traffic safety, however, was dynamic visual acuity. People with good dynamic visual acuity had substantially fewer traffic accidents and citations. It's likely that when you applied for your driver's license, you were tested on a measure of static visual acuity similar to the ones shown in Demonstration 4.2. Your motor vehicles department would have been wiser, however, to measure your dynamic visual acuity because that measure is a better predictor of traffic safety.

Figure 4.4 showed that visual acuity is

pyridoxine hydrochloride

pyridoxine hydrochloride

Figure 4.5   Print sizes used by Poulton.

much better for cones than for rods, and acuity is better with brighter lighting. Acuity is therefore relatively poor at night, and this factor accounts for many driving accidents. Leibowitz and Owens (1986) report that more than half of all traffic deaths happen at night, even though people drive fewer miles at night. When we take the mileage differences into account, the nighttime death rates are more than three times as high as the daytime death rates. Of course, factors such as drinking and fatigue may account for a portion of this discrepancy. However, the major problem is that we tend to drive at the same rate at night as during the day, even though our acuity is substantially lower under this less-than-ideal situation. Under the best possible conditions—using high beams on the headlights, with no glare from other traffic, and with a pedestrian wearing white—a driver can distinguish between the pedestrian and the dark background at a distance of about 300 ft (91 m). This distance may seem safe until we contemplate another piece of information. Considering reaction time and breaking distance, the average driver requires 317 ft (97 m) to stop a car traveling at 55 mph (88 km/h). With low beams on the headlights and a pedestrian wearing dark clothing, drivers can only see a pedestrian 100 ft (30 m) in front of them.

Our discussion of driving has revealed several facts. Designers of highways and highway signs need to consider the acuity of drivers, time limitations, word familiarity, and color contrast. Motor vehicle departments should assess dynamic visual acuity rather than static visual acuity. Finally, both drivers and pedestrians need to consider the information about nighttime acuity.

Two more applications of acuity are worth examining briefly. Some researchers have tried to determine whether athletes and non-athletes differ in their acuity. One study found no clear relationship between static visual acuity and athletic ability (Mizusawa, Sweeting, & Knouse, 1983), but another study showed a significant relationship between dynamic visual acuity and baseball players' hitting ability (Horner, 1982). It seems likely that dynamic visual ability may be a more valid measure in athletics, where movement is the goal of the game.

Many readers—both professors and students—who have tried to decipher tiny letters and numbers on photographic slides presented at lectures will appreciate the warning "Don't Crowd Your Slides!" provided by Hammerschmidt (1984). This author calculated on the basis of the Snellen chart that a slide should contain no more than 20 lines of print, with 12 lines closer to ideal. If you are presented with a slide containing too many lines, curse the lecturer rather than your own acuity!

Summary: Acuity

1. Visual acuity is the ability to see fine details, or the resolution capacities of the visual system.
2. An identification acuity task asks observers to recognize a target; an example is the Snellen chart.
3. A detection task asks observers to judge whether a target is present or absent.
4. A resolution task asks observers whether a separation exists between parts of a target.
5. A vernier acuity task asks observers to judge whether an upper line is to the right or left of a lower line.
6. Characteristics of the eye that influence acuity are focus, position on the retina, and (to a limited extent) pupil diameter.
7. Characteristics of the stimulus that influence acuity are lighting and glare.
8. Acuity has applications in the size of printing on packages, the design of road signs and other areas related to driving, athletics, and the presentation of photographic slides.

ADAPTATION

You have probably had an experience like this. You enter a movie theater in the middle of the afternoon. Outside the sun is shining.

Inside you seem to be temporarily blind, particularly if the movie has already started. You try to locate an empty seat, groping at what you hope are the backs of chairs rather than people's shoulders. You have not yet adapted to dark.

In our visual world we experience a wide range of light levels. As Hood and Finkelstein (1986) point out, the illumination from the noon sun is about 100 million times as intense as the illumination from the moon. Nevertheless, the visual system is so superbly designed that it allows us to function in both kinds of illuminations as well as the vast range in between. Except for the occasional encounters with dark movie theaters, however, we rarely appreciate the flexibility of our visual system. As Hood and Finkelstein (1986, pp. 5–45) remark, "Large changes in sensitivity take place as the sun sets and the ambient illumination passes from daylight through twilight to night. Because these changes occur slowly, one is not aware of them."

Adaptation is a change in sensitivity to a particular light intensity (Cohn & Lasley, 1986). **Dark adaptation** is an increase in sensitivity as the eyes remain in the dark. **Light adaptation** is a decline in sensitivity as the eyes remain in the light (Watson, 1986). Notice that the two kinds of adaptation can be remembered in terms of the *present* lighting conditions, either dark or light.

Dark Adaptation

Many laboratory studies have been performed on dark adaptation. Typically, studies on dark adaptation represent the performance of a single observer. In these studies the observer is first exposed to an intense light, called the **adaptation stimulus,** for several minutes. Then the light is turned off and the threshold for a small spot of light is measured; this spot of light is called the **test stimulus.** The threshold is measured using ascending series. The experimenter presents a low-intensity light and slowly makes it more intense. The experimenter records the intensity at which the observer reports seeing the test

stimulus; this point is called the threshold. The experimenter repeats the procedure, each time allowing a different amount of time in the dark before measuring the threshold. The curve shown in Figure 4.6 illustrates how one person's right eye adapted to light. Try Demonstration 4.5 to illustrate dark adaptation for yourself.

In Figure 4.6, look at the portion of the curve a few minutes after the light has been turned off. The light must be relatively intense for it to be detected. After about 30 minutes, however, dark adaptation is nearly complete; sensitivity is high, and threshold is low (that is, a low-intensity light can be detected). In fact, the eye is now about 100,000 times as sensitive as it was in the light. A **dark adaptation curve** such as the one in Figure 4.6 shows the relationship between time in the dark and the threshold, or the intensity of light that can barely be detected.

Notice the kink in the curve that occurs after about 5-10 minutes in the dark. This kink occurs consistently with many different observers who are being tested in many different conditions—it is not just an accident. Curves like this make researchers suspicious that two factors rather than just one must be

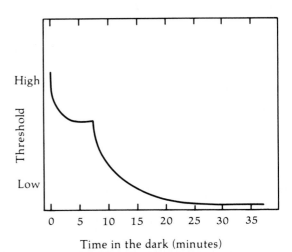

Figure 4.6 Dark adaptation as function of time in dark. Note that lower threshold means that eye is *more* sensitive.

Demonstration 4.5

Dark Adaptation

Find a flashlight that is opaque on all sides except where the beam of light shines through. Take about 15 index cards and the flashlight and go into a dark room where you can stay for 15 to 20 minutes. Place all the index cards over the beam of light. Remove the cards one at a time until you can barely see the light. Calculate the number of cards remaining on the flashlight. After a few minutes the light will look brighter to you. Add a card and see whether you can still see the light. If not, wait another minute and try again. Keep repeating the process for 15 more minutes. Notice that as time in the dark increases, you can detect an increasingly dim light.

involved in the dark adaptation process. In fact, one part of the curve represents the activity of cones, and the other part represents the activity of rods.

Figure 4.6 was obtained by shining the light on an area of the retina that contained both cones and rods. What would happen if only cones or only rods were involved? If we could shine the light only on the fovea, where there are cones but no rods, we might find a dark adaptation curve like that in Figure 4.7a.

Notice that there is a quick drop in the threshold during the first few minutes. Sensitivity levels off at this point, however, and the threshold remains relatively high.

On the other hand, notice what would happen if we could shine the light only on the periphery—about 20° out from the fovea—where there are many rods but few cones. The dark adaptation curve for rods, as shown in Figure 4.7b, is a different shape. The threshold is immeasurably high for about

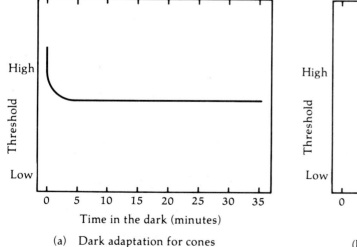

(a)   Dark adaptation for cones

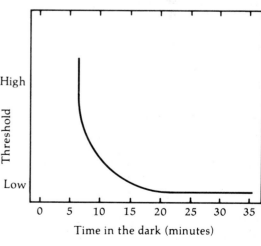

(b)   Dark adaptation for rods

Figure 4.7   Dark adaptation or (a) area in fovea having only cones and (b) area in periphery having only rods.

5 minutes, then decreases suddenly and later levels out.

Dark adaptation is usually complete after about 30 minutes, but a number of factors influence its rate. These include the size and shape of the test stimulus and whether it is exposed continuously or in a flashing on-and-off pattern. Other factors include the size of the pupil and the intensity, color, and duration of the adaptation stimulus. For example, an intense adaptation stimulus may prolong the dark adaptation process to 40 minutes (Hood & Finkelstein, 1986; Reeves, 1983).

The threshold stays high for the first few minutes of dark adaptation; only cones are active. After several minutes, however, the threshold drops abruptly and then levels out; only rods are active. Remember that rods are used in noncolored or **achromatic vision,** rather than color vision. You may have heard the saying, "In the night, all cats are gray." A marmalade-colored cat indeed looks orange in daylight, when cones can be used. At night, after dark adaptation has taken place and the rods are functional, that cat can only look gray.

Why does the eye become more sensitive to light as time passes in darkness during dark adaptation? The complete answer to this question is not known. Let's consider several factors. First of all, as you move from an intense light into darkness, your pupil dilates, or widens. When the pupil of the human eye is fully dilated, it lets in about 16 times as much light as when the pupil is small. The human eye can increase its sensitivity somewhat, then, by letting in more light. (For comparison's sake, you should notice the much more dramatic pupil size changes in a cat. In intense light the cat's pupils are tiny slits; at night the cat's pupils are huge.) Pupil size changes can increase the eye's sensitivity to light in a limited way. However, the dark-adapted eye is about 100,000 times more sensitive than the light-adapted eye. Pupil dilation is thus only a small part of the story.

A second factor that permits the eyes to be more sensitive in the dark is that dark-adapted eyes have a higher concentration of rhodopsin. As you'll recall from Chapter 3, rhodopsin is transformed in the presence of intense lights. When the lights are turned off, the level of rhodopsin rises again. The greater level of rhodopsin available to eyes in darkness is another part of the story, but this explanation is still insufficient. For example, researchers have found that the threshold changes less than 1 second after a light has been turned off. The level of rhodopsin could not change quickly enough to account for this rapid change in threshold.

The third, and perhaps most important, factor is the least understood. Researchers believe that neural processes at a higher level than the receptor cells must have a role in dark adaptation (Green & Powers, 1982). Dark adaptation is too spectacular a phenomenon to be accounted for by mere pupil dilation and changes in rhodopsin level. The details of these neural activities are still unclear, however.

Light Adaptation

In dark adaptation, eyes become more sensitive as they remain in the dark. In light adaptation, however, eyes become *less* sensitive as they are exposed to light. The surrounding illumination is intense, and our eyes do not need to be sensitive to dim spots of light. As you'll recall from Chapter 3, in well-lit or photopic conditions our eyes excel at acuity rather than sensitivity.

In a light adaptation study the observer is first completely dark-adapted. Then the experimenter turns on the lights. A typical illumination might be similar to a well-lit room. Now the experimenter measures the threshold for a small spot of light. As in dark adaptation, a low-intensity light is presented at first, and the intensity is increased until the subject reports seeing the light. The whole procedure is repeated many times to determine thresholds with different lengths of exposure to light.

During light adaptation the pupils quickly become smaller. As a result, less light enters the eyes. Shortly after the light is presented, the rods stop functioning. After all, the light changes the rhodopsin, so the critical chemical for rod vision cannot be used. Instead, the cones start to function. The chemical used in cone vision is changed by the light at first, but then more of this chemical is manufactured.

We said that light adaptation makes us less sensitive to light. However, at the levels of illumination we use during the day, we do not need to be light sensitive. It is more important to have acuity, and the cones active in light-adapted eyes allow us to have the impressive acuity discussed at the beginning of the chapter.

A striking difference between dark adaptation and light adaptation is the time required to complete the process. Dark adaptation takes about 30 minutes. In contrast, studies typically show that light adaptation is almost complete after 1 minute, although light adaptation requires substantially more time if the adaptation stimulus is extremely intense (Hood & Finkelstein, 1986).

Applications of Adaptation

An understanding of dark adaptation and light adaptation should alert you to applications in everyday life. For instance, it's unwise to hope that your eyes will be completely dark-adapted after a few minutes in the dark. A film on the Leboyer method of childbirth includes a segment in which an obstetrician points out how the mother and newborn appreciate the dim lighting specified by this method. He comments that the physicians' eyes quickly grow accustomed to the dark, so that they can see perfectly several minutes after the lights have been dimmed. The information you've learned in this chapter should make you skeptical about this claim. Mothers in labor should leap from the delivery table and turn the lights on!

In the section on acuity we discussed the visibility of highway signs. Naturally, at night a well-lit sign would be seen better than an unlit or poorly lit sign. However, now that you know about dark adaptation, consider the disadvantages of a sign that is too intensely lit. If you are driving at night and your eyes are fairly well dark-adapted, the intense light from a sign would require you to begin dark adaptation all over again (Forbes, 1972). Your sensitivity to other stimuli would be lowered.

In connection with night driving, you can probably guess why drivers are urged to use their dim lights, rather than their bright lights, when another car approaches. Drivers also find that they can retain their dark adaptation better by looking over to the right-hand side of their lane, avoiding looking into the headlights of the oncoming car.

Dark adaptation also has applications to certain professions. For example, radiologists who are viewing numerous films typically work in darkened rooms to enhance their sensitivity. If they must step outside the room for even a short period, they frequently wear red goggles. As it happens, the rods used in low illumination settings are not sensitive to red light. By wearing these red goggles, radiologists do not lose the benefit of their dark adaptation.

Summary: Adaptation

1. Adaptation is a change in sensitivity to a particular light intensity.
2. In dark adaptation the eye's sensitivity to light increases, as shown in a dark adaptation curve.
3. During the first 5 minutes in the dark adaptation the sensitivity of cones increases, but then their sensitivity remains constant.
4. Rods are insensitive to light for the first 5 minutes in the dark; then their sensitivity increases and levels off about 30 minutes after the lights have been turned out.
5. Factors that influence the rate of dark include attributes of the test stimulus, pupil size, and attributes of the adaptation stimulus.
6. Dark adaptation is caused by pupil dilation, the higher concentration of rhodopsin in dark-adapted eyes, and neural processes.
7. In light adaptation the eyes become less sensitive to light.

8. Light adaptation is complete after about 1 minute in most circumstances, but the process requires more time if the adaptation stimulus is intense.
9. During light adaptation the pupils become smaller, the light bleaches the rhodopsin, and the cones start functioning.
10. Adaptation has implications for driving and certain occupations, e.g., radiology.

EYE MOVEMENTS

Think about the number of different reasons you may have for moving your eyes. You watch a kite as it trembles and jerks on its way to a crash landing. You trace the smooth course of a robin as it approaches its nest. You move your eyes in small jumps along the page as you read this paragraph. You move your eyes inward to focus upon a fly landing on your nose.

To appreciate eye movements more thoroughly, imagine how your life would be limited if your eyes were "glued" in a stable position in your head. Imagine that you could change the direction of your gaze only by moving your entire head. This kind of system would be extremely awkward, inefficient, and time-consuming in a task such as reading. Fortunately, however, our eyes are attached to muscles that can move them independent of head movement.

Turn back to Figure 3.6 to examine the general appearance of these eye muscles, the structures in our visual system that perform so heroically in moving our eyes.

The accuracy, speed, and complexity of our eye movements are indeed amazing, giving further evidence for the impressive capabilities of our perceptual systems (Theme 2). Llewellyn-Thomas (1981) marvels about the performance of the visual system in connection with one representative task, keeping track of a fast-moving baseball:

It's astounding that any of us can hit [a baseball] at all. A ball is travelling a hundred miles an hour. A visual sample is taken from a bad angle in a single fixation from which the batter has to compute and extrapolate the ball's trajectory while initiating the voluntary muscle movements to guide a round club along a convoluted curve so it impacts the ball hard at a unique point in time and space! Impossible—all those differential equations to solve, and curves to plot in milliseconds! The fact that a good batter can hit a third of the pitches demonstrates how fantastically efficient our visual and neuromuscular systems are. But then a monkey's eye movement control system solves almost instantly problems in higher mathematics when it leaps from bough to bough! (pp. 318–319)

Eye movements can be classified in two basic groups, according to whether the angle between the lines of sight for the two eyes remains constant or changes as the eyes move. Before we discuss the classifications, take a moment to appreciate this distinction. First, look up at a boundary between a distant wall and a ceiling. Let your eyes trace along this line and notice how they move as a pair in the same direction. If you were to draw a line from each eye to the spot upon which it was focusing, the angle between the two lines would remain the same as you moved your eyes. **Version movement** is the term used for eye movement in which the angle between the lines of sight remains constant and the eyes move in the same direction.

In contrast, gaze at some distant spot and then turn your eyes inward to look at the tip of your nose. The angle between the lines of sight changes drastically as you perform this eye movement. There is a narrow angle when looking at the distant spot and a wide angle when looking at your nose. **Vergence movement** is the term used for eye movement in which the angle between the lines of sight changes and the eyes move toward or away from each other. You can remember which term is which because *vergence* sounds more like *changes*.

Version Movements

Several kinds of version movements depend upon the nature of the task that must be performed. We will consider three important kinds of version movements: saccades, pursuit movements, and involuntary eye movements.

Saccadic Movements

As your eyes glance over this sentence, become aware of how they are moving. Do they move smoothly and evenly across the page, or do they make a series of little jumps? Research has demonstrated that the eyes move in jumps rather than smooth movements. **Saccadic movement** is the term used to refer to these rapid movements from one fixation point to the next. These movements are necessary to bring the fovea of the eye (the region of the retina with the highest acuity) into position over the letters or words that you want to look at. During the **saccade** the eye moves from one location to the next. During the **fixation pause**—the pause between saccades—you read the letters or words.

Characteristics. Let's look at some important attributes of saccadic movement. First, saccades are probably the most frequent kind of eye movement (Bahill & Stark, 1979); they are used in activities such as reading and driving. We make several billion saccadic movements in a lifetime (Cumming, 1978). Second, saccades are jerky, rather than smooth. As noted, eyes jump in a saccade, whereas they glide in pursuit. Third, saccades are rapid—much faster than the relatively leisurely eye movements used in pursuing the flight of a bird or in vergence movement.

Let's look at the timing of the phases in saccadic movements. To plan a saccade requires about 250 milliseconds (about $\frac{1}{4}$ second). For example, if participants in a study are instructed that they must execute a saccade each time they see a specified signal, a delay of about 250 milliseconds occurs after the signal before the eye begins to move. This delay is longer than the time required for the saccade itself, which is only about 50 milliseconds (Hallett, 1986). The eye travels at an amazing speed during this brief saccade, reaching a velocity up to 600° per second (Hallett, 1986). The final stage of a saccade is the

fixation pause, which lasts about 200 milliseconds before the eye begins another cycle.

We have seen that saccades are frequent, jerky, and rapid—characteristics that are fairly obvious. The fourth characteristic is more subtle: Saccadic movements are ballistic. **Ballistic movements** have predetermined destinations. The path of a rocket, for example, is partially ballistic because the direction and the distance of its flight have been determined before the flight begins. Similarly, when the eyes take off on a saccadic jump, the brain has already programmed which direction they will move in and how far they will go. The eyes will reach their destination, even if some new information is added between the time of the programming and the time of the jump.

This programming of the ballistic movement has been described by Ditchburn (1973). Several studies have been conducted in which observers are asked to look at a target that is moved abruptly to a new location and then moved just as abruptly back to the original location. A fixation pause lasts 200 milliseconds ($\frac{1}{5}$ sec). What happens if the target is moved and returned in less than 200 milliseconds, say, 150 milliseconds?

Notice that it would be most efficient if the eye could remain in the same position because the target returns before the saccadic movement to the next location begins. Nonetheless, the eye has already been programmed to move, so it must obey the command, even though this command is no longer relevant. In a way, it is like the foolish, wasted arm movements we make in trying to swat a speedy mosquito. We see the mosquito land, we aim (that is, we program the ballistic movement of our hand), and we swat—even if the mosquito has departed $\frac{1}{10}$ second before the hand arrives.

The fifth characteristic of saccadic movements is that the eye muscles do not tire substantially during them. Fuchs and Binder (1983) asked several stalwart observers to make large (60°) saccades at the rate of one saccade per second for 31 minutes—close to 2,000 saccades. The velocity of these saccades had decreased only 10% by the end of this torturous session, and some hearty encouragement from the experimenter brought the velocity back to normal.

In summary, then, the eye movements that you are executing as you read this sentence are frequent, jerky, rapid, and ballistic. Furthermore, the movements do not produce fatigue. Let's examine in detail the research on eye movements in reading.

▶ IN-DEPTH:
EYE MOVEMENTS IN READING

The first major book on psychological processes in reading was published in 1908. When the same book was republished in 1968 (Huey, 1968), the introduction noted that no new information on eye movements in reading had been gathered during the half-century. As Banks (1985) points out, the major stumbling block was that behaviorists considered reading an unfit topic for study. With the recent interest in cognitive approaches, however, the topic of eye movements in reading has become extremely popular. In fact, entire books have been written on the subject (Groner, Menz, Fisher, & Monty, 1983; Rayner, 1983a). Obviously, then, our "in-depth" examination can cover only a small portion of this field.

To study eye movements in reading, researchers need to use fairly sophisticated equipment. One technique, for example, films eye movements with a television camera. A computer then identifies the movement of the eye by analyzing the image of the pupil. An alternative technique tracks the reflections from the cornea and the back of the lens (McConkie, 1982). These monitors provide useful information about a number of topics, including the control of eye movements.

Most of the textbook so far has concentrated on the remarkable capacities of our visual apparatus; the bottom-up approach has been emphasized. In the acuity section we discovered that the photoreceptors and other structures allow us to see fine details. In the section on adaptation, we noted that our vis-

ual system allows us to see in a wide variety of illumination conditions. With eye movements, however, we must stress a top-down approach consistent with Theme 4 of the book. As McConkie (1982) phrases it, "During reading the mind is sending the eyes to relatively precise locations in the text" (p. 36).

Determinants of saccade size. Let's explore some rules that the mind uses to decide where to send the eyes. First, the average saccade is about 5 to 10 letters (McConkie & Zola, 1984; Morrison & Rayner, 1981). Intriguingly, the size of the jump is relatively constant, whether the reading material is at a close, medium, or far distance. In other words, the brain doesn't simply move the eye a specified number of degrees; it pays attention to a relatively subtle factor, number of letters.

A second rule about eye movements is simple: Avoid the blank regions. When the eye jumps forward, it rarely moves to a blank space between sentences or between words (McConkie, 1983; McConkie & Zola, 1984). This strategy makes sense; there is no information to be gained from a white space.

A third rule is related to the second: Don't land on a word that provides little information. For example, the eye jumps past the word "the" (O'Regan, 1979). The eye also jumps past a word that is highly predictable in a sentence (Balota, Pollatsek, & Rayner, 1985).

A fourth rule is that a saccade will be shorter if the next word in the sentence is misspelled or if the next word is long (McConkie & Zola, 1984; O'Regan, 1980). If the material is puzzling or long, it would be unwise to make a large saccadic movement.

Perceptual span. A major portion of the research on eye movements in reading has examined the factors that determine the size of each saccadic movement. Another major research topic concerns the **perceptual span,** the region seen during the fixation pause. This research uses the gaze-contingent paradigm, developed by McConkie and Rayner (1975) and described in detail by Rayner (1983b) and Just and Carpenter (1987). The **gaze-contingent paradigm** involves tracking readers' eyes as they read material displayed on a cathode-ray tube and changing the text display as the readers progress through the text. With this method the researchers can selectively replace letters in certain regions of the display. For example, they can replace all letters more than 10 letters to the right of the letter the observer is viewing. The researchers note whether this alteration changed any measures of reading. If the measures changed, they can conclude that the letters in the altered region would normally be included in the perceptual span (Underwood & McConkie, 1985).

Let's look in some detail at a recent study by Underwood and McConkie that uses the letter-replacement method. Table 4.1 shows an example of some typical conditions similar to those used in their research. As you can see, participants in this study sometimes had no letters replaced on either side of the central fixated letter; this "none-none" condition therefore represents a control condition. The "none-8" condition shows text that has no replacements to the left of the fixated letter, but replacements for all text eight or more letters (or spaces) to the right of the fixated letter. Other replacement conditions are also illustrated. Unlike previous researchers, Underwood and McConkie often presented normal lines of text; the distorted versions only appeared occasionally. Whereas participants

in earlier studies might have changed their reading strategies because of the bizarre-looking text, participants in the Underwood and McConkie study probably used their normal reading patterns.

The researchers selected passages from newspaper articles and instructed the participants to read the passages silently. They recorded three measures of reading performance to determine what kinds of replacements interfered with normal reading. These measures were duration of fixation on the line with the error, size of the following saccade, and duration of fixation on the following line.

The results showed that replaced letters four or more positions to the left of the fixated letter had no influence on reading. Replaced letters eight or more positions to the right of the fixated letter likewise had no influence on reading. In other words, the bottom line in Table 4.1 would not be disruptive for a reader fixating the letter above the arrow.

Notice that the perceptual span is distinctly lopsided; only four positions are to the left of the fixated letter, whereas eight are to the right. Readers of English and other languages written from left to right are likely to search for reading cues (such as word length) from the upcoming text to the right. Pollatsek, Bolozky, Well, and Rayner (1981) tested readers of Hebrew, which is written from right to left. As you might expect, their per-

Table 4.1 Lines of Text Similar to Those Used by Underwood and McConkie (1985)

Condition	Appearance of a Line of Text
None-none	The judge dismissed the motion because they had not been ⤒
None-8	The judge dismissed the motion because thbw ejc kte awwd ⤒
8-none	Xfn okepf ovygottbe xfn jdtion because they had not been ⤒
8-4	Xfn okepf ovygottbe xfn jdtion because exbw ejc kte awwd ⤒
4-8	Xfn okepf ovygottbe xfn jdfavk because thbw ejc kte awwd ⤒

NOTE: Arrow indicates the fixated letter in each line of text.

ceptual span was distinctly lopsided in the opposite direction, with more positions to the left than to the right.

We have examined two major topics concerning eye movements in reading. The first topic concerned factors that determine the size of the saccadic movement, and we saw that the brain does not simply send the eyes forward a constant number of spaces; instead, the saccades are planned so that they carry the eyes to the next useful location. The second topic concerned the nature and size of the perceptual span. We saw that left-to-right and right-to-left readers differed in the distribution of the perceptual span with respect to the fixation point. The development of interest in research on reading—accompanied by the development of technology to assess eye movements used in reading—opens up numerous opportunities for exploration. ■

Pursuit Movements

We have examined saccadic eye movements in some detail because they are so common and because they have inspired the most research by people interested in perceptual and cognitive processes. We need to consider two additional version movements—as well as vergence movements. You use the version movement called pursuit movement when you watch a bird fly through the sky, a baseball being hit out of the ballpark, and a child gliding by on a bicycle. **Pursuit movements** are required to track something moving against a stationary background. They are necessary to maintain a stable picture of the moving object on the retina. It is much easier to identify an object if you can keep the picture of it in the same location on the retina than if its picture slides across the retina.

Pursuit movements have several important characteristics. They are relatively slow, with velocity typically ranging between 30° and 100° per second, substantially slower than the 600° per second velocities saccadic movements can reach (Hallett, 1986). Interestingly, however, the pursuit movements of professional baseball players—who have to track a speeding ball—reach velocities of up to 150° (Bahill & La Ritz, 1984). It's intriguing to speculate whether people with fast pursuit movements choose to become ball players, or whether they start with pursuit movements like the rest of us and perfect these skills during training. Research by Bahill and McDonald (1983) has demonstrated that nonathletes can learn to improve their pursuit movements, indicating that at least some training may be responsible.

A second attribute of pursuit movements is that they are smooth, in contrast to the jerky saccades. In fact, they are often called "smooth pursuit movements" to emphasize this important characteristic.

A third attribute is that they attempt to match a target's speed, although they have a general tendency to "underpursue" because the eyes cannot move as fast as the target (Hallett, 1986). As a result of underpursuit the object's image on the retina moves rather than remaining in a constant position on the retina. This movement of the retinal image makes it difficult to see details on moving objects. Details will be particularly blurry if the object is moving rapidly (Murphy, 1978).

Involuntary Eye Movements

Involuntary eye movements are the unavoidable small movements our eyes make when we try to hold them still to fixate on something (Ditchburn, 1981). We cannot consciously control these movements because they are involuntary and occur spontaneously. Try as hard as you can to look at the period at the end of this sentence. Notice how difficult this is! Sometimes your eye makes slow, miniature drifts away from the target. After the eye has drifted about 10 to 20 cones, the muscles give a tiny jerk to bring it back. The pattern of this alternation is a little like the pattern you might use if you were fishing in a slow-moving stream; you let the line drift slowly down the stream and then swiftly jerk it back to the target.

Your eye also makes miniature trembling motions, which you may have noticed as you were trying to keep your eye on the period. This movement is small—perhaps equivalent to 1 to 2 cones—but it is continuous. It seems that our eye "equipment" does not maintain the eye in an exact position for a long time.

Figure 4.8 illustrates these tiny eye movements. Notice that the direction, curvature, and length of these movements are random.

Fine eye movements, strange as it may seem, serve to improve vision rather than to reduce it. Procedures have been developed that stabilize the image projected onto the retina; these procedures are called **stabilized retinal image techniques.** One method that sounds particularly uncomfortable involves placing a contact lens on the cornea. This lens supports a small column, to which a tiny projector is attached. The projector presents a particular image back to the retina. If the eye moves, the contact lens and the projector move as well. Thus the projector continues to present the same stabilized image to the retina. This system effectively eliminates the variety of images that would be seen with normal eye movements.

What happens once the image has been stabilized? Gradually, the borders of the target fade, and the entire object disappears. Temporary blindness results. Apparently the retina requires a modest variety in its input to maintain shape perception.

Ditchburn (1981) points out that it is actually a major achievement that the eye moves as well as it does. The eyeball has three pairs of muscles that move it rapidly during saccadic movements and more slowly during pursuit movements, yet these muscles are also required to hold the eyeball still during fixations. He challenges us to try designing a similar system using six rubber bands and a ball bearing. Could we do nearly as well? Once again, we see that our perceptual equipment is remarkably well designed.

Try Demonstration 4.6 to make certain you understand the three kinds of version eye movements discussed in this section.

Vergence Movements

So far, we have been considering *version movements*, the three kinds of eye movements that keep the same angle between the lines of sight during eye movement. In contrast, recall that *vergence movement* involves eye movement in which the angle between the lines of sight changes.

More specifically, the eyes **converge,** or move together, to look at nearby objects. The eyes **diverge** or move apart, to look at distant objects. (**Convergence** and **divergence** are the nouns corresponding to those verbs; they refer to the act of moving together or moving apart. Notice that you can remember the general term **vergence** because it is a part of those two words.)

The purpose of vergence movements is to allow both eyes to focus on the same target. Try Demonstration 4.7 to show how you would have double vision if you avoided vergence movements.

Vergence movements are relatively slow; their velocities rarely exceed 10° per second (Hallett, 1986). The average vergence movement lasts about 1 second, which is a relatively long time in comparison to the saccadic eye movements. Demonstrate the speed of vergence movements to yourself by changing

Note: The numbered dots show the order of eye movement. The time interval between dots is about 1/5 second. The distance traveled between dots 1 and 2 is about 4 cones.

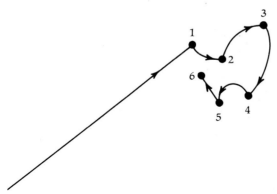

Figure 4.8 Example of involuntary eye movements. Numbered dots show order of eye movement. Time interval between dots is about ⅕ sec. Distance traveled between dots 1 and 2 is about four cones.

Demonstration 4.6

Three Kinds of Version Eye Movements

The next time you are driving, illustrate the three kinds of version eye movements for yourself. First, become aware of how you are using saccadic eye movements to keep track of the action around you and to keep your car in its proper lane. Next, notice when you use pursuit movements, for example, to follow the motions of a car passing you. Finally, notice how you also make small, involuntary eye movements, although these are usually not so conspicuous as the other two kinds of version movements. Still, when you are stopped at a traffic light, you might be concentrating on the bumper sticker in front of you or examining some detail on the traffic light. In each case try to recall as many characteristics as possible for each eye movement type.

Demonstration 4.7

Convergence

Hold your left finger as far as possible away from your body, and fixate both your right and your left eye upon the finger. Now slowly bring the finger in toward your left eye, but do not use convergence. That is, keep fixating upon your finger with your left eye, but keep your right eye in the same position it held when you first began fixating. (In other words, it will be looking generally straight ahead and should resist the temptation to turn inward.) As you move your finger inward, stop about 10 cm (about 4 inches) from your left eye. Notice that you will have double vision. Each eye will receive a different picture of your finger. Incidentally, you may find it extremely difficult to *avoid* convergence! We make vergence movements so automatically that it is difficult to work without them.

---

your fixation point from a nearby object to a distant object.

We saw that our eyes are remarkably resistant to fatigue when they make numerous saccadic eye movements. You may have wondered why your eyes feel tired when you've been steadily reading for several hours. The culprit is probably the muscle tension required to maintain convergence. Guth (1981) found that muscle fatigue during reading and keypunch work was three to four times

greater when the illumination was poor as when it was adequate. If people nagged you to turn on a light when you were reading as a young child, they were simply trying to save you from muscle fatigue due to convergence.

In Chapter 7 we will talk about vergence movements in connection with distance perception. As it happens, we may use the degree of convergence as one cue to determine the distance of an object. If our eyes have moved apart, we know we are looking at a distant object. If our eyes have moved together, we know we are looking at something close.

Summary: Eye Movements

1. Version movements of the eyes occur when the angle between the lines of sight remains constant; version movements include saccadic movements, pursuit movements, and involuntary eye movements.
2. Saccadic movements are the rapid movements of the eye from one fixation point to the next. They are frequent, jerky, rapid, and ballistic. Saccadic movements do not produce substantial fatigue.
3. The topic of eye movements in reading has inspired extensive research. One important topic is the rules that guide the size of the saccade: (a) saccades average 5 to 10 letters; (b) the saccade seldom ends on a blank space; (c) the saccade seldom ends on "the" and predictable words; (d) the saccade is shorter if the next word in a sequence is misspelled or long.
4. Another major topic concerning eye movements in reading involves the perceptual span, which is measured by determining the distance at which distortions in the text will not be detected. The span appears to extend from four spaces to the left to eight spaces to the right. Readers of Hebrew have perceptual spans that are lopsided in the opposite direction.
5. Pursuit movements are used to track moving targets; these movements are slow and smooth, and they attempt to match the speed of a target.
6. Involuntary eye movements are small eye movements that we make when we fixate upon something. Without these movements the borders of figures would slowly fade.
7. Vergence movements occur when the angle between the lines of sight changes. The eyes converge to look at nearby objects and diverge to look at distant objects. Vergence movements are slow. Continuous convergence for a period of time can produce eye muscle fatigue.

ACCOMMODATION

As Chapter 3 discussed, light entering the eye is first bent by the cornea, then it is bent still further by the lens. The cornea bends the light rays by a constant amount, but the remarkable lens can have its shape changed according to the distance of an object from the retina. More specifically, **accommodation** is a change in the shape of the lens that is necessary to keep an image in proper focus on the retina. Suppose that the lens were rigid and could not change its shape. Suppose also that the curvature of the lens were designed so that objects at a distance could be seen clearly. A problem would arise if you wanted to look at a nearby object. The light rays from that object would be focused on a point *behind* the retina rather than on the retina itself. The image of the object would be blurred. Fortunately, however, the lens is flexible, and its shape changes so that the light rays change their angle as they pass through the lens. As a result, the light rays end up on the retina, and the image of the object is sharp.

Normal Focusing

Let us first consider focusing in eyes with normal accommodation ability. People who have normal accommodation are called **emmetropic.** (An appropriate comment to yell at an irritating person who does not wear glasses is "You emmetrope!")

Imagine that a normal eye is looking at a white circle on a dark background. If that circle is far away, the light rays going from the circle to the eye are parallel—that is, they are the same distance apart. If the circle is close, however, the light rays are not parallel; instead, they diverge as they approach the eye. (The physics explanation underlying this phenomenon is beyond the scope of this book.)

Look at Figure 4.9. Let's first consider two situations in which the circle is far away and the light rays are parallel. If the light rays enter a thick lens, the thick lens bends them too much, and they gather in focus at a point

Note: If a circle is far away, a thick lens brings the light rays into focus in front of the retina; a thin lens focuses them on the retina. If a circle is close, a thick lens brings the light rays into focus on the retina; a thin lens focuses them behind the retina.

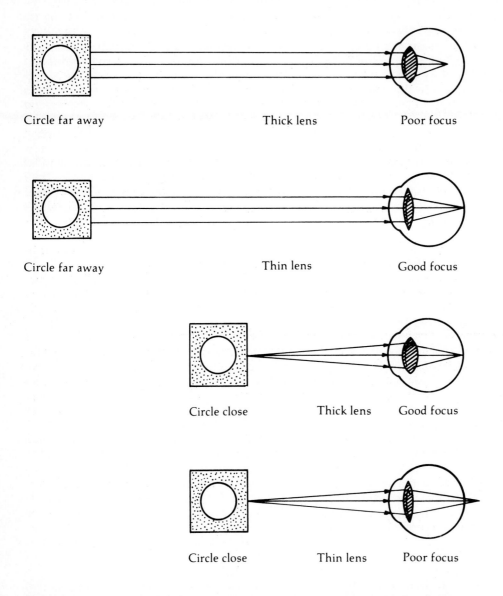

Figure 4.9 Focused and unfocused images. If circle is far away, thick lens brings light rays into focus in front of retina; thin lens focuses them on retina. If circle is close, thick lens brings light rays into focus on retina; thin lens focuses them behind retina.

in front of the retina. If the light rays enter a thin lens, however, they are bent just the right amount so that they gather in focus right at the retina.

Now consider two situations in which the circle is near, and the light rays are not parallel. If the light rays enter a thick lens, the thick lens bends them substantially, enough so that they gather in focus at the retina. If the light rays enter a thin lens, however, the thin lens does not bend them enough, and if light could pass through the retina, the rays would focus at a point behind the retina. Now try Demonstration 4.8, which illustrates accommodation.

Accommodation is performed by the **ciliary muscle,** a tiny muscle attached to the lens, to which you were introduced in Chapter 3. When this muscle contracts, the lens becomes thicker, and you can see things nearby. When this muscle relaxes, the lens becomes thinner, and you can see things far away.

Notice that accommodation involves a muscle inside the eye. All the eye movements talked about in the previous section involved muscles outside the eye.

Accommodation takes about .40 second. In the section on vergence we noted that convergence on divergence took approximately 1 second. Thus the focusing performed by the muscles inside the eye is faster than the vergence performed by the muscles outside the eye, even though both operations are used in shifting fixation from far objects to near ones.

A normal eye can bring into focus a point far away. It does not do as well with close objects. Nearby objects can be kept in focus until they are just a few centimeters away from the eye, but then the curvature of the lens has reached its limits. Try bringing your finger close to your eye to determine the limits of accommodation.

Focusing Problems

We have been discussing the capabilities of the normal eye. Unfortunately, the shapes of many people's eyeballs and lenses do not allow them to bring an image into clear focus

on the retina. Vision for a dot at a certain distance may therefore be blurred rather than a crisp point. People who are **myopic,** or **nearsighted,** can see objects nearby but cannot see objects clearly far away. They cannot focus on a point far away; in fact, they may not be able to see clearly any object farther than a meter away. (If you are like me, for example, you have to wear corrective lenses to look at your weight on the scale, or else perform gymnastics to get your eyes within 20 cm of the dial!) Nearsighted people have eyeballs longer than normal, or else their lenses are too thick. Figure 4.10 shows the situation in which the eye is too long. Notice that without correction, the image of objects is focused in front of the retina for nearsighted people. Remember, then, that *nearsighted* (myopic) people can see things *nearby,* and images are focused in *front* of the retina.

Nearsightedness can be corrected by wearing corrective lenses, as illustrated in Figure 4.10. Notice how this lens makes the light rays diverge more, so that after passing through the lens of the eye they end up exactly on the retina. The vision of a myopic person, when corrected, resembles the vision of an emmetropic person (Westheimer, 1986). Incidentally, the corrective lens is intended to correct vision for distant objects, but it also changes vision for nearby objects. Nearsighted people wearing corrective lenses cannot focus on objects as close to their eyes as they could without corrective lenses. If you are nearsighted and wear glasses or contact lenses, see how close you can bring your finger to your eye and still keep it in focus, both with and without corrective lenses.

Some interesting work by Young, Singer, and Foster (1975) indicates that myopic people tend to differ somewhat from other people in their personality characteristics. Myopic people are more likely to express an interest in academic achievement and creative efforts, and they are more likely to win academic awards. In contrast, people who are not myopic are more interested in outdoor activities and professions that require business skills. Furthermore, amount of time spent in reading is fairly strongly correlated

Demonstration 4.8

Accommodation

Stand in front of a window and hold a finger about 20 cm (8 inches) in front of your eyes. Focus upon your finger, forcing your lens to become thick. Notice how blurry all the objects are in the view from your window. With a thick lens, light rays from distant objects focus on a point in front of the retina.

Now focus upon a distant object, forcing your lens to become thin. Now your finger will look blurry. With a thin lens, light rays from nearby objects focus on a point that would be in back of the retina (if it were transparent, just as in the diagram in Figure 4.9).

If you have taken photographs, you know that it can be difficult to obtain clear images of both nearby and distant objects. The left picture shows clear images of nearby objects (but blurry distant objects), whereas the right picture shows clear images of distant objects (but blurry nearby objects). The next time you go to the movies, watch for this phenomenon. The camera focuses on the woman's face in the foreground, and the man in the background looks fuzzy. The focus may shift to provide a clear image of the man, but then the woman's face becomes blurry. (Photos by Ron Pretzer.)

with amount of myopia (Young, 1981). Young pursued this intriguing correlation by studying the development of myopia in monkeys. Since it seemed unprofitable to induce myopia in monkeys by teaching them to read, he forced them to have extensive experience with close objects by raising them in conditions where nothing was more than 50 cm from their eyes. After 3 years, the monkeys had become myopic. It is important to stress that you should not fling aside your textbook in the hope of avoiding myopia. The corre-

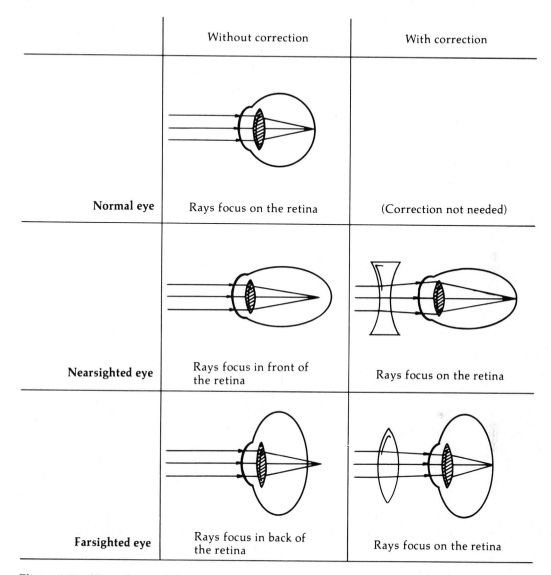

Figure 4.10 Normal, nearsighted, and farsighted eyes.

lation in humans is far from perfect, and a large component of myopia can be traced to heredity rather than experience with close objects.

People who are **hypermetropic,** or **far-sighted,** can see objects far away, but they cannot see nearby objects clearly. They have eyeballs shorter than normal, or their lenses are too thin. If light could pass through the retina, the image of the object would be focused behind the retina for farsighted people. Remember that *farsighted* (hypermetropic) people can see things *far* away, and images are focused *behind* the retina. They cannot read a book if it is held the normal distance from their eyes because the print is blurry.

With an appropriate corrective lens the light rays converge more. After the light rays pass through the lens, they end up on the retina.

People who have **astigmatism** have a cornea that is not perfectly round. Some areas of the cornea have more curvature than other parts. If the eye is focused for some parts of the cornea, it is out of focus for other parts. In most cases the astigmatism involves a cornea that is flatter in a horizontal direction than in a vertical direction. People with astigmatism require corrective lenses that have more curvature in some areas than in others.

Summary: Accommodation

1. Accommodation changes the shape of the lens to keep an image in proper focus on the retina. Without accommodation the light rays from an object would often be focused on a point either behind or in front of the retina rather than on the retina.

2. A person with normal focusing is called emmetropic.

3. Accommodation is performed by the ciliary muscles inside the eye.

4. People who are nearsighted (myopic) and cannot see distant objects have eyeballs longer than normal or lenses that are too thick; the image of the object is focused in front of the retina. They tend to differ from people who are not nearsighted in terms of several personality characteristics and time spent reading.

5. People who are farsighted and cannot see nearby objects have eyeballs shorter than normal or else lenses that are too thin; the image of the object would be focused behind the retina if light could pass through the retina.

6. People with astigmatism have corneas that are not perfectly round, so that an object in focus for some part of the eye is out of focus for another part.

Review

1. What are the five basic types of acuity? Identify the kind of acuity represented by each of these activities: (a) You are trying to read a sign across the ballpark, and you can't see whether it says HOT or HUT. (b) You just saw a car swipe the side of a parked car and speed away, but you cannot make out the number on the license plate. (c) The dial on your scale is clearly to the left of the 130-pound line rather than to the right. (d) One radiologist sees a tiny white spot on an X ray, but another radiologist does not see it.

2. Think about all the characteristics of the visual system and of a stimulus that could influence acuity. Combining all these factors, describe a situation in which acuity would be the best possible. Then describe a situation in which acuity would be the worst possible.

3. We discussed vision and driving in connection with two topics: acuity and dark adaptation. Summarize this information, emphasizing the practical applications.

Since driving uses saccadic eye movements, summarize this information as well.

4. Explain why dark adaptation curves make us suspect that two different factors must be responsible for dark adaptation. Discuss the experimental results on this topic.

5. What is light adaptation? Explain how acuity and sensitivity are related to vision in well-lit and poorly lit environments.

6. What are the four kinds of eye movements discussed in this chapter? Identify the kind of eye movement represented in each of these situations: (a) You watch a bird fly away from you in a diagonal direction, so that its flight is also from right to left. (b) You are staring into someone's pupils, but your eyes move slightly. (c) You are carefully examining a painting in art class.

7. The material on saccadic eye movements in reading mentioned the size of the perceptual span. What is this size, how is it

assessed, and what kind of information is picked up from the text that follows the fixation point?

8. For each of the following, supply an example that occurred today and identify whether the movement is slow or fast, smooth or jerky, and any other noticeable characteristics: vergence movements, involuntary eye movements, pursuit movements, and saccadic movements.

9. Describe the focusing process that takes place in normal eyes during accommodation, and then summarize how this focusing is abnormal in nearsightedness, farsightedness, and astigmatism. How can each of these disorders be corrected?

10. Contrast the focusing performed by the eye muscles during accommodation with the other eye movements mentioned in this chapter. Be certain to mention location of the muscle and speed of the movement.

New Terms

visual acuity	adaptation stimulus	stabilized retinal image techniques
visual angle	test stimulus	
static visual acuity	dark adaptation curve	converge
identification	achromatic vision	diverge
detection	version movement	convergence
resolution	vergence movement	divergence
resolve	saccadic movement	accommodation
vernier acuity	saccade	emmetropic
dynamic visual acuity	fixation pause	ciliary muscle
peripheral vision	ballistic movements	myopic
luminance	perceptual span	nearsighted
adaptation	gaze-contingent paradigm	hypermetropic
dark adaptation	pursuit movements	farsighted
light adaptation	involuntary eye movements	astigmatism

Recommended Readings

Boff, K. R., Kaufman, L., & Thomas, J. P. (Eds.) (1986). *Handbook of perception and human performance* (Vol. 1). New York: Wiley. *This volume is a necessity for any college library where students and faculty are seriously interested in perception. Chapters relevant to basic visual processes include those on sensitivity to light, the eye as an optical instrument, seeing spatial patterns, and eye movements.*

Just, M. A., & Carpenter, P. A. (1987). *The psychology of reading and language comprehension.* Newton, MA: Allyn & Bacon. *People who are interested in eye movements in reading—as well as topics such as vocabulary acquisition, the understanding of text, and speed reading—will want to use this clearly written, up-to-date summary of the literature.*

Rayner, K. (Ed.) (1983). *Eye movements in reading: Perceptual and language processes.* New York: Academic Press. *This book contains 29 chapters by prominent researchers in the area of eye movements in reading, and it covers some interesting topics such as eye movements and language processing and eye movements and reading disabilities, as well as excellent summary chapters by McConkie and Rayner.*

Note: I have not been able to locate full-length books suitable for undergraduates on the topics of acuity, adaptation, or accommodation. Students particularly interested in these topics may be most successful in pursuing more information in the journal *Vision Research.*

chapter 5
Color

Preview

Our examination of color perception begins with a discussion of the nature of color. We will see how color depends upon hue, saturation, and brightness. Then we will discuss two methods of mixing colors. The additive method is relevant when we combine different colored lights. The subtractive method, which produces different results, is relevant when we mix paints.

Color vision theory in its current form proposes two major stages in the processing of color information. In the first stage three kinds of color receptors, or cones, absorb wavelengths from somewhat different parts of the spectrum. In the second stage these color receptors pass the information on to ganglion cells. These ganglion cells operate according to opponent processes; they are exicted by some wavelengths and inhibited by others. The cortex contains cells that code information through an even more complicated double-opponent-process mechanism. Color vision theory accounts for many characteristics of color perception.

The third topic is color deficiencies, often mistakenly called color blindness. Most people have normal color vision; they are called normal trichromats. A significant number of people have relatively minor deficiencies; they are called anomalous trichromats. There are three kinds of more substantial color deficiencies; people with these disorders are called dichromats. A very small percentage of color-deficient people, called monochromats, are the only ones who are truly "color-blind." This section of the chapter also discusses the diagnosis of color deficiencies.

The final section of the chapter examines several color phenomena. These phenomena illustrate how color perception is influenced by other stimuli seen either at the same time or beforehand; sometimes we even see colors not present in the stimulus. Our memory for the typical color of an object can also influence color vision, as can the quality of the lighting. This section also examines some factors, such as stimulus size, that affect color vision. The chapter concludes with an in-depth discussion of research on color categorization, which demonstrates that colors at the center of categories (such as blue) are processed differently from colors at the boundaries of categories (such as blue-green).

Imagine eating dinner tonight and confronting a plate of purple chicken, red corn-on-the-cob, orange lettuce, and blue milk. It would be difficult to finish the meal with your eyes open! Color is so important that violations of our expectations are overwhelming.

We know that food colors are important to Americans because of the additives used to enhance color. Think also about the importance of the color of clothing. Toufexis (1983) describes how the Color Association of the United States tries to predict the long-range color preferences in women's fashion. If Princess Diana begins wearing melon pink, it's a good bet that American women will want to wear that color, too.

Color also has an important impact for other products. Eastman Kodak Company spends large sums to make certain that the quality of "Kodak yellow" is controlled within well-defined limits (Boynton, 1971). Detergent boxes must feature bold, primary colors to inspire images of cleanliness and strength (Toufexis, 1983). In fact, when people were tested on their reactions to detergents, they thought that the detergent in a yellow-orange box was too strong, the detergent in a blue box was too weak, and the ideal product came in a blue box with yellow-orange splashes (Kupchella, 1976). Furthermore, when people were asked to judge the capsule colors of drugs, they reported that white capsules suggested analgesic action, lavender suggested hallucinogenic effects, and orange or yellow were stimulants (Buckalew & Coffield, 1982).

Color has enormous social significance as well. Actors and actresses rise to stardom on the basis of the color of the irises in their eyes. Hair color is even more important. Skin color, of course, is most important. People have been enslaved, deprived, and killed because of the color of their skin.

The perception of color has been a consistently popular topic for researchers. In fact Haber (1985) argues that color is the single most studied topic in vision. We will consider four aspects of color: the nature of color, color

vision deficiencies, the sensory processing of color, and issues in color perception.

NATURE OF COLOR

Color, as we typically use the term, has several components. Three terms are used to describe our perceptions: hue, saturation, and brightness. Each of these qualities is generally determined by a physical component of light, as discussed in Chapter 3. A color's hue is determined by wavelength, saturation by purity, and brightness by the intensity of the light.

Let us first examine **hue,** which is the psychological reaction to wavelengths ranging from about 400 nm (seen as violet) to about 700 nm (seen as red). When we use the word *color* in everyday conversation, we typically mean *hue* instead.

The history of research on color vision might have been different if there had not been a plague in London in summer 1666. Isaac Newton escaped this plague by moving to Cambridge that summer, according to Wasserman (1978), and his major publications on the nature of light were based on his research there. Newton closed himself in a room that was entirely dark except for a beam of sunlight passing through a small hole in a shutter. Then he took a prism and held it up to the beam of light. The prism refracted, or bent, the white light from the sun into the rainbowlike spectrum you see in Color Plate 1 inside the front cover, with colors ranging from violet to red. Figure 5.1 illustrates how sunlight contains some portion of every wavelength from the visible spectrum. Notice, incidentally, that the light from a standard light bulb also contains all different wavelengths, but a greater proportion comes from the long wavelengths.

As Newton demonstrated, white light really consists of a combination of different colored lights, an observation that doesn't match our intuitive feelings about light. Another observation that doesn't match our in-

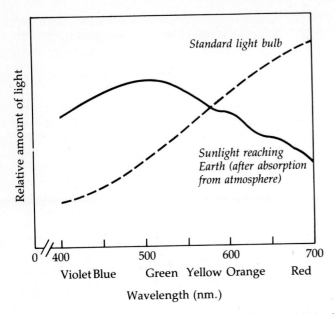

Figure 5.1 Wavelength composition of sunlight and light from light bulb.

tuitions is the fact that objects *look as if* they are colored, but they are really reflecting light from selected portions of the spectrum. Your jeans may look blue—and blueness seems to be a quality as inseparable from those jeans as their pockets. Nevertheless, the jeans are blue because their surface is absorbing all the long and medium wavelengths (from the red, orange, yellow, and green portion of the spectrum) and reflecting to your eyes only the light from the blue portion of the spectrum. Similarly, your white shirt is reflecting light to your eyes from the entire spectrum and your black shoes are reflecting almost no light.

We have two major topics in this section. We will first discuss the color solid as a scheme for organizing the three dimensions of color. Then we'll discuss how colors can be combined.

The Color Solid

One common way to organize colors is in terms of a **color wheel,** a circle with all the different wavelengths arranged around the edge. Figure 5.2 illustrates a color wheel. This figure shows several important aspects. Hues that seem similar are near one another. Yellow is near red and also near green. However,

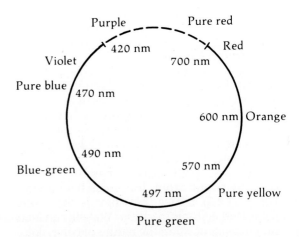

Figure 5.2 Color wheel.

red and green, which seem quite different, are separated on the color wheel.

Next notice the dotted line at the top of the color wheel. This part of the circle represents **nonspectral hues** that cannot be described in terms of a single wavelength from a part of the spectrum. Instead, these hues are produced by combining other hues. Purple is a combination of blue and red. Similarly, a red that people choose as the best example of red requires a little touch of blue, or it will look slightly yellow.

Notice also that some colors are not on the circle. Brown and pink aren't there, let alone the more exotic metallic colors such as silver and gold. In fact, you see on the wheel only a small proportion of the crayons you can buy in the extra-fancy, super-duper collection. Where is burnt sienna or carnation pink or periwinkle or mauve? The outside of the color wheel represents only the **monochromatic colors**—those which could be produced by a single wavelength—plus the true red and purple necessary to complete the circle.

We can change the color wheel so that the purity of the color can also be represented. The physical **purity** of a stimulus is determined by the amount of white light added to the monochromatic light. Colors high in purity and with no white light added are arranged around the edge of the circle. As we move toward the middle of the circle, we see the colors low in purity and with increasing amounts of light mixtures added. The center of the circle represents white or gray, an evenly balanced mixture of light waves, with no single wavelength dominant.

Figure 5.3 shows an example. Notice that as we move inward from blue to white, we move from a true, deep blue to more "washed out" shades of blue, such as sky blue and baby blue. As we have discussed, it is customary to refer to the physical characteristic as *purity*. The *apparent* purity of a color, however, is called **saturation;** purity is a term from physics, and saturation describes a psychological reaction. Thus we say that baby blue looks highly unsaturated because we are discussing our psychological reaction.

Now that we have added saturation to

hue, we can describe a large number of colors. However, one aspect of color is still missing: brightness. Remember from Chapter 3 that light waves can vary in their height as well as in their length. Intense or high-amplitude lights have high peaks on their waves, as Figure 3.3 showed; these lights are perceived as brighter and whiter. Lights with low peaks, in contrast, are perceived as darker. Thus **brightness** is the apparent intensity of a color; brightness describes our psychological reaction to the physical characteristic, intensity.

It is customary to represent brightness by adding a third dimension to the color wheel. This is illustrated in Figure 5.4, which is a picture of a color solid. A **color solid** or **color spindle** represents the hue, saturation, and brightness of all colors. Notice that the color solid looks like two cones joined together, with the color wheel represented at the broadest part of the figure, where there is the maximum saturation.

You may wonder why the color solid is pointed at both ends, rather than cylinder shaped. The answer is that some combinations of saturation and brightness are impossible. For example, you cannot have a dark or light color that is highly saturated. Look at

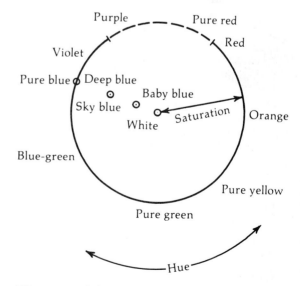

Figure 5.3 Color wheel with saturation added.

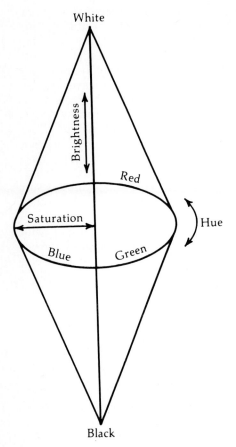

Figure 5.4 Color solid.

a dark color near you. It cannot look like a pure color; it has low saturation. In summary, high saturation is possible only when the brightness is intermediate, neither too dark nor too light.

Many versions of the color solid have been created for use by both psychologists and people in applied areas. Color Plate 2, inside the front cover, shows one example of a color solid. Notice how the colors in this illustration differ in hue, saturation, and brightness.

Color Mixing

What happens when we mix colors? There are two different ways to do this. The **additive mixture** method means that we add together beams of light from different parts of the spectrum. The **subtractive mixture** method means that we mix dyes or pigments, or we place two or more colored filters together. Additive mixtures combine colors from separate light sources, whereas subtractive mixtures involve only a single light source. We will discuss these two methods separately.

It is interesting to note, incidentally, how mixing colors differs from mixing stimuli relevant for some other senses. When you mix red and blue by either the additive or the subtractive mixture method, the result is a color of uniform shade. You cannot detect the separate parts that constitute the mixture because vision is a **synthetic sense** with respect to mixtures. Contrast this situation with the result when we combine two fairly different sounds, say a C and an A on the piano. Here, you can definitely separate the two notes when they are played together because audition is an **analytic sense**. Taste, as well as audition, is typically an analytic sense because we can detect the separate parts when we taste something. A chocolate mint mousse has two distinct, separable flavors—chocolate and mint.

Additive Mixtures

Let's consider the color wheel once more. Look at Figure 5.3 and notice that the wavelengths are not evenly arranged around the periphery of the wheel. The portion of the spectrum from 420 to about 500 clearly has more than its fair share. This unequal distribution is necessary to place complementary hues on exactly opposite sides of the color wheel. **Complementary hues** are those whose additive mixture makes gray. Notice, then, that when we add together two highly saturated complementary hues, the result is a color of low saturation. Figure 5.5 shows how an additive mixture would work if you mixed lights of the two complementary hues blue and yellow. (It should be noted that the hues must be carefully chosen or the combination may produce a color other than gray.)

If mixing equal amounts of complementary hues produces gray, what do you produce when you mix unequal amounts of other

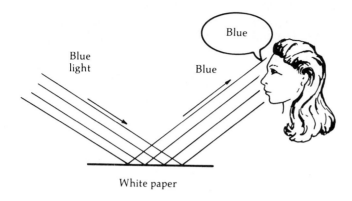

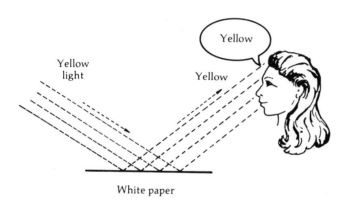

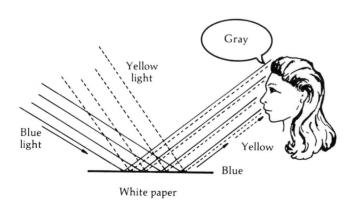

Figure 5.5 Additive mixtures for blue light and yellow light. (From Lindsay & Norman, 1977. Used with permission.)

colors? In general, you will produce a color between the two colors and low in saturation. Here is how you can predict the results. (1) Locate the two colors on the color circle and connect them with a line. (2) Place a dot along the line to represent the relative amount of each light in the combination. (3) Draw a second line from the center of the circle so that it passes through the dot and ends at the edge of the circle. (4) The point at which that line ends on the circle tells you the name of the color; the distance of the dot from the center tells you its saturation.

It's worth mentioning that an additive mixture cannot be highly saturated. Whenever we combine two colors additively, any point along the line connecting those two colors in a color circle cannot lie on the edge of the circle. Instead, it lies in the less saturated region. If the two colors are similar, the additive combination can still be fairly satu-

rated. If the two colors are complementary, however, and if the mixture uses equal quantities of both, the result is an extremely unsaturated mixture. Try Demonstration 5.1 to illustrate additive mixtures and clarify the issue of saturation.

The additive mixture process allows us to make **metamers**, pairs of lights that look exactly the same but are composed of physically different stimuli. Imagine two patches of color. The patch on the left is blue-green with medium saturation, and it is from a single light source. The patch on the right is created by mixing equal parts of highly saturated violet and green, as represented by the black dot in Demonstration 5.1. Our eyes could not distinguish between these two metamers, even though they are physically different.

We have been discussing mixtures of two colors. When equal parts of three colors are mixed together, the color can be predicted by

---

Demonstration 5.1

Predicting Additive Mixtures

What happens if we make an additive mixture of equal amounts of green and violet? We must place the dot halfway between green and violet. Notice that the result is blue, tending slightly toward green, with intermediate saturation. Try an additive mixture that is mostly violet, with just a little green. To do this, we must place the dot nearer to the violet side. Notice that we get blue. Similarly, try a mixture of mostly orange, with just a little green. Notice that the result is yellow. Finally, try an equal mixture of blue and a slightly orange yellow.

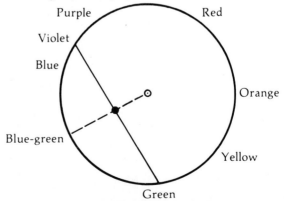

calculating the center point of a triangle produced by connecting the three dots representing each color. When the mixture is unequal, the resulting color shifts toward the color that contributes the largest portion—as you might expect.

A metameric match can be made for each color of the spectrum by mixing the correct amount of three colored lights. Most often, this is done by using the colors red (650 nm), green (530 nm), and blue (460 nm). Several resources describe how this procedure works (Mollon, 1982a; Wandell, 1982, 1985; Wright, 1972). Later in the chapter we will see the significance of being able to create all colors from three basic colors. This system allowed researchers to speculate that there are three types of color receptors.

In our everyday lives we do not often mix beams of lights of different colors. A more common way to produce additive mixtures is to place small patches of color next to one another. Color television produces its range of colors, for example, by using red, green, and blue dots. These dots are too small and too closely spaced to be discriminated with normal vision. Your eyes blend them together in what appear to be solid colors of assorted hues. Try Demonstration 5.2 to convince yourself that when you watch television, you are really watching spots in front of your eyes.

Artists can also produce additive mixtures with their paints. Georges Seurat, for example, didn't mix subtle shades on his palette. Instead, he used a technique called **pointillism,** in which discrete dots of pigments are applied to a canvas; these dots blend into solid colors when viewed from a distance. People who weave or do needlework are also aware of additive mixtures. Wasserman describes, for example, how 19th-century tapestry weavers tried to predict how a given thread would look on a given background. Observers looking at a tapestry from a distance would see a single color rather than two distinct colors. Additive mixtures are also relevant in theatrical lighting. A technician who plans to spotlight an actor by using blue and yellow lights may end up with a gray light.

Notice, also, how you make additive mixtures in everyday life. You look at an autumn hillside from a distance, and it looks brown, rather than patched with separate spots of gold, red, green, and brown.

Subtractive Mixtures

Subtractive mixtures, as we said before, involve mixing dyes or placing colored filters together. They are called *subtractive* because

---

Demonstration 5.2

Additive Mixtures and Color Television

The screen of a color television is like a miniature patchwork quilt consisting of many tiny dots. Typically, it has about 1 million dots of three types. When irradiated from behind the screen by a special beam, one type glows blue, another glows green, and another glows red (Boynton, 1979).

How can a patch on the screen look yellow? Take a magnifying glass and notice that a yellow patch is really tiny green and red dots of a carefully chosen hue. The dots are too small to be seen with the unaided eye when you sit at a normal distance from the television, but they are combined by additive mixture. With the magnifying glass, notice other blends of colored dots. See whether you can predict what they would look like from the normal viewing distance.

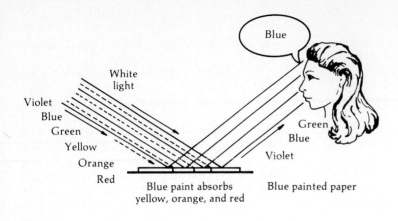

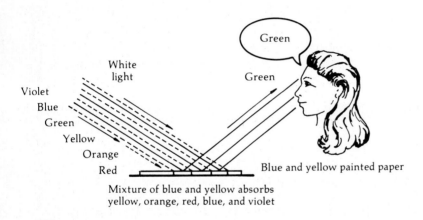

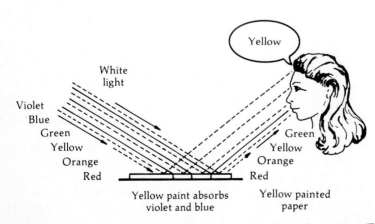

Figure 5.6 Subtractive mixtures for blue paint and yellow paint. (From Lindsay & Norman, 1977. Used with permission.)

Demonstration 5.3
_____

Two Mixture Techniques

First, try making an additive mixture. Take small pieces of blue and yellow paper. Cut the blue paper into narrow strips, then cut these strips into tiny squares. Arrange the squares in random order on part of the yellow paper, so that they cover about half the surface. Tape the squares in place, then tape the yellow paper on a wall at the end of a long hallway. Walk backwards down the hallway, looking at that paper, until you can no longer see the individual squares. The combination of yellow and blue should look gray.

To make a subtractive mixture, color a piece of white paper with yellow paint or crayon. Then color over this with blue paint or crayon. The combination should look green.

---

when a beam of white light passes through dyes or filters, parts of the spectrum are absorbed or subtracted. As Figure 5.6 shows, blue paint absorbs the yellow, orange, and red (the long wavelengths) from the white light. Only the light from the violet, blue, and green portion of the spectrum passes on to your eyes. However, yellow paint absorbs violet and blue (the short wavelengths). Consequently, when you mix blue and yellow, the only color *not* absorbed by either of the paints is green (a medium wavelength), so you report seeing green.

Remember that we are dealing with subtractive mixtures whenever we mix dyes or pigments. Thus artists work with subtractive mixtures when they mix pigments on a palette or when they put one color on top of another on the canvas. If you are repainting a room, you will also need to worry about subtractive mixtures, because yellow painted over blue may turn out a sickly green. Anyone who works with colored filters would also be concerned about subtractive mixtures. For example, a window display that uses various colors of cellophane might unintentionally reveal a new color if two colors overlap.

You may recall that when we mix blue and yellow in an additive mixture, we produce gray. However, when we mix blue and yellow in a subtractive mixture, we produce green. Thus the two mixture techniques produce different results. Try Demonstration 5.3 to illustrate the two techniques.

How can we predict what kinds of colors will result from the subtractive mixture technique? Unfortunately, there is no simple diagram such as the color wheel to help us. It is difficult to predict exactly what wavelengths will be absorbed by a particular pigment, and the pattern of absorption may be complex. For example, the light green you see on a cabbage absorbs the short and medium-long wavelengths but reflects the light from the medium and very long wavelength portion of the spectrum (Clulow, 1972). If we do not know exactly what wavelengths will be absorbed by the individual pigments, we cannot predict the results of the combination of pigments.

Summary: Nature of Color

1. Color has enormous importance in consumer psychology and personal interactions; it has also been a popular topic among perception researchers.
2. Hue corresponds to the length of light waves, and it can be represented by points along the edge of a color wheel. The color wheel also shows nonspectral hues such as purple and true red.

3. On a color wheel the saturation of a color is represented by the distance from the center of a circle.

4. A color solid represents hue and saturation on a color wheel. Brightness is represented along the vertical dimension. The solid is shaped so that the broadest portion occurs at medium brightness.

5. The additive mixture method means that we add together beams of different colored lights. We can predict the color of the resulting mixture by using a color wheel. The additive mixture method can produce metamers, pairs of lights that look identical but are physically different. Outside the laboratory additive mixtures can be accomplished by color television and an artistic technique called pointillism.

6. The subtractive mixture method means that we mix dyes or place colored filters together. Parts of the spectrum are subtracted or absorbed by the filters. It is difficult to predict the color of the resulting mixture because the patterns of absorption may be complex.

COLOR VISION THEORY

You are probably accustomed to theoretical arguments in many areas of psychology. Arguments are alive and well in perception, too. For example, in Chapter 7 you will see that there is a heated debate about distance perception. Some think that the stimuli reaching the eye are rich with distance information, whereas others think that these stimuli are impoverished. If I had written this textbook in the early 1970s, I would have described an equally fierce argument between the supporters of two color vision theories, the Trichromatic Theory people and the Opponent-Processes people. As Haber (1985) noted, this debate produced most of the excitement in the area of color vision research.

Happily enough, however, the argument has been satisfactorily resolved. Both theories are correct, but they apply to different zones of the visual processing system. Trichromatic

theory operates at the receptor level and applies to the cones, whereas opponent-process theory operates at the level beyond the receptors. Perhaps the best short description of current color vision theory has been supplied by DeValois and DeValois (1975): "Color vision requires, then, a limited number of receptors of different spectral sensitivity, plus a neural system that compares the output of different receptor types" (p. 119).

In this section we will first consider how color is coded by the receptors. Then we will see how this information from the receptors is interpreted by the neural system. Finally, we will see how this theory of color vision accounts for some color vision facts that we have discussed in the first part of the chapter.

Receptor Level

The **trichromatic theory** of color vision argues that there are three kinds of color receptors, each sensitive to light from a different part of the spectrum. The precise origins of this theory are not certain (Rushton, 1975; Wasserman, 1978). However, the founders of trichromatic theory include Sir Isaac Newton in the 1600s (whose work with prisms we mentioned earlier) and three researchers in the 1800s: Thomas Young, an English physician who also achieved fame by translating the Rosetta Stone; Hermann von Helmholtz, whose empiricist approach we will discuss later in the book; and James Clerk Maxwell, a Scottish physicist who conducted research on electromagnetic radiation.

About 100 years later, researchers began to produce physiological evidence in support of three kinds of color receptors. You will recall that we discussed in Chapter 3 the two kinds of receptors in the retina. Rods are used for black-and-white vision in poorly lit environments. Cones are used for color vision in well-lit environments. Whereas there is only one kind of rod, the evidence is now clear that there are three kinds of cones.

Rushton (1958, 1975) performed a landmark experiment in which he concluded that there were at least two kinds of cones. In this study he projected a beam of light into the eyes of human observers. Now when a light is shined on a cat's eye at night, the light reflected back is greenish; the light corresponding to other wavelengths has been absorbed. Similarly, Rushton measured absorption patterns for human eyes by comparing the composition of ingoing and returning light. He found two kinds of color receptors by this process. One kind absorbed mostly long wavelengths, and the other absorbed mostly medium wavelengths. However, he did not find any kind of receptor that absorbed mostly short wavelengths.

Marks, Dobelle, and MacNichol (1964) and other later researchers (for example, Dartnall, Bowmaker, & Mollon, 1983) used a different technique and discovered the missing third color receptor. They used a technique called microspectrophotometry, a term whose meaning is suggested by its components, "micro" (small), "spectro" (spectrum), "photo" (light), and "metry" (measurement). More precisely, **microspectrophotometry** is a procedure in which an extremely small beam of light from one limited portion of the color spectrum is passed through individual receptors in retinal tissue that has been freshly dissected. Naturally, the beam of light must be tiny to reach just one receptor. Using special equipment, the researchers can determine how much light is absorbed at each wavelength (Mollon, 1982a).

Research using microspectrophotometry has established that the three kinds of cone pigments have different but overlapping absorption curves. Figure 5.7 is an adaptation of a diagram by DeValois and DeValois (1975).

Incidentally, it seems that the short-wavelength-sensitive cones—the last ones to be discovered—differ from the other two cones because their absolute sensitivity is lower, they are more vulnerable to disease, and they are almost completely absent in the very center of the fovea (Mollon, 1982a, 1982b). It is likely that these short-wavelength–sensitive cones were difficult to discover because they were relatively rare in the fovea. In any event, the discovery was particularly welcome because, as discussed in connection with me-

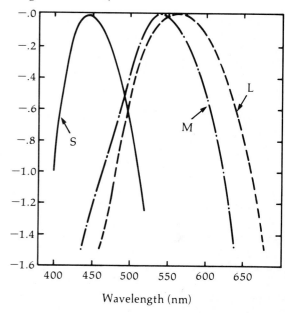

Figure 5.7 Absorption curves for three cone pigments. Each curve is plotted so that its maximum sensitivity is set at − .0, and other sensitivities are plotted relative to that maximum sensitivity, using logarithmic scale. For example, short cone pigment curve has maximum sensitivity at 450 nm; at wavelength of 400 nm its sensitivity is $\frac{1}{10}$ of maximum (because logarithim is − 1.0). (From DeValois & DeValois, 1975. Used with permission.)

tameric matches, all colors of the spectrum can be created from three basic colors. In contrast, if there were only two color receptors, it would be impossible to explain how our color vision system allows us to perceive certain colors.

Some books say that the short-wavelength curve in Figure 5.7 corresponds to the "blue" cones, the medium-wavelength curve to the "green" cones, and the long-wavelength curve to the "red" cones. However, this is misleading. As you can see, the medium- and the long-wavelength curves both absorb primarily in the yellow region. Notice, also, that the three curves overlap considerably. In other words, the curves do not differ much in their **spectral sensitivity,** or the region of the spectrum in which they absorb light. Finally, notice that the long and medium curves absorb some amount from nearly the entire spectrum, and the short curve absorbs from almost half the spectrum. Therefore, we will refer to these three kinds of cones as S (short wavelength), M (medium wavelength) and L (long wavelength), rather than by colors.

We have seen that there are three kinds of color receptors. You may remember from Chapter 3 that the rods contain a special chemical that breaks down into two components when light reaches the rods. Similarly, each of the three kinds of cones contains its own kind of chemical, each of which is most sensitive to a different wavelength (Mollon, 1982b). Thus the chemical in one kind of cone is most sensitive to the short wavelengths, the chemical in a second kind of cone is most sensitive to the medium wavelengths, and the chemical in a third kind of cone is most sensitive to the longest wavelengths. The specific nature of these chemicals and the genetic coding for these pigments have recently been identified (Nathans, Thomas, & Hogness, 1986).

So far we have discussed a mechanism in which a particular wavelength can be absorbed to differing extents by the different cone pigments. For instance, a wavelength of 500 nm has the highest absorption from the M cones, next most from the L cones, and least from the S cones. But what happens to this information about the relative absorption patterns? How is this information transmitted to the next stage in the visual processing system? Let us proceed to levels beyond the receptors.

Ganglion Level and Beyond

We have been discussing a visual system that processes color information in a way that seems entirely supportive of trichromatic theory. Trichromatic theory by itself cannot explain all the color phenomena that we will discuss throughout this chapter, however. There must be some mechanism beyond the receptor level that combines the information from the cones in a complex way. In particular, it seems that the visual system uses opponent processes. In its most general form the **opponent-process theory** specifies that cells respond to stimulation by an increase in activity when one color is present and by a decrease in activity when another color is present. For example, the activity rate might increase for a given cell when green is present and decrease when red is present. In other words, cells show activation to some parts of the spectrum and inhibition to other parts.

This activation-inhibition pattern is similar to a mechanism discussed in Chapter 3 for ganglion cells. On-center, off-surround ganglion cells, for example, show activation when light shines in the center of their receptive fields; however, they show inhibition when light shines in the surrounding portion of their receptive fields. You learned that the visual system has the capacity to respond to *spatial arrangements* by either increasing or decreasing the response rate. The visual system likewise has the capacity to respond to *color information* either by increasing or decreasing the response rate.

Ewald Hering, a German physician, developed the earlier work on the opponent-process theme into a formal theory. His work on the subject was published between 1878 and 1920. Hering incorrectly proposed that these opponent processes occurred at the receptor level rather than at higher levels in the nervous system. Thus the *original* version of opponent-process theory was incompatible with trichromatic theory.

Hering was puzzled by certain observations about color. For example, he had noticed that it was easy to report seeing color mixtures such as bluish green or yellowish red, but other color mixtures—such as greenish red or yellowish blue—were impossible. (Try for a moment to picture either of these mixtures.)

Hering suggested that there were six psychologically primary colors, which are assigned by pairs to three kinds of receptors. There is a white-black receptor whose response rate increases when white light is shown and decreases when no light is shown. There is a red-green receptor whose response rate increases to red and decreases to green. Finally, there is a yellow-blue receptor whose response rate increases to yellow and decreases to red.

Hering's theory did not receive a wide following until Hurvich and Jameson (1957) wrote an article called "An Opponent-Process Theory of Color Vision." The purpose of their psychophysical studies was to determine the amount of light of one color necessary to cancel all perception of the opponent color. For example, they showed a red light and measured the amount of green light that had to be added for observers to report that the light no longer looked red. (Remember from our discussion of additive color mixing that the right amounts of carefully chosen samples of red and green will make a neutral color, one that is neither red nor green, because red and green are complementary colors.) This procedure was repeated with different shades of red and with various shades of green, yellow, and blue. One very important contribution from this research, according to Wasserman (1978), was the development of a technique that allows us to directly measure opponent response functions.

The psychophysical studies were nicely supplemented by similar physiological findings. Researchers inserted electrodes into the retina of the goldfish to record responses at the level of the horizontal cells (Svaetichin, 1956; Svaetichin & MacNicol, 1958). (You may want to refresh your memory by returning to Figure 3.10; the horizontal cells receive information from the photoreceptors.) These researchers discovered that the wavelength of the light presented to the cones influenced the way that the horizontal cells responded. For example, one kind of cell increased its response rate when stimulated by wavelengths in the red range and decreased its response rate to wavelengths in the green region. Another kind of cell increased its rate in response to wavelengths in the yellow range and decreased its rate to wavelengths in the blue region. A third kind of cell re-

sponded to light intensity, similar to the white-black receptor that Hering had suggested. Thus, information about wavelength is passed on by the cones and processed in an opponent fashion by higher levels in visual processing.

DeValois and DeValois (1975) show how this opponent process might operate in humans at the level of the ganglion cell. It is important to emphasize how this treatment of opponent processes differs from Hering's original theory. DeValois and DeValois propose that opponent processes operate at the ganglion cells and beyond, rather than at the receptor level, as Hering had originally proposed. However, DeValois and DeValois's model *is* consistent with Hering's theory in its emphasis on the opponent processes that work in an antagonistic, push-pull fashion.

DeValois and DeValois suggest that there are six kinds of higher level cells, as illustrated in Figure 5.8. The first kind of cell, labeled $+B-Y$, is excited by blue wavelengths and inhibited by yellow wavelengths. At the top of the diagram are the three kinds of cones. As you will recall, one responds to short wavelengths, one to medium, and one to long.

When light of a particular wavelength reaches a cone, the cone passes on the information to at least two of the six kinds of higher level cells. Notice that the S cones pass on information to only two kinds of higher level cells, whereas the L cones pass on information to all six kinds.

Notice that the $+Wh-Bl$ cell receives only excitation. The $+Bl-Wh$ cell receives only inhibition. However, the other two sets of cells work in an interesting opposing, or mirror-image, fashion. The $+B-Y$ cells are stimulated by short wavelengths and inhibited by long; the reverse is true for the $+Y$ $-B$ cells. The same opposing operation holds true for the $+G-R$ and $+R-G$ system. Each of these four kinds of cells can therefore compare the excitation from one kind of cone with the inhibition from another kind of cone.

This information about the relative excitation and inhibition is coded in the ganglion cell. We know that the lateral geniculate nu-

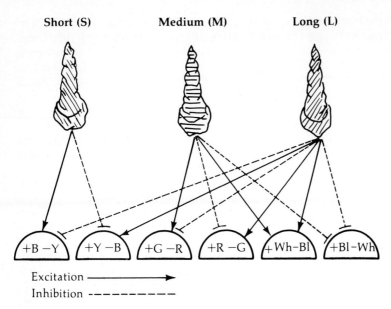

Figure 5.8 Model of how three cone types send information to higher level cells. (From DeValois & DeValois, 1975. Used with permission.)

cleus (LGN) encodes color in a similar opponent-processes fashion (DeValois, Abramov, & Jacobs, 1966; DeValois & DeValois, 1975, 1980), in other words, with little or no reorganization in the LGN (Gouras & Zrenner, 1981).

In the primary cortex many cells operate in the opponent-processes fashion, but these cells are not as common as in the LGN (Mollon, 1982a). Instead, the cortex seems to contain a large number of cells that process color information in a more complex fashion. You might recall the brief discussion of neurons picturesquely called "blobs"; they were mentioned in the "In-Depth" discussion of cortical columns in Chapter 3. These **blobs** are distributed at regular intervals throughout the column structure in the primary cortex; they respond to color and generally seem to be organized in a double-opponent-process cell fashion (Hubel & Livingstone, 1983; Humphrey & Hendrickson, 1980; Livingstone & Hubel, 1983).

So far we had been discussing a simple kind of opponent process in which a cell is

"turned on" by one kind of color and "turned off" by another kind. Figure 5.9 shows a **double-opponent-process cell,** which has a center that increases its response rate to one color and decreases its response rate to the complementary color and which also has a surrounding area that has exactly the opposite response patterns (Michael, 1978). Specifically, you'll notice that Figure 5.9 illustrates a cell in which the center of the receptive field shows activation to red and inhibition to green; in contrast, the surround of the receptive field shows inhibition to red and activation to green. The double-opponent-process for blob cells in the cortex may explain some color phenomena discussed at the end of the chapter, such as simultaneous color contrast. However, the blob cells are *not* sensitive to the orientation of a line, a topic discussed in Chapter 3 (Hubel & Livingstone, 1983; Mollon, 1982b).

Zeki (1980, 1981) has examined how color information is conveyed to even higher levels in the visual cortex. In brief the blob cells in the primary cortex send their information to

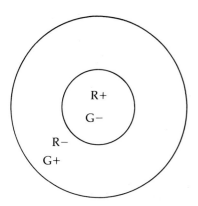

Figure 5.9 Double-opponent-process cell, sensitive to red and green.

the secondary cortex and to the additional areas in the visual cortex (see Figure 3.15). The neurons in these regions have complicated response patterns. Some neurons are also very selective about the wavelength that they "prefer." For example, a neuron might respond only to the green found at about 530 nm, but it might not respond at all to wavelengths shorter than 500 nm or longer than 550.

How the Theory Explains Features of Color Vision

So far we have seen three kinds of cones that differ in their spectral sensitivity. We have also seen that higher order nerve cells use the output from these three kinds of cones through an opponent-processes mechanism. Now we need to see why this two-level theory of color vision is appealing. Specifically, we need to explore why it accounts for some features of color vision already discussed. Later we'll discuss how it also accounts for other features in color perception.

One advantage of this two-stage color theory is that it can account for the colors in the color solid (DeValois & DeValois, 1975). Hue would be determined by the relative activity among the opponent cell types red-green and yellow-blue. The brightness could be determined by the activity rates of the white-black

cells. The saturation could be determined by which kinds of cells are most active. If the red-green and yellow-blue cells are more active, the color would be saturated. If the white-black cells are more active, the color would be unsaturated and would lie near the vertical center line in the color solid shown in Figure 5.4.

The opponent processes part of the theory also explains why some colors cannot coexist. Specifically, a color cannot coexist with its complementary color. As noted earlier, a greenish red cannot be visualized, nor can a bluish yellow. You can see a color, or its opponent, but not both. For example, we cannot see red and green at the same time because the red-green cells must respond only to green by activation or only to red by inhibition. It is impossible for the red-green cells to respond to both colors simultaneously. In contrast, the system *can* process a bluish green because blue and green can be processed by independent systems.

We have been discussing a color vision theory that consists of three kinds of color receptors. These color receptors pass on information to other higher level cells that work in terms of opponent processes. In the visual cortex are cells that operate in an even more complex double-opponent-process fashion, as well as cells that respond to only an extremely narrow band of wavelength from the spectrum. This complex system of color processing can explain the appearance of colors, the incompatibility of complementary colors, and other aspects of color. One additional aspect it can explain is color deficiencies, the focus in the next section.

Summary: Color Vision Theory

1. Until the early 1970s there was a disagreement between those who supported a trichromatic theory, with three kinds of color receptors, and those who supported the opponent-process theory, in which cells respond in opposite fashions to the members of a pair of colors. Now it is generally accepted that trichromatic theory applies at

the receptor level and opponent-process theory applies at levels beyond the receptor.

2. Trichromatic theory was developed in the mid-1800s, and physiological evidence to support the theory was presented by researchers about 100 years later. This research included absorption patterns for various wavelengths and microspectrophotometry at the level of the individual receptors.

3. Opponent-process theory was originally developed by Hering at the end of the 1800s. According to current theory, opponent processes operate at levels beyond the receptors. Green and red work in opposition, as do blue and yellow; two other kinds of cells handle information about black and white.

4. Information from the three kinds of cones is passed on the six kinds of ganglion cells, such as a $+B-Y$ cell activated by short wavelengths and inhibited by long. The cells can compare the activation from one kind of cone with the inhibition from the other kind.

5. Research support for the opponent-process theory comes from psychophysical observations and from recordings on the opponent processes in horizontal cells of goldfish.

6. The ganglion cells in the retina and the cells in the lateral geniculate nucleus encode color in an opponent-processes fashion; there are also cells in the primary cortex that use opponent processes.

7. Most cells in the primary cortex that encode color information operate in a more complicated double-opponent-process fashion. These cells are also known as blobs.

8. In the secondary cortex and in other areas of the visual cortex, the neurons have complex response patterns, and they tend to respond only to narrow bands of the spectrum.

9. Color vision theory explains the appearance of colors in the color solid, the incompatibility of complementary colors, and other topics in color vision.

COLOR VISION DEFICIENCIES

Some people cannot tell the difference between two colors that differ in hue. We often refer to those people as being "color-blind," but that term is much too strong. As you will see, only a few people are totally unable to discriminate colors. We will use the term "color vision deficiencies" instead. People with **color vision deficiencies** have difficulty discriminating different colors.

About 8% of males of European descent have some form of color vision deficiency, in contrast to about 0.4% of females (Jaeger, 1972). In other words, if you have 1,000 males and 1,000 females in a room, approximately 80 males and 4 females will have some trouble discriminating colors.

We need to discuss color vision deficiencies for two reasons. First, it is a fairly common problem. You may be color deficient yourself, and you probably have several friends who are color deficient. Second, color deficiencies have important implications for color theories, a topic discussed in the last section. In the present section we will consider the kinds of color deficiencies and their diagnosis.

Kinds of Color Deficiencies

The kinds of color vision are listed in Table 5.1. If you have normal color vision, you are

Table 5.1   Kinds of Color Vision, Normal and Deficient

Classification	Description
Normal trichromat	Normal color vision
Anomalous trichromat	Weak color vision
Dichromat	
Protanope	Insensitive to red
Deuteranope	Insensitive to green
Tritanope	Insensitive to blue
Monochromat	No color vision

a normal trichromat. A **normal trichromat** requires three primary colors, such as red, blue, and green, to match all the other colors. The word trichromat consists of two parts: *Tri*, which means "three," and *chroma*, which means "color"; the choice of the term makes sense.

In contrast to normal trichromats, anomalous trichromats have a mild color deficiency; the word *anomalous* means abnormal. An **anomalous trichromat** is similar to a normal trichromat in requiring three colors to produce all other colors, but this person will use different proportions of those three colors than the normal person. In the test for anomalous trichromacy, observers are required to match a yellow light by mixing together blue, green, and red lights. Most often, anomalous trichromats require more green or red in a mixture than would a person with normal color vision. The disorder was originally discovered by a physicist named John Strutt, who enterprisingly tested all his family members and found that some required much more green in comparison to others to match a yellow light (Alpern, 1981).

Anomalous trichromats cannot distinguish nearly as many hues in the spectrum as the normal trichromat, and they are confused by browns and dark greens (Rushton, 1975). It seems likely that anomalous trichromats have all three cone photopigments. However, at least one of these photopigments is abnormal in its absorption pattern (Mollon, 1982b).

A **dichromat** is a person who requires only two primary colors to match perception of all other colors. Note that the choice of the term makes sense because *di* means "two." The dichromat can see colors, but the range is narrow.

The dichromats fall into three groups. **Protanopes** are insensitive to long-wavelength reds; those colors look very dark to them. Their L cones seem to be filled with the photopigment appropriate for M cones (Carlson, 1986). **Deuteranopes** are insensitive to green colors; they appear yellowish. The M cones of deuteranopes seem to be filled with the photopigment appropriate for L cones (Carl-

son, 1986). Both protanopes and deuteranopes confuse red and green with each other.

You probably know several protanopes and deuteranopes. The third kind of dichromat is rare. Only about .005% (or 1 person in 20,000) of the population are tritanopes (Pokorny & Smith, 1986). **Tritanopes,** who have difficulty with blue shades, seem to lack the S cones.

How can we tell what the world looks like to a dichromat? Some evidence comes from a study by Graham and Hsia (1958). They located a woman who, amazingly enough, had normal vision in her right eye but was a deuteranope in her left eye. These researchers presented different hues to each eye and asked the woman to match colors. For example, they showed a red to her color-defective eye and asked her to adjust the color presented to the normal eye until it seemed to be the same hue. They found that her color-deficient eye saw all the colors between green and violet as blue and all the colors between green and red as yellow.

It is important to stress that dichromats have normal visual acuity. The retinas of protanopes and deuteranopes have the correct number of cones. In the case of tritanopes, the normal retina has so few of these "blue" cones that their acuity is not affected. Thus, these dichromats function normally on most visual tasks.

There are occasions, however, when dichromats face a real disadvantage. For example, isn't it unfortunate that traffic lights are red and green? Protanopes and deuteranopes manage to survive at intersections because they have learned that they must stop when the bottom of the three lights is illuminated. Obviously, they also have handicaps in certain professions. For instance, as a medical student taking a course in microbiology, my husband—a protanope—was assigned a proctor whose function was to look in the microscope and tell him the color of specified objects. Obviously, dichromat medical students should be discouraged from pursuing specialties such as dermatology, where it is essential to make precise discriminations about the colors of rashes and other skin

---

Demonstration 5.4

Color Deficiency

Turn to Color Plate 3, inside the front cover, and look at it under lighting a little less bright than you would use for normal reading. What number do you see?

---

problems. Similarly, people with color deficiencies should avoid careers in pharmacy, market gardening, laboratory technology, and butchery (Mollon, 1982a). Most dichromats survive well in everyday life, however, and they can learn to use a variety of color terms—perhaps mostly on the basis of brightness—even though they cannot discriminate these hues (Jameson & Hurvich, 1978).

The information on color deficiencies fits the color vision theory discussed earlier. As mentioned, people who cannot see red also have difficulty with green. Furthermore, the tritanopes who cannot see blue also have difficulty with yellow. If there is difficulty with one color, there is also difficulty with the opponent color. Color perception for other colors, however, may not be harmed. Thus, a person who cannot see red and green usually *can* see blue and yellow.

We have discussed trichromats, who make matches based on three colors, and dichromats, who make matches based on two colors. We now turn to the monochromats. A **monochromat** requires only one color to match perception of all other colors; the fragment *mono* means "one." Every hue looks the same to this person. Fortunately, this disorder is relatively rare, with an incidence of only about one in a million. The world of a monochromat is similar to your world when the lights are out—everything is a different shade of gray (Hurvich, 1981). Monochromats are the only people who are truly color-blind.

Diagnosis of Color Deficiencies

Many different ways of diagnosing color deficiency have been developed. One of the most common is the **Ishihara Test,** in which the observer tries to detect a number hidden

in a pattern of different colored circles (Davidoff, 1975). Demonstration 5.4 shows one example from the Ishihara Test. A person with normal color vision will see this number as 8. However, a person who has trouble distinguishing reds and greens may read the number as 3. Other tests allow more precise measurement (Boynton, 1979). For example, one test, which measures the amount of red and green required to match another color, distinguishes protanopes and deuteranopes.

Summary: Color Vision Deficiencies

1. Normal trichromats have normal color vision. Anomalous trichromats differ from normal trichromats in the proportions of the three primary colors they use to produce other colors.
2. A dichromat requires only two primary colors to match all other colors. The most common kinds of dichromats are protanopes, who are insensitive to deep reds, and deuteranopes, who are insensitive to greens. Tritanopes, a rare third kind of dichromats, are insensitive to blues. Dichromats have normal visual acuity. Information on dichromats is compatible with color vision theory.
3. A monochromat requires only one primary color to match all other colors; these people are truly color-blind.
4. Color deficiency tests often require observers to detect a different colored object within a similar background.

ISSUES IN COLOR PERCEPTION

This last section of the chapter discusses three topics. First we will look at several color phenomena; for example, humans can see particular colors even in the absence of appropriately colored stimuli. Second, we will examine some factors that influence color vision, such as the size of the stimulus and the region of the retina stimulated. Finally, an "In-Depth" section examines the categorization of color.

Color Phenomena

Throughout this book we will examine situations in which reality and perception differ. In general our perceptions are accurate, so occasional discrepancies are particularly intriguing. Chapter 7, for example, discusses stationary objects that seem to move. Chapter 8 examines illusions, such as those in which the true size of an object is different from its perceived size. In this part of the current chapter we will talk about color phenomena. An observer often reports seeing color when the stimulus is truly neutral in hue. Furthermore, an observer may report seeing a color different from the color actually shown. These color phenomena make it clear that

color is partly determined by factors other than wavelength, the intensity of light, and purity.

Simultaneous Color Contrast

Try Demonstration 5.5, which shows simultaneous color contrast. *Simultaneous* means "at the same time," so **simultaneous color contrast** means that the appearance of a color can be changed because of another color present at the same time. Notice in Demonstration 5.5 that the neutral color gray appears to be slightly yellow when a blue background is present. However, it appears to be slightly blue when a yellow background is present. Thus, "the color seen in a region of space is determined not only by the characteristics of the stimuli in that region, but also by those simultaneously present in surrounding regions" (DeValois & DeValois, 1975, p. 156).

How can we predict which hue a neutral color will adopt? Recall our discussion of complementary hues from the first part of this chapter. Complementary hues are opposite each other on the color wheel—blue and yellow, for example. As it turns out, the neutral

---

Demonstration 5.5

Simultaneous Color Contrast

For this demonstration you will need blue, yellow, and gray paper. Cut a large ring from the gray paper. Place the blue and yellow papers next to each other and place the ring so that it overlaps both other colors, as illustrated below. Draw two vertical lines on the gray circle, as indicated. Look at the color of the gray paper against the blue background and contrast it with the color against the yellow background.

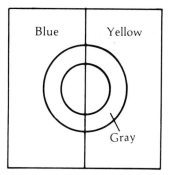

color tends to adopt a hue that is the complementary to the surrounding hue. Thus gray will look slightly blue when its background is yellow.

DeValois and DeValois (1975) suggested some time ago that color contrast must be produced at the level of the cortex. It seems likely, for example, that the double-opponent-process cells may be at least partly responsible for some simultaneous color contrast phenomena. Turn back to Figure 5.9 and think about how this cell would respond to the solid color red. A continuous red surface would produce activation in the center but inhibition in the surround. The net result would be a small response, if any. A continuous green surface would, in the same fashion, produce only a minimal response. However, notice what would happen if a red patch were placed next to a green patch, so that the red reached the center of the cell and the green reached the surround. In this case the excitation from the red in the center would be combined with the excitation in the surround. This cell would fire at its maximum rate, and the red would appear vivid. (You may have seen red and green giftwrapping, for example, in which the red looks especially intense.) However, part of simultaneous color contrast seems to occur prior to the cortex level. Boynton (1983) discovered that simultaneous color contrast is stronger when the stimuli are presented to the same eye rather than to different eyes. Thus, some of the activity probably occurs directly in the retina.

We may not know the precise explanation for simultaneous color contrast. However, the phenomenon itself has been well known for some time. It was first reported by Chevreul in the 1800s. Chevreul was in charge of dyes at the world-famous Gobelins tapestry works in France, and he became interested in special color effects when people began to complain that certain blacks in tapestries lacked depth and strength. Chevreul observed, in fact, that perception is greatly influenced by the surrounding colors (Birren, 1976).

Successive Color Contrast

Demonstration 5.6 is an illustration of successive color contrast. **Successive color contrast** means that the appearance of a color can be changed because of another color presented beforehand. For example, in Demonstration 5.6 part of the white paper seems to be somewhat yellow because you looked at a blue figure earlier. Thus, staring at a figure of a particular hue produces the complementary hue once that hue is removed.

Successive color contrast is one kind of negative afterimage. The term **negative afterimage** makes sense because it is an *image* that appears *after*wards, and it is the opposite, or *negative*, of the original image. Another kind of negative afterimage, other than successive color contrast, is called **achromatic afterimage** because it involves colorless or black-and-white stimuli. In special cases these afterimages may persist for hours and even days (Stromeyer, 1978). In both cases the afterimage is less intense than the original image, and it drifts and moves in the same direction the eyes move.

Successive color contrast can be traced to chromatic adaptation. **Chromatic adaptation** means that the response to a color is diminished after it is viewed continuously for a long time. Adaptation is a general phenomenon found in all our sensory systems; it is just one example of Theme 1 of this book, that the sensory systems share similarities. In the case of chromatic adaptation, either (or both) of two kinds of mechanisms may be involved. It may be that continuous exposure to a particular color depletes the photopigments associated with that color, leaving the other photopigment levels relatively high. Or it may involve adaptation at the opponent-process level. For example, staring at blue may weaken the blue response, leaving its opponent, yellow, relatively strong. As a consequence, an observer who has been staring at a blue patch will see a yellow afterimage.

Subjective Colors

Subjective colors are color impressions produced by black-and-white stimuli. Try Dem-

Demonstration 5.6

Successive Color Contrast

For this demonstration you will need blue, yellow, red, green, and white pieces of paper. Cut circles from each of the colored papers and arrange them on one piece of white paper, as shown below. Mark a dot in the middle of the sheet. Take a second sheet of white paper and keep it handy. Now stare at the dot in the center of the sheet with the colored circles for 2 to 3 minutes. It will get boring, but don't stop too soon. Then quickly transfer your focus to the plain sheet of white paper. The complement of each color should now appear, and the afterimage will look somewhat like a mirror-image version of the original.

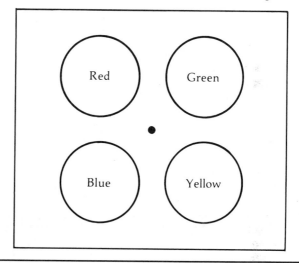

onstration 5.7 to see how uncolored figures can produce subjective colors. This pattern is often known as Benham's top, in honor of its 19th century-inventor. When this disc rotates at a rate of about 10 revolutions/second, desaturated colors appear along the curved lines (Wyszecki, 1986).

How can we be sure that the colors are really produced within our visual systems? Could it be that the whirling somehow causes white light to break down into its components, much as a prism separates the colors of the spectrum? As Fineman (1981) notes, the question can be answered by taking a color photograph of a spinning Benham's top. If the color really can be traced to different wavelengths in the stimulus, then the

color film should register the same color as our visual system. However, the photograph of the spinning top looks gray, rather than colored. The answer lies within the observer, not within the stimulus.

The nature of that answer is not clear, however. Festinger, Allyn, and White (1971) presented data to support an explanation that involves a kind of Morse code for color. Black-and-white flashes of certain intensities and durations may be a signal for particular colors. Other potential explanations, such as one involving the horizontal cells in the retina, are discussed by Wyszecki (1986).

Op Art is an artistic movement that developed in the United States and Europe in the 1960s. Op Art tried to produce a strictly

Demonstration 5.7

*Benham's Top
(Subjective Colors)*

Make a good photocopy of the design below. Cut it out and glue it to a piece of cardboard. Punch a hole in the center at the X spot, and place it on the end of a pencil or ballpoint pen. Hold the pencil with one hand and spin the edge of the circle with the other. When the speed is just right—neither too fast nor too slow—you should see pastel colors. If the top is turning clockwise, the bands should look somewhat blue (outside band), green, yellow, and red (inside band). If the top is turning counterclockwise, the bands should seem to be in the reverse order: red, yellow, green, and blue.

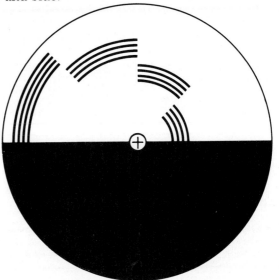

optical art, so it emphasized perceptual experiences. Many Op Art pictures have thin black lines in geometric designs on a white background, and they tend to vibrate and produce visions of pastel (Birren, 1976). Figure 5.10 shows an example. In some lights you'll see that the wavy regions in the middle appear yellow. I have an inexpensive East Indian rug that has elaborate black-and-white patterns. From a distance, parts look distinctly yellow, and I must keep reminding myself that the color is purely subjective.

Memory Color

The color phenomena we have been discussing can all be traced to some mechanism in

the visual system, although the specific details of those mechanisms may not be clear. In contrast, another color phenomenon can be traced to our expectations and cognitive processes. This phenomenon is called memory color. In **memory color** an object's typical color influences our perception of that object's actual color.

In a typical experiment Delk and Fillenbaum (1965) cut shapes out of one piece of orangish red cardboard. Two of the figures, an apple and a valentine heart, are typically orangish red, whereas two other figures, a bell and a mushroom, are typically not that color. Observers were asked to adjust a background field until it contained the same

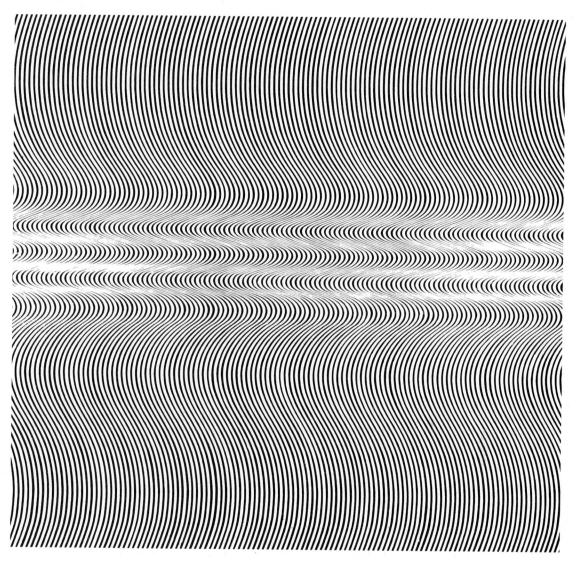

Figure 5.10 Example of Op Art: *Current,* by Bridget Riley. (Synthetic polymer paint on composition board, $58\frac{3}{8}'' \times 58\frac{7}{8}''$. From *Collection, The Museum of Modern Art, New York.* Phillip Johnson Fund. Used with permission.)

amount of red as each of the figures. The observers tended to select a redder background when they were trying to match the apple and the heart than when matching the bell and the mushroom. Our knowledge and expectation can often shape our perceptions. Consistent with Theme 4 of this book, top-

down processing may influence what we perceive.

Another demonstration of memory color employs the successive color contrast discussed earlier. White and Montgomery (1976) asked observers to stare at a design that resembled the American flag, except that it was printed in complementary colors (black stars on an orange background, with blue-green and black stripes). After fixating the target for 30 seconds, they then looked at a white card to produce an afterimage. They were instructed to quickly adjust a color-measuring device until it matched the colored (red) stripes in their afterimage. They also performed the same task with a pattern of isolated blue-green and black stripes that was identical to part of the complementary-color flag design described earlier. The results demonstrated that they perceived the afterimage to be a much brighter red when the stripes were part of the American flag, which everyone knows has red stripes. In contrast, isolated stripes produced no expectations about appropriate color—no "memory color."

Purkinje Shift

The color phenomena discussed so far have all concerned the hue dimension of color. In contrast, the Purkinje shift concerns brightness. Try Demonstration 5.8 to illustrate the Purkinje shift.

Johann Purkinje, a Czechoslovakian physiologist, was the first to describe this phenomenon in 1825, so it is appropriately named after him. According to the **Purkinje shift,** our sensitivity to various wavelengths *shifts* toward the shorter wavelengths as we change from photopic (cone) to scotopic (rod) conditions. Figure 5.11 will help clarify the Purkinje shift. When you tried Demonstration 5.8, you selected a blue and a red that were approximately equal in brightness in photopic conditions. In other words, your visual system was about equally sensitive to both samples. Note that the dotted lines cor-

responding to the red and blue wavelengths intersect the photopic-condition curve at about the same sensitivity. Now contrast the sensitivity under scotopic conditions. As you will note, the sensitivity is substantially higher for wavelengths in the blue range, so blues are brighter than reds.

Factors Affecting Color Vision

Let's briefly consider several factors that influence color vision. First, the region of the retina that is stimulated has an important effect on the perception of color. As you may recall from Chapter 3, cones are concentrated primarily in the central part of the retina, the fovea. As Jameson (1972) points out, most of the theorizing about color vision is therefore restricted to a 2° portion of the retina! Furthermore, if a color match is made for a stimulus that occupies 2° of the visual field, that match will not hold for either larger or smaller fields (Pokorny & Smith, 1986). Finally, stimuli presented in the far periphery will not reach the cones and will look uncolored (Boynton, 1971). In short, we cannot be precise in predicting color perception unless we know the portion of the retina on which the stimulus is registered.

Surprisingly, the size of the stimulus also affects color perception. Try Demonstration 5.9 to see how yellow and blue stimuli look colorless when they are small. Red and green stimuli can still be seen at this distance, although they will also look colorless if you back up further. This demonstration shows that we are all somewhat color deficient if the stimuli are small enough.

Wasserman (1978) remarks that it is ironic that many rubber lifeboats are yellow. Life-

---

Demonstration 5.8	Under brightly lit conditions, select an example of a red object and blue object that look equally bright to you. Now go into a darkened room and wait about 10 minutes until you are mostly dark adapted. Now compare the two objects to see which is brighter.
Purkinje Shift	

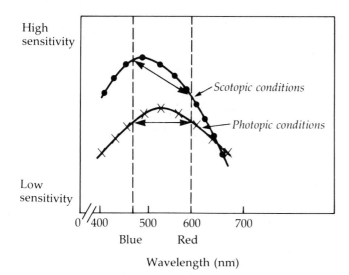

Figure 5.11 Purkinje shift. Under scotopic conditions, blue colors are brighter than red colors, whereas they are equally bright under photopic conditions.

boats should be designed so that they can be readily seen by airplanes flying overhead. These airplanes will be flying high enough that the lifeboat will be registered on only a small portion of the searchers' retinas. The lifeboat may therefore look colorless. Red or green would be better lifeboat colors, although green would be ruled out because the sea is sometimes green. If you are planning a cruise, check to make sure that your ship has red or fluorescent orange lifeboats!

Exposure time is another variable that influences color vision. With long viewing time the eye adapts to the color, and it may look different. On the other hand, stimuli also look different if they are presented for brief exposures $\frac{1}{20}$ second or less. In particular, small, dim stimuli may look white.

▶ **IN-DEPTH:**
CATEGORIZATION OF COLORS

Throughout this chapter the diagrams have represented wavelengths along the horizontal axis, showing a smooth continuum

---

Demonstration 5.9

Stimulus Size and Color Vision

For this demonstration you will need a piece of white paper and small pieces of yellow, blue, green, and red paper. Cut shapes about 1 cm from each of the colored papers and tape them onto the white paper. Tape the paper to a wall at the end of a hall. Walk backwards until you reach a distance at which you can still see the shapes of the cutouts. The yellow and blue shapes should look colorless. If you back up still further, the green and red should also look colorless.

between 400 and 700 nm. Indeed, if we consider simply the physical stimuli, there is a systematic, evenly spaced progression, with each wavelength consistently slightly longer than the wavelength to its left. However, as we stressed in the psychophysics chapter, there is often a discrepancy between physical stimuli and psychological responses. There is a similar discrepancy in color perception between the smooth progression of the physical stimuli and the categorical nature of the psychological response. Psychologically, as it turns out, certain portions of the spectrum clump together into categories of blue, green, yellow, and red (Bornstein & Monroe, 1980).

Marc Bornstein of New York University has been primarily responsible for the systematic and creative research on the categorization of colors. One of his goals in conducting this research has been to demonstrate the similarities between categories in color perception and categories in speech perception, a topic we will explore in later chapters. These similarities are additional evidence for Theme 1 of this textbook, that the perceptual processes share important similarities. Many of Bornstein's research questions were therefore inspired by research findings in speech perception.

First, let's consider the concept of **categorization:** When we categorize, we treat objects as similar or equivalent (Bornstein, 1984a). For example, when you categorize food into meats, vegetables, desserts, and so forth, you are treating all the items within one category as similar, despite their variations in appearance. Thus, green beans, okra, potatoes, and eggplant are all classified as vegetables, despite their obvious differences. Similarly, we can discriminate the differences in wavelength between many different colors in the short wavelength end of the spectrum, yet all these colors are classified as blue.

Several research studies by Bornstein and his colleagues demonstrated that all the members of a given color category are *not* created equal. In particular, the colors that fall near the center of color categories are somehow special, in comparison to colors that fall near the boundary between color categories. For

example, the pure blue found at 485 nm is responded to differently than the blue-green found at 500 nm.

In one series of studies, Bornstein and Monroe (1980) examined whether the location of a color in the category (category center vs. category boundary) influenced the time required to identify it. If all members of a given category are really equally important, then the 500 nm, boundary color should be identified as blue just as fast as the 485 nm, category center color. Bornstein and Monroe first tested all participants on the Ishihara Test for color deficiencies to make certain that everyone had normal color vision; this precaution was also taken in all subsequent studies. The observers were asked to indicate the name of the stimuli they would see by pressing a button labeled either ''blue'' or ''green.'' They then saw each of seven colors whose wavelengths ranged between 485 nm and 500 nm; each color was presented a total of 10 times. In each case the response time and the label (blue or green) were recorded.

Figure 5.12 illustrates both the response time and the label. Let's first discuss the response time, represented by the dotted line; the key for the response times is on the right of the diagram. You'll notice that the wavelength of 485 nm, the center color for all colors in the blue category, produced a quick response time. So did the wavelength of 500 nm, the center color for all colors in the green category. The closer a color approached a boundary, however, the longer the time required to decide whether the color was blue or green.

Now shift your attention to the color labels ''blue'' and ''green,'' represented by the solid lines; the key on the left indicates the percent of time each label was selected. Notice that nearly 100% of the stimuli with wavelengths between 485 nm and 489 nm are labeled ''blue.'' Similarly, nearly 100% of the stimuli with wavelengths between 493 nm and 500 nm are labeled ''green.'' Only in the narrow range between 489 nm and 493 nm is there a transition between color labels. In other words, observers divide the physical continuum of wavelength into two discrete hues;

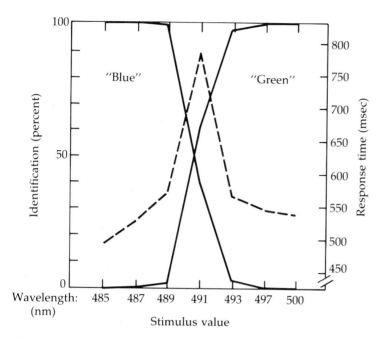

Figure 5.12 Response time (right margin) and label provided, in terms of percentage saying "blue" and percentage saying "green" (left margin). (From Bornstein & Monroe, 1980. Used with permission.)

the transition between the blue and green categories is abrupt rather than gradual. Furthermore, notice how nicely the transition point between the labels "blue" and "green" coincides with the very wavelength (491 nm) at which observers require the longest response time.

In other studies described in the same paper Bornstein and Monroe (1980) confirmed their findings and extended their conclusions to other regions of the spectrum. It seems that some colors are simply "better" than others, and they are identified more quickly. Furthermore, Raskin, Maital, and Bornstein (1983) discovered that the transition point between blue and green was similar across the lifespan. In that study the boundary between blue and green was consistently between 492 nm and 494 nm for 3- and 4-year-old children, for young adults, and for elderly people. The narrow boundary between categories, with rapid identification

for center stimuli and slow identification for boundary stimuli, is consistent with the results on speech perception that we will discuss later in the book.

Other research has established that babies prefer to look at colors in the center of the categories rather than at borderline colors (Bornstein, 1975). Furthermore, both Americans and people from an isolated tribe in New Guinea perform better on memory tasks involving central colors rather than borderline colors (Heider & Olivier, 1972; Rosch, 1978). It seems, as Bornstein (1985a) concludes, that not all stimuli in a category hold the same psychological status. Some colors are better than others because they are named faster, preferred for gazing, and remembered better. What are these colors? They are blue, green, yellow, and red. As you will recognize, these also happen to be the four colors that have been identified as crucial in opponent processing. Throughout this chapter we have mentioned color phenomena that support the opponent-processes portion of the color theory outlined in the second section. Once again we see a relationship. The way our visual system is "wired," with its dependence on four critical colors, seems to guarantee that these four colors will be treated differently. These four colors have special prominence in our sensory processes, and they also have special prominence in our psychological processes. ■

Summary: Issues in Color Perception

1. In simultaneous color contrast, the appearance of a color is changed because of another color present at the same time. For example gray looks slightly blue against a yellow background. The double-opponent-process cells may be at least partly responsible for some simultaneous color contrast phenomena.
2. In successive color contrast, the appearance of a color is changed because of another color presented earlier. For example, white looks slightly blue if you previously looked at yellow. The explanation may involve depletion of photopigments and/or adaptation at the opponent-process level.
3. Subjective colors are pastel colors resulting from black-and-white stimuli, such as Benham's top and Op Art pictures.
4. In memory color our expectations about an object's typical color influence our perception of that object's actual color.
5. In the Purkinje shift, the sensitivity of the visual system shifts toward the shorter wavelengths as we change from photopic to scotopic conditions.
6. Color vision is influenced by the region of the retina stimulated, the size of the stimulus, and exposure time.
7. In categorization we treat objects as similar or equivalent. For example, certain colors are all classified as blue, even though they differ somewhat.
8. Colors at the center of a category are named faster, are preferred by infants, and are remembered better. In contrast, colors at the boundaries between colors do not have this special prominence.
9. The colors at the center of their categories are blue, green, yellow, and red, which are also critical in opponent processes.

Review

1. The next time you are in a supermarket, notice the hue, saturation, and brightness of packages and commercially produced items, such as the colors of laundry detergent packages, wrapping papers, baby cards for boys, and baby cards for girls. Do these items tend to occupy different portions of the color solid?
2. Each of the following is an example of a color mixture; specify whether it represents an additive mixture or a subtractive mixture: (a) you wind strands of purple and blue yarn together to knit a sweater; (b) you paint a layer of green over a blue car fender; (c) you mix red food coloring into yellow egg yolks; (d) you cover one flashlight with green cellophane and another with red cellophane and then shine both of them on a white paper. Predict the color of the mixtures in as many of the combinations as possible. Why can't you make predictions for subtractive mixtures?
3. Summarize the trichromatic theory, as developed by Helmholtz, and the original form of the opponent-process theory, as developed by Hering. Why were the two incompatible, and what modification in the opponent-process theory made them compatible?
4. Think about the two-stage theory of color vision. Suppose you shine a monochromatic light having a wavelength of 460 nm in someone's eye. What kind of cones will respond? Which kind of ganglion cells will be excited? Which will be inhibited? Which will not be affected? How about a monochromatic light with a wavelength of 650 nm?
5. What are complementary hues? What

happens when you make an additive mixture of complementary hues? Why does this make sense, now that you know about opponent-process theory?

6. What is a normal trichromat, and how does this person's color vision differ from that of an anomalous trichromat?

7. Name the three kinds of dichromats, and point out some everyday kinds of color discriminations that they would find difficult. If you ask your female and male friends if they have color deficiencies, why are you likely to find more color-deficient males or females?

8. Suppose that someone who didn't know much about color vision asked the following questions about phenomena he or she had noticed. What explanation would you provide? (a) Why does a blue bird look gray when it's far away? (b) Why does a white shirt look a little green when worn with a red vest? (c) Why does the world look slightly yellow after taking off blue-tinted dark glasses? (a) Why does a red stop sign look uncolored if you look at it out of the side of your eye?

9. What is memory color? Describe the research studies discussed in the chapter, and point out why they provide support for the top-down view of perceptual processing. Finally, think of examples in which your expectations about an object's typical color influenced your perceptions of that color.

10. Discuss Bornstein's research on color categorization. How do we process colors from the center of a category differently from the colors at category boundaries? Finally, how is this research related to the idea of opponent processes?

New Terms

hue	metamers	deuteranopes
color wheel	pointillism	tritanopes
nonspectral hues	trichromatic theory	monochromat
monochromatic colors	microspectrophotometry	Ishihara Test
purity	spectral sensitivity	simultaneous color contrast
saturation	opponent-process theory	successive color contrast
brightness	blobs	negative afterimage
color solid	double-opponent-process cell	achromatic afterimage
color spindle	color vision deficiencies	chromatic adaptation
additive mixture	normal trichromat	Op Art
subtractive mixture	anomalous trichromat	memory color
synthetic sense	dichromat	Purkinje shift
analytic sense	protanopes	categorization
complementary hues		

Recommended Readings

Boff, K. R., Kaufman, L., & Thomas, J. P. (Eds.) (1986). *Handbook of perception and human performance* (Vol. 1). New York: Wiley. *This invaluable handbook has two relevant chapters, one on color appearance and one on color measurement.*

Hurvich, L. M. (1981). *Color vision.* Sutherland, MA: Sinauer Associates. *Leo Hurvich, together with Dorothea Jameson, was largely responsible for reviving interest in opponent-processes theory. His book is perhaps the most readable introduction to the field of color vision.*

Jacobs, G. H. (1981). *Comparative color vision.* New York: Academic Press. *The topic of the color vision capabilities of nonhuman animals was beyond the scope of your textbook, but this book should provide relevant information for those intrigued by vision in species such as frogs, pigeons, cats, and monkeys.*

Mollon, J. D., & Sharpe, L. T. (Eds.) (1983). *Color vision: Physiology and psychophysics.* London: Academic Press. *This volume is the proceedings of an international conference on color vision. It contains 55 papers, primarily on basic research in psychophysics and color physiology, but there are also several papers on color perception.*

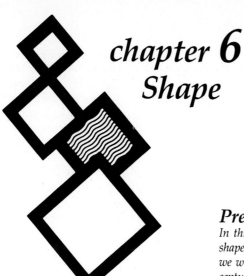

chapter 6
Shape

Outline

Contour
Aspects of contour
Masking
Illusory contour

Perceptual Organization
Laws of grouping
Law of Prägnanz
Figure-ground relationship
Problems with Gestalt approaches

Pattern Recognition
Theories of pattern recognition
Influence of context on pattern
recognition
In-Depth: Word-superiority effect
Picture and scene perception

Preview

In this chapter we will explore how our visual world is organized into shapes and patterns rather than random specks and patches. In particular, we will examine three aspects of shape perception: (1) contour, (2) perceptual organization, and (3) pattern recognition.

Contours or borders are the locations in the visual world in which there is a sudden change in brightness. Visual and motor disturbances occur when we are deprived of contours, and a physiological factor called lateral inhibition *causes an exaggeration of contour. One figure can also mask the contour of another. In addition, we can sometimes see contours even when they are not physically present.*

The section on perceptual organization considers the Gestalt approach to perception. We will look at several laws of grouping, which describe what figures will be perceived as belonging together, and at another Gestalt principle, which states that people tend to perceive figures that are good and simple rather than complex. We will also discover that several characteristics differentiate a figure from its background. Finally, some criticisms of the Gestalt approach will be discussed.

We will next look at three theories of pattern recognition. Then we will see how context can influence pattern recognition; in connection with this topic, an ''In-Depth'' section will consider how letter recognition is influenced by the context provided within a word. The final topic is research on picture recognition and scene perception.

Let's briefly review the visual system's many talents, as described in the previous chapters. In Chapter 4 we saw that the visual system can discriminate between two objects close together in space. The visual system also adapts to impressive ranges of dark and light, and it shows a variety of eye movements particularly tailored to our visual needs. Furthermore, it can focus so that we can see either distant or nearby objects. Chapter 5 examined how the elaborate processing of color information allows us to appreciate hues from all parts of the spectrum.

Impressive as these talents may be, they encompass only a fraction of the visual system's abilities. Look up from your book and glance around. Is your visual world a mass of random patches of light and dark, colored and uncolored fragments? In fact, your world is *not* chaotic because it is filled with objects having distinct shapes. Let's see, first of all, why contours are essential in perception of shape.

CONTOUR

A **shape** is an area set off from the rest of what you see because it has a contour. A **contour** is a location at which there is a sudden change in brightness. For example, draw an outline of a circle on white paper with a black marker. There will be a contour on the outside of the circle between the white paper and the black line. There will be another contour on the inside of the circle as well. In each case there is a sudden change in brightness. We need these contours to perceive shapes. However, if the brightness changes gradually over a region we are examining, then there is no distinct contour and we do not perceive definite shapes.

Aspects of Contour

In our everyday experience, contours are everywhere. Look around you for a moment and notice the many regions in which there is a sudden change in brightness. For example, as I sit here typing, numerous contours are formed by the letters on the sheet of paper, and the white paper forms a contour against the tan typewriter, which forms a contour against the black rubber mat, which forms a contour against the brown desk, which forms a contour against the blue rug.

The Ganzfeld

A visual field that has no contours is called a **Ganzfeld**, German for "whole field." I recall learning in an undergraduate perception course that we could make a Ganzfeld by cutting a Ping-Pong ball in half and taping one half over each eye. I didn't happen to have a Ping-Pong ball in my room—you probably don't, either. Coren, Porac, and Ward (1984) have offered a creative alternative—two plastic spoons. Place the bowl of one spoon over each eye while looking at a source of light. You will see uniform light without contours. Continue in this ridiculous position for several minutes and notice what happens. You will soon feel that you are blind—your eyes are open, yet you can see only gray. To see you need to have contours. You can restore your vision by restoring a contour, for example, by lifting your knee so that it casts a shadow over your visual field.

In the laboratory Ganzfelds are created with equipment more elaborate than plastic spoons or Ping-Pong balls. For example, observers may look through a glass cylinder filled with a fogging solution. The result is a uniform white field, resembling a "sea of light." Observers in a Ganzfeld often report a complete disappearance of vision after 15 minutes. They may also mention that they are uncertain whether their eyes are open. Motor system disturbances—such as loss of balance and coordination—are also common.

Contour is such a basic part of form perception that we tend to take it for granted. However, in the absence of contour—as in the Ganzfeld—vision is wildly distorted. Contour perception is therefore an extremely important aspect of vision.

Contrast and Mach Bands

Visual processes have a special feature that encourages the perception of contours. This feature is called **border contrast**, referring to the fact that the contrast at a contour seems much stronger than it really is. Try Demonstration 6.1 to see two examples of border contrast.

You may have examined Demonstration 6.1b and selected some area in the gray stripe that was second from the right. In fact, how-ever, all parts of each gray stripe are uniform throughout. You can prove this to yourself by placing white pieces of paper on each side of a stripe, isolating the stripe from the surrounding stripes. All of a sudden the light border on the left of the stripe and the dark border on the right of the stripe disappear. It is clear that each stripe actually has uniform brightness.

The bands that seem to appear at the contours are called **Mach bands** after Ernst Mach, an Austrian physicist and philosopher who

---

Demonstration 6.1

Mach Bands

a. Find a light bulb in a lamp where the shade can be removed, turn off all other lights in the room, and close the curtains. Move the lamp so that it is about 1 ft (0.3 m) from the wall. Use one hand to shade your eyes from the glare of the lamp, and use the other hand to hold up your textbook about 3 inches (7.1 cm) away from the wall between the wall and the lamp. Observe the area surrounding the shadow. Notice how the edge of the shadow is particularly dark looking and how the edge of the well-lit part of the wall nearest the shadow is particularly bright looking. Visual phenomena that resemble Mach bands are common in everyday life, although we seldon notice them.
b. Now look at the figure below, focusing on the region just to the right of the arrow. Find another shade of gray in a different stripe that seems to match that shade as closely as possible.

described them in 1865. As Ratliff (1984) describes a Mach band, people perceive bright and dark bands within a single stripe, yet—mysteriously—there is no corresponding variation in the physical distribution of light.

Mach bands are one example of border contrast because the contrast that already exists is exaggerated still further. Figure 6.1a

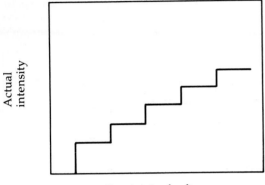

a.   The actual intensity of light at each point

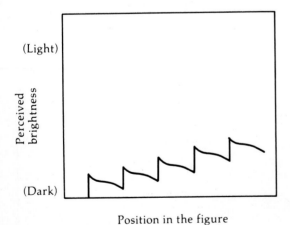

b.   The perceived intensity of light at each point

Figure 6.1   Actual intensity and perceived intensity for portions of Mach bands.

represents the actual intensity of the stripes at each position. Each step is flat, representing a uniform intensity at every point within each stripe. Figure 6.1b represents the *perceived* intensity of the stripes. The perceived intensity, or brightness, depends not only on an area's intensity but also on the intensity of the surrounding areas.

Mach bands can be explained by the principle of **lateral inhibition**, where *lateral* means "sideways": Whenever a light reaches one point on the retina, the neural activity for nearby points is inhibited. The more intense the light, the greater the inhibition. Let us examine this idea of lateral inhibition in more detail.

Research on lateral inhibition did not begin with the complex human retina. Instead, Hartline, Wagner, and Ratliff (1956) chose a much more primitive visual system, the eye of the Limulus, or horseshoe crab. In the Limulus each photoreceptor registers light independently and is attached to its own "private" neural cell. (In contrast, you'll recall from Figure 3.10, the human retina is arranged so that several photoreceptors "share" each neuron.) Each photoreceptor in the Limulus's eye is relatively large. Consequently, researchers can stimulate a single photoreceptor fairly easily without scattering the light to adjacent photoreceptors. Researchers can also select the neural cell corresponding to that photoreceptor, and they can record the electrical activity from that neural cell.

Hartline and his colleagues presented light to a photoreceptor at Point 1. The recording of the electrical activity at the corresponding neural cell is illustrated in Figure 6.2a. As you can see, the electrical activity is strong. Then these researchers presented simultaneous lights to photoreceptors at Points 1 and 2, as illustrated in Figure 6.2b. Notice that the electrical activity from the neural cell corresponding to Point 1 shows a clear *decrease*. When the intensity of the light at Point 2 was increased, the electrical activity from the critical neural cell decreased even further, as illustrated in Figure 6.2c.

a. Light presented only at Point 1

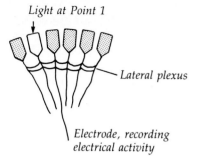

Light at Point 1

Lateral plexus

Electrode, recording
electrical activity

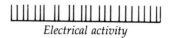

Electrical activity

b. Light presented at Point 1 and Point 2

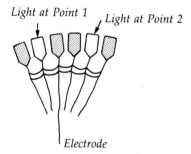

Light at Point 1

Light at Point 2

Electrode

Electrical activity

c. Light presented at Point 1 and intense light presented at Point 2

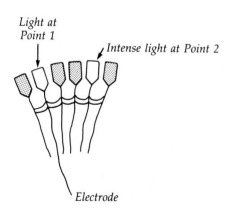

Light at
Point 1

Intense light at Point 2

Electrode

Electrical activity

Figure 6.2 Lateral inhibition in Limulus.

It seems then that the electrical activity of a Limulus photoreceptor depends not only on that photoreceptor's level of stimulation but also on the level of stimulation of nearby photoreceptors. The more these neighboring photoreceptors are stimulated, the lower the electrical activity of the neural cell. In other words, there is lateral inhibition. The mechanism for lateral inhibition in the Limulus is the lateral plexus, a primitive net that connects the photoreceptors and allows them to influence each other's electrical activity.

The human retina, although much more complex than the visual system of the Limulus, has a system of connections among photoreceptors that operates in a somewhat similar fashion. Turn back to Figure 3.9 and examine the horizontal cells, which connect the photoreceptors. At a somewhat more advanced stage of visual processing, you can see that the amacrine cells connect the ganglion cells with one another and also connect bipolar cells to each other. Thus, the cells in the human retina can communicate with each other and possibly inhibit each other's electrical activity, demonstrating lateral inhibition.

It seems likely that Mach bands, discussed earlier in this section, can be explained by lateral inhibition. The detailed mechanisms of lateral inhibition have not been determined, but let us consider a potential explanation, shown schematically in Figure 6.3.

Figure 6.3a illustrates the central two stripes from Demonstration 6.1b. For the sake of simplicity, let us imagine that a small horizontal segment that passes through those two Mach bands is stimulating four retinal receptors on the darker side and four receptors on the lighter side. Let's say that the light source—prior to any effects of lateral inhibition—produces 40 units of electrical activity on the dark side and 100 units of electrical activity on the light side (Figure 6.3b).

Suppose that the horizontal cells transmit inhibition from each receptor to its neighbor and that this inhibition equals 10% of the "sender's" electrical activity. Thus, a receptor that produces 40 units of electrical activity transmits 4 units of inhibition to each of its

neighbors, and a receptor that produces 100 units of electrical activity transmits 10 units of inhibition to each of its neighbors. Figure 6.3c shows how much inhibition each receptor receives from each of its two neighbors. (We won't discuss receptors *a* and *h* because their neighbors are less active than 40 and more active than 100, respectively; the diagram would be too complex.) The numbers in 6.3d show the total output after subtracting the inhibition. A graph of the total output appears in Figure 6.3e. Notice that it is similar to the central segment of Figure 6.1b, with decreased brightness on the left-hand side of the border and increased brightness on the right-hand side.

The crucial feature of lateral inhibition that needs to be stressed is that our visual system has the capacity to improve upon reality. Reality provides reasonably clear boundaries between light and dark. Consistent with Theme 2 of the book, the visual stimulus is rich with information. However, our visual system takes those reasonably clear boundaries and exaggerates them so that the dark side is even darker and the bright side even brighter. Objects are therefore more conspicuous because their contours are intensified. Consistent with Theme 3 of the book, the perceptual systems are extremely well designed to provide optimal perceptual experiences.

Masking

Suppose that someone presented very briefly a black square, as in Figure 6.4a. Then that square disappeared and was quickly replaced by the square-outline shape in Figure 6.4b, the shape being carefully constructed so that the square fit neatly inside its inner boundary. What would you see? Under appropriate conditions, you might not perceive the square that was initially presented.

Werner (1935) was the first to demonstrate the failure to perceive a shape, a phenomenon that has important implications for the perception of contours. Werner found that if he presented the black square very briefly, then a gray interval for about .15 second, then the square-outline shape, observers failed to

a. Light intensity

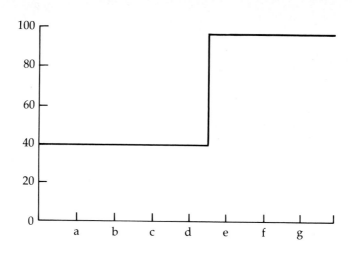

Receptors: a   b   c   d   e   f   g

b. Original electrical
   activity

| 40 | 40 | 40 | 40 | 100 | 100 | 100 | 100 |

c. Inhibition from left-
   hand neighbor

| | −4 | −4 | −4 | −4 | −10 | −10 | |

Inhibition from right-
hand neighbor

| | −4 | −4 | −10 | −10 | −10 | −10 | |

d. Total output

   (original activity *minus*
   inhibition)

| | 32 | 32 | 26 | 86 | 80 | 80 | |

e. Perceived brightness

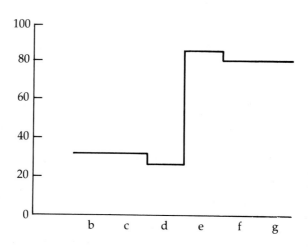

Figure 6.3 Schematic illustration of lateral inhibition in human retina.

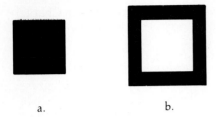

a.   b.

Figure 6.4   Shapes used in masking studies.

see the first square. Werner had discovered backward masking. In **backward masking**, "the accuracy for reporting a visual target is reduced by following the target with a spatially overlapping mask" (Liss & Reeves, 1983, p. 513). Notice that the second figure masks the first figure and that masking therefore works backwards.

Werner did not find **forward masking**, the tendency for the first figure to mask a second figure. When he presented the square-outline shape (Figure 6.4b) and then the black square (Figure 6.4a), observers perceived both figures. In general it is more difficult to demonstrate forward masking than backward masking.

Masking has been demonstrated by using other figures in addition to ones in which an inner contour of one shape matches the outer contour of another. For instance, backward masking can occur with flashes of light. The important attribute of masking is that when another stimulus interferes with the formation of a contour, the shape will not be seen.

Kolers (1983) points out that masking is in fact a general phenomenon frequently experienced in daily life:

> The underlying theme [in masking] is disruption in processing of one stimulus due to the insistence or salience or intensity of demand of a second. Suppose that a ringing telephone followed by a brief conversation interrupts an ongoing conversation. It is not uncommon, on finishing the telephone conversation, to find oneself temporarily lost as to the subject of the prior conversation; dealing with the telephone displaces a prior line of activity. Suppose that one is doing

some other thing and a pistol shot or a fire alarm or any other disruptive stimulus occurs; again, very often, perceptual contact with the antecedent task is lost, especially when the task was in process rather than completed (p. 143).

Kolers's parallel between backward masking and everyday kinds of interference is particularly helpful because, as Kolers points out, backward masking in visual perception violates our intuitive ideas about the way perceptual processes operate. Neither forward masking nor backward masking is a phenomenon that we expect.

Hochberg (1971a) points out that studies of masking must be concerned with *criterion*. As you may recall from Chapter 2, observers are sometimes eager to report that they have perceived something, and they will say that they have seen it even if it did not occur. At other times observers will not report something unless they are absolutely convinced it occurred. People therefore differ in the kind of criteria they use in reporting.

The criterion is relevant in studies of masking because observers see a figure for a brief period; they do not have a second chance. It is possible for answers to be biased, therefore, by observers' motivations. For example, people eager to impress the experimenter with their keen detecting abilities might say, "Yes, I saw the square" even if no square had been presented. Hochberg discusses possible methods of handling the criterion problem. For example, observers may be required to choose which of several letters had been used as the test stimulus; this method removes the criterion problem.

We have focused briefly on criterion because it is important to consider the dependent variable in perception experiments. As you may have learned, the **dependent variable** is a measure that describes the participant's behavior. In contrast, the **independent variable** is the variable the experimenters manipulate. The dependent variable in a masking experiment might be the probability that the observer will report seeing the square, and the independent variable might be the time lapse between the presentation of the first and second figure. Kahneman (1968) urged that people interested in perception must become more attentive to the dependent variable because "it is common practice in visual science to devote pages of text to the independent variable and to dismiss the dependent variable in a sentence" (p. 414).

We have examined some conditions in which masking operates. At this point you may be wondering, "*Why* does it operate?" Breitmeyer (1980) proposes some answers in an article appropriately titled "Unmasking Visual Masking: A Look at the 'Why' Behind the Veil of the 'How.'" He notes that the human eye has a foveal region that has high visual acuity. However, the fovea can take in only a small portion of the visual field. This causes a problem because we often want to look at things widely separated in space or things that move. For example, in the section on eye movement in Chapter 4 we discussed saccadic movements—those small jumps which serve to bring the next area of text into contact with the fovea. We mentioned that an important characteristic of saccadic movements is that vision is suppressed as the eyes leap from one location to the next. Suppose, instead, that the eyes were to pause for a fixation on an area of text, then move on to a second and a third area, pausing for a fixation each time. Suppose, also, that the pattern perceived during the first and second pauses happens to persist into the third pause. We would end up with an alphabet soup like the one in Figure 6.5a, with the new letter strings superimposed on the old ones.

Breitmeyer proposes that saccades have a second purpose in addition to changing the fixation point: They also inhibit any activity that remains from a preceding fixation interval. Thus as the eyes jump forward, the material from the preceding fixation is masked so that the next view is a clear one. As a result, we can clearly read the sentence at the bottom of Figure 6.5. Thus masking allows our eyes to wander freely without producing a big blur of superimposed images.

The research on forward masking and backward masking demonstrates the impor-

tance of time factors in perception. In Chapter 5 we saw that a color could influence the perception of another color presented immediately afterwards. Here we have seen that contour perception can be influenced by other shapes presented immediately beforehand or immediately afterwards. Shape perception does not occur instantaneously but requires a certain amount of time. A shape's contour may not be perceived if another shape is presented too soon after the original one.

As Kolers (1983) remarks, our information about perceptual experiences in the area of shape perception is not sufficiently well developed—and the relationships are too complex—to identify specific neural mechanisms. However, several researchers have begun to outline some relevant processes.

Breitmeyer's (1984) book on visual masking makes it clear that masking must involve at least two kinds of inhibition, though the details of the inhibition process are unclear. Breitmeyer emphasizes the distinction between X and Y ganglion cells. As you may recall from Chapter 3, the X cells are small and have a sustained response pattern and slow conduction. The Y cells are relatively large, respond in quick bursts, and have rapid conduction.

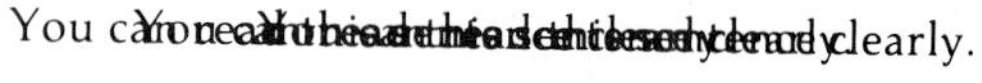

You can read this sentence clearly.

a. If material from every fixation pause were retained during the later fixation pauses, a sentence might look like this at the third fixation pause.

You can read this sentence clearly.

b. Fortunately, masking prevents the persistence of earlier material, and so we see a sentence that looks like this.

Figure 6.5 Fixation pauses and masking.

Breitmeyer's model proposes that both the target and the mask stimuli activate both X and Y cells. Each kind of cell demonstrates inhibition because of its center-surround receptive field; that is, stimulation in the center of some cells produces an increase in electrical activity, whereas stimulation in the surround of those cells produces a decrease. Other cells show the reverse pattern, with a decrease to center stimulation and an increase to surround stimulation. In addition to the inhibition within a single cell, there is also lateral inhibition between cells, with X and Y cells inhibiting each other's activity. As we discussed in connection with Mach bands, researchers have identified a probable general mechanism for contour phenomena. However, the details must wait until we know more about the physiology of contour formation.

Illusory Contour

Sometimes we can see a shape against a background, even when there is no concrete contour between the shape and the background. Notice, for example, that Figure 6.6 seems to

Figure 6.6 Example of illusory contour.

show a white triangle against a background of three circles and an outline triangle. Each side of the white triangle appears to be a continuous line, even though the true contour is only about 1 cm long at each corner of the figure. In **illusory contour** figures we see contours even though they are not physically present. Illusory contour figures have stimulus elements with true contours known as **inducing areas**. In Figure 6.6 the inducing areas include the boundary between the white and the black in the Pac-Man-shaped figures. Similarly, **inducing lines** are lines that encourage illusory contour. In Figure 6.6 the three V-shaped elements are inducing lines. The mystery, however, is that the contour of the illusory figure appears to extend between the inducing areas. Incidentally, another term that is frequently used as a synonym for illusory contour is **subjective contour**.

Try Demonstration 6.2 to illustrate how readily the shape of the illusory contour can be changed and how readily the illusory contour can disappear altogether. As Grossberg and Mingolla (1985) remark, it is most likely that an illusory contour will form in a direction perpendicular (at right angles) to the inducing lines. Notice, however, that Figure 6.6 featured a subjective contour not perpendicular to the ends of the V-shaped lines; Grossberg and Mingolla discuss in detail how these nonperpendicular subjective contours arise in some figures.

In illusory contours, the figure bounded by the illusory contour appears to be in front of the other figures. Frequently, it also seems to be brighter than the background, even though the intensity registered on the retina is identical (Kanizsa, 1976).

Why do we see subjective contours? Stanley Coren and his colleagues argue that we create subjective contours because we see simple, familiar figures in preference to meaningless, disorganized parts (Coren, 1972; Coren & Porac, 1983). Notice that in Figure 6.6 we *could* see three circles with wedges sliced out, alternating with three V-shaped lines. This interpretation of the picture is unnecessarily complicated. Instead, we use

---

<table>
<tr>
<td valign="top">

Demonstration 6.2
_____

Illusory Contours

</td>
<td valign="top">

Illustration a shows an illusory contour of a square. Using information from the description of illusory contours in the text, can you transform the illusory figure from a square into a circle while maintaining the inner tips of the inducing lines in their present position and only rotating the orientation of the lines? Experiment with illusory contours by drawing other line orientations that move outward from the dots shown in Diagram 6.2b. (You may want to trace over these dots on other sheets of paper if you'd like to try more than one variation.) Finally, try other line orientations for the dots shown in Diagram 6.2c in order to make the subjective contour disappear completely.

</td>
</tr>
</table>

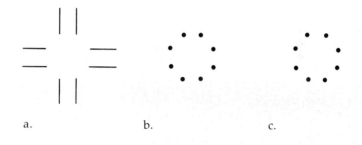

a.   b.   c.

---

depth cues (described in detail in Chapter 8) to sort out the picture, placing a simple white triangle in front of the background. This interpretation "explains" why there are peculiar gaps in the three circles—the triangle is merely hiding portions of them. As some authors have suggested, illusory coutours arise because the visual system essentially tries to solve a mystery or a problem as it attempts to sort out figure and ground (Parks, 1984, 1986; Rock & Anson, 1979). Notice that this depth-cue explanation involves cognitive processes. We use top-down processing, consistent with Theme 4 of the book, to make sense of an otherwise puzzling and disorderly jumble.

Coren and Porac supported their explanation with an experiment in which observers were asked to judge the distance of various parts of illusory contour figures. A special piece of equipment was used to present a spot that appeared to vary in distance from the observer. This spot could be located on any portion of the illusory contour figure, for example, within the white triangle in Figure 6.6 or in the area just above one of the partial circles (outside the illusory triangle). The researchers used the method of adjustment, discussed in the psychophysics chapter; observers moved the apparent distance of this spot back and forth so that it seemed to be at the same distance from them as the part of the stimulus (the figure or the background) on which it was superimposed. The selected setting for the figure was about 25% closer than the selected setting for the background.

However, the theory involving depth cues and other cognitive factors is not the only one proposed. As Diane Halpern and her coauthors cleverly state: "Every theory of illustory-contour (also called subjective-contour) perception has been both supported and refuted by research. The search for the best theory to explain the perception of contours that do not physically exist has proven as illusory as the nature of the contours themselves" (Halpern, Salzman, Harrison, & Widaman, 1983, p. 293).

Halpern and Salzman (1983) review several other major theories of illusory-contour perception. For example, it is possible that the feature detectors discussed in Chapter 3 could be triggered by the line segments in the designs. Another possibility is that illusory contours are caused by simultaneous brightness contrast. In Chapter 5 we discussed simultaneous color contrast, in which the appearance of a color can be changed because another color is present at the same time. Similarly, **simultaneous brightness contrast** means that the apparent brightness of part of a figure can be changed because another part is present at the same time. For example, a gray square looks brighter when it is surrounded by a black border than when it is surrounded by a light gray border. This explanation could apply to illusory-contour figures because the black partial circles in Figure 6.6, for example, make the white region in the center even whiter. A final explanation reviewed by Halpern and Salzman is that some illusory-contour figures can be explained by center-surround inhibition at the retinal level.

Which of these explanations is correct? Halpern and her coauthors (1983) asked observers to provide magnitude estimations for 24 illusory-contour figures, using a scale in which a real contour was assigned a value of 100. (As you'll recall, Stevens's magnitude estimation techniques was described in the psychophysics chapter.) Then a statistical method called factor analysis was used to determine the relative importance of the various explanations for illusory contour. The results of this analysis showed that each explanation had some validity for at least one of the illusory figures, and some of the figures were accounted for by two or three of the explanations. As these authors conclude, "The perception of illusory contours does not represent a single perceptual phenomenon" (p. 301). Instead, several factors combine to explain why contours sometimes appear when there are no physical boundaries.

Summary: Contour

1. Our visual worlds are not filled with randomly arranged stimuli. Instead, objects have distinct shapes.
2. Shapes are defined by their contours, which are locations that show a sudden change in brightness.
3. A Ganzfeld is created when there is no contour; a Ganzfeld produces strange disturbances in vision and in the motor system.
4. In Mach bands, the contrast at the boundary between two regions is exaggerated. Lateral inhibition, which has been examined in the eye of the Limulus, apppears to explain the Mach band phenomenon.
5. In backward masking, a second figure masks a first figure, if the interval between the two presentations is short enough; backward masking is easier to demonstrate than forward masking.
6. Masking is an example of a more general phenomenon in which one stimulus cannot be completely processed because of interference from a second stimulus.
7. The results of masking studies may depend on the criteria observers adopt.
8. Visual masking is essential in reading; otherwise we might see a blur of superimposed images when we move our eyes.
9. The physiological explanation for masking appears to involve at least two kinds of inhibition.
10. In illusory-contour figures, we see contours even though they are not physically present.
11. Explanations for illusory contours include the following: (a) illusory contours are created because simple, familiar figures are preferred to meaningless fragments; (b) illusory contours can be traced to feature detectors being triggered by line segments in the designs; (c) simultaneous brightness contrast makes the figure un-

usually bright; and (d) inhibition may operate at the retinal level.

12. According to research by Halpern and her colleagues, all four explanations have value in accounting for illusory contours.

PERCEPTUAL ORGANIZATION

Chapter 1 discussed the Gestalt psychology approach to perception. The **Gestalt approach** emphasizes that we perceive objects as well-organized "wholes" rather than separated, isolated parts. We don't see fragmented specks in disarray as we open our eyes to look at the world. Instead, we see large regions with definite shapes and patterns. The "whole" that we see is something more structured and cohesive than a group of isolated fragments; shape is more than a gathering of specks.

Gestalt psychology formed a strong contrast to another approach to perception that was dominant at the end of the 1800s and the beginning of the 1900s. This view was called **structuralism**, an approach that proposed that all experiences can be analyzed and broken down into their most basic sensations. We did not discuss structuralism in the history section of the first chapter because this approach no longer has many supporters (Lundin, 1984). Nearly a century ago, however, structuralism had a profound influence on the approach to perception in both Germany and the United States because of its emphasis on paying attention to the components of an object. Structuralists instructed observers to introspect and report about the variety of sensations associated with a particular object. For example, if you were asked to report on the appearance of your hand, you would note variations in color, brightness, and form—breaking down a shape into its component parts. Edward Titchener, a structuralist who lived in the United States, concluded that there were 43,415 different sensory experiences (Lundin, 1984).

In contrast to the structuralists, Gestalt psychologists maintained that "whole figures are not reducible to simple summations of local parts" (Palmer, 1982). The three psychologists most closely associated with the Gestalt approach—and whose work forms the basis for this section of the chapter—are Max Wertheimer (1923), Kurt Koffka (1935), and Wolfgang Köhler (1947). Gestalt psychologists investigated three areas that we will consider here: the laws of grouping, the "goodness" of figures, and figure-ground relationships. We will see that many of their ideas are still considered central to understanding perception, although the theories have certain limitations.

Laws of Grouping

Five major **laws of grouping**, describe why certain elements seem to go together, rather than remaining isolated and independent. These laws are illustrated in Figure 6.7:

1. The **law of nearness** (or the **law of proximity**) states that objects near each other tend to be seen as a unit.

2. The **law of similarity** states that objects similar to each other tend to seen as a unit.

3. The **law of good continuation** states that objects arranged in either a straight line or a smooth curve tend to be seen as a unit.

4. The **law of closure** states that when a figure has a gap, we tend to see it as a closed, complete figure.

5. The **law of common fate** states that when objects move in the same direction, we tend to see them as a unit. Since this law involves movement, it is difficult to illustrate on a motionless page. Try Demonstration 6.3 to appreciate the power of this law.

Notice, incidentally, that it is possible to see each of the designs another way, if you make a great effort. For example, you can force yourself, in the design of crosses and circles, to see seven columns. Nonetheless, an arrangement of rows is the pattern that emerges spontaneously.

Sometimes we can have a contest between two of the laws to see which is "stronger."

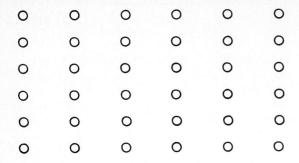

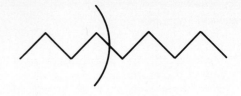

c. **The law of good continuation.** You will see a zigzag line with a curved line running through it, so that each line continues in the same direction it was going prior to intersection. Notice that you do not see that figure as being composed of these two elements:

a. **The law of nearness.** You will see this arrangement as a set of columns—not a set of rows. Items are grouped together that are near each other. Now notice the typing in this book. You see rows of letters, rather than columns, because a letter is closer to the letters to the right and left than it is to the letters above and below.

Look out the window at the branches of a tree, and focus on two branches that form a cross. You clearly perceive two straight lines, rather than two right angles touching each other.

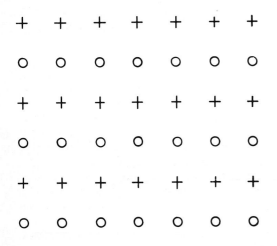

d. **The law of closure.** You will see a circle here, even though it is not perfectly closed. A complete figure is simply more tempting than a curved line! Now close this book and put your finger across one edge, focusing on the shape of the outline of your book. You will see a rectangle rather than a bent line with four angles.

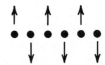

b. **The law of similarity.** You will see this arrangement as a set of rows, rather than columns. Items are grouped together that are similar to each other. Now look at this sentence that has a phrase in **boldface type.** Notice how those two words in heavier print cling together in a group, whereas the words in regular, lighter print form their own separate groups.

e. **The law of common fate.** If dots 1, 3, and 5 suddenly move up and dots 2, 4, and 6—at the same time—suddenly move down, the dots moving in the same direction will be perceived as belonging together. The next time you look at automobile traffic on a moderately busy street, notice how clearly the cars moving one direction form one group and the cars moving in the opposite direction form another group.

Figure 6.7 Laws of grouping.

Demonstration 6.3
_____

Law of Common Fate

Find a clear plastic report cover (typically sold as a folded sheet of plastic, with a detachable rigid spine). Cut the cover at the fold so that you have two separate pieces of plastic. Now cut about 10 small, random shapes from a piece of scrap paper and let them fall randomly on one sheet of plastic. Use transparent tape to affix the shapes to the sheet. Repeat the process with the other sheet. Now place one sheet on top of the other and notice that it is difficult to distinguish between the two groups of shapes. Now move the top sheet while keeping the bottom one motionless. Notice that the shapes quickly segregate into two groups. Incidentally, this demonstration was inspired by a study by Gibson, Gibson, Smith, and Flock (1959).

For example, try opposing the law of nearness and the law of similarity. Make a row of crosses and circles fairly close to each other. Underneath, at a distance greater than the distance between the crosses and circles, make another identical row of crosses and circles. Continue this process until you have six rows. Do you see rows or columns? You may be able to create a design in which no law of grouping is the clear-cut winner. The grouping will be unstable, and it will shift from one moment to the next. In contrast, try *combining* the laws of nearness and similarity. The grouping will be nearly permanent, and it will be extremely difficult to disrupt.

Max Wertheimer (1923) was the first to describe these laws of grouping. Although the grouping laws may be most obvious for visual perception (and that is why they are discussed in this chapter), Wertheimer noted that the laws of grouping occur with the other senses as well. For example, tap on the desk three times, pause, and tap again three times. The taps organize into groups on the basis of nearness. Now alternate soft and loud tapping; the loud taps will group together, and the soft taps will group together. Or suppose you are listening to a duet in which the singers at one point hit the same note and cross over; the law of good continuation may operate. Can you think of examples from non-

visual systems of the laws of closure and common fate?

Try to notice the laws of grouping and how they may be used commercially. For example, try to identify the laws of grouping shown in the fabric in Figure 6.8. Start to notice wallpapers, fabrics, and package designs.

Advertisers also use the laws of grouping (Zakia, 1975). Figure 6.9, an advertisement for Estée Lauder perfume, is particularly effective because of the law of similarity. Notice how the model tends to be grouped with the graceful swans in the background. Her dress is similar to them in color and brightness. Furthermore, the shape of her hairstyle and the curvature of her back are echoed in the shapes of the swans' necks. In fact, she becomes even more graceful because of her association with these swans. Cover the swans with your hand and notice how the photograph becomes less interesting.

The similarity in advertisements may be even more symbolic. For example, an ad for an air conditioner may show the rounded form of a curled-up sleeping cat next to the rounded form of the grid on an air conditioner. The viewer would tend to group the cat and the air conditioner because of the law of similarity. This grouping in turn encourages the association between the legendary quietness of the sleeping cat and the implied

Figure 6.8 Laws of grouping as illustrated in fabric. (Photo by Ron Pretzer.)

quietness of this particular air conditioner. Similarly, Loudon and Della Bitta (1979) note that advertisers show mentholated cigarettes in beautiful green, springlike settings to suggest freshness.

Zakia also urges us to look for Gestalt principles in other art forms such as paintings. Look closely at a painting you have surely seen before, Grant Wood's *American Gothic* (Figure 6.10). In particular, pay attention to the law of similarity. Notice how the three-pronged design in the shape of the pitchfork is repeated elsewhere in the picture. It is most obvious in the pattern in the bib of the man's overalls. You can also see it in the cactus on the porch. Less obvious, but still noticeable, is the trident shape of each of the two faces, with the lower portion of the faces echoing the outer portion of the fork and the long nose and lines above the mouth echoing the inner

portion. The three prongs are repeated in the man's shirt and the windows, and the curvature of the fork is repeated in the collars and the apron border. This classic picture of rural Americans brought an uproar from midwestern viewers when it was first shown at the Art Institute of Chicago in 1930. The pitchfork, after all, is symbolic of the devil, and symbols of the devil were not welcome in a portrait of upstanding citizens. Incidentally, also notice in *American Gothic* how the law of good continuation forces you to see the man's right shoulder continue in a smooth curve, despite interruption from the pitchfork.

Ideally, you will now be inspecting photos and paintings for evidence of Gestalt principles. Look at other art forms as well. Do the dancers in a ballet, for example, illustrate the law of common fate, as some move forward and some move backwards? Notice, also, how breaking a Gestalt law of grouping can be particularly effective. Several years ago, I saw Marcel Marceau, the pantomime artist, perform a sketch of David and Goliath. There was a small screen on stage, behind which "David" would disappear and emerge as "Goliath" on the other side. Now we are accustomed to seeing something disappear on one side of a screen and appear on the other side, but the law of good continuation demands that the nature of the thing remain the same. However, David on the left-hand side of the screen was tiny, nimble, and dancing, but the Goliath who emerged from the right-hand side of the screen was huge, muscular, and angry. The audience was clearly impressed and surprised by the transformation that violated the law of good continuation.

Law of Prägnanz

As Kurt Koffka described the **law of Prägnanz**, "Of several geometrically possible organizations the one will actually occur which possesses the best, simplest and most stable shape" (Koffka, 1935, p. 138). Thus in Figure 6.6, the best and simplest perception involved the creation of an illusory contour, a triangle that covers other shapes. According

Figure 6.9 Advertisement that makes effective use of law of similarity. (Reprinted with permission of Estée Lauder.)

to Gestalt psychologists, the preferred interpretation is the one that is the most efficient and the most economical (Attneave, 1982; van Tuijl, 1980). Figure 6.11 shows a design that could be interpreted in at least two ways. It could represent three squares, two of which have small squares cut out of the upper right corner, or it could represent three squares overlapping each other. The law of Prägnanz predicts that you will see three overlapping squares.

The law of Prägnanz also predicts that some geometric figures are "better" than others (Arnheim, 1986; Wertheimer, 1923). For example, Figure 6.12a, a right angle, is a bet-

ter figure than either Figure 6.12b or Figure 6.12c. As Arnheim observes, those other two figures are seen as being "not quite right" and unpleasantly off-key. In other words, all figures are *not* created equal. This concept should sound familiar. As you may recall from Chapter 5, all colors are not created equal. Some basic, central colors have a certain prominence in our perceptual processes, whereas other colors are "not quite right." Similarly, simple 90° angles, perfect circles, and perfect squares are good figures, in contrast to 80° angles, lopsided circles, and tilted squares.

The law of Prägnanz is a general principle

Figure 6.10   Painting illustrating Gestalt law of similarity: *American Gothic*, by Grant Wood. (Reprinted with permission of Art Institute of Chicago.)

that encompassess all other Gestalt laws (van Tuijl, 1980). In the last section we looked at the laws of grouping. These laws—nearness, similarity, good continuation, closure, and common fate—encourage the formation of good, simple, and stable shapes. Similarly, the law of Prägnanz encompasses figure-ground relationships, which will be considered in the next section.

Unfortunately, the law of Prägnanz is

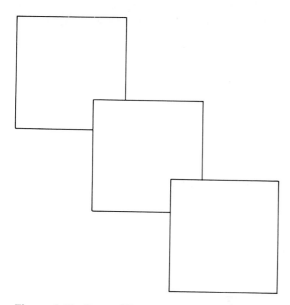

Figure 6.11 Law of Prägnanz, which predicts that this figure will be interpreted as three overlapping squares.

results showed that Figures b and d were almost always seen as three-dimensional. In two dimensions these figures were just too complex. Figure b, for example, has 16 line segments and 25 angles. This figure is not good and it is not simple, so the three-dimensional cube—a good, simple figure—will be perceived instead. Figure a is considerably simpler as a two-dimensional figure, in comparison to Figure b, so the two-dimensional figure can compete with the three-dimensional figure in perception. Figure a was seen as two-dimensional 60% of the time in the Hochberg and McAlister study.

In a later study Hochberg and Brooks (1960) made a further step toward measuring simplicity in an objective fashion. They derived a scale of complexity for two-dimensional figures, based on the number of angles, the number of continuous lines, and the number of different angles. Observers in this study saw a variety of figures and reported, as in the earlier experiment, whether they saw two or three dimensions. As the complexity score for the two-dimensional version increased, observers reported seeing the three-dimensional figure much more frequently. In summary, geometric properties of a design can be used to predict what we see. If the figure is simple in its two-dimensional form (as in Figures a and c), then we will often see the figure as a two-dimensional arrangement. On the other hand, if the figure is complex in its two-dimensional form and simple in its three-dimensional form (as in Figures b

rather vague. After all, how can we measure "goodness" or derive some index of "figure simplicity"?

Hochberg and McAlister (1953) wrote an article called "A Quantitative Approach to Figural 'Goodness'," in which they address the issue. Try a simplified version of their study in Demonstration 6.4. In their experiment, Hochberg and McAlister asked subjects to indicate their perceptions at random intervals during the 100-second viewing period. Their

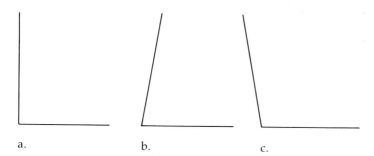

a.   b.   c.

Figure 6.12 Illustration of law of Prägnanz, which proposes that a right angle is "better" than other two angles.

Demonstration 6.4

Figural Goodness

Find a friend who will act as the observer. You will need a watch with a second hand. Cover up the last three figures, so that only the first one is exposed. Ask the observer to look at Figure a. Every ten seconds, give a signal to indicate that the observer should report whether the figure looks two-dimensional or three-dimensional. (Probably, the response "two" or "three" would be easiest.) Continue for 100 seconds, until you have 10 reports on the figure. Then repeat the procedure with each of the other figures.

Record the percentage of the time that the observer reports seeing a two-dimensional figure. Is the percentage about zero for Figures b and d, and about 50% for Figures a and c?

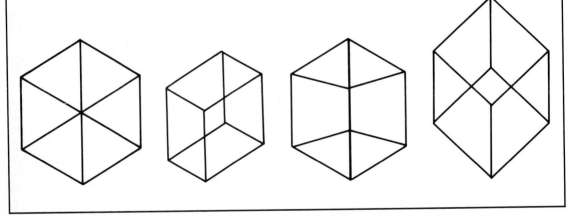

and d), then the figure will usually be seen as three-dimensional.

More recent research has focused on other properties of good figures. For example, Edmund Howe and his colleagues have found that people are better able to remember good figures (Howe & Brandau, 1983; Howe & Jung, 1986). These researchers propose that good figures are easy to encode into memory, in comparison to poor figures. As Hatfield and Epstein (1985) point out, simpler representations require fewer cognitive resources. You may recall that Bornstein and his colleagues concluded that good, central colors are, similarly, easier to remember than poor, boundary colors.

We saw that the laws of grouping could be applied when examining works of art. The

law of Prägnanz is also relevant to art. Deregowski (1984) points out the prevalence of symmetry in decorative arts, such as coats of arms and other heraldic designs. Simple, symmetrical patterns are preferred to unbalanced patterns, even though reality may have to be distorted to form a good design (Pomerantz & Kubovy, 1981). As Bornstein (1984b) observes, symmetry appears in art works of virtually every culture and period. Even modern art and high-tech designs provide illustrations of symmetry.

Hatfield and Epstein (1985) conclude that the law of Prägnanz, or the tendency toward simplicity, is well established for the perception of form under certain conditions. Nevertheless, the concept is somewhat fuzzy, and figures do not assume the simplest possible forms. As Pomeranz and Kubovy (1981) point out, it is ironic that Prägnanz—the law of simplicity—is not really as simple as it seems.

Figure-Ground Relationship

In the section on the laws of grouping, we saw that perceivers group parts of a design according to certain rules. In the second section, we saw that people tend to organize forms to produce a simple interpretation, such as three overlapping squares. Organization is not random; there are patterns in what we perceive. Parts of a design are also organized with respect to figure and ground. When two areas share a common boundary, the **figure** is the distinct shape with clearly defined edges. The **ground** is what is left over, forming the background. Look, for example, at a book (the figure) lying on a desk (the ground). The figure-ground relationship was one of the most important contributions of Gestalt psychologists.

Properties of Figure and Ground

Edgar Rubin (1915/1958), a Danish psychologist, was one of the first to try to clarify what constitutes the figure, as opposed to the ground. He reached four conclusions about figure and ground:

1. The figure has a definite shape, whereas the ground appears to have no shape. The figure is a "thing," whereas the ground is only a substance.

2. The ground seems to continue behind the figure. For example, try Demonstration 6.5.

3. The figure seems closer to us, with a clear location in space. In contrast, the ground is farther away, and there is no clear location in space; it is simply somewhere in the background. Try Demonstration 6.6 to illustrate this idea.

4. The figure is more dominant and more impressive than the ground; it is also remembered better and associated with a greater number of shapes. As Rubin states, the figure seems to dominate consciousness. If you were describing what you see in Demonstra-

tion 6.6, for example, you might say something like, "a black blob on a white piece of paper." The ground, on the other hand, seems to become part of the general environment.

Ambiguous Figure-Ground Relationships

As you stare at some figures against certain backgrounds, you may notice that an interesting reversal begins to occur. In Demonstration 6.5, for example, you probably began by seeing the radially marked cross as the figure. Perhaps, though, after a few seconds of looking at the figure, the concentrically marked cross popped out, forcing the radial markings into the background.

Ambiguous figure-ground relationships are situations in which the figure and the ground reverse from time to time, the figure becoming the ground and then becoming the figure again. These reversals often appear spontaneously, although you can also force the reversals to occur if you concentrate upon seeing a prominent shape in the ground. Figure 6.13 shows the vase-faces problem, one of the most famous examples of the ambiguous figure-ground relationship. One of my students, on viewing this illustration, reported that her brain seemed to be having a "tug-of-war" as she looked at it—a nice analogy! You can see either a white vase or two outlined faces. However, you cannot see both vase and faces at the same time.

Incidentally, the interest in ambiguous figures is not limited to European cultures. Carpenter (1980) describes how ambiguous figures (or, as he calls them, "visual puns") have been widely appreciated by people in other cultures, such as Eskimos, Melanesians, and Aztecs.

You may have seen some pictures of the Dutch artist, M. C. Escher, who enjoyed playing perceptual tricks on his viewers. In one picture, for example, light-colored horsemen and dark-colored horsemen take turns becoming figure and ground. You might wish to look at some of his pictures in a book, *The Graphic Work of M. C. Escher* (Escher, 1971).

Demonstration 6.5

Ground Continuing Behind Figure

Which is figure and which is ground in this picture? Probably, the cross with the radial marks looks like the figure, and the concentric circles look like the ground, continuing behind the figure. With some effort you can force the radially marked cross to become the ground and the concentrically marked cross to become the figure. However, this is difficult because the radial marks do not seem to continue behind the new figure.

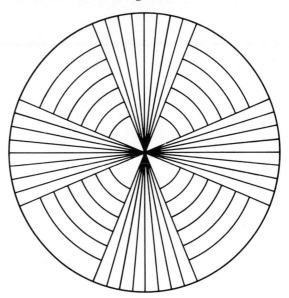

Demonstration 6.6

Figure Appearing Closer than Ground

Take a plain piece of rectangular white paper. Cut a small irregular figure from a piece of black paper. Look at the white paper for a moment. Now place the black figure quickly in the middle of the white paper. Suddenly, the white surface seems to recede. This illustrates how the ground seems to be farther away, with no clear location in space. Notice whether Rubin's other points regarding figure-ground apply in this case.

Figure 6.13 Vase-faces problem.

Ambiguous figure-ground relationships can be used effectively to convey a message. Figure 6.14 shows the cover of a disarmament booklet produced by a peace group, Coalition for a New Foreign and Military Policy. Notice how the weapons can be converted into peace doves.

In everyday life we do not see many examples of ambiguous figure-ground relationships. Sometimes, however, it is difficult to detect an animal concealed against a background of a similar pattern and design. We may even be unaware of the animal's presence until it suddenly scurries off. Regan and Beverley (1984) studied camouflaged figures in the laboratory and discovered that many could not be distinguished from the ground until the figure moved.

In the section on Gestalt laws of grouping, we discussed how the laws could help our appreciation of paintings and photographs. The figure-ground relationships are also important. Zakia (1975) points out how photographers use figure-ground relationships, which they would be more likely to call positive-negative space. For example, a scene in which figure and ground would be unambiguous in real life because of context, depth, and color cues can be rendered ambiguous in a photograph. In fact, you may have had the experience of taking a photograph of a friend against a background of trees. In real life the friend formed the figure against the ground of the trees. However, when you later inspect the photos, you notice that an oak tree appears to be growing out of your friend's head!

Similarly, look at a painting and force the background to become figure. Interesting shapes and textures appear, and you may find unusual details that you would have ignored if you had looked only at the figure. According to Gestalt principles, the figure is more thing-like and more impressive, so we must make a strong effort to overcome the tendency to ignore the background.

Although this is a chapter about vision, you might take a moment to think about ambiguous figure-ground relationships in the other sensory modes. As you taste a Chinese dish, for instance, you might notice how you can force the flavor of the garlic to become the figure, rather than the ground, and then you might concentrate upon the fresh ginger, causing it to become the figure. In listening to music, too, you can alternate between the singer and an accompanying instrument, reversing which is figure and which is ground.

Problems with Gestalt Approaches

As Grossberg and Mingolla (1985) observe, one of the great accomplishments of Gestalt psychologists was to suggest a short list of rules for perceptual organization. However, "as is often the case in pioneering work, the rules were neither always obeyed nor exhaustive" (p. 142). Let us consider some of the problems:

1. The major method in Gestalt psychology was phenomenological observation, a phrase clearly related to the more common word *phenomenon*. **Phenomenological observation** means that observers must look at their immediate experience and attempt to describe it completely, with as little bias or interpretation as possible (Lindauer, 1984;

Figure 6.14 Ambiguous figure-ground relationships on cover of disarmament booklet. (Reprinted with permission of Coalition for a New Foreign and Military Policy.)

Metelli, 1982; Pomerantz & Kubovy, 1981). However, modern experimental psychologists, often encouraged by behaviorist principles, tend to question any method that deals with private events. Thus, researchers may wonder whether observers really are providing unbiased, direct observations.

2. Gestalt theorists proposed a neurological explanation for their principles that involved electromagnetic fields in the brain. Research has not supported this explanation, and the original neurological aspects of the theory have been discarded (Hatfield & Epstein, 1985; Pomerantz & Kubovy, 1981).

3. The Gestalt laws are vague, and there is no clear-cut agreement among experts as to the exact list of laws. In fact, counts of the number of laws range between 1 and 114 (Pomerantz, 1986).

4. Most shapes we see are perceived as whole units already. A face, for example, seems to form a whole unit rather than a series of distinct parts. To use Gestalt principles to describe perception of the face, we would need to break the face into distinct parts and then demonstrate that Gestalt principles could be used to recombine the parts into a whole. This certainly doesn't sound like an efficient explanation!

5. Hints and suggestions can have an enormous influence on figure-ground perception. For example, Kennedy (1974) suggests that you think of the figure in Demonstration 6.5 as a beach ball rather than a cross. Probably you have no difficulty doing this. If conceptually driven processes can influence perception so strongly, argues Kennedy, then figure-ground perception cannot be very basic or primitive.

Despite these objections, Gestalt psychology has clearly *not* been abandoned by psychologists interested in perception. As Pomerantz and Kubovy (1981) conclude, "Gestalt psychology has now been with us well over half a century. Despite attacks upon it and periods of neglect, Gestalt thought continues to have an impact on theory and experimentation in perceptual psychology" (p. 455).

Summary: Perceptual Organization

1. The Gestalt approach emphasizes that we see objects as well-organized "wholes" rather than separate parts. This contrasts with the structuralist approach, which emphasized that experiences can be broken down into their most basic sensations.

2. The laws of grouping include the laws of nearness, similarity, good continuation, closure, and common fate. These laws have been applied in decoration, photography, advertising, painting, and other art forms.

3. The law of Prägnanz refers to the tendency to perceive figures as good, simple, and stable. People tend to see figures as three-dimensional if this interpretation is simpler than the two-dimensional interpretation.

4. The law of Prägnanz also points out that some figures are "better" than others, a conclusion that we also reached in connection with colors in the last chapter. Good figures are easier to encode into memory than poor figures.

5. In figure-ground relationships, the figure has a definite shape with clearly defined contours, in contrast to the ground, or background. The figure also seems closer and more dominant.

6. In ambiguous figure-ground relationships, the figure and the ground reverse from time to time. Figure-ground relationships are important in camouflage, the arts, and nonvisual perception.

7. Although Gestalt principles of organization are useful, their usefulness is limited by the methodology, by their vagueness, and by the organization inherent in many stimuli.

PATTERN RECOGNITION

In the previous two sections we have seen that contours are important in shape perception and that organizational processes influence the shapes we see. In this section we will discuss how we recognize certain patterns. Think about this for a moment. You see a picture in a yearbook, and you recognize that it is the person who sits next to you in biology. You look at each of the letters on this page and you can identify them. A dog runs up to you and you know that it is Spot, the next-door neighbor's dog. As Juola (1979) writes, "Pattern recognition is essential to almost all our waking activities. In fact, every living thing must recognize patterns when it interacts meaningfully with its world" (p. 493). **Pattern recognition** occurs when we identify a complex arrangement of sensory stimuli.

In this last section of the chapter we will consider three issues. First, we will look at several of the most important theories of pattern recognition. Then we will see how context influences pattern recognition, including an "In-Depth" section on how the context of a word helps in recognizing letters. The final topic is picture recognition.

Theories of Pattern Recognition

How do we manage to identify patterns? Several theories of pattern recognition have been developed. We will discuss three of the most important ones in this section.

Prototype-Matching Theory

According to the **prototype-matching theory**, we store abstract, idealized patterns in memory. When we see a particular object, we compare it with a **prototype**, or an ideal figure. If it matches, we recognize the pattern. If it does not match, we compare it with other prototypes until we find a match. For example, you have probably developed a prototype for your college president. This prototype represents a person of a certain height and body build and certain facial features. This prototype does not need to specify a particular facial expression or a particular kind of clothing—after all, a prototype is abstract. When you see the president, recognition occurs because the person in front of you matches the prototype.

Notice that the prototype-matching view is flexible. The prototype is a general pattern, not a specific one with every feature well-defined. After all, we can recognize a letter even when it is distorted. Consider the letter M, for example. Look at the assorted M's in Figure 6.15. You recognize those letters as M's even though they are all different. You can also recognize an M in various orientations like ꟽ and *M* and in various sizes like ᴍ and M.

Prototypes versus templates.   In contrast to the prototype-matching view, let us consider a similar but less flexible view, template matching. According to the **template-matching theory** we have many templates, or *specific patterns*, stored in memory. When we see a letter, for example, we see whether it matches one of the templates. If it matches, we recognize the letter. If it does not fit the template, we search for another template. In a way, the template is like a lock, and a letter is like a key. As you know, a key may be only a tiny bit different from the appropriate shape, yet it is different enough that it will not open the lock.

Now the idea of each pattern fitting into an appropriate template sounds interesting, but it has a clear drawback: We would need literally millions of templates to be able to recognize all the variations of all the letters and shapes. The system would have to be overwhelmingly bulky to store all the templates. Furthermore, it would be overwhelmingly time-consuming. To recognize a letter we would have to try the letter out with numerous templates. How could you ever read at an average rate of more than 200 words per minute if you had to struggle with dozens of templates for each letter?

Steven Pinker (1984) points out two additional problems with template models. Even if we could devise a modified template theory that was less bulky and more efficient, we would have difficulties with the third dimension. If you rotate Figure 6.15 so that one edge of this book is farther from you, the shape of the image on your retina changes drastically for each M. Nonetheless, you still

Figure 6.15 Variations of letter M.

recognize the letters. A template theory would need to suggest a different template for each rotation of a figure, a clearly unwieldy suggestion. Finally, template models only work for isolated letters and other simple objects presented in their entirety. Look up from your textbook right now and turn your head. You may see a complex array of fragmented objects that includes part of a book, a corner of a desk, and the lower edge of a lamp. Nonetheless, you can sort out this jumble and recognize the shapes. It's difficult to imagine how a template theory would include templates for lower edges of lamps and other fragments.

Because of the inefficiency of the template theory, we must abandon that view for the more flexible prototype matching. Remember that the prototype-matching theory says the patterns stored in memory are abstract, idealized, and not rigidly specific in their shape.

Research on prototype theory. Let's look at some studies on prototype recognition. Posner, Goldsmith, and Welton (1967), for example, examined prototype recognition for letters and figures. They created a prototype of a letter or a figure by placing nine dots in an arrangement on a sheet of graph paper that was 50 squares high and 50 squares wide. Then the original prototype was systematically distorted by moving each of the dots into neighboring squares on the graph paper. No-

tice that Figure 6.16b is close to the original M; as you proceed through the series, the forms become increasingly distorted until in Figure 6.16f the pattern of dots looks random. In addition to the letter M, observers saw the letter F, triangles, diamonds, and random dots.

During the experiment, the observers saw slides of the patterns, one at a time, and pressed a button to indicate whether the pattern was a triangle, a diamond, an M, an F, or random. The number of errors before observers mastered the task was about 20 times as great for patterns such as Figure 6.16f as for patterns such as Figure 6.16b. Recognition is easier when a pattern looks about the same as the prototype, but recognition errors are increasingly likely as the pattern deviates from the prototype.

A study by Franks and Bransford (1971) provides further information on recognition of prototypes, using geometric forms rather than dot patterns. Base designs, like those in Figures a, b, and c of Demonstration 6.7, were constructed by arranging four figures on a card. Observers in this study were told to look at each figure and then draw it; they were not told to remember the figures. Try Demonstration 6.7 before we proceed.

After a delay observers were shown more figures, some of which were the base designs

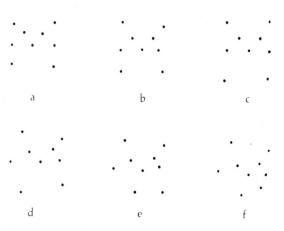

Figure 6.16 Stimuli similar to those used by Posner, Goldsmith, & Welton (1967).

Study each of these three figures, spending just five seconds on each figure. Then cover up these figures.

a.

b.

c.

Now do something else for five minutes. Then look at each of the figures below and mark on a sheet of paper which ones you have seen before.

d.

e.

f.

g.

h.

i.

Which ones looked familiar? Figures d and i were in fact the same as the original, and g was a minor transformation of b, with the right-hand two figures switched. Figures e and f involved more major transformations. Figure h involved the greatest transformations, and you probably judged that figure to be unfamiliar.

that had already been presented and some transformations of these base designs. The observers marked "yes" or "no" on an answer sheet to indicate whether they had seen each design before. The results showed that people were much more likely to recognize a design if it was not much different from the original (like Figure g). Transformations greatly different from the original (like Figure h) were seldom recognized. This study reinforces the findings of Posner and his colleagues (1967). Shapes are more likely to be identified and recognized if they are similar to prototypes.

Prototype-matching theory is an attractive approach to the problem of pattern recognition. It describes how shapes can be recognized readily, despite the variety of different representations of the same shape, the variety of orientations from which the shapes are viewed, and the fragmented view we often have of those shapes. However, the physiological details of this approach have not been developed. For example, how are the stimuli internally represented? How are prototypes related to the kinds of neuronal processes discussed in Chapters 3 and 5? How are the prototypes stored in memory? Are there templates for prototypes (Spoehr & Lehmkuhle, 1982)? The next approach that we will consider, distinctive-features theory, offers more precise answers to such questions. However, as we will also see, distinctive-features theory is not problem free.

Distinctive-Features Theory

One of the most widely accepted approaches to the recognition of patterns was developed by Eleanor Gibson of Cornell University to explain how we identify letters (Gibson & Levin, 1975). She argues that we can tell the difference between letters because of distinctive features. **Distinctive features** are characteristics of letters, such as straight versus curved lines. Thus the letter H has many straight lines, whereas the letter O has none.

Each letter has a pattern of distinctive features unique to itself. Some pairs of letters, such as G and W, are different from each other; they do not share any distinctive features. Other pairs of letters, such as P and R, are quite similar; they differ on only one distinctive feature, a diagonal line on the R. Distinctive features remain constant, whether the letter is typed or printed.

Gibson (1969) developed a chart that shows contrasting distinctive features for the 26 letters of the alphabet. Try Demonstration 6.8, which introduces you to Gibson's distinctive features. This list of features, which Gibson notes is probably not complete (Gibson & Levin, 1975), evaluates each letter with regard to each kind of feature.

Research on distinctive-features theory. Which kinds of distinctive features are most important? Which characteristics do we rely on the most when we are trying to identify a letter? Gibson, Schapiro, and Yonas (1968) asked college students to make rapid judgments about pairs of letterrs. A projector showed two letters at the same time on a screen. If observers thought the letters were the same, they pressed one button. If they thought they were different, they pressed a different button. The experimenters measured the **latency**, or the time taken to respond, as an index of similarity. If the latency was short, as it might be for G and W, then the two letters were considered very different from each other. If the latency was long, as it might be for P and R, then the letters were considered similar.

Gibson and her coauthors found that the first distinction people make is between letters that have only straight components (such as M, N, and W) and letters that have curved components (such as C, G, P, and R). Another important distinction is between round letters (such as C and G) and letters with an intersection in the middle (such as P and R).

Recent research on the distinctive-features theory has produced more complex mathematical models of letter recognition. Townsend and Ashby (1982) used four letters in their study of letter recognition. These stimuli were constructed of line segments of equal length, as Figure 6.17 shows. Participants in the study were instructed to watch as each letter was briefly presented and to report on

Demonstration 6.8

Distinctive Features

Below is a table of distinctive features, as proposed by Gibson (1969). Pay attentiton to just the top three kinds of features: straight, curve, and intersection. Notice, for example, how A and B share only one feature in these categories: intersection. Now look to see how similar M and N are. Do O and E have any features in common? Notice that B and P are identical with respect to these three categories, although they differ on other characteristics.

Features	A	E	F	H	I	L	T	K	M	N	V	W	X	Y	Z	B	C	D	G	J	O	P	R	Q	S	U
Straight																										
horizontal	+	+	+	+		+	+								+				+							
vertical		+	+	+	+	+	+	+	+	+				+		+		+				+	+			
diagonal /	+							+	+		+	+	+	+	+											
diagonal \	+							+	+	+	+	+	+	+								+	+			
Curve																										
closed																+		+			+	+	+	+		
open V																				+						+
open H																	+		+						+	
Intersection	+	+	+	+		+	+							+		+						+	+	+		
Redundancy																										
cyclic change		+							+		+					+									+	
symmetry	+	+		+	+	+	+	+			+	+	+	+		+	+	+			+					+
Discontinuity																										
vertical	+		+	+	+	+	+	+	+						+							+	+			
horizontal		+	+		+	+									+											

Source: Eleanor J. Gibson, *Principles of Perceptual Learning and Development*, © 1969, p. 88. Reprinted by permission of Prentice-Hall, Inc., Englewood Cliffs, NJ.

which line segments they had seen. (As you'll notice, these four letters are constructed from two vertical and three horizontal line segments.) Finally, the participants were asked to report which letter they had seen. The results of this study showed a clear-cut relationship between the line segment reports and the letter reports, indicating that letter recognition depends upon the recognition of isolated features.

One attractive aspect of the distinctive-features theory is that it could be compatible with physiological evidence. As you'll recall from Chapter 3, some neurons in the visual cortex respond most to horizontal lines, while others respond most to vertical or diagonal

Figure 6.17 Four letters used by Townsend and Ashby (1982).

lines. Clearly, the specifics of the connections between the stimulus configurations and the physiological responses must be complex. Still, the visual system is already appropriately "wired" to notice the kinds of differences that distinguish one letter from another.

Before we discuss the potential problems in distinctive-features theory, let's consider how distinctive-features theory differs from prototype-matching theory. Probably the most important difference is that distinctive-features theory proposes that pattern recognition results from detecting specific important parts of the stimulus. In contrast, prototype-matching theory emphasizes the importance of the entire shape of the stimulus (Naus & Shillman, 1976).

Problems with distinctive-features theory. Now let's consider some objections raised in connection with distinctive-features theory. First, notice how some patterns with completely different meanings may differ in only a single detail. For example, consider the letters Q and O. These two different letters may look more similar than two variations of the letter O (Haber, 1985). Furthermore, Pinker (1984) points out that the features-analysis approach was constructed to explain the relatively simple recognition of letters. Natural shapes, however, are much more complex. How can you recognize a horse? Do you analyse it into features such as its mane, its hooves, and its head? None of those features can be as precisely analyzed as the straight lines in Townsend and Ashby's four alphabetical letters.

Furthermore, consider an experiment by Pomerantz, Sager, and Stoever (1977). A modified version of their study appears in Demonstration 6.9. You probably noticed the deviant region much more quickly in part a than in part b. In fact, Pomerantz and his colleagues found that people took more than

---

Demonstration 6.9

Identification of Features in Simple and Complex Figures

Inspect the two diagrams below. In each diagram one region is deviant because the figure is different from the other three. Notice whether you identify the deviant region faster in part a than in part b.

a.

b.

twice as long to identify the deviant region for the simple figures in part a as for the more complex figures in part b. Distinctive-features theory proposes that we should process the diagonal lines the same way, whether they appear by themselves or in the context of a right angle. However, the study by Pomerantz and his coauthors suggests that we process more than simple isolated features; the triangle created in part b is a real figure, not just a diagonal line attached to a right angle. You'll notice that this argument is somewhat similar to the distinction between the structuralist and Gestalt approaches discussed in the last section. We'll reconsider the importance of context later in this chapter.

Theory of Spatial Frequency Analysis

The two theories discussed so far are different, but they seem like common-sense approaches to the problem of pattern recognition. The third approach, spatial frequency analysis, is not so intuitive. According to the **theory of spatial frequency analysis**, the visual system breaks the stimulus down into a series of narrow light and dark stripes. This approach to visual stimuli has been useful in research on visual sensitivity and it has also been applied to pattern recognition.

Fourier analysis.   Baron Jean Baptiste Joseph Fourier once traveled with Napoleon to Egypt, but vision researchers are more likely to know his mathematical contributions that form the basis of spatial frequency analysis. His work can also be applied to the analysis of sound waves, as we will see in Chapter 9, but we are now concerned with the analysis of visual stimuli. **Fourier analysis** involves analyzing a stimulus into its component sine waves. If you took a trigonometry course, you may recall that a **sine wave** is a smooth wave pattern resembling the light waves discussed in Chapter 3. As you can see in Figure 6.18a, the wave pattern is repeated at regular intervals, fluctuating from high intensity to low intensity and back. This sine wave corresponds to a narrow horizontal segment taken from Figure 6.18b. Figure 6.18b shows a **sinusoidal grating**, a set of blurry stripes that alternate between dark and light. (The dark

stripes represent the low-intensity areas of the sine curve; the light stripes represent the high-intensity areas.)

Figure 6.18a shows a single sine wave and how it corresponds to a stimulus that is a blurry set of stripes. Fourier analysis proposes that a stimulus can be analyzed into its component sine waves, so let's consider the kind of sine waves that might be the components for a horizontal strip taken from a set of clear stripes. Suppose that we add together a series of sine waves, a process known as **Fourier synthesis**. (We perform a Fourier *analysis* to analyze a stimulus into its component sine waves; we perform a Fourier *synthesis* for the reverse process of combining sine waves to represent the pattern in the stimulus.) Suppose we select a series of sine waves that have one, three, five, and seven cycles within the same horizontal distance, as shown in Figure 6.19. If we add these waves together, this Fourier synthesis results in the figure at the bottom of the diagram. You'll notice that it is similar to the square wave shown in Figure 6.20a. A **square wave** corresponds to a series of regularly repeating dark and light stripes that have crisp, not blurry, edges that are square rather than smoothly curved.

In short, Fourier analysis provides the tools for analyzing a pattern, such as a set of stripes, into its components. These components can be described mathematically in terms of sine waves. We have discussed a relatively simple stimulus, a narrow horizontal strip taken from a set of stripes. Repeating this procedure with a series of narrow horizontal strips would produce a two-dimensional striped pattern, as in Figure 6.20. By more complex combinations of sine waves, we can in fact construct the much more complex patterns that might be found in an ordinary black-and-white photograph (Graham, 1981).

Spatial frequency.   How can we describe a sinusoidal grating so that it is most useful in relation to visual processes? The grating in Figure 6.18b has a spatial frequency of about two cycles per inch. However, this system of measurement will not be useful when we

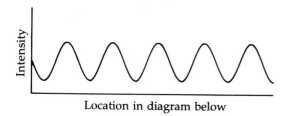

a. Sine wave

b. Sinusoidal grating

Figure 6.18 Sine wave and its corresponding sinusoidal grating.

want to discuss visual processes. If that pattern is presented 4 inches from your nose, the stripes are relatively broad; at a distance of 4 feet the stripes are relatively narrow. It is customary, therefore, to measure spatial frequency in terms of the number of cycles in each degree of visual angle.

Turn back to Demonstration 4.1 to review the concept of visual angle. Then return to Figure 6.18 and hold the book 35 cm (14 inches) from your eyes. Figure 6.18 shows a one-cycle grating at that distance. In other words, there is one complete cycle, including a dark and a light phase, in 1 degree of visual angle. Incidentally, if you move the book to a distance of 70 cm (twice as far away), you will achieve a 2-cycle grating. A 2-cycle grating could also be obtained by making twice as many stripes in the same horizontal distance.

Contrast sensitivity functions. The patterns you have seen so far have shown high-contrast stripes of black and white. The contrast can be reduced by alternating black and *gray* stripes. The contrast between the two kinds of stripes can be decreased even further until

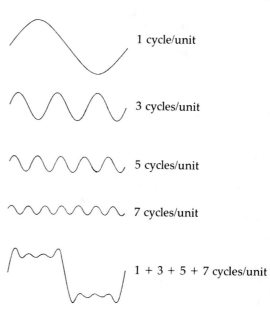

Figure 6.19 Addition of four sine waves produces an intensity distribution resembling that of square wave.

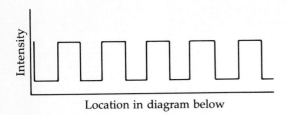

Location in diagram below

a. Square wave

b. Intensity distribution for a square wave.

Figure 6.20 Square wave and its corresponding intensity distribution.

an observer cannot distinguish between the stripes and a uniform gray patch. For example, a researcher might take the 1-cycle grating shown in Figure 6.18 and gradually lower the contrast until the observer reports, "I can't distinguish that figure from the gray patch." (You may recognize the psychophysical technique as the method of limits for discrimination.) This procedure could be repeated with a variety of gratings, perhaps representing spatial frequencies between 0.1 cycles and 50 cycles/degree.

Figure 6.21 shows a typical **contrast sensitivity function**, a diagram that shows the relationship between spatial frequency and sensitivity. Notice that the y-axis is labeled *sensitivity*. As you'll recall from Chapter 2, high sensitivity corresponds to low threshold. The sensitivity is highest for gratings with spatial frequencies of 6 cycles/degree. That means that observers are particularly good at discriminating between this particular grating and a gray patch. In fact, they are so good with this grating that the contrast between the black and gray stripes can be low. Spatial frequencies of 1 cycle/degree or less and spatial frequencies of 10 cycles/degree or

more require much higher contrast between the two kinds of stripes. The visual system simply doesn't process those gratings as well. Incidentally, if you want to know just what the grating looks like that you can see so well, turn back to Figure 6.18, prop up your book, and back up about 7 feet (2.1 m).

In the 1960s, two British researchers named Fergus Campbell and John Robson suggested that pattern perception could be described in terms of spatial frequency (Campbell & Robson, 1964, 1968). They proposed that our visual system has several sets of neurons, each of which responds best to a particular spatial frequency. The general idea of a "best stimulus" may be familiar to you; Chapter 3 discussed tuning curves, which demonstrate that simple cells in the visual cortex respond better to some orientations than to others. Similarly, there might be a number of **spatial frequency channels**, or channels sensitive to a narrow range of spatial frequencies.

For example, one set of neurons might respond best to a spatial frequency of .5 cycles/degree, another set to 1 cycle/degree, and other sets to frequencies such as 6, 10, and

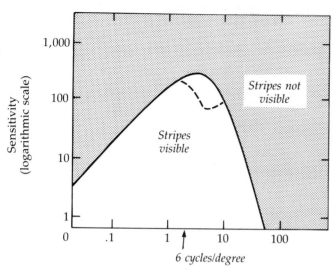

Figure 6.21 Typical contrast sensitivity function for human adult represented by solid line. Dotted line represents selective adaptation.

so on. The ideal combined frequency might be 6 cycles/degree, based on the contrast sensitivity functions of all the component neurons that make up the visual system.

How does the idea of spatial frequency channels—each having its own unique sensitivity function—fit with information on the physiology of vision? DeValois and DeValois (1980) conclude in their review of pattern vision: "Recent physiological studies agree in showing that most cortical cells are fairly narrowly tuned for spatial frequency and that the peak tuning of units within an area scatters over a considerable range" (p. 321). Thus, spatial frequency is registered in the cortex by cells such as the simple cells discussed in Chapter 3 (Hubel & Wiesel, 1965, 1979).

Furthermore, the response to stripes of various widths could be accounted for by the center-surround kind of organization also discussed in Chapter 3. For example, let's consider a particular cell that has an on-center, off-surround arrangement, as shown in Figure 6.22a. If a sinusoidal grating is presented so that the white portion stimulates

the center and the gray portion stimulates the surround, the cell will respond at a high rate. However, if the sinusoidal grating shows wide stripes (that is, low spatial frequency), the strong excitation of the center is cancelled by the strong inhibition of the surround; this situation is shown in Figure 6.22b. Finally, if the sinusoidal grating shows narrow stripes (that is, high spatial frequency), the moderate excitation of the center is cancelled by the moderate inhibition of the surround; this situation is shown in Figure 6.22c. To make certain that you understand these three situations, you may want to try to determine the response rate when an off-center, on-surround cell encounters (1) the sinusoidal grating shown in Figure 6.22a, but with the dark stripe centered over its center; (2) either the dark or the light portion of Figure 6.22b; and (3) any portion of Figure 6.22c.

Naturally, however, we manage to perceive sinusoidal gratings that have either higher or lower spatial frequency than the one in Figure 6.22a. There must be cells that correspond to other spatial frequency chan-

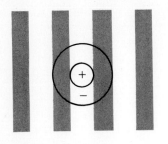
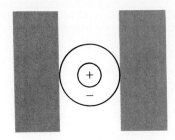

a. High response rate   b. Low response rate

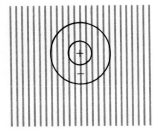

c. Low response rate

Figure 6.22   The nature of on-center, off-surround cell's response to sinusoidal grating depends upon spatial frequency of grating.

nels because they have either wider or narrower receptive fields. As mentioned, each set of neurons responds best to a particular spatial frequency. Remember, however, that a complex scene can be broken down into a number of sinusoidal gratings. Each grating then stimulates the cells with receptive field sizes "tuned" to respond maximally to that particular grating.

The theory of spatial frequency analysis is complicated. Let's briefly review before we consider the experimental evidence for this theory. By means of Fourier analysis, any complex scene can be broken down into its component sine waves, each of which corresponds to a set of blurry black-and-white stripes known as a sinusoidal grating. This grating is measured in by the number of cycles of grating included in one degree of vis-

ual angle. In general, people are most sensitive to gratings with spatial frequencies of 6 cycles/degree. However, each spatial frequency channel in the visual system seems to respond best to a different spatial frequency; some channels "prefer" frequencies higher than 6 cycles/degree, whereas other channels "prefer" lower frequencies. Furthermore, if cells with center-surround organization differ in the size of their receptive fields, this arrangement could account for the variety of spatial frequency channels.

Research evidence for the theory of spatial frequency analysis.   We have discussed how spatial frequency analysis *could* account for pattern perception. Now we need to consider whether the research suggests that this kind of sine-wave analysis actually occurs. A number of studies that both support and contradict the theory have been summarized elsewhere (e.g., DeValois & DeValois, 1980; Graham, 1981; Regan, 1982; Yellott, Wandell, & Cornsweet, 1984). Let's consider two of these studies.

One of the earliest studies on spatial frequency analysis is also one of the most convincing, according to DeValois and DeValois (1980). Blakemore and Campbell (1969) calculated the kind of contrast sensitivity function illustrated by the solid line in Figure 6.21. Then the observer looked at a 7.5 cycle/degree grating for 1 to 2 minutes, and the researchers again calculated a contrast sensitivity function. Intriguingly, the sensitivity to spatial frequencies decreased substantially around 7.5 cycles/degree. This decrease is represented by the dotted line in Figure 6.21. In other words, continuous exposure to a particular stimulus produces "fatigue" in the neurons that respond to spatial frequencies in the region of 7.5 cycles/degree. Other studies have used this **selective adaptation procedure** to demonstrate that continuous exposure to one spatial frequency decreases later sensitivity to that particular frequency. Incidentally, this is one example of a general phenomenon called *adaptation* that we will examine in other sensory systems later in the book. As Theme 1 proposes, the sensory systems have numerous similarities.

In another study on spatial frequency Harvey, Roberts, and Gervais (1983) compared the theory of spatial frequency analysis with the distinctive-features approach. They presented upper-case block letters, one at a time, for less than 50 milliseconds. In pretesting they had determined that exposures this brief allowed identification of the letters only 50% of the time. They were particularly interested in the kind of identification errors. For example, when observers saw the letter *M* and did not identify it properly, were they likely to say that they had seen another letter similar with respect to its distinctive features or with respect to its spatial frequency? The results showed that people were somewhat likely to substitute a letter with similar distinctive features, but they were substantially more likely to substitute a letter with similar spatial frequency. Obviously, we cannot conclude that people make *no* use of distinctive features and that the distinctive-features theory should be abandoned. However, this study does provide stronger support for a spatial frequency approach.

Naturally, there are some objections to the spatial frequency approach. Many criticisms of the distinctive-features theory also apply to the spatial frequency approach. As Graham (1981) observes, the psychophysical evidence for spatial frequency channels is not as clear-cut as some investigators might claim. Furthermore, Cutting (1987) points out that the spatial frequency approach guarantees that everything in the stimulus will be analyzed into sine waves; Fourier analysis is so unselective that even meaningless, unimportant, and irrelevant parts will be included in the analysis. Real perceivers, in contrast, are more selective; they can ignore the irrelevant portions of a pattern.

Chapter 5 pointed out that the current theory about color vision features the triumphant union of two theories once thought incompatible. Our knowledge about shape perception is not yet as advanced as our knowledge about color vision. However, as Graham (1981) concludes, it seems highly likely that shape perception is at least as complicated as color vision. It is possible that prototypes, distinctive features, and spatial frequency may all be involved. Furthermore, numerous alternate theories have been proposed in the last decade. For example, David Marr (1982) developed a complex theory involving three stages of image representation beyond the retina; his theory was based on computer simulation studies. Irving Biederman (1985) proposed that we recognize an object by segmenting its components into regular shapes, such as blocks, cylinders, wedges, and cones. In any event, most current theories rely almost exclusively on the information available in the stimulus; they use a data-driven or bottom-up approach. In the next section we will see how a conceptually driven or top-down approach facilitates pattern perception because context has an important influence on pattern recognition.

Influence of Context on Pattern Recognition

The section on contours at the beginning of the chapter concentrated on features of the stimulus and their influence on shape perception. For example, we saw how lateral inhibition produced exaggerated contrast beteen two surfaces. In the last section two of the theories particularly stressed the stimulus. The distinctive-features theory and the theory of spatial frequency analysis emphasize that the visual system performs a careful analysis of the stimulus, in terms of either isolated lines and curves or the underlying sinusoidal gratings. We mentioned this approach to perception, data-driven processing, in other parts of the book. As you will recall, the importance of the information in the stimulus is Theme 2, and the importance and capacities of our perceptual systems in processing this information is Theme 3. We now need to consider the data-driven processing approach more carefully, and we must contrast how it is coordinated with conceptually driven processing (Theme 4) to recognize patterns.

Integrating the Two Approaches

Let's first review the two approaches. The approach to perception that emphasizes the importance of the stimulus is called data-driven processing. **Data-driven processing** depends upon the arrival of data from the sensory receptors. The data arrive and set into motion the process of recognizing various shapes.

Conceptually driven processing is a different approach to perception; it emphasizes the importance of the observers' concepts in shaping perception. In conceptually driven processing, observers have expectations and concepts about how the world is organized. They believe that certain objects are likely to be found in certain situations. These expectations and concepts set into motion the process of recognizing various shapes.

Data-driven processing can be called **bottom-up processing**. We recognize simple, low-level features, and the combination of these simple features allows us to recognize more complex, whole patterns. Conceptually driven processing, on the other hand, can be called **top-down processing**. We begin by recognizing a whole pattern, which may be complex, and the recognition of the whole allows us to identify the simpler elements that are present in the whole.

Let's be more concrete. You are walking to class, and you recognize your professor for your course in perception. How did you manage to do that? If you used data-driven processing, recognition depended upon information about contours you received from the sensory receptors. Information was collected about the contour of the nose, the contrast between the eyebrow and the surrounding skin, and numerous other tiny features. These data about the parts allowed you to recognize the whole.

If you used conceptually driven processing to recognize your professor, recognition was prompted by your knowledge of the situation. In the past, you had seen your professor emerge from an office, turn right, and walk down the hall toward the classroom at 9:55 on a Tuesday morning. Context, expectancies, knowledge, and memory—concepts that you have as an observer—''drive'' the recognition process.

Palmer (1975a) pointed out a problem with accepting only the data-driven (bottom-up) or only the conceptually driven (top-down) approach:

> Which happens first: interpreting the whole or interpreting the parts? How can someone recognize a face until he has first recognized the eyes, nose, mouth and ears? Then again, how can someone recognize the eyes, nose, mouth, and ears until he knows that they are part of a face? This is often called the parsing paradox. It concerns the difficulties encountered with either a pure ''bottom-up'' (part-to-whole) or a pure ''top-down'' (whole-to-part) strategy in interpretive processing (p. 295).

Thus we have a puzzle in shape perception: We cannot recognize the parts without the context of the whole, yet we cannot recognize the whole without the information about the parts. How can we solve the parsing paradox? Palmer proposes that perception usually proceeds in both bottom-up and top-down directions at the same time. Both processes must occur simultaneously to guarantee quick and accurate recognition of shapes.

Palmer provides a useful example of the interactions of the two processing strategies. Look at each line fragment in Figure 6.23b. Each squiggle by itself is meaningless and unrecognizable. However, when each squiggle is placed within the context of a face, as in Figure 6.23a, the irregular bump is suddenly, unmistakably, a nose. In context, then, primitive, unrealistic lines can be recognized as features. Convince yourself of this by drawing a variety of lines to represent a mouth. Almost any segment of a reasonable length could pass for a mouth in the context of a face. You may have already discovered this if you are an enthusiastic pumpkin carver at Halloween. A mouth can be a circle, a jagged line, a series of curves, or a single curve. Similarly, a pumpkin eye can be a triangle, a crescent moon, or a perfect oval. Shapes can be recognized in context, although they would be meaningless out of context.

How can we recognize features out of context? If we supply internal structure for each feature adding realistic details, then the angular bump is clearly a nose, as in Figure 6.23c.

In summary, we can recognize the pattern in Figure 6.23a because of both bottom-up and top-down processing. We recognize the face as a whole because we recognize the parts, but we could not recognize the parts without the context of the whole.

We have discussed conceptually driven processing and looked at an example of how the context of a face might influence recognition of facial features. Let's now look at some research that demonstrates the importance of context.

One experiment by Palmer (1975b) explored the influence of "world knowledge" on recognition. You know that you are likely to find bread in a kitchen, a mailbox in a front yard, and a drum in a band. If you know what kind of a scene you are examining, you can rely upon important information about the

a. In context   b. Out of context, no detail

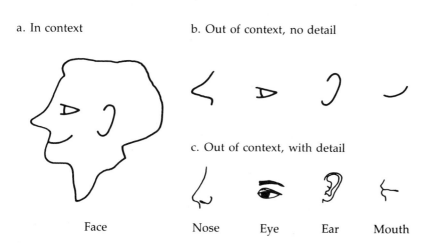

c. Out of context, with detail

Face   Nose   Eye   Ear   Mouth

Figure 6.23 Features in context and out of context. (From Palmer, 1975a, in David A. Norman and David E. Rumelhart, *Explorations in Cognition*. Copyright © 1975 W. H. Freeman and Company. Used by permission.)

kinds of objects you are likely to find in that scene. Similarly, if you are looking at a scene we could call "Psychology Building on a Tuesday Morning," you know that you are more likely to find your perception professor there than, say, Meryl Streep or William Shakespeare.

Palmer showed his observers scenes such as the one on the left in Figure 6.24. Then he very briefly showed them figures such as Figures 6.24a, 6.24b, and 6.24c. In some cases the figure was appropriate for the scene (such as the bread in Figure 6.24a); in others it was inappropriate, but its shape was similar to that of an appropriate figure (such as the mailbox in Figure 6.24b). In still other cases the figure was inappropriate, and the shape was different from the appropriate figure (such as the drum in Figure 6.24c). In a final condition, observers did not see any contextual scene; they were asked to identify the figure without any context. In each condition they were asked to name the object and to rate their confidence that their identification had been correct.

When the figure was appropriate for the scene, such as a loaf of bread in a kitchen, the observers were 84% accurate in their identification. They were substantially less accurate when they had no contextual scene. However, they were even less accurate when the figure was inappropriate for the scene, such as the mailbox or the drum in the kitchen.

Think about how you may have noticed the effect of appropriate context in your past experience. A friend whom you would recognize readily in an appropriate setting, such as a college classroom, is suddenly unrecognizable in your hometown supermarket or a New York City art gallery.

We have seen that an object can be more readily recognized if it appears in context. Numerous other experiments have been conducted to illustrate the importance of context in pattern perception. Perhaps the most extensive research on this topic involves the word-superiority effect, which is the topic of this next "In-Depth" section.

▶ IN-DEPTH:
WORD-SUPERIORITY EFFECT

According to the **word-superiority effect** (**WSE**), letters are perceived better when they appear in words than when they appear in strings of unrelated letters (Taylor & Taylor, 1983). For example, the letter *R* is easier to perceive when it appears in the word TIGER than when it appears in the nonword GIETR. The word-superiority effect, also known as the **word-apprehension effect**, was first demonstrated more than 100 years ago by Cattell (1886). He presented series of letters for 10 milliseconds and asked observers to report as many letters as they could. When random letters were presented, the observers usually reported only about four or five individual let-

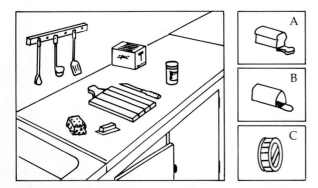

Figure 6.24   Context scene and target objects used in Palmer's experiment. (From Palmer, 1975b. Used with permission.)

ters. However, if English words were presented, the observers usually reported three or four complete words, that is, several times as many letters as in the random-letter condition.

The word-superiority effect was generally ignored for several decades, until Reicher (1969) revived interest in the phenomenon. In his study, observers first saw a stimulus, such as a four-letter word (for example, WORK) or a four-letter nonword (for example, ORWK) that was both meaningless and unpronounceable. This stimulus was presented for 50 milliseconds. Immediately afterward, a visual mask was presented that resembled the masks discussed earlier in the chapter. At the same time, off to one side, two letters appeared. These letters were placed in one of four letter positions, and the observers were asked to report which of the two letters had actually appeared in the stimulus. For example, the word WORK might be followed by the display $- - - \frac{D}{K}$. Observers had to specify whether they had seen a D or a K in the earlier stimulus. Notice that both letters form an acceptable English word. Thus, an observer could not receive a high score simply by guessing at a letter that would complete an English word. Furthermore, this experiment eliminated an accusation that could have been applied to Cattell's study: Perhaps observers can *perceive* the letters equally well in words and in isolation, but they *remember* the words better and therefore report more items. Reicher's experiment did not rely on observers' memories, however, because they simply chose between two alternatives. Thus, Reicher's study was designed to test whether the word-superiority effect would persist, even when two important advantages for words (guessing and memory) had been eliminated. The results showed that accuracy was between 65% and 77% higher when the stimuli were words.

Reicher also demonstrated that observers were more accurate in identifying a single letter when it was part of a word than when it appeared alone, an effect called the **word-let-**

ter phenomenon. At first glance this word-letter phenomenon doesn't make sense. Why should the letter K be easier to identify if it is part of the word WORK than if it appears all by itself? Adding extra material should make the task more difficult rather than easier! However, you may recall the experiment by Pomerantz, Sager, and Stoever (1977), illustrated in Demonstration 6.9. They showed that a diagonal line was easier to recognize if it was surrounded by a right angle than when it was shown by itself. Context appears to aid the perceptual stages of both letter and shape recognition.

After Reicher reopened the mystery of the word-superiority effect, dozens of additional studies were conducted. The WSE appears to be a remarkably general phenomenon. For example, it can be demonstrated with pseudowords, or nonwords that follow the general rules of English word construction. For instance, the letter K could be recognized more accurately in the pseudoword TORK than in the nonpronounceable string of letters RTOK. People also perceive words faster than nonwords on a matching task (Silverman, 1985) and on a search task (Staller, 1982). Thus, words provide a useful context for recognizing a letter, whether the task is identifying the letter (the WSE), seeing whether the letter matches another, or hunting for a letter.

In addition, the word-superiority effect has been demonstrated when the word appears as a mixture of upper-case and lower-case letters, such as WoRk (Taylor & Taylor, 1983). It also occurs when the stimulus is letter fragments (Solman, May, & Schwartz, 1981). In fact, it has even been demonstrated with Japanese symbols (Hung & Tzeng, 1981).

The word-superiority effect is so general that it is not limited to vision. Krueger (1982) demonstrated that the WSE can be obtained through another sensory mode—touch. People can identify letters in braille substantially faster if the letters appear in the context of words.

Unfortunately, there is no uniformly accepted theory to explain exactly how word context benefits the task of letter recognition.

However, interested readers may want to examine competing explanations (Chastain, 1986; McClelland & Rumelhart, 1981; Paap Newsome, McDonald, & Schvaneveldt, 1982; Rumelhart & McClelland, 1982).

Let's complete this "In-Depth" section with a closer look at a study representative of the recent research on the word-superiority effect. Chastain (1986) speculated that word context can sometimes interfere with letter recognition. When it provides an inappropriate context, a word can produce what we could call a "word-inferiority effect." A series of four experiments illustrated a word-superiority effect when the context was appropriate and a word-inferiority effect when the context was inappropriate. Chastain's basic manipulation was to alter a string of letters halfway through the exposure by either adding or dropping a letter.

Let's consider Chastain's first experiment, in which some three-letter words remained constant and some were changed into four-letter words by adding a single letter. For example, the word PAN could be changed to PAIN, and CAP could be changed to CHAP. Similarly, the nonwords PAH and RUJ could be changed to PAIH and RUNJ, respectively. In all cases the letters in the original word were spaced so that a new letter could be inserted in the middle without disrupting the location of any of the original letters. The words were exposed for an average duration of 87 milliseconds, with the word change taking place on half the trials after the exposure was half completed.

Figure 6.25 shows the results of this experiment. As you can see, when the word remained the same throughout its exposure, Chastain obtained the customary word-superiority effect. That is, people were able to identify the letter more accurately when it appeared as part of a word. For instance, the letter P would be recognized more accurately in PAN (a word) than in PAH (a nonword). Notice what happened to the recognition when a letter was added halfway through the exposure. Performance was much better when the letter appeared in a nonword than in a word. For instance, the letter P would be

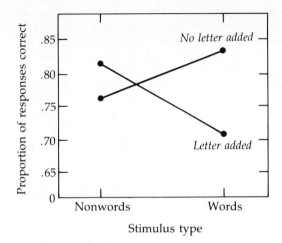

Figure 6.25 Results of Chastain's (1986) experiment, in which letter was either added or not added to nonword or word. (From Chastain, 1986. Used with permission.)

recognized more accurately when the nonword was changed from PAH to PAIH than when the word was changed from PAN to PAIN; there is a word-inferiority effect.

How does Chastain explain his results? He believes that his studies support Rumelhart and McClelland's model of excitatory and inhibitory effects, a model clearly based on the activities of neurons (McClelland & Rumelhart, 1981; Rumelhart & McClelland, 1982). According to this model there is an interaction between top-down and bottom-up processing. When a person sees fragments or features in a word, these features activate letter units. These in turn activate a word unit for that combination of letters, assuming that this word unit is present in a person's "mental dictionary." Once that word unit is activated, excitatory feedback helps in identifying individual letters. As a result, letters will be identified more quickly than if no word unit provided excitatory feedback. However, when the three-letter word was changed to the four-letter word (or the reverse), two words were activated at the same time. In the nervous system, the activation of two nearby cells can produce a mutual inhibition. Similarly, the activation of two words—which could happen when a person sees both a three-letter word and a four-letter word—could result in a decrease in the speed and accuracy of letter identification. Thus, the word-inferiority effect results when two or more words are activated simultaneously; the advantage of word context is then transformed into a disadvantage. ■

Picture and Scene Perception

Picture recognition is the subject of several books (e.g., Hagen, 1980) and many articles (e.g., Biederman, 1987). In this discussion we will see that people are highly accurate in identifying which pictures are familiar. We'll also see that scenes such as those found in pictures require certain relations to be considered normal. We'll discuss pictures again in Chapter 7 when we discuss the perception of depth and three-dimensionality in pictures. That chapter will also include a discussion of the perception of motion in static pictures.

Recognition Accuracy

Try Demonstration 6.10 to see how accurate you are in identifying which pictures you have seen in the early chapters of this book. One of the most impressive human abilities is our skill in picture recognition. For example, Shepard (1967) selected from magazines 612 pictures of familiar objects such as a typewriter, a wallet, and a flashlight. People viewed all 612 individual pictures by projecting them at their own rate on a screen. A recognition test followed in which 68 of the pictures were paired, one at a time, with a new picture. People were instructed to indicate which member of each pair they had previously seen. When they were tested immediately after the original viewing, their accuracy was 96.7%. When they were tested 2 hours later on a different set of old and new pairs, their accuracy was an incredible 99.7%! Even 4 months later, their recall was still impressive. Did you recognize Figures a, c, and f as familiar and b, d, and e as never having appeared before?

This study inspired other researchers to test the limits of human picture recognition. Standing (1973) found similar recognition rates with 10,000 pictures. Furthermore, Standing, Conezio, and Haber (1970) found that people were 63% accurate a *year* after viewing 2,560 pictures! In general, however, lower recognition rates are found in studies with a measure of recognition more stringent than the forced-choice method. (The **forced-choice method** asks observers to select between two stimuli; in this case they must select which picture they have seen previously.) Thus your accuracy on Demonstration 6.10 would have been even higher if you had been asked to select which members of several picture pairs were familiar.

Scene Perception

Irving Biederman has written extensively about the way we perceive a scence (Biederman, 1981, 1987; Biederman, Mezzanotte, & Rabinowitz, 1982). He points out that scene perception bears a striking resemblance to speech perception, an observation that adds further evidence to Theme 1 of this textbook. Both speech perception and scene perception are accomplished instantaneously and effortlessly. When you hear a scrambled sentence, it doesn't make sense; similarly, a scrambled scene doesn't make sense. Furthermore, you would be puzzled if you heard someone mention "the angry napkin" just as you would be puzzled if you saw a photo of a couch floating in the air.

Biederman (1987) specifies five important relations necessary for a scene to appear correct:

1. *Interposition*: An opaque object should cover the background.
2. *Support*: Most objects do not float in air.
3. *Probability*: Objects are more probable in some contexts than in others (as already noted in the study by Palmer, 1975b).
4. *Position*: Objects characteristically occupy specific positions—fire hydrants typically do not sit on top of mailboxes.
5. *Size*: Objects characteristically have familiar, expected sizes—ice-cream cones are not bigger than people.

Which of the following pictures and illustrations appeared earlier in this textbook, and which are new? The answers appear in the text.

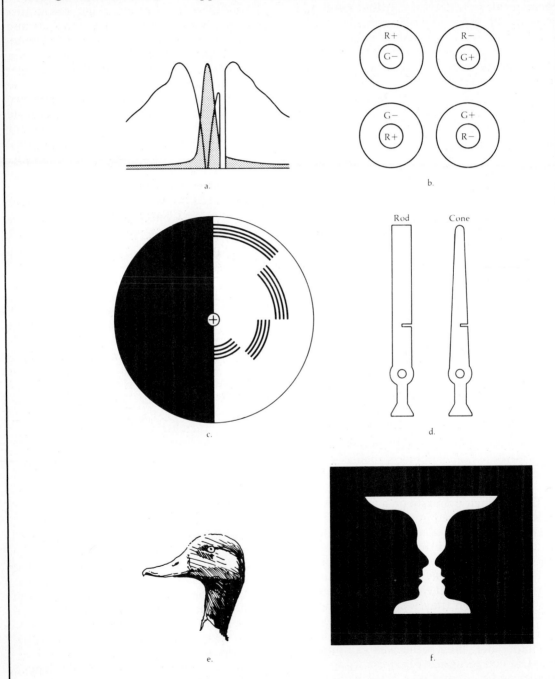

a.

b.

c.

d.

Rod   Cone

e.

f.

In other words, a scene that violates these five relations looks just like one of those "What's Wrong with this Picture" puzzles that you might have entertained yourself with as a child.

Biederman points out that a bottom-up model specifies that we must identify the elements of an object before we process more cognitive aspects of a scene, such as an object's probability or position. However, his research has shown that violations of these relations are extremely disruptive to scene perception. Instead, we seem to use the spatial relations among objects—without necessarily identifying the objects individually—to figure out whether a scene makes sense.

Summary: Pattern Recognition

1. Pattern recognition refers to the identification of a complex arrangement of sensory stimuli.

2. The prototype-matching theory of pattern recognition proposes that we compare an object with an ideal figure or prototype to see if it matches. Patterns similar to prototypes are easier to recognize.

3. The prototype-matching view is more flexible than the template-matching view, in which an object is compared to a specific pattern or template. The template-matching view is too inefficient, and it cannot handle the third dimension or fragmented objects, so it is no longer widely accepted.

4. The distinctive-features theory of pattern recognition proposes that we can distinguish among stimuli because of distinctive features. This theory has been useful in research on letter recognition, although it does have some problems.

5. The theory of spatial frequency analysis proposes that Fourier analysis can be used to break a complex scene into its component sine waves, each corresponding to a different sinusoidal grating. People are most sensitive to gratings with spatial frequencies of 6 cycles/degree, al-

though different spatial frequency channels have different ideal frequencies.

6. The theory of spatial frequency analysis can be compatible with the concept of center-surround cellular organization. Research evidence for this approach includes studies in selective adaptation and letter recognition.

7. Data-driven and conceptually driven processing probably occur simultaneously, guaranteeing rapid recognition of shapes.

8. Research has supported the importance of context in determining pattern recognition. Context can be helpful, but it can also be misleading.

9. According to the word-superiority effect (WSE), letters are perceived better when they appear in words than when they appear in strings of unrelated letters. The WSE was first demonstrated in 1886 and has been supported in numerous subsequent studies using a wide variety of experimental conditions and stimuli; it has also been demonstrated with braille.

10. If the context is inappropriate, a word-inferiority effect may be demonstrated.

11. People are impressively accurate in identifying which pictures they have seen before, even a year after the original exposure.

12. According to Biederman's theory of scene perception, five relations are required for a scene to appear correct: interposition, support, probability, position, and size.

Review

1. Why is contour important? Explain the physiological factors that are responsible for emphasizing contour.

2. Imagine that you are driving, using saccadic eye movements continuously. How would masking be important in that activity? Which would be most important—forward masking or backward masking?

3. Draw an example of a figure with a subjective contour. What are the explanations for the subjective contour in your drawing?

4. The laws of grouping apply in architecture, a topic discussed by Prak (1977). Examine the architecture and organizational structure of buildings nearby and try to find examples of as many of these laws as possible.
5. Select a magazine advertisement that illustrates a particular product against a background. Point out how the five properties of figure and ground are demonstrated in this advertisement. Similarly, look at a painting and discuss how the law of Prägnanz operates (or does not operate) in this painting.
6. Summarize the criticisms of the Gestalt approaches to perceptual organization. Where possible, think of an example to illustrate each criticism.
7. As you are driving along, you see a hand-lettered sign "EGGS FOR SALE." Describe how the following theories account for your recognition of letters in that sign: template-matching theory, prototype-matching theory, distinctive-features theory, and the theory of spatial frequency analysis.

8. Imagine that you must describe data-driven processing and conceptually driven processing to a student studying introductory psychology. Use your own words in this description, and use examples.
9. The importance of conceptually driven processing is emphasized throughout this book. In this chapter are several sections in which context is mentioned. Point out how context is important in: (a) the study by Pomerantz and his colleagues on identifying lines that either had or did not have a surrounding context; (b) the study by Palmer on object recognition; (c) the research on the word-superiority effect; and (d) Biederman's theory of scene perception.
10. Two related phenomena were discussed in the "In-Depth" section on the word-superiority effect. Define the terms word-superiority effect and word-letter phenomenon. In each case supply an example from some nearby stimuli. Explain how these phenomena facilitate reading.

New Terms

shape
contour
Ganzfeld
border contrast
Mach bands
lateral inhibition
backward masking
forward masking
dependent variable
independent variable
illusory contour
inducing areas
inducing lines
subjective contour
simultaneous brightness contrast

Gestalt approach
structuralism
laws of grouping
law of nearness
law of proximity
law of similarity
law of good continuation
law of closure
law of common fate
law of Prägnanz
figure
ground
ambiguous figure-ground relationships
phenomenological observation
pattern recognition

prototype-matching theory
prototype
template-matching theory
distinctive features
latency
theory of spatial frequency analysis
Fourier analysis
sine wave
sinusoidal grating
Fourier synthesis
square wave
contrast sensitivity function
spatial frequency channels
selective adaptation procedure
data-driven processing

conceptually driven processing

bottom-up processing

top-down processing

word-superiority effect

word-apprehension effect

word-letter phenomenon

forced-choice method

Recommended Readings

Beck, J. (Ed.). (1982). *Organization and representation in perception*. Hillsdale, NJ: Erlbaum. *This book is based on chapters written by participants at a conference on perceptual organization; it contrasts the Gestalt and information-processing approaches to this issue.*

Breitmeyer, B. G. (1984). *Visual masking: An integrative approach*. New York: Oxford University Press. *Breitmeyer is one of the most prominent researchers in the field of masking, and this book represents an extensive review of the literature and his theory of the physiological basis of masking.*

Halpern, D. F., & Salzman, B. (1983). The multiple determination of illusory contours: 1. A review. *Perception, 12,* 281–291. *This article provides a clear and comprehensive overview of the phenomenon of illusory contours.*

Kubovy, M., & Pomerantz, J. R. (Eds.). (1981). *Perceptual organization*. Hillsdale, NJ: Erlbaum. *This useful volume contains excellent chapters on the theory of spatial frequency analysis, figure-ground perception, scene perception, and a particularly helpful final chapter on perceptual organization.*

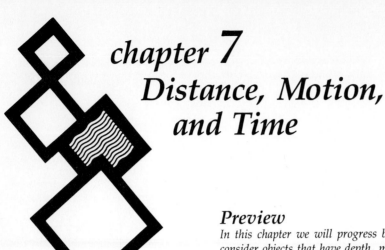

chapter 7
Distance, Motion, and Time

Outline

Distance Perception
Sources of information about
   distance
Theories of distance perception
Distance in art and movies

Motion Perception
Real movement
In-Depth: Event perception and
   biological motion
Illusory movement

Time Perception
Methodology issues in time
   perception
Research findings in duration
   estimation

Preview

In this chapter we will progress beyond flat, stationary objects as we consider objects that have depth, movement, and duration.

In the section on distance perception we will consider 12 sources of information about distance. Eight of these factors can be seen with just one eye and do not involve movement. Two factors can be seen with one eye and do involve movement. The last two factors are binocular and therefore require the use of both eyes. We will also consider two important theories of distance perception. Finally, we will see how art and movies can either use or ignore distance information.

Our visual systems encounter constant motion. Rather than a stationary retinal image, we almost always experience "retinal flow." In the section on motion perception we will see that the eyes are remarkably effective in detecting movement, even when that movement is very slow. The in-depth discussion of biological motion examines our extraordinary ability to interpret the movement of other humans, even when the only information about that movement comes from tiny lights attached to the joints. This section will also consider some aspects of people's perceptions of their own motions. We will next discuss some explanations for motion perception. The final portion of this section examines five kinds of illusory movement, situations in which people perceive that an object moves, even though it is really stationary.

The last section of this chapter considers time perception, a topic extensively researched but still puzzling. There are five common methods of measuring people's perception of time. After discussing the methods of research in this area, we will consider the results. It seems that time perception depends upon both qualities of the stimulus (for example, stimulus intensity) and activities of the participants (for example, whether the participant is simultaneously performing another task).

In Chapter 6 we considered the perception of shape. In general, we examined two-dimensional objects, simple figures whose shapes could be represented on a piece of paper. Furthermore, we only examined objects that stayed in the same place and did not move, and we only considered situations in which the observer did not move.

However, your visual world is astoundingly more complex than that. Except for reading, little of your visual activity is confined to flat shapes. You reach out in space toward a coffee cup and rotate the handle so that it is closer to you. You look out the window and see a car driving toward the horizon. You inspect a stuffed mushroom, which clearly has depth as well as height and width.

Your visual world also includes motion. You move around in the world, and your vistas change dramatically. This change is most spectacular when you are driving in scenic, mountainous country where each turn in the road presents a new view. On a more modest scale, look around you now; with a simple turn of your head, new objects pop into view. Furthermore, objects move in front of your eyes even when your own eyes are in a stable position. Look at an area with many people, such as a cafeteria, and notice the swirl of activity and motion as people move in different directions and at different speeds. There are also times at which something truly stable appears to move. Your visual world is in constant motion!

Finally, your visual world includes time. Some events are fleeting, lasting only a fraction of a second. In contrast, other events persist. As you'll learn later in the chapter, the perception of time is not constant or perfectly objective. Instead, it depends upon characteristics of the stimulus and our own activities.

Let's move beyond flat, stable shapes captured for a moment in time. We need to consider distance, motion, and time. We will discuss these three topics separately, but the separation is occasionally artificial. For instance, motion information helps us judge distance, and distance information is also related to the perception of motion. Furthermore, as you learned years ago, distance is equal to the speed of motion multiplied by time.

DISTANCE PERCEPTION

Distance perception is important in three kinds of situations. There is **egocentric distance,** which refers to the distance of an object from you, the observer. (You can remember the word egocentric because it literally means "self-centered.") When you estimate how far you are from the finish line in a race, you are judging egocentric distance. Second, there is **relative distance,** or how far two objects are from each other. When you decide that the library looks farther away than the gym, you are judging relative distance. Finally, there is **depth perception,** in which you perceive objects as three-dimensional; objects have depth or thickness in addition to height and width. Thus some parts of an object look farther away than other parts. You use depth perception as you notice the three-dimensional qualities of your desk lamp and this book. Distance is involved in all three kinds of situations, and psychologists do not emphasize the differences among these situations when they theorize about distance.

Notice how depth perception seems automatic, even unavoidable. Look at Figure 7.1, an example of an impossible figure. This figure would not be even mildly irritating if you could perceive it as a flat pattern, a random assortment of lines and curves. However, as Deregowski (1980) points out, the figure is seen as confusing or impossible because our perceptual processes interpret it as a representation of a solid figure.

Distance perception was one of the first topics to be studied by people interested in perception. Artists in the Renaissance faced a practical problem: How could they portray three-dimensional depths and distances on a two-dimensional canvas? Later, in the 17th century, philosophers wondered how hu-

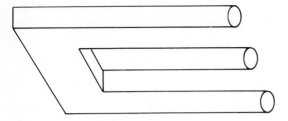

Figure 7.1   Impossible figure.

mans come to know about the world: How do we know that the world is three-dimensional if the eye appears to represent only two dimensions?

We will return to the ideas of philosophers and painters later in this section when we examine theories of distance perception and applications of distance perception. However, we will begin our discussion of distance perception by examining the sources of information about an object's distance.

Sources of Information about Distance

Before we examine psychologists' proposals about factors that influence distance perception, you may want to see how many you can identify on your own. Select two objects you can see from where you are sitting and list some reasons why you know that one object is closer than the other.

This section discusses 12 sources of information about distance. They are divided in two groups, a large group of monocular factors and a small group of binocular factors. Figure 7.2 provides a preview. Foley (1978, 1980) and Hochberg (1971b) discuss additional factors.

Monocular Factors

Most of our sources of information about distance are monocular. **Monocular factors** can be seen with one eye. Eight of these require no movement of either the object or the observer. Let us consider these first.

1. **Accommodation,** as you recall from earlier chapters in this book, is the change in the shape of the lens in your eye as you focus on objects at different distances. When you look at distant objects, the lens is relatively thin. When you look at nearby objects, the lens is relatively thick. Eye muscles that control lens shape therefore respond differently to objects at different distances. However, do we pay attention to the information that these muscles provide and use this information to make distance estimates? As Hochberg (1971b) concludes, "Seventy years of research . . . leave us with the conclusion that accommodation is, at best, a pretty weak cue to distance even at short distances" (p. 479).

Accommodation involves information provided by muscles. The remaining seven monocular, nonmovement cues have been called pictorial cues. **Pictorial cues,** or static cues, are cues that artists can use to represent distance in a picture. A **cue** is a factor that lets you make a decision automatically and spontaneously. Notice that we do not use the phrase "pictorial *clues*," because clues are factors that provide information but require a great amount of thought. (Sherlock Holmes discovered clues—not cues—and then sat down with his pipe and thought before reaching a decision.) When you see a pictorial cue, you automatically make a distance judgment.

2. **Interposition,** or overlap, means that one object overlaps or partly covers another. When interposition occurs, we judge the partly covered object farther away than the object that is completely visible. For example, your textbook looks closer to you than the desk that it partly covers. You may recall from the last chapter that Biederman (1987) proposed that a picture must obey the laws of interposition for the scene to appear correct. Furthermore, James Gibson (1982a) commented that children seem to be intrigued with interposition or concealment because they really enjoy games such as peek-a-boo and hide-and-go-seek. Both games exploit the concept of interposition, which seems to be one of the primary sources of information about distance; its value has been confirmed in perception experiments (Andersen & Braunstein, 1983).

3. **Size cues** refer to the influence of an

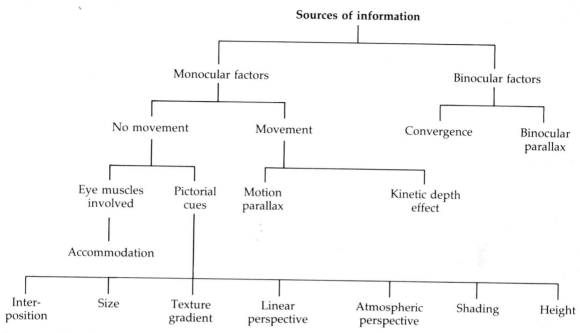

Figure 7.2   Twelve sources of information about an object's distance.

object's size upon distance estimates. If two similar objects are presented together, the object that occupies more space on the retina is judged closer. In a classic experiment, Ittelson and Kilpatrick (1951) asked people to judge which of two balloons was closer. The two balloons were actually the same distance away, and their size could be controlled by inflating them with bellows. Furthermore, the room was dark, so other distance cues were missing. People reported that the larger balloon appeared to be closer. As a balloon was inflated, it seemed to zoom forward in space. As the air was let out, it seemed to zoom backward. Thus **relative size**—an object's size relative to other objects—can be a helpful cue in telling us which of two objects is closer.

The **familiar size** of an object can also be a helpful cue because some objects are normally found in standardized sizes. For example, you know how big this textbook is. If it occupies a tiny space on your retina, you judge it to be far away. Of course, someone

might be able to fool you by showing you a giant-sized version of this book in a room with no other distance cues. You would probably estimate that it is closer than it truly is.

People who have participated in perception experiments have seen a wide variety of objects of abnormal sizes, all designed to test the effectiveness of size cues. For example, Epstein and Franklin (1965) showed photographs of three coins, a dime that was the size of a quarter, a normal-sized quarter, and a 50-cent piece the size of a quarter. Subjects judged the dime, which was bigger than normal, to be closer than the quarter. In contrast, the 50-cent piece, which was smaller than normal, was judged to be farther away.

Familiar size is an interesting topic to psychologists because some people believe that past experience is necessary for the perception of distance. Other people argue strongly that experience is irrelevant. If familiarity, or experience with an object, is an important distance cue, then the "past experience" position would be supported. Gogel (1976) has found that people's verbal reports about distances depend upon familiar size. However, when other, more subtle methods are used to obtain distance judgments from people, familiar size is not as important. In summary, familiar size is a helpful cue, but other cues are more helpful. This might strike you as strange, because most people without a background in perception think that size cues are the major factor in distance estimates. In fact, other factors that *seem* much more subtle and unimportant—such as motion parallax—are really more helpful.

4. **Texture gradient** refers to the fact that the texture of surfaces becomes denser as the distance increases, if we are viewing those surfaces from a slant. Texture gradients can be illustrated in a picture, but this source of

information has not been appreciated until recently (Gibson, 1979; Hagen, 1985; Neisser, 1981). You can also see examples of texture gradients in the picture in Figure 7.3, even though that is primarily an example of linear perspective.

Try Demonstration 7.1 to make you more aware of texture gradients in your visual world. The units that make up the texture are the same size throughout the scene, yet they look closer together in the distance than in the foreground.

James J. Gibson (1950) was among the first psychologists to emphasize texture gradients. In a way, the texture gradients provide a kind of scale by which we can measure objects. Thus a nearby object that hides three texture units is the same size as a distant object that

Figure 7.3 Examples of texture gradient and linear perspective. (Photo by Ron Pretzer.)

Demonstration 7.1

Texture Gradients

Select three places where the floor or the ground is covered with a textured surface. For example, you might choose a lawn, a room with a rug, a driveway, or a tiled floor. Look at the surface that lies immediately in front of you and note how the texture elements have distinct separations between them. Now look out toward the horizon and note how densely packed the texture elements are.

---

also hides three texture units—whether the texture units are floor tiles, strands of rug yarn, or pebbles.

Newman and his colleagues have demonstrated the importance of texture gradients. For example, Newman (1970) had subjects peek with one eye through a small hole in a viewing box. They saw two surfaces at an angle, a standard textured surface and a surface that was artificially constructed so that the texture changed rapidly from coarse to fine. When they were asked which of the two surfaces was longer, they chose the one with the rapidly changing texture. In other words, people used texture gradient as a cue to decide the distance of the far end of a surface. Newman, Whinham, and MacRae (1973) found that surface structure influenced judgments for six kinds of surfaces found in natural environments. This was true for three kinds of irregular textured surfaces (pebbles, concrete aggregate, and grass) as well as for three kinds of regular textured surfaces (paving stones, brick walls, and tiles).

5. **Linear perspective** means that parallel lines appear to meet in the distance. Look at Figure 7.3 for one example of linear perspective. The true distance between the railroad tracks remains constant, yet this distance occupies an increasingly smaller part of the retina as we see portions that are closer toward the horizon.

Cutting (1986) points out that linear perspective depends upon your point of view. If you stand on the ground and look toward the horizon, railroad tracks show linear perspective but telephone poles are parallel. Now imagine that you are in a low-flying airplane, looking down at the ground. From this different perspective, the railroad tracks are now parallel as you look straight down. However, the telephone poles now demonstrate linear perspective. The tops of the poles appear far apart, yet their bases appear close together.

6. **Atmospheric perspective,** or aerial perspective, refers to the observation that distant objects often look blurry and bluish, in contrast to nearby objects. This is because the air between you and the distant objects may not be perfectly clear. As Deregowski (1984) points out, atmospheric perspective resembles interposition. In interposition, a tree may cover part of a dog that is farther away from the viewer. In atmospheric perspective the objects that are performing this "covering" are tiny particles in the air. These accumulated particles partially obscure your view of a distant object.

Furthermore, the particles in the air slightly change the light reflected from objects, so that they appear bluish. The farther away the object, the blurrier and bluer it will appear. Color Plate 4 inside the front cover is an illustration of atmospheric perspective. Notice that the distant hills are softly blurred and faintly blue. If you look at realistic paintings of mountains, you'll see that they are also blue. This distance cue has been used by painters for centuries. For instance, Leonardo da Vinci discussed adding blue when painting distant objects.

We use atmospheric perspective as an informal scale to judge the distance of faraway places. Furthermore, we acquire a scale that is appropriate to the region in which we live. Easterners who live in humid areas and city dwellers who live in smoggy atmospheres develop a scale that does not work in the Rockies, for example. A mountain that looks blurry and blue enough to be 10 km away by their scale might really be 25 km away!

7. **Shading** is a cue provided by the pattern of light and shadows. Look at any object on your desk and notice how the lighting is definitely *not* uniform and constant across the entire surface. Shading, which provides information about parts of an object that stick out or cave inward and about flat or curved parts, gives the impression of solidity.

We are accustomed to overhead lighting. Except for the floor lights in theaters and discos, have you ever seen lighting from below? As a result, when a picture is ambiguous, we almost always assume that the lighting comes from overhead. Kevin Berbaum and his colleagues have been particularly active researchers in depth and distance perception. Their investigations have consistently demonstrated that observers looking at a picture assume that the lighting is from overhead (Berbaum, Bever, & Chung, 1983, 1984; Berbaum, Tharp, & Mroczek, 1983). Furthermore, Yonas, Goldsmith, and Hallstrom (1978) found that children as young as 3 can use information about shadows when they judge depth.

The assumption of overhead lighting can produce some intriguing results. Try Demonstration 7.2, for example, which illustrates the importance of shading in depth perception. When the picture is right side up, we see what appears to be a lake nestled in a volcano. When the picture is turned upside down, the dark shadowy area doesn't make sense as a convex shape if the lighting is from overhead. That assumption of overhead lighting is so strong that it forces the volcano to turn inside out. The shadowy area is now a concave shape from which a new, tiny volcano pops out, topped by a lake at its crest.

Just as we interpret shadowy regions as far away from a light source, we interpret highlighted areas as closer. Berbaum, Tharp, and Mroczek (1983) asked observers to judge

photographs. Their results demonstrated that apparent depth within a picture increases as the contrast between highlights and shadows increases. If you see a bright, gleaming area in one part of a figure and dark shadow in another part, you interpret that figure as having depth. In contrast, if the figure is uniformly lit, you interpret it as being relatively flat.

8. **Height cues,** or elevation cues, refer to the observation that objects *near* the horizon appear to be farther away from us than do objects *far* from the horizon. This statement may seem initially confusing, so look at Figure 7.4. Since the line represents the horizon, we interpret the triangles as resting on the ground. Notice that Triangle a is nearer the horizon, so we interpret it as being farther away from us than Triangle b. The same closeness-to-the-horizon rule applies to the clouds. Cloud a is nearer the horizon, so we interpret it as being farther away from us than Cloud b. Verify that this relationship holds true in "real life" by looking out a nearby window. Notice that objects near the horizon are far away, whereas objects far from the horizon (either at the top or bottom of your visual field) are nearby.

We discussed earlier that the texture-gradient cue was first described relatively recently. The height cue, in contrast, is literally as old as the Greeks. In fact, the first description of height cues can be traced to Euclid, a mathematician living in Greece about 300 B.C. (Cutting, 1986). Euclid is better known for developing the principles of geometry that you probably studied in high school.

Before we move on to other monocular sources of distance information, let's review the monocular/no-movement factors. The eight factors are accommodation, interposition, size, texture gradient, linear perspective, atmospheric perspective, shading, and height. Accommodation is different in that it is a muscular cue, whereas the other seven are pictorial cues. Interposition is perhaps the most basic of the pictorial cues; that's why it was discussed first. The next three factors are somewhat related to each other; faraway objects are smaller (size cue), faraway surfaces

Demonstration 7.2

Shading and Depth Perception

Look at this picture and decide which surface is closer to you (the observer). Now turn the picture upside down and decide which surface appears closer to you.

Cover from: 31 July 1970, Vol. 169, #3944. "Official USA Airforce photo by B. Pierson." Copyright 1970 by the AAAS.

have smaller distances between the texture elements (texture gradient), and faraway objects represent a fixed distance—such as the distance between railroad tracks—with a smaller space on the retina (linear perspective). Atmospheric perspective and shading are both factors that involve lighting. Finally, height cues involve the placement of objects in the visual field. This observation brings us full circle to the first of the pictorial cues, interposition, which also involves placement in the visual field.

All the depth-perception factors discussed so far involve rigid head positions and stable objects. In reality, most of our visual experience involves moving objects or moving retinas, as we turn our heads and move our bodies past objects. In fact, as Braunstein (1976) points out, motion is an extremely important source of information about distance and depth. Two kinds of distance factors involve motion: motion parallax and the kinetic depth effect.

You may not have been aware of these

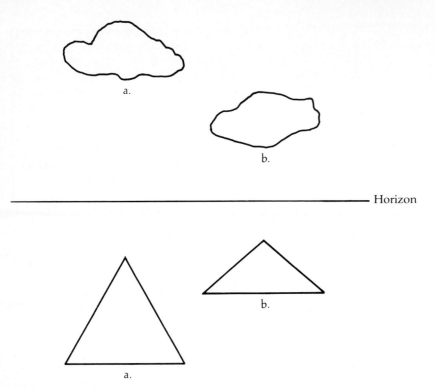

Figure 7.4 Height cues.

factors previously because they do not seem so important to nonpsychologists as some of the factors just discussed. Perhaps they are relatively unknown because they cannot be represented in a picture, and the only formal training most of us receive regarding depth perception is likely to be in elementary school art. You probably learned how to draw railroad tracks and to shade trees, but did you ever hear about the movement depth cues that cannot be drawn?

9. **Motion parallax** refers to the fact that as you move your head sideways, objects at different distances appear to move in different directions and at different speeds. *Parallax* means a change in position, so motion parallax is a change in the position of an object that is caused by motion.

Motion parallax is an excellent source of distance information (Johansson, 1974). For example, Wallach and O'Leary (1979) found that people could discriminate distances when their only available cue was parallax

caused by moving their heads. However, you may never have noticed how much information these head movements provide. Go to a window and focus on a part of the window frame. Hold your hand in front of your eyes. Now move your head to the left and notice that your hand seems to move in the opposite direction, to the right. In contrast, objects you can see out the window, which are farther away than the window frame upon which you are focusing, appear to move to the left. Thus they seem to move in the same direction as your head.

Notice that the direction in which objects appear to move is related to the fixation point, the part of the scene registered on your fovea. Objects closer to you than the fixation point seem to move in a direction opposite to your own movement. In contrast, objects farther away than the fixation point seem to move in the same direction as your own movement. When you were a child, did you ever notice that the moon seemed to be following you?

Like other distant objects, the moon often seems to move in the same direction as your own movement.

The next time you ride in a car or bus, fixate a point in the distance and notice how the speed of motion also depends upon distance. Posts on a highway that are relatively close to you seem to whiz past, whereas a billboard that is farther back—just in front of your fixation point—seems to move more slowly.

I mentioned earlier that these monocular factors that involve movement cannot be represented in a picture. As Pirenne (1975) has noted, spectators tend to move about in front of a painting. When they move, the various objects in the picture do *not* move in different directions at different speeds, as the objects in a real-life scene would. As you walk past a still life, for example, the bowl of fruit does not move to the left and the distant curtains do not move to the right. Because a picture cannot represent motion parallax, no artist can make a picture look perfectly three-dimensional to a roving spectator.

James J. Gibson (1966, 1982b) proposed that motion parallax is part of a more general motion pattern that he calls motion perspective. According to Neisser (1981), Gibson had developed an appreciation for perceptual information by the age of 8. His father worked on the railroad, so the future perceptual theorist observed with interest that the world seemed to flow inward when seen from the rear of the train, whereas it seemed to expand outward when seen from the locomotive.

According to Gibson, **motion perspective** refers to the continuous change in the way objects look as you move about in the world. As you directly approach a point straight ahead, objects on all sides seem to move away from that point. For example, as you walk between the rows of books in the library, staring straight ahead, you should have the sense of motion perspective illustrated in Figure 7.5. The importance of motion perspective in depth perception has been demonstrated experimentally (e.g., Braunstein & Andersen, 1981).

10. **Kinetic depth effect**, the second monocular-movement factor, involves the motion of objects rather than observers; a figure that looks flat when it is stable appears to have depth once it moves. Try Demonstration 7.3 to illustrate the kinetic depth effect with a rotating figure. The kinetic depth effect was first demonstrated with the shadows of rotating objects and has been explored in many other studies, according to Braunstein (1976). In one well-known set of experiments Wallach and O'Connell (1953) found that the two dimensional projection of solid blocks, wire figures, straight rods, and other figures looked flat when the objects were stationary and three-dimensional when they rotated. Similarly, a transparent sphere with dots on its surface looks solid when rotated (Braunstein & Andersen, 1984).

Notice that most other depth cues are missing in Demonstration 7.3. For example, cues such as interposition, shading, and texture gradient do not appear on the paper. Nonetheless, once the figure moves, you notice that some parts move faster than others, and they also move in different directions. This kind of movement compels you to conclude that the object casting the shadow must be three-dimensional. Once the movement stops, however, the object can be interpreted as two-dimensional.

Now that you have been introduced to all the monocular sources of information about depth, try Demonstration 7.4.

Binocular Factors

We first discussed eight factors in depth perception that did not involve movement. Then we talked about two factors in which movement was central. For all ten of these factors, however, one eye is sufficient. A person who is blind in one eye or who has lost one contact lens can perceive these ten depth factors to the same extent as a person with binocular vision. However, two binocular factors contribute to depth perception: convergence and binocular disparity. These binocular factors have been studied for more than 100 years (Foley, 1980). Like the motion-related factors discussed in the previous section, neither of these two factors can be represented in a single picture.

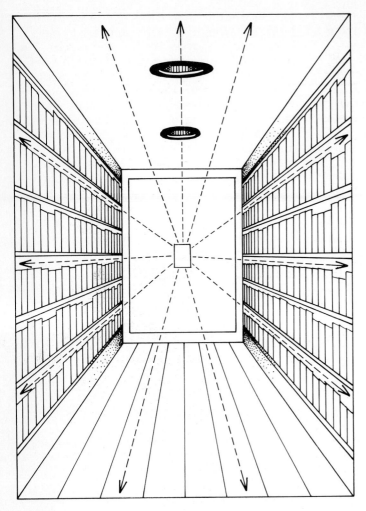

Figure 7.5 Motion perspective.

11. **Convergence,** as you may recall from Chapter 3, means that the eyes **converge,** or move together, to look at nearby objects. Demonstrate convergence for yourself by looking at a distant object on the horizon and then shifting your focus to the tip of your finger placed on the end of your nose.

If you had to design a visual system so that it would extract as much information about depth as possible from visual experiences, wouldn't it seem like a good idea to use this convergence information? Perhaps,

for example, we could calculate the distance of a particular object once we knew the distance between the eyes and the angle formed at the intersection of the two lines of sight— a wide angle for nearby objects and a narrow angle for distant ones. High school students calculate distances like these when they study trigonometry. Does your visual system calculate objects' distances in a similar fashion, although more automatically?

Actually, the answer to this question is not yet clear. There is evidence that some ob-

Demonstration 7.3

Kinetic Depth Effect

Take a pipe cleaner or a paper clip and bend it into a clearly three-dimensional figure. Find a piece of paper and a lamp. Place the figure between the lamp and the paper and notice that the figure, as seen through the paper, looks flat and two-dimensional. Now rotate the figure and notice how it suddenly appears to have a third dimension.

Demonstration 7.4

Monocular Sources of Information about Depth

Draw a picture to illustrate the pictorial distance cues. You should show a total of seven. Which monocular–no movement source of information cannot be represented in this drawing? Then turn on the television when a cartoon show is featured. Which pictorial distance cues are represented and which are not? Which monocular-movement sources of information are represented and which are not?

servers can use the information from convergence some of the time (Chung & Berbaum, 1984; Hochberg, 1971b; Yellott, 1981). However, this information is useful only for judging the distance of nearby objects. This makes sense because the degree of convergence does not change much as you change your fixation from an object 10 km away to one 9 km away. In contrast, the degree of convergence does change impressively when you change your fixation from an object 10 m away to one 10 cm away. In summary, convergence may sometimes act as a depth cue, particularly when other, more helpful cues are absent.

12. **Binocular disparity** is the second depth factor that uses information from both eyes. Your eyes are about 7 cm (3 inches) apart, certainly not a tremendous distance. Nevertheless, this distance guarantees that the two eyes will have slightly different views of the world whenever objects are at different

distances. This phenomenon is called binocular disparity.

You can illustrate binocular disparity by holding your left thumb about 15 cm (6 inches) from your eyes and your right thumb as far away as possible. Keep your head still, close your left eye, and open your right eye. Now close your right eye and open your left eye. Does your left thumb appear to jump back and forth in front of your right thumb? The reason that binocular disparity is important is that it provides the information needed to judge depth binocularly, an ability known as **stereopsis**.

Let's examine the concept of binocular disparity in more detail. Figure 7.6a shows two objects, labeled A and B, which are at different distances from the observer. Each object will be represented by an image on both retinas. However, notice that the distance between those two images is large in the case of the right eyeball but small in the case of the left eyeball. That is, the distance a_2b_2 is larger than the distance a_1b_1. There is a difference—or a *disparity*—in those two distances. Large disparities are created when two objects are far apart.

In contrast, look at Figure 7.6b, showing two objects, labeled c and d, which are equally distant from the observer. You can see that the distance between those two images is the same on both eyeballs. That is, the distance c_1d_1 equals the distance c_2d_2. There is no binocular disparity in this figure.

Figure 7.6a illustrates a large degree of binocular disparity, one that corresponds to a difference of several millimeters along the retina. Impressively, our visual system can detect differences in depth of two objects that correspond to a difference of 1 micrometer (μm) along the retina (Yellott, 1981). A micrometer is one one-thousandth of a millimeter, and a millimeter is approximately the thickness of the wire on a paper clip. One micrometer is therefore an impressively small difference, yet a binocular disparity of 1 μm can be detected. A practical application exploits our spectacular ability to detect binocular disparity: A real dollar bill can be presented to one eye, and a dollar bill suspected

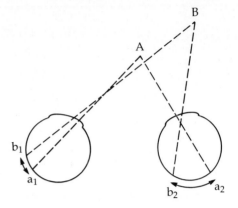

a. Binocular disparity

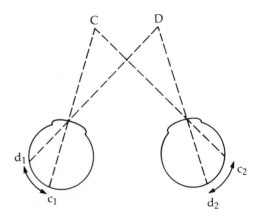

b. Zero binocular disparity

Figure 7.6 Relationship of two objects' distance from observer to binocular disparity. a, different distances, binocular disparity; b, same distances, no binocular disparity.

of being counterfeit can be presented to the other eye. If even the tiniest detail is different for the two bills, it can be detected immediately. Thus, our visual system is acutely sensitive to binocular disparity. Furthermore, Wallach (1985) argues that depth perception based on binocular disparity is innate—it is wired into our visual systems when we are born.

An important tool in exploring binocular disparity is the stereoscopic picture. We said earlier that binocular disparity cannot ordinarily be represented in a single picture. A **stereoscopic picture,** however, consists of two pictures, one for the right eye and one for the left eye. Notice how the two pictures in Demonstration 7.5 are slightly different. When each eye looks at the appropriate view and you manage to fuse the two images, you should have a sensation that one rectangle floats in front of the other.

The stereoscope was invented by Charles Wheatstone in 1838, and several authors describe the contribution of this instrument to our knowledge about depth perception (Foley, 1980; Mitchison & Westheimer, 1984; Ross, 1976). A **stereoscope** is a piece of equipment that presents two photographs of a scene taken from slightly different viewpoints—viewpoints separated to the same extent as human eyes. One photograph is seen by the right eye and other photograph by the left eye. When the two pictures are seen at the same time, they combine to make a three-dimensional scene. Stereoscopes became popular in the 19th century, and you may

have seen one in a museum. Perhaps you had a modern version of the stereoscope, called a "Viewmaster," when you were younger. If you can convince a child to lend you one, you will be impressed at the three-dimensional qualities of cartoons and landscapes.

You may recall the discussion in Chapter 3 of **strabismus,** which occurs when an object's image falls on different regions of the two retinas. If strabismus is not corrected, a person can develop **stereoblindness** (the inability to use binocular disparity information) and **amblyopia** (blurry vision in the weaker eye).

Ophthalmologists have developed a piece of equipment called an **amblyoscope** that is specially designed to test the degree to which people can fuse images presented to the two eyes (Vaughan & Asbury, 1986). For example, the amblyoscope might show a picture of a bird to one eye and a picture of a cage to the other. A person with good binocular vision will fuse these two images into a single picture of a bird in a cage.

Is binocular depth perception substan-

Demonstration 7.5

Stereoscopic Picture

Take a blank cardboard about 20 cm (8 inches) wide and line it up along the dotted line in the figure below. Rest your nose on the cardboard edge closest to you. Each eye should stare at the figure on the appropriate side of the cardboard. Try to fuse the two separate images into a single, unified image. You may find it helpful to try converging your eyes by looking slightly cross-eyed. When you achieve a single image, it should look three-dimensional.

tially more accurate than monocular depth perception? Try Demonstration 7.6 for an informal demonstration of the usefulness of binocular information. Now let's turn to the research.

One of the most active researchers in this area is John Foley at The University of California at Santa Barbara. Before discussing some of Foley's findings, it is worth returning to a point stressed in the last chapter: We need to pay attention to the dependent variable. As you will recall, the dependent variable describes the observer's behavior in the experiment. In distance perception research the dependent variable assesses the observer's estimate of the distance of a specified object. But how should these distances be estimated? One obvious dependent variable could be obtained by asking observers to report a perceived distance in either inches or centimeters. However, Foley (1977, 1985) compared these estimates with estimates obtained with another method. In this second method observers were asked to point to the apparent distance of the specified object. A horizontally placed board was located some-

---

Demonstration 7.6

Binocular versus Monocular Vision

Take an index card and cut it in half along the diagonal. Hold one piece in each hand so that the two sharpest angles are pointing toward each other. Hold both at arm's length, as shown in the illustration. Close your right eye and move the two triangles quickly toward each other, with the goal of touching the two points precisely together. Open your right eye and check your accuracy. Repeat the task with your left eye closed and again check your accuracy. Finally, repeat the task with both eyes open.

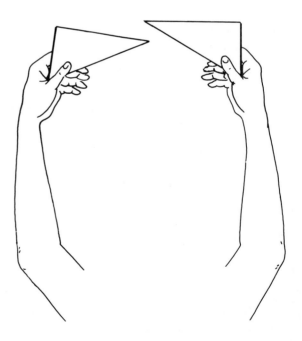

what below eye level so that observers could not see their own hands. Observers could reach out with an unseen hand and point to a particular position on the underside of the board. This pointing method produced much less variable scores, which makes it a wiser choice than verbal estimates.

Foley's research has shown that people perform significantly more accurately when they have binocular information than when they have only monocular information. This generalization, incidentally, is true whether the dependent variable is measured by pointing or by verbal estimates. However, even when people have binocular information, they are not completely accurate. Specifically, Foley (1980, 1985) found that people estimate nearby objects as farther away than they really are. In contrast, far objects are estimated as nearer than they really are.

Another group of researchers compared the accuracy of monocular and binocular depth perception by testing airplane pilots. Grosslight, Fletcher, Masterson, and Hagen (1978) asked pilots to land their planes with either normal binocular vision or with monocular vision (enforced by wearing an eye patch). The pilots were encouraged by prizes of up to $200 to be particularly accurate. The results demonstrated that monocular landings were just as accurate as binocular ones. However, the pilots judged the monocular landings to be poorer. They reported that the one-eyed landings were steeper, longer, and harder. A practical bit of advice from this study: If the flight crew members on your next plane trip are all sporting eye patches, check out the alternate flights!

It is safe to say that there is more research on binocular depth perception than in any other area in distance or depth perception. Some researchers have explored computer simulation of binocular depth perception (e.g., Marr, 1982; Poggio, 1984). Other investigations have focused on identifying the most effective kind of disparity; for example, Gillam, Flagg, and Finlay (1984) discovered that the visual system is more sensitive to vertical disparity than to horizontal disparity. Still others have tried to find explanations for

peculiar illusions in depth perception. For example, have you ever stared at a repeating wallpaper pattern—or rows of tiny dots on ceiling tiles—and discovered that part of the pattern seems to pop out toward you? Mitchison and McKee (1985) have shown that this phenomenon can be traced to a mismatching in the two retinas of repeating elements in the pattern.

DeValois and DeValois (1980) speculate that binocular vision is a particularly appealing research topic because of some potential physiological explanations for how this factor contributes to depth perception. For example, areas 17 and 18 of the visual cortex seem to have disparity-selective cells (Poggio & Poggio, 1984). As their name implies, **disparity-selective cells** have high rates of electrical discharge when stimuli are registered on different (disparate) areas of the two retinas. Some cells respond most to low levels of disparity, whereas other cells "prefer" high levels of disparity. However, disparity-selective cells have only a low response rate when they receive input from only one eye (Bruce & Green, 1985).

Now that we have discussed all 12 sources of information about distance and depth, it might be worthwhile to turn back to Figure 7.2 and review these 12 factors briefly. We began with the ten monocular factors, eight of which involved no motion (accommodation plus the seven pictorial cues) and two of which involved motion. We ended with the two binocular factors, the relatively unimportant factor called convergence and the relatively important factor called binocular disparity.

Theories of Distance Perception

There are two major theoretical approaches to distance perception, the empiricist position and the Gibsonian position. As you will see, the emphases of these two theories are different. The empiricist position stresses the contribution of memory and cognitive processes, which corresponds to Theme 4 of this book, but also acknowledges the contribution from the visual system, or Theme 3. The Gibsonian position stresses the richness of environmental input, which corresponds to Theme 2. Two other approaches to distance perception are discussed elsewhere; these include the Gestalt approach (Hochberg, 1978b; Michaels & Carello, 1981) and Marr's computational approach (Marr, 1982).

Empiricist Position

As discussed in Chapter 1, **empiricism** is a philosophical approach stating that all information is derived from sensory perceptions and experiences. We are not born knowing how to perceive distance, for example; we must acquire this skill by learning.

The empiricist position was outlined by George Berkeley in 1709 in an essay titled *An Essay Towards a New Theory of Vision*. Basically, the problem that Berkeley tackled was this: The stimulus registered in the eye has only two dimensions, height and width. Nonetheless, we also see depth or distance. How can we judge how far away an object is if "we cannot sense distance in and of itself . . ." (Berkeley, 1709/1957, p. 13)? We do have retinal *size* information—the amount of space an object occupies on the retina—but there is no equivalent way in which distance is registered on the retina. Still, we do perceive depth, so where does this perception come from?

Berkeley proposed that we can perceive distance by learning and experience. Specifically, we learn to associate various cues for distance with kinesthetic information about distance. **Kinesthetic information** is nonvisual information that includes all the muscular information we receive as we interact with objects. For example, we might feel a certain amount of muscle strain in our eyes as we look at an object close to our eyes. We receive muscular information as we reach out for an object a certain distance from our bodies or as we walk toward a distant object. Thus we know about distance indirectly because we link up kinesthetic information with various kinds of visual distance cues (the pictorial distance cues, for example). Notice that kinesthetic information is primary in Berkeley's theory, and vision is secondary.

As you might imagine, accommodation and convergence are important sources of distance information if kinesthetic information is basic to distance perception. The pictorial cues, such as interposition and linear perspective, are important learned cues. Familiar size, as we suggested earlier, is particularly relevant for the empiricist approach because of the importance of learning and experience.

According to the empiricist tradition, then, the visual world is sculpted from three spatial dimensions, whereas an image on the retina is limited to two dimensions. As Michaels and Carello (1981) summarize empiricism, "Traditional theory belittles the input, but at the same time praises the quality of the product. In such an analysis, the quality of the percept must come, in part, from the perceiver" (p. 5).

Empiricism was developed further by later theorists. Helmholtz, a 19th-century physiologist, applied the empiricist position to the issue of constancy, as we will see in Chapter 8. More recently Brunswik proposed that observers add the necessary mental structure to judge distance. For example, you perceive an object to be far away because of the converging lines in linear perspective. Depth cues act as symbols, and each depth cue is effective because it has been associated previously with other depth cues and with the kind of kinesthetic information just discussed. Sometimes the mental structure will be incorrect, and you will make errors. However, you will be right more often than you are wrong (Hochberg, 1978b).

Hochberg (1978b, 1984) has added to the depth perception theories developed by the empiricists and by Brunswik. His theory stresses the perceiver's active role in interpreting the visual world. Hochberg argues that we constantly interact with objects around us. As a consequence we develop certain expectations. When we encounter a new scene, we perceive what we *expect* to perceive. That is, we construct the most reasonable interpretation of the evidence before us, and this interpretation is what we actually see.

Many modern-day perceptual theorists

who have borrowed from the empiricist tradition prefer to call their approach a constructivist theory. According to the **constructivist theory,** the perceiver has an internal constructive (problem-solving) process that transforms the incoming stimulus into the perception (Cutting, 1986; Rock, 1983). Basically, constructivist theory proposes that the stimulus is often ambiguous, with no clear-cut interpretation. The perceiver's task is to solve the problem: What arrangement of objects in the environment is most likely to produce the stimulus registered on my retina? In Chapter 6 we saw that some theorists suggest that people "solve" illusory contour figures such as Figure 6.6 by reasoning that the most probable explanation is that a white triangle is covering the background figures. Similarly, constructivist theory proposes that people use their experience with objects at different distances to solve problems about depth perception.

This constructivist theory suggests a time-consuming process, and occasionally it is. However, as Rock (1983) explains, adult perceivers can solve perceptual puzzles rapidly because of their experience. A 4-year-old may have trouble tying shoelaces, but an adult does not because of experience. Similarly, adults can readily solve most puzzles involving distance. Notice, however, that everyday life occasionally presents distance puzzles; observe your thought processes as you attempt to solve the puzzle. Recently, for example, I saw two farm trucks in the road about one-half mile ahead of me. The scene didn't make sense; they were facing in opposite directions, yet neither seemed to change with respect to retinal image size. Were they moving slowly? Were they parked in the middle of the road? Finally, a car raced by at right angles to them both, temporarily blocking each of them from my view. Immediately, the problem was solved by this additional piece of information; two farmers had clearly parked their trucks in the middle of the road on the other side of an intersection. I was able to construct an interpretation of the scene that was consistent with all the information.

In summary, the empiricist position—in both its original and modern form—emphasizes that the visual stimulus that reaches the retina is impoverished and inadequate. Other kinds of cues and sources of information must be added for accurate distance perception.

Gibsonian Position

James J. Gibson proposed that the visual stimulus that reaches the retina is rich and full of information. Cutting (1986) summarizes the **Gibsonian** or **direct perception approach**: "Direct perception assumes that the richness of the optic array just matches the richness of the world" (p. 247). Gibson argued, in fact, that there is enough information in the stimulus to allow for correct perception. Visual information does not need to be supplemented by nonvisual information.

Gibson argued that most traditional cues—such as linear perspective, size, overlap, and atmospheric perspective—are not relevant for depth perception in real-world scenes (Gibson, 1979). He arrived at this conclusion after inspecting research on student pilots: Tests based on the cues for depth did not predict their success or failure. Therefore Gibson suspected that the traditional list of cues for depth was not adequate.

Gibson's early writing emphasized the importance of texture gradients as a source of information about distance (Gibson, 1950). As discussed earlier, texture gradients provide a scale whereby we can measure objects' distances from us.

Gibson's emphasis on texture gradients is part of his more general ground theory. According to **ground theory,** distance perception depends upon information provided by surfaces in the environment. The ground, floors, and building walls are all examples of surfaces that provide information. In the real world these surfaces help us know the distance of objects. As you look out your window, the objects you see do not float in air. Instead, the ground serves as their background, so distance can be seen directly (Gibson, 1979).

Gibson's early theories stressed the importance of texture gradients. His later work (e.g., Gibson, 1966) pointed out the importance of motion perspective, or the change in the way things look as we move through space. As we will note in the next section on motion perception, observers and objects are continually moving. This movement provides rich information about objects' depth and distance.

We have discussed the empiricist position on depth perception, which stresses how we enrich the visual stimulus with associations and expectations. This view proposes that perception involves thought, that it may occasionally be slow, and that it involves learning and awareness (Cutting, 1986). In contrast, the Gibsonian position stresses that the visual stimulus contains a wealth of information. This approach proposes that perception does not rely heavily on thoughtlike processes, that it is fast, and that it involves innate factors but not awareness.

It seems likely, as Ramachadran (1986) has pointed out, that these theories can be at least partly compatible rather than mutually exclusive. Indeed, the objects we see in natural environments probably contain much information about depth—more information than the empiricists originally envisioned. However, humans are thinking perceivers who use their associations and expectations to further enrich the visual stimulus, especially if it is ambiguous. Furthermore, both theories need to acknowledge the contribution from the visual system, as Theme 3 of this book stresses; for example, depth perception is enhanced by the cortical cells that are sensitive to binocular disparity. Depth perception therefore involves a visually rich environment, a visual system that is well equipped to register information about distance, and a thinking, problem-solving perceiver.

Distance in Art and Movies

The representation of distance in art has been widely discussed, and our survey will be relatively brief. However, if the topic interests you, chapters and books have been written by Arnheim (1974), Crozier and Chapman (1984), Deregowski (1984), Hagen (1986), and Pirenne (1975). Distance in movies has received much less coverage, but chapters by

Hochberg (1986) and Hochberg and Brooks (1978) have some discussion on this topic.

Art

As noted earlier in the chapter, artists in the Renaissance studied depth cues to help them portray distance on a flat canvas. For example, Leonardo da Vinci (1452–1519) was aware of practically all the distance and depth cues available to the painter (Hochberg, 1971b). Some artists, like Leonardo, use these cues extensively in their paintings. Other artists, however, have ignored them—either intentionally or unintentionally.

Paintings cannot take advantage of several potential distance cues. Accommodation, the two monocular-movement factors (motion parallax and the kinetic depth effect), and the two binocular factors (convergence and binocular disparity) simply cannot be represented in a flat picture that does not move.

We are left with "only" seven ways to represent distance in painting or other two-dimensional art. Distance or depth can nonetheless be portrayed effectively. Figure 7.7 is similar to a sheet of stationery sold by The Museum of Modern Art in New York; it provides the clear impression of raised surfaces appropriate for crumpled paper. Shading is the only depth cue shown, yet it provides the illusion of depth. The stationery is an example of trompe l'oeil art. **Trompe l'oeil** is French for "fool the eye," and it clearly fools the eye by creating an impression of depth when the surface is really just two-dimensional.

Now notice the painting of the woman by Constance Marie Charpentier in Figure 7.8, which uses a number of cues: size (the distant people are small), linear perspective (the lines on the distant building converge), shading (there is depth information in the woman's dress), interposition (her left arm covers part of the window and part of her body), and height cues (the distant couple is higher on the page than the woman). The full-sized picture may also show texture gradient and atmospheric perspective, but they are not obvious in this reproduction.

Figure 7.7 Example of trompe l'oeil art. (Photo by Ron Pretzer based on: *Crumpled Paper*. Designed by Judith Henry. Copyright © 1978 The Museum of Modern Art, New York. Courtesy, The Museum of Modern Art, New York.)

Other painters are not concerned about the representation of distance. Consider American folk artists. You are probably familiar with the work of Grandma Moses. A book titled *American Folk Art of the Twentieth Century* (Johnson & Ketchum, 1983) includes work by other artists as well. Figure 7.9 is a painting by Helen Fabri Smagorinsky. It shows impressive vitality and activity, but depth is not emphasized. The following cues are not shown: size (notice that the people in the background are the same size as those in the foreground), texture gradient, linear perspective, and atmospheric perspective. Shading is used to some extent. However, notice that interposition and height are clear distance cues.

Other painters deliberately try to break the rules of pictorial cues to present a dream-like, irrational image. For example, a surrealist painter may violate the interposition cue. A painting may show a faraway tree, which is close to the horizon, blocking a horse that is clearly nearby on the basis of all other distance cues.

Movies

Movies can show some depth cues that cannot be included in stationary paintings, but some depth cues are still missing. Movies offer no advantage over stationary paintings if we consider the eight kinds of monocular factors that require no movement. They cannot represent accommodation because you do not change your focus from mountains in the background to a cowboy in the foreground. However, interposition, size, texture gradient, linear perspective, atmospheric perspective, shading, and height can all be shown.

Movies also offer no advantage over paintings when we consider the binocular factors. After all, your eyes converge upon the movie screen, and they converge equally for all objects. Furthermore, except for the old 3-D movies, the same image is available for both the right and the left eye.

Movies do offer an advantage, however, when we consider the two monocular factors that involve movement. The camera can duplicate your head movements to create motion parallax. This is accomplished by a **tracking shot**, a special film technique in which the camera moves sideways along a track (Hochberg & Brooks, 1978). Figure 7.10 illustrates three representative shots from a series of frames that could be taken as the camera moves sideways. If the camera is focused on the man, the child in front of him seems to move to the left as the camera moves to the right. On the other hand, the picture on the wall seems to move to the right as the camera moves to the right.

We mentioned earlier Gibson's argument that motion parallax is part of a more general motion pattern called motion perspective, which was illustrated in Figure 7.5. Hochberg (1986) discusses how movies exploit motion perspective, so that near points move more

Figure 7.8 *Mlle. du Val d'Ognes*, by Constance Marie Charpentier. (The Metropolitan Museum of Art, Bequest of Isaac D. Oletcher, 1917. Mr. and Mrs. Isaac D. Fletcher Collection. 17.120.204.)

rapidly and far points move more slowly as the camera moves through a scene.

The kinetic depth effect is the second monocular factor involving movement, and it can also be illustrated in movies. The kinetic depth effect is most impressive when an object or a person looks two-dimensional, but then movement reveals the third dimension.

Figure 7.9 *Genesee County* (1981), by Helen Fabri Smagorinsky. (Jay Johnson, Inc., America's Folk Heritage Gallery.)

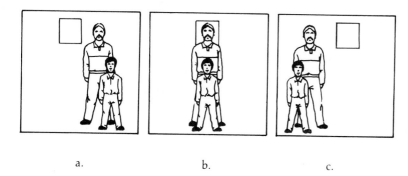

a.   b.   c.

Figure 7.10 Example of tracking shot.

In movies the picture seldom looks two-dimensional. Occasionally, however, you may see a shadow or a figure in an unlit corner that looks flat until it moves or rotates. Watch for this effect especially in horror movies.

Summary: Distance Perception

1. Most of our visual activity involves distance or depth perception.
2. Of the factors influencing distance percep-

tion, eight monocular factors do not require movement.

a. Accommodation, or a change in lens shape, is probably not an important factor.

b. Interposition means that we judge a partly covered object to be farther away than the object that covers it; it is a primary source of distance information.

c. Size (either relative or familiar) is important in laboratory studies of distance perception, but it is not vitally central.

d. Texture gradient, or the increase in surface density at greater distances, was emphasized by Gibson; its importance has been experimentally demonstrated.

e. Linear perspective, which means that parallel lines seem to meet in the distance, is an important pictorial cue.

f. Atmospheric perspective means that distant objects often look blurry and blue.

g. Shading conveys depth information because the lighting is not uniform across a surface and because objects far from a light source are more shadowy; the importance of this cue has been demonstrated in laboratory studies.

h. Height cues tell us that objects near the horizon are farther away from the observer.

3. Two monocular factors involve movement.

a. Motion parallax means that as you move your head sideways, objects at different distances seem to move in different directions; motion parallax is part of motion perspective.

b. Because of the kinetic depth effect, the two-dimensional projection of an object seems to have depth when the object rotates.

4. Two binocular factors influence depth perception.

a. Convergence, in which the eyes move together to look at a nearby object, can sometimes be a helpful source of depth information, at least for distances under about 20 ft (6.1 m).

b. Binocular disparity, in which the two eyes present two slightly different points of view, is an important source of information about distance. Binocular depth perception is more accurate than monocular depth perception. Disparity-selective cells in areas 17 and 18 of the visual cortex are probably responsible for registering binocular depth information.

5. The empiricist position on depth perception states that we perceive distance by associating various cues for distance with kinesthetic information; the visual stimulus itself is inadequate. Modern variations of empiricism, including constructivist theory, stress the importance of our expectations and problem-solving abilities in determining what we perceive.

6. Gibson's direct theory of depth perception argues that the visual stimulus is rich with information; texture gradients and motion perspective are particularly important.

7. Depth perception probably involves processes proposed by both the empiricist and Gibsonian approaches, combined with biologically based processes involving the disparity-selective cells.

8. Art can illustrate seven of the monocular–no movement factors: interposition, size, texture gradient, linear perspective, atmospheric perspective, shading, and height cues. However, painters can ignore these factors, either unintentionally or for special effects.

9. Movies can illustrate the seven monocular–no movement factors that can be shown in two-dimensional art, motion parallax (and its more general form, motion perspective), and the kinetic depth effect.

MOTION PERCEPTION

We have often used the term *retinal image* in discussing vision. However, many psychologists believe that *flow* is a better term (e.g., Johansson, von Hofsten, & Jansson, 1980; Lee, 1980). They believe that the kind of static perception implied by the term *retinal image* is artificial—it is interesting to study in the laboratory but does not describe perception in the real world. Lee (1980) describes this constant motion:

> An animal is constantly active when awake, moving around its environment, interacting with objects and other organisms, and so on. Even when simply sitting or standing still and looking at something, the body is always swaying slightly and the sway has to be actively kept in check. The result of this continual activity is that the head is always moving relative to the environment and so the animal's view of the world is constantly changing. This means that the ecological stimulus for vision is a globally changing optic array or optic flow field (p. 169).

James J. Gibson (1950) adds that our eyes are constantly changing their position in space when we walk, drive, ride, and change posture. He notes that probably the only time our heads could remain in a fixed position for any length of time is when they are artificially restrained. Outside of psychology laboratories and torture chambers, most of us don't spend much time wearing head vices.

Movement can arise from the movement of other people and objects in the world as well as from movement of the observer. As you are sitting here reading your perception book, there probably is not much movement except for your own eyes. After all, you probably chose a place to study in which there was little activity. However, think of the constant activity that you find in other situations. In the classroom the professor may walk around the room, people wiggle, and your pen moves across the notebook. In social situations we watch people approach us, move their mouths and bodies, and depart. Most entertainment involves motion—television, movies, sports, games, dancing, and so on. Try to observe the richness of movements in your visual world and notice how rarely you experience a frozen visual image!

There is also evidence that motion perception is an extremely basic aspect of vision. As Sekuler (1975) notes, "During evolution, motion perception was probably shaped by selective pressures that were stronger and more direct than those shaping other aspects of vision" (p. 387). Even in your relatively civilized life you have probably found that it is more important to respond quickly to a moving object than to recognize precisely what has moved. For example, if an object is being thrown toward your head, you detect the motion and duck. You probably don't stop to contemplate whether the object is a brick, a book, or a box. Sekuler suggests that our visual systems contain nerve mechanisms specialized for the analysis of motion because of this selective evolutionary pressure to detect motion.

Motion perception is so basic that it can be found in organisms that lack other visual skills. For example, babies can follow a moving object with their eyes as soon as they are born (Barten, Birns, & Ronch, 1971). Sekuler also remarks that sensitivity to the direction of visual motion is present in newborn mammals, although other visual functions require environmental stimulation to develop. Furthermore, he notes that when brain injuries in human adults cause the temporary loss of all visual functions, the first function to recover is often movement perception.

Motion perception is not only basic but also surprisingly accurate. When we walk, we typically do not bump into objects or fall into holes. When runners or swimmers compete, they usually do not collide. Airplane pilots almost always land on the appropriate locations in runways, and automobile drivers almost always avoid other cars. Cutting (1986) estimates that to walk without bumping into stationary objects, we need to be able to judge our direction of locomotion within 5° to 10° of visual angle. (Demonstration 4.1 can refresh your memory regarding visual angle.) Runners and automobile drivers require judgment accuracies of approximately 1°, and airplane pilots require even more precise judgment.

If you were asked to design a human visual system, how would you account for motion perception? One answer you might suggest is that we notice motion whenever the image of an object moves around on the retina. This answer is appealing, but it is incorrect. After all, the images of the words on this page are sliding all over your retina as you read, yet the page does not seem to wiggle. In this case, images move, yet we do not perceive motion. Furthermore, as your eyes follow the flight of a bird in smooth pursuit movement, the image of the bird remains on approximately the same part of your retina. In this case, images do not move, yet we perceive motion. Finally, we can sometimes see motion when the eye and the retinal image are both absolutely stationary; we will discuss this apparent movement at the end of the chapter. We must conclude that motion perception involves more than the movement of images on the retina. We will explore various mechanisms throughout this section on motion perception as we examine both real and apparent movement.

Real Movement

This part of the chapter is concerned with real movement, which involves either movement of the observer or movement of the objects and people being watched by the observer. We first need to discuss the limits of human skill in judging movement, that is, the thresholds for motion perception. Our next topic will be biological movement, or the detection of special movement patterns produced by moving humans. Then we will discuss movement of the observer. Finally, we will examine some explanations for motion perception.

Thresholds for Motion Perception

How good is the human eye in detecting motion? You cannot watch grass grow, or hour hands on clocks move, or bread rise. These movements are all too slow; the eye is impressive, but it isn't *that* good!

The **velocity detection threshold** is the minimum velocity that can be detected. It is usually expressed in minutes per second, or the number of minutes of angular velocity that an object moves in 1 second of time. Numerous methods exist for measuring velocity thresholds for a wide variety of targets (Bon-

If your head is 30 cm away from this book, you would notice motion if the circle in Figure 7.11a moved slowly from Point 1 to Point 2 during a 60-second interval.

a.

With a stationary background, you would notice motion if the circle in Figure 7.11b moved slowly from Point 1 to Point 2 during a 60-second interval.

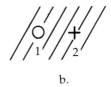

b.

Figure 7.11   Velocity detection thresholds.

net, 1982). Furthermore, thresholds are different for observers asked merely to detect motion rather than to report its direction (Bonnet, 1982; Sekuler, Ball, Tynan, & Machamer, 1982). In general, however, humans' velocity detection thresholds range between 10 and 20 minutes of angular velocity per second (Hochberg, 1971b). Figure 7.11a shows a concrete example of this threshold.

Several factors influence velocity detection thresholds. For example, moving targets are less visible when the observer is uncertain about which way the target will be moving (Ball & Sekuler, 1980). Furthermore, velocity detection thresholds are lower if there is a stationary background behind the moving object. When some parts of the visual field stay still, the velocity detection threshold for a moving object decreases to about 1 to 2 minutes per second; in other words, a background allows us to detect motion that is ten times slower than can be detected with no background. Figure 7.11b illustrates this velocity detection threshold. A children's game involves trying to move toward a goal with-

---

Demonstration 7.7

*Motion Detection in
the Periphery of
the Retina*

Stare at a point straight ahead. Hold the forefinger of your right hand directly in front of your eyes. Move it slowly toward your right, keeping the height at eye level, until you can no longer see it. Keep it stationary and make sure that you cannot see it at this location. Then wiggle your finger rapidly. It is likely that you *will* see it when it is moving.

---

out the leader's noticing. The leader can spot the movement readily because the children are moving in front of a stationary background.

Another variable that influences velocity detection thresholds is the region of the retina on which the movement is registered. You'll recall that acuity is much better at the fovea than at the periphery of the retina; this relationship was illustrated in Figure 4.2. You can tell the difference between the letter O and the letter C much better if the letter is registered on your fovea than on the edge of the retina. Usually, we are also more sensitive to motion in the fovea than in the periphery (e.g., Finlay, 1982). Occasional studies, however, cite velocity detection thresholds equally impressive in both regions. Summarizing a number of studies, Bonnet (1982) concludes: "Motion sensitivity never appears to be significantly better in the peripheral than in the central retina. In some extreme cases, motion sensitivity can be equal at different eccentricities" (p. 67).

We have said that the fovea is more sensitive to motion than the periphery. However, let's forget about the fovea for a moment and just discuss the periphery. In the periphery an object can be seen more readily if it is moving than if it is stationary (e.g., Finlay, 1982). Try Demonstration 7.7 to illustrate this point. Notice how often you tend to pay attention to things that move in your peripheral vision. For example, when you are driving, you can see a car approaching on the left or a pedestrian moving on your right. You also use your peripheral vision for moving objects in social situations and in sports. In

summary, then, velocity detection thresholds are not spectacular in the periphery, but people are much better at detecting moving objects than stationary objects in that region.

▶ **IN-DEPTH:
EVENT PERCEPTION AND
BIOLOGICAL MOTION**

The event perception approach to understanding motion was developed by James J. Gibson, a psychologist at Cornell University until his death (previous sections of this book have familiarized you with other areas of his work) and Gunnar Johansson from the University of Uppsala (Sweden), whose work in the area was first published in 1950 in a book called *Configurations in Event Perception*. Japanese researchers have joined other American and Swedish psychologists, so this area has a particularly international flavor.

Events are changes in structure over time (Warren & Shaw, 1985a). Consistent with Gibson's emphasis on natural environments, psychologists interested in event perception do not study artificial stimuli typically found in laboratories. A square of specified dimensions, color, and luminance—moving at a specified speed—would not interest them. These psychologists would point out that most motion patterns we watch in everyday life are much more complex.

For instance, Pittenger (1986) explains **event perception**:

Although there is no consensus yet on a precise definition of the field, theoretical and empirical work appearing under the name "event perception" typically involves two factors: change over time in the environment and perception of meaning. The changes over time can involve movement of objects, changes in an object's shape (as it bends, grows, breaks, etc.), and interactions among objects (as they collide, chase each other, etc.), as well as movement of the observer through the environment. This research often stresses perception of the meaning underlying motion, rather than perception of motion per se. Thus, workers in this area speak of perception of smiling rather than of change in the shape of the mouth, of collision rather than of objects moving to the same spatial location, and of walking rather than of change in limb position.

Consider the movement of humans. How does your friend's body move as she walks toward you? Her motion allows you to perceive not only movement closer to you but also more subtle changes in position as she moves her legs, swings her arms, tilts her head, and rearranges her facial features into a smile.

In this "In Depth" section we will discuss **biological motion,** or the pattern of movement of living things. We will examine how observers can guess what people are doing and who they are from subtle motion cues. We will see, too, that people are sensitive to facial movements that reveal emotions. These judgments are based on minimal information and very brief exposures, so our performance is particularly impressive.

The first research on biological motion perception was conducted by Johansson (1973, 1975), who attached small flashlight bulbs to the main joints of a male coworker; the man wore bright spots on his shoulders, elbows, wrists, hips, knees, and ankles. Johansson made a movie of this man as he moved around in a darkened room. Figure 7.12 shows the light tracks he made.

Figure 7.12 looks like meaningless streaks because it is a record of continuous movement. However, the movie showed isolated dots moving in patterns that observers could easily interpret. Johansson (1975) reports that

Figure 7.12 Projection of motion tracks made by lights fastened on head and joints of man walking in darkness. (Reproduced, with permission, from the *Annual Review of Psychology*, Volume 31. © 1980 by Annual Reviews, Inc.)

during the opening scene, when the man is sitting motionless in a chair, the observers were puzzled because they saw only a random set of lights. This pattern might have looked like a constellation of stars, but it had no meaning as long as the form was motionless. However, as soon as the man stood up and started to move, the observers instantly perceived that the lights were attached to a human being, who was invisible except for the lights. The observers could easily tell the difference between walking and jogging movements. Furthermore, they could recognize subtle peculiarities in the man's movement. For example, when he pretended to limp, they could detect it. Remember that observers can detect all this information from very few cues—just 12 tiny lights!

In another study, Johansson (1975) placed 12 lights on each of two dancers and filmed them performing a lively folk dance. Observers who watched the film immediately recognized that the 24 swirling dots represented a dancing couple! We do not need extra cues such as the contours of body parts or the continuous lines of the body to recognize complex movement. Mere spots, representing the body's joints, are sufficient.

In other work that Johansson (1975) summarizes, researchers found that one tenth of a second of watching a film was enough time to allow an observer to identify a familiar biological movement, such as walking. One tenth of a second is equivalent to two frames in a motion picture! Johansson concludes that the visual system must have fixed pathways from the retina to the cortex so that we do not have to decipher and sort out the movements each time we see a new pattern. Instead, we can recognize movements quickly, even before they reach consciousness.

Another film sequence Johansson used showed a pinpoint man doing push-ups. Johansson (1985) describes how viewers can clearly detect the elegant, forceful lifting of the body in the beginning of the sequence. As the push-ups continue, viewers note that the movement patterns change; the push-ups become increasingly shaky, slow, and irregular. Just ten dots represent the man's body, yet the actor's exhaustion is clear. Ten dots are sufficient to convey the difficulty of lifting one's body and straightening one's arms.

Johansson's intriguing findings on biological motion stimulated the interest of James Cutting, now at Cornell University, and his coauthors. Cutting and Kozlowski (1977) wondered whether people really could recognize their friends by walking styles. These researchers wrapped reflectant tape around six walkers' joints and videotaped their walking. Two months later the walkers watched the videotapes and tried to identify who was walking in each segment. Their guesses were far from perfect, but they were substantially above the chance level.

These results were intriguing, but the large number of factors underlying individual differences in gait made it a difficult topic for research. Gender seemed a more accessible factor. Barclay, Cutting, and Kozlowski (1978) selected females and males of about the same height and weight. These researchers fastened strips of reflectant tape around the wrists, arms, ankles, and legs of the walkers and attached additional strips at their waists and shoulders. The lighting was arranged so that only the tape showed, and Barclay and her colleagues took movies of each walker in motion.

The movies of the walkers were then shown to a group of viewers. Viewers, who saw each person for only 4.4 seconds, were able to guess whether the walker was male or female! Barclay and her colleagues also demonstrated that viewers identified genders accurately even when the movie image was so out of focus that all the lights blurred together.

Other research has determined a critical factor that distinguishes female from male walkers (Cutting, 1983; Cutting, Proffitt, & Kozlowski, 1978). This factor, the center of movement, is illustrated in Figure 7.13. If you stand up and walk around the room for a moment, you'll notice that your left arm stretches out with your right leg, and your right arm stretches out with your left leg; these movements cause stress lines along the diagonals of the body. The **center of movement** is the point where the stress lines cross. As Figure 7.13 shows, females have narrower shoulders and broader hips than males; as a result, females have a higher center of movement. The difference in centers of movement for males and females accounts for about 75% of the variation in gender judgments.

In other research Cutting (1978, 1983) constructed synthetic male and female walkers; the male had essentially Conan the Barbarian shoulders, and the female had unusually wide hips. Observers were even more accurate in identifying the superman as male and the superwoman as female than in identifying real people. Try Demonstration 7.8 to see the relationship between gender and gait.

If people can judge the motions of the body from a few lights, can they also judge facial emotion from such subtle cues? Think about a friend's face as it changes from a neutral expression into a smile. We tend to think that facial features on a motionless face are important cues to a person's feelings. For ex-

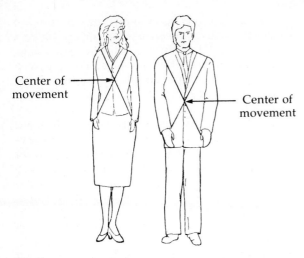

Figure 7.13   Females have higher centers of movement than males.

ample, you judge that your friend is happy if the outer corners of the mouth are raised. Indeed, static facial features do allow the recognition of emotion.

However, Bassili (1978) has argued that the motion of the face provides enough information for the recognition of emotion. Bassili adapted Johansson's techniques for use with the human face. He covered actors' faces with black makeup and scattered about 100 tiny white spots on each completely black face. Then he instructed each actor to portray six different emotions: happiness, sadness, fear, surprise, anger, and disgust. As in Johansson's studies, the camera recorded only the movement of the white spots.

Observers watched the movies and tried to judge which emotion was being portrayed. They were much more accurate than chance in their guesses. Recognition was highest for the expression of surprise and lowest for the expression of fear. Bassili describes the facial movement involved in the expression of surprise as "a sudden expansion of the lower part of the face (caused by the dropping of the jaw), along with an expansion in the lower area of the eyes (caused by the raising of the eyebrows) and a corresponding compression of the forehead" (p. 378). Thus, we watch changes as parts of the face move into new positions, and this information lets us identify an emotion.

The research discussed so far has demonstrated that people are able to use minimal

---

Demonstration 7.8

Gender Differences in Gait

Turn on a television set but turn off the volume so that you can ignore the program content. Select a program in which both males and females appear and are shown moving; a soap opera would be ideal. Notice whether you can detect observable differences in the gait of men and women. Can you detect differences other than center of movement?

information—supplied by a number of lights or dots—to draw conclusions about walking or facial expression. Runeson and Frykholm (1983), of University of Uppsala (Sweden), conducted six additional experiments that demonstrated humans' extraordinary abilities at identifying biological motion. Their first study involved judgments about people throwing a sand-filled bag. The researchers filmed a 14-year-old girl and a 34-year-old man throwing a sandbag to targets varying from 1.75 to 8.0 m (5.7 to 26.2 ft) away. As usual, they wore reflective tape at the joints, and their motions were videotaped. However, the videotape did not record the sandbag or its motion through the air. Later, observers watched the videotape and tried to guess, based only on the motion of the tape strips, how far the people had been trying to throw the sandbag.

Figure 7.14 shows the results of this study. As you can see, people are extraordinarily ac-

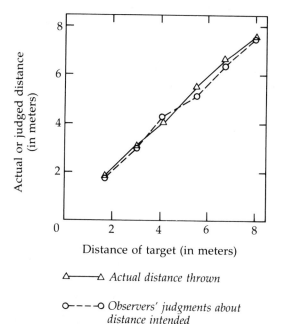

Figure 7.14 Actual distance thrown, compared with observers' judgments about intended distance to be thrown. (Based on Runeson & Frykholm, 1983.) Results are averaged for male and female throwers.

curate in their judgments; the observers' guesses almost precisely match the actual distance that the man and girl threw. An analysis of the films showed that no single feature distinguished the throws to nearby targets from the throws to distant ones. There were variations in the rotation at the elbow and wrist, in the shoulder rotations, and in the kneeling in the middle of the swing. Observers take in a rich variety of subtle information from the motion of a small number of strips of light.

In other studies in the same paper Runeson and Frykholm (1983) showed that observers can also guess (1) the weight of a box from the actor's movements before lifting it, (2) whether the actor is trying to deceive the observer about the weight of the box, and (3) additional subtle factors about gender.

Johansson (1985) points out the irony that biological motion is mathematically complex yet easy for our visual system to process. In contrast, motion that can be described with mathematically simple equations seems to be more difficult for our visual system. Furthermore, Johansson (1985) and Ullman (1983) note that biological motion is ecologically important for the survival of other species, not just for humans. Animals need to recognize the motion of other animals to recognize which animal is a potential mate, which a potential *dinner*, and which a potential *diner*.

At present, psychologists have accumulated a good number of studies testifying to humans' accuracy in judging biological motion. However, the state of our knowledge is more descriptive than explanatory (Lappin, 1985). Johansson (1975, 1985) has suggested that visual systems from the earliest stages of evolution are neurally organized to decode optic flow patterns in an efficient and accurate manner. But are humans born with the ability to appreciate biological motion? Is our visual system prewired to pick up subtle information about the way living organisms move? Researchers have determined that newborn babies do not seem to be sensitive to biological motion. However, at some time between 6 and 9 months babies can look at a display of moving lights and interpret the pattern as the motion of a person (Berthenthal, Proffitt, Spetner, & Thomas, 1985; Fox & McDaniel, 1982). Thus, the appreciation of biological motion seems to develop during the first year of life. ■

Movement of the Observer

So far we have discussed the movement of objects and the impressive ability of the human visual system to detect it. In this section we will examine situations in which the observer—rather than an object—is moving.

As Andersen (1986) notes in his review of self-motion, complex patterns of optic flow are created by object motion combined with observer motion. Even though these optic flow patterns are complex, the human visual system can usually determine what is moving—the observer, the object, or both.

Some of the most interesting research on observers' movements has examined people's perceptions of their movement speeds, particularly when they are driving. However, some researchers have examined how the movement of the observer can impair judgments about the speeds of other moving objects. For example, a study by Probst, Krafczyk, Brandt, and Wist (1984) contrasted motion perception for people driving on highways (and therefore moving) with motion perception for people in a laboratory. The people in the laboratory were not moving but had some of the visual information that had been available to the highway drivers. Probst and his colleagues found that when people ride in a vehicle, their thresholds for motion of other vehicles are substantially raised. These authors note that 50% of automobile accidents involving rear-end collisions occur when the difference in velocity between the two vehicles is less than 30 miles per hour (48 kilometers per hour). It seems that when people themselves are in motion, they are not sensitive to subtleties about the motion of other vehicles. Probst and his coauthors suggest that drivers should therefore pay particular attention to brake lights. They also recommend additional brake lights at eye level, a recommendation that some automobile manufacturers are now adopting.

We said that humans can usually determine from optic flow patterns whether they are moving or whether other objects are moving. However, this kind of distinction is sometimes difficult, and we can make mistakes. Perhaps this has happened to you. You may have stopped your car in traffic and then sensed that you were moving. You step on the brake firmly, yet you still appear to be moving. Then you look around and discover that other cars are moving, and your car is in fact stationary. You may have had a similar experience in a train, especially if you were expecting your own train to move soon. The perception that you are moving when you are really stationary—and other objects are moving—is sometimes called the **self-motion illusion** or visually induced self-motion. It was initially described by such illustrious early researchers as Mach—of the Mach bands—and Helmholtz (Andersen, 1986).

In general the self-motion illusion is more likely when other objects move in your peripheral vision than in your foveal vision (Dichgans & Brandt, 1978). This description may match your own experience with this illusion. When you are driving, your foveal vision may be directed toward the dashboard, and the optic flow pattern that convinces you that you are moving comes from the periphery of your retina.

In the self-motion illusion the optic flow information tells us we are moving, yet information from the vestibular system tells us that we are stationary. (As you will learn in Chapter 11, the vestibular system is responsible for your sense of upright posture and feeling of balance.) This mismatch of information from the two systems can result in motion sickness (Andersen, 1986). As Leibowitz, Post, Brandt, and Dichgans (1982) observe, passengers who ride in the back seats of automobiles are more likely than the driver to feel nauseated, since they experience mismatched information. They are primarily watching the interior of the car, which is not moving relative to their own eyes. Nevertheless, their vestibular system tells them they *are* moving. The driver, however, experiences optical flow from the panorama visible from the front seat, and this visual information matches the vestibular information. As a result, drivers seldom experience motion sickness.

In summary, we first explored the movement of the observer. We noted that motion perception is less sensitive when the observer is also moving. Then we discussed the self-motion illusion and saw that a conflict between visual and vestibular information can be, quite literally, a nauseating experience. Now that we have examined both the movement of objects and the movement of observers, we need to look at theoretical explanations for motion perception.

Theoretical Explanations for Motion Perception

Several explanations have been proposed for motion perception. Some emphasize that neurons register motion; others stress that the feedback from the body allows us to identify whether the observer or other objects are moving. Additional explanations emphasize the visual information available from the stimulus.

1. Motion-sensitive neurons. A physiological explanation for motion perception has not been completely developed. In comparison with our knowledge of the physiology of color vision, for example, we know relatively little about the physiology of the perception of movement in humans. Researchers are reasonably well informed about the perceptual experiences of humans and the physiology and anatomy of the visual system in animals such as the rabbit and the cat. However, these animals' visual systems are different enough from our own that information about rabbits and cats may be irrelevant (Berkley, 1982). Summarizing the literature on neural explanations for motion perception, Berkley believes that there is little coding of motion perception at the level of the retina. Moving to higher levels in the visual processing system, Berkley proposes that the superior colliculus has an important role in motion perception. For instance, cells in the superior colliculus respond to visual stimulation when the eye

is stationary but not when it is moving. These cells may help to distinguish between situations in which the observer is moving and those in which the stimuli are moving.

Complex cells in the cortex seem to respond only when a stimulus moves in a particular direction. Furthermore, cells in the higher levels of visual processing respond best to different velocities. The situation is clearly complex, however, because animals and humans with cortical lesions may be able to detect motion just as accurately as an observer with a normal cortex—even though they can no longer detect shapes (Berkley, 1982). Berkley concludes that motion perception clearly involves several neural areas, but more questions than answers now exist about their precise contributions.

2. Corollary discharge theory. A second class of explanations emphasizes information generated by the visual system. One such explanation is called corollary discharge theory. According to **corollary discharge theory**, the visual system compares the movement registered on the retina with any signals the brain might have sent regarding eye movement (Richards, 1975; von Holst, 1954). Corollary discharge theory specifically tries to explain why we *don't* perceive movement during normal eye movements.

Let's consider an example. Suppose you are looking at a picture and you decide to move your eyes to the right. The image of that picture will slide across your retina during eye movement; why don't you perceive the picture as moving? Corollary discharge theory argues that your brain sends a message to your eye muscles, commanding them to move to the right. At the same time the brain sends a copy of this message to a structure in the visual system. This copy is called a corollary discharge; the word *corollary* means "related." The structure in the visual system to which the corollary discharge is sent has not yet been identified by researchers; it is simply called *comparison structure* in Figure 7.15, which shows a simplified representation of the process. When the eyes actually move to the right, the movement produces a

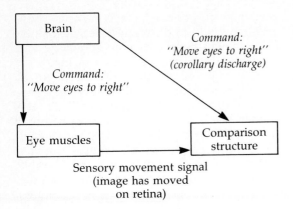

Figure 7.15   Schematic representation of corollary discharge theory.

sensory movement signal sent to the comparison structure. This structure compares the two messages (that is, the corollary discharge and the sensory movement signal); if they are identical, the sensory movement signal is cancelled. Because of this cancellation, the picture looks perfectly stable; no movement is perceived.

Suppose, however, that you are looking out the window and a car drives by; the image moves across your retina. Your brain did not send any message to the eye muscles or any corollary discharge. The comparison structure therefore receives only the sensory movement signal of the movement across the retina. Without a corollary discharge, that signal remains; movement is therefore perceived.

Corollary discharge theory suggests that you'll perceive movement if there is no corollary discharge. You can demonstrate this motion perception by placing your finger on your lower eyelid and pressing gently. Notice what happens when your eye is moved passively, by your finger, rather than through your brain's normal commands to the eye muscles. As Bridgeman and Delgado (1984) explain, there is a mismatch between the moving retinal image and the lack of corollary discharges. We saw earlier that a mismatch between visual and vestibular information causes motion sickness, an abnormal condition. Similarly, the mismatch that occurs

when you move your eye passively also causes an abnormal condition: A stable object appears to move.

Incidentally, corollary discharge theory is just one explanation that uses the concept of feedback in explaining motion perception. Others are discussed by Matin (1982) and Morrison (1984)

3. Information in the stimulus.   Gibson and others who favor the direct perception approach have argued that the stimulus is rich with information about movement, a claim consistent with the second theme of this textbook. In contrast, the first two kinds of explanations of motion perception (that is, motion-sensitive neurons and corollary discharge theory) offer praise to the visual processing system. (This praise is, of course, consistent with the third theme of this book.) In this current section we will examine six sources of information available from the stimulus.

For example, we can tell whether we are moving or whether an object is moving by noticing whether the object's background moves. Notice in Figure 7.16a that the woman is always in front of the painting. Because the woman does not move in relation to the painting, you conclude that she is stationary and you—the observer—are moving. In Figure 7.16b the woman is moving in relation to the background: In the first picture she is to the right of the painting, then she moves in front of the museum guard, and finally she moves in front of the doorway. As the observer you would conclude that she is moving and you are stationary.

Furthermore, moving objects show a systematic covering and uncovering of the background. Pick up your textbook and move it from right to left in front of your eyes. It systematically covers up the background on the left; this process is called **occlusion**. At the same time it systematically uncovers the background on the right; this process is called **disocclusion**. Occlusion and disocclusion tell us the direction of objects' movement (Gibson, 1979).

Objects that move toward us also show a systematic occlusion and disocclusion pat-

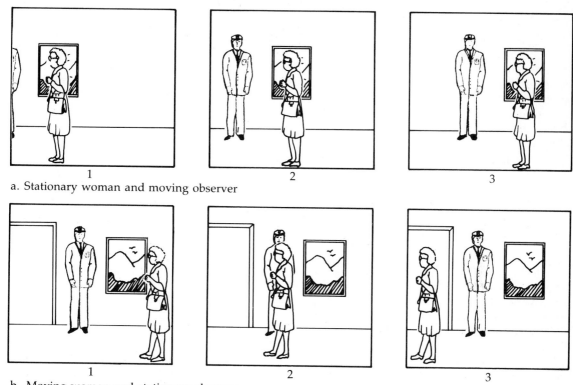

a. Stationary woman and moving observer

b. Moving woman and stationary observer

Figure 7.16 Information about motion that is available in stimulus.

tern. Pick up your textbook again and move it toward you so that it is about to hit your face. Notice how the occlusion occurs to the same extent on both the right and the left side of the book. When the occlusion is equal, we perceive that an object is coming directly toward us. Other times the occlusion is not equal—for instance, when you move your book toward your left ear. In this case the left side of the background becomes occluded at the same time as the right side becomes disoccluded. You perceive that the object will miss you. If the occlusion is extremely unequal, then the object will miss you by a large distance.

The next time you are playing a game such as volleyball, notice how this occlusion/disocclusion process works. You hold your hands in front of your face and move your body so that the occlusion pattern is equal on the right and the left. The ball appears to be coming directly at you. On the other hand, if

someone is throwing a snowball at you, you move your head so that the occlusion patterns are unequal, and the snowball will miss you. Notice, then, that you—the perceiver—can control what you perceive by adjusting your body.

The size of the image also increases as you approach objects and they approach you, as Regan, Beverley, and Cynader (1979) have described. Notice that image size is a monocular cue. Regan proposes that the strength of monocular cues such as image size explains how some pilots and ballplayers can continue to perform effectively after they have lost their vision in one eye. Their professions depend upon successful motion perception, yet they have enough information about motion from monocular cues. Have you ever noticed how motion is shown in cartoons? Someone falls off the cliff, and the features on the ground below expand suddenly until we see the final "splat!" from a side view. Thus cartoonists successfully exploit the image size cue for motion.

We discussed two other aspects of motion in the section on distance perception; both are relevant when observers are moving. Remember that motion parallax occurs when you move your head, and objects at different distances from your head appear to move in different directions. Goodson, Snider, and Swearingen (1980) have demonstrated that motion parallax is a very important cue to motion.

Motion perspective, also discussed earlier, is a more general term that includes motion parallax. As you drive down a road, motion perspective occurs as images of objects flow across your retina at different rates. If you look straight ahead, for example, nearby objects on either side of you flow by quickly; objects farther away flow slowly. Parts of the world expand and contract as you move around. The next time you are in a car, look straight ahead at a point on the horizon and notice how everything seems to expand outward from that point.

Motion perspective is clearly a useful source of information about motion. Even when we move so fast that the visual flow looks more like a visual blur, motion perspective is still useful (Harrington, Harrington, Wilkins, & Koh, 1980). However, there is a recent controversy among researchers because we sometimes gaze in a different direction from the one toward which we are moving (Regan & Beverley, 1982; Priest & Cutting, 1985; Regan, 1985). The resolution to this controversy is not yet clear. Nevertheless, motion perspective provides valuable information in most circumstances.

We have been discussing monocular cues so far. Corollary discharge theory can apply to one eye; background information, the occlusion/disocclusion process, image size, motion parallax, and motion perspective can also work with one-eyed vision. Regan and his coauthors (1979) point out that binocular cues are also helpful in motion perception. As a ball moves toward you, for example, the image moves at the same speed on both your right and left retinas. However, if the left ret-

inal image is moving more slowly than the right retinal image, then you perceive that the ball will pass toward your right side. Thus comparison of the speeds of the left and the right retinal images gives you information about the direction of movement. Regan and his coauthors describe several experiments that confirmed the usefulness of binocular cues when we watch moving objects.

In this discussion of explanations of motion perception we have mentioned many possible mechanisms. First we discussed a physiological mechanism, motion-detecting neurons. Then we talked about how the corollary discharge process could cancel the sensation of movement when your eyes move across a scene. Finally, we talked about six aspects of the stimulus that provide information about motion: the background, the occlusion/disocclusion process, image size, motion parallax, motion perspective, and binocular cues.

As you might expect, people disagree about which of these mechanisms are most important. Sekuler (1975), for example, argues that the physical aspects of the stimulus cannot fully explain motion perception: "We cannot reduce motion perception to obvious aspects of the stimulus. We must consider the contribution of our sensory apparatus" (p. 390). On the other hand, it is clear that aspects of the stimulus are sometimes sufficient to give the experience of motion, even when there are no muscular cues. For instance, have you ever seen a movie in Cinerama or on a very large screen? I recall seeing a Cinerama movie shot from a roller coaster. The audience gasped collectively at the sensation of motion we all felt.

These explanations for motion perception have stressed the richness of the stimulus (Theme 2) and the spectacular construction of the human visual processing system (Theme 3). In contrast, Theme 4 hasn't been mentioned yet. Where is the contribution from cognitive processes in motion perception? The answer is that cognitive processes such as memory and expectation may play a minor role in motion perception. However, motion perception takes place extremely rapidly, as the studies on biological motion demonstrated. Furthermore, motion perception can be fairly impressive, even in organisms with very primitive visual systems. Johansson (1982) asks us to consider the housefly, an organism not known for its impressive cognitive ability. Johansson describes how the male and female fly perform the mating procedure. The female partner circles around in a random path while the male partner follows the same pattern several inches above her. Johansson remarks that the male housefly's amazing accuracy in motion perception is far more perfect than that of airplane pilots. Certainly our cognitive processes are important in the interpretation of motion, but many aspects of motion perception clearly can be accomplished without thought or memory.

Illusory Movement

In our discussion so far we have stressed how observers and objects move continuously. For some reason, however, perception researchers have often been even more interested in illusory movement than in real movement. In **illusory movement** observers perceive that an object moves, even though it is really stationary. You'll recall that we discussed illusory perception in previous chapters. For example, in Chapter 5 we looked at subjective colors in which black-and-white stimuli create the impression of color. In Chapter 6 you learned that Mach bands create the impression of light and dark areas that are not really there. In that chapter you also saw that illusory contours could be created in designs that lack real ones.

Illusory movement is not very common in our everyday experiences, yet it occurs often enough to justify a brief discussion. In this section we will examine five kinds of illusory movement.

Stroboscopic Movement

Stroboscopic movement is the illusion of movement produced by a rapid pattern of stimulation on different parts of the retina. In a typical demonstration of stroboscopic movement, a light flashes on briefly at one lo-

cation. Less than a tenth of a second later another light flashes on briefly at a different location. Observers usually report that the light seems to move from the first location to the second. The first serious investigation of this phenomenon was initiated by Max Wertheimer, the Gestalt psychologist you read about in Chapter 6.

If the spatial separation and the timing of the two stimuli are just right, stroboscopic movement can be a powerful movement illusion, but the illusion won't work if the situation is not ideal (Burt & Sperling, 1981). The timing of the two light flashes must be precise. With some stimulus conditions, for example, an interval of about 60 milliseconds is ideal to produce the perception of an object moving through space. Intriguingly, an interval of about 100 milliseconds in those same conditions may the sensation of **phi movement,** in which observers report that they see movement, yet they cannot perceive an actual object moving across the gap. If the interval is longer than about 200 milliseconds, there is no apparent movement.

Motion pictures use stroboscopic movement to give the impression of movement (Anstis, 1978). Movie film is like a series of snapshots pasted together, as in Figure 7.17. Have you ever wondered how a series of isolated snapshots can give the impression of movement? Observers perceive movement because the movie projector exposes each frame in the series very quickly, so that there is stroboscopic movement of the dog's paw in Figure 7.17 from position 1 to position 2. You perceive movement from one place to the next, rather than a succession of static views (Hochberg & Brooks, 1978).

Naturally, the projector speed must be just right. If the speed is too fast, you may perceive a blur. If it is too slow, you will see the separate frames of the movie, and there will be a flicker. You can demonstrate the importance of projector speed if you have a movie viewer, an inexpensive piece of equipment that home movie makers use to review their movies. You control the speed of the movie by hand, and the impression of movement is achieved by finding the ideal speed,

Position 1

Position 2

Figure 7.17 Stroboscopic movement from frames of movie film.

less, Brer Hedgehog was at the 1-mile mark ahead of him. Brer Rabbit ran even faster over the second mile, but once again Brer Hedgehog reached the 2-mile mark first. At every milestone along the track Brer Hedgehog arrived first, so Brer Rabbit lost the race. Brer Rabbit did not realize that there were really six hedgehogs, Brer Hedgehog, Mrs. Hedgehog, and four hedgehog children. Brer Rabbit's movement was real, but the hedgehog's movement was illusory. That illusory movement depended crucially on the fact that all hedgehogs look enough alike to correspond to one another.

Perception researchers do not typically use hedgehogs for experimental stimuli; geometric figures are more common. Berbaum, Lenel, and Rosenbaum (1981) found that observers saw smooth illusory movement when the two figures were highly similar to one another (for example, a square and a parallelogram). The movement was significantly less smooth when the figures were dissimilar (e.g., a square and a triangle).

Other researchers have been interested in the interaction between real and apparent movement. Real movement can enhance the strength of apparent movement when the two movements are in the same direction (Green, 1983). In other conditions, real and apparent movement can cancel each other out (Gregory & Harris, 1984). In addition, Berbaum and Lenel (1983) discovered that real objects, placed in the path of apparent movement, may deflect motion from a straight path: The apparent movement takes a curved path around the object.

Autokinesis

Autokinesis occurs when a stationary object, with no clear background, appears to move. Try Demonstration 7.9 to see whether you can experience autokinesis. Hochberg (1971b) notes that the autokinesis effect was first reported by astronomers who found that the stars they watched through telescopes seemed to drift. Incidentally, Sharma and Moskowitz (1972) reported that the autokinesis effect increased after their observers had smoked marijuana.

One explanation for autokinesis is that it

intermediate between the blurs and the flickers. Also, some children's books show cartoon characters in a sequence of frames in the upper corner. If you thumb through the pages at just the right speed, you may see a mouse juggling.

Anstis (1980) tells an Uncle Remus story to illustrate how we can obtain an impression of illusory movement even when the stimuli are somewhat different from one another. You may recall the story in which Brer Rabbit challenged Brer Hedgehog to a 5-mile race. Both animals started at the same time, and Brer Rabbit ran as fast as he could. Nonethe-

---

Demonstration 7.9

Autokinetic Movement

Find a flashlight that has opaque sides so that light shines out only through the front. Take a piece of opaque cardboard and poke a tiny hole in it with a pin. Attach it to the flashlight so that the only visible light shines through the pinhole. Find a totally dark room and turn on the flashlight. Place it about 2 m (6.6 ft) from you so that you can clearly see the tiny spot of light. Fixate the light steadily for about 2 minutes. The light may appear to move slightly.

---

is caused by the spontaneous tiny movements of the eyes. Do you remember the involuntary eye movements discussed in Chapter 4—particularly the miniature drifts when you try to fixate on something? If your eyes drift without your voluntarily controlling them, there will be no corollary discharges to cancel out the perception of movement. As a result, you will see movement.

Other evidence for the eye-movement explanation of autokinesis comes from a study by Pola and Matin (1977). These researchers placed a contact lens on the eye and recorded eye movements. They found a systematic relationship between the direction of the target's apparent movement and the eye movements they recorded.

As you might expect, the autokinesis effect is reduced if another, similar stimulus is nearby. For instance, when a second stimulus is 1 degree from the fixated stimulus, autokinesis is reduced by about 50% (Post, Leibowitz, & Shupert, 1982). Also, when observers were told to expect movement in a certain direction, the stimuli did actually tend to move in that direction (Leibowitz, Shupert, Post, & Dichgans, 1983).

Would you believe that personality psychologists have also been interested in autokinesis? Rechtschaffen and Mednick (1955) presented a pinpoint of light and told observers that the moving light would write words. In fact, the light was really stationary. The observers were encouraged to guess whenever they could not make out every letter of a word. All the observers reported words being written by the point of light—an average of 15 words per person. Some observers reported an astonishing number of words. One person reported that the light "wrote":

> When men are tired and depraved, they become mean and callous individuals. When men learn to master their souls, the world will be a more humane and tolerant place in which to live. Men should learn to control themselves (p. 346).

The autokinesis effect seems to be an interesting projective technique in which people respond to relatively unstructured and ambiguous stimuli. It's like a combination of a Rorschach inkblot test and a Ouija board!

Induced Movement

Induced movement occurs when a visual frame of reference moves in one direction and produces the illusion that a stationary target is moving in the opposite direction. The next time the moon is bright and there are some clouds in the sky, see whether you notice any induced movement. The moon is essentially stationary, yet the clouds are moving in front of it. Consequently, the moon many appear to move in a direction opposite to the clouds' motion.

Many astronomers believe that induced movement, perhaps in combination with autokinesis, is responsible for the majority of Unidentified Flying Object reports. People look up at a star against the background of moving clouds, and it appears to drift noticeably.

In the section on autokinesis we discussed how involuntary eye movements may at least partially explain this phenomenon. Post and

Leibowitz (1985) have developed a theory to explain autokinesis, induced movement, and other phenomena, which involves another kind of eye movement. These authors suggest that whenever our eyes make the kind of smooth pursuit movements discussed in Chapter 4, the visual system produces a neural signal (similar to the corollary discharges mentioned as an explanation for motion perception). Suppose your eyes are tracking a robin streaking through the sky. The presence of this neural signal—in combination with the stationary image of the bird on a particular part of your retina—tells you that the bird is in motion. However, Post and Leibowitz argue that these smooth pursuit movements can explain the perception of illusory movement as well as real movement. They cite research to indicate that the pursuit system is activated during autokinesis and induced movement. A neural signal is produced when this pursuit system is activated. As with real movement, the presence of this neural signal—in combination with the stationary image of the stimulus on a particular part of the retina—tells you that the stimulus is in motion. This theory is recent, and it will be interesting to see whether further research continues to support the argument that similar mechanisms can explain both real and illusory movement.

Movement Aftereffects

Movement aftereffects occur when you have been looking at a continuous movement and then look at another surface; that surface will seem to move in the opposite direction. You might try to demonstrate movement aftereffects if you can visit a waterfall. Stare for several minutes at the waterfall, then turn your gaze toward the nearby bank. The rocks and plants will seem to move upward in a compelling fashion. Try Demonstration 7.10 to see another example of movement aftereffects.

Movement aftereffects resemble the successive color contrast and achromatic afterimages discussed in Chapter 5. The explanation for those phenomena probably involves some kind of adaptation or fatigue of cells involved in visual processing. A similar kind of adaptation may be involved in movement aftereffects. The response rate of motion-sensitive cells may be depressed after they have been stimulated for a long time (Sekuler, 1975). However, movement aftereffects cannot be entirely explained by simple, low-level mechanisms, because at least in some cases, a higher-level, less peripheral process must be involved (Weisstein et al., 1982).

Movement in Pictures

In the comics section of your newspaper you have probably seen illustrations of static figures that show motion. However, as Friedman and Stevenson (1980) note, researchers have generally ignored the topic of movement in pictures. Of course, movement occurring over time cannot really be captured in a static representation. We cannot really be fooled by pictorial movement as we might be fooled by pictorial depth. Still, a picture can often convey some sense of movement, as in Figure 7.18.

If you are interested in art, read Friedman and Stevenson's article on the perception of movement in pictures. They examined paintings from many cultures and many historical periods to look for consistencies and differences in the depiction of movement. They found, for example, that Greek vase paintings were particularly likely to show movement.

Photographs can also convey motion. If you enjoy photography, you should look at Zakia and Todd's (1969) book, *101 Experiments in Photography*. One section tells how to adjust the shutter speed of your camera to give the impression of movement.

In this section we have examined five kinds of illusory movement: stroboscopic movement, autokinesis, induced movement, movement aftereffects, and movement in pictures. In all these cases the object and the observer are stationary. Nonetheless, movement is perceived. In apparent movement effects, our perceptions do not match the true qualities of objects. We will see other examples of the differences between our perceptions and reality in the next chapter, "Constancy and Illusions." First, however, we must consider time perception.

Demonstration 7.10

Movement Aftereffects

Make a photocopy of the spiral shape. Glue it onto firm cardboard and cut out the spiral. Poke a hole in the center and place the figure on a phonograph turntable. Turn on the phonograph at a speed of 33⅓. Stand directly over the rotating figure and fixate it for 1 to 2 minutes. Then turn off the phonograph and hold the turntable stationary. The spiral should seem to be moving in a direction opposite to its previous motion, even though nothing is really moving.

Summary: Motion Perception

1. In the real world, static perception is rare; motion perception is an important aspect of vision. It is both basic and accurate.
2. Velocity detection thresholds are influenced by several factors:
   a. uncertainty about direction of movement;
   b. presence of a stationary background; and
   c. region of the retina on which the movement occurs.
3. The event perception approach to motion perception focuses on the change in the environment over time and the perception of meaning; biological motion perception is a representative research area.

4. Observers can quickly identify a person's actions by watching the movement of lights attached to the person's main joints; they can also recognize friends by their walking styles.
5. Observers can identify a person's gender by his or her walking style; an important factor appears to be gender differences in the center of movement.
6. Observers can judge facial emotion, the distance that an object will be thrown, and the weight of a box that is going to be lifted on the basis of information conveyed by spots of light.
7. When observers are moving, they are less able to judge the movement of other objects.
8. The self-motion illusion is generally more

Figure 7.18 Apparent movement in static picture.

likely to occur when objects move in peripheral vision.

9. Two explanations for motion perception involve motion-detecting neurons in the visual cortex and corollary discharge theory, which proposes that the visual system compares the movement registered on the retina with any signals the brain may have sent about eye movements.

10. A third explanation for motion perception involves information available from the stimulus: background information, the occlusion/disocclusion process, image size, motion parallax, motion perspective, and binocular cues.

11. Five kinds of apparent movement include the following:
    a. Stroboscopic movement is produced by

sequential presentation of stimuli at different locations on the retina; the distance and timing between the stimuli are crucial, but the stimuli can have somewhat different shapes.

b. Autokinesis, or spontaneous apparent movement of a stationary object, can be influenced by nearby stimuli and by instructions.

c. Induced movement occurs when a visual frame of reference moves; autokinesis and induced movement may both be caused by factors related to eye movements.

d. Movement aftereffects occur after watching continuous movement.

e. Movement can also be represented in pictures, although the movement is generally not convincing.

TIME PERCEPTION

Time is an essential variable in perception. The timing of the stimuli must be precisely correct for backward masking to occur, for example. The timing of the two stimuli in stroboscopic movement studies must be equally precise; the phenomenon is lost if the interval between the two stimuli is too long or too short. Careful regulation of the interval length can produce the impression of an object moving through space or—by extending the interval by less than one tenth of a second—the impression of movement unaccompanied by an object (phi movement). Virtually every experiment in perception specifies how long a stimulus was exposed to observers, how long observers were allowed to dark adapt, the number of cycles that a sound wave completes in 1 second (a variable related to pitch, as we'll see in the chapters on hearing), or some other characteristic related to time.

However, until now, time has been on the periphery of our discussion. Now we'll make it our central issue. Two topics in this section are methodology issues in time perception and research findings in the estimation of duration.

Methodology Issues in Time Perception

Perhaps you had an uneasy feeling as you began to read about time perception. Color perception, shape perception, and distance perception all refer to tangible attributes. Even motion perception seems reasonably concrete. But time perception? The topic refers to something invisible and fleeting. In the last section I apologized that psychologists know little about the neural coding of motion; we know even less about the neural coding of time. In Chapter 5 we saw how three kinds of photoreceptors register information about color, yet no receptor registers information about the passage of time. And consider the stimulus for time perception. A square or a red patch *exists*, yet as Fraisse (1984) points out, "Duration has no existence in and of itself" (p. 2).

Despite the invisibility of time, the topic is intriguing. For example, a bibliography on time uncovered 1,652 references between 1839 and 1979 (Eisler et al., 1980). The annual average between 1900 and 1960 was only about 15; the dominant behaviorist influence was not tolerant of an area in which both stimuli and responses are so elusive. Since 1970, however, about 150 studies have been published each year on the subject.

A basic research issue in time perception studies involves the dependent variable. How shall we measure people's impression of the passage of time? Suppose, for example, that you would like to determine whether there is any truth to the saying, "Time goes quickly when you're having fun." You would need to locate a task that is pleasant and a task that is unpleasant, according to specified criteria; these tasks would constitute the two levels of the independent variable. The more challenging task would be to select the dependent variable. As Fraisse (1984) emphasizes, "Results are neither comparable nor homogeneous across methodologies" (p. 10).

Let's look at five dependent variables that could be chosen. The first is straightforward: Participants in the study could simply estimate time passage in either seconds or minutes. Suppose, for example, that people worked on each of the two tasks—pleasant and unpleasant—for 2 minutes. Immediately after each time period, participants would estimate time passage. A second dependent variable involves time production. Participants could work on each task and indicate, for example, when 2 minutes had passed. A third dependent variable requires participants to reproduce a given time period. The experimenter could present a time interval of a certain duration, perhaps 2 minutes, without telling the participants the number of minutes that had passed. The participants would be required to reproduce this time interval while working on a pleasant task and an unpleasant task.

The other two dependent variables are somewhat different. Time estimation could be assessed using the **magnitude estimation technique** discussed in the psychophysics chapter. Rather than estimating the number of minutes or seconds that had passed, participants could assign a number value to the duration. You'll recall a variant of the magnitude estimation technique used **cross-modality comparisons;** participants could draw a line to indicate the time duration. Finally, a dependent variable might be assessed with a rating scale. For example, the two ends of the rating scale might be labeled "short time interval" and "long time interval." Alternately, the ends might be labeled "time passed quickly" and "time passed slowly" (e.g., Jourbert, 1984).

Think about how these five dependent variables—and their variants—might yield different results. For example, it might initially seem that time would be rated as passing quickly during a pleasant event, and therefore participants would also be likely to rate that period as a "short time period." However, you've probably had the experience of an event that seemed to pass quickly, yet it also (in contradiction) seemed to last a long time. Because the experimental results depend so heavily on the exact nature of the dependent variable, research on time perception often seems to produce contradictory results. Let's now turn to the research findings in duration estimation.

Research Findings in Duration Estimation
Characteristics of the Stimulus

We will begin by looking at qualities of the stimulus that influence duration estimation. For example, stimulus intensity is important. Fraise (1984) concludes that more intense sounds and lights are judged longer than less intense stimuli. This phenomenon is particularly true for vision. Furthermore, when participants look at a display of dots, the perceived duration depends upon the number of dots (Mo, 1975). The greater the number of dots, the longer the time interval seems to be!

Stimulus complexity also influences duration estimation. Poynter and Homa (1983) presented flashing lights, which flashed on and off in either a simple, regular pattern or a more complex, irregular pattern. Using the reproduction technique of duration estimation, participants provided longer estimates for the more complex patterns.

Duration estimates also depend upon whether the interval is segmented or unsegmented. Poynter (1983) prepared two kinds of tape recordings. Both consisted of 27 nouns and the names of 3 U.S. presidents, and each recording lasted 170 seconds. However, in the unsegmented recording, all 3 presidents' names appeared first, followed by the 27 nouns. In the segmented recording the three presidents' names appeared in positions 10, 20, and 27, thereby creating three segments, or parts, in the recording. Poynter used the magnitude estimation technique. Participants heard a 30-second reference time interval in which no words were presented; they were told that this time interval corresponded to a 30-mm (1.2-inch) line drawn on the response sheet. They were instructed to indicate, by placing an arrow on a 300-mm (11.8-inch) line, the duration of the recording with the nouns and the presidents' names. The average line length was only 106 mm (4.2 inches) for the unsegmented recording, in contrast to

132 mm (5.2-inches) for the segmented recording.

Notice, then, that stimulus characteristics can have an important influence on duration estimates. A time period is judged longer if it is intense, complex, and segmented. Some stimuli require more cognitive processing, and we may judge time on the basis of the amount of sensory information or cognitive "work" that occurs during an interval (Luce, 1984). These findings are consistent with Ornstein's (1969) theory that time estimation depends upon the number of stimulus events stored in memory during an interval.

Activities of the Participants

We have discussed how characteristics of the stimulus can influence duration estimation. The activities of the participants themselves also influence time perception. For instance, one study asked people to estimate time passage, in number of seconds, for a tone sounded while they were performing another task (Tsao, Wittlieb, Miller, & Wang, 1983). When the other task was extremely demanding, they were more likely to underestimate time. For example, a 63-second interval was estimated as 38 seconds when the other task was extremely demanding, in contrast to 49 seconds when there was no other task.

You've heard the proverb, "A watched pot never boils." This saying has inspired several studies to determine whether people overestimate time when they are waiting for an event. For example, Cahoon and Edmonds (1980) told participants in their study that the experiment would start after a delay; the experimenter said he would return later. One group was told to call the experimenter when the water in a glass coffee pot started to boil, whereas a control group did not receive these instructions. In both cases the experimenter returned 4 minutes later and asked the participants to estimate how long he had been gone. The duration estimates were significantly longer for participants in the "watched-pot" group. Try Demonstration 7.11 to determine whether the same results can be obtained with two different dependent variables.

Demonstration 7.11

Testing the Watched-Pot Phenomenon

Since time estimates tend to vary widely from one person to another, this study might best be conducted by your entire class so that the data can be pooled. You will need a hotplate or stove and a container for water that permits the observers to readily determine whether the water is boiling. You will test four conditions in all, asking for their judgments about a 4-minute interval. In two conditions participants will make duration estimates while watching a pot that is about to boil; in the other two conditions, there is no anticipated event. In addition you will use two different dependent variables (one for each of the two watched-pot conditions and one for each of the two control conditions). One dependent variable is time estimation; ask participants to estimate the number of minutes and seconds that have passed. The other dependent variable uses a rating scale; ask people to rate their perception of the interval on a 7-point rating scale where a rating of 1 is "time passed quickly" and 7 is "time passed slowly."

After the data have been gathered (ideally with at least ten people in each of the four conditions), compare the watched-pot group with the control group. Perform a separate comparison for each of the two dependent variables. Do the time estimation results confirm the findings of Cahoon and Edmonds (1980)? How do those results compare with the time-passage ratings?

Finally, let's discuss the results on that other proverb mentioned at the beginning of this section, "Time goes quickly when you're having fun." Given that probably close to 2,000 studies have been conducted on time estimation, we might expect several dozen on the effects of pleasantness on time estimation. However, when I reviewed the literature on this topic several years ago (Matlin & Stang, 1978), I discovered only one study. Thayer and Schiff (1975) asked female participants to estimate duration in a neutral condition and then in an experimental condition in which they gazed at another person. This other person was either male or female, and either smiling or scowling. The duration of the interval was either 12 or 36 seconds, and participants were asked to reproduce the time interval on a masked stopwatch. The time estimates were significantly longer when the

face was scowling than when it was smiling. This finding was particularly true when the face was female rather than male.

In summary, it seems that when people pay attention to time, the duration estimates are longer. We are more likely to pay attention to time if there is nothing else to do, if we are waiting, and if time is dragging because an event is unpleasant.

Summary: Time Perception

1. Time perception has been a popular topic for research, particularly in recent years.
2. In time perception research, there are several options in choosing a dependent variable: (a) time estimation; (b) time production; (c) time reproduction; (d) magnitude estimation, including cross-modality comparisons; and (e) rating scales.

3. Stimulus characteristics influence duration estimates; a time period is judged longer if it is intense, complex, and segmented.
4. Activities of the participants influence duration estimates; a time period is judged

longer if people are not performing another task simultaneously, if they are waiting for an event, and if the situation is unpleasant.

Review

1. Find a painting or a photograph that seems fairly lifelike. Identify at least one example of each of the seven kinds of monocular factors without movement that can be represented in a picture.
2. List the five distance factors that cannot be represented in a picture. Describe why a picture cannot effectively illustrate these five factors.
3. Some sources of information about distance, such as size cues, would be included in a "common-sense" list of factors. Other sources of information, such as binocular disparity and shading, would be omitted. Describe each of these factors, discuss some research conducted on them, and point out their importance in theories about distance perception.
4. Summarize the empiricist position and Gibson's theory with regard to distance perception. Now return to the discussion of these two theories in the first chapter and review their capsule summaries to clarify the contrast between the two approaches.
5. William Shakespeare wrote, "Things in motion sooner catch the eye than what stirs not." How is this relevant to your peripheral vision? Compare your peripheral vision and vision in your fovea with respect to velocity detection thresholds.
6. Imagine that an industrial employee has been instructed to report whether a dial on a piece of equipment moves the slightest amount. Describe how uncertainty and the background behind the dial might be important, and mention why apparent movement might be a problem. Finally, describe how the employee's time perception might be influenced by this task.
7. Summarize the studies on biological motion discussed in the "In Depth" section.

What kinds of information about motion can we pick up readily without seeing an entire organism? What variables, other than gender, do you think might be interesting to investigate using this research technique?

8. Suppose you are playing baseball and you are up at bat. How would Gibson's theory explain your perception of motion as the ball is being pitched toward you? Suppose you are pitching and you quickly move your head to determine whether the person on second base is trying to steal toward third. How might corollary discharge theory account for the stability, despite the motion of images across your retina?
9. Name the kind of apparent movement represented in each of these situations.
    a. On a dark night you see a single small light in a neighbor's house, and you know that the neighbor is on vacation. The light appears to move and you suspect a burglar.
    b. A billboard has a line of light bulbs that turn on and off in rapid succession. The light appears to travel across the billboard.
    c. In a planetarium the star show ends with the stars whirling swiftly about in a clockwise direction for several minutes. Out in the lobby a minute later, the room around you seems to be whirling in the opposite direction.
    d. On a dark night you watch a plane fly over a radio tower. For a brief moment the plane seems to be stationary and the tower light seems to move.
10. Describe a situation in which time would pass as fast as possible, and a situation in which time would pass very slowly. Describe characteristics of the stimulus and

the activity of the person who is estimating duration. Now imagine that you would like to conduct research in the area of time perception. Select an independent variable not mentioned in the discussion of time perception and describe the five methods that could be used to measure the dependent variable.

New Terms

egocentric distance	convergence	velocity detection threshold
relative distance	converge	events
depth perception	binocular disparity	event perception
monocular factors	stereopsis	biological motion
accommodation	stereoscopic picture	center of movement
pictorial cues	stereoscope	self-motion illusion
cue	strabismus	corollary discharge theory
interposition	stereoblindness	occlusion
size cues	amblyopia	disocclusion
relative size	amblyoscope	illusory movement
familiar size	disparity-selective cells	stroboscopic movement
texture gradient	empiricism	phi movement
linear perspective	kinesthetic information	autokinesis
atmospheric perspective	constructivist theory	induced movement
shading	Gibsonian approach	movement aftereffects
height cues	direct perception approach	magnitude estimation technique
motion parallax	ground theory	cross-modality comparisons
motion perspective	trompe l'oeil	
kinetic depth effect	tracking shot	

Recommended Readings

Cutting, J. E. (1986). *Perception with an eye for motion*. Cambridge, MA: The MIT Press. *This book offers an advanced-level discussion of distance and motion perception, although it does not examine the topic of biological motion, an area to which Cutting contributed substantially.*

Deregowski, J. B. (1984). *Distortion in art: The eye and the mind*. London: Routledge & Kegan Paul. *Of many books on the topic of perception and pictures, this is one of the most readable.*

Fraisse, P. (1984). Perception and estimation of time. *Annual Review of Psychology, 35*, 1–36. *French researcher Paul Fraisse is perhaps the foremost figure in the area of time perception. This chapter offers an excellent review of the literature.*

Reed, E., & Jones, R. (Eds.). (1982). *Reasons for realism: Selected essays of James J. Gibson*. Hillsdale, NJ: Erlbaum. *This collection of Gibson's writing includes both published and unpublished papers from the approximately 40-year span of his research.*

Warren, W. H., Jr., & Shaw, R. E. (Eds.). (1985). *Persistence and change: Proceedings of the First International Conference on Event Perception*. Hillsdale, NJ: Erlbaum. *In 1981, prominent researchers in the area of event perception gathered to present papers and discuss critical topics. This volume includes those papers and the syntheses of those discussions; the paper by Johansson is particularly useful.*

Wertheim, A. H., Wagenaar, W. A., & Leibowitz, H. W. (Eds.). (1982). *Tutorials on motion perception*. New York: Plenum. *This book is the product of an international symposium on motion perception. It contains much valuable information on topics such as velocity thresholds and the neural basis of motion perception, but the lack of careful editing makes it challenging to read.*

chapter 8
Constancy
and Illusion

Preview

This chapter investigates two areas in which our perceptions do not correspond to the patterns registered on our retinas: constancy and illusion.

The first section considers constancy, the tendency for the properties of objects to seem constant and stable despite the circumstances in which we view them. For instance, objects seem to stay the same size, even though we view them from different distances. Also, objects seem to stay the same shape, even though we view them from different orientations. Furthermore, objects seem to stay the same brightness, even though we view them in different illuminations. We'll also briefly consider several other constancies: color constancy, motion constancy, position constancy, and existence constancy.

The second section is concerned with illusions, or incorrect perceptions. Although psychologists disagree about whether illusions are important in our daily lives, the volume of research on illusions has been impressive. In this section we discuss size illusions, including an in-depth examination of the moon illusion. For centuries observers have noted that the moon looks much larger on the horizon than when it is overhead; however, the explanation for the moon illusion has been elusive. Although size illusions are most common, other illusions involve the perceived direction of lines or the shape of lines and geometric objects. Several theories for the illusions have been proposed. However, it seems that each illusion requires more than one theory to explain the effects.

What is the relationship between the patterns registered on our retinas and our perceptions of them? In many cases our perceptions match those retinal patterns. However, when we examine constancy and illusion, we find that we often "see more than meets the eye."

The section on constancy emphasizes that objects seem to stay the same to viewers, even though the representation of those objects on the retina changes enormously. For example, a boy 3 feet tall produces an image on the retina that is fairly large if he is standing in front of you. As that same child walks down the street, the image on your retina shrinks. However, you perceive the child as staying the same height. The perceived sizes do not correspond to the retinal sizes. In the case of constancy, the perceived size corresponds to the object's true size—the child *seems* to stay the same size, and in fact the child's true size does stay the same.

In the section on illusion you will see that two objects may seem different to viewers, even though the representations of those objects on the retina are just the same. One line may look much longer than another in the Müller-Lyer illusion (see Figure 8.6). Nevertheless, the actual lines are exactly the same length, and their retinal images are also identical. In the case of illusions the perceived size does not correspond to the object's true size.

We need to have some vocabulary to refer to the objects "out there" and the objects as they are registered on the retina. The term **distal stimulus** refers to the objects "out

there" in the world, such as a phonograph record. A distal stimulus has no contact with a sense organ, such as the retina. The term **proximal stimulus** refers to the representation of objects in contact with a sense organ. Thus the size, shape, and brightness represented by the phonograph record on your retina are examples of proximal stimuli. Incidentally, you can remember which term is which by thinking of distal as "in the distance." Table 8.1 outlines the size relationships for both constancy and illusions.

Don't get the wrong impression from the names "constancy" and "illusion." It is tempting to think that constancy is a normal process, whereas illusions are abnormal. However, illusions are universal. Age and cultural experience influence the magnitude of some illusions, but everyone experiences them to some extent. Illusions are also predictable; we can tell in advance what kind of distortion people will perceive. As Coren and Girgus (1978) have argued, illusions are not special or rare cases of deviant perception. Instead, they are part of normal perception, and in fact they may be an inevitable product of normal perception. Thus any discussion of perceptual processes must include information about illusions.

CONSTANCY

As you move around in the world, you change your distance from objects, approach-

Table 8.1 Constancy and Illusion

	True Sizes (Distal Stimuli)	Retinal Sizes (Proximal Stimuli)	Perceived Sizes
Constancy (e.g., two identical objects at different distances from viewer)	Same	Different	Same
Illusions (e.g., two identical objects with different surrounding lines)	Same	Same	Different

ing them and then moving away. An image of these objects is registered on your retina. However, that image will vary from time to time—it may be large or small, round or elliptical, bright or dark. Nonetheless, properties of objects seem to stay the same, or constant, even though we view them in different conditions.

Consider a phonograph record, for example. If you hold it close to your eyes, it takes up nearly the whole view, and the image on your retina is large. If you stand across the street, however, the image on your retina may be as small as a period on this page. The shape of the image can also change, from round to elliptical to a straight line. The brightness of the record also changes, because it reflects much more light to your retina if you are looking at it in bright sunlight than if you are in a candle-lit room. Still, a record is a record. The visual qualities of the record seem to stay the same. The phenomenon operating is **constancy,** the tendency for qualities of objects to seem to stay the same despite changes in the way we view the objects.

Consider another example, Demonstration 8.1. How many right angles did you count? When I first saw this demonstration,

I systematically began counting four angles for each of the three sides I could see. However, there really are no right angles in this diagram! Because of constancy, we believe that this diagram represents a cube, placed at an angle. We count the number of right angles that would appear in a cube, ignoring the stimulus that is really in front of us.

One reason that constancy is an interesting phenomenon is that the distal stimulus is often different in size, shape, and brightness from the proximal stimulus. For instance, the round shape of a phonograph record may be represented by an ellipse on your retina. Nonetheless, we tend to perceive the *true* shape (distal stimulus) rather than the shape on the retina (proximal stimulus). This section of the chapter will discuss how we are able to perceive "more than meets the eye." We will consider size, shape, and brightness constancy in some detail. There are also several other constancies that we will discuss briefly because they demonstrate how general the constancy phenomenon is.

Size Constancy

Size constancy means that an object seems to stay the same size despite changes in its dis-

---

Demonstration 8.1

*An Example of
Shape Constancy*

Count the number of right angles in the figure below.

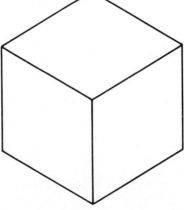

tance. Notice, then, that the proximal size of an object can shrink and expand, yet the distal size of the object seems to stay the same. Try Demonstration 8.2 to help you notice how the visual angle and retinal size change as an object moves away from your eye. **Visual angle,** a term used in Chapter 4, means the size of the arc formed on the retina by an object. **Retinal size** refers to the amount of space the object occupies on the retina. Visual angle and retinal size are closely related terms.

Think about how size constancy operates in the real world. As your professor steps forward to make a particularly important point, he or she does not expand magically before your eyes. As a car drives away from you, you don't believe that it is shrinking to matchbox size. As a dog plays "fetch the stick" with you, it does not expand and contract. The next time you get up from reading this book, notice how objects seem to stay the same size as you move away from them.

You might argue that you have size constancy because you know how big your professor, a car, and Rover are. Yes, familiarity may help to preserve size constancy (Leibowitz, 1971), but size constancy operates for unfamiliar objects as well, as long as distance information is present. If you cut a random shape out of white paper and changed your distance from that shape, it would also seem to stay the same size.

Distance Information and Size Constancy

In everyday life you have substantial information about distance that can tell you how far away an object is. Theoretically, you could combine knowledge about an object's distance and knowledge about its retinal size to determine how big an object "really" is—that is, its distal size.

A classic experiment demonstrated the importance of distance information in determining size constancy (Holway & Boring, 1941). As Figure 8.1 shows, observers were seated so that they could look down either of two darkened hallways. Down the right-hand hallway a standard stimulus could be placed at any distance from 10 to 120 feet (3 to 36 m). The standard stimulus was a circle whose size could be systematically varied to produce a visual angle of 1°. (Consequently, the circle was much bigger at the 120-foot distance than at the 10-foot distance.) Down the left-hand hallway, 10 feet away, was a comparison circle, which observers were instructed to adjust until it matched the size of a particular test stimulus.

This study had four experimental conditions:

1. Normal, binocular viewing with all distance information present.

Demonstration 8.2 *Size Constancy*	Take your pen and hold it about 3 cm (1 inch) in front of your eyes. Notice the size of the visual angle that it occupies and think about how big the retinal size must be for a pen held this close. Now move the pen out to 30 cm (12 inches). Notice how the visual angle is much smaller; the retinal size is also much smaller. Now prop up the pen and walk across the room. The visual angle is now extremely small, and the retinal size is also extremely small. Think about how the pen looked to you. Did it seem to shrink to doll-sized proportions as you walked away from it? In fact, it seemed to stay a constant size, despite the fact that the retinal size was much, much smaller when the pen was viewed from across the room.

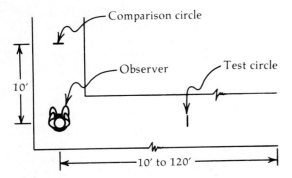

Figure 8.1 Setup for Holway and Boring experiment (looking down).

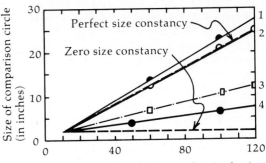

Figure 8.2 Performance on Holway and Boring experiment as a function of viewing conditions, 1–4.

2. Monocular viewing with all other distance information present.

3. Monocular viewing through a peephole, which removed the distance information available from motion parallax (the head-movement factor).

4. Monocular viewing through a peephole with drapes along the hallway, which removed almost all distance information.

Notice that the amount of distance information available to observers differed in the four conditions.

Figure 8.2 shows the observers' performance in the four conditions. First look at the two dotted lines, placed on the figure as guidelines. One dotted line represents how people would perform if they had perfect size constancy and the object seemed to stay exactly the same size, no matter how distant it was. The other dotted line represents how people would perform if they had absolutely no (zero) size constancy—if in judging its true size they considered only retinal size and not the distance of the object.

Now notice how people performed in the four conditions. In the normal viewing condition (1), people showed a little **overconstancy**; they overcorrected for distance and actually made overly large estimates for distant objects. In the monocular condition (2), people showed almost perfect size constancy. In the monocular/peephole condition (3) and in the monocular/peephole/drapes condition (4), people showed **underconstancy**; they

provided estimates that were too small for distant objects. Without information about distance, people do not show much size constancy.

Photographs and paintings can look bizarre if they reduce distance information. Figure 8.3 is a photograph from an angle highly unusual in Western tradition (Hagen, 1986). Since there is so little distance information, size constancy cannot be preserved, and the feet in the foreground look unusually large.

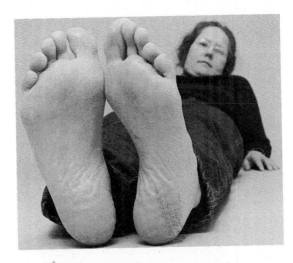

Figure 8.3 Difficulty of preserving size constancy in photograph taken from unusual angle. (Photo by Ron Pretzer.)

Emmert's Law

Try Demonstration 8.3 to illustrate Emmert's law, which is related to size constancy. You'll notice that this demonstration uses a negative afterimage. Staring at the circle in Demonstration 8.3 leads to adaptation; as you look away from the black circle, a white circle appears. However, the perceived size of the circle depends upon the background against which it is viewed. **Emmert's law,** named after the man who discovered it in 1881 (Boring, 1942), states that an afterimage actually appears bigger if it is projected on a more distant surface. In terms of an equation, Emmert's law can be stated as:

$$\text{Perceived Size} = K \text{ (Retinal Image Size} \times \text{Perceived Distance).}$$

This equation, in which K represents a constant, says that the perceived size is a function of both the size of the retinal image and the perceived distance of the object. Notice how this equation explains Demonstration 8.3. Since K is a constant, it stays the same; the portion of the retina that has experienced adaptation also stays the same. The only terms that change when you look from a nearby surface to a faraway surface are perceived size and perceived distance. Specifically, an increase in the perceived distance (when you look off at the faraway surface) means that the perceived size must increase as well. As a consequence, perceived size is larger on the faraway surface.

Size constancy can be illustrated using the Emmert's law equation. Size constancy means that perceived size does not change—even though retinal image size changes—as an object is seen at varying distances. As the neighbor's dog trots away from you, the retinal image size grows smaller, but the perceived distance grows simultaneously larger. In fact, these two changes balance each other out, so that the perceived size does not change. The dog doesn't seem to shrink magically. We will see that this equation is important in one explanation for size constancy.

Explanations for Size Constancy

More research has been conducted on size constancy than on the other constancies (Leibowitz, 1971). Nevertheless, psychologists disagree about what factors are responsible for this phenomenon.

Several factors have been proposed, and it seems likely that each may be involved in some aspects of size constancy. We mentioned already that familiar size may be helpful. If you know how big a pencil is, you can guess its size even when the distance varies. As Leibowitz (1971) points out, this differentiation is learned; young children misidentify a man in the distance as a boy and a distant large animal as a dog.

A second explanation of size constancy is the size-distance invariance hypothesis. This explanation applies to both familiar and unfamiliar objects. According to the **size-dis-**

Demonstration 8.3

Emmert's Law

Attach a white paper to a surface several feet from where you are sitting. Now fixate the center of the circle below for about a minute, making certain that your eyes do not move significantly. Then look at the white surface to the right of the circle; you should see a bright-looking afterimage. Note the size of the afterimage. Now transfer your gaze to the white paper and note whether the afterimage seems to have grown. Incidentally, if the afterimage seems to fade during this demonstration, a rapid blink will restore it.

tance invariance hypothesis, a viewer calculates an object's perceived size by
combining an object's retinal size and its perceived distance. This definition is a restate-
ment of Emmert's law. Notice another pre-
diction that can be derived from Emmert's
law. If two objects have the same retinal size,
the object that looks as if it is farther away
will be perceived as larger. This classic theory
was originally proposed by Helmholtz (1866),
the empiricist whose views we discussed in
Chapter 7. Do not take this principle too literally, however. You don't take out a pocket
calculator to figure the objective size. In fact,
you probably are rarely aware of this process.
Even animals seem to be guided by this principle (Gogel, 1977), so it cannot involve elaborate conscious calculations.

The size-distance invariance hypothesis
has recently been updated by Irwin Rock of
Rutgers University. Rock (1983) uses the term
unconscious inference, which Helmholtz also
used. When we make an inference in logic,
we draw a conclusion based on the evidence
and we are *conscious,* or aware, of the infer-
ential process. In unconscious inference, we
arrive at a perception in a somewhat similar
fashion, beginning with evidence and arriv-
ing at a conclusion. However, in perception
the process is *not* conscious; furthermore, the
result is a perception rather than a logical conclusion. For example, an observer might inspect a scene in which the retinal image size
of one pencil is roughly twice the size of another pencil. The observer might reason, un-
consciously, "The retinal image size for pencil
A is twice that of pencil B. However, the distance for pencil A is half that of pencil B.
Therefore, their perceived sizes are equivalent."

Some researchers have tried to figure out
exactly what distance information people
take into account in the size-distance invariance hypothesis. Leibowitz, Shiina, and Hennessy (1972), for example, have discovered
that the distance factors of accommodation
and convergence led to size constancy for objects closer to the eye than 1 m (3.3 ft). Other
researchers have found that the size-distance
invariance hypothesis is not perfectly relia-

ble. For example, Vogel and Teghtsoonian
(1972) found that judged size was related to
distance in different ways in three different
conditions they tested. Thus the relationship
between size and distance was variable rather
than invariant.

Another explanation for size constancy
concerns the relative sizes of objects being
judged (Rock & Ebenholtz, 1959). According
to this relative-size explanation, people notice the size of an object, compared to other
objects. For example, look at your pen on the
desk. Now get up and walk across the room.
The image of the pen grows smaller, but the
image of the desk also grows smaller. In fact,
the ratio of the retinal sizes remains constant.
The retinal size for the pen may be one tenth
as long as the retinal size for the desk,
whether you are 1 m or 10 m away. Thus objects seem to stay the same size as we move
away from them because they keep their
same size relative to other objects near them.
Notice that in this theory the viewer does not
need to take distance into account. All the
information necessary for constancy is
present in the relationship among the stimuli.

One other explanation is also concerned
with the relationship among stimuli. According to Gibson's direct perception explanation, we can directly perceive the environment from the information in the stimulus
(Gibson, 1959). For example, people notice
the size of an object by comparing it to the
texture of the surrounding area. As you may
recall from Chapter 7, Gibson emphasized
texture in distance perception; texture is
equally important in his theory of size constancy. Try Demonstration 8.4 to illustrate the
importance of texture in size constancy.

We have mentioned that Gibson's emphasis on the information available in the
stimulus provides support for the second
theme of this textbook. The stimulus registered on the retina is not an impoverished
representation of reality; it is rich with useful
information about the environment. A Gibsonian concept particularly relevant to the
constancies is invariants. Invariants are aspects of perception that persist over time and
space and are left unchanged by certain kinds

Demonstration 8.4

*Influence of
Surrounding Texture
on Size Constancy*

Select a long, flat area that has noticeable texture patterns, such as a tile floor, a sidewalk, or a rug with a regular geometric pattern. Take two same-sized sheets of paper and place them about 1 m and 5 m away from you. Notice how the paper covers the same number of texture units in both cases. For example, it may cover $1\frac{1}{4}$ tiles; this coverage is the same whether the paper is near or far from you.

---

of transformations (Epstein, 1977; Michaels & Carello, 1981). Whereas most other theories propose that the mechanisms for constancy are located within the viewer, the direct perception approach proposes that the explanation is located within the stimulus. For example, in Demonstration 8.4 the relationship between the two sheets of paper and the texture units surrounding them provides enough information to establish size constancy.

The discussion of distance perception in Chapter 7 concluded that explanations from both the empiricist and the Gibsonian traditions are probably valid. We can assess distance relatively accurately because we can take advantage of a wide variety of information sources about distance. Similarly, we will conclude the discussion of size constancy by noting that several factors are probably responsible for our remarkable accuracy in preserving size constancy: Objects seem to stay the same size because of familiarity, the size-distance invariance hypothesis, the relative size of other objects, and the texture of the surrounding areas.

Shape Constancy

Shape constancy means that an object seems to stay the same shape despite changes in its orientation. The proximal shape of an object is the same as the distal shape *only* if the object is exactly perpendicular to your line of view. In all other cases the proximal shape is distorted.

Notice what happens to the proximal shape of a familiar object, such as an index card, as you change its orientation. In fact, when an index card is viewed at an angle, the proximal shape is a trapezoid rather than a rectangle.

Get up from your chair and walk around the room. Look at a particular object, such as a window, and view it from different angles. Notice that the shape registered on your retina is a trapezoid from every orientation except when you are facing it directly. Observe how the rim of a cup usually forms an ellipse rather than a perfectly round circle. Nevertheless, the window seems to stay rectangular and the rim of a cup seems to stay circular. Objects do not grow distorted and then normal-shaped again as we change our orientation to them.

Notice also how shape constancy is related to size constancy. Stand next to one side of the window and notice the proximal shape of the window frame. As we said before, it is a trapezoid. Notice that one of the most striking aspects is that the side nearest to you has a bigger retinal size than the farther side. As in the case of size constancy, objects closer to you have a bigger retinal size.

We saw in the discussion of size constancy that observers showed less-than-perfect constancy when information about depth is reduced. Epstein, Hatfield, and Muise (1977) reasoned that a reduction in information could also produce less-than-perfect shape constancy. Their technique for reducing information involved backward masking, a method you learned about in Chapter 6. Specifically, a masking stimulus was introduced on some trials to provide a precise method for controlling the amount of time that observers could process a stimulus. If you simply present a stimulus and then turn it off, observers continue to process that stimulus. However, if a new stimulus—the masking stimulus—is introduced, observers cannot process that original stimulus because they are busy processing this new stimulus.

Epstein and his coauthors presented elliptical shapes (such as the dotted-line figure on the inside of Figure 8.4). A masking stimulus, consisting of a random arangement of scraps of white paper on a black background, was presented shortly afterwards on some trials. The results showed that when observers had less time to process the information about shape, they showed less shape constancy. In the laboratory, at least, shape constancy is not an immediate and automatic process. Instead, it requires processing time in order to appreciate that an object can retain its shape even when it is viewed from different orientations.

Shape Constancy in the Laboratory and in Real Life

In many laboratory studies observers have shown underconstancy—even when processing time is adequate. In other words, when asked to judge the true shape of a circle they are viewing at a slant, they do not believe that it is a perfect, round circle. Instead, they respond that it is somewhat elliptical, as in Figure 8.4. Thus their response is a compromise between the true shape of the circle (distal stimulus) and the image registered on their retina (proximal stimulus).

Why don't observers in the laboratory demonstrate more shape constancy? Carlson (1977) proposes that one problem may be that the instructions are not clear. If I show you a slanted circle and ask you to judge what you see, you may not know whether I want you to respond in terms of what is registered on your retina or what you think the shape really is. Also, you might think that the answer "a circle" would be too simpleminded! Carlson cites studies that demonstrate that people have excellent shape constancy if the instructions are precise, specifying that they must

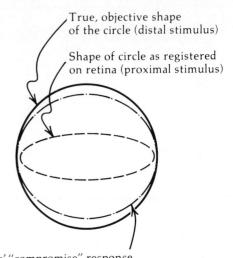

True, objective shape of the circle (distal stimulus)

Shape of circle as registered on retina (proximal stimulus)

Subjects' "compromise" response

Figure 8.4   When subjects view circle from slant, their response is compromise between distal and proximal stimulus.

respond in terms of the true, objective shape of the figure.

Another reason that observers in the laboratory do not demonstrate more shape constancy is that the laboratory conditions have been too deprived. Lappin and Preble (1975) argue that laboratory studies on shape constancy typically show circles, rectangles, and simple geometric forms in plain, uncluttered backgrounds with most of the potential depth information missing. You may recall from the section on size constancy that people show much less constancy when depth information is missing. Consequently, those laboratory studies probably underestimate observers' true ability for shape constancy. Lappin and Preble believe that it would be more useful to study shape constancy in more complex environments—ones with more ecological validity. (**Ecological validity** means that the results we obtain in the laboratory also hold true in "real life.") Laboratory environments are unnatural, without all the useful clutter that real-life environments have. Thus it may be difficult to generalize from the laboratory environment to the real world.

Lappin and Preble made up photographic slides of complex and meaningful scenes, such as a messy office desk. Included in the scene was an octagon (eight-sided figure), which was placed in the picture at a specified angle. Lappin and Preble found that people were accurate in guessing the true shape of the octagon. Thus when people have the information available that they would have in real life, they show excellent shape constancy.

Explanations for Shape Constancy

In the section on size constancy we discussed possible explanations for constancy in some detail. Fortunately, some of the same ideas can be modified slightly to explain shape constancy. Familiarity, for example, has a role in shape constancy. Since you know that a phonograph record is round, you know that the true shape of the record is round, even when it is seen at a slant.

The size-distance invariance hypothesis, used for size constancy, can be translated into the shape-slant invariance hypothesis. (Notice that distance, the potential distorter for size, is translated into slant, the potential distorter for shape.) According to the **shape-slant invariance hypothesis,** a viewer calculates objective shape by combining information about an object's retinal shape and its slant. According to Rock's (1983) more recent unconscious-inference interpretation of shape constancy, we arrive at shape constancy by a reasoning-like process in which information about an object's retinal image shape and slant are combined in the same fashion as two premises in a logical proof. Thus when a phonograph record is tilted away from the observer, he or she makes the inference that the true shape has not changed.

A potential problem Lappin and Preble (1975) found, however, is that people had trouble judging objects' retinal shape. (For the record, remember that Lappin and Preble found that people were excellent at judging objects' *true* shape.) If observers cannot judge objects' retinal shape accurately, their calcu-

lations of objective shape should be inaccurate. However, these retinal shape judgments may not be adequate assessments of observers' knowledge about those shapes. People often know more than they reveal in an overt response. For example, I can hear Beverly Sills's trilling soprano voice distinctly in my "mind's ear," but any attempt to reveal that knowledge by trying to duplicate that voice with my singing would be laughable! Researchers in shape constancy will find it challenging to find alternate methods of obtaining overt responses about retinal shape.

Let's now consider James J. Gibson's direct perception approach to shape constancy. You'll recall he proposed that people take texture into account to maintain size constancy. Gibson (1950) suggested a similar explanation for shape constancy. When an object with a distinct texture is slanted, the texture units farther away from the viewer are compressed. Try Demonstration 8.5 to help you understand the relationship between slant and compression of texture units.

Brightness Constancy

Brightness constancy means that an object seems to stay the same brightness despite changes in the amount of light falling on it. For example, the white paper on this page looks equally bright whether you are reading indoors or outdoors. Similarly, the black letters on this page look equally dark whether you are reading indoors or outdoors. The amount of light reflected from the page and the letters is vastly different in the two cases, with perhaps 100 times as much light reflected when you are outdoors on a sunny day (Hurvich & Jameson, 1966). Try Demonstration 8.6 to show how objects appear to be equally bright under different illuminations.

Nature of Brightness Constancy

Let us examine brightness constancy in more detail. It is important to keep in mind throughout this section that there is a difference between the physical characteristics of

Demonstration 8.5

Relationship between Slant and Compression of Texture Units

Look at the two pieces of waffle in the picture below. You are looking straight at one of the pieces, but the other one is viewed at a slant. Which one is at the slant? Is the top part of *a* or *b* farther away from you? (Notice that both are cut into unfamiliar shapes, so you cannot use a familiar rectangular or oval shape as a cue for slant.) (Photos by Ron Pretzer.)

objects and our psychological reactions to them. We describe objects in terms of the intensity or amplitude of light waves. In contrast, we describe our psychological reactions in terms of **brightness.** Thus an intense light *generally* looks bright to us. However, the phenomenon of brightness constancy demonstrates that perceived brightness also depends upon other factors.

Here is another way to look at brightness constancy. The amount of light falling on an object changes from one situation to the next, for example, as you move a book from indoors to outdoors. However, an object always reflects the same *proportion* of that light. Figure 8.5 illustrates how a constant proportion of light can be reflected in different lighting situations. The black record may reflect only 10% of the light falling on it, whereas the

white label may reflect 90% of the light falling on it. The term **albedo** refers to the proportion of light reflected by an object. For example, the printing on this page might have an albedo of 3%. Albedo is a property of an object that stays the same even when the amount of light falling on the object changes.

Strangely, a black object can sometimes reflect more light than a white object. For example, suppose you are looking at a black record on a sunny day, when the illumination is 1000 units (in some unspecified light measurement system). If the record has an albedo of 10%, it will reflect 10% of the 1000 units, or 100 units. In contrast, suppose you are looking at the white label indoors, where the illumination is 10 units. If the label has an albedo of 90%, it will reflect 90% of 10 units, or 9 units. Your eye receives 100 units from

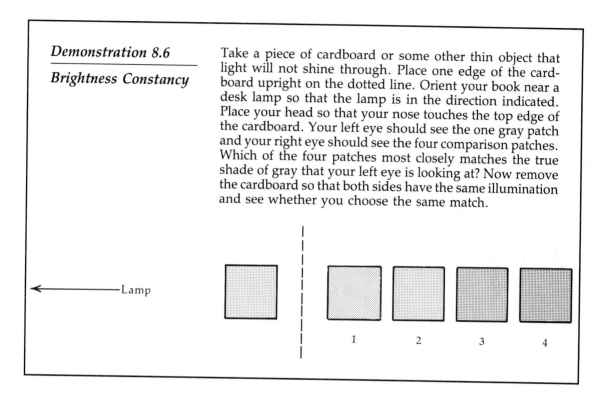

Demonstration 8.6

Brightness Constancy

Take a piece of cardboard or some other thin object that light will not shine through. Place one edge of the cardboard upright on the dotted line. Orient your book near a desk lamp so that the lamp is in the direction indicated. Place your head so that your nose touches the top edge of the cardboard. Your left eye should see the one gray patch and your right eye should see the four comparison patches. Which of the four patches most closely matches the true shade of gray that your left eye is looking at? Now remove the cardboard so that both sides have the same illumination and see whether you choose the same match.

the black record outdoors and 9 units from the white label indoors. However, you would certainly say that the white label *looks* brighter. We do not make brightness judgments on the basis of the amount of light reflected into our eyes. The proximal stimulus is not what we "see," even though it is registered on our retinas. Instead, we see the properties of objects. Ordinarily, what we see resembles the distal stimulus and is related to qualities of that stimulus such as its albedo.

Explanations for Brightness Constancy

There are three basic theories of brightness constancy. According to the explanation based on Helmholtz's (1866) theory, we take illumination into account when we judge brightness. This "taking into account" explanation should sound familiar, because it resembles the theory that people take distance into account when judging size and slant into account when judging shape. What kinds of information do people use in judging illu-

mination? One factor is the position of the object in relation to the light. In Demonstration 8.6 you knew that the left-hand side was near a light and the right-hand side was hidden from the light. Shadows provide further information; we know that an object in a shadow receives less illumination. On the other hand, bright spots on metal or other shiny objects tell us that an object is in a bright light.

Notice that Helmholtz's theory involves a large amount of mental activity. The information is not directly available in the stimulus. Instead, we judge brightness by first figuring out the illumination. Then we assess how much light an object is reflecting onto our retina and take illumination into account to calculate brightness. One reason that Helmholtz's explanation is not widely accepted is that people are not very accurate in judging how much light an object reflects onto their retinas (Beck, 1974). (Remember that this was also a weakness with the similar

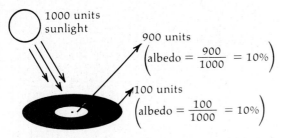

1000 units of sunlight strikes a black record and its white label. The record reflects only 100 units; its albedo is therefore 10%. The label reflects 900 units; its albedo is therefore 90%.

Figure 8.5 Albedo. Note that 1000 units of sunlight strike a black record and its white label. Record reflects only 100 units; its albedo is therefore 10%. Label reflects 900 units; its albedo is therefore 90%.

shape constancy explanation; people are not very accurate in judging retinal shape.) Without that information they could not calculate brightness very accurately.

The second explanation for brightness constancy is called contrast theory. According to **contrast theory** the important factor that determines how bright an object looks is the stimulus intensity of that object in comparison to other objects in the scene. Thus the label on the record looks bright because it is surrounded by a dark region. The label looks relatively brighter, whether the record is seen in sunlight or in a dark room.

Gelb (1929) performed a classic experiment to demonstrate that judgments of brightness depend upon the intensity of nearby objects. To perform this study he created an unusual situation. Observers sat in a dark room and looked at a circle made of black velvet. From a hidden projector Gelb projected a bright beam of light that fell precisely upon the black velvet circle. The observers reported that they saw a white circle. After all, the illuminated black circle was lighter than the surrounding darkness; in contrast, the circle looked light. Then Gelb placed a little slip of white paper in front of the circle, so that the light was shining on it. Presto! Observers suddenly reported that the circle was black. The circle may have been light in comparison to the dark background, but next to a white slip of paper it was dark!

When I first heard of this study, I suspected that Gelb probably could not have fooled his observers for long. Now that they knew that the circle was truly black, they would certainly remain convinced that it was black, wouldn't they? However, Gelb found that when he removed the slip of paper, people again reported seeing a white circle. In social psychology we are accustomed to thinking that we cannot fool a person twice—once someone is aware of a deception, he or she will not fall for the same trick again. However, in Gelb's experiment the contrast between the dark background and the relatively light circle was so convincing that the observers were willing to ignore what they knew and report only what they saw.

According to the contrast theory of brightness constancy, observers pay attention to the relative intensity of the stimuli rather than the absolute intensity. An object may be objectively dark, but it will appear bright as long as it is brighter than other objects. Brightness constancy occurs because the relative intensity of an object remains the same when illumination varies. Your white sweater therefore looks bright in the moonlight because it is the brightest object in sight. Your dark shoes look dark in the noonday sun because they are the darkest objects in sight.

Notice that contrast theory, unlike Helmholtz's theory, allows the viewer to gather all the necessary information from the world "out there." In this respect, contrast theory is similar to some theories discussed in connection with the other constancies. For example, remember the theory that size constancy is caused by noticing how big an object is in comparison to other objects. In both these theories the relationship among the stimuli provides enough information for us to maintain constancy.

Although contrast theory is quite popular, some studies have shown that this explanation may be too simple. For example, experiments by Gilchrist (1977, 1980) have shown that brightness judgments depend upon the relative intensity of objects perceived to be the same distance from the viewer. On the other hand, the relative intensity of objects merely next to each other in the retinal image (but perceived to be at different distances from the viewer) is less important. In other words, it seems that viewers must make depth perception judgments before they make brightness judgments. Brightness judgments therefore involve more than simple contrast.

Other explanations of brightness constancy argue that the phenomenon can be explained at the level of the retina. These theories, summarized by Gilchrist (1980), propose that either lateral inhibition or opponent processes can account for the fact that an object seems to stay the same brightness in different illuminations. All these explanations hold that perceived brightness can be explained on the basis of the stimulation on the retina, without input from any higher level information (such as knowledge about an object's distance from an observer or knowledge of the illumination conditions). However, as we just noted, participants in Gilchrist's (1977, 1980) studies responded differently when objects in a stimulus were perceived to be the same distance away than when the objects were perceived to be at varying distances. Even though the stimulation on the retina did not differ in the two conditions, the observers' brightness constancy judgments *did* differ. Some process beyond the retina must be at least partially responsible for brightness constancy.

So how can we explain brightness constancy? It seems that none of the theories can adequately explain it! The answer probably is that none of the theories alone can offer a sufficient explanation, but some combination may work. Brightness constancy probably depends on some contribution from all three factors. Consistent with three of the themes of this book, the stimulus, the perceptual processing system, and complex mental processes are all involved. In the case of brightness constancy we must consider the contrast in the stimulus, physiological processes at the level of the retina, and perceivers' knowledge about distance, illumination, and other important factors that are relevant in making decisions about an object's brightness.

Other Constancies

Most research on the constancies has been conducted on size, shape, and brightness. However, constancy invades almost every area of perception, and we should consider other constancies briefly.

Consider color constancy, for example. As Maloney and Wandell (1986) write, "When evening approaches, and daylight gives way to artificial light, we notice little change in the colors of objects around us. The perceptual ability that permits us to discount spectral variation in the ambient light and assign stable colors to objects is called color constancy" (p. 29). Because of **color constancy,** then, we tend to see the hue of an object as staying the same despite changes in the color of the light falling on it. For example, a rose remains red even under a green light bulb.

However, color constancy is not like the other constancies we have considered; the color may not remain very constant. In particular, we seem to have difficulty maintaining color constancy when the shift in color involves the red-green opponent processes. In contrast, we maintain color constancy reasonably well for the blue-yellow opponent processes (Worthey, 1985).

We can draw some practical conclusions from the observation that color constancy is far from perfect (Worthey, 1985). For example, if you are buying fabric, you should take the bolt of material outside if you want to see the colors under natural light rather than under the fluorescent lights in the stores, since these cast a blue color on objects. Makeup mirrors are available with special lighting that duplicates natural sunlight, fluorescent light, and dimly lit rooms. Presumably an eye shadow that is attractive by candlelight might look quite different in a fluorescent-lit office.

Motion constancy means that an object seems to maintain the same speed despite changes in its distance from us. However, motion constancy occasionally breaks down. For me, this is most striking when I am waiting for a subway. The tiny dot of light seems to approach so slowly when the train is far away, but it races toward me over those last few yards.

Position constancy means that an object seems to stay in the same place despite the body's movement relative to it. For example, I can get up from my desk and walk off to the right. The image of my typewriter formerly in the center of my retina is now on the left of my retina. Nonetheless, my typewriter does not appear to jump across the room to the left.

Existence constancy may be the most general constancy of all. **Existence constancy,** or object permanence, means that objects still seem to exist, even if they are no longer in our vision. For example, if you cover your pen with your hand, you know that the object is still in existence, even if it is no longer registered on your retina. You may have learned about this constancy if you had a course in human development, because Piaget (1954) and his followers have studied it extensively. However, it is usually considered a part of cognition, rather than perception, because it relies more heavily on knowledge than on visual information. (Incidentally, if you are as frustrated by lost objects as I am, you might use this remedy: Temporarily stop believing in object permanence!)

We have been considering only the visual constancies. There are constancies for the other senses as well, although information on them is certainly scarce. For example, consider what we could call taste constancy. The taste of lemon juice seems to retain its tartness, whether you are eating lemon meringue pie or a French restaurant's garlicky veal in lemon sauce. Constancy also operates in hearing. You might be startled to hear a tune on a music box that you originally heard played by a huge symphony orchestra. Nonetheless, you recognize it. The tune remains constant despite changes in its loudness, tone, and pitch. In the chapter on smell we will discuss how the intensity of an odor remains the same despite the volume of air you inhale. Can you think of a constancy for touch? These constancies, which we will examine later in the book, offer evidence for Theme 1: The perceptual systems share important similarities.

We have looked at a large number of constancies in this chapter. Constancies simplify our perceptual world enormously, yet we often fail to appreciate them. Take just a moment to fantasize what a nightmare life would be without all these constancies! Think about the chaos you would live in if everything grew and shrank, became regular in shape and then irregular, and grew light and dark as you moved about in the world. Without constancy, objects could change their colors from one moment to the next, and we would have to devise another color name system. Objects would seem to change their speed as they approached and passed us. They would move every time we moved. And, as a final insult, they would disappear as soon as we stopped looking at them. Fortunately, constancies provide stability in a changing world.

Summary: Constancy

1. In constancy, objects seem to stay the same even though their representations on the retina change. In illusions, objects look different even though their representations on the retina stay the same.
2. Size constancy means that an object seems to stay the same size despite changes in its distance from the observer.
3. In experiments in which distance information is removed, people do not show substantial size constancy.
4. Emmert's law states that an afterimage appears larger if it is projected on a more distant surface.
5. Four explanations for size constancy are familiar size, the size-distance invariance hypothesis (including Rock's updated version of unconscious inference), the relative-size explanation, and Gibson's theory, involving invariants, about the texture of the surrounding area.
6. Shape constancy means that an object seems to stay the same shape despite

changes in its orientation toward the observer.

7. People show less shape constancy if they are not allowed adequate time to process the stimulus.

8. In the laboratory, people do not show much shape constancy, probably because they may not understand the instructions and because the laboratory conditions convey minimal information.

9. Two explanations for shape constancy are the shape-slant invariance hypothesis and Gibson's theory that people use information about the compression of texture units.

10. Brightness constancy means that an object seems to stay the same brightness despite changes in illumination.

11. Three explanations for brightness constancy are (a) Helmholtz's theory that we take illumination into account when we judge brightness, (b) contrast theory, and (c) retinal-level processes.

12. Other constancies include color constancy, motion constancy, position constancy, and existence constancy.

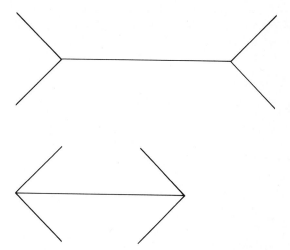

Figure 8.6 Müller-Lyer illusion.

ILLUSION

An **illusion** is an incorrect perception. In an illusion what we see does not correspond to the true qualities of an object. In the Müller-Lyer illusion in Figure 8.6, for example, the line on the bottom looks longer than the line on the top. If you use a ruler to measure the "true qualities" of the lines, you will discover that the two lines are exactly equal in length.

Actually, there are two kinds of illusions or incorrect perceptions: those due to physical processes and those due to psychological processes. Illusions due to physical processes include mirages and distortions caused by water. **Mirages,** according to Fraser and Mach (1976), are caused by the optical properties of the atmosphere. In one famous example of a mirage, explorers at the North Pole thought they saw beautiful scenery in front of them, including hills, valleys, and snow-

capped peaks. They then tramped 30 miles (48 km) over arctic ice to discover that the scene had been a mirage. You may have seen a more modest mirage, such as a pond of water on a hot highway. Also, you have probably noticed distortions caused by water. For example, a stick dipped partway into water looks bent at the point where it enters the water. In all these cases a physical condition such as water or water vapor distorts an image before it reaches the retina. The image recorded on the retina, however, corresponds to our perception. Thus the psychological processes are accurate. In this chapter we will be concerned only with illusions due to psychological processes. With this kind of illusion the image recorded on the retina does not correspond to our perception.

Psychologists disagree about whether illusions are important. Gibson (1950) believes that we are seldom misled by illusions in our everyday lives. As Epstein (1977) summarizes Gibson's position, "Gibson separates himself from the rest by insisting that illusions are peculiarities that occur only under special conditions having little in common with normal conditions of stimulation. Accordingly, the principles that determine illusory perception are not the principles that govern veridical perception" (p. 7).

In contrast, other psychologists argue that illusions occur frequently and that they reveal important information about perceptual processing. For example, Coren and Girgus (1978) write in their book, *Seeing Is Deceiving: The Psychology of Visual Illusions,* "Illusory phenomena are extremely prevalent in the world outside the laboratory" (p. 24). Wolfe (1986) remarks that the study of illusions is valuable: "Illusions are of great use in the study of perception because, in examining the failures of the visual system, we may be able to determine the rules that govern its normal behavior. A visual illusion may literally be the exception that proves the rule" (p. 80). This section of the chapter should encourage you to conclude that illusions are both widespread and useful.

One aspect of illusions is *not* controversial: People enjoy studying illusions! Gillam (1980) notes that more than 200 illusions have been discovered. Coren and Girgus (1978) report that more than 1,000 articles had been written on illusions before the publication of their book in 1978. Impressively, most of the common illusions date back to Helmholtz (Robinson, 1972). However, new illusions and variants of old ones are still being discovered (e.g., Coren, 1981; Leguire, Blake, & Sloane, 1981).

Despite extensive research on illusions, psychologists are still struggling to find a satisfactory method for classifying them. As Wade (1982) concludes, every classification system has been plagued by exceptions. Coren and Girgus (1978) lament the lack of a classification system because most sciences develop a classification system and then add items to the system with new research. An advantage with this kind of system is that researchers can notice gaps and conduct research to fill them. Unfortunately, however, illusions are more difficult to classify than rocks or chemical elements. There are two major reasons for this difficulty. First, people vary somewhat in their responses to illusions. Second, any distortion may involve several explanations rather than just one.

Coren, Girgus, Erlichman, and Hakstean (1976) tackled the problem of developing a classification system by asking 221 observers to make judgments about 45 illusions. An analysis of the data showed that people divide illusions into two basic categories: illusions involving size and illusions involving shape and direction. Let's consider several illusions in each of these two categories.

Size Illusions

The category of size illusions can conveniently be divided into two further subcategories, illusions in which the length of a line or a distance is misjudged, and illusions in which the area of an object is misjudged.

Illusions Involving Line Length or Distance

Figure 8.6 shows one of the most famous illusions, the Müller-Lyer, first demonstrated in the late 1800s. In the **Müller-Lyer illusion** the two lines are actually the same length. Nonetheless, the line on the bottom with the wings pointing outward looks about 25% longer than the line with the wings pointing inward.

Coren and Girgus (1978) estimate that more work has been done on the Müller-Lyer figure than on all other illusions combined. As you would expect, psychologists have tried many variations of the figure, including those in Figure 8.7. Impressively, the illusion remains strong in all these variations.

In fact the Müller-Lyer illusion can even be demonstrated with a single figure that captures both the wings-inward and wings-outward versions simultaneously. Figure 8.8 shows one such figure, which was studied by Tsal (1984). He instructed observers in the wings-inward condition to ignore the outer wings; observers in the wings-outward condition were told to ignore the inner wings. The wings-outward instructions produced longer estimates for the length of the shaft, in contrast to the wings-inward instructions, although the difference was not as noticeable as when observers viewed the classical illusion (Figure 8.6). Thus, the Müller-Lyer illusion can be at least partly created by encouraging observers to selectively attend to certain portions of the design.

The Müller-Lyer illusion can also be demonstrated with a variety of psychophysical methods. Although it is usually customary to employ the classical psychophysical techniques, McClellan, Bernstein, and Garbin (1984) found that the Müller-Lyer illusion could be effectively demonstrated using the magnitude estimation technique. McClellan and her coauthors supplied their observers with a comparison line, which was assigned

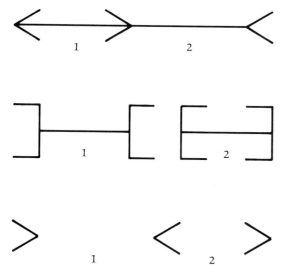

Figure 8.7 presents part of the figures. (continued)

a value of 100 units. The observers were told to supply judgments for the Müller-Lyer figures relative to that norm. In one condition, for example, the observers supplied an average magnitude estimate of 99 for the wings-inward version and 112 for the wings-outward version. (Incidentally, this study also reinforced earlier studies that concluded that the Müller-Lyer illusion is primarily due to the expansion of the wings-outward version rather than the contraction of the wings-inward version.)

One final version of the Müller-Lyer illusion is particularly effective. Figure 8.9 works especially well because depth information has been added.

Another line-length illusion is the **Sander parallelogram,** presented in two versions in Figure 8.10. Students in my classes are usu-

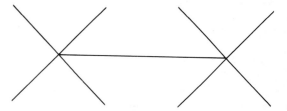

Figure 8.8 Combined wings-inward and wings-outward version of Müller-Lyer illusion, in which observers were instructed to attend to either wings-inward or wings-outward version. Figure similar to ones studied by Tsal (1984).

Figure 8.7 Variations of Müller-Lyer illusion; in each case, segment 1 is equal in length to segment 2.

Figure 8.9 Variant of Müller-Lyer illusion.

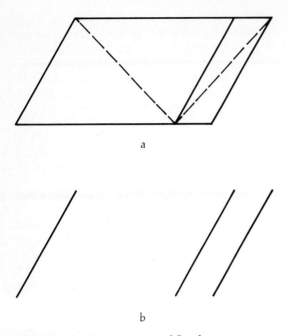

a

b

Figure 8.10 Two versions of Sander parallelogram; a, two dotted diagonal lines are equal length; b, two diagonal lines that you can imagine in the same location as in *a* are also equal length.

ally convinced that I have drawn this one incorrectly until they measure it with a ruler.

A third line-length illusion is the **horizontal-vertical illusion,** illustrated in Demonstration 8.7. This illusion, also called the inverted-T illusion, is effective for two reasons. First, vertical lines look longer than when they are presented alone, and horizontal lines look shorter than when they are presented alone (Masin & Vidotto, 1983). Second, when a line is interrupted by another line, we judge the interrupted line to be shorter. To make a "pure" horizontal-vertical illusion, therefore, neither line should be interrupted. If you try drawing an L so that the two lines are of equal length, you will find that you will be more accurate than you were in Demonstration 8.7.

Think about applications of the horizontal-vertical illusion. I once looked at my sleeping daughter and speculated that she had shrunk. Then I recalled that the horizontal-vertical illusion guaranteed that she would look smaller when horizontal than in the upright orientation in which I view her more often. Similarly, if you want to photograph a fish you have just caught, by all means hold it vertically!

Demonstration 8.7
_____

Horizontal-Vertical Illusion

Extend the vertical line upward until it seems equal in length to the horizontal line. Then measure the two lines and check your accuracy.

Coren and Girgus (1978) point out other natural occurrences of the horizontal-vertical illusion. People overestimate the height of vertical objects such as parking meters, lampposts, and buildings, often by as much as 25%. A tree looks shorter when it has been cut down than it did when it was standing. One of the most famous architectural examples of this illusion is the Gateway Arch in St. Louis (Figure 8.11). Only by measuring can you convince yourself that the height and the width are equal. In reality, both height and width are 630 ft (192 m).

The **Ponzo illusion** is shown in Figure 8.12. Notice how the figure on the top creates the impression of linear perspective, even though it is drawn with only a few lines. On the bottom, additional distance cues convince you that the distant bar must be larger be-

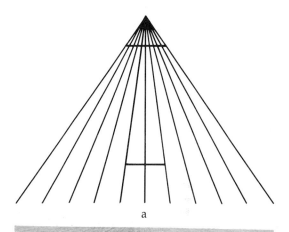

a

b

Figure 8.11 Gateway Arch in St. Louis, Missouri—example of horizontal-vertical illusion. (Photo courtesy of St. Louis Regional Commerce & Growth Association.)

Figure 8.12 Ponzo illusion. Two horizontal lines are actually same length in a; two bars are same length in b. (Photo by Ron Pretzer.)

cause it has the same retinal size as the closer figure. We can call the figure on top an illusion. The figure on the bottom, however, shows the appropriate use of size constancy. As you can see, the boundary between "inaccurate" perception in illusions and "accurate" perception in size constancy is extremely thin. Suppose the observer interprets certain cues in a line drawing to be depth cues, although no instructions specified to do so. In this case, judging two equal figures unequal in objective length is called an illusion. When there are more depth cues present, judging two equal figures unequal in objective length is called size constancy. Indeed the distinction between illusions and size constancy does sound rather arbitrary!

So far we have considered illusions involving line length. Several similar illusions do not involve estimating the length of an actual line; instead, they involve estimating the distance between two objects. For example, a distance that is filled seems longer than a distance that is unfilled, an illusion called the **filled space–open space illusion.** Demonstration 8.8 illustrates this phenomenon, which is an example of an illusion that has real applications in everyday life. When I am typing a page for this book, for example, I occasionally decide to revise several lines of text, which requires placing a blank piece of paper over those lines. Inevitably, the piece of paper I cut is about 20% too long.

Notice the similarity between the filled space–open space illusion and two observations in the last chapter with respect to time. We noted that a time interval seems longer when people are looking at a large number of dots (Mo, 1975) and when the interval is segmented (Poynter, 1983). Similarly, a visual space seems longer when it is filled rather than empty. Consistent with one of the themes of this book, the perceptual processes often share similarities. In this case, time duration estimation is similar to visual length estimation.

Let's explore one final kind of illusion in this section. Coren and Girgus (1980) wondered whether the Gestalt laws of perceptual organization—examined in Chapter 6— might produce illusions. Specifically, would

the distances between two elements in a good figure be judged smaller than the distances between one of those elements and another element outside that figure? For example, the law of nearness states that items are grouped together that are near each other. In Figure 8.13a, dots 1 and 2 would be grouped together by the law of nearness; in Figure 8.13b, dots 2 and 3 would not be grouped together. In reality the distances between each pair of dots are equivalent. However, Coren and Girgus demonstrated that observers tend to underestimate distances within a Gestalt, in comparison to distances involving an element outside the Gestalt. For instance, the distance between dots 1 and 2 in Figure 8.13a was judged somewhat smaller than the distance between dots 2 and 3 in Figure 8.13b. This same tendency was also demonstrated for the laws of similarity, closure, and good continuation. These authors suggest that the spatial distortions could be called the *Gestalt illusions.*

Explanations for the line-length and distance illusions. I mentioned earlier that over 1,000 articles have been written about more than 200 illusions. Most of these articles are about the illusions just discussed. As you can imagine, we will not be able to conclude that there is one simple explanation for all these illusions. Let's therefore summarize several of the most widely accepted current theories.

The discussion of the Ponzo illusion hinted at one of the most popular explanations, the theory of misapplied constancy. According to the **theory of misapplied constancy,** observers interpret certain cues in the illusion as cues for maintaining size constancy. Therefore they make length judgments on the basis of size constancy, and a line that looks farther away will be judged longer (Gillam, 1980). This explanation is particularly relevant for the Ponzo illusion. Check back to Figure 8.12 and notice how the top line does indeed look farther away. Because it looks farther away, we conclude that it is longer.

The theory of misapplied constancy argues that people are sensitive to distance cues in the illusions because they have had experience with cues such as converging lines.

Demonstration 8.8

Filled Space–Open Space Illusion

Locate a medium-length paragraph on this page, and cut a piece of white paper so that it is the same width as one column of the text. Now, holding the paper at least 6 inches (15 cm) away from the book, cut it so that it appears to be the same length as the paragraph. Your final piece of paper should look as if it would precisely cover that paragraph. Finally, place the piece of paper over the paragraph to check the accuracy of your estimation. Repeat this task with size estimations for other paragraphs.

People therefore use this experience inappropriately in making judgments about the Ponzo illusion. According to this view, then, *experience* is a crucial factor, and people who have had less experience should be less deceived by the illusion.

Leibowitz (1971) discusses two groups of people who lack experience with linear perspective, young children and people living in areas with few perspective cues. Leibowitz summarizes studies that demonstrate that the Ponzo illusion has no effect for children 5 years of age and younger. The magnitude of the illusion then increases dramatically; it is as effective for 10- to 15-year-olds as it is for adults.

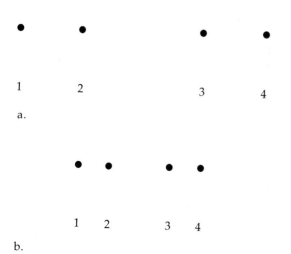

Figure 8.13 Gestalt illusion of nearness.

Leibowitz summarizes his research with people living on the island of Guam, where there are no railroads and where the perspective cues are far less prevalent than in the United States. Leibowitz compared English-speaking undergraduates at the University of Guam with undergraduates at Pennsylvania State University. Both groups judged the illusions drawn with straight lines. They also judged the illusions in photographs, one with texture depth cues and one with perspective depth cues plus texture depth cues. For the Guam students, adding the depth cues of texture and perspective did not increase the magnitude of the illusion. For the Pennsylvania students, adding these cues increased the magnitude of the illusion by about 200%. Experience with depth cues therefore makes it more likely for people to use these cues in judging some illusions. Ironically, the more knowledge and experience we acquire, the less accurately we perform on some illusions!

Other illusions require more elaborate variations of the misapplied constancy theory. For example, the Müller-Lyer illusion might be due to our experience with similar-looking figures in architecture. In Figure 8.14, notice how the corner on the left looks like the "wings-inward" version of the Müller-Lyer and the corner on the right looks like the "wings-outward" version. Gregory (1973) has suggested that when we look at the Müller-Lyer illusion, we are reminded of our experiences with corners. Therefore we recall that the vertical line is farther from us in the "wings-outward" version. We misapply size

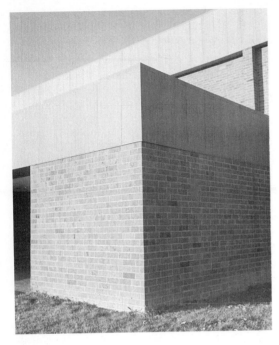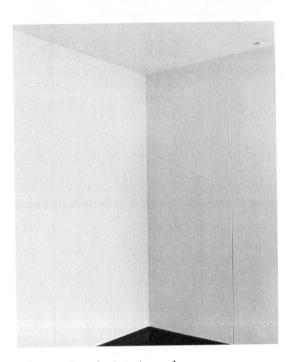

Figure 8.14 Müller-Lyer illusion in corners; architectural examples of wings-inward and wings-outward versions of Müller-Lyer illusion. (Photos by Ron Pretzer.)

constancy and conclude that the line is longer in the "wings-outward" version.

In general, research has supported the misapplied constancy theory explanation for the Müller-Lyer illusion (e.g., Madden & Burt, 1981; Pedersen & Wheeler, 1983). For example, Pedersen and Wheeler examined the Müller-Lyer illusion among two groups of Navajos in an experiment conceptually similar to the one by Leibowitz (1971). One group of Navajos had lived all their lives in rectangular houses, where they would have frequent encounters with corners such as those in Figure 8.14. The other group of Navajos had lived at least the first 6 years of their lives in the traditional Navajo round house, called a hogan. Consequently, their early lives were less likely to involve encounters with the kind of corners represented in Figure 8.14. All the participants were tested on the Müller-Lyer illusion. Those who had lived in rectangular houses were significantly more

susceptible to the illusion. In matching a wings-inward line 2.30 cm (0.9 inches) long, the participants who had lived continuously in rectangular houses adjusted the wings-outward comparison figure so that the line was 4.53 cm (1.8 inches), in contrast to a line length of only 2.60 cm (1.0 inches) for those who had lived at least 6 years in hogans.

You'll notice that this theory of misapplied constancy is related to two theories discussed in connection with other topics in this book. According to the constructivist theory of distance perception, we need to solve a puzzle when we perceive distance; we use our experiences with objects at different distances to draw conclusions about distance. Similarly, according to Rock's (1983) approach to explaining constancy, we use unconscious inference to gather information and draw conclusions about constancy. As Hoffman (1983) explains in connection with visual illusion: "The visual system apparently organizes ambiguous retinal images according to rules of inference that exploit certain regularities in the external world. . . . Evidently the visual system does more than passively transmit signals to the brain. It actively takes part in organizing and interpreting them'' (p. 154). In short, the misapplied constancy theory of illusions emphasizes the contribution of our cognitive processes during perception, an emphasis consistent with Theme 4 of this textbook.

The theory of misapplied constancy is intuitively appealing in explaining the Ponzo illusion, and it is reasonable—although perhaps not as intuitive—in explaining the Müller-Lyer illusion. Ward, Porac, Coren, and Girgus (1977) tested whether this theory could explain a variety of illusions. Their results showed that it could indeed explain some, such as the Ponzo illusion; however, it could not handle others, such as the horizontal-vertical illusion. Clearly, as mentioned earlier, we cannot hope to find just one explanation for over 200 very different kinds of illusions.

The **eye-movement theory,** an alternative explanation, states that illusions can be explained by differences in eye-movement patterns. For example, this approach to the Müller-Lyer illusion suggests that the distortion in line lengths can be traced to systematic mistracking of the two stimuli (Coren, 1981). The eyes trace a longer path in the wings-outward version than in the wings-inward version, and therefore people judge the wings-outward version to be longer. As Wade (1982) points out, the eye-movement theory sometimes argues that illusions can be traced to differences in the *extent* of eye movements (as in the Müller-Lyer illusion) and sometimes can be traced to differences in the *effort* of eye movement. For instance, it has been argued that the horizontal-vertical illusion can be explained by the potentially greater effort required to move the eye in a vertical direction than in a horizontal one.

Most research on the eye-movement theory has concentrated on differences in the *extent* of eye movements. However, Coren (1981) complained that most research—his own included—was correlational. Researchers began with a well-known illusion in which it was observed that people judged one line longer than another. Then the researchers measured the extent of eye movements for the two lines and discovered that the eye movements were longer for the line that had been judged longer. These researchers, having established a correlation between eye movements and judged length, then—inappropriately—concluded that the longer eye movements for one line *caused* the line to be judged longer. Coren points out that another explanation is possible because correlations typically have more than one potential explanation. In the case of the Müller-Lyer, for example, observers who see an apparently longer line may respond by making longer eye movements along that line. Rather than eye movements causing line-length differences, it may be the other way around: Line-length differences may cause eye-movement differences.

Coren argues that it is more scientifically legitimate to try to experimentally create differences in eye-movement patterns and then determine whether these differences produce differences in estimated line length or distance. For example, he showed observers the two kinds of designs illustrated in Figure 8.15. Previous research had determined that when people have been instructed to fixate a target stimulus, their true fixation point is drawn away toward an irrelevant nearby stimulus. For example, if observers were told to fixate the dot on the left side of Figure 8.15a, their eyes would be drawn inward slightly, toward the irrelevant **X**. Notice, then, that observers asked to shift their glance in Figure 8.15a, from the left-hand dot to the right-hand dot, will end up moving their eyes a shorter distance than those who shift their glance in Figure 8.15b. Coren predicted that observers would judge the distance between the two dots in Figure 8.15a shorter than the distance between the two dots in Figure 8.15b, and in fact they did. Thus, there is some support for an eye-movement explanation for the Müller-Lyer illusion.

The **incorrect comparison theory** states

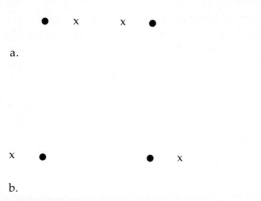

a.

b.

Figure 8.15   Figures similar to those Coren used in studying eye movements in visual illusions.

that observers base their judgments on the incorrect parts of the figures. This explanation of the Müller-Lyer illusion argues that observers are unable to separate the lines from the wings in this figure. As a result, they compare the distances between the ends of the wings. Experimental evidence supports this theory. For example, Coren and Girgus (1972) asked people to judge Müller-Lyer illusions in which the wings were a different color from the lines, so that the wings would not be likely to enter into the comparison. The magnitude of the illusion was greatly reduced. You'll notice that the incorrect comparison theory is somewhat similar to the eye-movement theory; neither relies on the experiences of the viewers to explain the illusions.

Incidentally, you may notice that none of these three explanations suggests that the illusions can be explained at the retinal level. Some theorists had suggested that physiological effects, such as lateral inhibition, might be responsible. However, as Gillam (1980) concludes, the current evidence compellingly argues that the illusions do not originate in the retina. She argues that studies have demonstrated that illusions can still be produced when part of the figure is presented to one eye and another part is presented to the other eye. Therefore, the explanation must originate at a point in the visual system more central than the lateral geniculate nu-

cleus, the earliest step in visual processing at which the inputs from the two eyes first come together.

None of the three dominant theories—misapplied constancy, eye movement, or incorrect comparison—can handle all the line-length illusions by itself. Each illusion probably depends upon at least one of these explanations, as well as other factors that no one has yet developed (Beagley, 1985). It would make life simpler if we could believe in just a single explanation. However, the one-explanation approach to illusions is, in fact, another illusion!

Illusions Involving Area

The illusions we have considered so far have focused on linear distance, involving either the length of a line or the distance between two points. Thus, they involve a single dimension. Other illusions involve area, or two

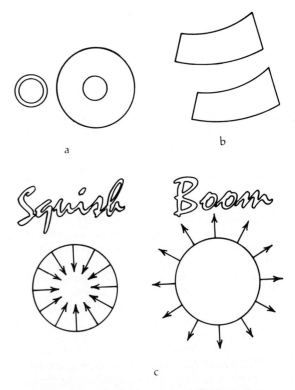

Figure 8.16   Miscellaneous area illusions; in each case two figures are equal in area.

dimensions. Several miscellaneous area illusions are shown in Figure 8.16. However, the most famous area illusion is the moon illusion, the subject of the next in-depth section.

▶ IN-DEPTH:
THE MOON ILLUSION

On a clear evening, watch the moon rise from its position on the horizon and notice the impressive change that appears to occur in the moon's size, even a mere 15 minutes later. The transformation is particularly striking if there are objects, such as trees or buildings, on either side of the moon. In the **moon illusion,** observers generally report that the moon at the horizon looks about 30% bigger than the moon at the zenith, or highest position (Baird & Wagner, 1982; Rock & Kaufman, 1962).

Although the moon illusion is both ancient and impressive, the explanation for this phenomenon is not clear. In this section we will examine a number of proposals that have been suggested, and we will also see why some have been rejected.

Early research on the moon illusion was conducted by Holway and Boring (1940a, 1940b), whose work on size constancy we examined in the first section of this chapter. These researchers proposed that the moon illusion can be traced to the fact that our eyes look upward to see the moon in its zenith position, whereas they look straight ahead to see the moon on the horizon. However, later research demonstrated that the angle of eye elevation did not affect estimated size (Kaufman & Rock, 1962). It is now generally accepted that eye and head position are not worth pursuing as possible explanations for the moon illusion (Baird & Wagner, 1982; Hovde, 1978).

Furthermore, the moon illusion is not a mirage. It cannot be explained by atmospheric conditions, for example. Photographs taken of the horizon moon and the zenith moon show that the moon occupies the same visual angle in both cases. (The visual angle is surprisingly small—only about 0.5°. A nickel held at arm's length will form an image on the retina comparable to the image of either the horizon moon or the zenith moon.) Other experiments have also ruled out differences in color and brightness as possible explanations for the moon illusion (Hershenson, 1982; Kaufman & Rock, 1962).

We know, then, that the moon occupies the same area on the retina in both its horizon and zenith positions. The explanation must therefore be psychological. Several explanations have been proposed, and no single theory has yet won the majority vote.

Let us first examine a theory that had widespread popularity until several years ago. This theory is called the **apparent-distance theory** because it argues that the moon seems to be farther from the viewer when it is on the horizon than when it is at the zenith; the two positions of the moon may differ in their apparent distance from the viewer. An early form of this theory was proposed in the 11th century (Ross & Ross, 1976), but the modern version was developed by Kaufman and Rock (1962).

In Kaufman and Rock's research, observers were asked to report whether an imaginary point at the horizon seemed nearer or farther away than a similar point at the zenith. Almost all observers said that the point seemed farther away when it was at the horizon. On the basis of these observations Kaufman and Rock concluded that people perceived the sky as somewhat flattened, almost Frisbee-shaped. The dotted line in Figure 8.17 represents how Kaufman and Rock's observers seemed to perceive the sky.

Kaufman and Rock related this finding about the apparent shape of the sky to the size-distance invariance hypothesis, which we considered earlier in this chapter in connection with constancy. As mentioned earlier, the moon keeps the same retinal size, whether it is at the zenith or at the horizon. According to the size-distance invariance hypothesis, then, people should think that the moon is larger when they believe the sky is farther from them. If they believe that the sky is Frisbee-shaped, then, as Figure 8.17 shows, the moon should be larger when it is on the horizon because the horizon sky is so far

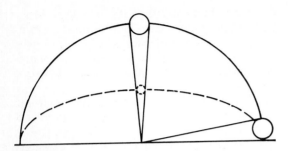

Figure 8.17 Effect of apparent distance of moon on judgments of moon size. Solid curve represents true path of moon in sky; dashed curve represents apparent path of moon against flattened sky. Solid circle represents true size of moon at horizon and at zenith; a dashed circle represents apparent size of moon at zenith. (At horizon, apparent size equals true size.)

away. In contrast, when the moon is at the zenith, people should believe the moon is relatively close to them. If the moon is close to them and the size is still the same, then it looks small. Rather than maintaining its horizon size, the zenith moon appears to shrink down to the dotted-moon size shown in Figure 8.17. (Notice that this explanation is similar to Emmert's law, which says that an afterimage will be smaller if you shift your gaze from a far to a nearby background.)

The apparent-distance theory is complicated enough already, but there was an additional problem. The *moon* itself seems closer, rather than farther away, when it is on the horizon, even though the *surface* to which the moon is attached may seem farther away. Potential answers to this puzzle were proposed, however, and people were generally satisfied with the apparent-distance theory for 20 years.

In 1982, Baird and Wagner decided to test the apparent-distance theory more rigorously. They were concerned because of the apparent contradiction in the theory and also because Kaufman and Rock's (1962) data were gathered on a small number of observers who made judgments under daylight conditions rather than at night. Therefore, Baird and Wagner asked a larger number of ob-

servers to make judgments about the sky's distance in two separate experiments. These judgments were made at night, when the moon was not in view, and the magnitude estimation technique was used. Baird and Wagner's results showed great individual variation among observers' responses. However, the sky at the zenith was judged somewhat farther away than the sky at the horizon. In other words, these results directly contradicted the results of Kaufman and Rock. The sky does *not* seem Frisbee-shaped, and the size-distance invariance hypothesis is not relevant.

Another theory that had been proposed to explain the moon illusion had been receiving relatively little attention, even though it sounded plausible. This theory is similar to one of the other theories of size constancy. You may remember the theory that proposed that size constancy occurs because observers notice an object's size relative to other objects around it. Similarly, Restle (1970) proposed a relative-size explanation for the moon illusion; people judge the size of the moon relative to other objects around it. For example, Kaufman and Rock (1962) had found in connection with their other research that terrain cues next to the horizon were necessary for the moon illusion to occur. All the hills, trees, and buildings that clutter the horizon are necessary if the moon is to look larger there.

Specifically, then, Restle proposed that when the moon is on the horizon, it is judged relative to other objects that have tiny retinal sizes. Looking at the horizon moon in the country, for example, we see objects such as leaves on trees, a distant tractor, and a signpost. Compared to the small retinal sizes of these objects, the moon looks large. When the moon is overhead, it must be judged relative to a huge, uncluttered dome of sky. Compared to that vast sky, the moon looks small.

The relative-size explanation has been updated and modified by John Baird of Dartmouth College, who had also provided evidence that the apparent-distance theory was incorrect. Baird's (1982) theory, called **reference theory,** proposes that both the sky and the ground are important referents when observers judge the size of the moon. More specifically, the first assumption of reference theory is that observers compare the apparent size of the moon with objects on the ground. Those comparison objects are in the vicinity of the point where a weighted line, dropped from the apparent location of the moon, would hit the ground. However, these comparison objects become less important as the moon rises higher and higher above the horizon.

The second assumption of reference theory is that another important referent in judging the moon's size is the empty expanse of the sky. The sky becomes increasingly important as the moon rises above the horizon. Baird proposes four possible models for how these two referents, the ground and the sky, can be combined. The model that Baird believes is best able to match the data on moon-size judgments is a complex trigonometric equation that depends upon both the ground and the sky when the moon is closer to the horizon than the zenith and it depends only upon the sky when the moon is closer to the zenith than the horizon.

In recent years several other explanations for the moon illusion have been explored (Gilinsky, 1980; Hershenson, 1982; Iavecchia, Iavecchia, & Roscoe, 1983; Smith, Smith, Geist, & Zimmerman, 1978). However, the most recent suggestion about the moon illusion is called the terrestrial passage theory (Loftus, 1985; Reed, 1984, 1985). According to the **terrestrial passage theory,** the moon illusion occurs because observers mistakenly treat the moon as if it were an object in terrestrial passage, that is, an object moving through the earth's atmosphere. Consider an airplane flying overhead at a constant elevation above the earth's surface. Suppose that this airplane is flying toward you. As it approaches, its visual angle increases and its distance above the horizon (with respect to the observer) also increases. Thus we are accustomed in everyday experiences to objects growing larger in terms of visual angle as they pass overhead. When objects fail to grow larger, we conclude that they have moved farther away from the earth; for instance, the plane might increase its el-

evation. (We reject the option that the plane has shrunk.)

Now consider the moon. As its distance above the horizon increases, its visual angle does *not* increase. We conclude that the moon has moved farther away (consistent with Baird's interpretation). We also conclude that the moon has decreased in size. You'll note that we specifically rejected the possibility that the plane could shrink. Why is this option possible for the moon? As Reed (1985) explains, a problem with this theory is that "it abandons the object-constancy that is characteristic of human perception of natural objects. But perhaps celestial objects are exceptions" (p. 122).

Unfortunately, we do not have any data about whether people are willing to abandon size constancy when they watch the moon. Personally, I find this explanation perfectly acceptable. Recently, I had spent a frustrating day trying to unravel the mystery of the moon illusion, and I was muttering to myself while driving home that the moon illusion probably didn't deserve all this scientific attention. Suddenly, over to my right, the moon appeared on the horizon. It was monstrous, far more dramatic an illusion than I had recalled. I stopped and watched the moon rise. A mere 5 minutes later, the moon seemed much smaller. It truly appeared to have shrunk. Its lack of size constancy did not bother me. I would be bothered if my daughters or my typewriter or an airplane appeared to truly shrink within a 5-minute period because these are people and things I've been physically close to. I've never been close enough to the moon to know how big it really is, so I'm not greatly disturbed to abandon size constancy.

We have discussed several approaches to the moon illusion. Kaufman and Rock's theory that people perceive the sky as flattened—previously the most popular explanation—must now be rejected. The remaining two theories that seem to have generated the most enthusiasm are that observers compare the moon to both the sky and the ground and that observers judge the moon—inappropriately—the same way they judge the passage of objects through the atmosphere. We can hope that future researchers will reconcile these two approaches; the approaches may even be compatible. However, it is clear that in the discussion of the moon illusion, researchers have been reluctant to gather data. Admittedly, it is difficult to study an illusion that appears for only a short time on nights when the moon is full and the sky is cloudless. In contrast, the Müller-Lyer illusion can be examined in nearly every possible testing situation. Still, it is alarming that Baird's (1982) reference theory had to be tested using moon-illusion data gathered 20 to 40 years earlier. Furthermore, as Loftus (1985) complains, we really have no systematic data to describe the moon distance illusion (that the moon appears closer at the horizon than at the zenith). Also, as mentioned earlier, it would be useful to gather data about observers' willingness to abandon size constancy in the case of the moon illusion. Baird (1982) notes that many studies have examined the perception of a *simulated* moon; however, how realistic can that simu-

lation be when the real moon is so much farther away than any artificial moon created in laboratory studies? In summary, it might be wise to stop theorizing about the moon illusion until we have gathered more data on real observers watching the real moon. ■

Direction and Shape Illusions

So far we have focused on size illusions, which included both line-length/distance illusions (such as the Müller-Lyer illusion) and area illusions (such as the moon illusion). Clearly the size illusions have attracted far more attention than the other major class of illusions, those which involve direction and shape.

One of the most familiar of the direction and shape illusions is the Poggendorf illusion (see Demonstration 8.9). In the **Poggendorf illusion** a line disappears at an angle behind a solid figure. It appears on the other side of the solid figure at a position that seems wrong. In the classic version of the Poggendorf illusion, the "solid figure" is simply two

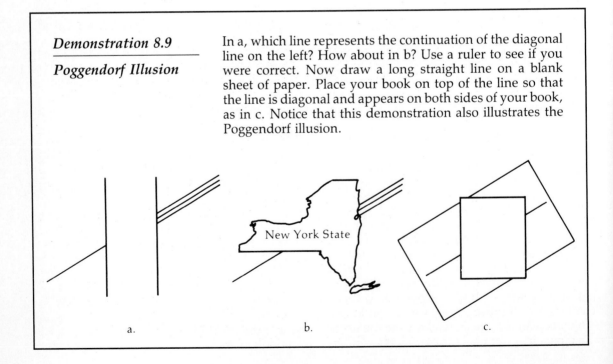

Demonstration 8.9

Poggendorf Illusion

In a, which line represents the continuation of the diagonal line on the left? How about in b? Use a ruler to see if you were correct. Now draw a long straight line on a blank sheet of paper. Place your book on top of the line so that the line is diagonal and appears on both sides of your book, as in c. Notice that this demonstration also illustrates the Poggendorf illusion.

New York State

a.   b.   c.

lines. However, the Poggendorf illusion can be produced by placing almost anything in front of a thin line. A map of the state of New York and your own textbook both work well.

Coren and Girgus (1978) point out that the Poggendorf illusion has many important applications in everyday life. A surgeon may use a probe to try to remove a bullet. In an X-ray the probe, a bone, and the bullet might be arranged as in Figure 8.18. Although it looks as though the probe is lined up so that it will touch the bullet, the Poggendorf illusion is at work—it will miss it completely. Architects also need to be concerned with this illusion. A line hidden behind a column will look displaced when it emerges on the other side.

The final example of Coren and Girgus's book is particularly chilling. In 1965, two airplanes were preparing for landing in the New York City area. A cloud formation was between them, and because of the Poggendorf illusion they seem to be headed for each other. Quickly, the two pilots changed their paths to correct for what they thought was an error. With the revised routes, the two planes collided. Four people died and 49 were injured, and only an illusion was to blame.

Gillam (1980) uses a variation of the misapplied constancy theory to explain the Poggendorf illusion. She argues that an observer sees the display as a solid figure facing forward, with the line receding in space. For example, in Demonstration 8.9a, the lower left end of the line might be nearer to you than the upper right end. If the line really were receding in space, then it should emerge from the other side of the solid figure at a place several millimeters lower than it does. On the other hand, Coren and Girgus (1978) argue that much of the Poggendorf illusion can be traced to anatomical and physiological factors, such as blur and lateral inhibition. As we have mentioned with other illusions, more than one explanation may be necessary to produce the effect.

Several effective illusions can be constructed out of lines that look as though they are made of twisted cords. Demonstration 8.10 shows both a tilted line illusion and a shape illusion. A quilt maker working with checkered gingham fabric should be very cautious about using a decorative trim. Any trim resembling a twisted cord should be pretested!

Other illusions distort the shape of lines or other geometric figures. For instance, the lines in Figure 8.19a are parallel to each other, yet they appear to bulge outward in the middle. In contrast, the parallel lines in Figure 8.19b appear to be closer to each other in the middle. Figures 8.19c and 8.19d show a circle and a square that are distorted by the surrounding lines. You may notice that Figure 8.19d is a variation on the Ponzo illusion because the top line is perceived to be more distant, and therefore larger.

Finally, look at Figure 8.20. The wood grain in this frame is very noticeable. As a result, the frame looks as if it is badly warped. A woodworker should beware of highly visible wood grains unless he or she wants chair legs to look crooked and tables to look lopsided.

This section on illusions has demonstrated that illusions can cause distortions in line length, area, direction, and shape. In many cases the illusions seem to be governed by the same rules that govern the constancies. Furthermore, they have practical importance in many applied areas. We discussed the use of illusion in several applied areas, but readers who are interested in illusions in painting and

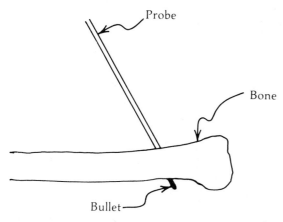

Figure 8.18 Example of Poggendorf illusion.

Demonstration 8.10

Twisted Cord Illusions

In a, convince yourself that the letters are oriented straight up and down. Either measure the distance of the top and bottom of a letter from one of the sides or notice that the top and bottom of each letter are located along the same column of dark diamonds in the checked pattern. In b, place your finger at any point along the "spiral" and trace around, trying to get to the center of the design.

a

b

other art should pursue the topic in several books: *Illusion in Nature and Art* (Gregory & Gombrich, 1973); *Illusion in Art* (Mastai, 1975); *Illusions, Patterns and Pictures: A Cross-Cultural Perspective* (Deregowski, 1980).

Summary: Illusions

1. An illusion is an incorrect perception; theorists disagree about whether illusions are important. It is difficult to classify illusions.
2. The line-length and distance illusions include the Müller-Lyer illusion (and its many variants), the Sander parallelo-

gram, the horizontal-vertical illusion, the Ponzo illusion, and the filled space–open space illusion. In addition, there are illusions based on the Gestalt laws of perceptual organization.
3. A popular explanation for some illusions is the theory of misapplied constancy, in which cues in the illusion are interpreted as cues for maintaining size constancy. Research has demonstrated that experience with depth cues and rectangular stimuli enhances these illusions, a finding that supports the theory of misapplied constancy. However, this theory cannot explain all the illusions.

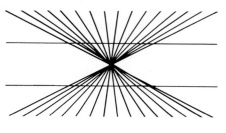

a.

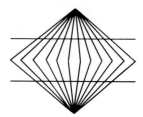

b.

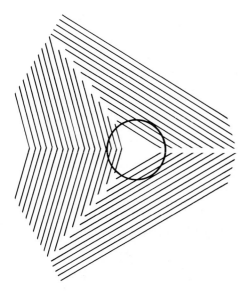

c.

d.

Figure 8.19 Distortions of shape.

4. According to the eye-movement theory illusions can be traced to differences in eye-movement patterns. For example, the eyes may move more in the wings-outward version of the Müller-Lyer illusion than in the wings-inward version.

5. The incorrect comparison theory proposes that illusions occur when observers base their judgments on the incorrect parts of the figures. This theory, like the other two, proposes that illusions do not originate in the retina.

6. The most famous area illusion is the moon illusion, in which the moon looks about 30% bigger when it is at the horizon than when it is at the zenith.

7. There is no clear explanation for the moon illusion. Some proposals that have been rejected include the idea that the illusion occurs because the zenith moon is viewed from a different angle of eye elevation, the mirage explanation, and theories involving color and brightness. Kaufman and Rock's theory, based on the perceived shape of the sky, has also been rejected.

8. Restle proposed that people judge the

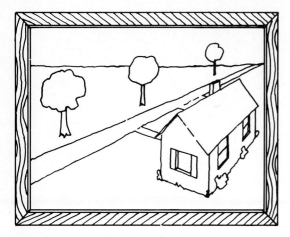

Figure 8.20 Illusion in which shape is distorted by wood grain in picture frame.

size of the moon relative to other objects around it, and this theory has been up-

Review

1. Suppose you have two lines of identical length. You place one line 1 m (3.3 ft) from yourself and the other 5 m (16.4 ft) from yourself. Compare the retinal sizes and the perceived sizes of the two objects. You draw wings pointing inward on one of the lines and wings pointing outward on the other. If they are the same distance from you, compare the retinal size and the perceived sizes. Which situation is constancy and which is illusion? How does the theory of misapplied constancy interrelate the two topics?

2. In the discussion of size constancy we saw that the removal of distance cues leads to a reduction in size constancy. Discuss how this effect could be explained by each of these three theories: (a) the size-distance invariance hypothesis; (b) the relative size explanation; and (c) Gibson's direct perception explanation.

3. What is Emmert's law and how is it related to one of the theories of size constancy, specifically, the size-distance in-

dated in the form of Baird's reference theory. In this theory, observers compare the moon with both the sky and objects on the horizon when it is relatively close to the horizon, and they compare the moon with the sky when it is relatively close to the zenith.

9. Other theories of the moon illusion include the terrestrial passage theory, which proposes that observers judge the moon's passage through the sky the same way they judge the passage of terrestrial objects.

10. The moon illusion has produced many theories but no abundance of data; it is difficult to explain the illusion unless we have more information about observers' judgments.

11. Direction and shape illusions, such as the Poggendorf illusion, can have important applications in daily life.

variance hypothesis? Explain how Rock's development of that hypothesis proposes that perception involves thoughtlike processes.

4. MacDonald and Hoffman (1973) studied messages written on road pavement. They were written either in normally proportioned letters or in tall letters (so that when a driver viewed them from the typical slant of the automobile, the retinal images were normally proportioned). From what you know about constancy, which kind of letter would you guess would be recognized more accurately? What kind of constancy is this?

5. Suppose that you wear a black-and-white striped shirt and emerge from a darkened movie theater into the bright sunlight. How would Helmholtz's theory and contrast theory account for the brightness constancy you experience when you look at your shirt? Albedo should be discussed in this explanation. Try to think of examples from your recent experience to il-

lustrate each of the following constancies: motion constancy, position constancy, color constancy, and existence constancy.

6. Discuss why the empiricist explanations for the three major constancies—size constancy, shape constancy, and brightness constancy—are similar to one another.

7. Gibson (1950) argued that humans and animals react to the spatial environment with enormous accuracy and precision and that our visual worlds agree very closely with the environment. How does this argument correspond with his views on the importance of illusions?

8. This chapter argues that the major distortions in illusions do not occur at the retinal level. Discuss this issue and point out how the cross-cultural research on illusions also supports this conclusion.

9. Explain the Müller-Lyer illusion in terms of each of the following theories: (a) misapplied constancy, (b) eye movement, and (c) incorrect comparison.

10. Imagine that a friend who is a college student but not a psychology major discovers that you are taking a course that covers illusions. Suppose that this person asks the question you dread: Why is the moon so big at the horizon and so small when it is overhead? Give a simple, clear summary of the two current theories most extensively discussed in this chapter. Now suppose that this friend recalls reading in an introductory textbook that the illusion could be traced to something about the shape of the sky. What would you reply?

New Terms

distal stimulus
proximal stimulus
constancy
size constancy
visual angle
retinal size
overconstancy
underconstancy
Emmert's law
size-distance invariance
  hypothesis
unconscious inference
relative-size explanation
direct perception explanation

invariants
shape constancy
ecological validity
shape-slant invariance
  hypothesis
brightness constancy
brightness
albedo
contrast theory
color constancy
motion constancy
position constancy
existence constancy
illusion

mirages
Müller-Lyer illusion
Sander parallelogram
horizontal-vertical illusion
Ponzo illusion
filled-space–open-space illusion
theory of misapplied constancy
eye-movement theory
incorrect comparison theory
moon illusion
apparent-distance theory
reference theory
terrestrial passage theory
Poggendorf illusion

Recommended Readings

Coren, S., & Girgus, J. S. (1978). *Seeing is deceiving: The psychology of visual illusions.* Hillsdale, NJ: Erlbaum. *This clearly written book emphasizes that illusions are part of the normal perceptual processes. Theories and applications of illusions are also discussed.*

Epstein, W. (Ed.). (1977). *Stability and constancy in visual perception: Mechanisms and processes.* New York: Wiley. *I am not aware of any more recent book written specifically about the constancies. This book contains 13 chapters on topics such as stereoscopic depth constancy, the effect of instruction on constancy judgments, and a history of the study of constancy.*

Michaels, C. F., & Carello, C. (1981). *Direct perception.* Englewood Cliffs, NJ: Prentice-Hall.

This book is one of the clearest and most concise summaries of Gibson's ideas about perception, including the constancies.

Rock, I. (1983). *The logic of perception.* Cambridge, Ma.: The MIT Press. *According to Rock, perceptual issues such as constancy involve an unconscious inference; to perceive is to solve a problem regarding* the characteristics of the distal stimulus. This book is a convincing summary of his position.

Wade, N. (1982). *The art and science of visual illusions.* London: Routledge & Kegan Paul. *This book is primarily a collection of illusions; the text itself is brief. It contains some elegant Moiré patterns and other Op Art designs and some interesting variations of the classical illusions.*

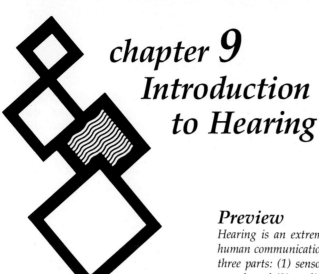

chapter 9
Introduction to Hearing

Preview

Hearing is an extremely important perceptual system, and its role in human communication is vital. This introduction to hearing consists of three parts: (1) sensory aspects of hearing, (2) perceptual responses to sound, and (3) applications of hearing research.

The sounds we hear can be described in terms of sound waves that differ in their frequency and amplitude. This section of the chapter examines the auditory system, including the three sections of the ear, the pathway from the ear to the brain, and the auditory cortex. It also considers two theories about how frequency is registered in the auditory system and how these theories can be reconciled.

The second section looks at psychological qualities related to the physical features of sound. Although the correlations are less than perfect, pitch is roughly correlated with frequency, and loudness is roughly correlated with amplitude. Timbre, or a tone's quality, is the characteristic that distinguishes the tone of an oboe from the tone of a flute; timbre depends largely upon the complexity of sound waves. The next topic in this section is the perception of tone combinations. Depending upon the physical characteristics of the tones, the combination may be heard either as a single tone or as two tones, which are either pleasant or unpleasant in combination; one tone may also mask the other. The final topic is an in-depth examination of how we determine the direction from which a sound is coming.

In the final section we consider two applications of hearing research, noise pollution and hearing impairments. The discussion of noise pollution includes how thresholds can shift after a loud noise, how noise pollution influences human behavior, and how noise pollution can be reduced. The examination of hearing impairments focuses on two kinds of deafness, conduction deafness and nerve deafness.

Take a minute to appreciate the variety of sounds you hear nearby. There may be voices and music, rattles, thuds, whines, buzzes, squeaks, roars, and drips. Some sounds are loud and some are soft. Some are high, some low. Sounds also vary in their apparent location.

We assume that vision is our most important perceptual process, assigning hearing to second place. However, consider the variety of ways in which hearing provides us with information about the world. Nathan (1982) points out the evolutionary importance of hearing, which was essential in detecting the approach of predatory animals and in locating the flow of streams. Even in the twentieth century, hearing can be critically important in informing us of danger. We hear a barking dog, a car horn, and a shout of "Fire!"

Hearing is also vital to human communication because it is central in social interactions and in transmitting knowledge. This is why Evans (1982a) argues that hearing is even more important than vision for humans. As he notes, "It has been said that a blind person is cut off from the world of *things*, whereas one who is deaf is cut off from the world of *people*" (p. 239). Furthermore, hearing is a major source of entertainment in music, movies, and plays.

We will begin this chapter by examining sensory aspects of hearing; then we will consider perceptual qualities of sound and two applications of hearing research. The next chapter will consider two topics concerned with complex auditory perception—music and speech.

SENSORY ASPECTS OF HEARING

Chapter 3 introduced the visual stimulus—light—and the structure of the visual system. Now we need to examine the equivalent topics for hearing: the auditory stimulus—sound waves—and the structure of the auditory system.

Auditory Stimulus

The auditory stimuli we hear are caused by tiny disturbances in air pressure. Something vibrates, and the vibration causes molecules of air to change their positions and collide with each other, causing sound waves.

Perhaps the easiest way to visualize these sound waves is to consider how air molecules respond to a vibrating diaphragm on the speaker of a stereo. Try Demonstration 9.1 to appreciate how this diaphragm vibrates impressively by moving forward and backward.

Similarly, the speaker diaphragm influences the surrounding air molecules. When the diaphragm moves forward, it shoves the surrounding air molecules close together. The density of the air molecules next to the diaphragm increases. (Imagine how the density of people standing in a room would increase if one wall were to move inward.) When the diaphragm moves backward, a partial vacuum is created and the surrounding air molecules move apart. The density of the air molecules decreases. (Imagine how the density of people in a room would decrease if one wall were to move outward.) This change in the density of air molecules produces a corresponding change in atmospheric pressure.

When your stereo plays a typical note, the speaker diaphragm could repeat the cycle of moving forward and backward a total of 500 times in 1 second. In other words, the atmospheric pressure next to the diaphragm could increase and decrease 500 times in the time it takes you to blink your eye. (As we'll see later, it could also vibrate as seldom as about 20 times a second or as often as 20,000 times a second.)

Each individual air molecule moves very little during this process. Instead, a wave of pressure moves continuously outward from the vibrating diaphragm. Notice in Figure 9.1 the areas of high atmospheric pressure, represented by the high density of air molecules, and the areas of low atmospheric pressure, represented by the low density of air molecules. (Of course, this diagram is schematic, since the air molecules are invisible.) This

---

---

wave of pressure resembles the ripples created when you throw a stone into a pond, with the ripples traveling outward from the source of the disturbance.

Now suppose that we were to measure the atmospheric pressure near the speaker diaphragm, recording this pressure as it increases and decreases during one cycle. Figure 9.2 illustrates a typical diagram of a sound wave. You can see that the shape of the sound wave resembles the sine wave functions discussed in Chapters 3 and 6 in connection with light waves.

The wave of pressure traveling outward

from your stereo will ultimately reach your eardrum. The rapid increase and decrease in atmospheric pressure will cause your eardrum to move backward and forward, also in a sine-wave fashion. These successive pressure changes are called **sounds**.

You hear a sound because of tiny disturbances in air pressure. This seems incredible. How can the movement of invisible air molecules possibly be strong enough to cause your eardrum to move? The truth is that they need to displace your eardrum by only a miniscule amount—about .000000001 cm (.0000000004 in) (Green, 1976). The distance is difficult to imagine; it is one billionth of a centimeter!

We have discussed how sound travels through air, where it moves at a speed of about 340 m (1115 ft) each second. Sound can also travel through other media. For example, it travels more than 4 times as fast through water and nearly 15 times as fast through steel. However, most of our hearing occurs with our heads in the air rather than immersed in water or encased in steel. Therefore most of this chapter will examine sound moving through air. Let's examine how sound waves can vary in their frequency and their amplitude. Demonstration 9.2 illustrates these two qualities.

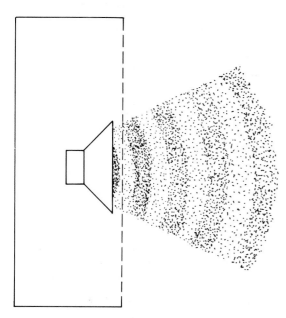

Figure 9.1 Areas of high and low atmospheric pressure created by vibrating diaphragm in stereo.

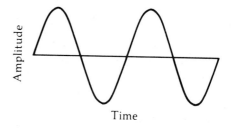

Figure 9.2 Sound wave.

Demonstration 9.2
_____

Frequency and
Amplitude of
Sound Waves

Place a rubber band over an open box. By plucking the rubber band gently or vigorously, you can vary the amplitude or height of the sound waves associated with the sound of the rubber band. By pulling the rubber band tightly on the side of the box, you can vary the frequency of the sound waves associated with the sound of the rubber band.

Frequency

Frequency is the number of cycles a sound wave completes in 1 second. For example, middle C on the piano has a frequency of 262 cycles per second, or 262 Hz. (The abbreviation **Hz** is derived from the name of Heinrich Hertz, a German physicist.) Frequency generally corresponds to the psychological experience of pitch, although we'll discuss later in the chapter why the correspondence is far from perfect. Thus, middle C on the piano, with a frequency of 262 Hz, sounds higher than the lowest note on the piano, which has a frequency of about 27 Hz. Also, the sound wave in Figure 9.3a has a higher frequency (the sound source vibrates more frequently) than the one in Figure 9.3b and will probably sound higher.

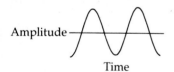

Amplitude

Time

a.

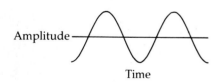

Amplitude

Time

b.

Figure 9.3 Two sound waves differing in frequency.

Table 9.1 shows five kinds of measurement units used in this chapter and the next. They are listed in the same order in which they are introduced in the chapter. As you can see, some units (such as Hz) measure the physical attributes of sound; others assess its psychological dimensions.

What range of frequencies can humans hear? Young adults can typically hear tones with frequencies as low as 20 Hz and as high as 20,000 Hz (Gelfand, 1981). Older adults, as we will see in Chapter 15, may have difficulty hearing tones as high as 20,000 Hz. Most of our auditory experience, however, involves only a small fraction of that 20 to 20,000 Hz range. For example, singers at a concert are unlikely to sing a note with a basic frequency below 75 Hz or above 1000 Hz.

Let us examine detection thresholds for tones of various frequencies; **detection thresholds** measure the smallest amount of a stimulus that can be detected 50% of the time. Humans are more sensitive in detecting tones in the 3000-Hz range than they are in detecting higher or lower tones (Gelfand, 1981; Sivian & White, 1933). Intriguingly, the frequency of agonized human screams may reach as high as 3000 Hz.

The frequency of a tone influences discrimination as well as detection. You may recall that psychophysical techniques can be used to measure a difference threshold. A **difference threshold** is the smallest change in a stimulus that can produce a difference noticeable 50% of the time. We can notice differences more readily in the low-frequency range. For example, a 60-Hz tone can be dis-

Table 9.1 Measurement Units Used in Audition

Quality Measured	Name of Unit	How Measured	Page on Which Quality is Discussed
Physical:			
Frequency	Hz (Hertz)	Number of cycles completed in one second	p. 268
Sound pressure	dB (decibel)	Ratio of two pressures (20 log P_1/P_0)	p. 270
Psychological:			
Pitch	Mel	1000 mels = 1000 Hz at 60 dB (Other pitches are assigned other mel values.)	p. 284
Loudness	Sone	1 sone = 40 dB tone of 1000 Hz (Other loudnesses are assigned other sone values.)	p. 286
Loudness	Phon	40 phons = loudness equal to 40 dB tone of 1000 Hz (All equally loud tones—on an equal loudness contour—have the same number of phons.)	p. 287

criminated from a 62-Hz tone about 50% of the time; thus, the difference threshold in that region is 2 Hz. However, a 3000-Hz tone cannot be discriminated from a 3002-Hz tone. Tones in this high-frequency range require a difference threshold of about 16 Hz. Thus, a 3000-Hz tone could be discriminated from a 3016-Hz tone about 50% of the time.

Data on difference thresholds can be expressed in terms of Weber's fraction, in which the difference threshold is divided by the frequency of the tone. The Weber's fraction is particularly remarkable in the intermediate frequency range, which is the range you are likely to hear in a concert (about 500 to 2000 Hz). We are so sensitive to changes in frequency in this range that the Weber's fraction can be as small as 0.3% (Evans, 1982b). In other words, we need to change a tone's frequency by only 0.3% to notice a difference. In contrast, we are relatively insensitive to change when judging taste (where Weber's fractions are usually about 20%) and smells (where Weber's fractions are usually about 25%—roughly 100 times less sensitive).

So far our discussion of frequency has included only **pure tones**, which are most likely to be encountered in laboratory settings. Most sounds we hear in our everyday lives—including musical instruments and speech—are **complex tones**, tones that cannot be represented by one simple sine wave. For example, look at the complex tone illustrated in Figure 9.4, which represents the combination of several different tones. We will consider these more complex auditory stimuli in the discussion of timbre later in this chapter and in Chapter 10.

Amplitude

This chapter has described the frequency of sound waves. Now let's consider their **am-**

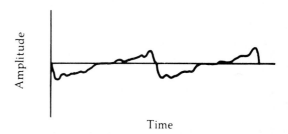

Figure 9.4 Example of complex tone.

plitude, or the change in pressure created by the sound waves. In general, amplitude corresponds to the psychological experience of loudness. That is, a high-amplitude sound wave moves your eardrum more than a low-amplitude sound wave, and the sound seems louder. Thus, the sound wave in Figure 9.5a has a higher amplitude than the one in Figure 9.5b, and it will usually also sound louder.

The frequency of sound waves can be described in direct, obvious units—number of cycles per second. Unfortunately, the units used to describe amplitude are more indirect and difficult to understand. The reason is that the range of amplitudes we can hear is impressively extreme. The most intense sound we can tolerate is about 1,000,000,000,000 more intense than the weakest one we can detect. Using a direct, unconverted scale would involve measurements such as 875,934,771. Instead, we use a scale that involves a logarithmic transformation. As you'll recall from earlier chapters, a logarithmic scale is useful in shrinking large numbers.

Decibels, which measure the amount of pressure created by a stimulus such as a sound wave, are measured in terms of the following equation:

Number of decibels $= 20 \log(P_1/P_0)$

According to this formula for decibels (or **dB**), we multiply 20 times the logarithm of the ratio

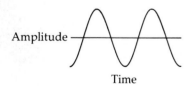

Amplitude

Time

a.

Amplitude

Time

b.

Figure 9.5   Two sound waves differing in amplitude.

of P_1 to P_0, where P_1 is the sound pressure level of the stimulus we want to measure in decibels and P_0 is a standard reference level researchers have agreed upon. Specifically, this reference level sound is a 1000 Hz tone that can just barely be heard under ideal conditions. This threshold, reference-level sound is usually set at 0.0002 dynes/cm². (Air pressure is often measured in terms of this unit called **dynes**, for each square centimeter.)

Logarithmic transformations shrink the large numbers drastically, but they have more modest effects on small numbers. Thus, the amplitude of heavy automobile traffic could be given as 10,000,000,000 (in comparison with a barely detectable, reference-level sound). However, the logarithmic scale shrinks this large number to 100 dB, a manageable number. The amplitude of a soft whisper, which could be given as 100, is converted to 20 dB—a much more modest change.

Table 9.2 shows some representative decibel levels for sounds that humans can hear. Notice that decibels are standardized so that 0 dB represents the weakest sound you can hear. Values above 120 dB are painful and can cause permanent hearing loss.

We discussed our impressive ability to discriminate differences in frequency. Humans are also spectacular in their ability to discriminate differences in amplitude. The human auditory system is so remarkable that it can discriminate two complex sounds, each consisting of 21 tones of identical frequencies, but *a single tone* being somewhat greater in amplitude in the second sound. Despite the subtlety of the difference between the two sounds, observers can tell that they are not identical (Green, 1983; Green, Kidd, & Picardi, 1983).

Auditory System

We have been discussing sound pressure changes. Once these sound pressure changes have been transmitted to a human observer, certain changes must occur in the auditory system to transform the physical energy into a kind of energy that can be transmitted by

Table 9.2 Some Typical Amplitudes of Various Noises, Measured by Decibel Scale

Level	dB	Example
	160	Loudest rock band on record
Intolerable	140	Jet airplane taking off
	120	Very loud thunder
Very noisy	100	Heavy automobile traffic
Loud	80	Loud music from radio
Moderate	60	Average conversation
Faint	40	Quiet neighborhood
	20	Soft whisper
Very faint	0	Softest detectable noise

neurons. What happens to sound waves when they reach the ear, and how do the various parts of the ear contribute to the transformation process?

There are three anatomical regions in the ear. Their names, fortunately, are refreshingly straightforward: the outer ear, the middle ear, and the inner ear. As Nathan (1982) points out, all three parts develop in the human embryo out of the surface epithelium, the covering that will later become the skin. We will see that the receptors in the inner ear resemble the receptors in the skin because they detect pressure and movement. As stressed in the first theme of this textbook, the perceptual systems share important similarities.

This section first discusses the three regions of the ear, and then examines how frequency and amplitude are registered in the inner ear. Finally, it considers higher levels of auditory processing.

Outer Ear

The most obvious part of the outer ear is what people ordinarily refer to as "*the* ear." The technical name for this flap of external tissue is the **pinna**. In humans the pinnae protect the inner parts of the ear, and they slightly increase the sound amplitude (Scharf & Buus, 1986). They also help somewhat in determining the direction from which a sound is coming, as we'll discuss later in the chapter. However, other animals—such as dogs, horses, owls, and bats—have more useful pinnae (Stebbins, 1983; Stokes, 1985). Their ears can be moved around to help localize sounds. Even your Uncle Fred, who can wiggle his ears entertainingly at family reunions, cannot move his pinnae enough to improve his localization ability.

Figure 9.6 shows other structures in the outer ear. Notice the tube, called the **external auditory canal**, that runs inward from the pinna. The external auditory canal is about 0.8 cm (0.3 inches) in diameter and 2.5 cm (1 inch) long. This structure helps keep insects, small objects, and dirt away from the sensitive eardrum (Scharf & Buus, 1986). Furthermore, this canal behaves somewhat like a resonant tube, such as an organ pipe, and can amplify some frequencies impressively. The maximum amplification is about 11 dB for frequencies of about 4000 Hz (Warren, 1982). If you can barely hear the piccolo in a symphony orchestra, thank your external auditory canals!

Finally, there is the **eardrum**, or **tympanic membrane**, the thin piece of membrane that vibrates in response to sound waves. This membrane is the most important structure in the outer ear.

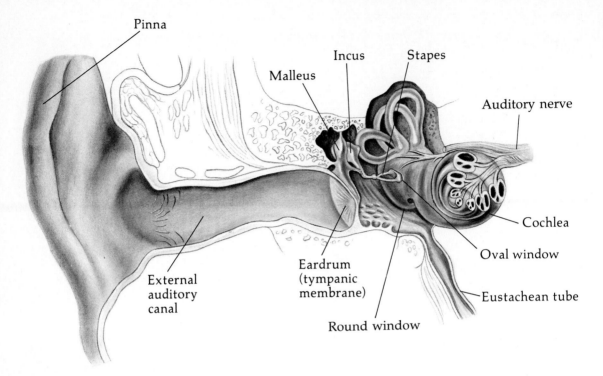

Figure 9.6   Anatomy of ear.

Middle Ear

The middle ear is the area on the outer side of the eardrum, occupying only about 2 cm³ (.1 cubic inches). The middle ear contains three bones known as the **ossicles**, the smallest bones in the human body. They are individually called the **malleus** (or hammer), the **incus** (or anvil), and the **stapes** (or stirrup), all referring rather poetically to their shapes.

The ossicles are not merely decorative structures but are critical in solving a basic problem faced by the auditory system. Sound waves travel through the air until they reach the inner ear. Air doesn't offer much opposition to the flow of sound waves. Within the inner ear, however, sound waves must travel through liquid, a medium that *does* offer opposition to their flow. This resistance to the passage of sound waves is known as **impedance** (Gelfand, 1981). You can demonstrate the differences in impedance for air and water by trying Demonstration 9.3. When the impedances for two media differ, **impedance mismatch** results, and sound waves cannot be readily transmitted from one medium to another. When the sound in air reaches a liquid, there is a loss of about 30 dB, or about 99.9% of the power. Most of the sound energy is simply reflected back into the air (Warren, 1982).

Three important processes help solve the impedance mismatch problem by increasing the efficiency with which sound is transmitted to the inner ear (Warren, 1982):

1. The eardrum is somewhat curved, which makes it respond more efficiently.

2. The three ossicles act like a lever, which offers a small but important mechanical advantage.

3. The force of the relatively large tympanic membrane is transmitted to the much

---

Demonstration 9.3
───────────────
**Difference in
Impedance for Air
and Water**

For this demonstration you'll need to be in a swimming pool (or a less satisfactory substitute, a bathtub). With your head out of water, identify a noise that is approximately at threshold. Now see whether you can hear the noise with your head below the surface of the water. Repeat the comparison with sounds varying in loudness.

---

smaller region where the stapes meets the oval window of the cochlea, a relationship you can see in Figure 9.6. In fact, the ratio of the size of the tympanic membrane to the size of the stirrup is about 17 to 1.

When these three factors are combined, the magnitude of the sound waves is increased by a factor somewhere between 20 and 100 (Gelfand, 1981). In short, then, the auditory system is well designed to recover a good part of the energy lost because of impedance mismatch. As stressed in Theme 3 of this book, our perceptual systems are impressive structures that are typically ideally set up to accomplish perceptual tasks.

Each middle ear also contains a **eustachian tube**, which connects the ear to the throat. The eustachian tubes help equalize the air pressure in the auditory system. When you swallow, for instance, the eustachian tubes open up and allow air to flow into or out of the middle ear. You've probably heard your ears "pop" when you change altitudes in an airplane or in an elevator in a tall building; the tiny explosion represents the sudden flow of air during a dramatic change in pressure.

Inner Ear

The major structure in the inner ear is the bony, fluid-filled **cochlea**, which contains receptors for auditory stimuli. Its name means "snail" in Latin, appropriately describing its coiled shape. It is small, only about half the size pictured in Figure 9.6.

The stapes rests directly on a location in the cochlea known as the **oval window**, a membrane that covers an opening in the

cochlea. When the stapes vibrates, the oval window vibrates, creating pressure changes in the liquid inside the cochlea. Figure 9.7 shows a close-up of the cochlea, including the relationship between the stapes and the oval window. If the cochlea were uncoiled, it would be about 3.5 cm (1.4 inches) long.

Figure 9.7 also shows that the cochlea has three canals running through its entire length. The one on which the stapes rests is called the **vestibular canal**. At the far end of the vestibular canal is a tiny opening called the **helicotrema**. Here the fluid can flow through to the other canal, the **tympanic canal**. You'll notice that the tympanic canal has its own membrane-covered opening, the **round window**. Excessive pressure on the stapes can displace liquid along the vestibular canal, through the helicotrema, and back along the tympanic canal, where the round window can bulge outward from the extra pressure.

Although the round window's bulging may serve as a release in cases of extreme

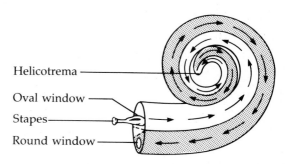

Figure 9.7 Schematic drawing of cochlea (partially uncoiled).

Helicotrema
Oval window
Stapes
Round window

pressure, another mechanism is more common and more important for hearing. Specifically, pressure from the stapes on the vestibular canal pushes on the elastic partition between the vestibular canal and the **cochlear duct**, the third of the three canals in the cochlea and the one that houses the auditory receptors. When the stapes causes the oval window to vibrate, the vibration is transmitted to the membrane beneath the vestibular canal. This vibration in turn stimulates the auditory receptors. Thus, the auditory system includes an appropriate distribution of bony structures and elastic structures to guarantee that the sound pressure (which the middle ear works so hard to maintain) is ultimately transmitted to the auditory receptors. At this point in your reading, jargon shock may have reached an advanced state. Keep in mind, however, that each of these tiny structures has an important function in enabling you to hear.

Now let's enter the cochlear duct, which holds several even more important structures. Figure 9.8 shows an enlargement of the triangular-shaped cochlear duct and the organ of Corti. The **organ of Corti** contains the receptors that change the pressure energy from a sound wave into the kind of electrical and chemical energy that can be carried through the higher pathways in the auditory system.

The organ of Corti has two important membranes, the **basilar membrane**, which is on the base of the organ of Corti, and the **tectorial membrane**, which rests at the top. (It may help to remember that *b*asilar is the *b*ottom and *t*ectorial is the *t*op.) The organ of Corti also includes the **hair cells**, the actual

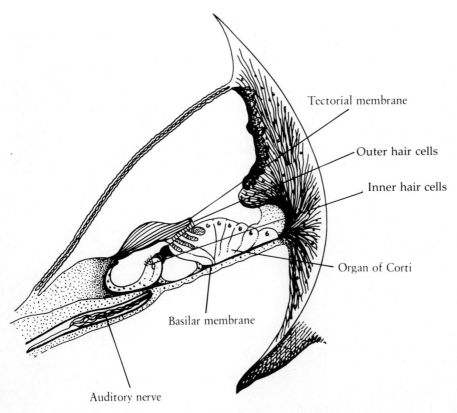

Tectorial membrane

Outer hair cells

Inner hair cells

Organ of Corti

Basilar membrane

Auditory nerve

Figure 9.8 Cross-section of cochlea showing organ of Corti.

receptors for hearing. The basilar membrane in the inner ear therefore resembles skin, as mentioned earlier in the chapter, because hairs protrude from its surface.

There are two kinds of hair cells, just as there are two kinds of vision receptors. You'll be pleased to learn that their names are straightforward: inner hair cells and outer hair cells. Figure 9.9 shows an electron micrograph of these structures after the tectorial membrane has been removed. The **inner hair cells** are on the inner side of the organ of Corti, and they are relatively scarce. There are two rows of inner hair cells. The **outer hair cells** are on the outer side of the organ of Corti, and they are relatively abundant. There are three to six rows of outer hair cells. Now, as you may recall from the discussion of the visual receptors, there are more rods than cones, and many rods have to "share" a ganglion cell, whereas there are relatively few cones for each ganglion cell. Similarly in the auditory system, the inner hair cells and the outer hair cells do not share the auditory nerve fibers equally. Specifically, the relatively scarce inner hair cells have the luxury of "owning" about 90% of the auditory nerve fibers. In contrast, the relatively abundant outer hair cells must share the remaining 10% of the auditory nerve fibers. In the organ of Corti, as in life itself, resources are distributed unequally.

The two kinds of hair cells differ in another characteristic. The inner hair cells are attached only to the basilar membrane and not to the upper tectorial membrane. Their **cilia**, or tiny tufts of hair, float free. In contrast, the outer hair cells are attached to both

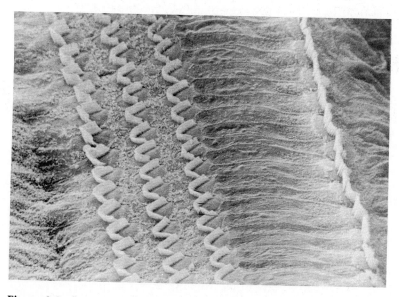

Figure 9.9 Inner and outer hair cells. (Photograph courtesy of Dr. David Lim.)

the basilar and the tectorial membranes. Their cilia are imbedded in the membrane above them (Lim, 1980).

With so many differences between these two kinds of hair cells, we should expect them to perform different functions. The research on this subject is not nearly so clear-cut as with the two kinds of visual receptors, but there are some tentative conclusions (Dallos, 1981; Ryan, Dallos, & McGee, 1979). In studies on experimental animals either the inner hair cells or the outer hair cells have been destroyed, and then the animal's auditory capabilities are measured. It seems likely on the basis of this research that the inner hair cells are sensitive to a tone's frequency, whereas the outer hair cells are responsible for detecting sounds near threshold. Thus the inner hair cells (which have the largest share of auditory nerve fibers) perform the refined task of conveying frequency information. The outer hair cells, in contrast, perform the relatively coarse task of simply identifying whether a tone is present. The inner hair cells are similar to the visual system's cones, which convey information about color. The outer hair cells are similar to the visual system's rods, which are sensitive to weak stimuli such as dim lights.

We've introduced the main structures in the organ of Corti; now let's see what they do. You'll recall that the vibrations on the oval window were transmitted to the membrane between the vestibular canal and the tympanic canal. In turn, this vibration produces a displacement in the basilar membrane. This displacement bends the cilia on the hair cells. The cilia on the inner hair cells, attached only to the basilar membrane, are bent like the hairs on your arm when you swim through water. The cilia on the outer hair cells, attached to both the basilar and the tectorial membranes, are bent because the two surfaces are displaced relative to each other when the basilar membrane moves (Scharf & Buus, 1986).

It is generally believed that the bending of the cilia on the hair cells stimulates these cells. This stimulation produces electrical charges that apparently release neurotrans-mitters, chemicals picked up by the nerve endings leading to the auditory nerve (Dallos, 1978; Scharf & Buus, 1986). The **auditory nerve** is a bundle of nerve fibers that carries information from the inner ear to higher levels of auditory processing. At long last, then, all this pushing of membranes, sloshing of liquids, and bending of hair-cell cilia ultimately activates the auditory nerve. We'll examine the auditory nerve and higher levels of auditory processing after discussing how frequency and intensity are registered in the auditory system.

Registration of Frequency

We have examined how sound waves are transmitted into the inner ear, but how does the inner ear register frequency? When middle C is played on the piano, you hear a different pitch than if, say, the note A is played. How can the elaborate process just investigated possibly account for the subtle kinds of distinctions we make with respect to sound? The two most popular approaches to this mystery are called the place theory and the frequency theory.

Place theory. The **place theory** proposes that each frequency of vibration causes a particular *place* on the basilar membrane to vibrate. This theory has existed since the 1600s, but its modern versions can be traced to Hermann Helmholtz (1863), a 19th-century researcher whose work is discussed throughout the book. Helmholtz proposed that the basilar membrane consists of a series of segments, with each segment resonating to a tone of a particular frequency. The details of Helmholtz's theory are not accurate, but the spirit of his theory was further developed by Georg von Békésy, whose research earned him the Nobel Prize in 1961.

Békésy (1960) proposed that the vibration pattern of the basilar membrane leads to the stimulation of different places along this membrane. Békésy determined that the width of the basilar membrane increases as we move from the area near the stapes toward the area near the helicotrema. This increase is not intuitive because the cochlea itself decreases in diameter as we move toward the helicotrema. Figure 9.10 shows a diagram of this relationship. The membrane is about 100 times stiffer near the stapes than at the helicotrema. Because of this systematic variation in stiffness, vibration in the cochlea produces a pressure wave that travels from the stapes to the other end of the cochlea; this wave is called a **traveling wave**.

Figure 9.11 illustrates a typical traveling wave. The shape and pattern of the traveling wave shift from moment to moment, just like the waves in the ocean. However, for each traveling wave a point can be located on the membrane at which the displacement is the greatest. The location of this maximum-displacement point has been shown to depend upon the frequency of the auditory stimulus. For example, a low-frequency tone of 25 Hz produces the greatest displacement in a region near the helicotrema, about 3.5 cm (1.4 inches) from the stapes. In contrast, a high-frequency tone of 1600 Hz produces the greatest displacement in the middle of the basilar membrane, about 1.8 cm (0.7 inches) from the stapes. In other words, if someone nearby is playing a scale on a piano, running from low to high notes, the displacement is initially greatest at the inner tip of the cochlea; by the end of the scale, the area closest to the stapes shows the greatest displacement.

Let's relate Békésy's observations to the auditory receptors. Suppose that a 1600-Hz tone is sounded, producing maximum displacement 1.8 cm (.7 inches) from the stapes. At this location the cilia in the hair cells of the organ of Corti will be bent the most. These particular cilia will therefore produce the highest rate of electrical charges, which will ultimately be picked up by the auditory nerve.

You may recall that the lateral geniculate nucleus (LGN) and the visual cortex show retinotopic organization; points near each other on the retina tend to be represented near each other in the LGN and the cortex. Similarly, the basilar membrane shows a **tonotopic organization**; there is a systematic relationship between the frequency of tones and their location on the basilar membrane. We will see that this tonotopic relationship is also preserved at higher levels of auditory processing.

Frequency theory. According to **frequency theory** the entire basilar membrane vibrates at a frequency that matches the frequency of a tone. For example, the membrane vibrates 25 times each second for a 25-Hz tone and 1600 times each second for a 1600-Hz tone. The vibration rate in turn causes nerve fibers in the auditory nerve to fire at a matching rate, for example, 25 times each second.

Frequency theory can be traced back to the 19th century (Rutherford, 1886), but Wever (1949) has been its primary advocate in this century. In particular, Wever proposed an answer to a serious flaw in the earlier frequency theory. Here is the problem with the original theory. Each neuron has a **refractory period**, a time immediately following a response during which it cannot produce another response. This refractory period restricts the

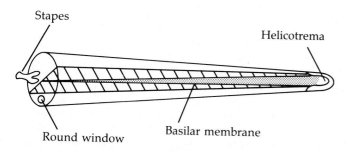

Figure 9.10 Schematic drawing of uncoiled cochlea.

Stapes end of ————————→ Helicotrema end of
basilar membrane *Direction of movement*   basilar membrane

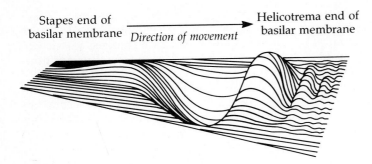

Figure 9.11   Traveling wave as proposed by Békésy.

maximum number of responses to 1000 each second—still an impressive rate. If a neuron is limited to 1000 responses a second, how can we hear frequencies of up to 20,000 cycles per second, a rate 20 times as fast?

Wever (1949) proposed a **volley principle** whereby clusters of neurons share in producing the required firing rate. Consider an analogy. Suppose for some obscure reason you wanted to produce one scream each second for about a minute. This task would be impossible for you alone, but with the appropriate community effort you and four friends could organize your screams so that you would take turns; each of you would need to produce only one scream every 5 seconds—a manageable task. The net result, however, would be the required one scream per second. Similarly, a 1000-Hz tone could be registered if each of five neurons fired 200 times each second—again, a manageable task.

Research has demonstrated that nerve fibers in the auditory nerve can indeed fire at a rate to match some tones (e.g., Rose, Brugge, Anderson, & Hind, 1967). Fibers in a group tend to fire irregularly, rather than neatly taking turns as Wever had suggested, but they do consistently fire when the amplitude of the sound wave is at its maximum. Thus, a group of nerve fibers can represent a particular tone frequency by "cooperating" to produce a given firing rate. However, even with the addition of the volley principle, the system cannot handle frequencies above about 4000 Hz.

Conclusions about registration of frequency. We have seen that frequency theory has difficulty explaining how we hear high-frequency tones. As it happens, place theory has difficulty explaining how we hear low-frequency tones; we can make discriminations between two tones that are more precise than could be predicted by minor differences in displacement of the basilar membrane by a 100-Hz tone and a 105-Hz tone, for example.

A compromise seems to be called for. You may recall that in Chapter 5 we concluded the discussion of the color-vision battle between opponent-process theories and trichromatic theories by proposing that both theories could live happily with each other. The same conclusion applies to the discussion of how frequency is registered. Frequency theory explains how low-frequency tones are registered, and place theory explains how high-frequency tones are registered. In the middle range that we use for most daily activities, both theories probably apply, as Figure 9.12 illustrates. In this region, perhaps between 500 and 4000, frequency is registered in terms of neuronal firing rate and location on the basilar membrane. We will see in Chapter 10 that this frequency range is particularly important in music and speech perception. One theme of this book is that the perceptual systems are well designed to perform perceptual tasks. In the case of hearing, the perceptual system appears to be so splendidly designed that two separate mechanisms work together to register the frequency of tones we encounter frequently.

Registration of Amplitude

The theoretical research on how frequency is registered in the auditory system has been abundant. In contrast, there is little information on how amplitude is registered. How does the auditory system code a near-painful 110-dB rock band, in contrast to the faint, 25-dB sounds when a record of that band is played on a stereo at the other end of a long hallway? As Scharf and Houtsma (1986) state quite bluntly, "A direct physiological interpretation [of loudness] is not feasible because the neural code for intensity is not known" (pp. 15–16).

Scharf and Houtsma point out that researchers in auditory perception often assume that the neural correlate of amplitude is the number of neuronal impulses generated each second. However, this very plausible notion has not yet been confirmed experimentally. Furthermore, physiological data gathered from the auditory system indicate that the mechanism is complex. Nevertheless, Sharf and Houtsma believe that the assumption is appealing. They propose that as stimulus amplitude increases, a greater number of neural fibers are active and each neural fiber fires more often. Consider an analogy: The noise in an elementary-school cafeteria is a function of both the number of children who talk and how much each of these children talks.

Higher Levels of Auditory Processing

We left the auditory stimulus back in the cochlea while we paused to consider how frequency and intensity are registered. Let's now discuss the processing of auditory information beyond the cochlea, although little is known about this topic, in contrast to higher levels of visual processing.

First, let's consider the auditory nerve. About 30,000 auditory nerve fibers are associated with each cochlea (Warren, 1982). Electrical impulses can be recorded from an individual fiber in the auditory nerve to determine the frequency to which the fiber is most sensitive. You may recall that we discussed single-cell recording from a simple cell in the visual cortex to determine an orientation tuning curve, a graph showing the relationship between the orientation of a line and the cell's response rate. Similarly, a **frequency tuning curve** is a graph showing the relationship between the frequency of an auditory stimulus and an auditory nerve fiber's response rate. This information can be graphed in several ways. Figure 9.13 shows a typical frequency tuning curve, with stimulus frequency along the x-axis and the intensity of sound (in dB) required to produce neural firing along the y-axis. As you'll note, lower decibel values are associated with greater sensitivity. The nerve fiber in this diagram is particularly sensitive (has the lowest threshold) to a stimulus around 1000 Hz, a frequency often found in speech. Other auditory nerve fibers have frequency tuning curves with sensitivities in other frequency ranges.

After leaving the inner ear, the auditory nerve travels to the **cochlear nucleus**, which

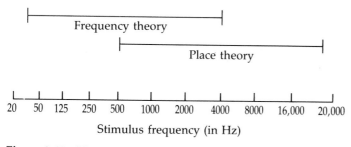

Figure 9.12 Hypothetical ranges of operation of frequency theory and place theory as function of stimulus frequency.

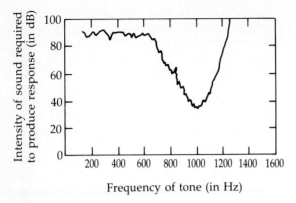

Figure 9.13 Typical frequency tuning curve.

is at the bottom of the back part of the brain. (This route is shown schematically in Figure 9.14.) In the cochlear nucleus the auditory nerve cells transmit their information to new cells.

You may recall that the visual system has a complex mechanism for ensuring that the information from each eye is distributed to each side of the brain. Similarly, in the auditory system each of the two cochlear nuclei sends its information to two structures on different sides of the brain. At lower stages in auditory processing, audition is **monaural** because a tone sounded only in the right ear involves structures for only that ear (*mono* means "one"). Beyond the cochlear nuclei, however, audition is **binaural** because a tone sounded only in the right ear involves structures for two ears (*bi* means "two").

The name of the structure at the level beyond the cochlear nucleus sounds like the name of a mystical cult—the superior olivary nucleus. Because of its binaural input the **superior olivary nucleus** can compare the information it receives from the two ears. We will discuss the significance of this comparison in the section on localization.

Each superior olivary nucleus sends its information to an **inferior colliculus**, which is just below (or inferior to) the superior colliculus discussed in the anatomy of the visual system. It is possible that information in the auditory system is compared with the nearby

information in the visual system during this stage in processing.

From the inferior colliculus, information passes on to the **medial geniculate nucleus** of the thalamus, a structure near the lateral geniculate nucleus of the visual system. Incidentally, it should be mentioned that frequency tuning curves have been reported for the cochlear nuclei, the superior olivary nuclei, the inferior colliculi, and the medial geniculate nuclei (Moore, 1982). In other words, at all these points between the cochlea and the cortex, each nerve fiber is particularly sensitive to a fairly narrow frequency range.

Information from the medial geniculate nucleus now travels to the **primary auditory cortex**, which is in a deep groove on the temporal lobe of the cortex (at the side of the brain). Its inaccessible location makes it quite challenging to study. Another difficulty is that when experimental animals are anesthetized, the responses of the cortical neurons are changed. Researchers in the 1980s have discovered an impressive amount about the structure and function of the auditory cortex, but methodological problems have hampered a complete understanding of this structure. For example, researchers have not yet been able to completely map the auditory cortex in any primate species (Brugge & Reale, 1985).

We have pointed out several similarities between auditory processing and visual processing, similarities that provide additional

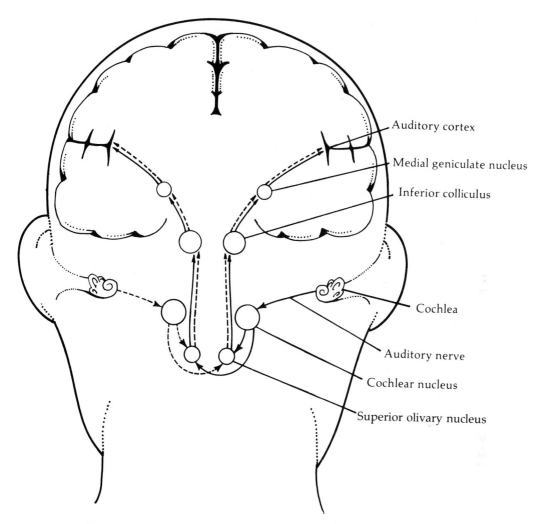

Auditory cortex

Medial geniculate nucleus

Inferior colliculus

Cochlea

Auditory nerve

Cochlear nucleus

Superior olivary nucleus

Figure 9.14 Pathway from ear to brain (schematic representation). Only structures on right side of head have been labeled; notice corresponding structures on left side of head.

evidence for Theme 1 of this book. There is a further similarity at the level of the cortex. You'll recall that cells in the visual cortex are arranged retinotopically; there is a correspondence between the area of the retina stimulated and the area of the cortex on which that stimulation is registered. Similarly, there is some evidence for a tonotopic organization in the auditory cortex, although the evidence is not as clear as in visual processing (Gelfand, 1981; Moore, 1982).

There is an additional similarity at the cortical level. You'll recall that some cells in the visual cortex respond optimally to certain visual features, such as the orientation of a line or its movement pattern. Similarly, some cells in the auditory cortex frequently respond to more complex characteristics of stimuli than simple frequency and intensity (Moore, 1982). In fact, many cortical neurons do not respond to pure tones that have unvarying intensity. Many neurons, for example, respond only to complex stimuli such as bursts of noise, clicks, and sounds resembling kissing. Some neurons respond to tones, but only if their frequency is changing—a situation similar to the cells in the visual cortex that respond only to a moving line. In the auditory cortex some cells are most responsive to a sequence of tones that moves from low to high frequency, and some are most responsive to the reverse pattern. The rate of change in frequency may also influence a cell's response rate (Evans, 1982c).

How essential is the auditory cortex? People with disorders in this region have difficulty discriminating changes in the timing within a sequence of sounds. Speech perception is usually a major problem. They also have difficulty with sound localization in space. Thus, the auditory cortex is essential for more complex kinds of auditory tasks.

Summary: Sensory Aspects of Hearing

1. Hearing can inform us of danger, and it is extremely important in human communication.
2. Sound waves can be described in terms of their frequency and their amplitude; ultimately, they cause the eardrum to vibrate.
3. Frequency is the number of cycles that a sound wave can complete in 1 second, abbreviated Hz; frequency is an important determinant of pitch.
4. We hear tones with frequencies between 20 and 20,000 Hz.
5. We detect tones best in the 3000-Hz range, but we discriminate tones best in the low-frequency range, where the Weber's fraction can be as small as 0.3%.
6. Complex tones represent the combination of several different tones.
7. Amplitude is the change in pressure created by sound waves, often measured in decibels; amplitude is an important determinant of loudness.
8. The outer ear consists of the pinna, the external auditory canal, and—most important—the tympanic membrane.

9. The middle ear contains three bones—the malleus, the incus, and the stapes, important in solving the impedance mismatch problem, and the eustachian tube.
10. The inner ear contains the cochlea, which houses the organ of Corti, a structure that contains the auditory receptors, or hair cells; the organ of Corti also includes the basilar membrane and the tectorial membrane.
11. There are relatively few inner hair cells, although they monopolize most of the auditory nerve fibers; they are sensitive to a tone's frequency.
12. There are relatively many outer hair cells, although they share a small number of the auditory nerve fibers; they identify whether a tone is present.
13. Two major theories explain how the ear registers frequency information: (a) The place theory proposes that each sound wave frequency causes a traveling wave, which makes a particular place on the basilar membrane vibrate to a greater extent than other places. (b) The frequency theory proposes that sound wave frequency is matched by the vibration rate on the basilar membrane, which then causes nerve fibers in the auditory nerve to fire at a matching rate (with the volley principle added to explain high frequencies).
14. The two theories may be compatible. Place theory may explain how we hear high frequencies, and frequency theory may explain how we hear low frequencies; both theories may hold for hearing intermediate frequencies.
15. The physiological mechanism for registering amplitude is not known; however, greater stimulus amplitude may be associated with a greater number of active neural fibers, each of which fires at a faster rate.
16. The auditory nerve has nerve fibers sensitive to particular frequencies; this nerve travels to the cochlear nucleus. The auditory pathway continues to the superior olivary nucleus, then to the inferior colliculus, then to the medial geniculate nucleus, and finally to the auditory cortex.

17. There is a tonotopic organization in part of the auditory cortex; furthermore, some cells in the auditory cortex respond to complex characteristics of sounds. The auditory cortex is essential for sound localization, speech perception, and other complex auditory tasks.

PERCEPTUAL RESPONSES TO SOUND

Listen to a sound right now and think about the perceptual qualities you notice. The sound is high or low (pitch) and loud or soft (loudness). It also has a sound quality (timbre); for example, the tone of a flute is different from that of a clarinet. In addition, the sound appears to be coming from a particular direction. All these qualities are subjective or psychological qualities of sound, as opposed to the physical qualities such as frequency and amplitude discussed in the last section.

Pitch

Relationship between Frequency and Pitch

As mentioned in the discussion of frequency, high-frequency tones are generally associated with high pitch, whereas low-frequency tones are generally associated with low pitch. In other words, there is a relationship between frequency and **pitch**. However, as Wightman (1981) points out, the relationship is by no means a simple one.

For example, pitch perception can depend upon the amplitude of the sound. In experiments using pure tones, the pitch of low-frequency tones (e.g., 300 Hz) seems lower as the amplitude of the tone is increased. In contrast, the pitch of high-frequency tones (e.g., 3000 Hz) seems higher as the amplitude of the tone is increased (Gelfand, 1981). However, the pitch of complex tones is relatively unchanged by variations in amplitude. In

other words, when a conductor instructs a band to play louder, the pitch of the piccolo and the tuba will not be substantially distorted because musical instruments produce complex tones.

The pitch of a tone can also be influenced by a previous tone (Scharf & Houtsma, 1986). This effect can be observed when the previous tone is similar (within 5%) to the test tone and it is presented for at least a minute. The pitch of the test tone shifts away from the pitch of the previous tone. That is, if the test tone is higher in frequency, the pitch is perceived as still higher; if the test tone is lower in frequency, the pitch is perceived as still lower. The magnitude of this effect from the previous tone is not large, but the effect does suggest that the auditory system provides for a process that may be similar to adaptation.

Another reason that pitch is not perfectly correlated with frequency involves the case of the missing fundamental. Admittedly, this term sounds like the latest in a series of teenage mystery stories. However, the **case of the missing fundamental** refers to the fact that listeners report the pitch of certain complex stimuli as being the pitch of a tone that was never even presented.

To explore this point more fully, we have to examine complex sound waves briefly. A complex sound wave may be broken into a series of components. The component of a complex sound wave that has the lowest frequency is called the **fundamental frequency**. Thus 100 Hz is the fundamental frequency in a complex tone representing 100 Hz, 200 Hz, and 300 Hz. The other components of a complex tone are called **harmonics**; harmonics therefore have higher frequencies than the fundamental. In this example, 200 Hz and 300 Hz are harmonics.

Let's now consider an example of a missing fundamental. Suppose that an experimenter presents a complex tone that contains 700-Hz, 800-Hz, 900-Hz, and 1000-Hz tones. In other words, this complex tone is missing the 100-Hz fundamental for which these four tones represent harmonics. Even though this fundamental is missing, listeners report that they hear a pitch appropriate to the frequency that is absent from a complex tone. In this case, people hear a 100-Hz tone.

In a way the case of the missing fundamental is similar to visual illusions (van den Brink, 1982). Just as the visual system can see an illusory contour that is not there, the auditory system can hear a tone that is not there.

One further reason that the correlation between frequency and pitch is not perfect is that characteristics of the observer can influence pitch. For example, arousal can influence pitch perception (Thurlow, 1971). If you are sleepy, a tone will sound lower in pitch than it would if you were alert.

Is pitch related to the frequency of a tone? Yes, it definitely is. However, the relationship is complex because pitch perception can be influenced by the following factors: amplitude, the previous tone, the missing fundamental, and characteristics of the observer such as arousal. In the psychophysics chapter of this book, we stressed that physical stimuli are often related in complex ways to psychological responses. Similarly, we saw that wavelength and hue are complexly related to each other. The information on the less-than-perfect relationship between frequency (a physical quality) and pitch (a psychological quality) adds further evidence about complexity in perceptual processes.

Measurement of pitch. We talked about the units of measurement used to scale the physical attribute, frequency. As Wightman (1981) notes, we can determine the frequency of a sound with an accuracy of better than 0.1% by using modern laboratory equipment. However, Wightman continues, there is no such thing as a pitch meter. Pitch cannot be measured directly because it exists only in a listener's head.

Musicians and psychologists have both tackled the problem of a scale for pitch. Musicians use the term **octave**, which is represented by the distance between two notes that have the same name. Thus there is an octave between one C and the next higher C or the next lower C on the piano.

In describing pure tones, psychologists often use the mel scale, which was suggested by Stevens, Volkman, and Newman (1937). You may recall Stevens's name from the discussion of Stevens's power law and magnitude estimation in the psychophysics chapter. This magnitude estimation technique is used to obtain the mel scale of pitch. In the **mel scale** a 1000-Hz pure tone with an intensity of 60 dB is arbitrarily assigned a pitch of 1000 mels. Then listeners are asked to adjust a comparison tone until it seems to be half as high as this 1000-Hz tone; this tone is assigned a value of 500 mels. Other points in the scale are filled in by asking listeners to locate comparison tones that represent other fractions and multiples of the standard 1000-Hz tone. Try Demonstration 9.4 to illustrate an informal construction of a mel scale.

Loudness

Relationship between Amplitude and Loudness

As noted earlier, **loudness** is roughly determined by a tone's amplitude. However, as in the case of pitch and frequency, we find that the correlation between loudness and amplitude is not perfect. For example, loudness perception depends upon the duration of a tone. If a tone lasts longer, it sounds louder (Evans, 1982b). Loudness also depends upon other physical qualities such as background sounds.

A third factor that complicates the relationship between amplitude and loudness is the observers themselves. As Scharf (1978) notes, the loudness of a sound depends upon whether we pay attention to it or merely hear it as background noise. Perceived loudness also depends upon whether our ears are "fresh" or recently exposed to sound. Try Demonstration 9.5 to illustrate the influence of previous sounds upon loudness perception.

A fourth factor may be the most important of all: Perceived loudness depends upon the frequency of a tone. We noted in the last section that pitch perception depends upon the amplitude of a tone. Similarly, loudness perception depends upon the frequency of a

Demonstration 9.4

Informal Construction of a Mel Scale

You'll need a piano for this demonstration, since this instrument has the widest range in frequency among the standard musical instruments. (A true mel scale is created with pure tones; however, the piano has complex tones.) Also locate a volunteer who can either play appropriate notes on the piano while you scale them or who can provide the scaling judgments while you play.

First play the C two octaves above middle C. (Its frequency of 1046 Hz is reasonably close to the 1000-Hz tone used in formal experiments.) Assign this note the value of 1000 mels. Now play on the piano the notes listed below, in the specified order. Ask the listener to supply a judgment in terms of mels for each note. Just before each judgment, play the standard C so that this reference tone can be kept in mind. Run through the sequence twice and take an average of the two values for each note. (Each C is recorded in terms of its position on the keyboard, so that the lowest C, three notes from the bottom, is 1, the standard C is 6, and the highest C is 8. You may want to place these numbers, written on masking tape, on the keys before you begin so that they can be located quickly and accurately.)

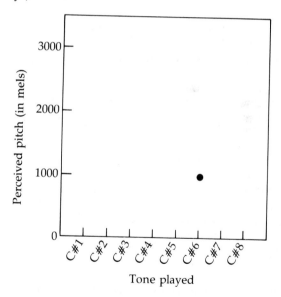

After you have calculated an average mel value for each note, record the average value on the graph above. The value of C6 was set at 1000, so this point is already recorded on the graph. What is the relationship between notes on the scale, as represented by octaves, and the way these notes are judged in mels?

Demonstration 9.5

Influence of Previous Noises on Loudness

Find a watch that ticks and place it where you can clearly hear it; the ticking should definitely be above threshold. Then turn on a record player or a radio so that it is loud but not painfully loud; leave it on for 10 minutes, then turn if completely off. Return to the location from which you originally heard the ticking watch. Judge its loudness relative to your original judgment. We will talk more about the influence of previous noises on hearing in the section on noise pollution.

---

tone. Each of these important physical characteristics of sound complicates the relationship between the *other* physical characteristic and psychological responses. We'll explore this topic again in the next section when we consider equal loudness contours.

Measurement of loudness.   We saw in the discussion of pitch that musicians and psychologists have both developed methods for measuring loudness. Musicians, for example, scale loudness in terms of a seven-level marking system that ranges from ppp for the very softest sound (about 30 dB) through fff for the very loudest sound (about 90 dB) (Pierce, 1983).

Psychologists measure loudness in a number of different ways. One of the most widely used systems is the sone scale (Stevens, 1955). The **sone scale** is a scale of loudness obtained by the magnitude estimation technique. (You'll recall that the mel scale is a scale of *pitch* obtained by the same kind of magnitude estimation technique.) In the sone scale, a 40-dB pure tone at 1000 Hz is arbitrarily assigned a loudness of 1 sone. Listeners judge the loudness of other tones in relationship to this standard tone. Thus a tone that appears to be twice as loud would be judged as 2 sones, and a tone that appears to be half as loud would be judged as .5 sone.

In general, Stevens found that the amplitude of a tone had to be increased by 10 dB for listeners to judge it twice as loud. Thus a 50-dB tone appeared to be twice as loud as a 40-dB tone; the 50-dB tone would therefore equal 2 sones.

A positive feature of the sone scale is that the measures correspond to our everyday perceptions of sound in a more meaningful fashion than the decibel system. For example, suppose that you are working in a quiet office where the noise level is measured at 40 dB, or 1 sone. The company may wish to bring in a new kind of equipment that will raise the noise level to 50 dB. This 10-dB increase would not strike most people as substantial, and they would not be alarmed at the prospect of such a change. However, you now know that this increase represents an increase from 1 sone to 2 sones. The new noise level would really sound *twice* as loud, which represents a major increase in perceived loudness.

Despite its advantages, the sone scale has been criticized because people's judgments are heavily influenced by the order in which stimuli are presented, the range of stimuli, and other biasing factors (Moore, 1982). Nevertheless, many researchers support the use of this sone scale. For example, Algom and Marks (1984) discovered that individual differences are remarkably small when a single method of judgment is used in a magnitude estimation study. As these authors conclude their article: "To be sure, magnitude-estimation scales of loudness show diversity, individuality, and idiosyncrasy; but beneath lies a common core of uniformity in sensory-perceptual processing of sound intensity and, at one stage of processing at least, in the underlying scale for loudness" (p. 591).

We noted that 1 sone is the loudness of a 40-dB tone at 1000 Hz. Earlier, it was hinted that a tone's frequency has an important influence on loudness perception, and we noted at the beginning of the chapter that people are particularly sensitive in detecting tones in the 3000-Hz range. In other words, that 40-dB tone may sound louder for a 3000-Hz stimulus than for a 1000-Hz stimulus.

The relationship between stimulus frequency and loudness perception is most often explored in equal loudness contours. The basic procedure for determining an equal loudness contour is simple: One tone (for example, a 1000-Hz tone) is presented at a constant intensity level (for example, 40 dB). It serves as a reference tone throughout the experiment. A comparison tone of a different frequency is then varied in amplitude until the listener judges its loudness to be equal to that of the reference tone; this amplitude is recorded. Then the procedure is repeated with tones of other frequencies. The relationship between tone frequency and the number of decibels required to produce a tone of equal loudness is called an **equal loudness contour**; as the name suggests, all the points along an equal loudness contour sound equally loud. Figure 9.15 shows an equal loudness contour where the reference tone is a 1000-Hz tone at 40 dB. Notice that this curve is labeled 40 phons, which means that all points along this curve have a loudness level of 40 phons. A

phon is another measure of loudness perception. All sounds that are equal in **phons** have the same perceived loudness, even though they may be different in terms of decibels (Gelfand, 1981). In other words, similar psychological responses (in terms of loudness) can be produced by different physical stimuli (in terms of decibels).

The experiment can be repeated by using other reference tones that differ in amplitude. For example, a second equal loudness contour can be generated by using a 1000-Hz tone at 60 dB (rather than 40 dB) as the reference tone. Figure 9.16 shows how this experiment could be repeated so that there are seven equal loudness contours, using reference tones that vary between 0 dB and 120 dB. As you can see, these equal loudness contours are approximately parallel.

In Figure 9.16, think about the meaning of the 0 dB curve. This curve represents the hearing threshold. All the area below this line is essentially inaudible. For example, a tone of 20 Hz could not be heard if its intensity were less than about 60 dB. Also, you can see that the hearing threshold is lowest around 3000 Hz, consistent with the earlier discussion.

Now shift your attention to the curve at the top of Figure 9.16 representing 120 phons. At this level, sounds are painful. Notice that

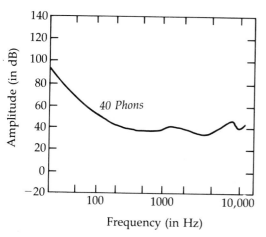

Figure 9.15 Equal loudness contour for 40 phons.

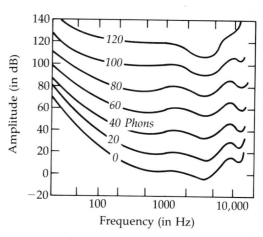

Figure 9.16 Equal loudness contours.

considerably lower decibel levels are required to produce a painful sound in the 3000-Hz region than in the region below 100 Hz. If a piccolo could be amplified to about 120 dB, its sound would be more painful than the lowest notes of the bass tuba, played at the same decibel level.

Timbre

Pitch and loudness are familiar concepts. Timbre is also a familiar concept, although the term itself may be unfamiliar. **Timbre** is a tone's sound quality. Two sounds may have the same pitch and the same loudness yet differ in quality. A piece of chalk squeaking across a blackboard seems different in quality from the sound produced by a valuable violin, and they both seem different from the voice of a soprano—even though the three may be nearly identical in pitch and loudness. Furthermore, two male voices of equivalent pitch and loudness may be quite different in timbre. Timbre involves qualities such as richness, mellowness, brightness, and so on (Evans, 1982b).

If pitch is related to frequency and loudness is related to amplitude, what physical feature of sound is related to timbre? The psychological quality, timbre, corresponds to the physical quality of complexity.

As mentioned earlier, complex tones cannot be represented by a simple sine wave; instead, they must be represented by complex wave forms. The specific nature of the complexity is related to the tone quality, or timbre. Figure 9.17 illustrates the sound waves associated with the complex tones produced by several instruments.

Complex sound waves such as those in Figure 9.17 can be analyzed into their component sine waves by **Fourier analysis**. Fourier analysis was considered in some detail in connection with shape perception in Chapter 6; you may wish to review that portion of the theory of spatial frequency analysis. Our auditory system is designed to perform a Fourier analysis for complex tones. It can isolate several simple sound waves when we hear a complex tone. Auditory perception involves

more than a simple Fourier analysis, however, because tone combinations produce complex perceptions, as will be seen in the next section.

In connection with the case of the missing fundamental, we mentioned that the lowest-frequency tone in a complex sound wave is called the fundamental frequency, whereas the higher-frequency tones are called harmonics. Musical instruments have harmonics

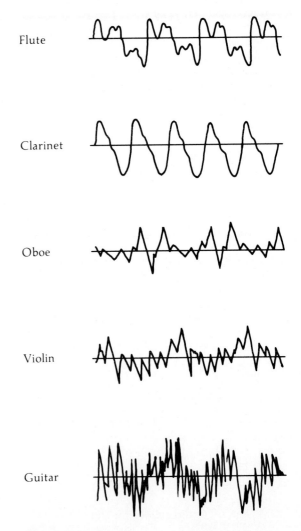

Flute

Clarinet

Oboe

Violin

Guitar

Figure 9.17 Sound waves of several kinds of complex tones produced by musical instruments.

(also known as **overtones**) that are multiples of the fundamental frequency. For example, if you play the A above middle C on the piano, the fundamental frequency of 440 Hz is produced. In addition, however, the overtones of 880 Hz (2 × 440) and 1320 Hz (3 × 440), as well as higher-frequency overtones, are also produced.

The fundamental frequency contributes the greatest amplitude to the tone, but the harmonics also contribute substantially. Suppose that you play this A above middle C on a variety of instruments. The fundamental frequency of 440 Hz will be produced in each case, so the pitch will be identical for all instruments. However, one instrument may emphasize the overtone of 880 Hz; this overtone may have a greater amplitude than other overtones. In contrast, a different instrument may emphasize the overtone of 1320 Hz.

Our ears can analyze complex tones and detect which overtones are emphasized. We can therefore distinguish among the sounds made by different instruments. Some instruments, such as the flute, have very few overtones, and any overtones that do exist have relatively low amplitude. As a consequence, the tones produced by the flute sound pure. In contrast, other instruments, such as the guitar, have many high-amplitude overtones. As a consequence, the tones produced by the guitar sound thick and rich.

We were able to discuss psychological aspects of pitch and loudness in some detail. This is not possible with timbre, the third dimension of hearing. Scharf and Houtsma (1986) point out that the advance of computer music and electronic musical instruments makes it important to understand timbre, yet we have little knowledge or theory in this area. As they complain, "Hardly more than a handful of studies on timbre exists" (pp. 15–31). It's clearly an important attribute of sound. Consider how useful timbre is in identifying a friend on the telephone; pitch and loudness would not be sufficient clues. Opera enthusiasts can readily tell from a recording whether the soprano in *Norma* is Montserrat Caballé, Joan Sutherland, or Thelma Schlump. However, the dimensions

of timbre that underlie this identification process haven't really been studied.

Perception of Tone Combinations

So far we have discussed how a single complex tone can consist of several component tones. Now let's consider a related question. What happens when we add together several different tones? In Chapter 5 we considered the perception of color mixtures. A combination of a red light and a yellow light, as we saw, produced an orange light, rather than the separate components of red and yellow. What happens when we combine two tones? The answer depends upon the similarity of the two tones.

When two tones are sounded that are similar in frequency, we do not hear two distinct components. Instead, we hear a single strange tone whose quality depends upon the difference in frequency between the two notes. According to Nordmark (1978) and Warren (1982), there seem to be three distinct kinds of combination tones:

1. When the tones differ by less than 6 Hz (for example, 400 Hz and 404 Hz), we hear a single tone that surges up and down in loudness.

2. When the tones differ by 6 Hz to 24 Hz, we hear a single tone that appears to be a series of distinct impulses; the number of impulses per second equals the difference in frequency. Thus a 400-Hz tone and a 412-Hz tone would produce 12 impulses per second.

3. When the tones differ by 25 Hz to about 10% of the frequency, we hear an unpleasant roughness rather than distinct impulses. For example, a 400-Hz tone would produce roughness with any tone between 425 Hz and 440 Hz (Nordmark, 1978).

The changes in loudness found in the first and second categories—either the tone that surges up and down or the distinct impulses—are called **beats**.

What happens when we combine two tones that differ substantially? When two tones differ in frequency by more than 10%, we can hear two distinct tones. A **consonance** is a combination of two or more tones, played at the same time, judged to be pleasant. In general, tone combinations are consonant if the ratios of the frequencies of the two tones are simple fractions. For example, if you strike the A above middle C (440 Hz) and the A one octave higher (880 Hz), the combination is very pleasant. Notice that the ratio of their frequencies is 2/1, a simple fraction. Other frequency ratios such as 3/2 and 4/3 also sound consonant.

In contrast, a **dissonance** is a combination of two or more tones, played at the same time, judged to be unpleasant. In general, when the ratio of two tones is not a simple fraction, the combination sounds dissonant. Consonance and dissonance are the result of matches and mismatches among the notes' overtones. More information about consonance and dissonance can be found in a chapter by Risset (1978).

We discussed visual masking in Chapter 6. In some conditions the presence of one visual stimulus prevents the perception of another. The same **masking** phenomenon occurs in audition; in some tone combinations one tone masks another. Once again, then, we see a resemblance between vision and audition, an observation consistent with the first theme of the book.

If one sound is intense and another is very weak, it seems obvious that the loud sound should mask the softer sound. However, auditory masking phenomena are very complex, as discussed in reviews of the literature (Patterson & Green, 1978; Warren, 1983; Zwislocki, 1978). In fact, masking depends almost as much on the frequencies of the tones as on their intensities. In general, a tone masks other tones higher in frequency than itself to a greater extent than those lower in frequency than itself (Evans, 1982b).

In connection with shape perception, it was mentioned that backward masking was easier to demonstrate than forward masking. In other words, a mask presented *after* the test stimulus was more effective in blocking perception than a mask presented *before* the text stimulus. However, in audition both forward and backward masking can be demonstrated

(Jesteadt, Bacon, & Lehman, 1982; Kallman & Massaro, 1979; Kallman & Morris, 1984). That is, a tone can block you from hearing another tone presented either earlier or later. It seems that we need *time* to perceive; audition doesn't occur instantaneously.

▶ **IN-DEPTH:**
SOUND LOCALIZATION

You reach out in the darkness of early morning to turn off the ring of the alarm clock, and your hand locates the source of that unpleasant noise. A button pops off and rolls away, but you can trace it from its sound effects. The human auditory system allows us to identify with some accuracy where a sound is coming from; in other words, we show localization.

Compared to some other animals, humans are not particularly impressive in their ability to locate the direction from which a sound is coming. For example, bats hunt for insects at night and have such exquisitely developed sensitivity to their own echoes that they are able to detect frequency changes as small as .01% (Neuweiler, Bruns, & Schuller, 1980). It could be argued, of course, that we don't need the bat's echolocation ability. We don't typically hunt bugs by night using our auditory system; we pursue our food by day using our visual system. Still, we are fairly accurate; we can sometimes locate a sound within 1 degree of its true location (Phillips & Brugge, 1985).

Researchers have been continually intrigued by the sound localization ability of humans and other animals. One reason that sound localization is so mysterious is that auditory space is not represented directly on the basilar membrane (Oldfield & Parker, 1984). Frequency, amplitude, and complexity are all represented, but there is no way in which the basilar membrane can indicate, for example, that a dog is barking directly behind your head. The auditory system must encode this information in another fashion.

In our discussion of vision, we saw that binocular vision offers a distinct advantage in trying to determine where an object is. In discussing localization, binaural audition is even more important; it is extremely useful to have two ears when we try to localize sounds. (In contrast, pitch, loudness, and timbre can all be appreciated with monaural hearing.) In fact, the major portion of our ability to localize sounds can be traced to the fact that our ears are some distance away from each other, so they receive somewhat different stimuli from the sound source (Phillips & Brugge, 1985).

In this discussion we will begin by considering the sources of information for sound localization; then we will examine factors that influence localization accuracy. The final topic will be the physiological basis of sound localization.

Sources of Information for Sound Localization

Why is it advantageous, with respect to sound localization, to have two ears located some distance apart? As Figure 9.18 illustrates, a sound coming from the left will have to travel different distances to the two ears. This difference in distance has two conse-

quences: (1) the sound will arrive at one ear before the other, producing an **onset difference**; (2) the sound will be at different phases within a cycle when it arrives at the two ears—perhaps at the maximum point in its cycle for the right ear and at the minimum point for the left ear, producing a **phase difference**. These two components produce the interaural time difference. The **interaural time difference**, therefore, is a cue to sound localization that is produced by the different arrival times at the two ears. (Notice, however, that there is no interaural time difference when the sound comes from in front of the head.)

The onset difference is a useful source of information for sounds throughout the entire frequency range. Figure 9.19 shows typical findings on the relationship between the direction from which the sound is coming and the size of the onset difference. As you can see, when the sound comes directly from the side (for example, straight out from the right ear), the sound reaches one ear about 0.6 milliseconds before it reaches the other ear. Ob-

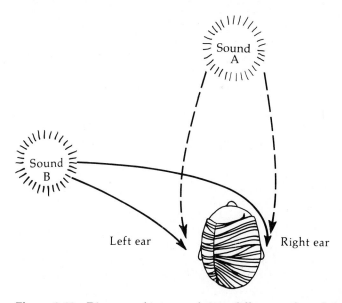

Figure 9.18 Diagram of interaural time difference. Sound A, directly in front of observer, reaches two ears at same time. Sound B, off to side, reaches listener's left ear before right ear.

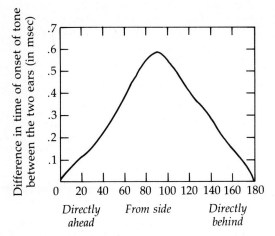

Direction of source of sound (in degrees)

Figure 9.19 Relationship between direction of sound and size of onset difference.

viously, this is not an enormous discrepancy, but the auditory system can detect this difference and make use of it in sound localization.

The phase difference is *not* useful throughout the entire frequency range; it is an effective clue only for low-frequency sounds. The human auditory system cannot discriminate phase discrepancies when the waves come close together at the higher frequencies in *pure* tones. In everyday life, however, this inability is not a major disadvantage because most natural, complex sounds contain both high- and low-frequency components (Phillips & Brugge, 1985).

However, the interaural time difference—with its two components of onset difference and phase difference—is only one of the two major binaural factors that provide information for sound localization. The second factor is called **interaural intensity difference** because the sound reaches the two ears at different intensities. For example, the left ear is closer than the right ear to Sound B in Figure 9.18, so the sound is slightly more intense. More important, however, is the fact that the head produces a **sound shadow**, or a barrier that reduces the intensity of the sound. We

are accustomed to a reduction in intensity when something large—such as a bedroom door—separates us from a sound source. However, even your head blocks some of the sound coming from sources on the opposite side.

This shadow effect is particularly strong for the high-frequency sound waves, which have difficulty bending around the head. In other words, the difference in intensity between the two ears, or interaural intensity difference, is especially strong for high-frequency tones. (As you'll recall, the interaural time difference was a particularly useful cue for *low*-frequency tones.) For example, for high-frequency tones above about 4000 Hz, the difference in intensity may be close to 30 dB (Phillips & Brugge, 1985). That is a substantial difference!

What happens when a sound is coming from a source directly in front of you? In this case, the tone reaches both ears simultaneously and at the same phase within the sound wave; furthermore, the tone reaches both ears with the same intensity. The same is true for sounds directly above your head or directly behind you. For this reason, it is often difficult to determine whether a sound is coming from ahead or behind. (You may have discovered this if you were driving and trying to figure out the location of an ambulance siren.) For other locations away from this midline, however, there will be interaural time differences and interaural intensity differences.

There is an additional potential ambiguity. Figure 9.20 illustrates something called the cone of confusion. At every location on the surface of this **cone of confusion** the auditory system should theoretically receive the same set of information about the source of the sound. That is, the interaural time differences and the interaural intensity differences will be similar. For example, a sound from every point on that surface might reach the left 0.4 milliseconds faster than the right ear.

Obviously we manage to surmount the problems involving the midline and the cone of confusion because we can localize sounds

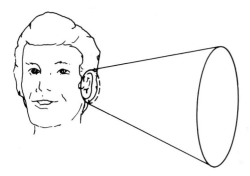

Figure 9.20 Cone of confusion.

fairly accurately, even within potentially ambiguous regions. There seem to be two major ways in which the auditory system solves these problems.

1. The discussion so far does not take the pinnae into account. Those generally useless flaps of external ear help to resolve the confusion. It's worth a trip to the mirror to inspect the structure of your pinnae; they have ridges and valleys and interesting twists. As it turns out, these features force the sound waves to bounce around slightly before entering the ear. The pattern of delay depends upon the original location of the sound (Batteau, 1967; Moore, 1982). Thus, the pinnae contribute to the encoding of sound location and help resolve ambiguities.

2. We move our heads and our bodies. For example, suppose that a sound is reaching your two ears at the same time and the same intensity, so that you don't know whether its source is ahead or behind you. Simply rotate your head a few inches, and you create interaural time differences and interaural intensity differences. This process is fairly automatic; we don't pause, contemplate the ambiguity, and reason that we could create interaural differences by head rotation! We sometimes take even more active steps to resolve ambiguities, however, by moving our bodies and exploring. This point is stressed by theorists who encourage psychologists to apply Gibson's ecological approach to audition. As Noble (1983) observed, "An ecologically oriented form of study of [localization]

replaces the model of a static and passive receiver of stimuli with one of an active, exploring *agent*, a listener with powers to discover the whereabouts of sources of sound" (p. 331).

Localization Accuracy

In general, humans can identify the location of sound quite accurately—within 1 degree, according to some reports (Phillips & Brugge, 1985). However, several factors can influence this accuracy. For example, information in the visual modality can influence activity in the auditory modality (Bohlander, 1984). You may have noticed how vision can bias auditory localization while watching a movie in a theater. The sound is really coming from speakers on both sides of the screen, yet it appears to be coming from the actors' lips.

Vision can sometimes increase localization accuracy. Let's explore a study on this topic in some detail. Shelton, Rodger, and Searle (1982) tested the influence of vision and head movements on the accuracy of sound localization. Half the participants in this study wore opaque goggles so that there were no visual cues, and half had unobstructed vision. Half of each of those groups were instructed to use a bite-bar so that their heads remained in a stable position; half were encouraged to move their heads freely.

Participants in the study sat in a chair with eight sound speakers arranged in an arc on their left; four speakers were arranged between 0° and 45° from the front, and four were between 45° and 90°. They were instructed to press one of eight switches in a hidden response box to indicate which of the speakers had produced a sound. On each trial the experimenter recorded the number of degrees of error for the participant's choice. Figure 9.21 shows the results.

As you can see, vision and head movement influence the listeners' ability to locate the sound source. For example, people generally perform much more accurately in the vision condition than in the no-vision condition. Head movement generally improves accuracy by only a small amount, except that the improvement is dramatic when people are in the vision condition and are judging sound sources from 45° to 90°. The reason that head movement seems to be helpful in this experiment is that it permits listeners to turn their heads to look toward the sound source; if they are already facing the sound source or if they can't see because they are wearing opaque goggles, head movement isn't useful. Previous researchers had suggested that head movement was useful in resolving ambiguities in the signals to the two ears, but this study shows that a more important function of head movement may be to help people *see* where the sound is coming from.

What effects does the position of the sound source have on localization accuracy, under normal conditions where people can move their heads and use visual cues? According to Oldfield and Parker (1984), people are relatively accurate in identifying locations in front of them, as opposed to locations in back of the head.

How accurate are people in monaural conditions, when they have information from only one ear? Oldfield and Parker (1986) replicated earlier research by demonstrating that

listeners were substantially less accurate when they lacked information from two sound sources. Try Demonstration 9.6 to illustrate the accuracy of monaural sound localization. Oldfield and Parker's observers, however, still had the ability to make rough judgments about sound localization. To some extent the cues provided by the pinna may be helpful in these monaural judgments (Musicant & Butler 1984; Phillips & Brugge, 1985).

Physiological Basis of Sound Localization

As mentioned earlier, the basilar membrane does not record information about the direction of a sound source. How is sound localization processed? As you may recall, information from the two ears remains segregated until it reaches the superior olivary nucleus. This structure seems to be critical in sound localization. The superior olivary nucleus is a structure composed of several smaller cell groups, two of which are important in sound localization. One of these cell groups, the **medial superior olivary nucleus (MSO)** is specialized for processing low-frequency infor-

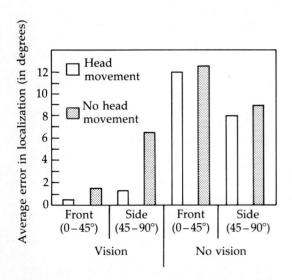

Figure 9.21 Average error in localization as function of vision condition, head movement condition, and speaker position. (Based on Shelton, Rodger, & Searle, 1982.)

> **Demonstration 9.6**
>
> **Monaural Sound Localization**
>
> Ask a friend to help you with this demonstration. Close your eyes and turn around several times. Then ask your friend to make a noise of very brief duration. Point to your friend's location and then open your eyes to determine your accuracy. Now place your index finger in one ear, or use an earplug. (Caution: Do not insert other foreign bodies into the auditory canal.) Repeat the demonstration, and try it several other times in both binaural and monaural conditions. Were you more accurate with information from two ears?

mation. Research has demonstrated that cells in this area are sensitive to interaural time differences, which—as mentioned earlier—is a more effective cue for low-frequency information. Another cell group, the **lateral superior olivary nucleus (LSO)**, is specialized for processing high-frequency information. Research has also demonstrated that cells in the LSO are sensitive to interaural intensity differences, a particularly effective cue for high-frequency information (Phillips & Brugge, 1985).

It is difficult to record neural activity in the superior olivary nucleus, so most of the physiological research is conducted on the higher levels in auditory processing. For example, the superior olivary nucleus sends its information on to the inferior colliculus. In a classic study Rose, Gross, Geisler, and Hind (1966) discovered a group of neurons within the inferior colliculus that were sensitive to a specific interaural time difference. Their work has been replicated more recently in research demonstrating that interaural time differences of less than .25 milliseconds produced optimal responses (Yin & Kuwada, 1983). Phillips and Brugge (1985) also summarize research on neurons sensitive to interaural intensity differences. Thus, the auditory system can take advantage of information from the two ears, in terms of both the timing of the two sounds and their intensity. Researchers have also examined the role of the auditory cortex in sound localization, but the conclu-

sions are not yet clear (Jenkins & Merzenich, 1984; Phillips & Brugge, 1985).

In this section on sound localization we have examined the sources of information that help identify the location of a sound source. The two ears receive different information about the sound's timing and the sound's intensity, and other cues are also available if that information is ambiguous. We also looked at accuracy on sound-localization tasks; factors such as vision, head movement, the location of the sound, and binaural versus monaural cues are all important determinants of accuracy. Finally, we saw that the superior olivary nucleus is where information about sound localization seems to be registered, although the auditory cortex may also be important. Sound localization occurs almost effortlessly. The richness of information about sound that is available in the stimulus (Theme 2) and the impressive capacity of our auditory systems to make use of this information (Theme 3) combine to accomplish this task of identifying the direction of a sound. ■

Summary: Perceptual Qualities of Sound

1. Pitch depends mainly upon frequency, but it also depends upon (a) amplitude, (b) previous tones, (c) the missing fundamental, and (d) the arousal of the perceiver.

2. Pitch can be measured by octaves, a measurement system used by musicians, and by the mel scale, a measurement system based on magnitude estimation.

3. Loudness depends mainly upon amplitude, but it also depends upon (a) duration, (b) background noises, (c) characteristics of the perceiver, and (d) frequency.

4. Loudness can be measured by an eight-level musical system devised by musicians, and by the sone scale, a measurement system based on magnitude estimation.

5. Equal loudness contours show the relationship between tone frequency and the number of decibels required to produce an equally loud tone. All sounds that are equally loud in phons have the same perceived loudness.

6. Timbre, a tone's sound quality, corresponds to complexity, which involves the combination of sound waves. The auditory system performs a Fourier analysis to analyze a complex sound wave into its components.

7. The nature of the overtones is one determinant of the timbre of musical instruments and the timbre of human voices.

8. When two tones are combined, the resulting sound depends upon the difference in frequency between the two tones; we can hear beats, roughness, or two distinct tones.

9. The combination of two distinct tones can sound consonant if the ratios of the frequencies of the two tones form a simple fraction; otherwise, the combination sounds dissonant.

10. One tone can mask another in a tone combination, depending upon the relative amplitude and frequency of the two tones.

11. Sound localization involves identifying the direction and the distance of a sound. One cue to the direction of a sound comes from the fact that a sound has to travel different distances to the two ears, creating an interaural time difference with two components, an onset difference and a phase difference. The interaural time difference is particularly useful for low-frequency sounds.

12. A second cue to the direction of a sound comes from the fact that a sound reaches the two ears at different intensities, creating an interaural intensity difference. The interaural intensity difference is particularly useful for high-frequency sounds.

13. There are potential ambiguities when the auditory system has only information about interaural time difference and interaural intensity difference; information based on pinnae contours and head or body movements helps to resolve these ambiguities.

14. Localization accuracy is influenced by vision, head movement, the position of the sound source, and monaural conditions.

15. The superior olivary nucleus is an important structure in sound localization. Within that structure the medial superior olivary nucleus processes low-frequency information and is sensitive to interaural time differences. The lateral superior olivary nucleus processes high-frequency information and is sensitive to interaural intensity differences. The role of the auditory cortex in sound localization is not clear.

APPLICATIONS OF HEARING RESEARCH

Research in hearing has particularly important applications in two areas, noise pollution and hearing impairment. As we will see, the two areas are related; noise pollution frequently leads to hearing impairment.

Noise Pollution

Think about the noise pollution you customarily experience in your daily life. **Noise** is irrelevant, excessive, or unwanted sound (Kryter, 1985). Of course, people differ with respect to their judgments about noise. A sound that is irrelevant, excessive, and unwanted to you may be sweet music to a friend.

In recent years psychologists, engineers, and audiologists have become increasingly concerned about noise pollution at home, entertainment places, and work. For example, people whose homes are near airports may experience a 120-dB sound every time a nearby jet takes off or lands. Rock groups can produce 110- to 120-dB music, nonstop, for several hours. Virshup (1985) measured the noise at various exclusive restaurants in New York City. They ranged from 66 dB at the classic "Four Seasons" to 94 dB at the currently trendy "America."

Consider the noise that can be produced in work settings. A jackhammer produces sounds of 120 dB, for example. In some cases, noise at work has produced deafness. Weavers in a mill were exposed to a sound level of about 100 dB for an 8-hour day. This level was so intolerable that the weavers were partially deaf—even on weekends—after several years of employment (Taylor, Pearson, Mair, & Burns, 1965).

This section on noise pollution has three parts: (1) techniques for studying noise pollution, (2) the consequences of noise pollution, and (3) reducing noise pollution.

Technique for Studying Noise Pollution

For ethical reasons psychologists cannot study noise pollution by presenting extremely loud noises to humans. A common approach is therefore to present loud, but safe, tones to humans for short periods and to observe the changes that occur in hearing ability.

To discuss these changes in hearing ability we need to examine the difference among three terms: masking, auditory adaptation, and auditory fatigue. Masking, a term discussed in the previous section, occurs when a tone cannot be heard because another tone is presented simultaneously or briefly before or after. In contrast, auditory adaptation and auditory fatigue concern the inability to hear a tone because of sustained previous tone

stimulation. Specifically, **auditory adaptation** occurs when one tone is presented continuously; the perceived loudness of that tone decreases as time passes. In normal ears, a 1-minute exposure to a continuous tone produces loudness adaptation of 15 to 20 dB (Evans, 1982b; Moore, 1982). The auditory system therefore shows an adaptation similar to the adaptation in other perceptual systems, consistent with the first theme of the book.

However, the *magnitude* of auditory adaptation is not large; the decrease in apparent intensity of odors, tastes, and skin sensations is much more dramatic. As Scharf (1983) observes, loudness adaptation can only be demonstrated in some conditions; it is not inevitable. In other words, your neighbor's stereo may still sound just as loud after 5 hours of continuous noise.

Whereas auditory adaptation involves the continuous presentation of the same tones, **auditory fatigue** occurs when a loud tone is presented and then turned off, causing a change in threshold for *other* tones. For example, when people are exposed to a complex noise having an intensity of 120 dB for 5 minutes, their threshold for a 4000-Hz test tone presented 2 minutes later may shift by 40 dB (Miller, 1978). Before exposure to the loud noise they could have barely heard the tone if it were presented at 0 dB. After the loud noise the tone would have to be presented at 40 dB (the loudness of a quiet neighborhood) to be heard at all. Keep this in mind if you are planning on hearing a 120-dB band this weekend!

Auditory fatigue can lead to two kinds of changes in hearing threshold. **Temporary threshold shift** is a temporary increase in a hearing threshold as a result of exposure to noise. It may take several hours or days for the threshold to recover completely (Evans, 1982b). In the laboratory, temporary threshold shifts in humans are studied because of the insights they may provide regarding permanent threshold shifts.

A **permanent threshold shift** is a permanent increase in a hearing threshold as a result of exposure to noise. Sometimes a permanent threshold shift is produced by a single loud noise, such as an extremely loud firecracker explosion. This shift has also been produced when a ringing cordless telephone is placed near the ear (Orchik, Schumaier, Shea, & Moretz, 1985). More often, permanent threshold shifts are a result of repeated exposures to noise on a regular basis, as in the case of the weavers mentioned earlier, or in the case of people who regularly visit discos. Hartman (1982) tested college students who regularly visited two discos where the decibel level ranged between 123 and 129. He found that 32% of these students showed substantial hearing loss in the high-frequency range.

Effects of Noise Pollution

The most dramatic effect of noise pollution is hearing loss, an area we will discuss in the last section of this chapter. Other important effects occur in (1) physical health, (2) mental health, (3) task performance, and (4) social behavior.

Noise pollution has some effect on physical health. For example, children from noisy schools have higher blood pressure than children from similar but quiet schools (Cohen, Evans, Krantz, & Stokols, 1980). Adults who live in noisy areas are more likely to contact a physician because of cardiovascular disease and high blood pressure (Kryter, 1985). Furthermore, noises are likely to cause industrial accidents, often because workers in noisy environments cannot hear warning shouts or sirens (Wilkins & Acton, 1982).

Since loud noises influence blood pressure and other measures associated with stress, we would expect noise pollution to be related to mental illness. In fact, industrial workers exposed to loud noises are more likely than other workers to report headaches, anxiety, sexual impotence, and other disorders (Cohen, Glass, & Phillips, 1977). Other studies demonstrate that people who live in noisy communities are more likely to require admission to psychiatric hospitals (Kryter, 1985).

Loud noise also influences task performance. For example, children who attend noisy schools are more likely to perform poorly on

cognitive tasks and are more likely to give up on a task before the allotted time (Cohen, Evans, Krantz, & Stokols, 1980). Although the results are not perfectly consistent, noise has also been found to influence performance on tasks such as arithmetic computation, memory, and reaction time (Loeb, 1981). However, performance on tests of general intelligence and some other kinds of cognitive abilities are sometimes unaffected (Kryter, 1985).

Finally, noise can influence social behavior. People in noisy environments sit farther away from each other. Noise also increases aggression and decreases helping behavior (Bell, Fisher, & Loomis, 1978).

In summary, then, noise pollution can have a substantial effect on humans. Their health, psychological well-being, cognitive performance, and social interactions can all be affected.

Reducing Noise Pollution

Current government regulations prohibit industries from exposing their workers to more than a 90-dB sound level for 8 hours a day. Even though this sound level may produce some hearing loss, special interest groups continually pressure the government to reduce or eliminate these limits. Thus, factory workers still need to be concerned about the possibility of hearing loss. Guidelines and standards set by governmental agencies are discussed by Kryter (1985).

One approach to the problem is to provide earplugs or earmuffs to workers exposed to loud noises. However, these devices are uncomfortable and interfere with work. Furthermore, people report that they feel lonely and excluded from the normal audible world when they wear these protective devices (Noble, 1983).

Some efforts have been made to modify noise at its source. For example, the design of some jet airplanes has been changed to reduce their noise at takeoff and landing. Furthermore, some companies have included sound absorbers, either on machines or in walls. However, these absorbers are much more effective for high-pitched sounds than for low rumbles. Ultimately, as Bershader (1981) says, "Quiet is a commodity that costs money" (p. 74). Individuals and industries will have to decide how much must be paid to reduce the noise in our environment.

Hearing Impairments

Several kinds of disorders can occur in the auditory system. For example, **tinnitus** is a high-pitched ringing in the ears that can be caused by a high fever or ear infection (McFadden, 1982). Tinnitus can also be caused by taking large doses of aspirin. This medication that once seemed so innocent also can increase the magnitude of a temporary threshold shift (McFadden & Plattsmier, 1983), so it should be used cautiously.

Ear infections themselves are another common disorder, especially among young children. In an **ear infection** the eustachian tube becomes swollen, cutting off the middle ear from the respiratory tract. Bacteria may multiply in the middle ear, resulting in a painful earache and temporary hearing difficulties. Children who frequently have ear infections may have difficulties developing normal language (Eimas & Kavanagh, 1986).

The major kind of hearing impairment, however, is deafness. In the United States there are approximately 13 million hearing-impaired people, of whom perhaps 300,000 cannot be helped by a conventional hearing aid (Moore, 1977).

Deafness can be assessed by a variety of techniques. One is called **electric response audiometry**; it involves recording electrical activity at locations in the auditory pathway in response to auditory stimulation (Catlin, 1984). However, deafness is more commonly assessed by **audiometry**, or the measurement of the sensitivity of audition. One technique is to present a series of pure tones, perhaps at frequencies of 250, 500, 1000, 2000, and 4000 Hz. The audiologist measures the decibel difference between a persons' threshold at each frequency and the average threshold of a normal population (Green, 1976). Other hearing tests measure the perception of speech sounds. Let us consider how three hy-

pothetical people might respond to a standard audiometry test. Figure 9.22 illustrates the hearing of a normal person and two hearing-impaired people. Notice that Person A shows a consistent loss of about 35 dB at all the tested frequencies. In contrast, Person B shows no loss at the lower frequencies but substantial loss at the higher frequencies.

Person A and Person B are respresentative of two different kinds of hearing problems, known as conduction deafness and nerve deafness. **Conduction deafness** involves problems in conducting the sound stimulus; the problem occurs in either the external ear or the middle ear. Person A in Figure 9.22 shows conduction deafness and would be helped by a hearing aid, which would make sounds of all frequencies louder. This person can hear sounds conducted through the bone but cannot hear sound waves that travel through the air. (Try Demonstration 9.7 to illustrate the two ways in which sound waves can travel.) A hearing aid would be useful for people with moderate levels of conduction deafness. The hearing aid can channel airborne sound waves to the bony part of the skull below the ear, making it vibrate and stimulate the cochlea.

The other kind of deafness is called nerve deafness. Person B in Figure 9.22 has nerve deafness. In **nerve deafness** the problem occurs either in the cochlea or in the auditory nerve. For example, if the ear is exposed to extremely loud noises—the kind we discussed in the previous section—the hair cells in the organ of Corti may be destroyed. (Look back at Figure 9.9.) If all the hair cells are damaged, there are no receptors to transmit the sound waves. Thus neither airborne sound nor bone-conducted sound can be transmitted; the person is deaf. A simple hearing aid would not help someone with complete nerve deafness, just as a pair of glasses would not help someone who has a detached retina.

What can be done to help a person with nerve deafness? A method of stimulating the auditory nerve electrically is being developed. Furthermore, if some hair cells are intact, the hearing aid can be modified so that it differentially amplifies the different fre-

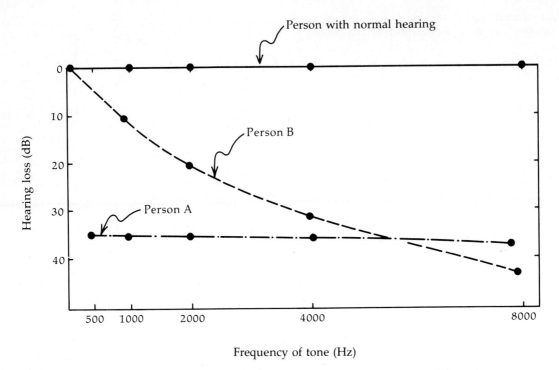

Figure 9.22   Hearing loss in two hearing-impaired people, in comparison with person with normal hearing.

quencies. For example, Person B does not require amplification of the low-frequency tones but does require amplification of the high-frequency tones. However, people with nerve deafness also show a disorder related to loudness perception, called recruitment.

Recruitment is a condition in which a deaf person perceives very loud sounds normally; this person's perception does not differ from a normal, hearing person's perception if we only consider loud sounds. However, very weak sounds are not heard at all. Thus, the

---

Demonstration 9.7
_____

*Sound Waves
Traveling through
the Bone and through
the Air*

Tape record your own voice and play it back. This recording captures the sound waves from your voice that travel only through the air. Now talk in a normal voice; you hear both the sound waves that travel through the air and the sound waves that travel through the bony part of your skull. Finally, plug your ears so that no sound waves can travel through the air and pass into your external auditory canal; you hear only the sound waves that travel through the bony part of your skull.

design of a hearing aid for a nerve-deaf person has to take care of two problems: a differential sensitivity to the various pitches and a differential sensitivity to the various loudnesses.

Summary: Applications of Hearing Research

1. Noise, or unwanted sound, is an increasing problem in modern society.
2. Auditory adaptation, or a decreased perceived loudness for a tone that is presented continuously, is generally small. In contrast, the auditory system does show auditory fatigue; when a loud noise is presented and then turned off, other tones are difficult to hear.
3. Auditory fatigue can lead to a temporary threshold shift or a permanent threshold shift. Psychologists study temporary threshold shifts to gain insight about permanent threshold shifts.
4. Noise pollution leads to a hearing loss and a deterioration in physical health, mental health, task performance, and social behavior.
5. Noise pollution effects can be reduced by limiting workers' exposure to loud noises, providing earplugs or earmuffs, and modifying noise at its source.
6. Three kinds of hearing impairments are tinnitus, ear infection, and deafness.
7. A person with conduction deafness shows a consistent loss of hearing at all frequencies; the sound stimulus is not properly conducted, and this person can be helped by a hearing aid.
8. A person with nerve deafness shows a hearing loss at certain frequencies, although hearing may be normal for other frequencies.
9. A person with nerve deafness shows recruitment; very loud sounds are perceived normally, whereas very weak sounds are not heard at all.
10. It is difficult to design a hearing aid for nerve-deaf people because of their differential sensitivity to various pitches and loudnesses.

Review

1. Describe the auditory stimulus with respect to frequency, amplitude, and complexity. Then turn back to Chapters 3, 5, and 6 to compare the auditory stimulus with the visual stimulus.
2. Summarize your knowledge about psychological reactions to tones of various frequencies. Mention (a) the range of frequencies that humans can hear, (b) the tones they can most readily detect, (c) the tones they can most readily discriminate, and (d) the relative loudness of tones of various frequencies.
3. Discuss why pitch is not perfectly correlated with frequency. Consider the factors that influence pitch and describe the conditions that would make the pitch abnormally high and the conditions that would make it abnormally low. Repeat this same process with the relationship between frequency and loudness.
4. Draw a rough sketch of the auditory system, identifying the parts of the outer ear, middle ear, inner ear, and the pathway from the ear to the brain. Point out the similarities between the higher levels of auditory processing and the higher levels of visual processing.
5. In a way, the path between the external ear and the cochlea resembles a real-life board game, in which points are lost because of some events and points are gained because of other events. Describe this "board game."
6. Discuss the two kinds of hair cells and point out how each kind resembles one of the two kinds of receptors in the visual system.

7. Discuss the two theories of how frequency is registered in the inner ear, and point out how the two theories can be reconciled. Be certain to include concepts such as the traveling wave and the volley principle in your description.

8. Notice a sound in your present environment and list the cues that help you judge the direction of the sound source. What are the factors that could help you resolve potential ambiguities about the location of that sound?

9. Point out the differences among masking, auditory adaptation, auditory fatigue, temporary threshold shift, and permanent threshold shift. Which of these terms are relevant for the study of noise pollution?

10. Suppose that you know two people who are deaf. One has conduction deafness and the other has nerve deafness. List various ways in which the perceptual experiences of these two people would differ.

New Terms

sounds
frequency
H$_z$
detection threshold
difference threshold
pure tones
complex tones
amplitude
decibels
dB
dynes
pinna
external auditory canal
eardrum
tympanic membrane
ossicles
malleus
incus
stapes
impedance
impedance mismatch
eustachian tube
cochlea
oval window
vestibular canal
helicotrema
tympanic canal
round window
cochlear duct
organ of Corti
basilar membrane

tectorial membrane
hair cells
inner hair cells
outer hair cells
cilia
auditory nerve
place theory
traveling wave
tonotopic organization
frequency theory
refractory period
volley principle
frequency tuning curve
cochlear nucleus
monaural
binaural
superior olivary nucleus
inferior colliculus
medial geniculate nucleus
primary auditory cortex
pitch
case of the missing
    fundamental
fundamental frequency
harmonics
octave
mel scale
loudness
sone scale
equal loudness contour
phons

timbre
Fourier analysis
overtones
beats
consonance
dissonance
masking
onset difference
phase difference
interaural time difference
interaural intensity difference
sound shadow
cone of confusion
medial superior olivary nucleus
    (MSO)
lateral superior olivary nucleus
    (LSO)
noise
auditory adaptation
auditory fatigue
temporary threshold shift
permanent threshold shift
tinnitus
ear infection
electric response audiometry
audiometry
conduction deafness
nerve deafness
recruitment

Recommended Readings

Barlow, H. B., & Mollon, J. D. (Eds.) (1982). *The senses.* Cambridge: Cambridge University Press. *Three chapters by Evans provide a solid overview of the nature of sound and sensory aspects of the auditory system.*

Gelfand, S. A. (1981). *Hearing.* New York: Marcel Dekker. *Of the three textbooks in this list, Gelfand's has the most detail on the psychophysics of auditory perception.*

Moore, B. C. J. (1982). *An introduction to the psychology of hearing* (2nd ed.). London: Academic Press. *Moore's book is an advanced-level presentation, with more emphasis on perception than sensation.*

Phillips, D. P., & Brugge, J. F. (1985). Progress in neurophysiology of sound localization. *Annual Review of Psychology, 36,* 245–274. *This review chapter summarizes the current sound localization literature, with a particular emphasis on its physiological basis.*

Warren, R. M. (1982). *Auditory perception: A new synthesis.* Elmsford, NY: Pergamon. *Warren's book is a concise and well-written introduction to the topic, with more emphasis on perception than sensation.*

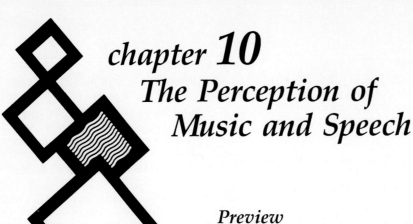

chapter *10*
The Perception of
Music and Speech

Outline

Preview

In this chapter we move beyond the relatively simple perceptual characteristics of auditory stimuli, such as their pitch, loudness, and timbre, to consider two major applications of hearing: music perception and hearing perception.

In the discussion of music you'll see that there are important interrelationships among tones that differ in pitch. For example, two tones separated by an octave can be more psychologically similar than two closer tones. The section on perceptual qualities and music will also examine topics such as concert-hall acoustics, how musical instruments differ in timbre, and the complications of trying to predict which tone combinations will be consonant. Other portions of the section on music perception discuss the Gestalt principles as applied to music, musical constancy, and musical illusions.

Speech perception is a challenge for researchers to explain because we must account for our ability to recognize so many thousands of words, when our pronunciation is so variable and the boundary among the words is often unclear. This half of the chapter examines how speech is produced and how speech sounds are classified, how people tend to perceive speech sounds as belonging to a small number of categories, and how top-down processing aids speech perception. The final topic in the chapter is theories of speech perception.

The introduction to hearing in the previous chapter explored the physical characteristics of sound, the anatomy of the auditory system, and the basic psychological reactions to sound. These reactions involved judgments such as "that tone has a higher pitch than the previous one" and "that sound came from a position directly in front of me." In general, the sounds were isolated rather than sequential, and the psychological reactions we discussed were not complex. In our daily lives, however, we perform sophisticated analyses of sound. Furthermore, we do not hear sounds in isolation but in meaningful patterns. This chapter examines two important areas of complex auditory perception: music and speech.

MUSIC PERCEPTION

It would be difficult to present a convincing argument that music perception is more vital for humans than speech perception. Certainly speech perception has a more major role in human relationships, work settings, and daily living. Still, take a moment to consider how often music plays a part in your everyday life. For instance, the day after beginning this chapter, I realized that my major activities on that day had concerned music. My husband and I had driven our teenage daughter and her friend to a rock concert, but being less than enthusiastic about that kind of music, we had spent the intervening time seeing a movie in which music from the 1950s figured prominently, hearing jazz in a restaurant, and listening to the opera *Fidelio* on the tape recorder. The trip home was accompanied by such camp classics as "Found a Peanut." Try Demonstration 10.1 to become more aware of the frequency and importance of music in your own life.

For many years research on hearing was concerned only with detection, discrimination, and scaling (Deutsch, 1986)—the kinds of perceptual responses discussed in the previous chapter. More recently, psychologists

and others have begun to explore higher-level processing of music. As Krumhansl (1985) describes:

> When listening to music, we hear the sounded elements not as disconnected units but in relation to one another. The individual tones are perceived in terms of their functions in the broader context of pitch and rhythm, and we achieve a sense of the underlying organization of the composition. Describing this process is the goal of research in music perception, an increasingly active area of interdisciplinary study. For psychologists studying mental capabilities, music is interesting because it requires the listener to perceive and remember complex events occurring over a period of time. Its study may uncover new principles of perception and cognition, as well as aspects held in common with other domains of human behavior" (p. 371).

In this section of the chapter, we will begin by exploring some of the perceptual qualities discussed in the previous chapter—pitch, loudness, timbre, and tone combinations—but this time with an emphasis on the importance of these qualities in music.

Perceptual Qualities and Music

In the last chapter we saw that perceptual qualities such as pitch and loudness are more complex than they might initially seem. For example, pitch depends upon many variables other than the frequency of a sound's wavelength, and loudness depends upon many variables other than the amplitude of a sound's wavelength. However, we will see in this chapter that these perceptual qualities are even more complex when we consider music perception. There are complex similarities among tones of widely varying pitch, for example, and timbre can convey such subtle psychological qualities as emotion. Let's now explore the interrelationship between perceptual qualities and music.

Pitch

In Chapter 9 we saw that humans can hear frequencies in the range of 20 to about 20,000

Demonstration 10.1

*Music in Everyday
Life: A Music Journal*

For the next 3 days, keep an informal music journal. Record each time you hear any form of music. You'll notice that music is sometimes central to your activities, as when you attend a concert or a dance or hear selections in a music course. Sometimes music is peripherally important, for example, when there is background music on the late-night movie. Still other times you encounter music unintentionally, from a friend singing in the hall, the stereo next door, or the "easy listening" music in the dentist's office. This journal should make you aware that it is difficult to *avoid* music in our culture!

Hz. Music represents a substantially narrower range of pitches, particularly at the upper end. Figure 10.1 shows that the the fundamental frequencies on the piano range from 27.5 to 4186 Hz. As you can also see, each instrument in an orchestra or human voice range is still more limited, typically less than half the range of the piano.

In Western cultures pitch is probably the most essential attribute of music (Cross, Howell, & West, 1983; Krumhansl & Kessler, 1982). In other cultures rhythm may be more important, so the emphasis on pitch is not universal. However, our culture emphasizes pitch and the relationships among tones with different pitches. Let's explore those relationships.

Figure 10.1 shows an arrangement of tones from low to high, an arrangement that suggests that pitch is one-dimensional. However, this view of pitch ignores the fact that the tones in that diagram have regular cycles, with each tone resembling a tone in the previous cycle. Figure 10.2 illustrates these repeated cycles. **Tone chroma** refers to the similarity shared by all musical tones that have the same name; for example, all Cs on the piano sound similar, even though they are separated by many other tones. **Tone height** refers to the increase in pitch that accompanies an increase in frequency; the highest C on the piano has greater tone height than the other Cs.

To discuss Figure 10.2 more thoroughly, we need to examine the musical concept of the octave more thoroughly. As mentioned in Chapter 9, an **octave** is the distance between two tones that have the same name. Thus there is one octave between two adjacent Cs on the piano. There is an important relationship between octaves and wavelength frequency. Specifically, each tone on the scale of the piano has exactly double the frequency of the previous tone with the same name. Let us follow the musical convention and use subscripts to represent a tone's position on the piano, so that C_1 is the lowest C, C_2 is the next higher C, and so forth, up to C_8. Since C_1 has a frequency of 32.7, C_2 has a frequency of 32.7×2, or 65.4. Thus, the perceived similarity of tones an octave apart has a physical basis; the frequency of the higher tone is twice the frequency of the lower tone.

Diana Deutsch, a prominent researcher in the psychology of music, performed a classic experiment to demonstrate the similarity of tones an octave apart. Deutsch (1973) presented one tone, which listeners were instructed to compare with another tone. In between these two tones, however, she presented six irrelevant tones, which listeners were instructed to ignore. They were told to pay attention to the two important tones and to judge whether these tones were the same or different. An important factor that influenced listeners' accuracy was

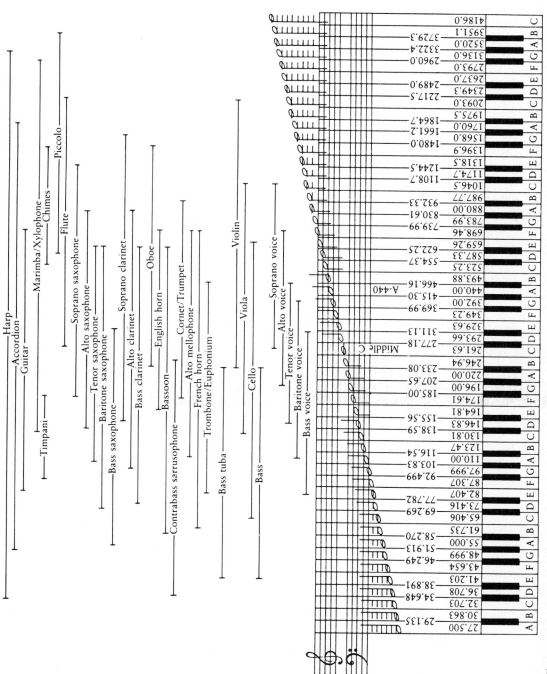

Figure 10.1 Pitch of musical instruments, with piano as reference. (From *The Science of Musical Sound* by John R. Pierce. Copyright © 1983 Scientific American Books. Adapted from a figure published in *Musical Acoustics: An Introduction* by Donald E. Hall. Published by Wadsworth.)

Tone height

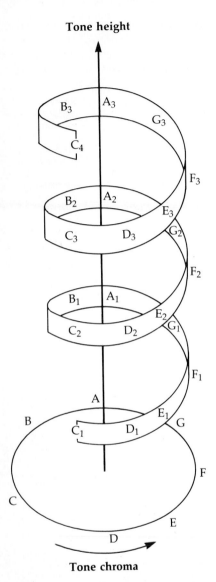

Tone chroma

Figure 10.2 Schematic diagram of pitch, showing tone chroma and tone height.

ditory system regards that irrelevant tone as equivalent as long as it matches in chroma, and it does not need to be identical in tone height. This concept is often called **octave generalization** because tones separated by one octave are in some respects musically equivalent (Burns & Ward, 1982). Thus, a tone may have more in common with another tone an octave away than it does with a closer neighbor. Pitch is not a one-dimensional characteristic with a simple progression from low tones to high tones.

Other evidence against the one-dimensional view of pitch comes from research on tonality. **Tonality** is the organization of pitches around one particular tone. This tone, known as the **tonic**, is one of the 12 pitches within an octave; in Western music, the tonic is the same as the key of a piece of music (Krumhansl, 1985).

Carol Krumhansl used a method called the probe-tone technique to examine tonality in music (Krumhansl, 1983, 1985; Krumhansl & Kessler, 1982). In the **probe-tone technique** listeners first hear a musical chord or a scale, either of which provides sufficient information to establish a key. Then a single pitch, or probe tone, is presented; this tone is one of the 12 tones found within the octave of the key being examined. The listeners are instructed to rate how well that tone fits within the scale or chord presented earlier. For example, in a typical trial, listeners might first hear a scale in the key of C major. Then they might hear the probe tone of F and be asked to judge how well that F fits within the framework of the C major scale. Incidentally, the listeners who were tested in this research had each studied a musical instrument for at least 5 years, although they had received little instruction in musical theory.

The results showed, as expected, that some tones were judged to fit much better than others within a given key. For example, in the key of C major the tone that received the highest rating was C, which is the tonic for this key. The next "best" tone for this key was G, followed in order by E, F, A, D, and B. All the five tones with sharps (C#, D#, F#, G#, and A#, which would be repre-

whether one of the irrelevant tones matched the comparison tone. If it did, listeners frequently made errors. The major implication of this study for the concept of octaves, however, was that the irrelevant tone could produce errors if it was one octave higher or lower than the comparison tone—it did not need to be precisely the same tone. Our au-

sented by the black keys on the piano) were judged equally unsuitable for the key of C. A C# might be right next to a C on the piano, but *psychologically* it doesn't belong within the key of C.

Krumhansl was curious to see whether these ratings of probe tones were correlated with the use of these tones in classical music. Luckily, statistical analyses have been conducted on several pieces by composers such as Mozart, Schubert, and Strauss. These analyses list the frequency of occurrence of each tone and often include additional information about the total duration of each tone (because some tones are short and some are long). Krumhansl found a high positive correlation between probe-tone ratings and the total du-

ration of the tones. That is, tones that were judged to fit well in a particular scale were also likely to occur often and to be the longer tones in a musical composition in this key. The most remarkable correlation occurred for Schubert's *Moments Musicaux* (op. 94, no. 1). The correlation between the probe-tone ratings and the total duration of the tones for this particular piece was + .97. (Correlations have a maximum value of 1.00; psychologists in many disciplines are elated by correlations in the neighborhood of + .40, so a correlation of + .97 is astonishingly high). The relationship between these two measures is illustrated in Figure 10.3. As you can see, since the piece is in the key of G, this tone of G is the most highly rated and also the tone that

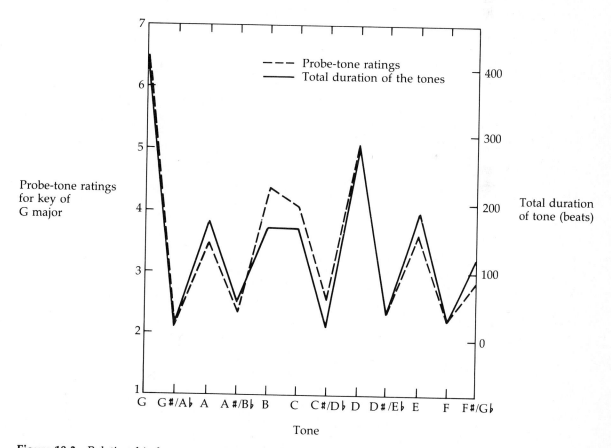

Figure 10.3 Relationship between probe-tone ratings and total duration of the tones, for Schubert's op. 94, no. 1. (From Krumhansl, 1985, Figure 2. Used with permission.)

has the longest total duration. Now try Demonstration 10.2 to see whether you find a similar relationship for the key of C with introductory-level exercises.

Loudness

We saw in the previous chapter that researchers have not been eager to theorize about physiological explanations for loudness; pitch has monopolized their attention. Similarly, psychologists and other researchers interested in music have not been overly intrigued with loudness.

As you can imagine, the various instruments in an orchestra differ in the amplitude of the sound they produce. A clarinet, for example, has a maximum amplitude of 86 dB, whereas a trumpet's maximum is 94 dB and a trombone's is 107 (Pierce, 1983). Remember, though, that loudness involves qualities other than amplitude; in a symphony orchestra, a clarinet sometimes seems louder than a trombone.

One application of loudness in music is concert-hall acoustics. To those of us who are not professional musicians, this might not seem like a complex subject. However, when music is played in an enclosed space, we need to consider both direct sounds and indirect sounds, which reach the listener after bouncing off the walls. These indirect sounds influence not only the loudness of music but also the impression of spaciousness (Rasch & Plomp, 1982).

One of the most dramatic demonstrations of the subtleties of concert-hall acoustics occurred with Philharmonic Hall in New York City. This hall was designed by an architectural firm, which issued a statement about "the care taken in planning the Philharmonic Hall in Lincoln Center. Lady Luck has finally been supplanted by careful analysis and the

---

Demonstration 10.2

Relationship between Average Rating of Probe Tones and Their Frequency of Occurrence in Music

For this demonstration you will need a beginning book for the piano or some other instrument; select only pieces in the key of C. Go through as many selections as time permits, recording the number of times that each tone occurs. (Count all Cs as equivalent, all Ds as equivalent, and so forth.) Tally the total frequency of occurrence for each tone and enter it in the table below, next to the average rating of probe tones, as established by Krumhansl (1985). In general, did you find that the tones rated best for the key of C also tended to appear most often in the music?

Tone	Average Rating for Key of C	Frequency of Occurrence in Your Music Sample
C	6.4	
G	5.2	
E	4.3	
F	4.1	
A	3.7	
D	3.4	
B	2.9	
$F^{\#}$	2.7	
$G^{\#}$	2.6	
$A^{\#}$	2.6	
$D^{\#}$	2.4	
$C^{\#}$	2.2	

painstaking application of new but firmly grounded acoustic principles'' (cited in Pierce, 1983, p. 143). When the hall opened in 1962, it was clear that the acoustics were disastrous. The members of the orchestra could hear neither themselves nor others. In some seats there were echoes. Mysteriously, the low frequencies could not be heard by the audience; musicians played the cello and the double bass, but their music never spread throughout the hall! Later, Philharmonic Hall was completely redesigned with a new ceiling, seats that absorbed less sound, and elements on the side walls to scatter the sound. It opened some time afterwards under a new name, Avery Fisher Hall, and the acoustics of this new hall have been highly praised.

Timbre

Timbre, like loudness, has received much less attention than pitch. As Chapter 9 discussed, timbre is a tone's sound quality. Deutsch (1986) points out, "Timbre may be described as that perceptual quality of a sound that distinguishes it from other sounds, when simple attributes such as pitch and loudness are held constant" (pp. 32–34). For example, a flute and an oboe may both play the same tone at the same loudness, but you can still distinguish between the nasal quality of the oboe and the pure quality of the flute.

As discussed earlier, an important determinant of timbre is the harmonics or overtones that supplement the fundamental frequency. Figure 10.4a shows the fundamental

frequency and harmonics for one of the higher tones in the oboe's range. Notice that the harmonics are relatively high amplitude, in comparison to the fundamental frequency, and there are eight for this particular tone. Contrast this distribution of harmonics with that of the flute, in Figure 10.4b, for one of the higher tones in the flute's range. Impressively, this tone has only a single harmonic, and its amplitude is so low that you might miss it on first inspection. An important characteristic of the flute's distribution of energy is that when a tone in the high range is played, the fundamental frequency carries almost all the energy output; the harmonics are practically nonexistent. As a result, the sound in this range is clear and pure (Olson, 1967). If you play a musical instrument, you'll be interested in examining the distribution of harmonics for that instrument in Olson's (1967) book, *Music, Physics, and Engineering*.

Helmholtz's classical view of timbre proposed that differences in the sound quality of musical instruments could be entirely traced to the distribution of harmonics (Deutsch, 1986; Risset & Wessel, 1982). However, more recent theories stress the importance of an additional factor, the attack. A musical tone has three sections during the time it is played: (a) the **attack**, or the beginning buildup of a tone; (b) the **steady state**, or the middle portion of a tone; and (c) the **decay**, or decrease in amplitude at the end of a tone.

Helmholtz and his followers analyzed only the harmonic components of the steady-

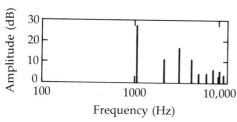

a. Note with frequency of 1046 Hz, played on the oboe

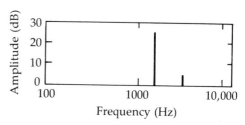

b. Note with frequency of 1568 Hz, played on the flute

Figure 10.4   Fundamental frequency and harmonics for note on oboe and on flute. (From Olson, 1967, Figures 6.25 (top) and 6.19 (top). Used with permission.)

state portion of a tone. However, it is clear that listeners use additional information when they identify instruments. For example, when your 10-year-old nephew plays a middle C on his flute, the harmonics are much different from the same tone played by Jean-Pierre Rampal. However, you can identify that both tones have been produced by a flute. Furthermore, when a listener moves around a room while an instrument is being played, the pattern of harmonics changes completely. Still, the instrument can be readily identified (Risset & Wessel, 1982).

As mentioned, more recent work on timbre has identified that the specific details of the attack portion of a tone are important. Certain harmonics appear quickly, perhaps .02 seconds after the initiation of a tone, whereas other harmonics may not appear until .04 seconds after initiation. Most important, each instrument has a distinctive pattern within the attack portion of a tone. We know that this portion is critical to instrument recognition because recognition accuracy drops when the attack portion of a tone has been eliminated from a recording or when a tone is played backwards (Deutsch, 1986; Risset & Wessel, 1982). Interestingly, the decay segment of a tone doesn't seem to add much information. Listeners don't attend to the speed with which the harmonics fade (Deutsch, 1984).

Perception of Tone Combinations

Chapter 9 discussed how two tones could be combined to produce either consonant or dissonant combinations. Let us examine how the frequencies of the tones in a consonant tone combination tend to form a ratio that is a simple fraction. For example, you know that if a tone is combined with another tone exactly one octave lower, the first tone is twice the frequency of the second tone; the ratio is a simple 2/1. Try Demonstration 10.3 to illustrate various consonant and dissonant tone combinations. This demonstration also lists the commonly used names for the musical intervals.

Musicians have been aware of these ratios for literally thousands of years. For example,

a Babylonian tablet from earlier than 1000 BC has been discovered that describes the 4/3 ratio in tuning (Pierce, 1983). Pythagoras, whose Pythagorean theorem about the sides of triangles you studied in high school, also developed theories in the sixth century BC about the ratios of the lengths of vibrating strings (Warren, 1982).

It is clear that the consonance of tone combinations largely depends upon whether the frequency of two tones forms a simple ratio. However, it is equally clear that this ratio is not the only determinant of consonance. You might have expected this conclusion because you know that perceptual experiences do not tend to be related to physical stimuli in a simple fashion. For example, pitch depends upon more than frequency, loudness depends upon more than amplitude, and timbre depends upon more than the nature of the harmonics.

Shepard (1982a) points out why consonance is less than perfectly related to simple ratios:

1. Listeners cannot discriminate between a simple 3/2 ratio and a highly complex one such as 29,998/20,000, with a similar numerical value.

2. Listeners who make judgments about the ideal octave select a ratio slightly larger than the theoretical 2/1; the ratio of the frequencies they select is much more complex than 2/1.

3. Listeners who make judgments about the pleasantness of tone combinations usually prefer a 5/4 ratio over a numerically simple 4/3 ratio.

It is clear, also, that the perception of consonance and dissonance depends upon individual differences and cultural backgrounds. For example, an American who hears East Indian music for the first time may judge the combination of notes dissonant and unpleasant. Many musical intervals in Indian music do not correspond to simple ratios; however, the combinations do not sound unpleasant to Indians. Instead, the music sounds rich and extremely varied in mood (Moore, 1982). Similarly, cultural preferences

Demonstration 10.3

Consonant and Dissonant Tone Combinations

Locate a piano. You do not have to know how to play it to try this demonstration, but you do need to be able to locate middle C. The figure below illustrates the notes included in this octave. Musicians have provided names for many of the intervals or tone combinations, as listed below. Play each of the first seven tone combinations and judge the pleasantness of each of these pairs. Now try the three dissonant tones whose combinations form complex fractions. You may want to experiment with other possible combinations.

Name of Interval	Notes (in C major key)	Frequency Ratio
Octave	C–C	2/1
Major third	C–E	5/4
Minor third	E–G	6/5
Fourth	C–F	4/3
Fifth	C–G	3/2
Major sixth	C–A	5/3
Minor sixth	E–C	8/5
(Dissonance)	C–C$^\#$	262/277
(Dissonance)	C–D	262/294
(Dissonance)	C–D$^\#$	262/311

change as a function of time. The music of Stravinsky was condemned as unpleasant dissonance 60 years ago, yet it sounds pleasant to most of us today.

Pattern and Organization in Music

Our discussion of music has primarily concentrated on isolated tones. However, few of us would attend a concert at which only a single tone was played. Music is a sequence of tones occurring over time, yet we do not typically hear these as disconnected. Instead, the tones group together. For example, in the tune "Yankee Doodle," the two tones corresponding to "Yankee" seem to belong together. Like the visual stimuli discussed earlier in the book, Gestalt laws of grouping and the figure-ground relationship can be applied to audition.

Let us first discuss the laws of grouping. Consider the law of similarity, for example, which states that similar objects tend to be seen as a unit. Deutsch (1982b) points out that classical music compositions can exploit this law. Look at the music by Beethoven in Figure 10.5. This is a melody played by a single instrument. As you see, the tones alternate between two different pitch ranges. In ordinary music, listeners tend to group a tone with adjacent ones because of the law of proximity. However, when this music is played fast enough, listeners prefer to group a tone with tones from approximately similar pitch ranges. As a consequence, listeners report hearing two simultaneous melodic streams—one high and one low—rather than a single melody that flutters between high and low pitch. At slower speeds, listeners still tend to group in terms of similarity, rather than proximity, although the grouping is not nearly so compelling. Other research indicates that listeners group not only in terms of pitch similarity but also in terms of similarity in loudness, timbre, and spatial location (Deutsch & Feroe, 1981).

See if you can think of examples in music of the laws of proximity, good continuation, closure, and common fate. For example, consider how the law of good continuation is important; an instrument playing a scale will play a melody that is clearly perceived as a unit because it continues in a consistent direction. Research has demonstrated, incidentally, that good continuation is important in music perception, but similarity is even more important (Tougas & Bregman, 1985).

Another important Gestalt principle involves the figure-ground relationship. As Sloboda (1985) points out, in music only one melodic line can be heard as "figure" at any given time. We focus our attention on this line so that we can notice relationships within the melody and recognize it. In contrast, the other melodic line (or lines) forms the background. We are aware of these other lines, but they merely add interest. Like the famous vase-faces illustration in Figure 6.13, we cannot concentrate on both the figure and the ground at the same time. However, it is usually possible to force ground to become figure. You might want to turn on the radio and notice whether you can readily force a guitar melody to become the figure, while the singer's melody retreats into the ground.

Dowling (1973) examined listeners' ability to separate two melodies and perceive figure-ground relationships. He presented two familiar tunes, "Mary Had a Little Lamb" and "Three Blind Mice." However, in this unusual presentation, the tones in the two tunes were interleaved, so that "Three Blind Mice" was played for tones 1, 3, 5, and so on, and "Mary Had a Little Lamb" was played for tones 2, 4, 6, and so on. When the two tunes were presented in similar pitch ranges, observers were unable to perceive two different tunes; in fact the tunes needed to be about an octave apart before the separate melodies could be recognized. Once the melodies were recognized, however, listeners reported an interesting figure-ground relationship. When they attended to "Three Blind Mice," for example, "Mary Had a Little Lamb" became background; the two melodies could not be simultaneously perceived as figures. Similarly, attending to "Mary Had a Little Lamb" forced "Three Blind Mice" into the background.

In summary, the Gestalt laws of grouping and the figure-ground relationship are not limited to the visual system. Auditory processing also shows the tendency to find patterns on the basis of qualities such as similarity and the tendency for a distinct figure to be seen against a less prominent background.

Figure 10.5 Melody typically heard as two melodic streams on basis of law of similarity. (From Beethoven's *Six Variations on the Duet* "Nel cor piu non mi sento" from Paisiello's *La Molinara*.)

Constancy in Music

If you've seen the classic Bogart film *Casablanca*, you'll surely recall the scene in the bar where Ingrid Bergman says "Play it, Sam" and sings the melody of the song that Sam used to sing for her and Bogart. Sam launches into the memorable tune "As Time Goes By." Edworthy (1985) points out that Sam does not play the same intervals that Bergman sings, yet Sam, Bergman, and the filmgoers are all equally unperturbed by the discrepancy. Both sets of intervals share the same contour, so the correspondence satisfies us all. The fact is that we can readily recognize tunes that are not exact duplicates of each other (Dyson & Watkins, 1984).

Early Gestalt psychologist Von Ehrenfels (1890) pointed out that melodies can retain their perceptual identities even when they are transposed to different keys, as long as the relationships between adjacent tunes in the melody remain constant (Deutsch, 1986). In a similar fashion, we recognize a shape if it is moved nearer or farther away, or if it is tilted at an angle. However, the similarity between visual and auditory processing is not perfect. For example, size constancy is preserved if your friend walks toward you, increasing the size of the retinal image by perhaps 100 times. What happens if we greatly increase the size of the intervals in a melody, for example making one *octave* between each of the first three tones in "Three Blind Mice"—rather than just one tone? The tune is unrecognizable. Thus, there are limits to constancy in music.

Illusions in Music

One of the themes of this book is that the perceptual processes share important similarities. We have seen that music, like vision, shows pattern, organization, and constancy. Similarly, a number of musical illusions have been described by psychologists and others interested in research on music; illusions are not limited to visual processes. One of the earliest illusions was created by Shepard (1964), who used a computer to produce a series of tones that seem to increase endlessly in pitch. Each tone seems to be distinctly higher in pitch than the previous tone, yet after numerous tones you are back to the tone where you began! By carefully manipulating the harmonics, we have the illusion of increasing pitch. This illusion is worth hearing in the record that accompanies Pierce's (1983) book. Variations of the original illusion have also been created (e.g., Burns, 1981; Pollack, 1978).

Another remarkable illusion, illustrated in Figure 10.6 and created by Deutsch (1983), is called the **octave illusion**. One tone is presented to one ear and another tone an octave away is simultaneously presented to the other ear. For example, the first combination presented to the listener in Figure 10.6 is G_4 (392 Hz) presented to the left ear and G_5 (784 Hz) presented to the right ear. In the next tone combination, however, the tones are shifted between the ears, so that G_4 is presented to the right ear and G_5 is presented to the left ear. Surprisingly, listeners do not perceive the stimuli accurately; most listeners perceive a single tone, G_5, in the right ear, followed by a single tone, G_4, in the left ear, and continuous alternation so that the right ear hears only high tones and the left ear hears only low tones. This illusion is also included in the record accompanying Pierce's book.

A musical passage can be described in terms of two pressure waves reaching the two auditory canals, with variations in frequency, amplitude, and complexity. However, a description of these two soundwaves would

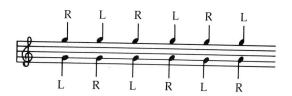

R = Tone presented to right ear
L = Tone presented to left ear

Figure 10.6 Octave illusion.

have little correspondence with our perceptual experience (Shepard, 1982b). We perceive pitches that show patterns not revealed in a simple analysis of stimulus frequency. We perceive loudness that depends upon the room in which we hear the music. We perceive timbre that depends upon complex properties of the beginning of a tone. We perceive consonance and dissonance in tone combinations, although it is difficult to predict the determinants of these judgments. Furthermore, Gestalt organizational properties give the music cohesiveness, and both constancy and illusions can be demonstrated. In a complex process such as music perception, our perceptual experience is a complex transformation of the physical stimulus.

Summary: Music Perception

1. Two aspects of pitch are tone chroma and tone height.
2. Two tones separated by an octave are psychologically similar in some respects. Listeners are confused when they try to identify a tone if a tone of the same name, but from a different octave, is presented afterwards.
3. The importance of tonality has been demonstrated by the probe-tone technique; in any given key, some tones seem to fit better than others. These tones are also found more often in musical selections in that key.
4. Researchers have attempted to study the subtleties of concert-hall acoustics, which are extremely complex.
5. Musical instruments differ in their pattern of harmonics, which is an important component of timbre. Another important characteristic is the attack component of an instrument's musical tone.
6. Consonant tone combinations tend to be simple fractions; these ratios have been known for about 3000 years. However, consonance depends upon factors other than just forming a simple ratio. Also, perceptions of consonance and dissonance depend upon individual differences and cultural experience.

7. Music shows pattern and organization, as in the laws of grouping. For example, the law of similarity can be demonstrated when listeners perceive two simultaneous streams of music because they group together tones that are similar in pitch. The law of good continuation is also important, although it does not seem to be as critical as the law of similarity.
8. The figure-ground relationship can be observed in music; this effect can also be demonstrated when two tunes have been combined.
9. Musical constancy holds in many cases, but not when the transformation is too drastic.
10. Researchers have devised some musical illusions such as the octave illusion and an illusion in which tones seem to increase endlessly in pitch.

SPEECH PERCEPTION

On the surface, speech perception doesn't appear to be a particularly impressive accomplishment. If someone says the word *cat*, for example, wouldn't it be rather simple to analyze the auditory information in that word and identify those sounds as *cat*? Unfortunately, speech perception is much more complicated than that. For example, consider that the average high-school graduate can understand about 50,000 words—not counting variations of the same word (Huggins, 1981). The size of our vocabularies means that any theory involving template-matching would require hundreds of thousands of templates; the theory would have difficulty explaining how we perceive speech so quickly.

In addition to the problem of the sheer size of our vocabularies, there are two additional obstacles to speech perception: the variation in the speech stimulus and the lack of segmentation between words (Cole & Jakimik, 1980). Let's consider these issues separately.

The fact is that a particular word is *not* consistently pronounced in a constant fashion by all speakers on all occasions. The variation is overwhelming! Consider, for example, how speakers differ. Physical differences in the vocal apparatus create variety; when the word *cat* is spoken by a 6-year-old boy, the physical characteristics of the sound waves may be entirely different in amplitude, frequency, and complexity from when that same word is spoken by his 60-year-old grandfather. Even among adults, the length of the vocal tract, which is used to produce speech, is 15% longer in males than in females (Jusczyk, 1986). As a consequence, there is an upward shift in the compounds of speech for female speakers. Nonetheless, the average listener does not find it challenging to understand speech in conversations when some speakers are female and some are male.

Think about the other ways in which speakers differ in their pronunciations. Consider how your friends differ in their *rate* of speaking, yet notice that listeners have little difficulty adjusting for speaking rate (Miller, Aibel, & Green, 1984). Also, you have little trouble understanding English spoken with southern, British, or Caribbean accents, even though the rhythms and pronunciations of specific sounds vary tremendously. As Levinson and Liberman (1981) point out, individual differences are so strong that analyses of speech sound waves may show that two words spoken by the same person are more physically similar than the same word spoken by two different people. Nonetheless, we do not find the task extraordinarily challenging.

Even a single speaker shows considerable variability in pronunciation. Think how the pitch of your voice would change if you wanted to say the sentence "Isn't that just marvelous?" with sarcasm, as opposed to enthusiasm. It is clear that emotions can change the speech stimulus (Huggins, 1981; Scherer, 1986). For example, when people smile, their vocal tracts shorten somewhat, which raises the pitch of their voices. Emotions can also influence speaking rate, pauses, and the amount of pitch variation. Of course, pronunciation can also be influenced by what the speaker is doing while talking. It is impressive that you can interpret a spoken message, even when the speaker is eating a cookie,

chomping on a pipe, or brushing his or her teeth.

Still one other source of variability in pronunciation is our own sloppiness. If people are asked to read a list of isolated words, their pronunciation is reasonably precise and standardized. However, almost all speech perception involves fluent speech—and pronunciation of words in fluent speech is both imprecise and variable. Cole and Jakimik (1980) point out how the word *what* can be pronounced numerous ways in the sentence "What are you doing?" They include the variants "Whacha doing?"; "Whadaya doing?" and "Whaya doing?" You may be able to add other possibilities. Out of context, pronunciation is often so sloppy that it is impossible to identify a word or phrase. For example, in a classic study Pollack and Pickett (1964) recorded the conversation of people waiting for an experiment to begin. Later, these same people were asked to identify isolated words and phrases from their own conversations. People who heard a single word were only about 50% accurate, and recognition rose to only about 70% when two or three words were presented.

In short, any given word can be pronounced in a wide variety of ways because of differences in the age and gender of the speaker, other sources of individual differences, dialect, emotions, and sloppiness. And yet—miraculously—we generally manage to perceive the stimulus accurately. Speech perception is somewhat similar, in this respect, to two visual processes. You'll recall that our discussion of pattern recognition pointed out that we are able to identify the letter *M*, even when it is written in a variety of sizes and styles. Furthermore, the discussion of constancy pointed out our ability to perceive qualities of an object, even though the distance, angle of orientation, and brightness differ from one viewing to the next. It seems to be an inherent property of perceptual systems that we can extract important information out of irrelevant clutter that could be misleading.

So far, we have discussed how speech perception is difficult because of vocabulary size and because of the variability in the speech stimulus. An additional problem is that the speech we hear often lacks segmentation between words. If you have ever heard people speaking a foreign language, you have probably noticed that the words seem to flow on in a stream. There seem to be no segments or boundaries dividing words into the neat little bundles of letters we see on the printed page. Usually, however, we are able to perceive the boundaries among words in our own spoken language, even when the speech stimulus lacks any clear, crisp pauses (Cooper, 1983).

Listeners occasionally do make mistakes. Bond and Garnes (1980) catalogued several kinds of "slips of the ear," or cases in which we misperceive speech. One common kind of misperception involves word-boundary errors, which take three forms. Sometimes the word boundary is deleted; "Get a pill out" was heard as "Get a pillow." Other times the boundary is shifted; "There's some iced tea made" was heard as "There's a nice teammate." Still other times, a word boundary is inserted; "Oh, he's Snoopy in disguise" was heard as "Oh, he's Snoopy in the skies."

An interesting example of a boundary error (of the boundary shift variety) was mentioned by Safire (1979). A grandmother who was more familiar with intestinal disorders than with psychedelic experiences heard the line "the girl with kaleidoscope eyes" in the Beatles' song "Lucy in the Sky with Diamonds." She perceived the line as "the girl with colitis goes by."

In fact, it is amazing that we do not make more mistakes in the perception of word boundaries. Cole and Jakimik (1980) estimate that a physical event, such as a pause, marks a word boundary less than 40% of the time. As Cohen and Grossberg (1986) observe, even an individual word can present several potential groupings; "myself" can be a single word, two words, or extra sounds plus "elf." Interestingly, however, the boundary between words seems to be more distinct for adults who can read than for adults who cannot (Morais, Cary, Alegria, & Bertelson, 1979).

The mystery, then, is that we can perceive speech quickly and with a generally high degree of accuracy when there are so many potential words to recognize, when those words are pronounced with such variability, and when there are usually no clear boundaries between the individual words. To examine why speech perception is so efficient, we first need to consider more details about the speech stimulus. The other topics we'll consider in this half of the chapter include categorical speech perception, top-down processing, and theories of speech perception.

Speech Stimulus

There are two topics in this section: how we produce sounds and how the auditory characteristics of speech are represented in speech spectrograms.

Producing Sounds

If we are concerned about speech *perception*, why should we begin with speech *production*? Gelfand (1981) points out that the two subjects are inherently related: "We must be able to speak what we can perceive, and we must have the ability to perceive the sounds that our speech mechanisms produce" (p. 323).

People interested in research on speech characteristically begin with the phoneme. A **phoneme** is the basic unit of speech, that is, the smallest unit that makes an important difference between speech sounds. Thus, /h/ and /r/ are both phonemes in English because it makes a difference whether you say you want to wear a *hat* or a *rat*. (Notice, incidentally, that a phoneme is written with slashes on either side.) A phoneme can also be viewed as a group of sounds classified as the same by people who are native speakers of a language (Gelfand, 1981). For example, try pronouncing the words *pie* and *tip*, attending to the pronunciation of the phoneme /p/. When you pronounce the /p/ in *pie*, you release a small puff of air; no air puff is released for the /p/ in *tip*. The two sounds are actually slightly different, and this difference may be important in other languages. However, native speakers of English classify both of these sounds as belonging to the same /p/ phoneme category (Gelfand, 1981).

Let us examine how the basic phonemes in English are produced. Figure 10.7 shows the major features in the **vocal tract**, the anatomical structures involved in speaking that are above the vocal cords. We speak by allowing air to pass through the vocal tract in a fashion that uniquely specifies the various phonemes. Table 10.1 shows how the tongue is important in producing vowels. For example, notice that when the front part of your tongue is raised high in your mouth, you can produce either the *ee* sound in *tree* or the *i* sound in *hid*.

The consonant sounds involve a greater variety of structures. The consonants vary along three dimensions, as illustrated in Demonstration 10.4. These three dimensions are (1) **place of articulation**, which specifies where the airstream is blocked when the consonant is spoken (for example, blockage by the two lips pressed together); (2) **manner of**

Table 10.1   Producing Vowel Sounds

| *Part of Tongue Used* | Height of Raised Portion of Tongue | | |
	High	*Medium*	*Low*
Front	Tree hid	Late Let	Fat
Middle	Carry	Sofa	Nut
Back	Root Nut	Coat Sought	Top

Note: This table shows how 13 vowel sounds are produced. For example, notice that when the front part of your tongue is raised high in your mouth, you can produce either the *ee* sound in *tree* or the *i* sound in *hid*.

articulation, which specifies how completely the air is blocked and where it passes (for example, complete closure or blockage); and (3) **voicing**, which specifies whether the vocal

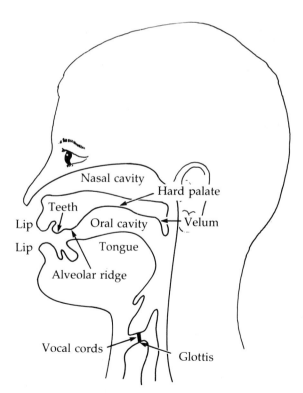

Figure 10.7   Major features in vocal tract.

Demonstration 10.4

Pronouncing the Consonant Sounds

Look back at Figure 10.7 to guide you in pronouncing the consonants. The "place of articulation" in the diagram below shows the portion of the vocal tract involved in making a particular sound; the place of articulation is illustrated in Figure 10.7. The rows in the diagram below are labeled "manner of articulation," for example whether there is a complete closure or a more modest narrowing of the passageway. Finally, the top member of each pair of words is voiceless, and the bottom member is voiced. Pronounce each of these consonants to appreciate the variety of ways in which these sounds can be produced.

	Place of Articulation						
Manner of Articulation	*Two Lips*	*Lip + Teeth*	*Tongue + Teeth*	*Tongue to Alveolar Ridge*	*Tongue to Palate*	*Tongue to Velum*	*Glottal*
Complete closure	*p*in			*t*oe	*ch*ip	*k*ilt	
	*b*in			*d*oe	*j*am	*g*ive	
Narrowing at point of articulation		*f*it	*th*ick	*s*ave	*sh*are		*h*ill
		*v*igor	*th*is	*z*ebra	a*z*ure	—	
Mouth closed; nasal cavity opened	—			—		—	
	*m*ice			*n*ice		si*ng*	
Glides and laterals	*wh*ere			—	—		
	*w*ere			*l*ess	*y*es, *r*im		

cords vibrate. In Demonstration 10.4, the top member of each pair of words is a **voiceless consonant**, which means that the vocal cords do not vibrate. Hold the palm of your hand on your throat as you pronounce the phoneme /p/; there is no vibration. In contrast, the bottom member of each pair of words in Demonstration 10.4 is a **voiced consonant**, and the vocal cords *do* vibrate. With the palm of your hand on your throat, contrast the vibration for the phoneme /b/ as opposed to /p/.

Speech Spectrograms

We have discussed one way in which speech stimuli can be classified; this classification method involves the way in which the phonemes are produced. A second classification method frequently used in research on speech perception emphasizes the physical qualities of the sounds themselves. A **speech spectrogram** or **sound spectrogram** is a diagram that shows the frequency components of speech. Figure 10.8 shows a speech spectrogram produced when a speaker said the word *dough*. As you can see, a spectrogram represents the passage of time along the x-axis (with the word *dough* requiring somewhat less than one half second to produce) and the frequency of the sound waves along the y-axis.

Notice that Figure 10.8 shows horizontal bands of concentrated sound called **formants**. In this figure, a first formant is located at about 500 Hz, and a second formant is initially located at about 1500 Hz, but it moves

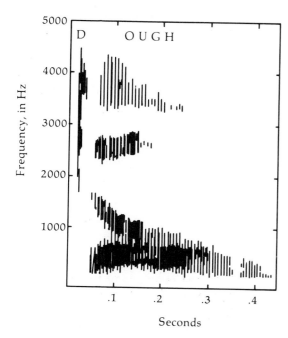

Figure 10.8 Speech spectrogram of the word *dough*. (Speech spectogram courtesy of Speech Science Laboratory, Department of Speech Pathology and Audiology, SUNY at Geneseo.)

downward a mere one tenth of a second later. You can also see a third formant at about 2500 Hz and a fourth formant at about 3800 Hz.

Analyses of speech spectrograms have revealed some interesting characteristics of human speech. For example, we might guess that the phonemes of a spoken word would appear as discrete units in time, rather like beads on a string. For example, it might seem logical to expect that the word *dog* would have a spectrogram with three segments, with /d/ first, then /o/, and finally /g/. However, speech spectrograms typically reveal that the phonetic segments overlap considerably (Jusczyk, 1986). Some acoustic energy from the final /g/ sound is present even before the energy from the initial /d/ sound has faded completely. As Hockett (1955) picturesquely described spoken language, the stimulus reaches the listener not in the form of beads on a string but like a row of uncooked colored

Easter eggs run through a wringer! This tendency for some of the sounds in a syllable to be transmitted at about the same time—that is, in parallel—rather than one at a time is called **parallel transmission**. Each phoneme is not pronounced in isolation because its sound is modified by the surrounding phonemes.

Because of parallel transmission, speech sounds flow together. As a result, a small segment of speech cannot carry all the acoustic information about one phoneme because that information is distributed across several segments. Furthermore, a phoneme's sound can change, depending upon which phonemes precede and follow it. In other words, phonemes often do not have a single, constant pronunciation. The information in Demonstration 10.4 implied that a consonant phoneme always has a consistent pronunciation, for example, that an /s/ always requires the same placement of tongue and lips, restriction of airflow, and vibration of vocal cords, no matter what word uses the /s/ phoneme. However, notice the shape of your mouth for the /s/ sound when you say the words *seat* and *sorry*. The corners of your mouth are stretched far apart in *seat*, but they are close together in *sorry*. Your mouth anticipates the letters that follow the /s/ sound.

Spectrograms confirm that a single phoneme has varying sounds as a result of the context of other sounds in the word. Nonetheless, we hear the sounds as similar even though they are physically different. Earlier in this section, we discussed three reasons why it should be difficult to perceive speech: vocabulary size, variability in the pronunciation of words, and the lack of segmentation between words. We now need to add a fourth reason—individual phonemes that constitute words do not have consistent pronunciations because pronunciation is influenced by surrounding phonemes.

Categorical Speech Perception

In Chapter 5 we discussed how the smooth continuum represented by the color spectrum that runs between 400 and 700 nm does not produce a smooth continuum in our perception. Instead, we tend to categorize the colors of the spectrum. For example, there is an abrupt boundary in the region of 490 nm that separates the greens from the blues. On one side of the boundary, we consider the colors green; on the other side, we consider colors blue.

Marc Bornstein, whose research we examined in detail in Chapter 5, has pointed out the remarkable similarities between the perceptual categories in vision and in audition (Bornstein, 1987). He compares these two separate disciplines—each providing dozens of studies about categories in perception—and concludes that the similarities are striking. Consistent with the first theme of the book, the perceptual systems share important similarities.

Let us look at these categories in speech perception. In general **categorical perception** is said to occur when we have difficulty discriminating between members of the *same* category but we are readily able to discriminate between members of *different* categories (Jusczyk, 1986; Moore, 1982). When we consider speech sounds, for example, listeners should find it easy to discriminate between sounds from two different categories, such as /p/ and /b/. However, their discrimination between two different examples of /p/ from the same speaker should be poor.

The classic experiment on categorical perception in speech was conducted by Liberman, Harris, Hoffman, and Griffith (1957), using synthesized speech sounds. Specifically, they created artificial speech representing a series of sounds between /b/ and /d/ and between /d/ and /g/. Try for a moment to produce a /b/, then something halfway between /b/ and /d/, then /d/. (In all likelihood, even if you could produce a halfway-between phoneme with your vocal tract, you could not *perceive* it as halfway between—which is the point of categorical perception!)

These artificially created phonemes were then presented to listeners for two different kinds of judgments. One task involved simple identification; listeners were asked to de-

cide whether a particular sound was a /b/, a /d/, or a /g/. The other task involved the **ABX paradigm**, in which three stimuli are presented in a row, with A different from B and X identical to either A or B. Listeners are asked to judge whether the X matches the A or the B sound.

The results of the study demonstrated that people have abrupt boundary lines when they identify letter sounds, just as they do when they identify color names. Sounds from the continuum between /b/ and /d/ are consistently labeled as /b/ until a certain point is reached, and then sounds on the other side of that point are consistently labeled as /d/. Another finding was that—consistent with the definition for categorical perception discussed earlier—people had difficulty discriminating between members of the same category but could readily discriminate between members of different categories.

Subsequent research, summarized by Stevens (1980, 1981), has extended the conclusions about categorical perception. Liberman and his colleagues demonstrated that listeners make distinct categories on the basis of place of articulation (as shown in Demonstration 10.4, the /b/ is articulated with two lips, the /d/ with tongue to alveolar ridge, and the /g/ with tongue to palate). However, you know that consonants vary in other dimensions. Categorical perception has also been demonstrated for the distinction between voiced and voiceless phonemes and between nasal and nonnasal sounds. Furthermore, Jusczyk (1986) points out that there have been several reports of categorical perception of musical stimuli, so the phenomenon may not be limited to speech.

Some researchers question the entire concept of categorical perception. For example, Massaro and his colleagues are skeptical about whether the evidence for categorical perception is sufficiently compelling (e.g., Massaro, 1987; Massaro & Cohen, 1983a). In addition, categorical perception seems to apply only to consonants, and not to vowels. Also, under some conditions listeners can make distinctions between two synthetic speech sounds that belong to the same phoneme category (Pisoni & Tash, 1974). Further research may strengthen the argument of those who oppose the categorical-perception position. However, at present the majority of researchers seem to favor the idea that people divide the wide variety of consonant sounds into a limited number of distinct categories.

You may recall that we have occasionally pointed out that our psychological experience often differs from the physical stimulus. This observation was made frequently in the psychophysics chapter, for example. We also remarked in Chapter 9 and in the discussion of music in this chapter that pitch is different from frequency, that loudness is different from amplitude, and that timbre is different from complexity. Similarly, the perception of speech sounds does not seem to correspond perfectly with the physical characteristics of the stimulus. Stimuli can be artificially created that show a steady and continuous progression between two phonemes. Listeners, however, don't appear to perceive this continuum because they seem to divide the stimuli into two distinct categories, as indicated in Figure 10.9.

It is worth mentioning, incidentally, that categorical perception may not be limited to the rather basic perceptual processes we have discussed. For example, humans have an overwhelmingly strong tendency to divide people and personal characteristics into two simple categories, masculine and feminine, even though the boundary is really very blurry (Bem, 1985; Matlin, 1987).

Top-down Processing in Speech Perception

Our discussion of auditory perception in Chapter 9 and in this chapter has primarily focused on physical characteristics of sound stimuli and how these stimuli can be transformed by the auditory system. However, we have not formally mentioned how higher mental processes influence hearing. According to Theme 4 of this book, our prior knowledge, context, and expectations are critical in shaping our perceptions. Our perception of speech, for example, will be aided by top-down processing as well as bottom-up processing. That is, we perceive speech because of the combination of our cognitive processes and the information available in the auditory stimulus. Let's discuss the variety of ways in which top-down processing aids speech perception, including an in-depth investigation of the phonemic restoration effect. This effect, as you will see, bears a resemblance to the word-superiority effect found in visual

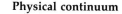

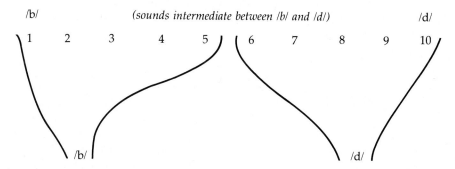

Figure 10.9   Categorical perception of speech sounds on a physical continuum.

perception, which we discussed in the in-depth discussion in Chapter 6.

There are a number of ways in which top-down processing facilitates speech perception; these factors involve both global and specific kinds of information:

1. *Listeners perceive better if they know they will be hearing speech.* This principle was best demonstrated in a study by Remez, Rubin, Pisoni, and Carrell (1981). They recorded a spoken sentence, "Where were you a year ago?" and then transformed the sentence by eliminating some of the acoustical information. One group of listeners was told nothing about the nature of the sounds; they were simply asked to report their impressions of the stimuli. Most did not realize that it was speech, and only 2 people out of 18 correctly identified the sentence. Another group of listeners was told that they would hear a sentence produced by a computer; half the people correctly identified the sentence in this condition. If we are oriented toward hearing speech, we are more likely to perceive it.

2. *Listeners perceive better if the phonemes appear in a word.* In an often-cited study, Rubin, Turvey, and Van Gelder (1976) demonstrated that listeners could detect a target consonant, /b/, more quickly when it began a word such as *bit* than when it began a nonword such as *bip*. (Notice that these findings are directly comparable to the word-superiority effect.) The word provides a context in which recognition is facilitated. If we perceive speech just as a sequence of phonemes in order, with no interrelationships among them, then a word should offer no particular advantage over a nonword—the /b/ should be identified equally quickly in both conditions. However, people took only 593 milliseconds to locate the target phoneme in a word, in contrast to 644 milliseconds to locate that same phoneme in a nonword. As the authors conclude, "Higher order properties of a speech event affect the detection of its constituent parts" (p. 396).

3. *Listeners perceive better if the words appear in a phrase or sentence.* This principle is clearly related to the previous one; context is im-

portant in identifying either phonemes or words. We already discussed one study supporting this principle. You'll recall that Pollack and Pickett (1964) found that people listening to fragments of their own previous conversations were much better at identifying words if two or three words were presented, rather than an isolated word.

Furthermore, Cole and Jakimik (1980) discuss several studies about the helpfulness of contextual information, even when words are carefully pronounced. For example, Morton and Long (1976) showed that people were faster in identifying a phoneme that occurred in a word that was highly likely in a sentence than in a word that was highly unlikely. For instance, you would more quickly identify the /b/ in a sentence "The sparrow sat on the *branch*" than in the sentence "The sparrow sat on the *bed*."

4. *Listeners perceive better if they know the topic of conversation.* Reddy (1976) presented sentences that had unusual word orders, and he asked listeners to repeat the sentences. The sentence "In mud eels are; in clay none are" (read without substantial intonation) was heard as "In model sar; in claynanar" by a typical listener. The sentence "In pine tar is; in oak none is" was heard as "In pyntar es; in oak nonus." However, if the listeners had been told that the first sentence concerned the habitats of amphibians and that the second sentence concerned the properties of trees, accuracy would have been higher. Again, context helps in perceiving speech, whether that perception involves the detection of phonemes or location of word boundaries.

5. *Listeners perceive better if they can see lip movements.* Dodd (1977) found that listeners could use visual information as an aid in speech perception when masking noise made hearing difficult. Interestingly, listeners who received contradictory auditory and visual information were not able to ignore one of the two inputs. Instead, they often combined the inputs. For example, when the voice was saying *tough* but the lips were saying *hole*, the listener reported hearing a blended word, *towel*. We spoke about the importance of vis-

ual information when listeners want to determine the location of a sound source. Similarly, Massaro and Cohen (1983b) observed that vision can bias perception when we watch a ventriloquist: "Ventriloquists do not throw their voices; rather a listener's percept is thrown by the visual input of the apparent speaker" (p. 753). In their own research, Massaro and Cohen specifically instructed listeners to report what they heard rather than what they saw. Nevertheless, the listeners relied heavily on lip movement. We don't realize the helpfulness of this visual information until we listen to a man with less-than-perfect articulation whose moustache partly conceals his lips.

▶ IN-DEPTH: PHONEMIC RESTORATION

Suppose that you go out to dinner with a group of friends. You make a screeching sound with your chair as one friends asks you to pass the salt. You perceive her message as an intact utterance nonetheless, with no missing phonemes. Another friend asks the waiter for the check. Even though a crash in the nearby kitchen masked part of one word, the waiter does not perceive a segment to be missing. Every day, in every possible setting, portions of our utterances are concealed by both unintentional and intentional noises of short duration. Still, we perceive speech accurately, without lamenting the missing sounds. In everyday life—and also in the laboratory—we demonstrate **phonemic restoration**, which occurs when a speech sound is replaced or masked by an irrelevant sound, and the perceptual system restores or fills in the gap appropriately. In most cases phonemic restoration works so well that the listener cannot identify which speech sound was missing.

Richard Warren, one of the principal researchers in the area of phonemic restoration, points out that phonemic restoration is really an auditory illusion. We have discussed illusions at several points in this textbook, principally in connection with illusory contour, visual illusions, and musical illusions.

For example, in a pattern with an illusory contour, the contour appears to extend across the distance between two actual contours. In reality, there is a white space in the pattern, yet we may perceive a dark line. Similarly, in phonemic restoration speech appears to extend across the irrelevant noise, as if it were uninterrupted.

Richard Warren and Roslyn Warren (1970) reported the classic study on the phonemic restoration effect. They recorded the sentence, "The state governors met with their respective legislatures convening in the capital city." Then they carefully cut one phoneme out of the recorded sentence, specifically, the first /s/ in *legislatures*. A coughing sound was inserted to fill the gap. (Thus, in the laboratory studies, a phoneme is actually missing, rather than concealed.) When listeners heard this revised sentence, they experienced a compelling auditory illusion. They reported that the /s/ sound was just as clear as were any of the phonemes that were actually present. Even when they listened to the sentence repeatedly, they judged the sentence to be intact; the cough seemed to supplement the sentence, rather than replacing any speech sounds (Warren, 1983).

Furthermore, one group of listeners was told that the cough had completely replaced a speech sound, and they were asked to locate the missing phoneme. They were unable to do so; they could not even identify precisely where the cough appeared in the sentence (Warren, 1983). Intriguingly, however, when a phoneme was simply deleted and a silent gap appeared in the middle of the word, listeners were highly accurate in locating the gap and noting that a phoneme was missing completely. In other words, phonemic restoration cannot occur when a phoneme is replaced by silence.

Why should phonemic restoration operate in one condition and not the other? As Warren (1983) proposes, it may be that listeners perceive the silent gap as being intrinsic to the actual speech—the speaker is leaving something out. In contrast, a cough superimposed upon the sentence is perceived as extrinsic and irrelevant to the flow of speech.

In the study in which the word *legislatures* was interrupted, the phonemes are so highly constrained that *s* is the only possible missing sound. What happens when there are several possibilities? In other research, Warren and Warren (1970) played four sentences to their listeners. In these sentences, the asterisk symbol, *, represents the loud cough that replaced a phoneme.

1. It was found that the *eel was on the axle.
2. It was found that the *eel was on the shoe.
3. It was found that the *eel was on the orange.
4. It was found that the *eel was on the table.

Using tape recorders, Warren and Warren produced four sentences that were identical except for a different word spliced on at the end of each sentence. Thus all the above sentences were physically identical, up through the final *the*.

What did the listeners report hearing? Warren and Warren found that the interpretation of the ambiguous word **eel* depended upon which final word they had heard. Listeners reported hearing *wheel* in the first sentence, *heel* in the second, *peel* in the third, and *meal* in the fourth. Context clearly influenced speech perception.

Notice that in phonemic restoration studies, context does not increase the accuracy of identifying the physical stimulus; people did not report hearing "cough-eel." As Warren (1984) observed, phonemic restoration is a kind of illusion; "these perceptual reconstructions do not correspond accurately to the sounds at the listeners' ears" (p. 381). However, under normal listening conditions, phonemic restoration does enhance accuracy. There really *is* a phoneme hidden underneath the screech of a chair or the crash of a dropped platter; in ordinary life, it is useful to cancel out the interference from the extraneous noise (Warren, 1983). In the laboratory, phonemic restoration is an illusion; in real life, it's a good strategy! You may recall a sim-

ilar situation with the Ponzo illusion. Turn back to Figure 8.12 and notice that the top figure, constructed in the laboratory, is an illusion; the bottom figure, a real-life cornfield, illustrates the use of a good strategy (in this case, size constancy).

After Warren's original research he and several other researchers found additional evidence for the phonemic restoration effect (e.g., Layton, 1975; Obusek & Warren, 1973; Warren & Sherman, 1974). For several years the phonemic restoration effect was frequently cited but seldom investigated. Then Arthur Samuel decided to explore the phenomenon once more, using a different kind of methodology.

As Samuel (1981) noted, there are potential problems in the way phonemic restoration had been studied. For example, one index of phonemic restoration had been that listeners made errors in locating the irrelevant noise; a listener might claim that it appeared at the location of the final *s* in legislatures. However, Samuel pointed out that a person who locates the cough six phonemes away from the true location is not really demonstrating stronger phonemic restoration than a person who locates the cough three phonemes away; *both* listeners are restoring a missing phoneme.

The other index of phonemic restoration (or, more properly, *lack* of phonemic restoration) in the earlier studies was simply the "hit rate," that is, the listener's correct detection of a missing phoneme. However, there is a drawback to this measure; there is no comparable false-alarm rate. That is, there is no measure that tells us how often a listener reported that something was missing when nothing was. The earlier studies included a missing phoneme in every sentence. A listener who reported "phoneme missing" on every trial might be doing so because his or her criterion is biased in the direction of *reporting* missing phonemes, rather than because this listener is highly accurate in *detecting* them. As discussed in Chapter 2, the signal detection approach emphasizes that criterion and sensitivity should both be assessed in perception research.

Samuel (1981) used a signal detection approach in a series of studies on the phonemic restoration effect. He contrasted listeners' performance on two kinds of stimuli: (1) a word in which a sound replaces a phoneme, with the phoneme really missing, and (2) the same word, but with the sound *added on* to the phoneme. Samuel's rationale is that people in laboratory studies of phonemic restoration report that a phoneme seems to be present; the cough or other irrelevant noise is merely added on. If this really is the listeners' perception, they should not be able to discriminate between the two kinds of stimuli. With this methodology Samuel was able to calculate a hit rate (the number of times listeners reported phonemic replacement when the phoneme was indeed replaced) and a false-alarm rate (the number of times listeners reported phonemic replacement when the phoneme was really there).

Let us consider Samuel's (1981) experiment in some detail. He constructed "replaced" and "added" versions of 90 words, which represented four factors: word frequency (high versus low), word length (two-, three-, and four-syllable words), phonetic class of the replaced or added phoneme (five kinds), and position of the replaced or added phoneme (beginning, middle, and end). One additional feature of this experiment was that Samuel obtained hit rates and false-alarm rates on the isolated segments; he sliced out the portion of the word in which the sound either replaced the phoneme or was added on to it. It would make a particularly strong argument for phonemic restoration if (1) listeners were highly *inaccurate* in discriminating between a word with a sound replacing a phoneme and a word with a sound added onto a phoneme, and if (2) listeners were highly *accurate* in discriminating between the two brief segments presented out of context.

Let's see what Samuel discovered. In general, the d' values, which were used as an index of discrimination, were around 1.0 for the words and between 2.0 and 3.0 for the segments. This means that listeners treated words with a phoneme missing not much differently from words with the sound added to

the phoneme; the listeners really are experiencing phonemic restoration. However, in isolation those two brief segments are definitely distinguishable; the d' is high.

Three of the four variables also influenced the strength of the phonemic restoration effect. For example, it was stronger for high-frequency words than for low-frequency words. Figure 10.10 shows the modest effect of word length, the second variable. As you can see, longer words produce greater phonemic restoration; the greater the context, the greater the phonemic restoration. (Keep in mind that low d' values on the words indicate greater phonemic restoration; words with missing phonemes are not distinguishable from words with a sound added to the phoneme.)

Samuel examined two other variables in this study. Phoneme class had an important effect on d'. Phonemes in the first two categories of the table in Demonstration 10.4 (phonemes such as /p/, /d/, and /f/) were particularly likely to show phonemic restoration, probably because these sounds were most similar to the extraneous noise. In contrast, phonemes in the last two categories of Demonstration 10.4 (such as /m/, /n/, and /l/), as well as vowel sounds, were less likely to show phonemic restoration. Finally, the position of the critical phoneme did not influence phonemic restoration; there was no systematic tendency, for example, for phonemes in the middle of a word to be restored more often than phonemes at the beginning or the end.

Samuel's experiment shows the influence of top-down processing. As Figure 10.10 shows, top-down processing increases as the amount of context increases. However, bottom-up processing is also important, because phoneme data—the phoneme class of the critical sound—had a large influence on whether listeners restored a phoneme. If, for example, the extraneous noise replaced a vowel, listeners were reluctant to conclude that the noise was simply superimposed upon the vowel; they *were* willing to draw that conclusion if the phoneme resembled the extraneous noise. As you can see, Samuel's conclusion that both processes operate is

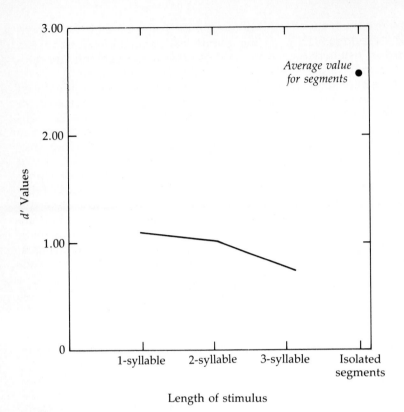

Length of stimulus

Figure 10.10   *d'* values for one-, two-, and three-syllable words and for segments in phonemic restoration study. (Based on Samuel, 1981.) Note: lower *d'* values indicate greater phonemic restoration.

compatible with our conclusion in Chapter 6 that top-down and bottom-up processing must both operate in visual pattern recognition.

Samuel and Ressler (1986) propose that phonemic restoration occurs because the configurational properties of a word prevent listeners from paying attention to the individual phonemes. They argue that phonemic restoration is similar to the celebrated Müller-Lyer illusion, in which observers' attention is diverted to the arrowheads. Impressively, extensive training on the phonemic restoration task does not suppress the restoration effect. Also, Samuel (1987) demonstrated that phonemic restoration is particularly likely if more than one restoration is possible. (For example, "*egion" could be restored as either "le-

gion" or "region," whereas "*esion" could be restored as only "lesion.") Furthermore, Samuel (1987) found that phonemic restoration was particularly likely when the initial syllable of the word was relatively unique; if you hear a word that begins with "veg-" you are likely to complete that word and restore any missing phoneme. However, if a word begins with "sub-", phonemic restoration is not nearly so compelling.

In summary, then, a series of experiments by Warren and Samuel has illustrated that top-down processes are important in speech perception. When we hear a word, we are likely to restore a missing phoneme. Phonemic restoration is more common in some circumstances than others, however, and it is clear that bottom-up processes are important as well. However, the phonemic restoration effect demonstrates that we do not need to hear every phoneme distinctly to perceive speech. Any theory that attempts to explain the mystery of speech perception must therefore point out that speech perception is clearly facilitated by top-down processing. Consistent with Theme 4 of this book, our expectations have an important influence on perception. ■

Theories of Speech Perception

Unfortunately, the theories of speech perception—that is, auditory pattern perception—are not nearly so developed as the theories of visual pattern perception. One interesting basic question, however, is whether speech perception is somehow different from other kinds of auditory perception, so that it may require a different kind of explanation. For example, Jusczyk (1986) points out that speech sounds are different from other auditory stimuli because the relationship between sounds and meanings is arbitrary and symbolic. There is no logical or necessary connection between the sounds in a word and its meaning. In English, we call a certain kind of pet a *dog*, but it is called *perro* in Spanish, and it could just as easily be called a *murj*. In contrast, most other auditory stimuli have a logical connection with the forces that produce them; when your car collides with a telephone pole, the "crash" sound is not arbitrary. In fact, the same noise would result if your car collided with a telephone pole in Madrid! So speech is different because these speech symbols must somehow be processed to decode the messages they symbolize.

Another difference between speech and nonspeech stimuli is the rate at which the two can be processed. For example, we can perceive speech at rates as fast as 25 to 30 segments per second and perhaps as fast as 400 words per minute. The ear is unable to resolve nonspeech stimuli presented at this rate; they are perceived as a continuous buzz (Jusczyk, 1986).

In the early research on speech perception it was argued that speech stimuli were processed much faster by the left hemisphere of the brain, whereas nonspeech stimuli were processed much faster by the right hemisphere. If subsequent research had continued to support this difference, we would have clear evidence for a "speech is different" conclusion. However, the current conclusion is that there is no simple difference in hemispheric processing (Halperin, Nachson, & Carmon, 1973; Jusczyk, 1986).

More compelling evidence comes from studies in which listeners heard synthetic speech, much like the passages created in the study by Remez and his coauthors (1981) that was discussed in connection with top-down processing. Best, Morrongiello, and Robson (1981) found that people performed much differently on identification and discrimination tasks if they perceived the stimuli as speech sounds rather than nonspeech sounds. (In both cases, it should be mentioned, the stimuli were the same.) Once we know that a stimulus is a word, we may switch into a "speech mode" and process it differently.

Liberman (1982) is one of the major current supporters of the "speech is different" view. As he proposes, humans have specialized processes that allow them to perceive phonemes. Liberman's argument is related to his earlier **motor theory of speech perception** (e.g., Liberman & Studdert-Kennedy, 1978). According to this motor theory, humans have a specialized device that allows them to decode speech stimuli and permits them to connect the stimuli they hear with the way these sounds are produced by the speaker. For example, you can hear the phoneme /t/ in any word and immediately recognize that it was made by pressing the tongue against the alveolar ridge, thereby blocking air passage while not vibrating the vocal cords. It is important to stress that this recognition occurs automatically and without cognitive analysis. This explanation is somewhat similar to the explanation proposed by Johansson and others for our immediate perception of biological motion (Johansson, 1985). It may be that our perceptual systems are specially designed to process messages from other human beings, whether those messages represent body movement or speech. Consistent with Theme 3, our perceptual processes are well suited to the tasks they must accomplish.

Many theorists have been concerned with how we decode the specific phonemes in speech. Cole and his colleagues are concerned about speech at the phonemic level, but they also discuss the process by which phonemes are integrated into words and higher units (Cole & Jakimik, 1980). First, let's consider a point Cole makes about phonemes, then we'll move to higher levels of speech processing.

You'll recall that a potential problem in speech perception is that the phonemes are not pronounced consistently. As discussed in the section on speech spectrograms, a phoneme's sound can change, depending upon which phonemes precede and follow it; the /s/ in *seat* is different from the /s/ in *sorry*. Cole and Scott (1974), however, argued that phoneme variability is not a major problem. Specifically, all consonant phonemes possess some features that do not vary from one word to the next; these are called **invariant features**. For instance, the phoneme /s/ always has a hissing sound, even though the shape of our lips varies when we pronounce the /s/ in *seat* versus *sorry*. Furthermore, the phoneme /s/ has a consistently higher pitch than the phoneme /z/. The invariant features allow us either to identify the phoneme precisely or else to narrow down the possibilities to two or three phonemes.

Cole and Jakimik (1980) propose a model of speech perception that addresses the issues of word boundaries, mentioned at the beginning of this speech perception section, and context, discussed in connection with top-down processing. There are four important assumptions in their theory. The first assumption emphasizes that words are recognized through the interaction of data from the speech stimulus and our previous knowledge:

> Fluent speech is an ambiguous stimulus. A given stretch of speech can often be parsed into words in more than one way, and because of phonological variation, the

acoustic information that accompanies an intended word may be insufficient, by itself, to uniquely specify its identity. The first assumption of the model, that words are recognized through the interaction of sound and knowledge, is an attempt to come to grips with the fact that words are often recognized from partial acoustic information. The assumption is that words are constrained both by their acoustic structure and the context in which they occur, and that listeners use both sources of information to recognize words from fluent speech (p. 139).

Cole and Jakimik's theory contains three other assumptions. The second assumption is that we process speech sequentially, or word by word. The recognition of one word accomplishes two purposes: (1) it locates the beginning of the next word in the sequence, and (2) it provides constraints that limit the number of possibilities that would be appropriate for the correct grammar and meaning of the sentence. For example, consider the phrase *green grass*. Once you recognize the word *green*, you realize that a boundary must follow (unless you are talking about obscure topics like greengage plums or British greengrocers). Furthermore, the word *green* constrains the grammatical forms of the word that follows; it will probably be a noun, though it might be another adjective. The word *green* also constrains the meaning of the word that follows; unless you are hearing something like Dr. Seuss's *Green Eggs and Ham*, the word will be something that customarily is green. Thus Cole and Jakimik's second assumption addresses both the word-boundary problem and the influence of context.

Cole and Jakimik propose two additional assumptions: We identify words from their beginning sounds rather than their middle sounds or their final sounds. Furthermore, we recognize a word when our analysis of its acoustic structure narrows down the possibilities to only a single candidate. In summary, their theory proposes that "word recognition is conceptually guided, but data driven'' (p. 150). As we saw in the discussion of visual pattern recognition in Chapter 6, an adequate explanation of speech perception must involve both data-driven and conceptually driven processing.

Summary: Speech Perception

1. Speech perception is difficult to explain because our vocabularies are large, there is variability in the speech stimulus (such as pitch, speaking rate, and pronunciation—both between and within speakers), and there is seldom true segmentation between words. Nonetheless, people can recognize words and identify the boundaries between them.
2. A phoneme, the smallest unit that makes a difference between speech sounds, is produced by a unique combination of characteristics such as place of articulation, manner of articulation, and voicing.
3. A speech spectrogram illustrates the frequency components of speech. Speech spectrograms reveal that sounds in a syllable show parallel transmission. In addition, a phoneme's sound can change, depending upon the surrounding sounds.
4. There is evidence that we tend to perceive consonant speech sounds in categories, rather than as sounds varying slightly from each other along a smooth continuum. The phenomenon appears similar to the categorical perception of hues in the color spectrum.
5. Top-down processing facilitates speech perception because listeners perceive better (a) if they know they will be hearing speech; (b) if the phonemes appear in a word; (c) if the words appear in a phrase or sentence, (d) if they know the topic of conversation, and (e) if they can see lip movements.

6. Phonemic restoration occurs when the perceptual system fills in a missing phoneme that has been replaced by an irrelevant sound; according to Warren, listeners are unable to locate the position of the missing phoneme, and phonemic restoration is influenced by the nature of the sentence.
7. Samuel has conducted several studies on phonemic restoration using a signal detection design. Listeners have difficulty discriminating between a word with a phoneme replaced by a noise and a word with the same phoneme supplemented by a noise, although the critical segments are clearly discriminable when presented in isolation out of the word context.
8. Factors that influence phonemic restoration are word frequency, word length, and phoneme category. Furthermore, it is more likely to occur with multiple possible restorations and when the initial syllable is relatively unique.
9. There is some evidence that the auditory system treats speech sounds differently from other auditory stimuli: (a) speech sounds, unlike other sounds, are arbitrary and symbolic; (b) speech sounds are processed faster; and (c) people perform differently on perception tasks when they know that the material consists of speech sounds. It may be that humans have specialized perceptual processes that allow them to process phonemes faster than other auditory stimuli.
10. Cole and his colleagues have developed a theory that people can detect the invariant features of phonemes. According to this theory, word recognition involves an interaction of data from the speech stimulus and our previous knowledge; speech is processed sequentially; words are identified from their beginning sounds; and word recognition occurs when the possibilities have been narrowed down to a single candidate.

Review

1. Why is pitch more complicated than a simple arrangement of notes from low to high? Be certain to mention the concepts of the octave and tonality. Then discuss

how notes with similar tone chromas from different octaves are similar to each other.

2. Much of this chapter concerned the observation that psychological reactions often cannot be predicted by a simple analysis of physical stimuli. Discuss as many examples of this observation as you can recall from both music perception and speech perception.

3. Imagine yourself at a concert of your choice. Discuss how the material in the music perception portion of the chapter might make you more aware of perceptual qualities of the music. Be certain to mention pitch and tonality, loudness, timbre, and tone combinations.

4. What information do we have that auditory perception is similar to visual perception with respect to perceptual organization, constancy, and illusions? Are there areas where there are differences?

5. What factors make speech perception difficult to explain? Provide examples where applicable.

6. Cognitive psychologists propose that people often operate according to a small number of heuristics, or rules of thumb, that often work well in solving problems in everyday life; however, these heuristics often lead us to incorrect answers when we face special kinds of situations in the laboratory. Why would this information be relevant to the material on phonemic restoration?

7. Imagine that you have just heard a sentence on television that was part of a news report. You heard all of it distinctly except for one blurred phoneme in one word. Discuss how each of the five factors mentioned in the top-down processing section could help you identify the phoneme.

8. Discuss the original setup for phonemic restoration studies, as designed by Warren. Then note how Samuel changed the methodology of these experiments. List as many factors as you can that influence the strength of phonemic restoration.

9. Is speech somehow special? Discuss the evidence for this point of view.

10. Describe the theory developed by Cole and his colleagues and point out how this theory can help resolve some mysteries of speech perception.

New Terms

tone chroma	octave illusion	formants
tone height	phoneme	parallel transmission
octave	vocal tract	categorical perception
octave generalization	place of articulation	ABX paradigm
tonality	manner of articulation	phonemic restoration
tonic	voicing	motor theory of speech perception
probe-tone technique	voiceless consonant	invariant features
attack	voiced consonant	
steady state	speech spectrogram	
decay	sound spectrogram	

Recommended Readings

Boff, K. R., Kaufman, L., & Thomas, J. P. (Eds.). (1986). *Handbook of perception and human performance* (Vol. 2). New York: Wiley. *This hand-book includes chapters by Deutsch and Jusczyk that provide current and reasonably detailed overviews of music perception and speech perception.*

Cole, Ronald A. (Ed.). (1980). *Perception and production of fluent speech.* Hillsdale, NJ: Erlbaum. *This volume contains a number of relevant papers, including the interesting chapter summarized at the end of the section on theories of speech perception; it also describes computer models of speech perception, a topic beyond the scope of this textbook.*

Deutsch, D. (Ed.). (1982). *The psychology of music.* New York: Academic Press. *Deutsch's volume includes papers on topics such as timbre, pitch combinations, melodic processes, and other issues related to psychological reactions to music.*

Pierce, J. R. (1983). *The science of musical sound.* New York: Scientific American. *Pierce's book focuses more on the physical nature of sound, in contrast to Deutsch's. The recordings included in this volume are particularly well done.*

Samuel, A. G. (1981). Phonemic restoration: Insights from a new methodology. *Journal of Experimental Psychology: General, 110,* 474–494. *Research articles in perception are often difficult to read; Samuel's article provides a model of a sophisticated design that is clearly described.*

Warren, R. M. (1982). *Auditory perception: A new synthesis.* New York: Pergamon. *Warren's book provides two relevant chapters, one on perceptual restoration of missing sounds (including sounds other than phonemes) and a fine overview of speech perception.*

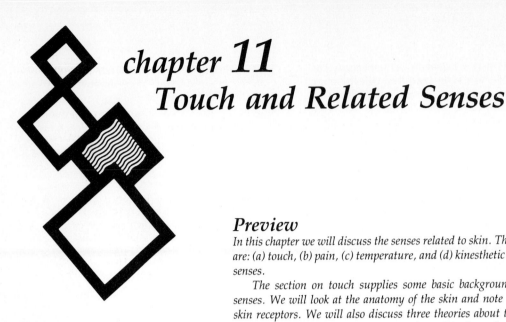

chapter 11
Touch and Related Senses

Outline

Preview

In this chapter we will discuss the senses related to skin. The four sections are: (a) touch, (b) pain, (c) temperature, and (d) kinesthetic and vestibular senses.

The section on touch supplies some basic background on the skin senses. We will look at the anatomy of the skin and note many kinds of skin receptors. We will also discuss three theories about the skin senses and the two systems that transmit information from the skin receptors to the brain. Passive touch occurs when an object is placed on a person's skin; our discussion of passive touch examines touch thresholds, adaptation to touch, and more complex passive touch perception. Active touch occurs when a person actively explores the environment by touching objects; it is more useful in everyday life than passive touch. As you'll discover in the in-depth section, we usually trust our vision more than our sense of touch when there is a conflict between the two. An important practical application of active touch is that it can provide blind people with alternatives to visual material.

In the section on pain we will look at pain thresholds and pain tolerance, and then we will see that pain adaptation occurs only for mildly painful stimuli. We will also discuss three theories of pain perception, including the currently popular gate-control theory. The final topic is pain control. Some pain-control methods include medication, the body's own production of pain-relieving substances, acupuncture, and techniques used by psychologists.

The discussion of temperature points out that the body is well equipped to maintain its temperature at about 33° C. We will also examine temperature thresholds and adaptation to temperature changes. Adaptation explains why a swimming pool seems icy when you first jump in, yet the temperature is pleasant after just a few minutes.

Kinesthesia is the sensation of movement and the sensation that your body parts are in a particular position. The vestibular senses are concerned with body orientation, such as whether you are standing upright or slanted. The vestibular senses also provide information about how fast you are going, for example, when you are traveling in a car. Much less is known about these last two senses than about touch or pain, but clearly they are important sources of information about our bodies.

Your skin represents the largest sensory system you own. In fact, your skin has about 2 square meters of receptive surfaces (Sherrick & Cholewiak, 1986). Contrast this size with the relatively miniscule receptive surfaces for vision and hearing.

Despite its impressive size, we often ignore the importance of the skin. Vision and hearing seem highly important to us, and we may contemplate how our lives would be changed if we were blind or deaf (Loomis & Lederman, 1986). However, have you ever contemplated what your skin and the skin senses can accomplish? Consider the protective value of the skin, for example. The skin senses inform you that you must go around large barricades, rather than through them, that a potentially suffocating object is covering your face, and that you should not try to fit through a narrow opening. The skin senses protect you from potential tissue damage when you feel pain. Furthermore, the skin senses protect you from extremely hot or extremely cold temperatures. Finally, two related senses—the kinesthetic sense and the vestibular sense—inform you about whether you are standing upright or tilted and where your body parts are in relation to each other. (In fact, without those specialized senses, we might see a new breed of bumper stickers asking, "Do you know where your toes are tonight?")

Also consider the importance of the skin senses in social interactions. Touching is important to both infants and their parents in the development of infant-parent attachment (Brown, 1984). Furthermore, think about the variety of ways in which another adult might touch you: a pat on the head, a handshake, a hearty punch in the arm, or an arm around your waist. The effects of even a subtle touch can be substantial. For example, students rated a library's staff and facilities more positively if the clerk touched their hands just briefly while returning their library cards (Fisher, Rytting, & Heslin, 1976). Consider, too, how the message of a pat or a handshake differs from a hostile punch in the nose. Fi-

nally, the importance of touch in sexual interactions is obvious.

Other evidence of the importance of touch is conveyed by the phrases we use to talk about emotions and social relations, many of which involve aspects of touch. Thayer (1982) lists several dozen items, including the following: he's touchy, a gripping experience, handle with kid gloves, to be deeply touched, the personal touch, rub someone the wrong way, be on your toes, makes my skin crawl, and rubbing shoulders with. Touch is so important that it serves as a frequent metaphor for subtleties in our social interactions.

Elementary school teachers tell their students that there are five senses: vision, hearing, touch, smell, and taste. Aristotle used this classification system more than 2300 years ago, and it is probably still the most common one. Nonetheless, current researchers typically expand beyond five senses by subdividing the touch category. In this chapter we will subdivide this category into what we commonly mean by touch as well as several other topics, including pain, the temperature senses, and kinesthetic and vestibular senses. Although these topics are diverse, they belong in one cluster. As Stevens and Green (1978) remarked, when we feel an object such as a tennis ball, an ice cube, or a piece of sandpaper, the experience seems unitary. We do *not* break down the experience into the various attributes such as temperature, roughness, size, and pressure.

TOUCH

Touch includes the sensations produced by deformation of the skin. That is, your skin becomes slightly distorted when you touch an object or an object touches you. The first topic in this section is sensory aspects of touch. Then we'll discuss passive touch and active touch.

Sensory Aspects of Touch

Three components of our discussion of the sensory aspects of touch are the skin's structure, theories about the skin senses, and how touch information is transmitted to the brain.

Skin's Structure

In addition to its function in sensation, the skin performs many other important services. Skin holds our body fluids inside its remarkably elastic boundaries. It regulates body temperature with the aid of blood vessels and sweat glands. It also protects us from the sun's radiation and from harmful microorganisms.

Figure 11.1 shows a diagram of **hairy skin**, the kind that covers most of your body and contains either noticeable or almost invisible hairs. Another kind of skin, called **glabrous skin**, is found on the soles of your feet, the palms of your hands, and on the smooth surfaces of your toes and fingers. Glabrous skin is similar to hairy skin except that its epidermis is thicker, it has relatively fewer receptors with free nerve endings, and there is a more complex mixture of receptors. This complexity is probably related to the fact that these areas are sensitive to stimulation and that we use these areas of skin in our hands to actively

explore the physical qualities of objects (Carlson, 1986; Vallbo, 1981).

Notice that the skin in Figure 11.1 can be divided into three layers. The **epidermis**, on the outside, has many layers of dead skin cells. The **dermis** is the layer that makes new cells. These new cells move to the surface and replace the epidermis cells as they are rubbed off. Underneath the dermis is the **subcutaneous tissue**, which contains connective tissue and fat globules. Also notice that the skin contains an impressive array of veins, arteries, sweat glands, hairs, and receptors. The skin varies greatly in thickness, with facial skin being about 0.5 mm thick (as thick as a page of this book) and skin on the sole of your foot being about ten times as thick (Sherrick & Cholewiak, 1986).

Let us examine the receptors in the skin. Recall that visual receptors in the retina come in two styles, rods and cones, each with its own specialized function. In contrast, skin receptors come in an impressive variety of styles, each style bearing its own name. However, all skin receptors are the endings of neurons that carry information from the skin to the higher processing levels.

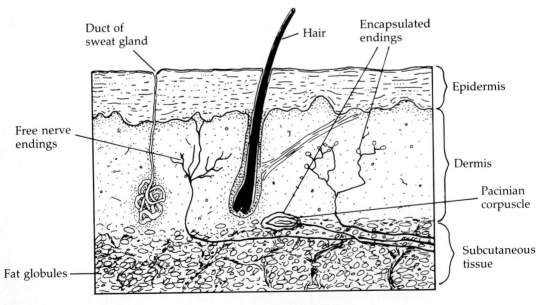

Figure 11.1   Cross-section of segment of hairy skin (schematic).

Some skin receptors have **free nerve endings**; as Figure 11.1 shows, these receptors do not have any small bulbs or capsules on the end nearest the epidermis. In contrast, skin receptors with **encapsulated endings** have small capsules on the end nearest the epidermis. These endings differ in their size, shape, and degree of organization.

The most widely studied skin receptors with encapsulated endings are the Pacinian corpuscles. The **Pacinian corpuscles** are the largest sensory end organs in the body (about 0.5 mm wide and 1.0 mm long), and they are extremely sensitive to skin indentation. Each Pacinian corpuscle consists of about 70 layers assembled in an onionlike fashion on the end of an axon. It seems that the unusual layered structure permits the successive layers to slip over each other so that this receptor is more sensitive to a change in touch than to sustained touch. Thus, a Pacinian corpuscle in the sole of your foot would not continue to send out signals after you have been standing at a party for 3 hours, deforming the structure continuously. However, the structure of this receptor would be sensitive to a *change* in stimulation, so that it could readily detect the vibrations of a subway rumbling under the apartment in which you have been standing (Carlson, 1986; Iggo, 1982; Vierck, 1978). These impressive receptors seem to be strategically located, with about 1000 to 1500 Pacinian corpuscles on the palm side of each hand (Sherrick & Cholewiak, 1986). Details on other kinds of encapsulated-ending receptors can be found elsewhere (Darian-Smith, 1982; Gottschaldt & Vahle-Hinz, 1981; Iggo, 1982; Sherrick & Cholewiak, 1986).

There does not seem to be a perfectly clear-cut relationship between skin-receptor type and function. Early researchers should be praised for the suffering they endured in the attempt to locate a correspondence between the kind of receptor stimulated and the kind of sensation produced. In a typical study a researcher might take a sharp needle and poke around on his or her own skin until a tiny region of skin was found that was particularly sensitive to the pain. Then this brave researcher would snip out that small region of skin and use a microscope to determine what kind of receptor it was. The procedure was repeated to locate receptors that might be associated with either touch or temperature. Early investigations tended to discover that pain was typically associated with free nerve endings. However, these mutilated researchers eventually concluded that the type of receptor often seemed unrelated to the type of sensation. Even today, the correspondence between receptor type and sensation is far from clear.

Theories about the Skin Senses

How does the skin operate to provide us with information? The three basic theories about the skin senses are specificity theory, pattern theory, and the combined approach.

The specificity theory was responsible for the experiments just discussed about the relationship between skin receptors and sensation. Specificity theory was based upon the **doctrine of specific nerve energies**, an idea proposed by an early 19th-century physiologist, Johannes Müller, that different sensory nerves have their own characteristic type of activity and therefore produce different sensations. A later researcher named von Frey extended the doctrine of specific nerve energies by suggesting a particular type of receptor structure for touch, warmth, cold, and pain. Thus **specificity theory** states that each of the different kinds of receptors responds exclusively to only one kind of physical stimulus (for example, pain) and each kind of receptor is therefore responsible for only one kind of sensation. However, we have just seen that the research did not provide complete support for this aspect of the theory.

A second theory, **pattern theory**, suggests that the pattern of nerve impulses determines sensation. According to pattern theory each kind of receptor responds to many different kinds of stimulation, but it responds more to some than to others. Thus a particular receptor might respond vigorously to a cold stimulus, less vigorously to a touch stimulus, even less to a pain stimulus, and very little to a hot stimulus. The brain can eventually interpret a code in terms of the relative strengths of the receptors' responses.

More recently Melzack and Wall (1962) incorporated some aspects of each theory into their proposal. As Sherrick and Cholewiak (1986) noted even more recently, their paper is now regarded as a landmark in the theory of skin sensitivity, and the basic assumptions of the theory still appear correct. These authors rejected the idea that each different receptor is specifically matched to a particular sensation. However, they accepted the idea that the receptors differ. Specifically, each kind of receptor is specialized so that it can convert a particular kind of stimulus into a particular pattern of impulses. We feel pain if the impulses in one kind of nerve fiber are dominant. However, we feel other sensations such as warmth, cold, or pressure if the impulses in another kind of nerve fiber are dominant. Melzack and Wall developed their theory in more detail for painful stimuli, so we will discuss this issue further in the section on pain.

From the Skin to the Brain

The chapters on vision and hearing discussed the pathways from the visual receptors and the auditory receptors to the brain. In each case the receptors occupied a relatively small, compact space. In contrast, the skin receptors are distributed over the entire body, so the task is more challenging and complicated. Details can be found in other resources (Carlson, 1986; Sherrick & Cholewiak, 1986).

One important aspect of neuronal transmission is that there are two systems by which information travels from the skin receptors to the brain: the lemniscal system and

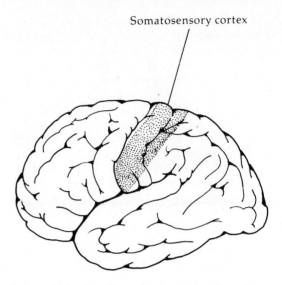

Somatosensory cortex

Figure 11.2   Location of somatosensory cortex.

the spinothalamic system. Table 11.1 shows some important characteristics of the two systems. As we have noted in discussing both the visual and the auditory processes, our sensory processes often divide the tasks between two systems, each of which has a function it performs best. As you can see, for example, the **spinothalamic system** has smaller nerve fibers and slower transmission. (In fact, it may be helpful to recall that the *spino*-thalamic system is *small* and *slow*, whereas the *lemniscal* system is *large*.) The **lemniscal system**, however, has much more precision than the spinothalamic system. This lemniscal system could determine that your skin is being stimulated by two drops of water, a few millimeters apart, whereas the spinothalamic

Table 11.1   Lemniscal and Spinothalamic Systems

	System	
Characteristic	*Lemniscal*	*Spinothalamic*
Nerve fiber size	Large	Small
Speed of transmission	Fast	Slow
"Acuity"	Relatively good	Relatively poor

system might erroneously interpret the two drops as a single large drop.

Both the lemniscal and the spinothalamic systems eventually pass on their information to the somatosensory cortex. The somatosensory cortex is shown in Figure 11.2.

For many years researchers have tried to discover the relationship between points on the body and points on the cortex. Their efforts have been only moderately successful for the part of the cortex associated with the spinothalamic system, but some fairly precise mapping has been obtained for the lemniscal system. For example, Penfield and Rasmussen (1950) obtained information on patients whose skulls were opened up for tumor removal. Penfield and Rasmussen electrically stimulated various points on the somatosensory cortex. Then they asked the patients, who were alert because they had only local anesthetics, to identify the part of their body that tingled.

Figure 11.3 shows the correspondence they found. Notice that this distorted creature has its body parts scattered along the edge of the cortex in a pattern that bears little resemblance to your own body; its thumb is next to its eye. Furthermore, some large body parts, such as the leg, receive much less cortex space than some much smaller body parts,

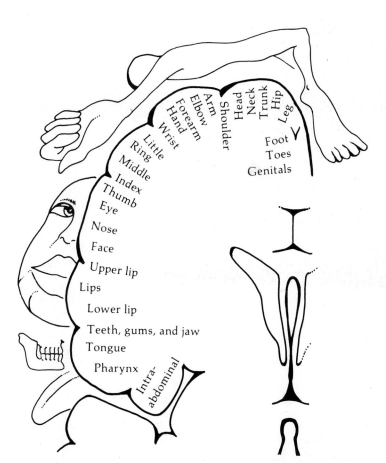

Figure 11.3 Correspondence between parts of somatosensory cortex and body part. (Reprinted with permission of Macmillan Publishing Co., Inc. from *The cerebral cortex of man* by Wilder Penfield and Theodore Rasmussen. Copyright 1950 by Macmillan Publishing Company, Inc., renewed 1978 by Theodore Rasmussen.)

such as the lip. In the next section we will see that the amount of space occupied on the cortex is related to thresholds of the various body parts.

More recent research has revealed more details about the organization of the somatosensory cortex. You will recall that the visual cortex is organized in columns. Similarly, a columnar arrangement was discovered in the somatosensory cortex even before it was discovered in the visual system (Carlson, 1986; Mountcastle, 1957). Furthermore the somatosensory cortex appears to be divided into between five and ten different maps of the body surface. Within each of these maps cells respond to stimulation of a particular kind of receptor. For example, one such map might correspond exclusively to the Pacinian corpuscles (Carlson, 1986; Dykes, 1983).

Passive Touch

In **passive touch** an object is placed on a person's skin; in contrast, **active touch** involves a person's actively seeking interactions with the environment by exploring objects and touching them. Active touch will be examined later; let's first explore passive touch.

Thresholds for Touch

In classic studies on passive touch researchers measure thresholds for the detection of a single skin indentation. Try Demonstration 11.1 to illustrate how parts of your body differ in their sensitivity. The cotton was probably particularly noticeable when it touched your cheek, yet its impact on the sole of your foot was so minimal that you probably had to check visually to be certain that you were really touching it. As you may recall, a **de-**

tection threshold is the boundary point at which something is reported half the time. The most extensive research on thresholds was conducted by Weinstein (1968). He examined both men and women, touching them on 20 different body parts with a nylon hairlike strand for which the force could be precisely measured. Figure 11.4 shows the sensitivity for females, and Figure 11.5 shows the sensitivity for males. Notice three features of these diagrams: (1) Women are significantly more sensitive to touch than men (that is, their thresholds are lower); (2) the parts of the body vary in sensitivity—for example, people are more sensitive in the facial area than around the feet; and (3) women and men differ in their specific patterns of sensitivity— for example, women's bellies and backs are nearly as sensitive as parts of their faces, but these body parts are relatively insensitive for men.

We have been discussing detection thresholds. Another kind of threshold is a **two-point discrimination threshold**, which measures the ability to notice that two points on your skin, rather than a single point, are being touched. Typically, two-point discrimination thresholds are assessed by selecting two blunt but narrow-diameter prongs and placing them perhaps 2 cm (0.8 inch) apart. The observer is asked to report whether he or she feels one or two stimuli; on descending trials the distance between the two stimuli is decreased until the observer consistently reports one stimulus. On ascending trials the distance between the two stimuli is systematically increased, as you might expect from the methodology described in the psychophysics chapter.

Try Demonstration 11.2 to illustrate two-

Demonstration 11.1 *Threshold for* *Touch for Various* *Body Parts*	Take a small piece of cotton (or a fragment of a tissue) and lightly touch it to the following parts of your body: the thick part of the sole of your foot, your calf, your back, your nose, and your thumb. Notice that the parts of your body are not uniformly sensitive to touch.

point discrimination thresholds. It is worth mentioning, incidentally, that if you ever visit a neurologist for an extensive neurological examination, you are unlikely to escape without a test similar to this demonstration. It is also worth mentioning that people's performance on this task can be substantially improved by practice (Sherrick & Cholewiak, 1986). Demonstration 11.2 points out how two-point discrimination thresholds vary as a function of body location. When two toothpicks touch your calf, you feel one single touch rather than two. However, on your nose there are two distinctly separate touch sensations.

Weinstein (1968) measured two-point discrimination thresholds as well as the detection thresholds discussed earlier. Again, the face was generally more sensitive than other regions. However, Weinstein also found that the fingers and toes are extremely sensitive in detecting two separate touch sensations. Our fingers and toes, which show relatively high detection thresholds in Figures 11.4 and 11.5, have low thresholds for determining that a stimulus is touching two points rather than a single point.

Figure 11.3 illustrated that certain body parts correspond to large areas on the cortex, whereas other body parts correspond to smaller cortical areas. Weinstein discovered a consistent relationship between measures of cortical area and the size of the two-point thresholds. For example, a large space on the cortex is devoted to the lip, and the lip is also very sensitive in its two-point discrimination threshold. In contrast, relatively little space on the cortex is devoted to the leg, and our discrimination is also poor in this area.

You may recall a similar relationship from Chapter 3. The largest space on the visual cortex is devoted to the fovea, which also happens to be the area in which discrimination is best. Thus there is a uniform pattern; when a large region of the cortex is devoted to information from a particular area of skin surface, we are usually able to make precise discriminations when that area of skin is touched. This similarity between touch and vision, another illustration of Theme 1 of this textbook, can also be found in other phenom-

ena. For example, other resources describe how touch demonstrates certain principles discussed in connection with visual perception. These principles include illusory movement, masking, and figure-ground relationships (Berlá, 1982; Craig & Sherrick, 1982; Loomis & Lederman, 1986; Sherrick & Cholewiak, 1986).

Adaptation to Touch

We discussed adaptation in the vision and hearing sections of this book. In **touch adaptation** the perceived intensity of a repeated tactile stimulus decreases over time. This morning when you first put on your clothes, you might have noticed the pressure of your waistband, your socks, and your watch. Very quickly, however, the sensations disappeared. You probably were not even aware of pressure from your clothes until you read this paragraph.

We seem to notice a stimulus as long as its weight moves our skin downward. However, when the skin movement stops, we no longer notice it. Once the stimulus is removed, though, our skin moves upward, and we notice pressure sensations once more. Skin movement is therefore an important factor in touch perception.

Try Demonstration 11.3 to illustrate touch adaptation. This powerful phenomenon has not been extensively studied; the most extensive series of studies was conducted by Nafe and Wagoner (1941), who examined the hairy skin on the thigh next to the knee. There has likewise been no extensive study of glabrous skin, which could yield very different results (Sherrick & Cholewiak, 1986). However, Carlson (1986) points out that adaptation to touch cannot be explained by "fatigue" in the receptor processes. Instead, adaptation can probably be traced to the mechanical construction of the receptors. For example, the Pacinian corpuscle mentioned earlier responds once when the receptor is bent under pressure and again when it is released. Under constant pressure, however, the nerve ending simply floats within all the protective onionlike layers, and it does not continue to produce signals following the initial stimulation.

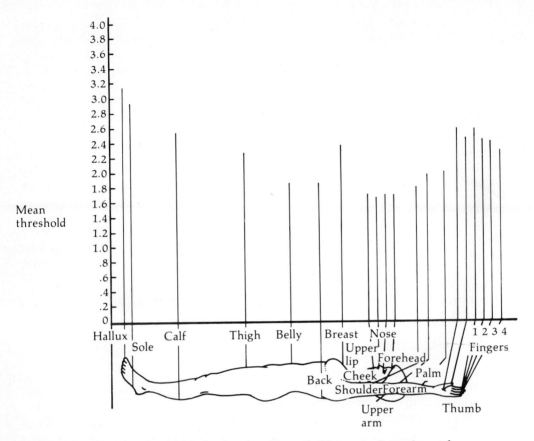

Figure 11.4   Detection thresholds for females. (From S. Weinstein, Intensive and extensive aspects of tactile selectivity as a function of body part, sex, and laterality. In D. R. Kenshalo (Ed.), *The skin senses*, 1968. Courtesy of Charles C Thomas, Publisher, Springfield, Illinois.)

Perception of Complex Passive Touch

In general, studies of passive touch assess thresholds either for a single touch or for vibrations. One area in which more complicated perception is assessed concerns people's ability to read letters and numbers traced on their skin. A neurologist's examination, for example, might include a test in which the examiner traces a series of letters on your fingers or foot, asking you to identify them one at a time. Heller's (1980) research on the topic of passive "reading with the skin" demonstrates that people have fairly

poor digit spans. They can recall only about three items in a row when they are written on the same area of skin, whereas visual digit spans are usually about twice as long. Heller's most interesting result, however, was a phenomenon that by now should seem familiar: People are better at recognizing letters when they appear in words than when they appear in a random letter sequence. Thus, the word-superiority effect has been demonstrated for vision, hearing, and touch. As Theme 1 of this textbook proclaims, the perceptual systems demonstrate similar effects. In this case, all three word-superiority effects are encouraged

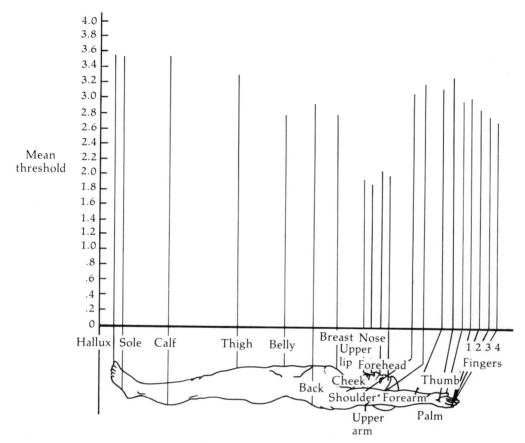

Figure 11.5 Detection thresholds for males. (From S. Weinstein, Intensive and extensive aspects of tactile sensitivity as a function of body part, sex, and laterality. In D. R. Kenshalo (Ed.), *The skin senses*, 1968. Courtesy of Charles C Thomas, Publisher, Springfield, Illinois.)

because our cognitive processes—expectations about sequences of items—influence perception. In this case Theme 1 is demonstrated because of the importance of Theme 4 in all the perceptual systems.

Active Touch

So far we have discussed situations in which a person sits patiently, waiting to be prodded, poked, and drawn upon. However, many touch experiences are much more active. Right now, your fingers may be twisting around a curl in your hair. You may also use

active touch to figure out how to fasten a button at the back of your neck, to determine which peach is the ripest, and to see whether the shelf with the honey jar is still sticky.

The active aspects of touch have been particularly emphasized by Gibson (1966), whose work is discussed frequently throughout the book. He emphasizes how we humans actively seek contact with things:

The hand can grope, palpate, prod, press, rub, or heft, and many of the properties of an object can thus be detected in the absence of vision. The properties we call "tangible"

Demonstration 11.2

Two-Point Discrimination Thresholds

Find two toothpicks and hold them so that their points can both touch your skin at the same time. Separate the toothpicks by about 1 cm (0.5 inch). Touch your cheek with the toothpicks and describe the sensation. Now touch your calf with the toothpicks and notice whether the sensation is different. Move the toothpicks closer together and touch your cheek once more. How close can they be moved toward each other before you perceive only a single touch? Now move the toothpicks farther apart and touch your calf once more. How far apart can they be moved before you perceive two separate touches?

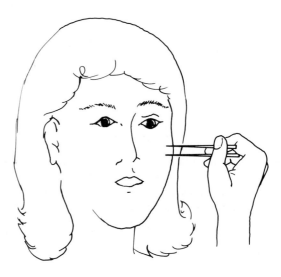

Demonstration 11.3

Touch Adaptation

Place a 1-cm² piece of paper on the hairy-skin side of your hand and notice how long it takes until you can no longer feel the paper. Repeat this exercise with the glabrous-skin side of your hand. Continue these comparisons in touch adaptation by trying stimuli of different sizes and weights and different regions of both sides of your hand. Compare touch adaptation in both locations and—more important— notice the general phenomenon of touch adaptation.

are (1) geometrical variables like shape, dimensions and proportions, slopes and edges, or curves and protuberances; (2) surface variables like texture, or roughness-smoothness; and (3) material variables like heaviness or mass and rigidity-plasticity (p. 123).

We are accustomed to believing that vision is such an important sense that we ignore the capabilities of active touch. For example, consider the usefulness of active touch in determining the "feel" of an object. If you were buying a new mattress for your bed, would you trust your visual sense or your tactile sense?

Active touch is also important in identifying the characteristics of surfaces. For example, if a surface is smooth and cool, you may judge it wet. You may also notice whether a surface is regular or irregular, slippery or firm, and granular or plain. Think about the feel of velvet compared with the feel of sandpaper or motor oil.

The perception of objects by touch is called **haptic perception**. Haptic perception occasionally involves holding a hand against an object without any movement. More often, we seek additional information, and so we move our hands around, actively exploring an object's characteristics. Try Demonstration 11.4 to illustrate haptic perception.

Our discussion of active touch has three sections. First, we will compare active and passive touch. Our next topic is an in-depth consideration of the relative dominance of touch and vision. Finally, we will consider some important applications of active touch.

Active versus Passive Touch

It probably will not surprise you to learn that active touch is more precise and useful than passive touch. For example, when a tiny raised dot is pressed against the skin, people can detect a dot about 10 micrometers high. (A micrometer is one-*thousandth* of a millimeter.) This perceptual ability is fairly impressive until it is compared with the threshold for active touch, which can be even lower than 1 micrometer (Johansson & LaMotte, 1983). When people are allowed to stroke their fingers across a surface, they are much more sensitive to a tiny irregularity in that surface.

James Gibson was an important influence on theories of vision, and he also was central in pointing out the importance of active touch. Consistent with his general approach to perception, Gibson proposed that the study of active touch would provide more information about people's daily activities, whereas information about passive touch would be far less useful. Gibson (1962) compared active and passive perception for six small metal cookie cutters shaped like a teardrop, a star, a triangle, and so forth. When the cookie cutter was pressed against the palm of the hand (passive perception), accuracy was only 29%; however, when people were encouraged to feel each cookie cutter (active perception), accuracy soared to 95%.

Heller's more recent research has extended Gibson's findings. Heller (1984a) used nine cookie cutters to test three kinds of touch: (1) active exploration with an index finger, (2) passive touch, in which a cookie-cut-

---

Demonstration 11.4	Assemble ten miscellaneous objects that you find in your room, such as a small paperclip, a large paperclip, a rubber band, a ring, and so forth. Place them on your desk and close your eyes. Touch an object and identify it by exploring with your active touch. Repeat the process, removing each object from the display after you have identified it. Did you make any errors?
Haptic Perception	

ter outline was rotated over a passive finger-tip, and (3) static stimulation, in which the cookie-cutter was pressed onto a passive fingertip. Two exposure periods, 5 seconds and 30 seconds, were used for each condition. Heller's results showed that active touch produced much higher identification accuracy. In fact, people with only 5 seconds of active touch exposure were more accurate than people in either of the two passive groups who had a full 30 seconds of exposure. Heller proposes several explanations for the results. For example, the skin may simply have poor "acuity" when it is immobilized and passive. Furthermore, people may experience more aftersensations with passive touch than active touch; that is, the skin may still tingle slightly after it has been passively touched, a sensation that may disrupt attention to new stimuli. In any event, we can conclude that active touch provides useful information about objects, even when the exposure is brief.

▶ **IN-DEPTH:**
RELATIVE DOMINANCE OF TOUCH AND VISION

Suppose that your eyes saw one object, but—simultaneously—your hands felt a somewhat different object. Which sense would you trust more? Reviews of a large number of studies have noted that when there is a discrepancy between vision and touch, people generally trust their vision (Power, 1981; Rock, 1983; Welch, 1978). As Rock concludes, visual "capture" typically occurs when there is a conflict between the two modalities; vision wins and tactile perception is recalibrated so that it matches what we see.

Let us examine one of the more recent studies in this area. Roderick Power of Macquarie University in Australia decided to determine whether visual capture could occur with familiar objects. In one experiment Power asked people to examine a 20-cent Australian coin (roughly the size of our 50-cent piece). Each participant wore special lenses that distorted the shape of the coin. Rather than appearing perfectly round, the coin looked oval. Half the participants saw

the vertical axis as 80% longer than the horizontal axis, and the other half saw the horizontal axis as 80% longer. While looking at this distorted coin, they actively felt the object. They were then instructed to draw the object on graph paper. The drawings showed an average distortion of 75%; people drew what they saw, not what they felt.

In another study in the same paper Power (1981) demonstrated that various distortions of familiar cubic objects—dice—also produced visual capture. In both studies, in fact, observers made verbal comments reinforcing that vision was dominant. For example, one visiting psychologist who tried the demonstration commented, "You must have a magnificent workshop to produce such a coin" (p. 32). The visual experience was so compelling that people—even normally suspicious psychologists—were convinced that the coin was really an oval counterfeit that had been produced in the laboratory. In both of Power's studies, then, vision was dominant—so dominant that it overpowered touch even when the objects were clearly familiar.

Can a situation be created where touch is dominant over vision, where touch "captures" vision? Morton Heller (1983) of Winston-Salem State University created touch dominance by reducing visual accuracy. Specifically, participants viewed forms through stained glass, a situation that created substantial blurring. Under several different conditions Heller demonstrated that tactile qualities were dominant over visual ones. Heller pointed out a potential real-life application of this series of studies. When people see an object in their peripheral vision, the blurring is equivalent to the blurred vision obtained in his study with stained glass. Under normal foveal vision, we may trust the information provided by our eyes; under peripheral vision, we may trust the information provided by our hands.

We have seen that under normal conditions, vision is dominant over touch. When provided with conflicting information, people place more weight on vision. However, according to Bill Jones and Sandra O'Neil (1985) of Carleton University in Canada, "dominance" can have an additional meaning. Specifically, we can say that a sensory mode is dominant if we judge objects more *efficiently* in that mode. For example, we could say that vision is dominant over touch if we can explore objects more accurately or more rapidly with vision than with touch.

Jones and O'Neil examined this second kind of dominance using a test that involved texture perception. Participants in their study judged squares of abrasive sandpaper that differed in their "grit" value. They were presented with two samples and asked to select which had the rougher texture. Some participants were allowed only visual information, some only tactile information, and some visual plus tactile information.

The results showed that the sensory condition did not have a significant effect on the number of items correctly guessed; however, the condition *did* influence the decision time. Specifically, as shown in Figure 11.6, people made the fastest judgments in the vision-only condition and the slowest judgments in the tactile-only condition. As you can see, this same advantage in the vision-only condition held true for both the correct and the incorrect items.

In another study in the same paper Jones and O'Neil asked participants to judge whether the samples were the same or different, a modification of the earlier study. Once again, people were equally accurate in the three conditions, although they again tended to be faster in the vision-only condition. Finally, in a third study the authors found that participants in the condition in

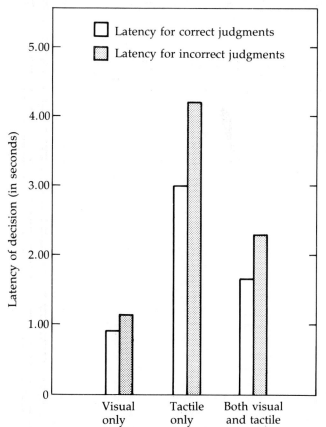

Figure 11.6 Latency of decisions about which surface was rougher, given only visual information, only tactile information, or both visual and tactile information. (Based on data from Jones & O'Neil, 1985.)

which vision and touch were combined did not treat these two sources of information as independent clues about texture. Instead, they seemed to average the two information sources.

Jones and O'Neil's findings on accuracy are surprising in two respects. First, if vision is generally dominant over touch, we might expect visual judgments to be more accurate. Second, we would suspect that if two heads are better than one, then two senses would be more accurate than one. Nonetheless, that was not the case in Jones and O'Neil's studies. Research by Heller (1982) also discovered no difference between vision and touch in judgment accuracy for samples of rough paper. However, congruent with expectations, people were more accurate when vision and touch were combined than when either mode was used alone. It is not clear why these two studies differ with respect to the usefulness of combining both senses.

In summary, the research on vision and touch reveals that the two kinds of judgments are indeed correlated. When people make shape judgments and the two sources of information are in conflict, they pay more attention to vision than to touch, unless the visual information is not helpful. In other kinds of tasks, vision and touch may be equally helpful in providing accurate information about texture. However, people judge more quickly if given visual information than tactile information. Finally, it is not clear whether accuracy can be improved by combining information from both sensory modes. ■

Applications of Active Touch

An important application of active touch is the development of material for blind people. The best-known system was developed by Louis Braille, a blind Frenchman who lived in the 19th century. He was discouraged by the difficult task of trying to read the limited number of books specially prepared with raised versions of standard letters. After all, our visual system can readily distinguish a *P* from an *R*, but the task is much more challenging for our tactile system.

Figure 11.7 illustrates the letters in the **braille** alphabet; notice that each letter con-

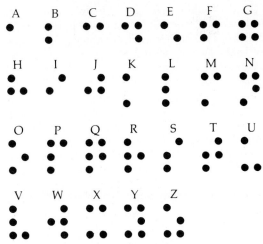

Figure 11.7   Braille alphabet.

sists of raised dots. Braille is difficult for the novice; if you have access to a book in braille and a copy of the braille code, it's well worth trying to decipher a portion. Most blind people never learn braille. However, a person who has mastered braille can read about 100 words a minute, a speed that is impressive but considerably slower than the rate of about 250 words a minute for sighted people reading standard print (Foulke, 1982).

Several electronic devices have been designed to increase the options for blind people. For example, the **Optacon** converts material on a printed page into electrical impulses that produce a vibration pattern on the tip of the index finger (Bliss, Katcher, Rogers, & Shepard, 1970; Bliss & Moore, 1974; Craig & Sherrick, 1982).

Another device, the **Tactile Vision Substitution System** (TVSS) (Craig & Sherrick, 1982; White, Saunders, Scadden, Bach-y-Rita, & Collins, 1970) uses a television camera to record a scene, then converts the image into vibrations applied to a person's back. People can control the scanning pattern of the television camera and can thus appreciate complex arrangements of objects. The TVSS requires less practice than the Optacon or braille to achieve reasonable levels of accuracy (Heller, 1984b). With experience, users can perceive more complex objects and appreciate depth information.

Other tactile aids for blind people also

have been developed. For example, haptic pictures are two-dimensional plastic or paper sheets with markings on them, such as raised lines and grooves (Kennedy, 1982). Mobility maps have also been designed to represent the physical layout of streets in a town, pedestrian subways, and shopping centers (James, 1982).

Touch can be useful for deaf people as well as blind people. For example, using the **Tadoma method**, a deaf or deaf-blind person places his or her hand on the lips and jaw of the speaker to pick up tactile sensations of speech such as airflow, lip and jaw movement, and vibration (Loomis & Lederman, 1986). Several systems have also been developed to present tactile displays of speech patterns, somewhat analogous to the Optacon and the TVSS (Kirman, 1982).

A final but extremely important application of active touch occurs in medicine. A physician must palpate a patient's skin to determine the location, size, and shape of a fetus inside a pregnant woman's uterus or a swollen appendix (Loomis & Lederman, 1986). Consider, also, the usefulness of active touch in detecting breast cancer. In 1985, approximately 119,000 women developed breast cancer and 38,400 died from this disease (Diem & Rose, 1985). However, early detection of cancer makes survival more likely. Since breast self-examination is a risk-free procedure, it is routinely recommended for all women over the age of 20. Statistics suggest that a woman who examines her breasts once a month for possible lumps will reduce her chances of dying from breast cancer by about 15% (Foster, Costanza, & Worden, 1985).

Touch may not be so central to our lives as vision or hearing. However, it is useful in many phases of daily life, and it also has important applications for helping people who are blind or deaf and for early detection of breast cancer.

Summary: Touch

1. Skin is the largest sensory system; it has protective value and is important in social interactions.

2. Skin has three layers: epidermis, dermis, and subcutaneous tissue.

3. There are many kinds of skin receptors, which have either free nerve endings or encapsulated endings. One kind, the Pacinian corpuscle, is extremely sensitive to skin indentation. However, there is no perfectly clear-cut relationship between the type of skin receptor and its function.

4. Specificity theory is based on the doctrine of specific nerve energies; specificity theory states that each of the different kinds of receptors responds to only one kind of physical stimulus.

5. Pattern theory proposes that the pattern of nerve impulses determines sensation.

6. Melzack and Wall's (1962) theory combines specificity and pattern theory; the basic assumptions of this theory are widely accepted.

7. Two systems convey information from receptors to the brain: the spinothalamic system and the lemniscal system. The spinothalamic system has smaller nerve fibers and slower transmission. The lemniscal system has larger nerve fibers, and it has more precision than the spinothalamic system.

8. Both the lemniscal system and the spinothalamic system pass their information on to the somatosensory cortex; mapping studies have shown a correspondence between body parts and cortex region.

9. Studies of passive touch show that thresholds are different for females and males and for various body parts.

10. Two-point discrimination thresholds are also different for various body parts; these correspond to the amount of space occupied by that body part on the cortex.

11. Humans show touch adaptation, or a gradual decrease in touch sensation as a result of prolonged stimulation.

12. The word-superiority effect operates for passive touch as well as for vision and hearing.

13. Active touch is important when we explore objects and try to discover their properties; this is also called haptic perception. Active touch is more precise and useful than passive touch.

14. When there is a conflict between touch and vision, people generally trust their vision. When the visual image is blurred, people trust their touch more. In other tasks, vision and touch may be equally helpful. However, visual information may produce faster judgments than tactile information. Finally, it is not clear whether accuracy can be improved by combining information from both sensory modes.

15. Applications of active touch include braille, the Optacon, the Tactile Vision Substitution System—all designed to help blind people—and the Tadoma method, designed to help deaf people. Active touch is also important in medical diagnosis.

PAIN

How would you define pain? If you have difficulty in formulating an objective definition, you are in good company. For example, the March 1985 issue of *Behavioral and Brain Sciences* contains articles by 28 prominent researchers or research groups, all struggling with the task of defining pain (e.g., Rachlin, 1985). The definition we will use was provided by Carterette and Friedman (1978): **pain** "involves (a) the perception of actual or threatened tissue damage; and (b) the private experience of unpleasantness ('that which hurts')" (p. xiv). This definition stresses that pain has two important components, a sensory component and an emotional component.

Pain is more strongly linked with emotion than any other area of perception. A visual perception, such as a beautiful sunset, seems to exist *out there* in the environment; we feel we can share those perceptions readily with other people. In contrast, a perception of pain, such as a toothache, seems to exist *in here* within the confines of our own bodies; we feel that these perceptions are difficult to share with others (Verillo, 1975). As Wall (1979) observes, pain seems to be unlike seeing and hearing, which are stimulated by external events; it has more in common with hunger and thirst, which are stimulated by internal events.

Early definitions of pain often stated that pain was the result of an overstimulation of either touch or temperature receptors. If a cold receptor was mildly stimulated, we felt cold, but if it was stimulated too much, we felt pain. These early definitions are now acknowledged to be inadequate because pain is often unrelated to degree of stimulation. That is, pain often occurs with only a mild stimulation, and a strong stimulation often produces no pain.

You may wonder why pain is necessary. Vision, hearing, and other perceptual activities all seem to have a purpose. However, when you have just scraped your knee, pain may seem entirely pointless. In many cases, though, pain has survival value; it serves to protect your body from further damage.

Sternbach (1978) describes the horrible things that can happen to people who have certain pain perception disorders and cannot feel pain. Initially, this might sound like an enviable condition. However, children who are born with pain insensitivity have picked away their nostrils and bitten off their tongues and fingers by mistake. Adults may suffer from a ruptured appendix, a fractured bone, or cancer, yet not detect the problem early enough to seek adequate treatment. In fact, one woman died because of damage done to her spine when she did not make the usual kinds of posture adjustments that we routinely make when our muscles and joints begin to ache (Sternbach, 1968). Another person felt only a mild headache when an axe was buried in his skull (Dearborn, 1932). Yes, pain is uncomfortable, but consider the dangers we would encounter without its warning capacity!

This section on pain has four parts. The first two sections discuss pain thresholds and pain adaptation. The third section considers theories about pain perception. The last section examines a variety of methods of relieving pain.

Thresholds for Pain

Sherrick and Cholewiak (1986) describe the stimuli used to test pain thresholds and related measures:

> The full array of devices and bodily loci employed in the study of pain would bring a smile to the lips of the Marquis de Sade [from whose name the word "sadism" is derived]. . . . Mechanical, thermal (conductive and radiant), chemical, and electrocutaneous stimuli have been applied to or injected into the limbs, torso, genitalia, face, cornea, palate, scalp, and tooth pulp of humans and animals in an unremitting search for either the conditions of stable production of pain or of reliable relief from it (pp. 12–39).

The **pain threshold** is the intensity of stimulation at which an observer says, "It's painful" half the time and "It's not painful" half the time. Notice, then, that the pain threshold differs from other kinds of thresholds, which involve responses such as "It's present" or "It's absent." When we measure pain thresholds, we ask people to judge the *quality* of a stimulus. In contrast, when we measure a hearing threshold, for example, we ask people to judge whether a sound is present or absent (Sternbach, 1978).

Pain thresholds depend upon many different factors. You may recall that the in-depth section in the psychophysics chapter examined factors that influence both sensitivity and criterion in the perception of pain. Also, different parts of the body have different sensitivities to pain, an observation that is not surprising if you recall that sensitivity to touch depends upon the part of the body stimulated. The cornea, the back of the knee, and the neck region are particularly sensitive, whereas the sole of the foot, the tip of the nose, and the inside lining of the cheek are particularly *in*sensitive. You have probably already discovered that parts of the body differ in their sensitivity if you have ever compared the pain of a tiny paper cut under a fingernail with the pain of a large gash on the sole of your foot.

A term related to pain thresholds is **pain tolerance**, the maximum pain level at which people voluntarily accept pain. Ethical problems in research on pain tolerance are discussed elsewhere (e.g., American Psychological Association, 1981; Matlin, 1979; Sternbach, 1983).

Both pain threshold and pain tolerance show enormous variation from one individual to another. A particular stimulus may be perceived by one person as being below his or her pain threshold, whereas the same stimulus may be perceived as above another person's pain tolerance. Researchers have tried to identify personality characteristics that might be related to pain thresholds and pain tolerance. Some factors that have been studied are anxiety, extraversion, and depression (Liebeskind & Paul, 1977; Sternbach, 1978; Weisenberg, 1977).

Many researchers have wondered whether there are ethnic differences in pain tolerance. For example, a large-scale study by Woodrow, Friedman, Siegelaub, and Collen (1972) tested 40,000 individuals as part of their routine physical examinations. They found that whites tolerated more pain than blacks, who tolerated more pain than Orientals. However, Weisenberg (1977) notes that the testers were probably white; black or Oriental testers might obtain different results. Another study examined various ethnic groups for their tolerance for pain and found the following ranking, from most tolerance to least: Protestants of British descent, Jews, Irish Catholics, and Italian Catholics (Sternbach & Tursky, 1965). In some cultures people are taught to endure pain as long as they possibly can, whereas in other cultures people are encouraged to avoid a painful situation when it becomes unpleasant.

Adaptation to Pain

Think about the last time you had a severe pain, such as a headache or a burn. If you took no medication, did the intensity of the pain seem to decrease over time? Most people report that the pain seems just as excruciating after half an hour as it did initially. In other words, pain adaptation does not seem to occur for intense pains.

However, adaptation does occur for mild pains. Try Demonstration 11.5 to illustrate how you can adapt to a mildly painful cold stimulus, particularly when only a small area of skin experiences pain. As Kenshalo (1971) points out, there is a physiological reason why we can adapt to painful cold stimuli; the chilling of nerve tissue blocks receptor activity and the conduction of impulses.

Adaptation also occurs for other mild pains, such as a pinprick and mildly painful hot stimuli. For example, we show adaptation for hot water temperatures up to about 46°C (115°F). However, we show little or no adaptation for hot water temperatures above 46°C (Hardy, Stolwijk, & Hoffman, 1968). If your doctor advises you to soak an infected finger in water as hot as you can tolerate, keep the temperature at about 46°C.

Theories of Pain Perception

At the beginning of the chapter we discussed three theories about the skin senses: specificity theory, pattern theory, and a theory that combined specificity theory and pattern theory. Let us now see how each of the three theories accounts for pain perception.

The **specificity theory of pain perception** states that pain is produced by the stimulation of specific pain receptors, which transmit information directly to a pain center in the brain. Supporters of this theory believe that the specific pain receptors responsible for pain perception are the free nerve endings, illustrated in Figure 11.1. According to this specificity theory, there is a direct connection from the free nerve endings to the part of the brain where we feel pain. Thus when the re-

ceptors are stimulated, we must *always* feel pain, and we must *only* feel pain—rather than any other sensation.

There is a major difficulty with the specificity theory of pain perception, however; the specificity theory cannot account for the fact that many psychological variables influence the amount of pain that people report. For example, Beecher (1959) describes ''soldiers who have been seriously wounded in battle who are clear mentally, not in shock and with normal blood pressure, having had no narcotics for a period of four hours or more and some not at all, [yet they] state on direct questioning that they do not have wound pain great enough to require medication'' (p. 166).

Apparently, these soldiers are so relieved to have survived the ordeal that their perception of wound pain is drastically reduced.

One soldier's report is particularly graphic:

> He was a raw recruit from Parris Island, taking a beachhead in the Pacific. He was scared to death. Heavy enemy fire was killing his buddies all around him. When a shell burst nearby, he felt an excruciating pain and the sensation of blood pouring down his leg. There was a call for a corpsman, and he was carried to a medical station, where doctors discovered he had indeed been hit—on his canteen. They sent him back out. More shells, more bombs. Suddenly, he felt a sharp pain in his head, hit the sand, rolled over and ran his hand across his forehead. Sure enough, there was blood. Again they carried him to the medical station. The doctor took some tweezers, picked out a few fragments of metal from his face, slapped on some adhesive bandages and sent him back to fight once more. By

Demonstration 11.5	Take a glass of cold water and add several ice cubes. Place your index finger in the water. Notice that you feel mild pain in your finger initially. Leave your finger in the water for several minutes. Do you still notice the pain?
Adaptation to Pain	

then, almost his entire company had been wiped out. For the third time, a shell burst near him. It tore off his leg. He did not feel a thing (Wallis, 1984, p. 66).

Additional evidence that people may not feel pain when the damage is severe comes from a study by Melzack, Wall, and Ty (1982). They questioned 138 patients who came to an emergency clinic at a hospital. All of them had fairly severe injuries, but 51 of them reported that they did not feel pain at the time of injury. In other words, more than one third of these patients had suffered substantial damage to their bodies, but there was no perception of pain! Clearly, these data are damaging to specificity theory.

Specificity theory also cannot account for **phantom limb pain**, which is perceived pain in an amputated arm or leg. The pain may be as intense in this "phantom limb" as when the limb was intact (Rivlin & Gravelle, 1984). How could someone feel pain in a missing arm when there are no longer any specific pain receptors in the skin to be stimulated? Clearly there must be higher-level processes, in addition to pain receptors on the skin, that can either reduce or increase the perception of pain.

The **pattern theory of pain perception** states that pain is produced by particular patterns of stimulation; specifically, the stimulation of receptors must be added together, and the stimulation must reach a critical level for the pain to be perceived. Theorists who support the pattern theory have argued that no specialized receptors receive only pain information. However, the physiological evidence here supports the specificity theory— rather than the pattern theory—because the free nerve endings *do* seem to be responsible for pain perception (Verillo, 1975).

The most popular current theory of pain perception combines the specificity theory and the pattern theory, and it also emphasizes the importance of psychological factors in pain perception (Weisenberg, 1984). Ronald Melzack and his colleagues have argued that specificity theory ignores psychological factors and pattern theory ignores physiological evidence (Melzack & Wall, 1965, 1982;

Melzack & Dennis, 1978). Their **gate-control theory** proposes that pain perception is a complex process in which the neural fibers interact, and the brain also has an important influence on pain perception.

To understand the gate-control theory, consult Figure 11.8. Admittedly, this diagram may look only slightly less complicated than the map of the New York City subway system; pain perception is not a simple process. Let's begin with the two kinds of neural fibers in the lower left corner; one kind is large in diameter, and the other is small. They ultimately have different influences on the gate-control system. Notice first that both of these have a direct effect on the **transmission cells**, located in the spinal cord. Both the large fibers and the small fibers stimulate (+) the transmission cells.

However, the neural fibers have an additional function: They influence another part of the system, also located in the spinal cord, called the **substantia gelatinosa**. The large fibers stimulate the substantia gelatinosa, whereas the small fibers inhibit (−) it. Let's look at this process in more detail. You'll note that signals from the substantia gelatinosa inhibit the transmission cells. As a consequence,

1. When the *large* fibers stimulate the substantia gelatinosa, this substance inhibits the transmission cells. As a result, the gate is closed, and the transmission cells contribute less to the perception of pain.

2. When the *small* fibers inhibit the substantia gelatinosa, this substance sends less inhibition to the transmission cells. As a result, the gate is open. (Inhibiting the inhibition is like multiplying a negative number times a negative number in algebra; the result is positive.) With the gate open, the transmission cells are more active, so the perception of pain is increased.

In summary, the basic operation of the gate-control system shows that when there is substantial large-fiber activity, the perception of pain is decreased. When there is substantial small-fiber activity, the perception of pain is increased.

However, two other portions of the sys-

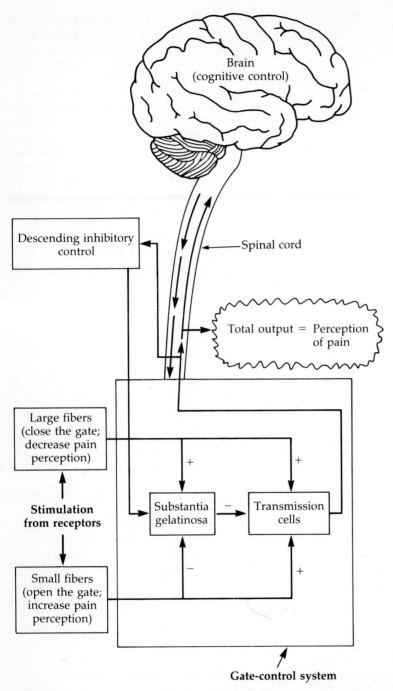

Figure 11.8   Gate-control theory of pain. (Based on Melzack & Wall, 1965, 1982.)

tem can influence pain perception. Notice that the brain can have an influence. We have repeatedly emphasized the importance of cognitive processes in perception, and cognitive control is an important part of the gate-control theory. Signals from the brain feed into the box labeled "gate-control system." As we will note later in the chapter, treatments for pain often involve cognitive processes. Melzack and Wall (1982) recently added a feature called the *descending inhibitory control*. It seemed appropriate to add this feature because of evidence that the brain could influence the system at a step beyond the transmission cells. As you can see, the descending inhibitory control has an influence on the substantia gelatinosa.

In summary, the entire system has mechanisms by which neural fiber activity can increase and decrease pain. Furthermore, there are two mechanisms by which central processes can also influence the perception of pain. Pain perception is much more than simple stimulation of the free nerve endings!

Have you ever noticed that a painful stimulus often seems to produce two different kinds of pain? For example, if you scrape your knee, you may at first feel a sharp "bright" pain, followed by a different kind of pain that is more dull and nagging. This sharp pain followed by dull pain is known as **double pain**. Although the support is not entirely clear (Sherrick & Cholewiak, 1986), the sharp pain may be due to stimulation of the large, fast fibers. According to research by Campbell and LaMotte (1983), for example, this "first pain" may be felt 400 milliseconds after stimulation, which means that the nerves signalling first pain must have conduction velocities greater than 6 m (20 ft) per second. Impulses travel more slowly through the small fibers; they are responsible for the delayed, dull pain.

Pain Control

About one third of the people in the United States have chronic pain, either persistent or recurrent. In all, Americans spend about $70 billion each year in medical costs and compensation for lost working days (Wallis, 1984). A variety of methods can be used to relieve pain. For example, neurosurgeons can cut the nerve pathways to relieve pain. Surprisingly, however, less drastic methods, such as hypnosis, can be more effective (Melzack, 1973; Rachlin, 1985). In this section, we will consider medication, endorphins, counterirritants, and procedures used by psychologists.

Medication

When you have a headache, you may take an aspirin. Aspirin is an **analgesic medication**, a drug specifically designed to relieve pain. Analgesics also include Novocain (which your dentist may inject before filling a cavity in your tooth), codeine (which is stronger than aspirin and classified as a weak narcotic agent with low addiction potential), and morphine (which is stronger than codeine and has high addiction potential). Details on these medications and their harmful side effects are discussed by Elton, Stanley, and Burrows (1983).

Psychological factors have an important impact on the effectiveness of analgesics. For example, analgesics can be ineffective if they are administered in a laboratory rather than in a doctor's office.

Furthermore, pain can often be reduced by giving a patient a placebo. A **placebo** is an inactive substance, such as a sugar pill, that the patient believes is a medication. If a doctor gives a patient a placebo and announces that it is a sugar pill, the pill will not have any pharmacological action. However, if the placebo is believed to be an analgesic, it may reduce pain significantly. In fact, it has been suggested that the history of medicine up to the 1600s is really the history of the placebo effect, since none of the treatments was inherently helpful (Critelli & Neumann, 1984). More recently, however, the term placebo has been extended so that it applies to other kinds of treatments in addition to medication.

Endorphins

In the early 1970s, researchers noticed that certain parts of the brain are particularly sensitive to opiates such as morphine (Pert & Snyder, 1973). These **opiate receptors** are specific locations on the surfaces of brain cells that respond to opiate drugs in a fashion similar to a lock and a key (Feuerstein, Labbé, & Kuczimerczyk, 1986). This finding may not seem particularly significant until you consider this point: Opiate drugs do not occur naturally inside the human body, so why should our brains be so cleverly designed to match the structure of opiates? Researchers realized that there must be some similar substance that naturally occurs inside our bodies, in other words, some *endogenous* substance. Indeed, some endogenous substances were discovered soon afterwards (e.g., Goldstein, 1976; Snyder, 1977), and they were called **endorphins**, as a shortened name for endogenous morphinelike substances. Feuerstein and his coauthors describe the discovery of additional endorphins. These substances have analgesic effects that resemble morphine's impressive ability to reduce pain (Bolles & Fanselow, 1982).

There is additional evidence that these endorphins are similar to the opiate drugs. A drug named **naloxone** is a powerful antagonist for opiate drugs such as morphine. (In fact, naloxone is sometimes given to people who have taken overdoses of morphine.) Intriguingly, naloxone also blocks the pain relief normally produced by other mechanisms. For example, placebos normally lessen pain; however, when naloxone is given in addition to a placebo, the placebo is no longer effective (Levine, Gordon, & Fields, 1979). Furthermore, we will discuss a Chinese pain-relief method called *acupuncture*; when naloxone is taken simultaneously, the acupuncture is no longer effective. It seems that certain pain-control procedures must release endorphins. Furthermore, repeated stress can also produce these endorphins, thereby providing analgesic effects (Willer, Dehen, & Cambier, 1981). Clearly, these findings have important implications for treating pain because they may suggest a therapy less dangerous than addictive drugs (Watkins & Mayer, 1982). However, at present researchers know little

about the natural conditions that activate endorphins in humans (Akil et al., 1984).

Counterirritants

You may have discovered that the intensity of pain from a wound can be reduced by scratching the surrounding skin. Several methods of pain control involve **counterirritants**, which stimulate or irritate one area to diminish pain in another.

One kind of counterirritant is the classical Chinese technique called acupuncture. **Acupuncture** involves the insertion of thin needles into various locations on the body. In some cases the needles may be heated or twirled. Figure 11.9 shows a typical acupuncture diagram. Each of these locations is carefully charted, and stimulation of these locations relieves a particular symptom. Often the stimulated point is far away from the painful area. For example, surgery for removal of the stomach is accomplished with four acupuncture needles in the pinna of each ear (Melzack, 1973).

Physicians in the United States have been reluctant to accept acupuncture as a method of controlling pain. In fact, most Americans were not interested in acupuncture until an American columnist, James Reston, had his appendix removed with the aid of acupuncture in an operation in China (Hassett, 1980). Melzack (1973) reports that a large proportion of patients in China—perhaps as high as 90%—undergo surgery with the acupuncture method. Patients who experience surgery with acupuncture are reported to be fully conscious during the operation. They chat pleasantly with the doctors, eat pieces of orange, and are keenly interested in the procedures of the operation. In China acupuncture is part of an entire approach to medicine that involves rapport, explanations, and expectations (Liebeskind & Paul, 1977). Naturally, it is difficult to duplicate these conditions in Western medical practice.

The mechanisms of acupuncture are not clear. It seems likely that endorphins are involved (Han & Terenius, 1982; Mayer, Price, Rafii, & Barber, 1976). Gate-control theory is

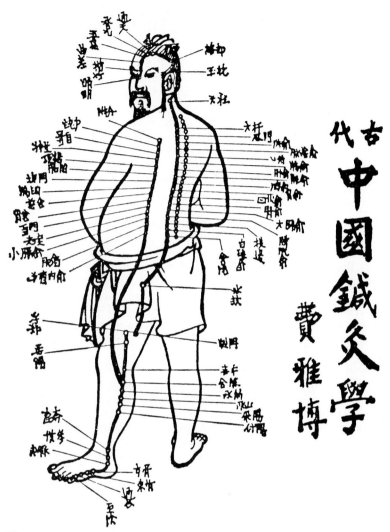

Figure 11.9 Acupuncture diagram. (From Ronald Melzack, *The puzzle of pain* (London: Penguin Education, 1973), Figure 38, p. 186. Copyright Ronald Melzack, 1973. Reprinted by permission of Penguin Books Ltd.)

also a likely explanation. Acupuncture may stimulate the large fibers, thus closing the gate (Rachlin, 1985). However, it is likely that more central factors must also be involved because acupuncture is so successful when needles are inserted at locations far removed from the pain.

Recently psychologists and others interested in pain control have begun to explore another kind of counterirritant method called stimulation-produced analgesia. **Stimulation-produced analgesia** involves the electrical stimulation of certain regions of the brain, which leads to analgesia, or a loss of sensitivity to pain. According to Cannon, Liebeskind, and Frenk (1978), stimulation-produced analgesia is as effective as high doses of morphine for suppressing pain in experimental animals. Furthermore, stimulation-produced analgesia has been demonstrated to increase the threshold for dental pain by 187% (Chapman, Chen, & Bonica, 1977). Perhaps in several years, your dentist may offer you a stimulating alternative to Novocain!

Procedures Used by Psychologists

So far we have seen that pain can be controlled by swallowing analgesics and sugar pills, by endorphins, and by being prodded with sharp needles and electrical stimulation. Now let us look at some procedures that psychologists use: hypnosis, cognitive-behavioral therapy, and modeling.

Hypnosis is an altered state of consciousness in which a person is susceptible to suggestions made by the hypnotist (Barber, 1986). It has been used to help people suffering from chronic pain and to prevent pain in patients undergoing surgery. It can provide dramatic relief in some cases. For example, Bellisimo and Tunks (1984) cite the case of a man suffering from painful cancer of the throat. Under hypnosis he was told that he would feel a pleasant tingling sensation, similar to a weak electric current, whenever he started to sense pain in his throat. The patient successfully substituted the pleasant tingling for the pain. Bellisimo and Tunks describe numerous other uses of hypnosis in pain treatment. For example, hypnosis can be used to distort time, so that the "time in pain" appears to pass more quickly.

It should be stressed that some researchers are skeptical about hypnosis. Typically they acknowledge that hypnosis may indeed relieve pain, but they argue that people typically show as much pain reduction when provided with pain-reduction suggestions under waking conditions as they do when hypnotized (Barber, 1982). The results suggest that hypnosis produces effective pain relief, although it may not be any more successful than the less mysterious techniques such as

those used in cognitive-behavioral techniques.

Cognitive-behavioral approaches to pain focus on helping the patient develop more adaptive cognitive and behavioral reactions to a physical problem (Feuerstein, Labbé, & Kuczmierczyk, 1986). They include a wide variety of techniques. Some techniques that emphasize the cognitive aspect include teaching the patient to identify negative thoughts related to pain, substituting more adaptive thoughts, and using coping strategies such as distraction to minimize suffering. Cognitive-behavioral approaches also borrow from behaviorism; patients are frequently taught operant conditioning principles, in which behavior not related to pain—for example, increased physical activity—is reinforced.

The cognitive-behavioral approach is thoroughly described in a book by Turk, Meichenbaum, and Genest (1983). They discuss, for example, how the approach is used for patients with cancer. Treatment includes education about the disease, relaxation training, and help in clarifying feelings.

A common component of cognitive-behavioral treatment involves **distraction**, or a refocusing of attention toward something other than the pain. McCaul and Malott (1984) reviewed the studies on the effectiveness of distraction. These authors concluded that distraction is indeed more effective than a placebo control condition in relieving pain. Furthermore, distraction techniques are particularly effective if they require a high level of attention rather than being just slightly distracting. Distraction is particularly effective for low-intensity pain.

Cognitive-behavioral techniques are prominently featured in prepared childbirth. For example, the **Lamaze method** focuses on educating women about the anatomy and physiology of childbirth and controlled muscular relaxation and on teaching them to pay attention to something other than pain (Wideman & Singer, 1984). The studies on this technique have demonstrated that women who have received prepared childbirth training are more tolerant of pain and require less medication during childbirth.

A final procedure used by psychologists is a modeling approach, a technique that could probably be successfully combined with cognitive-behavioral techniques. According to the **modeling approach** people learn both positive and negative behavior by simply watching another person in a situation; they do not have to perform the behavior themselves. For example, children learn that the dental setting is painful by watching their parents' reactions. Parents who report being extremely anxious in a dentist's office tend to have children who are negative and uncooperative during dental examinations (Craig, 1978). Edwards, Zeichner, Kuczmierczyk, and Boczkowski (1985) discuss a variety of other studies in which similar correlations between parental behavior and children's pain reactions have been demonstrated for recurrent stomach pain, lower back pain, and chronic headaches. These authors also found that students with frequent pain were likely to have a large number of family members who complained about pain, thereby serving as pain models.

Notice that modeling theory accounts for the ethnic differences in pain tolerance discussed earlier in this section. It also helps explain why acupuncture may be more effective in China than in the United States. Chinese patients have been exposed to others who have had successful acupuncture experiences. In fact, new patients are encouraged to talk to people who have previously experienced acupuncture (Craig, 1978).

Modeling therapy has been successfully used in dental care. For example, children saw a film in which a model was initially fearful but controlled his fear and received verbal praise and a toy at the end of a dental session. These children were much less anxious and disruptive during their own dental session than children who had not seen the film. Similarly, you may have heard about hospital programs in which children awaiting surgery see a movie about another child's experience in surgery. Experiments have confirmed the effectiveness of this kind of modeling program (Craig, 1978).

It is interesting to speculate why these procedures used by psychologists are effective in pain relief. Specifically, do these psychological procedures decrease sensitivity, or do they alter the criterion for reporting pain? Clearly, signal-detection methods would provide useful answers to this question.

Summary: Pain

1. Pain involves the perception of tissue damage and the personal experience of unpleasantness. It often has survival value, protecting us from further damage.
2. The pain threshold is the lowest intensity of stimulation at which we perceive pain.
3. Pain tolerance is the maximum pain level at which people accept pain; there seem to be ethnic differences in pain tolerance.
4. Humans adapt to mild pains but not to severe ones.
5. The specificity theory of pain perception states that pain is transmitted directly from pain receptors to a pain center in the brain; this theory cannot account for the fact that psychological variables influence the amount of pain that people report.
6. The pattern theory of pain perception states that pain is produced by a particular pattern of stimulation from the receptors; this theory cannot account for the physiological evidence that free nerve endings do seem to be responsible for pain perception.
7. Melzack and his colleagues proposed a gate-control theory in which pain perception is hypothesized to be the result of complex interactions of large fibers and small fibers with the substantia gelatinosa and the transmission cells. In addition, cognitive control from the brain has an important influence on pain perception.
8. Pain can be controlled by analgesics, such as aspirin, codeine, and morphine; placebos may also relieve pain.
9. Endogenous opiatelike drugs have been found in humans; these endorphins appear to be released by acupuncture and stressful experiences.
10. Counterirritants, which diminish pain in one area by stimulating or irritating an-

other area, include acupuncture and stim-
ulus-produced analgesia.
11. Techniques used by psychologists in controlling pain include hypnosis, cognitive-
behavioral approaches such as distraction, and modeling.

TEMPERATURE

This section discusses the perception of
warmth and cold. In particular, we will examine four topics: (1) body temperature regulation, (2) warm and cold spots, (3) temperature thresholds, and (4) adaptation.

Body Temperature Regulation

Think about how hot or cold you feel right
now. Probably you feel reasonably comfortable. Your body has an impressive ability to
regulate its own temperature and keep it at
about 37°C (98.6°F). If you are in a snowstorm

and your body temperature starts to drop,
you shiver, a useful process for making more
heat. Also, the blood vessels near the surface
of the skin shrink in diameter so that less of
the warmth from your blood will be lost on
the surface. If you are playing a fierce tennis
game in the hot August sun, you sweat, and
that cools your skin. Also, the blood vessels
expand in diameter, so that more of the
blood's warmth can be disposed of. Poulton
(1970) notes that we may lose consciousness
if our body temperature falls below 33°C or
rises above 41°C. Thus the skin's role in temperature regulation is not merely a pleasant
luxury; it is absolutely necessary. Other aspects of temperature regulation in vertebrates
are discussed by Heller, Crawshaw, and
Hammel (1978).

Generally, we find that a surrounding
temperature of about 22°C (72°F) is most comfortable. Figure 11.10 shows ratings of discomfort associated with various temperatures. Hancock (1986a) reviewed a number of
studies on the relationship between sur-

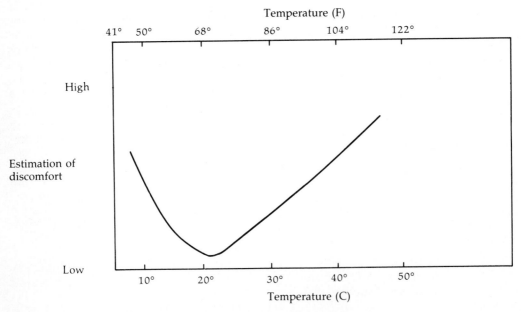

Figure 11.10   Amount of discomfort as function of temperature.

rounding temperature and performance. He concluded that people's performance generally decreases at temperatures greater than 29°C (85°F). This decrement is particularly strong for people who are not very skilled at a task. Thus the temperature of your surroundings can influence both how comfortable you feel and how well you perform.

Warm and Cold Spots

The section you are reading is labeled "temperature," so it might be tempting to think that we have just one kind of temperature sense. However, we really have separate systems for a warmth sense and for a cold sense. Researchers concluded that there are two separate systems because they were able to identify separate warm and cold spots on the skin. For example, Dallenbach (1927) took a stimulus the size of a pinhead, cooled it, and touched it to various precise locations in a 2-cm² (.3 square inches) patch of skin. The same procedure was repeated for the same patch of skin using a heated stimulus. He found no correspondence between areas that responded to the cool stimulus and areas that responded to the warm stimulus. (Also, as you might have guessed from our earlier discussion, he found no correspondence between the type of sensation and the type of receptor underlying the skin at the stimulation point.) Thus we should not speak of a "temperature sense" as if it were a single sense; the warmth sense and the cold sense are really separate. Subsequent research has established that these warm and cold spots

are about 1 mm (.04 inches) in diameter (Hensel, 1982).

Has this ever happened to you? You put your hand out to test the temperature of the shower water before entering. A few drops convince you that the water temperature is chillingly cold. However, a moment later you realize that the water is really scaldingly hot. If so, you have experienced paradoxical cold. A paradox is a puzzle, and **paradoxical cold** occurs when a hot stimulus produces the sensation of cold when it stimulates a cold spot. The ideal temperature to produce paradoxical cold is about 45°C (113°F) (Sherrick & Cholewiak, 1986). It may be that cold spots are active in that temperature range as well as in colder temperatures.

Incidentally, you may wonder whether there is a corresponding sensation called paradoxical warmth. Sherrick and Cholewiak reviewed several studies about the quest for paradoxical warmth, but this phenomenon has not yet been demonstrated in other than a few isolated reports. It appears that the warm spots are active only in the higher temperature range.

Thresholds for Temperature

Try Demonstration 11.6 to illustrate how temperature sensitivity varies greatly for different parts of your body. According to Stevens, Marks, and Simonson (1974), the forehead is particularly sensitive to heat. The chest, stomach, shoulder, and arm are less sensitive, and the calf is the least sensitive. Perhaps you have noticed the difference in tem-

Demonstration 11.6	Find a metal fork or spoon. Touch the bottom of the handle to your forehead, chest, stomach, shoulder, arm, foot, and calf. Notice that the handle feels cold when you touch some parts of your body, but its temperature is not noticeable on other body parts. Now run hot water on the utensil handle, wipe it off quickly, and touch it to your forehead. Repeat the heating, drying, and touching process for your other body parts. Where is the heat most noticeable?
Threshold for Temperature of Various Body Parts	

perature sensitivity if you have sat at a camp fire trying to warm your hands. Your forehead probably felt much hotter than your hands, even though it was farther away from the fire.

There are also body-region differences in sensitivity to cold. Stevens (1979) found that the trunk was most sensitive, an observation you can appreciate if a doctor has placed a cold stethoscope on your chest. Arms and legs are somewhat less sensitive to cold, followed by the cheeks, and finally the forehead.

We can often detect small changes in temperature, as minute as .003°C (.006°F) (Kenshalo, 1978). However, no single value can be supplied as the absolute threshold for warm and cold sensations because the threshold depends upon several factors. For example, the larger the portion of skin exposed to the warm or cold stimulus, the smaller the threshold; it makes sense that we can detect a tiny change more readily on an entire arm than on a pinpoint-sized dot of skin. Also, if the temperature changes quickly, we are more likely to notice it than if the change is gradual (Kenshalo, Holmes, & Wood, 1968). Kenshalo (1978) discusses other factors that influence threshold, such as current skin temperature, phase of the menstrual cycle in women, time of day, and stress.

Taus, Stevens, and Marks (1975) found that people are poor at localizing temperature sensations for above-threshold stimuli. They asked people to judge whether a stimulus was presented below or above a particular reference point on their arm. Even with the warmest stimulus, accuracy ranged between 80% and 95%. In contrast, *touch* localization was 99% for a hair that was just barely perceptible. Thus we are better at identifying where something touched us than where something warmed us.

Adaptation to Temperature

When you first sit down in a hot bath, the temperature may seem unpleasantly hot. After a few minutes the temperature seems comfortable. However, if you slide down further into the water so that your back is submerged, the temperature of the water surrounding your back is—once again—unpleasantly hot. The rest of your body had adapted to the hot temperature, but the newly immersed skin had not.

As you know, adaptation occurs when a stimulus is presented continuously; the perceived intensity of the stimulus decreases over time. **Thermal adaptation** is therefore a decrease in the perceived intensity of a hot or cold temperature as time passes. Thermal adaptation is usually studied by placing warm or cold stimuli on the skin and asking the subject to report when the temperature sensation disappears. For example, Kenshalo (1971) reports that people seem to be able to adapt completely to temperatures on the skin in the range of about 29°C to 37°C (84°F to 99°F), starting from a normal skin temperature of approximately 33°C (92°F). Outside this range the temperature will seem persistently cold or warm, no matter how long the stimulus is left on the skin.

Try Demonstration 11.7 to illustrate an adaptation effect that John Locke reported in the 17th century. Notice that your left hand, which has adapted to the hot water, feels cold in the neutral-temperature water. In contrast, your right hand, which has adapted to the cold water, feels warm in the same neutral-temperature water. Our skin is not an accurate thermometer; we perceive relative, rather than absolute, temperature. A particular temperature can feel cold or hot, depending upon the temperature we have become accustomed to.

People seem to be able to adapt fairly well to cold stimuli. Hensel (1981), in his book *Thermoreception and Temperature Regulation*, describes research on people who are repeatedly subjected to cold conditions. For example, if you were to place your hand in ice water, your blood pressure and heart rate would increase. However, if you repeated this process several times with room-temperature intervals in between, you would respond less dramatically. Studies on people re-

Demonstration 11.7

Temperature Adaptation

Locate three bowls. Fill one with very hot tap water (but not so hot that it is painful). Fill the second bowl with very cold tap water. Fill the third with a mixture from the other two bowls. Arrange the three bowls as illustrated below. Place your left hand in the hot water and your right hand in the cold water. Leave your hands in these bowls for approximately 3 minutes and quickly transfer both your hands to the middle (lukewarm) bowl. Notice the apparent temperature of each hand.

Right hand   Left hand

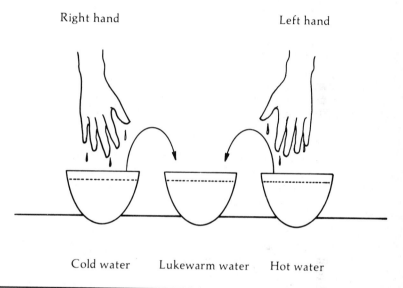

Cold water   Lukewarm water   Hot water

peatedly exposed to cold conditions, either because of the region they live in or their profession (e.g., fishing), show they feel little or no pain when their hands are exposed to cold (Hensel, 1981).

Summary: Temperature

1. The body has several mechanisms for regulating its temperature.
2. A temperature of about 22°C (72°F) is generally most comfortable to the majority of people.
3. There are separate warm and cold spots on the skin.
4. Paradoxical cold occurs when a hot stim-

ulus produces the sensation of cold; there does not appear to be a comparable paradoxical cold phenomenon.

5. Thresholds for temperature are influenced by factors such as body part, amount of skin exposed, and speed of temperature change. People are poor at localizing touch.
6. Thermal adaptation is a decrease in the perceived intensity of a hot or a cold temperature as a function of repeated exposure.
7. People can adapt fairly well to cold stimuli, for example, if their living conditions or occupations require repeated contact with cold.

KINESTHETIC AND VESTIBULAR SENSES

There is abundant information on touch, and researchers have also been active in investigating pain. There is somewhat less information about the perception of temperature, but this is abundant compared to the information about the last two areas to be covered in this chapter. We know relatively little about the kinesthetic and vestibular senses, which give us information about movement and about maintaining upright posture. These senses are similar in that we are seldom aware of them. We are seldom conscious of how our hand moves downward and toward the right to pick up a pen, and we are seldom aware that we are standing upright rather than tilted at a 15° angle.

Kinesthetic Sense

Kinesthesia is derived from a Greek word meaning "perception of movement." As it is usually employed today, **kinesthesia** refers to the sensation of movement or the sensation of static limb position (Clark & Horch, 1986). In its broadest sense kinesthesia includes sensations that come from the position and movement of body parts; this movement can be active or passive. A similar term typically used interchangeably with kinesthesia is **proprioception**.

The central nervous system has two methods for obtaining information about the position and the movement of body parts: (1) It can monitor the commands it sends to the muscles, on the assumption that the muscles carry them out or (2) it can receive information from appropriate sensory receptors. In fact, the central nervous system uses both sources of information. Just as the visual system uses more than one source of information to determine the distance of an object, as you learned in Chapter 7, the kinesthetic system uses more than one source to determine the position of the body parts. If you stretch your arm out to the right in the direction of a pen, your central nervous system knows where your arm is because it sent that arm on this particular errand and because feedback from the arm tells your central nervous system where the arm is. These two kinds of kinesthetic information are supplemented by other senses. For example, your vision informs the central nervous system about the location of your arm, your touch senses let you know when your finger makes contact with the pen, and even your hearing may contribute information about the slight scrape that the pen makes on the desk surface as your hand reaches its destination (Clark & Horch, 1986).

Let's briefly examine the receptors that provide kinesthetic information. We discussed in the section on touch the variety of receptors found in the skin. Several of these receptors respond to the stretching of skin, so they are potential candidates for supplying information about kinesthesia. However, these receptors are spread so sparsely across the skin's surface that it seems unlikely that they could provide precise information about the location of a body part. Instead, it is more likely that the receptors in the ligaments and joints provide this information (Burgess, Wei, Clark, & Simon, 1982; Clark & Horch, 1986).

The kind of receptor most extensively researched is the Golgi tendon organ. The tendon is the tough, fibrous material that attaches the muscle to the bone. **Golgi tendon organs**, located in these tendons, respond when the muscle exerts tension on the tendon (Carlson, 1986). The Pacinian corpuscles, mentioned earlier in connection with the skin receptors, are also in the muscles. These receptors respond to deep pressure on the muscles. Also, the free nerve endings associated with pain can provide information when body movement is accompanied by pain.

Researchers have explored a number of topics within kinesthetic perception: ability to judge whether lines are straight or curved, based on feeling them; ability to judge distance, based on the distance traced by fingers (Loomis & Lederman, 1986); judgments about the width of wood blocks (Baker & Weisz,

1984); and discriminations about an object's weight (Brodie & Ross, 1984).

One area of kinesthesia research is related to our earlier in-depth examination of the relationship between touch and vision. In particular, this kind of research investigates what happens when there is a discrepancy between kinesthetic information and information from one of the other senses. You'll recall that when tactile and visual information are in conflict, people tend to trust their vision. There are similar results with kinesthesia, when the discrepancy is created by using prism lenses (Welch & Warren, 1980). If you looked through lenses that showed your hand several inches away from its true location, your vision would strongly bias your sense of where your hand was. However, vision cannot completely influence kinesthesia, because kinesthetic information has a modest influence on judgments of the location of body parts when visual and kinesthetic information conflict.

You may recall that Chapter 9 included an in-depth examination of auditory localization, which involves judgments about the direction of a sound source. What happens when there is a discrepancy between kinesthetic information and auditory information? Welch and Warren (1980) conclude that kinesthetic information has a stronger effect. In other words, kinesthesia biases audition more strongly than audition biases kinesthesia.

Kinesthesia is certainly not a prominent sensory or perceptual system. Nonetheless, this brief description may make you more conscious of your ability to judge body position and movement. To help increase this appreciation, try Demonstration 11.8.

Vestibular Sense

The **vestibular sense** provides us with information about orientation, movement, and acceleration. Like kinesthesia, the vestibular sense is something we seldom appreciate. Typically, we notice it only when our sensory receptors are stimulated in an unusual fashion, for example, if you have been spinning around for an extended time—perhaps on a ride in an amusement park—and come to a sudden halt (Benson, 1982). Try Demonstration 11.9 to appreciate the vestibular sense more thoroughly.

The other senses examined in this chapter involved large receptive surfaces covering the entire body. In contrast, the receptors for the vestibular sense are very small; in fact, they are actually next to the two cochlea within the ear. More information on these receptors can be found in Carlson (1986) and Benson (1982).

Researchers interested in the vestibular

Demonstration 11.8 *Importance of Kinesthesia*	Close your eyes and extend your arms out at your sides. Point your index fingers, folding your thumb and remaining fingers into a fist. Now bring your index fingers quickly toward each other in front of your body. See whether you can make them touch—without looking. Try this several times and assess your success. Then close your eyes and use an index finger to touch each of your toes. Repeat this exercise several times and assess your success. You might also be interested in seeing whether you are equally successful touching your index fingers together *behind* your back; most people are somewhat less accurate.

Demonstration 11.9

Importance of Vestibular Sense

Stand up and lift one leg. Notice how your body automatically adjusts to retain your balance in this somewhat precarious position. (Incidentally, you may also want to repeat this exercise with your eyes closed; you will find that the postural adjustments are larger and that the task is more difficult. Vision clearly aids the vestibular senses in maintaining body balance.)

---

sense have examined a variety of topics. Some have studied how animals such as rabbits and cats manage to land on all four feet when they fall from an upside-down position (Howard, 1986). Researchers interested in the vestibular sense in humans have looked at thresholds for the detection of movement and the self-motion illusion, which was mentioned in Chapter 7 (Howard, 1986).

A number of studies have been conducted on the perception of the upright (Howard, 1986). In some experiments people sit in a chair that can be tilted from side to side, and the chair is centered in a small room that can also be tilted from side. If you were a participant in the tilted-room experiment, you would be asked to adjust your chair until it is perfectly upright. Suppose that the surrounding room had been tilted so that it was at a 20° angle. Would you adjust your chair to match the up-down orientation of the walls of this room or to line up straight with the force of gravity?

There are individual differences in how people resolve this discrepancy between visual cues and vestibular cues. People who rely on the orientation of the room (visual cues) are called **field dependent**, whereas people who rely on the orientation of their bodies (vestibular cues) are called **field independent**. In view of the significant individual differences in this area, it's surprising that individual differences have not been examined in the way people resolve conflicts between the other touch-related senses and vision. For example, it would be interesting to know

whether some people consistently pay attention to touch, whereas others consistently pay attention to vision in the kinds of experiments discussed in the in-depth section earlier in the chapter.

Summary: Kinesthetic and Vestibular Senses

1. Kinesthesia refers to the sensation of movement and the sensation of static limb position. Sources of information about kinesthesia include monitoring of commands sent to muscles and information from sensory receptors, supplemented by visual, auditory, and tactile information.
2. Kinesthetic receptors include Golgi tendon organs, Pacinian corpuscles, and free nerve endings.
3. One topic studied in kinesthesia is the response to discrepancies between kinesthetic information and visual information; people rely more on vision than on kinesthesia.
4. When kinesthetic information and auditory information conflict, people rely more on kinesthesia than on audition.
5. The vestibular senses are concerned with orientation, movement, and acceleration.
6. The vestibular receptors are near the cochlea of the auditory system.
7. When vestibular information and visual information conflict, there are individual differences in the response; some rely more on vestibular information, and some on visual information.

Review

1. In this chapter we discussed thresholds and two-point discrimination thresholds for touch, pain, and temperature (both warmth and cold). We saw that each of these thresholds varied from one part of the body to another. Summarize the findings on these various kinds of thresholds and note the similarities and differences.

2. Adaptation was also a recurring theme in this chapter. Discuss adaptation to touch, pain, and temperature. Think of an example of each of these kinds of adaptation from your own recent experience. Can you think of an occasion when adaptation did not occur?

3. Discuss specificity theory and pattern theory, both in their application to the general skin senses and in their application to pain perception. Then discuss the gate-control theory in as much detail as possible.

4. Refer to material in the chapter to explain each of the following observations about touch:

   a. Something touches your leg, and you have no idea what shape it is; then it touches your face, and its shape seems clear.

   b. The fabric on a chair seems rough against your arm when you first sit down, but you do not notice it after 5 minutes.

   c. You've placed your sleeping bag on a surface without noticing that there is a twig underneath. In reality, the twig has two prominent points, yet when some parts of your body rest on the twig, it seems like a single point.

5. At three points in this chapter, there was discussion about how people respond when there is a conflict between two senses. Discuss each of these topics, providing particular detail on the vision-touch conflict.

6. What is pain, why does it differ from other perceptual experiences, and why

are its thresholds different? What function does pain serve?

7. Melzack and his colleagues emphasized that psychological processes influence pain perception; pain is more than the perception of the impulses that flow from the receptors to the brain. Explain why each of the following topics documents the importance of central psychological processes in pain perception: (a) ethnic differences in pain tolerance, (b) phantom limb pain, (c) placebo action, (d) acupuncture, (e) cognitive-behavioral approaches, and (f) hypnosis. Then discuss how endorphins may be relevant for placebo and acupuncture therapy.

8. Refer to material in the chapter to explain each of the following observations about temperature perception:

   a. You stand too close to a kettle full of boiling spaghetti sauce, and a drop splatters on your wrist; surprisingly, it seems cold.

   b. Maria has been sitting in front of the fire, and the kitchen seems cold to her; Pat has been outside in the snow, and the kitchen seems warm to her.

   c. Your internal temperature remains at about 37°C, whether you spend your winter in Vermont blizzards or the Caribbean sunshine.

   d. You know a man who works for hours at a time with frozen foods, without gloves, and he claims that the cold doesn't bother his hands.

9. Compare the senses discussed in this chapter with vision and hearing. Mention, for example, (a) the size of the receptive system, (b) the kind of receptors, (c) the ability to discriminate, (d) sensitivity, and (e) the nature of the stimuli.

10. Suppose you know a student taking introductory psychology. The chapter on perception in that student's textbook does not mention the kinesthetic and vestibular senses. Briefly summarize the nature of these senses and how they are important in daily life.

New Terms

hairy skin

glabrous skin

epidermis

dermis

subcutaneous tissue

free nerve endings

encapsulated endings

Pacinian corpuscles

doctrine of specific nerve
   energies

specificity theory

pattern theory

spinothalamic system

lemniscal system

passive touch

active touch

detection threshold

two-point discrimination
   threshold

touch adaptation

haptic perception

braille

Optacon

Tactile Vision Substitution
   System (TVSS)

Tadoma method

pain

pain threshold

pain tolerance

specificity theory of pain
   perception

phantom limb pain

pattern theory of pain
   perception

gate-control theory

transmission cells

substantia gelatinosa

double pain

analgesic medication

placebo

opiate receptors

endorphins

naloxone

counterirritants

acupuncture

stimulation-produced analgesia

hypnosis

cognitive-behavioral
   approaches

distraction

Lamaze method

modeling approach

paradoxical cold

thermal adaptation

kinesthesia

proprioception

Golgi tendon organs

vestibular sense

field dependent

field independent

Recommended Readings

Bellissimo, A., & Tunks, E. (1984). *Chronic pain.*
   New York: Praeger. *This book reviews clinical material, relevant research, and theory of pain. Pain-
   control techniques are discussed in detail.*

Boff, K. R., Kaufman, L., & Thomas, J. P. (Eds.).
   (1986). *Handbook of perception and human performance* (Vols. 1 and 2). New York: Wiley. *Several relevant chapters cover the following topics: the
   vestibular system, skin sensitivity, kinesthesia, the
   perception of the upright, and tactile perception.*

Elton, D., Stanley, G., & Burrows, G. (1983). *Psychological control of pain.* Sydney, Australia:
   Grune & Stratton. *In addition to pain-control techniques discussed in this chapter, Elton and her coauthors include topics such as biofeedback, the methodology of pain research, and personality
   characteristics related to pain perception.*

Feuerstein, M., Labbe, E. E., & Kuczmierczyk,

A. R. (1986). *Health psychology: A psychobiological
   perspective.* New York: Plenum. *The chapter in
   this volume most related to Chapter 11 is the last
   one, on the topic of pain; it is a superb, brief overview
   of the topic. Additional chapters in this volume relate
   pain to the topic of stress.*

Hensel, H. (1981). *Thermoreception and temperature
   regulation.* London: Academic Press. *Hensel's
   book reviews the sensory basis of temperature and
   some aspects of temperature perception; its primary
   emphasis is temperature regulation.*

Schiff, W., & Foulke, E. (Eds.). (1982). *Tactual perception: A sourcebook.* Cambridge: Cambridge
   University Press. *This well-written sequence of
   chapters includes an introduction to tactual perception and an overview of the psychophysics of touch;
   its most valuable feature is the discussion of applications of touch.*

chapter 12
Smell

Preview

Smell is still rather mysterious, and there are many unanswered questions about this topic. Our examination of smell covers three areas: (1) sensory aspects, (2) olfactory processes, and (3) applications of research.

The discussion of the sensory aspects of smell begins with the nature of the odor stimulus. We first consider what kinds of substances have noticeable odors and what kinds of systems have been devised to classify them. Then we examine the olfactory system, beginning with the receptor cells and moving on to the brain.

The section on olfactory processes notes that people can detect impressively tiny amounts of an odor, but they have difficulty distinguishing between two different concentrations of it. Also, humans adapt rapidly when they are continually exposed to a particular odor; after about 1 minute, their sensitivity is greatly reduced. The in-depth section examines the recognition of odors; these odors include familiar odors found around the house as well as the odor of other people. Constancy and illusion are also examined.

The final section, on applications of research on smell, covers the control of odor pollution. It also considers the use of smell as a diagnostic tool in medicine; certain diseases are associated with particular odors. Another application of olfactory research is the manufacturing of perfumes. Finally, chemical signals called pheromones play an important role in reproduction among lower animals, and they may be involved in aspects of human behavior.

The sense of smell is both important and mysterious. Although we may not always be aware that smell is influential, it can still be important in everyday behavior. For example, you meet someone at a party and dislike him instantly because his after-shave lotion reminds you of someone you loathe. You smell a piece of fish and decide to throw it out because of the spoiled odor. You pause in the doorway of a new Chinese restaurant and decide to enter because the aroma contains the appropriate mix of garlic, ginger, and sesame oil. You visit a friend's house, and one whiff immediately makes you think of your grandmother's attic, which you have not visited in 10 years.

Smell, also known as **olfaction,** is particularly important in the way food tastes, as we will explore more thoroughly in Chapter 13. Usually, we say that something *tastes* good, when in fact we should be commenting on its smell. (Smell and taste are frequently grouped together under the name **chemical senses** because the receptor cells for smell and taste are both sensitive to chemical stimulation.) Smell is even more important for nonhuman animals because it is used to locate food, identify the enemy, and engage in mating.

Despite its importance, we do not know much about smell. Gesteland (1978) wrote that olfaction is the most mysterious of the senses. As we will discuss in this chapter, researchers have not developed a classification system for the different smells. They also cannot accurately predict a substance's smell on the basis of its chemical structure, and they are not certain whether smell is a factor in human sexual relations. Teghtsoonian (1983) claims that vision and hearing are like the two pampered daughters, whereas smell is the Cinderella of perception. To support this statement she points out that her survey of journals in perception revealed that about 50% of the articles concerned vision, 25% concerned audition, and only 2% concerned smell.

Why should smell suffer such neglect? As Teghtsoonian notes—and we will discuss in more detail later—it is difficult to classify the stimuli for smell, whereas it is easy to specify the dimensions of visual and auditory stimuli. In addition the field of perception currently emphasizes cognition and information processing. It is easy to see how vision and hearing are important in our thought processes, but the relationship between smell and thought is more remote. As Trygg Engen points out in his important book *The Perception of Odors* (1982), smell is more closely linked with emotion. If the discipline of psychology in general—and perception in particular—were to place more emphasis on emotion than on cognition, we would probably see a blossoming of research on the topic of odor.

There are three parts to this chapter. The first part, on the sensory aspects of smell, examines the nature of the odorous stimulus and the olfactory apparatus. The second part, called "Olfactory Processes," is concerned with thresholds, adaptation, recognition, and constancy and illusion. The final part discusses applications of research on smell in areas such as perfume manufacturing, pollution control, medicine, and communication.

SENSORY ASPECTS OF SMELL

A discussion of smell should begin with an examination of the sensory aspects of smell. In particular, what is the nature of the smell stimulus, or **odorant,** and how can odors be classified? Furthermore, what is the structure of the sensory receptors, and how is information about smell transmitted to higher levels?

Stimulus

Description

For substances to be smelled they must be volatile. **Volatile** means that something can evaporate, or change into a gas form. However, we cannot smell all the volatile substances. Water, for example, is volatile because it can evaporate, and the vapor form of water bathes our nasal cavities every time we take a shower. However, pure steam has no odor. Thus volatility is necessary but not sufficient to permit smelling.

Another necessary but not sufficient characteristic of substances that can be smelled is that they have a particular molecular weight. As you have learned in previous chapters, we can accurately specify the nature of stimuli that we see and hear. For example, the visible spectrum includes only the wavelengths from 400 nm to 700 nm. We can hear sounds only in the frequency range of 20 Hz to 20,000 Hz. In general, we can detect only the smells of substances that have molecular weights between 15 and 300 (Carlson, 1986). The **molecular weight** of a substance is the sum of the atomic weights of all the atoms in the molecule. For example, the molecular weight of the alcohol in a gin and tonic is 46. (The formula for ethyl alcohol is C_2H_5OH. Each of the two carbon atoms has an atomic weight of 12, each of the six hydrogen atoms has a weight of 1, and oxygen has a weight of 16; $24 + 6 + 16 = 46$.) Thus you can smell alcohol, but you cannot smell table sugar ($C_{12}H_{22}O_{11}$), which has a molecular weight of 342. In summary, the substances that we smell must be volatile and must typically have molecular weights between 15 and 300. There are probably additional factors that have not yet been identified.

Classification

As Engen (1982) notes, in no other perceptual system has classification played as dominant a role in research as it has in smell. Indeed, it is an impressive challenge to establish a system for classifying odorants. A sound, for example, can be precisely described as being a pure tone of 1000 Hz and 40 dB. With odorants, we must settle for qualitative descriptions such as minty, goaty, and spicy.

The issue of smell classifications has intrigued many people, probably beginning with Aristotle (Cain, 1978a). We will look at two of the many systems that have been proposed, although neither is perfectly satisfactory.

One commonly discussed system of classi-

fications was proposed by Henning (1916). Figure 12.1 illustrates the prism-shaped figure he constructed to show how smells can be defined in terms of six basic odors.

Now try Demonstration 12.1. See how accurate you are in placing odors on the prism in relation to the square that contains the floral, fruity, spicy, and resinous odors. Notice, incidentally, that cooks in the Western hemisphere use only certain portions of this square. We use the side between floral and spicy, the spicy portion of the spicy-resinous side, and the fruity portion of the fruity-resinous side. Greeks, however, use resinous substances to flavor their wine called retsina (which tastes almost as if you were drinking a pine tree) and orange blossom water to flavor their pastries. East Indians flavor their desserts and drinks with rose water. We are depriving ourselves of some interesting sensory experiences!

Henning proposed that simple odors must be located on the surfaces of the prism. They could not be located somewhere inside the prism. Thus a simple odor could not be partly burned, partly spicy, and partly fruity be-

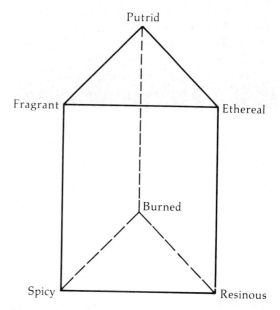

Figure 12.1 Smell prism devised by Henning.

Cover the diagram on the bottom before you begin. Here
is the front face of Henning's prism, taken from Figure 12.1.
A few of the odors have been filled in to provide guidelines.
From your knowledge of various odors, see how many of
the following you can add: roses, orange blossoms, ginger,
thyme, turpentine, jasmine, cloves, cedarwood, strawberry, spruce, and vanilla.

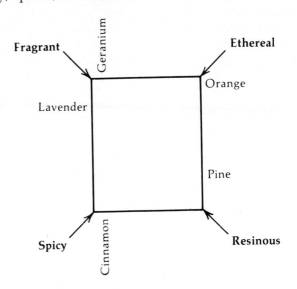

ANSWERS:

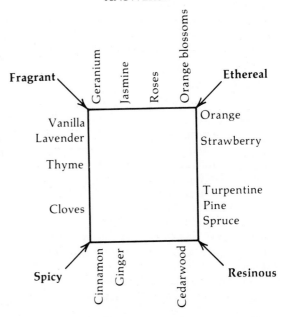

cause this combination of odors would be located inside the prism. However, a *complex* odor (such as burned apple–cinnamon pie) could be represented inside the prism. Cain (1978a) discusses some of the problems with Henning's model. For example, people differ enormously in their odor judgments. One person might agree with the system, but another might disagree strongly.

Amoore (1970) has proposed a different classification system. Whereas Henning's system emphasized perceivers' reactions to odors, Amoore's system focuses on the chemical structure of odors. According to Amoore's **stereochemical theory,** odorous molecules have definite shapes that determine the kind of odor we smell. For example, minty fragrances have somewhat oval molecules. Fragrances that resemble mothballs are much rounder. He proposed that receptor sites are related to the shapes of molecules, the same way lock shapes are related to key shapes.

Amoore asked people to compare certain fragrances with five different standards. Fragrances judged to smell like the standards also resembled them in their chemical structure. Amoore suggested a limited number of primary odors. Table 12.1 shows one version of the list of primaries, together with examples. In a more recent version, Amoore (1977) has expanded the total number of human primary odors to 32.

Amoore's theory is controversial. For example, Schiffman (1974) obtained judgments about various odors and found they were often vastly different for two molecules of similar size and shape. Furthermore, Wright (1982) noted that two nearly identical complex molecules had extremely different fragrances, one smelling like spearmint and the other like caraway. Thus, any correspondence between the shape of a molecule and its smell is very complex. Of course, these two approaches are not the only attempts to classify odorants. There have been at least six other general classifications proposed since the 1700s (Amoore, 1977).

In summary, a satisfactory method for classifying odors has not yet been developed. Henning's model of six primary odors does not match everyone's perceptual experiences. Amoore's theory—that molecular shape is closely related to odor—is too simple, and there are too many exceptions. Vision has its primary colors and taste, as you will learn, has its primary sensations, but odors are too complex to be organized into any current classification system.

Olfactory System

Figure 12.2 illustrates the anatomy of the nasal (or nose) area. First, look at the region called the **nasal cavity,** the hollow space behind each nostril. Air containing odors reaches the nasal cavity through two routes. Most obviously, we sniff and inhale to bring in the outside air. However, air can also come up from the back of the throat when we chew or drink. Trace the pathway from the mouth, up the throat, to the nasal cavity. Notice the importance of this throat passage the next time you are eating food with a strong odor. Plug your nostrils and notice its blandness. Suddenly release your fingers. A current of air will quickly flow from your mouth, carrying odor molecules with it, up the throat and into the nasal cavity. Instantly, you will experience a burst of flavor.

Notice the three bones neatly lined up in the nasal cavity, called the **turbinate bones.** (Think about how these bones would cause *turbulence* in the airstream, similar to rocks in a river.) Notice that they are positioned so that they force most of the air you breathe in

Table 12.1 Primary Odors Suggested by Amoore

Odor	Example
Camphoraceous	Mothballs
Pungent	Vinegar
Floral	Roses
Ethereal	Dry-cleaning fluid
Minty	Peppermint stick
Musky	Musk perfume
Putrid	Rotten egg

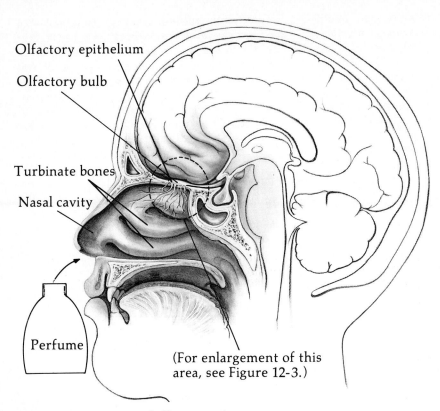

Olfactory epithelium

Olfactory bulb

Turbinate bones

Nasal cavity

Perfume

(For enlargement of this
area, see Figure 12-3.)

Figure 12.2   Anatomy of olfactory system.

to go down your throat. Thus only a little of
the air will make its way up to the smell receptors at the top of the cavity.

As you can imagine, the hidden location
of the smell receptors makes them difficult to
study. Also, as will be discussed shortly, their
hidden location guarantees that only a small
portion of the inhaled molecules will reach
this surface. However, the air that does travel
up to the top of the cavity has most of the
dust cleaned away by the time it arrives.

At the top of the nasal cavity is the olfactory epithelium. The word *epithelium* refers to
skin, so **olfactory epithelium** is the kind of
skin you smell with! The size of the olfactory
epithelium is about 2.5 cm² for each nostril
(Engen, 1982). The olfactory epithelium contains the smell receptor cells. These are illus-

trated in Figure 12.3, which is an enlargement
of a portion of Figure 12.2.

Let's examine these receptors. Unlike the
receptors in vision, hearing, and the skin
senses, smell has only one kind of receptor.
There are about 5 million for each nostril, a
number that sounds impressive until Engen
(1982) points out that dogs have 20 times as
many smell receptors. An important feature
of each receptor is the tiny **cilia,** or hairlike
fringes, protruding out of each receptor cell
into the mucus. (**Mucus** is the thick secretion
you normally have in small qualities but is
produced too abundantly when you have a
cold.) It seems highly likely that the action
between the odorant and the receptors takes
place on these cilia (Lancet, 1984). Notice,
then, the direct contact between the stimulus

and the receptor in the case of smell. In vision, the cornea and other structures block direct contact, as does the eardrum in hearing and the epidermis in touch (Gibbons, 1986); in smell, there is no such barrier.

One important theme of this book is that many attributes of the perceptual systems are similar, and this is generally true. However, the receptors for smell differ from the others with respect to a second attribute in addition to their direct contact with the stimulus. The neurons in the other systems are irreplaceable. In fact, this is true of the mammalian nervous system in general. That is, a neuron develops early in life, performs its functions, and then dies—without being replaced. However, receptor cells in the olfactory epithelium are continually formed throughout your life. Each functions for less than 8 weeks and is then replaced (Gesteland, 1982).

The smell receptors are the most important receptors in the olfactory epithelium, but these patches of skin also store a second kind

of receptor, which is not illustrated in Figure 12.3. The **trigeminal nerve** has free nerve endings that extend into the olfactory epithelium, and these endings register sensations important in both smell and taste. As Cain (1981) describes the role of these receptors,

> These register the "feel" of cigarette smoke during inhalation, the "bite" of chili pepper, the "burn" of ammonia, the coolness of menthol, and so on. . . . They may lack the qualitative range and richness of odors or tastes, but can nonetheless add much to the enjoyment of eating, drinking, and smoking, and even of fresh air. Crisp, invigorating air often gains its sensory character from concentrations of ozone sufficient to trigger common chemical sensations (p. 109).

Let's return to Figure 12.3. Notice that a structure located above the receptor cells is labeled the olfactory bulb. The **olfactory bulb** performs the first processing on the signals

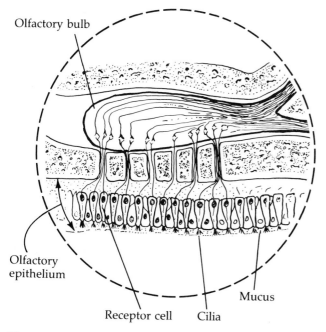

Olfactory bulb

Olfactory epithelium

Receptor cell   Cilia   Mucus

Figure 12.3 Enlargement of part of olfactory system.

from the smell receptors. Figure 12.3 illustrates that the endings of the receptor cells synapse with new neurons in the olfactory bulb. The olfactory bulb is actually the enlarged ending of the olfactory lobes at the front of the brain, so your brain is more intimately and directly involved in smell than in the other senses (Engen, 1982). There are several pathways for the neurons out of the olfactory bulb, including the olfactory cortex and the hypothalamus, a structure important in the regulation of food intake. The details of these pathways are still unclear.

Summary: Sensory Aspects of Smell

1. Smell and taste are called the chemical senses; there is far less research on smell than on vision or audition.
2. For substances to be smelled they must be volatile and have a molecular weight between 15 and 300.
3. The search for a classification system has dominated research in smell.
4. One classification system, proposed by Henning, shows a prism-shaped structure in which smells are defined in terms of six basic odors.
5. Amoore proposed a classification system in which the shape of the odor molecule determines the odor.
6. Neither Hemming's nor Amoore's system appears perfectly satisfactory.
7. The nasal cavity is the hollow space inside the nose, and the three turbinate bones are lined up in the nasal cavity.
8. The olfactory epithelium at the top of the nasal cavity contains the smell receptor cells. These cells are in direct contact with the stimulus, and they are able to renew themselves periodically, unlike the cells in the other sensory systems discussed so far. The cilia of the receptor cells make contact with the odorants.
9. The olfactory epithelium also contains the free nerve endings, which register sensation of pungency, such as the burning sensation of chili, ammonia, and other chemicals.
10. The olfactory bulb processes information

from the smell receptors, and information is then transmitted to the olfactory cortex and other areas.

OLFACTORY PROCESSES

This section discusses several important aspects of olfactory perception. The first topic is smell thresholds for both detection and discrimination. The second topic covers adaptation, an issue familiar from other chapters. The third topic is an in-depth exploration of the recognition of odors. Our final topic in this section is a brief discussion of constancy and illusion.

Thresholds

As you'll recall, a **detection threshold** is a boundary point at which something is reported half the time. In the case of smell, the detection threshold would be the concentration of a chemical for which a person says, "Yes, I smell it" half the time and "No, I don't smell it" half the time. For example, a person may be able to detect a chemical that has a concentration of 11.0 mg of the chemical per liter of air. Detection thresholds can be measured by the standard techniques discussed in Chapter 2 as well as by some modified techniques sensitivity can also be assessed with signal-detection techniques (Semb, 1968).

Detection thresholds are difficult to measure. Cain (1978a) discusses the various kinds of equipment invented for presenting smells. Many have been based on the **olfactometer**, which literally translates as "smell-measurer"; an early version is shown in Figure 12.4. The bent ends of the tubes are inserted into the nostrils. The large tube contains the odor stimulus being studied. The kind of equipment used has an enormous influence on the threshold (Cain, 1978b), so different researchers may report vastly different thresholds for the same chemical.

The situation is even more complicated because it is difficult to know just how much

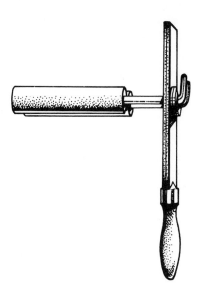

Figure 12.4 Early example of olfactometer.

of a chemical substance actually reaches the smell receptors. Mozell (1971) points out that many molecules that enter the nose will be absorbed by the nose lining before they reach the receptors. Also, you already know that the turbinate bones effectively block many molecules from reaching the receptors. In fact, Mozell estimates that in a normal breath, approximately 2% of the odorous molecules entering the nose will reach the olfactory epithelium. The next time you smell a skunk or a particularly repelling locker room, be grateful that only a small fraction of those odor molecules can reach your smell receptors!

Incidentally, it should be mentioned that people's "sniffing habits" have been examined, and these have implications for threshold measurement. First, individuals differ markedly in their sniffing patterns when they are sampling the odorants (Laing, 1982). Furthermore, people seem to obtain the necessary information on the first sniff, and additional sniffs serve merely to confirm the original judgments (Laing, 1983).

Detection Thresholds

Humans are impressively sensitive to some odors. For example, when *National Geographic* was preparing its "smell survey" (Gibbons, 1986), it distributed several scratch-and-sniff panels to readers. Humans are so sensitive to one of these unidentified odorants that the publishers required less than 1 ounce of the substance to encapsulate it on the approximately 11 million copies of the survey! Several thresholds for different odorants appear in Table 12.2. To place some of these impressive thresholds in perspective, let's translate the threshold for the musky odorant into more concrete terms. A peanut weighs about 1 g. Imagine dividing that peanut into 10 *billion* parts and dispersing one of those parts through 1 liter of air. This invisible fragment of a peanut still weighs more than the amount of that musky chemical that you can detect in a liter of air!

Naturally, humans are not that sensitive to all smells. For example, we need more than 4 mg of carbon tetrachloride per liter of air to detect that odorant. We are also remarkably insensitive to the smell of some dangerous gases, such as carbon monoxide. Furthermore, humans are less sensitive to odors than some animals. For example, dogs are about 100 times more sensitive than humans to some smells (Gibbons, 1986; Mozell, 1971).

Table 12.2   Some Representative Thresholds for Odorants

Odorant	Smell	Concentration at Threshold (in mg/L air)
Carbon tetrachloride	Sweet	4.533
Amyl acetate	Banana oil	0.039
Hydrogen sulfide	Rotten eggs	0.00018
Citral	Lemonlike	0.000003
Ethyl mercaptan	Decayed cabbage	0.00000066
Camphor	Mothballs	0.000000113
Trinitro-tertiary-butyl xylene	Musk	0.000000075

Source: Based on Engen, 1982; Wenger, Jones, & Jones, 1956.

Therefore we use bloodhounds to track down villains and pigs to sniff for gourmet truffles. Experienced police dogs only require a sniff at a fingerprint to search for a thief (Wright, 1982). In those situations, animal noses are superior to human noses. Still, the average human is better at detecting odors than is a physical sensor such as a smoke detector (Engen, 1982).

Many factors influence thresholds. First, it is important to consider the wide individual differences among people in their smell sensitivity. We are accustomed to the fact that people differ in their visual sensitivity. However, people also differ in their sensitivity to odors. Try Demonstration 12.2 to illustrate some individual differences in smell sensitivity. Individual differences may be in the range of 20 to 1 (Rabin & Cain, 1986). Thus, if you test a group of people, the "best smeller" might detect 0.05 mg of a substance per liter of air, whereas the "worst smeller" might re-

---

Demonstration 12.2

Individual Differences in Smell Sensitivity

For this demonstration you will need paper, tweezers, perfume or shaving lotion, and five containers. Cut a strip about 1 cm wide from the piece of paper. Cut this strip into pieces so that you have tiny pieces 1 cm, 2 cm, 3 cm, and 4 cm long. Take one container, fill it with water, and add one drop of perfume or shaving lotion. With the tweezers, dip each of the tiny pieces in the scented water, swirl it around, and place it in one of the four remaining containers. Place the containers in order, from strongest odor (longest piece of paper) to weakest odor (shortest piece). Ask four friends to sniff the containers, progressing from weakest to strongest, and identify which container contains the threshold concentration of the scent. See whether they differ substantially in their choices. (Incidentally, you may have to adjust the concentrations if your scent is too strong or too weak.) Save the containers so that you can use them again in Demonstration 12.5.

quire 20 times as much, or 1.0 mg, before it can be detected.

Did you notice any sex differences in Demonstration 12.2? Several studies have demonstrated that females are more sensitive to odorants than males (Koelega & Koster, 1974). Furthermore, the sex differences were larger for odorants that might be considered biologically meaningful. We will discuss sex differences further in a later section of this chapter.

Let's review this information on detection thresholds. Sensitivity to odorants depends upon the equipment used to measure thresholds, the substance studied, and the species. There are substantial individual differences among people in their smell sensitivities, and there are also sex differences.

Difference thresholds. In the section on detection thresholds we saw that the nose can detect impressively tiny concentrations of certain substances. Our difference thresholds are generally much less impressive. As you will recall from Chapter 2, the **difference threshold** is the difference between two stimuli that a person can just barely tell apart. For example, one study discussed by Mozell (1971) examined acetic acid, which has a vinegar odor. Two samples of acetic acid must differ by about 26% to be detected. Thus, you should be able to tell the difference between 100 g of vinegar and 126 g of vinegar.

The ability to detect a difference of 26% might sound reasonably sensitive until you compare the difference thresholds for smell with similar thresholds for other senses. For example, people can tell the difference between two sounds if they differ by as little as 0.3%, a difference threshold roughly 100 times as sensitive.

Why are the difference thresholds relatively crude? As Wright (1982) points out, difference judgments are generally not important for biological survival. It's difficult to imagine a situation in which a person is more likely to survive because of the ability to tell that one odorant is stronger than another. However, difference thresholds obviously

have their application in cooking and eating and other tasks of civilized life.

Adaptation

You have probably had this experience. You walk into a room in which onions have been frying, and the odor is overpowering. If you stay in the room for several minutes, however, the smell seems fainter and fainter. After a while, you hardly notice any odor at all. You have experienced **adaptation,** the temporary loss of sensitivity as a result of continued stimulation (Beets, 1978). The power of adaptation is particularly impressive if you leave the room in which you have become adapted to an odor and then return to it. The odor is once again overwhelming. Try Demonstration 12.3 to illustrate the adaptation process.

Adaptation has both advantages and disadvantages in everyday life. If you are sitting in a room crowded with sweaty bodies, be thankful for adaptation! Adaptation will also reduce the odor from a neighboring chemical plant. On the other hand, perfumes seem to fade after a few minutes, and this property may be due to our noses as well as to the perfumes. A burning smell from an automobile may be unnoticeable after a short period of driving, when it may be a warning sign for electrical problems. More dangerously, we may not notice a poisonous gas if we have adapted to the odor.

Cain (1978b) points out that adaptation reduces our sensitivity to an odor, but it does not eliminate the sensitivity completely. We still smell *something*. On the average, the perceived magnitude of an odor decays at the initial rate of about 2.5% each second. After less than a minute, adaptation is essentially complete. At this point, the perceived magnitude of an odor is about 30% of the initial magnitude. Thus the perceived magnitude certainly does not decrease to zero. Nonetheless, a 70% reduction is impressive.

What physiological explanations can account for this enormous reduction in sensitivity? The answer is not clear. One nice, in-

Demonstration 12.3 *Adaptation*	Find a substance with a strong odor, such as an onion, nail polish remover, shaving lotion, or carbon paper. Place it near your nose as you read your book for the next 10 minutes. Notice how much fainter the odor seems after that time. Remove the substance for the next 5 minutes, then bring it back for a final whiff. At this point the odor should seem just about as strong as it did when you first smelled it.

tuitive answer might be that the receptors simply become tired after high levels of stimulation. Olfactory receptors probably play some part in adaptation, yet the greater part of adaptation seems to occur at higher processing levels. Mechanisms for adaptation are probably in the brain, but these have not yet been identified. Try repeating Demonstration 12.3, but plug your left nostril as completely as possible. After 2 minutes, quickly plug the right nostril and unplug the left one. You will find that the sensitivity in the left nostril is fairly low, even though the smell receptors in that nostril received only minimal stimulation when it was plugged. Some mechanism must have ''turned off'' your sensitivity at a level more advanced than the receptors.

We have seen that adaptation is the temporary loss of sensitivity to an odor when that odor is presented for several minutes. This process is often called self-adaptation to distinguish it from another process called cross-adaptation. **Cross-adaptation** means that exposure to one odor influences the threshold for other odors. Have you experienced cross-adaptation? When someone has been frying onions, are you less sensitive to the odor of frying garlic? When you have been smelling one perfume at a cosmetics counter, do you then notice another perfume less? Does exposure to an acid in a chemistry lab reduce the odor of another acid?

A typical study concerning cross-adaptation was conducted by Engen (1963), who studied chemicals in the alcohol family. He first presented either an odorless liquid or an alcohol liquid. Then he presented a different

alcohol liquid and measured people's thresholds. Engen found that the thresholds for these new alcohol liquids were much higher when the people had first smelled an alcohol liquid rather than the odorless liquid. That is, exposure to one alcohol reduced their sensitivity to another alcohol.

Recall from the beginning of the chapter that many researchers have tried to devise some method of grouping similar odorants. It would seem that cross-adaptation should be a useful tool. However, Engen (1982) and other researchers have concluded that no clear relationship exists between the extent of cross-adaptation and the similarity of the odorous qualities.

▶ **IN-DEPTH:**
RECOGNITION OF ODORS

How good are humans at recognizing odors? If you were presented with a common odorant, such as vinegar or an orange, could you unfailingly supply its name? If several odorants were presented at the beginning of an experimental session, could you reliably indicate 10 minutes later which ones you had smelled earlier and which were new? Finally, how accurate would you be in identifying other people based only on their odors? Let's first examine the recognition of familiar odors and then move on to the recognition of humans on the basis of their odors.

Recognition of Familiar Odors

Try Demonstration 12.4 to illustrate an informal variation of experiments that assess the

---

Demonstration 12.4

Recognizing Smells

For this demonstration you will need about a dozen odorous substances. Use your imagination to find them. Some suggestions are pencil shavings, a green leaf, mud, partly chewed gum, carbon paper, cinnamon, ground coffee, cheese, onion, and mustard. Take each of the substances and cover it with a sheet of paper. (If you can find opaque containers, they would be even better.) Invite several friends to see if they can identify the odors. See which odors are easiest and which are most difficult. Also notice whether your friends differ in their overall accuracy.

---

recognition of familiar odors. A typical study on this subject was conducted by Desor and Beauchamp (1974), who presented people with common, everyday odors such as fried liver, popcorn, and motor oil. People were fairly accurate for odors such as coffee, paint, banana, and chocolate. However, fewer than 20% of the participants correctly identified smells such as cigar, cat feces, ham, and sawdust. Furthermore, people were less accurate on items they rated unfamiliar. It seemed that people made mistakes because they could not give the correct label, not because they confused the odors with other odors.

Desor and Beauchamp also tested the effects of practice. In the second part of the study people were trained on 32 different odors. Every time they smelled a particular odor, the name was supplied if they did not spontaneously supply it. They were trained extensively until they could identify all the odors correctly on two successive trials. Five days later they returned to the laboratory; their performance was nearly perfect. Furthermore, these same people later learned to correctly identify 64 different odors. When people have had practice, the recognition of odors can be impressive.

How much information do we need to identify an odor? When I try a variant of Demonstration 12.4 in the classroom, students typically sniff each mystery odorant several times, as if each additional whiff will provide more clues. However, Laing (1986) has demonstrated that odors can generally be iden-

tified with a single sniff. Furthermore, we don't require a lengthy inhalation to reach the goal; the shortest sniff that can be physically achieved (less than half a second) seems to be perfectly sufficient.

Often, though, we smell a particular odorant and are certain that the smell is familiar, although the name escapes us. For example, if your friends tried Demonstration 12.4, they might have experienced this phenomenon with pencil shavings or carbon paper. The ability to recognize an odorant as familiar, combined with the inability to recover its name, has been called the **"tip-of-the-nose" phenomenon** (Lawless & Engen, 1977). It resembles the more familiar "tip-of-the-tongue" phenomenon in which we *know* that we know the word for which we are searching, yet the word remains perched on the tip of the tongue, refusing to be spoken.

We mentioned earlier that females are somewhat more sensitive than males to various odors; they have lower thresholds. Similarly, females are more accurate on odor-identification tasks. For example, Cain (1982) discovered that females are better at identifying the name of stereotypically feminine substances such as baby powder and nail-polish remover. Furthermore, they are better at identifying virtually all foods, which are presumably neutral with respect to gender associations. Finally—and most surprising—females are also better at identifying stereotypically masculine substances such as cigar butts and machine oil. It's not clear whether females' superiority in odor identification is due to superior discrimination abilities, to deliberate attempts to learn about odors (for example, in food preparation), or to some other factor (Cain, 1980).

The kinds of tasks discussed so far require the participant to supply a name for an odorant. In contrast, another kind of task asks people to judge whether a particular odor is familiar; no labels are required. Let's consider a study by Engen and Ross (1973), who presented an odorant to participants, then several seconds later presented a pair of odorants. The participants were instructed to indicate which of the two odorants was "old" and which was "new." The participants' accuracy was only about 70%, which is particularly dismal when that performance is compared with an accuracy of 99.7% for visual stimuli (Shepard, 1967).

What happens with the passage of time? Visual recognition memory declines rapidly. Surprisingly, however, there was little further decline in the recognition of odors (Engen & Ross, 1973). Even after a year, there was only an additional drop of 5%. A full 12 months later, people are still better than the 50% chance level in selecting which member of the pair they had smelled before.

Let's examine one other study in this area in more detail. Michael Rabin and William Cain (1984) of Yale University studied familiar odorants such as chocolate, leather, popcorn, and soy sauce. Participants in this study first rated the familiarity of these odorants and tried to supply labels for them. Then, after 10 minutes, 1 day, or 7 days, the participants were assigned a second task. They were supplied with 40 items, 20 of which were among the "old" odorants and 20 of which were "new." They were instructed to respond either "old" or "new" to each item, and they were also asked to rate their confidence about each decision. These confidence ratings allowed the researchers to perform a signal-detection analysis of the data.

There were a number of interesting findings in the study. First, the average accuracy in supplying a correct label for odorants in the first phase of the study was 41%. If "near-miss" answers were also included—for example, when a participant supplied the name "raspberry" for "strawberry"—accuracy rose to 63%. However, we are primarily concerned with participants' ability to judge whether an odorant was old or new. Their accuracay was assessed by the signal-detection index d', which was discussed in Chapter 2. When d' is used in memory experiments, high d' values indicate high accuracy. After a 10-minute delay, d' had an average value across all conditions of about 2.25. After a 1-day delay, d' was 0.2, and it fell to about 1.6 after 7 days.

Are people more accurate in recognizing whether they have smelled a particular odorant if they were able to supply a name for the substance? Figure 12.5 illustrates these results. As you can see, when the d' values were averaged across all three retention intervals, accuracy was substantially higher when people had been able to recall the accurate name.

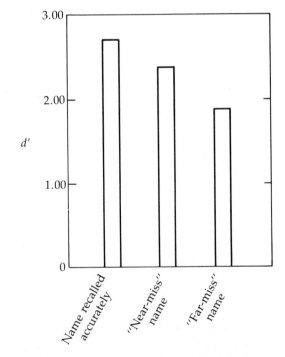

Figure 12.5 Accuracy of odor recognition as function of whether name was recalled accurately, was a near miss, or was a far miss. (Based on Rabin & Cain, 1984.)

It was lower when they had supplied a "near-miss" label, and it was much lower when the label was a "far miss" (such as "paint thinner" for soy sauce).

Furthermore, not surprisingly, recognition accuracy depended upon familiarity. The d' values were much higher for substances that had been rated high in familiarity than for substances that had been rated low.

Rabin and Cain's (1984) study demonstrates for odors a principle that had previously been demonstrated on visual and verbal material. As they write,

> A familiar odor, like a familiar face, connects with existing information in memory and, as a result of interacting with that information, may leave a very discriminable memory trace. The degree to which an odor connects with experience, as indexed by rated familiarity, or label quality . . . appears to be directly related to subsequent recognition performance (p. 325).

Recognition of Humans

Can we recognize other humans on the basis of their odor? Studies attempting to answer this question have focused on two issues: (1) Can people identify the gender of other humans on the basis of their smell? and (2) Can people identify specific other humans on the basis of their smell?

One of the first studies on gender identification was conducted by Russell (1976), who asked college students not to wash themselves for 24 hours prior to the experiment, then to wear a plain white T-shirt for the next 24 hours. The dirty T-shirts were then collected and placed in individual containers. Each person was presented with three containers. One held the person's own T-shirt, another held an unfamiliar female's T-shirt, and a third held an unfamiliar male's T-shirt. One interesting finding was that 22 out of 29 people correctly identified their own T-shirts, a result significantly better than chance. However, people were also accurate in guessing gender. In an additional test, 22 out of 29 correctly identified which of the two other T-shirts belonged to the male and which

belonged to the female. However, other subsequent research on guessing gender from odor has produced mixed results (Doty, Green, Ram, & Yankell, 1982; Doty, Orndorff, Leyden, and Kligman, 1978).

Richard Porter and his colleagues at Vanderbilt University have been exploring whether people can recognize their relatives on the basis of their odors. In the first study Porter and Moore (1981) asked 12 pairs of siblings to wear white T-shirts to bed for three nights. The following morning, each child was presented with two containers. One held the child's sibling's T-shirt, and the other held a T-shirt that had been worn by an unrelated child. The children were instructed to guess which of the two containers held their sibling's T-shirt. The results showed that 19 out of 24 children guessed correctly. Nine mothers agreed to participate in the study as well. Since each mother had two children, these mothers made 18 comparisons; they were correct in 17 of the 18 comparisons, a highly significant result. In a further test parents correctly identified which T-shirt belonged to which of two siblings in 16 out of 18 comparisons. Thus, parents can distinguish between their own children on the basis of smell, as well as distinguishing between their own children and strangers.

Richard Porter, Jennifer Cernoch, and Joseph McLaughlin (1983) extended these findings to the recognition of newborns. Sixteen out of 20 mothers guessed which T-shirt had been worn by their newborn, who was between 2 and 6 days old. Furthermore, even mothers who had limited exposure to their newborns (because the babies had been delivered by Caesarean section) were more accurate than chance in identifying their babies' T-shirts. These studies demonstrate impressive accuracy, given that our sense of smell is relatively poorly developed (Halpin, 1986.)

As you can see, the research on recognition of odors supplies us with many interesting individual pieces of information, but no overall pattern so far. The following factors are related to accuracy in identifying familiar odors: (a) nature of the substance, (b) amount of practice, (c) gender of the person making the judgments, (d) supplying an accurate label, and (e) apparent familiarity of odorant. With respect to the question of humans recognizing other humans, we are sometimes accurate in identifying gender on the basis of body odor. Furthermore, people seem to be fairly accurate (although certainly not perfectly accurate) in identifying their relatives on the basis of body odors. It seems likely that research in all these areas—but especially human odor—has been inhibited by the fact that smell is indeed the Cinderella sister in perception. If you were a researcher, would you prefer to tell people that you were studying the columnar organization of the visual cortex or that you were asking people to sniff dirty T-shirts? Our ignorance about olfaction is unfortunate because there are important potential applications of research on odor identification in areas such as food technology, the perfume industry, and even family relationships. ∎

Constancy and Illusion

Constancy and illusion are such popular topics in the area of visual perception that they merited an entire chapter in this book. In contrast, there has been little research on constancy and illusion in connection with smell.

The major investigation of odor constancy was conducted by Teghtsoonian, Teghtsoonian, Berglund, and Berglund (1978). They wondered if stronger sniffs produce stronger smells. These authors therefore trained the participants in their study to breathe odors at two different "sniff vigors," one twice as strong as the other. Then the participants sniffed various odors using either strong or weak sniff vigors. Each time they made magnitude estimations by supplying a number to correspond with the strength of the sensation.

Figure 12.6 shows the magnitude estimations for different concentrations of one odor. People supply larger numbers for greater concentrations; thus they can detect differences. What is more interesting, however, is that at each concentration the estimates are almost identical for the weak and

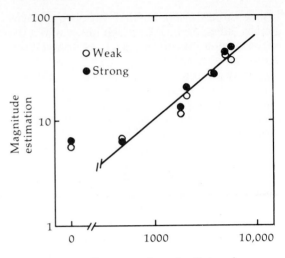

Figure 12.6 Magnitude estimation as function of odor concentration and sniff vigor. (From R. Teghtsoonian, M. Teghtsoonian, B. Berglund, & U. Berglund, Invariance of odor strength with sniff vigor: An olfactory analogue to size constancy, *Journal of Experimental Psychology: Human Perception and Performance*, 4 (1978), 144–152, Figure 4. Copyright 1978 by the American Psychological Association. Reprinted by permission of the author.)

the strong sniff vigors. The two dots are actually touching each other at six of the seven concentrations. People therefore supply equivalent judgments for a weak sniff and a sniff that is twice as strong, even though the stronger sniff presumably brings in twice as many molecules.

These researchers propose that the results can be explained by odor constancy. **Odor constancy** means that the perceived strength of an odor remains the same despite variations in sniff vigor. Odor constancy is therefore similar to the visual constancies. For example, in size constancy, the size of the object remains the same despite variations in distance. Teghtsoonian and his colleagues suggest that information about the number of odor molecules is combined with information about sniff vigor so that the resulting perception of odor strength remains constant. Try

Demonstration 12.5 to see whether you can find evidence for odor constancy.

We discussed visual illusions in detail. It is also possible to produce a smell illusion (O'Mahony, 1978). At the end of a television show about the chemical senses, viewers were told that it was possible to transmit smell by sound. The lecturer presented an elaborate description that involved vibrating molecules and even the basics of Fourier analysis. Viewers were specifically told that when a particular sound was presented, they would smell a pleasant country fragrance. They were urged to write to the television station, reporting their reaction. The station received a total of 179 responses. Twenty-four respondents reported that they did not smell anything. (This number would clearly be an underestimate because those who smelled nothing would be much less likely to respond.) The remaining 155 viewers reported smelling hay, grass, flowers, trees, and fruits!

This chapter has devoted several pages to the description of the stimulus for smell and several additional pages to a discussion of the olfactory apparatus. Themes 2 and 3 in this book emphasize the importance of both stimuli and sensory equipment in perception. Theme 4 stresses the importance of cognitive factors in perception, but this theme seems to have fewer applications in the area of smell than in the other senses. However, it is clear that smell illusions arise from cognitive processes. When there is no stimulus and the sensory receptors cannot be stimulated, the suggestions about smell give rise to expectations. These expectations can lead us to report odors that have not even been presented!

Summary: Olfactory Processes

1. It is difficult to measure detection thresholds for smell. However, detection thresholds are extremely low for some substances.
2. Factors influencing detection thresholds include kind of odorant, type of equipment used to measure thresholds, species, individual differences, and gender.
3. Difference thresholds are relatively large in everyday life.
4. Adaptation typically involves a 70% reduction in sensitivity. The explanation involves higher neural levels in addition to the receptors.
5. In cross-adaptation, exposure to one odor influences the threshold for other, similar odors. Cross-adaptation is not clearly related to the amount of similarity between odorants.
6. Some odors can be readily recognized, whereas others cannot. Practice influences accuracy, but the length of the inhalation does not. People report having a "tip-of-the-nose" phenomenon when they are unable to identify an odor.
7. There are sex differences in the accuracy of odor identification.

Demonstration 12.5

Odor Constancy

Using the containers with the 2-cm, 3-cm, and 4-cm strips from Demonstration 12.2, take a large sniff of the 2-cm container, so that you estimate you are taking in about twice as much air as normal. Now take a normal sniff of each of the three containers. Try to identify which of the three has the same intensity as your first large sniff. If you have odor constancy, the 2-cm container should smell constant in its intensity, despite changes in sniff vigor. If you have no odor constancy, the 4-cm container may be your choice. If you have partial constancy, you may choose the 3-cm container.

8. People are only about 70% accurate in identifying whether they smelled a particular odor several seconds earlier, but their accuracy does not decline drastically with the passage of several days.

9. People are more accurate in identifying an odor if they have supplied an accurate label and if the odor seems familiar.

10. People can sometimes identify gender on the basis of body odor.

11. People seem to be fairly accurate in identifying their relatives on the basis of body odors.

12. People seem to show odor constancy; that is, the perceived strength of an odor remains the same despite variations in sniff vigor.

13. Under certain conditions smell illusions can be demonstrated in which people report certain smells that were never presented.

APPLICATIONS OF OLFACTORY RESEARCH

Research in smell has particular importance in four areas: pollution control, medicine, perfume manufacturing, and communication among members of a species. Other applications, including the use of police dogs in criminal cases and the breeding of salmon, are discussed by Wright (1982).

Odor Pollution Control

Odor pollution means that unpleasant odors escape from a source and linger in the atmosphere (Moskowitz, 1978a). Common sources of odor pollution include animal-rendering plants, paper mills, oil refineries, and numerous other industries (Cain, 1978b). Odor pollution can occur on a smaller scale within your home as well as in a community. It is an important issue, not only because it affects the quality of life but also because air pollution can damage olfactory receptors (Halpern, 1982). There are other health hazards as well, such as allergies, nausea, and breathing disorders (Wright, 1982).

How can odor pollution be controlled? Cain (1978b) discusses several kinds of procedures, such as burning the waste, adsorption with charcoal, and chemical conversion. One of the most common methods of trying to control odor pollution is odor mixture. In an **odor mixture** two odors that do not cause a chemical reaction are presented at the same time. When you spray a room with an air freshener to get rid of the smell of boiled cabbage, you are actually making an odor mixture. Think about what happens when we make mixtures of visual or auditory stimuli. Remember, for example, that when we mix a yellow dye with a blue dye, we get a green dye—we can no longer sense the yellow and the blue components. When we mix several notes in music, however, we usually *do* hear the individual components.

When we mix odors, it is very difficult to predict just what the result will smell like (Gregson, 1984). In some cases we find that the result is ideal for odor pollution control because one smell masks another. In **masking,** one odor conceals an odor so completely that it cannot be detected. We hope that the air freshener will mask the cabbage odor, instead of the cabbage odor masking the air freshener!

More often, the two odors blend together. In a **blend** the mixture resembles both components, and it is nearly impossible to separate the two parts. A blend of odors is therefore like the visual experience of a blend of colored dyes. On other occasions the two odors in some other mixtures can sometimes be perceived separately, like the mixture of notes in music. Finally, some mixtures of odors produce an interesting alternation of odors. You smell first one odor, then the other. Try Demonstration 12.6 to see whether the mixtures produce masking, blends, separate odors, or alternation.

So far we have seen that the *quality* of the odor mixture is unpredictable. How about the *quantity*, or the intensity of the odor? When two odors are added together, how strong does the result smell? Laing, Panhuber, Willcox, and Pittman (1984) confirmed earlier results that the mixture's intensity is interme-

Demonstration 12.6 *Odor Mixtures*	For this demonstration you will need some perfume or shaving lotion and, if possible, some air freshener and several odorous substances such as some of the stronger ones used in Demonstration 12.4 or strong-smelling food. Permeate the air with the perfume or shaving lotion, then stand different distances away from one of the odorous substances. Notice whether the distance influences how the mixture smells. Do you sometimes observe a masking, sometimes a blend, and other times separate odors or alternation? Repeat this with other odorous substances. After the perfume or shaving lotion has faded, try the demonstration once more with air freshener.

diate between the intensities of the two components. Thus if you mix a strong air freshener with a weak burnt-toast odor, the intensity of the mixture should be moderate.

We tend to think only of the negative side of unpleasant odors, and certainly most of the consequences of unpleasant odors are negative. However, there are some areas in which unpleasant odors are useful. For example, an unpleasant odor can be added to an odorless but poisonous gas so that gas leaks can be detected readily.

Medicine

The importance of olfaction in medical diagnosis has a long history, and physicians are still urged to pay attention to how their patients *smell*, as well as how they look and sound (Smith, Smith, & Levinson, 1982). For example, the breath odor of a person with stomach cancer may resemble fermentation. Typhoid was often diagnosed by its smell, which was similar to baking bread. German measles resembled plucked feathers, and yellow fever smelled like a butcher shop (Gibbons, 1986). More recently, it has been noted that schizophrenics may emit a distinctive odor (Wright, 1982).

Obviously, laboratory tests and more refined medical techniques have greatly reduced the frequency with which physicians diagnose illness on the basis of smell. Gib-

bons quotes Lewis Goldfrank, M.D., chief of emergency services at Bellevue Hospital, New York City, who nevertheless maintains that smells can provide valuable information: "We get people we don't know, or who can't speak, so we've got to use all our senses. Odor is important. The breath of a diabetic in coma smells sweet, like apples, although a fruity odor can also mean starvation. The odor of garlic may mean a spaghetti dinner or arsenic poisoning. Turpentine in the urine smells like violets. The odor of peanuts may tell you a kid has swallowed a rodenticide" (p. 351).

Perfume Manufacturing

During 1981 more than $2 *billion* was spent to purchase perfumes and other fragrances for women. Brady (1982) describes how the French fashion designer Yves Saint Laurent spent several hundred thousand dollars to promote a new fragrance. He invited prominent people in the fashion circle and flew them to Paris for an evening of dance by Nureyev, followed by dinner at Maxim's. In terms of publicity and finances, perfume manufacturing is clearly the most important application of olfaction research.

A fascinating section on perfumery appears in the *Handbook of Perception* (Moskowitz, 1978a). One portion describes the development of a new fragrance, which may eventually be used as an additive to soaps, creams, or cosmetics, as well as a perfume. In the early stages the perfumer must consult the **fragrance library,** a room containing many small bottles of different fragrances at high concentrations. The library may have 30 to 50 chemicals that smell somewhat similar but show subtle differences. Each of these fragrances is as chemically pure as possible. Furthermore, the contents of the bottles are replaced frequently because many chemicals change their odors as they age. Natural fragrances, which constitute only about 5% of the fragrances used by perfumers, are particularly likely to change their odors as they age.

The perfumers gather periodically to evaluate recently developed or synthesized chemicals. During these evaluation sessions a blotter is dipped into the chemical. The perfumers pay particular attention to three aspects of the fragrance. The **top note** is the first impact of the fragrance. Typically, the top note is light, perhaps involving a citrus smell like lemon or a green, leafy smell. If the chemical is pure, the top note is the only fragrance. However, if it is not pure, there will be a middle note and an end note. The **middle note** follows after the top note has disappeared; this is frequently a flower fragrance such as carnation or lilac. The **end note** is the fragrance that remains for a long time after the top note and the middle note have evaporated. Thus the noticeable fragrance on the blotter changes substantially as time passes.

Perfume evaluators must have developed good memories, as you can imagine from the discussion in the last section. In fact, Jones (cited by Cain, 1979) tested two perfumers who could identify 100 and 200 different perfume fragrances. The perfumer must also be able to imagine how the particular fragrance would interact with other chemicals that might be added to create the perfume.

In the creation of a perfume the perfumers are inspired either by a natural product or by a synthetic product. They first make a basic mixture of four or five components. With the hundreds of fragrances in the fragrance library, literally a million different combinations would be possible. Thus perfumers must use educated guesses to find the right fragrances to combine. Once they find a mixture that brings out the smell to the best advantage, they experiment further to find an exact combination with the desired characteristics. The final result must have an appropriate top note, middle note, and end note.

Smell and Communication

Smell has an important role in communication among members of a species. Researchers are especially intrigued by substances called **pheromones,** which act like chemical signals in communicating with other members of the same species. The name *pheromone* looks like *hormone,* which is a chemical used to send communications from one part of the body to another. Hormones are internal, though, and pheromones are external. Pheromones are excreted in the urine and by various sweat glands. The importance of pheromones to lower animals is well established; the importance of pheromones in humans is still controversial.

Pheromones and Lower Animals

A female dog, horse, or cow releases pheromones when she is in heat. These odors attract the sexual interest of the males of the species. Pheromones also have an important role in pregnancy in some species. Research on mice has shown that if an unfamiliar male mouse is placed near the cage of a newly pregnant female, she is likely to abort the fetuses (Parkes & Bruce, 1961; Rogel, 1978).

Pheromones are also crucial in insect communication. This has important applications, for example, in controlling the destructive gypsy moth. Beroza and Knipling (1972) describe how a sex-attractant pheromone, called disparlure, can be used to lure male gypsy moths inside special traps. With the males captured, they cannot breed with the females, and the population of moths declines (Nathan, 1982).

Are There Pheromones in Humans?

It is unclear whether there are pheromones in humans and—if there are—whether they influence behavior. As discussed earlier in the chapter, males and females differ in their sensitivity to various odors. The sex differences are particularly striking for odors that have a sexual significance, such as steroid sex hormones. Some researchers have found that sex differences in detecting these sexually significant odors may not appear until adulthood. For example, Le Magnen (cited by Vierling & Rock, 1967) studied a chemical that smells very musky and is used as a fixative in perfumes. Sexually mature women perceived this odor very intensely. However, mature males, as well as immature females and immature males, barely noticed it.

One of the most striking demonstrations of the possibility of pheromone activity was demonstrated by a college student. Martha McClintock was a senior at Wellesley College when she examined the folk belief that if women live together, their menstrual cycles become similar (McClintock, 1971). She studied 135 women who lived in a dormitory and asked them to keep track of the dates on which their menstrual cycles began. She found at the beginning of the school year that close friends and roommates differed by 8 to 9 days in the date of the cycle onset. The difference decreased as the school year progressed. By March their cycles began an average of 5 days apart. Some kind of chemical messages must be exchanged among women who see each other frequently, and these messages influence their menstrual cycles.

McClintock hinted that pheromones might be involved in the regulation of the menstrual cycle. A study by Russell, Switz, and Thompson (1980) seemed to point even more clearly to the importance of pheromones in the menstrual cycle. These researchers took gauze pads that women with regular menstrual cycles had worn under their arms and at regular intervals rubbed them on the upper lips of women volunteers. After several months the menstrual cycles of these volunteers shifted significantly toward the cycles of the "donor" women. This research created excitement about the importance of human pheromones, but later critics pointed out that the volunteers had been told about the nature of the experiment, so their expectations may have influenced the results

(Doty, 1981; Filsinger & Fabes, 1985). We can probably conclude that pheromones *may* be important in the menstrual cycle, although their importance has not yet been established.

In her 1978 review of pheromones in humans Rogel proposed that pheromones were more likely to be involved in menstrual-cycle regulation than in any other aspect of human behavior. As she concluded, "It seems unlikely that chemical communication plays any significant role in the control of higher primate reproductive and sexual behavior" (p. 810). For example, it is questionable whether pheromones are involved in determining the frequency of sexual relations in married couples (Engen, 1982; Filsinger & Fabes, 1985; Rogel, 1978).

Nevertheless, a number of companies suspect that there may be money in human pheromones. The Monell Chemical Senses Center has filed applications for four pheromone patents (Leo, 1986). Furthermore, the perfume industry—as you might expect—has entered the competition. A recent advertisement, for example, proclaims the potency of their two new fragrances: "The first pheromone-based fragrances, scientifically created to attract. . . . Two powerful bands of fragrance energy. One for him. One for her. Each capable of triggering an intense magnetic reaction between the sexes." Amusingly, the ad sounds somewhat like the description given to television viewers in O'Mahony's smell-illusion demonstration! Clearly, this application of olfaction research is premature.

Summary: Applications of Olfactory Research

1. Odor pollution is an important environmental problem, but it is difficult to study.
2. One procedure for controlling odor pollution is to produce an odor mixture in which one odor may mask another. However, it is difficult to predict what will happen in an odor mixture. Instead of masking, a mixture may produce a blend, separate odors, or alternation.
3. The intensity of an odor mixture is generally intermediate in strength.

4. A patient's smell may be important when a physician is making a medical diagnosis.
5. Perfume manufacturing begins with the fragrance library, which contains hundreds of chemicals that differ slightly.
6. Perfumes are evaluated in terms of their top note, middle note, and end note.
7. Pheromones are chemical signals important in communication with others belonging to the same species. They are excreted in the urine and by the sweat glands.
8. Pheromones are important determinants of the behavior of nonhuman animals. For example, the odor of unfamiliar males can cause spontaneous abortions in a newly pregnant female mouse. Pheromones can also be used to trap male moths and thereby control moth populations.
9. There are sex differences in sensitivity for sexually significant odors. These differences do not appear until sexual maturity.
10. Pheromones released by underarm sweat glands may influence the onset of menstrual periods for a woman's close associates, but the research in this area is not conclusive. It is also uncertain whether pheromones are important in other aspects of sexual behavior.

Review

1. What are the important characteristics of stimuli that determine whether they are odorous? Suppose you smell an orange and a lemon and they smell similar. How would Henning's and Amoore's systems explain the similarities?
2. Reach for something nearby that has an odor, and hold it close to your nose. Trace the pathway that information about odor will take from the moment it enters your nasal cavity.
3. In a laboratory at your college a professor measures a student's threshold for a particular odor, and it is high. In a laboratory at another college a different professor measures a different student's threshold for a second odor, and it is low. Identify as many factors as possible that might explain the different results.
4. Compare smell with vision on the following dimensions: (a) amount of research performed; (b) nature of the stimulus; (c) nature of the receptors; (d) memory for stimuli. Also suggest any other characteristics that you think provide a useful comparison.

5. Point out aspects of the following topics that might be relevant for a perfumer: detection thresholds, difference thresholds, adaptation, cross-adaptation, odor recognition, and odor constancy.
6. How would adaptation and cross-adaptation be important in pollution control?
7. Suppose you have a friend who teaches home economics. What would you tell your friend about the recognition of odors that might be relevant in teaching cooking? What suggestions would you make for improving recognition ability?
8. Two portions of this chapter discussed humans smelling other humans—the section on smell recognition and the section on pheromones. Summarize the results of these two sections. Point out how sex differences are important in these areas.
9. What is odor constancy, and how might it be relevant in your everyday life?
10. Describe the four areas of applied research discussed in this chapter. What other topics covered in this chapter could have important applications in industry or in other aspects of daily life?

New Terms

olfaction

chemical senses

odorant

volatile

molecular weight

stereochemical theory

nasal cavity

turbinate bones

olfactory epithelium

cilia

mucus

trigeminal nerve

olfactory bulb

detection threshold

olfactometer

difference threshold

adaptation

cross-adaptation

"tip-of-the-nose" phenomenon

odor constancy

odor pollution

odor mixture

masking

blend

fragrance library

top note

middle note

end note

pheromone

Recommended Readings

Carterette, E. C., & Friedman, M. P. (1978). *Handbook of perception*, Vol. 6A (Tasting and smelling) and Vol. 10 (Perceptual ecology). New York: Academic Press. *The second half of Volume 6A concerns topics such as history of research on smell, theories of odor perception, and applications. Volume 10 includes a chapter on odor control and perfumes.*

Engen, T. (1982). *The perception of odors.* New York: Academic Press. *Engen's first-rate book is readable, clear, and comprehensive. The book includes information on anatomy, psychophysics, anosmia, practical problems in odor perception, and odor mixtures.*

Gibbons, B. (1986). The intimate sense of smell. *National Geographic, 170 (3),* 324–361. *This popularized introduction to the topic of smell includes information on human odor identification, perfume manufacturing, smell in medicine, and other applications.*

Wright, R. H. (1982). *The sense of smell.* Boca Raton, FL: CRC Press. *Wright's book contains 52 short chapters on selected topics. It is more difficult to read than Engen's book, but it provides interesting coverage of one theory of smell, some material on thresholds and other psychophysical issues, and coverage of smell in fish and in police dogs.*

chapter *13*
Taste

Preview

The chapter on taste contains three sections: (1) sensory aspects of taste, (2) taste processes, and (3) applications of taste.

The first section emphasizes that the term taste *should really only be applied to the perceptions resulting from the stimulation of special receptors in the mouth. However, people informally use the term* taste *to include other perceptual experiences, such as smell and texture. Most psychologists agree that humans can taste four basic categories: sweet, bitter, salty, and sour. This section also discusses the anatomy of the taste system, how spicy substances are registered, and the regions of the tongue and mouth that are particularly sensitive to each of the four basic tastes.*

The section on taste processes first considers factors that can influence thresholds, such as smoking, food color, and temperature. The next topic is adaptation; in the laboratory, sensitivity to a taste decreases after continuous exposure, but adaptation may be less dramatic in real life. Exposure to a particular taste can sometimes influence people's sensitivity to other substances. For example, after drinking lemon juice, plain water tastes sweet. Several taste modifiers can also transform the taste of other foods. This section examines the way smell influences flavor perception and the factors that can influence people's judgments about whether a food is pleasant.

The last section discusses applications of taste research. Food technologists working in taste-test laboratories use three kinds of tests— discrimination, affective, and descriptive—to assess different foods. We will also discuss wine tasting and tea tasting in this section.

Paula Wolfert's Moroccan cookbook describes a remarkable dish called bisteeya, which Wolfert calls

the most sophisticated and elaborate Moroccan dish, a combination of incredibly tasty flavors representing the culmination of all the foreign influences that have found their synthesis in Moroccan culture. Bisteeya is a huge pie of the finest, thinnest, flakiest pastry in the world, filled with three layers—spicy pieces of pigeon or chicken, lemony eggs cooked in a savory onion sauce, and toasted and sweetened almonds—and then dusted on top with cinnamon and sugar (1973, p. 2).

If you were to eat bisteeya, you would actually *taste* very little. **Taste** refers only to the perceptions that result from the contact of substances with the special receptors in the mouth (Bartoshuk, 1971). When psychologists speak about taste, they mean only a very limited portion of the perceptions involved in the everyday usage of the word *taste*—only perceptions such as sweet and bitter.

Let us discuss the difference between taste and another characteristic often used to describe the taste experience, because the distinction is important. The word *flavor* is used to refer to the wide variety of perceptions we experience when we eat. **Flavor** includes smell, touch, pressure, pain, and so on, in addition to taste (McBurney, 1978).

Thus the *taste* of bisteeya combines several taste qualities—the sour of the lemon, the sweet of the sugar, the bitter of the toasted almonds, and the salt of the chicken—although each of these qualities is quite mild. However, the *flavor* of bisteeya includes additional richness and complexity. Among the smells are the buttery fragrance from the pastry, the strong overtones of onion and garlic, and the delicate hints of saffron and cinnamon. The flavor also involves the tactile qualities of food in the mouth, such as its temperature and its texture. The texture of bisteeya is richly varied, with the crisp flaky pastry, the hard nuggets of almonds, the chewy chicken, and the fluffy eggs. (Another

flavor quality of food—its painfulness—is not present in bisteeya, but you are certainly familiar with this possibility if you have tasted the right recipe for chili.)

We have discussed the theories of James J. Gibson in many parts of this book. Gibson characteristically examined perceptual issues from novel angles. For example, when most psychologists interested in vision were examining the anatomy of the visual system, Gibson instead examined the nature of the visual *stimulus*. Most psychologists interested in touch conducted research on passive touch, yet Gibson emphasized the importance of active touch. In Gibson's (1966) work on flavor, he emphasized the variety of information we can obtain about food—information other than taste and odor.

Consider, for instance, how we process surface texture properties such as the slippery surface of butter, the rough surface of bread crust, and the smooth surface of noodles. When we chew, we can register a substance's consistency. We note the thickness of a substance; it may be thin broth or the thick, rubbery texture of the 3-day-old gelatin dessert served in a high-school cafeteria. The consistency may also be elastic, soft, hard, or brittle. In addition we can register the shape, size, weight, and granularity of a substance. Try Demonstration 13.1 to illustrate these characteristics. A section at the end of this chapter considers these additional dimensions of flavor in more detail.

The first section in this chapter discusses sensory aspects of taste. The next section examines a number of taste phenomena. The last section highlights some applications of taste and flavor.

SENSORY ASPECTS OF TASTE

In this section we will first discuss the stimulus for taste, particularly with respect to efforts to classify taste stimuli. The next topic is taste receptors, followed by the relationship between taste and tongue region and the problems of taste coding. The final topic is the pathway from the receptors to the brain.

Demonstration 13.1

Texture Characteristics of Foods

Bring this textbook to your next meal or copy the list below. Judge everything you eat and drink by checking the appropriate choice in each category.

		Foods and Beverages									
		Toast									
Surface texture	Slippery										
	Rough	✓									
	Smooth										
Substance thickness	Very thin										
	Thin	✓									
	Medium										
	Thick										
	Very thick										
Consistency	Elastic										
	Soft										
	Hard										
	Brittle	✓									

Stimulus

An important issue in the last chapter concerned the classification of smell stimuli. Stimuli we see can be described in terms of wavelength, and stimuli we hear can be described in terms of frequency. However, as discussed, the stimuli we smell seem to resist neat categories or measurement systems. For-

tunately, the stimuli we taste are somewhat more cooperative than the stimuli we smell. Although there is some controversy, most psychologists tend to agree that we taste four basic kinds of stimuli: sweet, bitter, salty, and sour.

The search for the basic categories for taste dates back to Greek history. For example, Aristotle proposed this list of basic categories:

sweet, bitter, salty, sour, astringent, pungent, and harsh. Bartoshuk (1978) discusses the history of other kinds of classification systems. Hans Henning (1927) is generally credited with promoting the idea of four basic tastes. Remember that Henning proposed a six-sided prism to represent the six basic odors. Similarly, Henning proposed a **taste tetrahedron**, a four-sided figure with one of the basic tastes at each of the four corners. Figure 13.1 illustrates Henning's taste tetrahedron.

Although the classification based on four primary tastes is currently dominant, some researchers argue that there are more than four primaries. For example, Schiffman and Dackis (1975) used *multidimensional scaling*, discussed in the psychophysics chapter, which involves asking people to judge the similarity of two tastes. The results of these judgments allow researchers to determine the similarities among different tastes. Schiffman and Dackis found evidence for the traditional four tastes (sweet, bitter, salty, and sour), but they also found evidence for three other taste qualities: alkaline, sulfurous, and fatty. Other researchers have argued that studies are likely to confirm the four-primaries theory because they use stimuli from only these four categories and because experimenters bias

participants by using the words sweet, bitter, salty, and sour in the instructions (O'Mahony & Thompson, 1977). Interestingly, in Japan tasters add a fifth label, corresponding to the taste of Ac'cent, which is used frequently in their cooking (O'Mahony & Ishii, 1986). Still other researchers argue that more than four primary tastes are possible because mixtures (for example, sweet and salty) tend to taste different from their components (Erickson, 1982; Schiffman & Erickson, 1980).

Supporters of the traditional, four-primary classification system interpret those results differently. For example, Bartoshuk (1980) maintains that the components of taste mixtures can be individually recognized; mixtures do not create new taste sensations. McBurney and Gent (1979) strongly support the four-primary model: "We argue that the four taste qualities together exhaust the qualities of taste experience" (p. 151). We will discuss some of their evidence later, such as the different taste that water has following adaptation to different substances, the influence of taste modifiers on taste perception, and the results of cross-adaptation studies. McBurney (1978) has also stressed that other proposed taste qualities, such as alkaline, are due to sensations from mechanisms other than the taste buds.

Throughout the chapter on taste, it is important to remember that when you taste a food, it may contain several different tastes. The bisteeya mentioned at the beginning of the chapter has a mixture of sour, sweet, bitter, and salt. Similarly, we will see in the discussion of wine tasting later in the chapter that an ideal substance contains an appropriate balance of tastes. Specifically, wine tasters judge a wine in terms of the extent to which the sour, sweet, and bitter components are balanced, without a single taste being dominant.

Taste Receptors

The basic receptor for taste stimuli is called the **taste bud.** Taste buds are visible only with a microscope. They are located throughout the mouth, not just on the surface of your

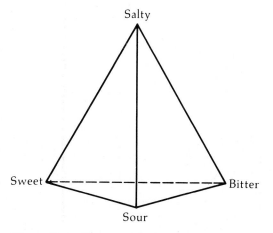

Figure 13.1   Taste tetrahedron proposed by Henning.

tongue. For example, there are taste buds inside your cheeks, on the roof of your mouth, and in your throat (Oakley, 1986). Most of the research and discussion, however, examines the taste buds on the upper surface of the tongue.

The taste buds are on little bumps on the tongue known as **papillae**. Each papilla is small, but it can be seen with the unaided eye, as Demonstration 13.2 shows. There are at least four kinds of papillae (Keverne, 1982). They seem to have somewhat different functions, although these are far from clear-cut. The smallest papillae, for example, do not have any taste buds; we will be concerned only with the larger kind that do contain these taste receptors. Figure 13.2 shows an enlarged picture of a papilla. Note that taste buds are lined up in the pits on either side of the papilla. Thus the taste buds are *not* on the actual tongue surface.

Figure 13.3 shows an enlargement of a taste bud from Figure 13.2. This pear-shaped taste bud contains several receptor cells arranged like the segments of an orange. The tips of the receptor cells reach out into the opening and can touch any taste molecules in the saliva that flows into the pit. The tips of the taste receptors are **microvilli**, and the opening of the taste bud is the **taste pore**. Researchers currently think that the taste stimuli in the saliva interact with molecules in the membranes of the microvilli; the stimuli do not seem to actually enter the receptor cells (Keverne, 1982).

Humans have about 10,000 taste buds (Bartoshuk, 1971). Other species differ widely; for example, chickens have only

about 24 taste buds (Kare & Ficken, 1963), so a fine wine would be wasted on them. On the other hand, consider the catfish, which has more than 175,000 taste buds (Pfaffmann, 1978). Most of these taste buds are on the external body surface, so the catfish can "taste" the water it is swimming in without even opening its mouth.

As you sit here reading this book, your taste buds are dying rapidly. Beidler and Smallman (1965) demonstrated that the life span of the average cell in the taste bud is only about 10 days. Thus the cells in the taste bud that responded to the chocolate mousse you ate last night will be long gone by next month. Beidler and Smallman write such a depressing passage about the life of taste buds that you may be ready to go collecting door-to-door for the Taste Bud Relief Fund:

> The taste buds on the surface of the tongue are constantly assaulted by abrasion against the teeth and hard palate; by exposure to extremes of temperature; and by flooding the tongue with various solutions. This is particularly true in man who daily abrades his tongue by talking and chewing, and subjects the taste buds frequently to draughts of hot tobacco smoke, hot coffee or tea, ice-cold alcoholic drinks. . . (p. 263).

How do the taste buds renew themselves? It seems that the cells surrounding the taste bud move into the taste bud and migrate toward the center, replacing the dead cells (Beidler & Smallman, 1965).

In the chapter on smell, we discussed the free nerve endings of the trigeminal nerve;

Demonstration 13.2

Looking at the Papillae on Your Tongue

Take a small glass of milk or a spoonful of ice cream and stand in front of a mirror. Coat your tongue with the milk or the ice cream and immediately look at your tongue in the mirror. You will notice rounded bumps that rise above the milky surface of your tongue. These are the papillae that contain taste buds. The smaller bumps do not contain taste buds.

Taste bud

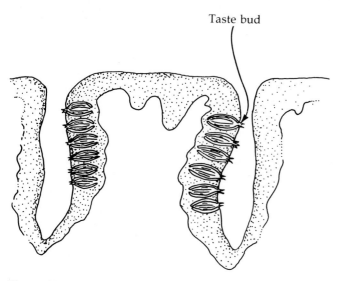

Figure 13.2 Enlargement of papilla, containing many taste buds.

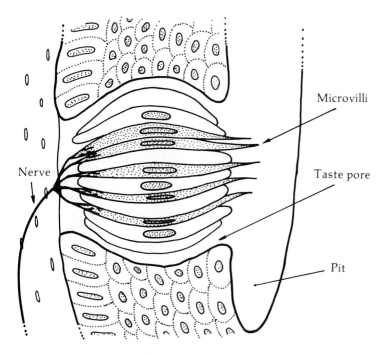

Microvilli

Taste pore

Nerve

Pit

Figure 13.3 Enlargement of taste bud.

stimulation of these free nerve endings (for example, by ammonia) produces a sensation of pungency. Similarly, there are free nerve endings of the **trigeminal nerve** located in the mouth. For example, one kind of papilla has even more free nerve endings than it has taste buds (Lawless, 1984). These free nerve endings register spiciness when you eat chili peppers; we'll mention the perception of spiciness again later in the chapter. However, there is speculation that the irritation produced by eating chili peppers may encourage the brain to release endorphins. This could explain the enthusiasm with which some of us pursue spicy foods (Naj, 1986).

Relationship between Taste and Tongue Regions

You can probably remember learning that different regions of the tongue are sensitive to different taste qualities. In fact, McBurney (1978) speculates that this concept is probably the most generally known fact about taste. Until recently, however, the only research evidence for this belief was the work of Hanig (1901).

In 1974, Collings conducted a careful study of the regions of the tongue and the **soft palate,** a region on the upper part of the mouth, just above the back of the tongue. Tasters in her study rinsed their mouths with distilled water and then extended their tongues. Collings dipped a tiny piece of filter paper into a solution and then placed it on the tongue or soft palate. There were four kinds of solutions: salty, sour, bitter, and sweet. The participants then pointed to a card indicating the name of the taste quality. They rinsed their mouths thoroughly and then tested another stimulus. By repeating this technique, Collings was able to determine thresholds for regions of the tongue and the palate.

She found that sour tastes were most noticeable on the sides of the tongue. Salty and sweet tastes were most noticeable on the front of the tongue. Bitter tastes turned out to be most noticeable on the soft palate. However, within the regions of the tongue alone, bitter tastes were most noticeable on the front, *not* on the back, as is commonly believed. Demonstration 13.3 may produce similar results, although these results may be difficult to duplicate without refined technology.

How did the middle of your tongue react to the flavors in Demonstration 13.3? Actually, it should have been relatively insensitive to all the flavors. The middle of the tongue lacks taste buds, so it could be called a "blind spot." Like the blind spot on your retina, there are no receptors at this location.

Did the two sides of your tongue respond the same to the various flavors? Researchers have always assumed that the sides are similar, and Kroeze (1979) demonstrated their equivalence.

Problem of Taste Coding

You may recall that color-coding mechanisms include three kinds of color receptors and higher-level cells that use opponent processes. Unfortunately, our knowledge of taste coding is not nearly so detailed, and there are still many uncertainties.

Researchers in the area of taste once searched for four different kinds of taste receptors, which might operate the same way as the three kinds of color receptors. Some earlier researchers produced data that they felt could support the existence of four kinds of papillae, each sensitive to only one taste. However, more recent experiments contradict those data. For example, Arvidson and Friberg (1980) found that some papillae indeed did respond to only one taste quality. However, other papillae responded to two, three, and even all four taste qualities. Obviously, taste coding is not simple.

Still, we know there must be some relationship between the taste buds on the papillae and the code for taste. We need some explanation for the fact that the regions of the tongue respond differently to the taste qualities. There must be a reason, for example, why the taste buds at the tip of the tongue are particularly responsive to sweet stimuli. Currently, most researchers believe that each taste bud can respond to at least one taste

Demonstration 13.3

Taste and Tongue Regions

For this demonstration you will need to assemble four kinds of substances: sour (vinegar or lemon), salty (salt), sweet (sugar), and bitter (unsweetened quinine water or unsweetened extra-strength coffee with caffeine). Dissolve the salt and the sugar in water (separately). Take a piece of absorbent white paper and cut it into 25 to 30 small squares. Divide the squares into four piles and place each pile in one of the substances.

It is best to use tweezers to place each square on your tongue; if you use your fingers, be careful to let drops of the solution drain off before proceeding. Place a drained square of one solution—one at a time—on each of these regions of the tongue and mark the location where the taste is most noticeable.

Region of the Tongue

		Front	Middle	Back	Left Side	Right Side	Palate
	Sour						
Taste Quality	Salty						
	Sweet						
	Bitter						

quality. However, each taste bud responds *most vigorously* to only one taste. For example, Figure 13.4 shows the relative thresholds for a hypothetical taste bud that is particularly sensitive to a bitter taste; it could be called a "bitter-best" taste bud. Notice that this taste bud (perhaps one on your palate) is most sensitive to bitter tastes, least sensitive to sweet tastes, and moderately sensitive to salty and sour tastes. Some other taste buds may have little or no sensitivity to a particular taste. For example, a taste bud might be floating in vinegar and refuse to respond.

In summary, it seems that most taste buds do not restrict their responses to a single stimulus. However, they probably respond better to one kind of stimulus than to any other. The higher levels of stimulus processing, beyond the receptor level, must somehow take into account these relative response rates to code tastes (Logue, 1986). Unfortunately, the details of this process have not been established.

Pathway from Receptors to Brain

The discussion of vision provided reasonably detailed information on the pathway from the receptors to the brain. However, this kind of detail is simply impossible in a discussion of the pathway for taste. We know relatively little about what happens to information about taste once the information leaves the taste buds.

Figure 13.3 shows a nerve receiving information from the taste cell. The nerves in the mouth and throat gather into three bundles, one from the front of the tongue, one from the back of the tongue, and one from

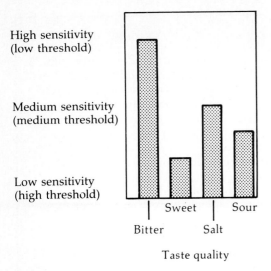

Figure 13.4   Sensitivities for hypothetical taste bud sensitive to bitter.

the throat. These three nerves travel from the mouth to an area in the base of the brain called the **thalamus.** From there, information travels to several regions in the cortex, primarily the **somatosensory cortex,** the part discussed in connection with touch.

We also know little about how the cortex handles information about taste. Three Japanese researchers found that most cortical taste cells responded to three or four of the four basic taste stimuli; however, like the taste buds, they respond most vigorously to only one or two of these stimuli (Yamamoto, Yuyama, & Kawamura, 1981). Other research has suggested that the cortex may not be essential to the most primitive kinds of taste reactions. For example, newborns with birth defects so severe that they lack a cortex still manage to make the same kind of negative facial expressions that normal babies make when they taste sour and bitter solutions (Keverne, 1982; Steiner, 1979).

In summary, the information travels from the taste receptors to the thalamus and then to the cortex. However, we know remarkably little about the exact mechanisms of the higher levels of processing for taste. This ig-

norance is particularly regrettable since taste figures so prominently in our everyday lives.

Summary: Sensory Aspects of Taste

1. Taste refers only to perceptions resulting from substances in contact with special receptors in the mouth. Flavor refers to the broader variety of perceptions associated with eating; as described by Gibson, for example, it includes textural qualities as well.
2. Although there is controversy, most psychologists believe that humans can taste four basic kinds of stimuli: sweet, bitter, salty, and sour.
3. The taste receptors are called taste buds; they are on the sides of some of the papillae of the tongue.
4. Taste buds have a life span of about 10 days; they are constantly being replaced.
5. The free nerve endings of the trigeminal nerve register the spiciness of chili peppers and other pungent substances.
6. Sour tastes are most noticeable on the sides of the tongue, bitter on the soft palate, and salty and sweet on the front of the tongue; the middle of the tongue is relatively insensitive to all tastes.
7. Each taste bud responds to at least one kind of taste, but it responds most vigorously to only one.
8. The nerves from the mouth and throat travel to the thalamus, and taste information is then transmitted from the thalamus to the somatosensory cortex. The cortex may not be essential for the most basic kinds of taste reactions.

TASTE PROCESSES

In this section we will first discuss thresholds for taste and various factors that may influence them. Then we will examine adaptation, the decrease in sensitivity when a stimulus is presented continuously. The following section illustrates how adaptation to one substance often influences the reaction to other substances. Finally, we will see how taste and smell interact in perception.

Thresholds

A **detection threshold**, as we have discussed in previous chapters, is the boundary point at which something is reported half the time. For example, suppose that 1 gram of a particular substance is added to a liter of water, and you taste this solution. You might say "Yes, I taste it" half the time and "No, I don't taste it" half the time. We have already discussed one aspect of detection thresholds— the fact that they vary across the regions of the tongue. Thus a particular concentration of a solution may be just at your threshold on the side of your tongue, way above threshold on the tip of your tongue, and way below threshold in the middle of your tongue.

As you might expect, thresholds vary from one substance to another. Bitter quinine sulphate is easy to detect in small quantities. In contrast, relatively large quantities of sweet glucose are necessary for detection. You can test your thresholds for table sugar by trying the demonstrations in Chapter 2.

McBurney (1978) notes that psychologists often make a distinction between the detection threshold and the recognition threshold. The detection threshold, as we said, is the boundary point or concentration of a solution at which something is reported half the time. The **recognition threshold** is the concentration of a solution that can be recognized by quality. In other words, the recognition threshold specifies the amount of a substance that must be added to distilled water for tasters to recognize whether the taste is salty, bitter, sweet, or sour. As you can imagine, tasters require a relatively strong concentration of a substance to recognize that it is, for example, salty. Thus recognition thresholds are generally higher than detection thresholds.

As discussed before, the **difference threshold** is the difference between two stimuli that a person can just barely tell apart. Difference thresholds have not been thor-

oughly studied in the area of taste (Mc-Burney, 1978). Psychologists have shown little interest in this area, perhaps because we do not seem to make much use of intensity information when we taste.

The research conducted, however, indicates that our difference thresholds are not impressive. In general, the concentration of a substance must be increased by 15 to 25% for us to notice a difference in its taste. Thus if you have added 5 teaspoons of lemon juice to a sauce, you need to add about 1 more teaspoon to make it noticeably more sour. You may recall that our difference thresholds for smell are similarly unimpressive, about 20 to 30%.

One interesting finding about taste thresholds concerns the amount of time required for judgments. As Kelling and Halpern (1983) remark, we can see a remarkable amount during one lightning flash, and we can also hear an identifiable sound in the fraction of a second during which a twig snaps or a person gasps. These researchers decided to discover what people could identify in a "taste flash," a taste presented for a fraction of a second. Even when a salty or sweet taste was presented for as short a period as one tenth of a second, people could reliably discriminate these tastes from water. Thus, we don't seem to need an extended period of contact between a taste stimulus and the receptors in order to judge its quality.

In the remainder of this section on thresholds we will look at some factors that could influence thresholds. We'll divide these factors into two categories, characteristics of the taster and qualities of the stimulus.

Characteristics of Taster

Several characteristics of the taster, such as smoking and insensitivity to certain substances, can influence threshold judgments. It is commonly believed that smoking dulls the sense of taste; in fact most researchers exclude smokers from taste experiments. However, McBurney and Moskat (1975) noticed that previous research on the relationship between smoking and taste had been inconclusive. They conducted four experiments in which they compared smokers and nonsmokers on their detection and recognition thresholds. The studies showed no consistent differences between smokers and nonsmokers. For example, nonsmokers and heavy smokers—at least 15 cigarettes a day—were asked to judge whether a liquid was bitter, sour, salty, or sweet. The two groups did not differ significantly on any of the four substances.

However, before you conclude that smokers experience the same *flavor* sensations as nonsmokers, remember that McBurney and Moskat studied only taste. Smokers and nonsmokers may indeed differ in their sensitivity to smells, textures, and other components of flavor. Furthermore, these researchers studied only college students. Older people who have been smoking for a longer time might indeed be less sensitive to tastes.

Finally, some people appear to be unable to taste certain substances. We have seen that some individuals respond abnormally to some stimuli in every sensory system. We know most about color deficiences in vision, but this book has also discussed deafness and insensitivity to pain. Hall, Bartoshuk, Cain, and Stevens (1975) discussed a similar phenomenon, often called *taste blindness*, in taste perception. The name is somewhat misleading, like the term *color blindness.* We saw in Chapter 5 that most people with color deficiencies are not really color blind because they can see some colors but not others. Similarly, "taste-blind" people really can taste most substances, but they are insensitive to some particular tastes; these people are called **nontasters.**

Notice, then, that we have additional evidence for Theme 1, the similarity among the perceptual systems. Each is associated with a particular disorder or insensitivity, although clearly visual blindness is more disabling than insensitivity to certain tastes.

One of the most commonly tested substances in these experiments with nontasters is phenylthiocarbamide (**PTC**). The ability to taste this bitter substance is genetically acquired, just like eye color or height. Hall and

her coauthors found that PTC-nontasters could taste PTC if the concentration was strong enough—about 300 times the normal concentration. These researchers found that PTC-nontasters were also much less sensitive to the bitter taste of caffeine than PTC-tasters.

In another study Gent and Bartoshuk (1983) studied people who are nontasters of a different bitter substance, 6-n-propylthiouracil (**PROP**). These researchers used the magnitude-estimation technique discussed in the psychophysics chapter. They discovered that PROP-nontasters were less sensitive to the sweet tastes of sucrose and saccharin than people who could taste PROP. Gent and Bartoshuk are uncertain about the explanation for their results, but they speculate that nontasters may have a smaller number of receptors for both bitter and sweet substances.

Qualities of Stimulus

We have seen that characteristics of the taster may influence thresholds for taste. The threshold could also be influenced by attributes of the stimulus, such as its color, temperature, and spiciness.

The color of a substance can influence the accuracy of taste discriminations. For example, Maga (1974) examined how the four basic tastes can be influenced by adding food coloring. In general taste thresholds were higher—and sensitivity was therefore lower—when color had been added. However, salty solutions were not influenced by color. Other studies have found that the addition of food coloring influences recognition thresholds for fruit-flavored beverages, birch beer (which has a flavor similar to root beer), and cake (DuBose, Cardello, & Maller, 1980; Hyman, 1983). If you'd like your lemon pudding to have a recognizable flavor, then, it's best not to add green food coloring!

Perhaps you have noticed that temperature influences taste. A wine expert comments about the relationship between temperature and taste:

> While sugar can conceal and disguise certain faults in wine, its power to do so is limited. If you are evaluating a chilled white wine

and the sugar is getting in the way of your taste, let the wine warm up to room temperature. The winemaker's errors will fairly leap out at you! (Kovi, 1980, p. 12)

Thus certain tastes that may be below threshold when you taste a chilled wine will be above threshold when the wine warms up.

Although most researchers agree that temperature does influence taste, they often disagree about the exact nature of this relationship. McBurney (1978) states that the majority of studies show that people are most sensitive to tastes when the substance is served at about room temperature or body temperature. Typical results are shown in Figure 13.5. Notice that sour substances are less affected by temperature than salty, sweet, or bitter substances. However, all the curves show a maximum sensitivity (that is, a lowest threshold) at a point between 22° and 32° Centigrade. Now try Demonstration 13.4 to see if you notice the same effect.

Think about the practical applications of the relationship between taste and temperature. Cookbooks frequently mention that the final seasoning of a dish must be performed when the food has reached the temperature at which it will be served. Suppose that you salted a soup when its temperature was about 25°C and then you heated it to 40°C. According to Figure 13.5, you would now be less sensitive to its saltiness—it might not taste salty enough. On the other hand, suppose you were preparing a lemon pudding. If you adjusted the amount of sugar and lemon so that it tasted just right when it was very hot, it would taste too sweet and too sour when it cooled down.

Quinine shows particularly dramatic changes in threshold as a function of temperature. Paulus and Reisch (1980), for example, found that people could detect bitterness when 9 mg of this substance was added to a liter of water when the solution was at 10°C, 6 mg at 20°, and 44 mg at 60°. As you may know, quinine is the substance that gives tonic water its bitter taste; an iced gin-and-tonic is very bitter. It is clear, however, that a creative chef who is concocting a gin-and-tonic soup to be served at around 60°C would have to add about five times the amount of quinine for the bitterness to be tasted.

A final stimulus quality that can influence

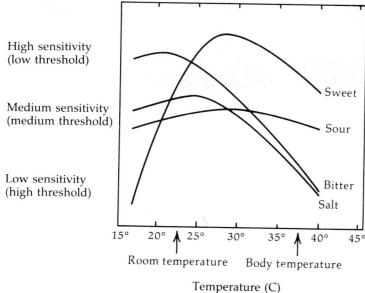

Figure 13.5 Relationship between temperature and taste.

Demonstration 13.4

Temperature and Taste

Take four small (4-oz) glasses and place two pinches of sugar in each. Fill the first two with cold water from the tap. Stir until dissolved and add an ice cube to glass 1. Add lukewarm water to glass 3 and very hot water to glass 4. Now taste each of the four solutions. Do glass 2 and glass 3 contain the sweetest-tasting solutions?

---

thresholds is spiciness. The Nirvana Indian restaurant in New York City asks its patrons not to request that certain dishes be prepared with extra chili pepper, since the chili might mask the other tastes. This warning has some merit, because Lawless, Rozin, and Shenker (1985) report that both frequent and infrequent eaters of chili peppers rated sweet, salty, bitter, and sour substances as less intense when chili had been added.

Let's review the factors that can influence thresholds. Smoking does not appear to influence taste thresholds, although different results might be obtained with long-term smokers. Also, some people are insensitive to certain tastes. Stimulus qualities that affect thresholds include color, temperature, and spiciness.

Adaptation

Remember that when a smell is presented continuously, sensitivity to that smell decreases. **Adaptation**, or a decrease in sensitivity following the continuous presentation of a stimulus, also occurs for taste. In other words, when a specific substance is placed on your tongue, your threshold for that substance increases—you require a stronger concentration of the substance to taste it. The threshold reaches it maximum in about 1 minute. This relationship is illustrated in Figure 13.6. Notice that when the substance is removed, the threshold rapidly recovers to normal.

Try Demonstration 13.5 to see one example of how adaptation works. When your tongue is adapted to the salt in your own sa-

liva, your threshold for salt is relatively high. However, when you rinse your mouth out with distilled water or tap water, your tongue becomes adapted to a salt-free environment. Your receptors are now more sensitive to salt; in other words, your threshold is relatively low (Bartoshuk, 1980; O'Mahony, 1984).

Adaptation works for spicy substances as well as for the four standard taste qualities. Lawless (1984) found that spicy peppers and ginger were judged less intense when they followed a strong substance than when they followed a weak one.

These laboratory studies on adaptation may not accurately describe everyday encounters with substances. For example, tastes last longer when people sip a solution than when it is poured on their tongues, which is the more common practice in the laboratory (Lawless & Skinner, 1979). It seems likely that the tongue movement involved in sipping may prolong the taste. Also, in the laboratory the taste stimulus is placed on a small area of the tongue. However, when you eat a salty cracker at lunch, your chewing movements and your tongue movements shift the salty substance around so that it comes into contact with many different receptors. Thus a single receptor is unlikely to have prolonged, constant stimulation.

Halpern and Meiselman (1980) point out another difference between the laboratory and everyday eating experiences. When you are drinking your lemonade, you sip the liquid, swallow at least once, then may pause before sipping again. In other words, the receptors experience noncontinuous stimulation. Halpern and Meiselman tried duplicat-

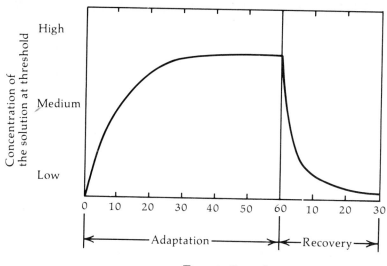

Figure 13.6 Adaptation to specific taste.

Demonstration 13.5

Adaptation to Salt in Saliva

Take a quart jar, fill it with water, and add ½ teaspoon of salt. Stir the solution until the salt dissolves. Take four small glasses and fill the first glass with the solution. Fill the second glass three fourths full, the third glass one half full, and the fourth one fourth full. Add water to these last three glasses until they are full and mix the solutions thoroughly.

Take a sip of the solution in the fourth glass, swish it around in your mouth, and see whether you detect any trace of saltiness. If you do, mix up several glasses of increasingly diluted salty water; wait several minutes before proceeding.

If you do not taste saltiness in the fourth glass, test the third glass to see if you detect salt. Continue with the second and first glasses until you can just barely notice the salt. Record the number of the glass that contains a barely noticeable amount of salt.

Now rinse your mouth thoroughly with water. Use distilled water if possible because tap water may be somewhat salty. Keep rinsing for about a minute. Repeat the threshold-measurement process. Your threshold should now be lower, so that you detect lower concentrations of salt.

ing more closely the natural alternation between taste stimulus and no stimulus by presenting alternate spurts of salt water and "artificial saliva." (This substance—probably less commercially profitable than cola drinks—contains the important chemicals of real saliva.) People who tasted alternating spurts of salt water and saliva experienced no decrease in the intensity of the salt, whereas people who tasted only spurts of salt water reported a sizable decrease in intensity. For a variety of reasons, then, we show less adaptation in everyday life than in typical laboratory studies.

We have seen in this section that adaptation affects both thresholds and judgments of intensity, for both the four traditional taste qualities and for spicy substances. However, adaptation is less likely in everyday experiences because when we normally eat or drink, we sip, move our tongues, and pause to swallow.

Cross-Adaptation and Cross-Enhancement

Cross-adaptation and cross-enhancement both refer to the effects that adaptation to one substance can have on the taste of another substance. **Cross-adaptation** means that adaptation to one substance *raises* the threshold for another substance; we will be less sensitive to the second substance. **Cross-enhancement,** which is just the opposite, means that adaptation to one substance *lowers* the threshold for another substance; we will be more sensitive to the second substance. (You can recall which is which by remembering that adaptation is a decrease in sensitivity, whereas enhancement means an increase in sensitivity.)

Think of situations in which you have experienced cross-adaptation and cross-enhancement. For example, if you have been drinking tea with lemon, the vinegar marinade on the ribs will not taste so sour; you have experienced cross-adaptation. However, if you have been eating a sweet roll at breakfast, the orange juice tastes unpleas-

antly bitter; you have experienced cross-enhancement.

In general, cross-adaptation is specific to a particular taste quality (Bartoshuk, 1974). For example, if you are adapted to a sour taste, you will be less sensitive to other sour tastes. However, your sensitivity to salty, sweet, and bitter tastes will not be decreased because these tastes represent different taste qualities. In fact, your sensitivity to these other substances may be increased through cross-enhancement.

McBurney and Gent (1979) point out how the results on cross-adaptation support the theory that there are four basic taste qualities. Since there is little cross-adaptation across qualities, it seems likely that there must be separate receptor mechanisms for each taste quality.

In a representative study on cross-adaptation, Lawless and Stevens (1983) found that the sweet taste of sucrose induced cross-adaptation for other sweeteners such as saccharin and aspartame. However, the cross-adaptation was not consistently symmetrical. For example, aspartame induced only partial cross-adaptation for sucrose and no cross-adaptation for saccharin. Saccharin induced only partial cross-adaptation for aspartame and no cross-adaptation for sucrose. If there were only one kind of sweetness receptor, then every sweet substance should have provided cross-adaptation for every other sweet substance. The authors argue that there seem to be several receptors that mediate the taste of sweetness, but the details of this theory have not yet been specified.

Now let's turn to cross-enhancement. Kuznicki and McCutcheon (1979), for example, focused on the influence of sweet tastes on later sour tastes. These authors asked the participants to stick out their tongues, then placed a tiny drop of a substance on an individual papilla that was sensitive to both sweet and sour. These careful techniques minimized the spread of the substance. First a drop of a sweet liquid was presented, followed 15 seconds later by a drop of a sour liquid. In the control condition a drop of water, rather than sweet liquid, was presented prior to the sour liquid. In each case people used a magnitude-estimation technique, supplying a number to indicate the intensity of the sour liquid. (The magnitude-estimation technique was discussed in Chapter 2.) People judged the intensity of the sour solution to be greater when it had been preceded by a sweet taste than when it had been preceded by water. Kuznicki and McCutcheon favor an explanation for cross-enhancement that involves chemical interactions on the surface of the receptors.

Cross-adaptation and cross-enhancement are involved in several other taste processes. Two of these are the taste of water and taste modifiers.

Water Taste

What could be as tasteless as water? Actually, water can have a distinct taste when your tongue has been adapted to another taste; this phenomenon is called **water taste.** Try Demonstration 13.6 to show how water can acquire a specific taste that depends upon what you have previously eaten. In general, sour and bitter substances produce a sweet water taste, and sweet or salty substances produce a sour or bitter water taste. Incidentally, urea (a component of human urine) is one of the few substances that produce a salty water taste.

McBurney and Shick (1971) examined the water tastes of 26 compounds. They wanted to determine whether there was some relationship between the taste of a compound and its water taste that was as clear-cut as the opponent-process relationship we saw for color vision in Chapter 5. Unfortunately, their data did not support an opponent-process view; many relationships were not comple-

---

Demonstration 13.6

Water Taste

There are three ways to produce a sweet water taste with an adaptation procedure. Try as many of these ways as possible.

1. Take a mouthful of diluted vinegar and swirl it around in your mouth for 30 to 40 seconds. Spit it out and then take a drink of plain water.
2. Repeat this procedure with strong coffee that contains caffeine. (A teaspoon of instant coffee dissolved in a small amount of water works well.)
3. Eat some artichokes (canned ones work well), making sure that they are thoroughly spread throughout your mouth. After swallowing them, sip some plain water.

There are two ways to produce a sour or bitter water taste:

1. Dissolve a teaspoon of salt in a small amount of water. Swirl it around in your mouth for 30 to 40 seconds, spit it out, and sip some plain water.
2. Repeat this procedure with sugar.

You may find it difficult to decide whether the water tastes produced by salt and sugar are sour or bitter, but the taste is definitely *not* salty, sweet, or neutral.

mentary. However, this study provided interesting information about the *intensity* of the water taste. In general, the water taste was about one third as strong as the taste of the substance itself. For example, the intensity of a solution of salt water was judged about 32, and the intensity of the water tasted afterwards was judged about 12. Try to notice the nature and the intensity of various water tastes by drinking water with your meals. This amazing low-calorie beverage can assume many disguises!

Taste Modifiers

Several special substances change the flavor of other food by modifying the receptors on the tongue; these are called **taste modifiers.** The one you are most likely to have tasted is monosodium glutamate (MSG), which is frequently sold with spices in grocery stores under the trade name Ac'cent. It is used extensively in Oriental cooking. By itself, **MSG** has an unusual taste that seems to combine the four taste qualities; when added to other foods, however, the thresholds for sour and bitter tastes are reduced (Moskowitz, 1978b). In other words, if a Chinese hot-and-sour soup contains MSG, the chef will not need to add as much vinegar for the sour taste to be detected.

Another taste modifier is **gymnema sylvestre,** a climbing plant found in India and Africa. A British officer stationed in India first reported its effects in the Western literature after noticing that after chewing the leaves of the plant, he could not taste the sugar in his tea. Bartoshuk (1974) notes that after one tastes *gymnema sylvestre,* sugar crystals are indeed tasteless and feel like sand on the tongue.

A third substance, popularly called **miracle fruit,** changes the taste of sour substances. Africans have used miracle fruit to sweeten sour wines and beers (Bartoshuk, 1974, 1980). Linda Bartoshuk lectured on taste modifiers several years ago and distributed samples of miracle fruit. This amazing substance had the potential to transform the pure lemon juice that we drank afterwards into the most delicious sweetened lemonade. The name "miracle fruit" is appropriate because a taste of this substance imparts a sweet taste to everything eaten in the next hour (Henning, Brouwer, Van der Wel, & Francke, 1969).

Bartoshuk (1974) discussed some practical applications of these taste modifiers. Foods made from yeast and algae are extremely nutritious, but their taste is reported to be loathsome. Special diets designed for patients with particular diseases are similarly unappealing. In these cases it is often impossible or undesirable to use conventional flavorings, but it is possible to control the taste of food by temporarily altering the taste receptors. Furthermore, substances such as miracle fruit could be explored as alternatives to nonnutritive sweeteners such as cyclamates and saccharins, chemicals that may have undesirable side effects.

Interaction of Taste and Smell

This textbook includes separate chapters on smell and taste, and this separation of topics might lead you to conclude that these perceptual systems are largely independent. However, as Burdach, Kroeze, and Koster (1984) point out, we rarely encounter "pure" taste stimuli—independent of their odors—outside the laboratory. When you sit down to consume a pizza, the odors of the crust, the oregano, and the mozzarella combine with the salty taste to produce the familiar flavor. Often, as in the case of pizza, smell is even more important than taste in determining flavor. Demonstration 13.7 illustrates the contribution of smell to flavor.

The importance of smell in flavor thresholds has been experimentally tested. Hyman, Mentzer, and Calderone (1979) presented solutions of orange juice, vinegar, and chocolate syrup. In some cases participants were allowed to taste and to smell the stimuli, but in other cases they wore swimmers' nose clips to block the smell of the stimuli. These authors used the **forced-choice method**; one cup contained the stimulus, and the other cup (presented either before or after the stimulus) contained only water. Participants were in-

Demonstration 13.7
_____

Importance of Smell
for Taste Experiences

Take a piece of each of the following: apple, onion, and potato. Close your eyes, plug your nose, and take a bite out of each of them. Notice how the tastes for all three of them are remarkably similar. They all have crisp textures, so that if you are deprived of odor cues, there are no important characteristics to distinguish among them.

structed to tell which cup contained the stimulus (detection) and what it was (recognition).

The results of this study showed that the participants were much more accurate in judging orange juice and chocolate syrup when they were also allowed to smell these stimuli. For vinegar, however, the "taste plus smell" group performed no better than the "taste only" group. In other words, smell is often—but not always—helpful.

How does the intensity of a smell-taste combination compare with the intensity of a smell and the intensity of a taste, judged separately? The research fairly consistently concludes that the whole is *less* than the sum of the parts (Enns & Hornung, 1985; Hornung & Enns, 1987; Murphy, & Cain, 1980; Murphy, Cain, & Bartoshuk, 1977). For example, Enns and Hornung (1985) worked with almond extract, which participants smelled, tasted, or simultaneously smelled and tasted. In each case they supplied magnitude estimations of the substance's intensity. On the average the estimates of overall intensity (both smell and taste) were 33% less than the sum of the separate estimates for smell and taste.

▶ **IN-DEPTH:**
HEDONICS OF FOODS

Hedonic preferences, or **hedonics**, involve judgments of pleasantness and unpleasantness, which are central in our perceptual responses to food. For example, suppose you have just lifted your spoon to your mouth to consume the first bite of maple-pecan-fudge-ripple ice cream. The

issue of thresholds might be important if you contemplate whether you can detect the maple, which may be partly masked by the fudge sauce. Adaptation may be important because subsequent spoonfuls might be perceived as less sweet. Cross-adaptation should be considered because if your prior cup of coffee contained aspartame, the ice cream may taste less sweet than if the coffee contained saccharin. However, the perceptual reaction that really matters most is, "Does this taste good?"

We will examine factors that influence hedonic judgments, divided into the two categories, characteristics of the taster and qualities of the stimulus. This organization will provide some continuity with the earlier section on thresholds.

Characteristics of Taster

Clearly, tasters differ. The topics we will consider in this section include obesity, smoking, use of salt, and food aversions.

It may surprise you to learn that obesity does not influence flavor hedonics in any consistent fashion. For example, Drewnowski, Grinker, and Hirsch (1982) reviewed the previous research on hedonic preferences for sweet solutions. One study found that obese people liked these solutions more than normal-weight people. Another study showed no relationship between body weight and preferences. Three additional studies demonstrated that obese people liked these solutions *less* than normal-weight people. In their own study these authors found no relationship between body weight and preferences. As they note, the substantial individual differences among the obese people and among the normal-weight people are at least partially responsible for finding no consistent differences between the two groups.

How does cigarette smoking affect hedonic judgments? In the section on thresholds, we saw that research had *not* demonstrated substantial differences between smokers and nonsmokers. Similarly, research on hedonics indicates few differences in smokers' and nonsmokers' judgments of taste pleasantness, although one difference may have important implications. Kathleen Redington (1984) of Cornell Medical College compared nonsmokers, smokers who were not allowed to smoke, and smokers who were allowed to smoke. These individuals rated the pleasantness of sugar, salt, and quinine solutions, using 5-point scales that ranged from +2 to −2. The results showed that these ratings did not differ for the three groups.

In the second phase of the experiment Redington asked the participants to consume a sugary drink. About 40 minutes later the participants performed three additional taste ratings. The three categories of people did not differ in their ratings of salty and bitter solutions. However, they did have different hedonic reactions to the sweet solutions, particularly the most intensely sweet solution. Figure 13.7 shows how the three groups rated this stimulus. As you can see, the nonsmokers found it somewhat pleasant, the smokers who had not smoked found it closer to neutral, and the smokers who had smoked rated it mildly unpleasant.

Notice, then, that the combination of cigarette smoking and the sugary drink influences the results. This might sound like a rather trivial finding until you consider that smokers who decide to quit smoking often gain weight. Those who continue to smoke may find sweet food less pleasant, after they have already eaten, so they may consume less. However, those who have stopped smoking find sweet food appealing after they have already eaten, so they may consume more. Hedonic ratings of salty and bitter substances are not affected, but these foods are less likely to be high in caloric content. Thus, smoking does not consistently influence he-

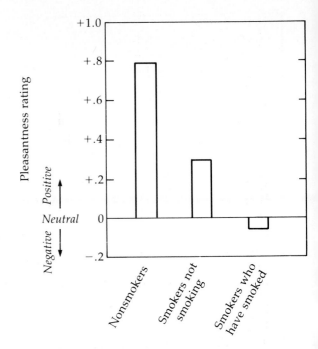

Figure 13.7   Pleasantness rating for very sweet solution, for nonsmokers, smokers not smoking, and smokers smoking. (Based on Redington, 1984.)

donics, but the one condition in which it does have an effect has some important applications for everyday life.

Bertino, Beauchamp, and Engelman (1982) examined how the use of salt can influence hedonic judgments about salty foods. In particular, a group of young adults maintained a low-sodium diet for 5 months; a control group continued on their normal moderate-sodium diet. For 2 months prior to the change in diet and during the 5 months of the diet, the participants were asked to rate the pleasantness of water, soup, and crackers, all presented with varying concentrations of salt. At the end of the diet period the participants who had restricted their sodium intake showed a substantial shift in their food preferences. They tended to prefer much less salty food than before. The control participants, in contrast, did not show a shift in preferences. You probably know people who have been advised by their doctors to reduce their salt intake so that their blood pressure can be lowered. Ask them whether they have noticed any change in their preferences for salty food; they are likely to tell you that potato chips and ham now taste unpleasantly salty.

Finally, tasters differ in their food aversions. Eleanor Midkiff and Ilene Bernstein (1985) of University of Washington distributed questionnaires to introductory psychology students asking whether they had any learned food aversions. Demonstration 13.8 is based on their questionnaire. Midkiff and Bernstein found that 57% of the respondents reported at least one aversion. Intriguingly, most of the food aversions involved foods that are sources of protein. People were likely to report learned aversions to chicken or meat but unlikely to report learned aversions to orange juice or chocolate chip cookies. The authors point out an important consequence of their study. When people undergo chemotherapy to treat cancer, they often develop food aversions to foods eaten around the time of their chemotherapy. If these food aversions involve protein foods—and this research indicates it is likely—cancer patients may develop nutritionally deficient diets.

Qualities of Stimulus

As you can imagine, qualities of food have a significant impact on hedonic judgments.

Moskowitz (1978c) summarizes some of those qualities. Food color is one important quality. Moskowitz reports on a study conducted by Moir (1936), who prepared a buffet of foods for a group of food scientists. However, many of the foods were inappropriately colored. Some of the diners complained about the off-flavor of many of the foods, and several reported feeling ill after eating. We saw earlier that color can influence thresholds, and it also influences hedonic responses.

Temperature also influences hedonics, although there may be individual differences in the suggested ideal temperatures. For example, I have heard Americans travelling to Greece report that the food they ate occasionally tasted less than ideal because it was served close to room temperature rather than steaming hot. To a Greek the moussaka might be best at 25°C, but an American might prefer it at 45°C.

Texture is also important. Consumers are negative, for example, in their reactions to the thin, watery texture of pancake syrups that have been sweetened at least partially with artificial sweeteners rather than more viscous substances (Moskowitz, 1978c). You may have noticed that low-calorie syrups are now available that mimic the viscosity of the high-calorie alternative; their slow-pouring quality makes them seem more genuinely sweet.

As mentioned earlier, aroma is important as a determinant of flavor. Moskowitz reports

---

Demonstration 13.8	Interview your friends to determine whether their food aversions are similar to those reported by Midkiff and Bernstein (1985). Ask each person the following question:
Learned Food Aversions	"People who become sick after eating a specific food may develop an intense dislike for that food, even if it was not really responsible for the illness. For example, a 4-year-old might come down with the flu several hours after eating a particular food, and the child might avoid this food for several years, even though he or she knew that the food did not cause the illness. Have you ever had an experience like this, which produced a strong dislike for some food or beverage?"

that foods lose both their flavor and attractiveness without aroma. A final important stimulus quality, of course, is the nature of the ingredients. We each can identify spectacular cookies and loathesome cookies, for example. The sad news, however, is that humans generally prefer foods high in sweetness and fat content (Drewnowski & Greenwood, 1983). An informal analysis of my favorite cookie recipes supports this finding. The recipe for butterscotch brownies with $\frac{1}{2}$ cup of butter and 1 cup of sugar for every cup of flour is marked "Great!" whereas "Aunt Martha's chocolate brownies," with $\frac{1}{4}$ cup butter and $\frac{3}{4}$ cup sugar for every cup of flour is marked "Aunt Martha is a loser."

In this in-depth investigation of the hedonics of food we saw that characteristics of the taster such as obesity may have little effect on hedonic judgments; however, they sometimes have inconsistent effects, as in the case of smoking. Characteristics of the taster that do have consistent influences on hedonics include salt intake and food aversions. Qualities of the stimulus that can influence hedonics include food color, temperature, texture, aroma, and specific ingredients.■

Summary: Taste Processes

1. The detection threshold, the boundary point at which something is detected half the time, depends upon some characteristics of the taster. Smoking does not appear to influence taste thresholds. Nontasters are insensitive to certain tastes.
2. The detection threshold also depends upon some characteristics of the stimulus, such as color, temperature, and spiciness.
3. Adaptation is a decrease in sensitivity when a stimulus is presented continuously. Laboratory demonstrations of adaptation may not accurately describe our everyday experiences, where we seem less likely to show taste adaptation.
4. Cross-adaptation occurs when adaptation to one substance raises the threshold of another substance; cross-enhancement oc-

curs when adaptation to one substance lowers the threshold of another substance.
5. Various substances can modify the taste of water; for example, after vinegar, water tastes sweet.
6. Three taste modifiers are MSG (which lowers the threshold for sour and bitter tastes), *gymnema sylvestre* (which makes sugar tasteless), and miracle fruit (which makes sour substances taste sweet).
7. Smell contributes significantly to flavor perception; the intensity of a smell-taste combination is about 33% less than the sum of the separate estimates for smell and taste.
8. Some characteristics of the taster such as obesity may have little influence on hedonic judgments; smoking has inconsistent effects on hedonic judgments; salt intake and food aversion do affect hedonic judgments.
9. Some qualities of the stimulus that influence hedonic judgments include food color, temperature, texture, aroma, and specific ingredients such as fat and sugar content.

APPLICATIONS OF TASTE RESEARCH

We have already hinted at some applications of taste research. For example, taste modifiers are important in food technology, and the issues raised in the section on the hedonics of food can be applied in both the manufacturing of food products and in restaurant and home food preparation. In this portion of the chapter we will focus more specifically on these real-world applications. First we will see how food technologists have developed systems of evaluating foods. Then we will look at beverage testing, examining the tasting of wine and tea.

Food Tasting

As discussed at the beginning of chapter, the phrase "food tasting" is really inaccurate, just as inaccurate as the phrase "wine tasting" that will be considered later in the chapter. In our culture we are accustomed to judging food in terms of its flavor rather than its taste. As we said, flavor includes smell, touch, pressure, and pain, in addition to taste. In other cultures, visual and auditory components of food may be even more important than in the United States. For example, in Japanese cooking the visual appearances of the food are particularly stressed (Steinberg, 1969). When Japanese food is served, colors, shapes, and textures are contrasted. Often the items on a plate are arranged in a special design. One dish, which is made for the spring fish festival, consists of tuna, cucumber, radish, and lotus root—all arranged to suggest the flowers, rivers, trees, and mountains of Japan in springtime.

When you cook, you may consider how the dish will *look*, but have you ever considered how the dish will *sound*? Lang (1979) points out the auditory components of food in Chinese cooking:

> Some foods are loved in China because they can be heard while you eat them, thus giving pleasure to another sense. (Eating crunchy jellyfish is a perfect example; in Western cuisine, celery perhaps comes close to it.) Chinese taste is much more complex than taste in the West; the cuisine includes texture foods which are frequently flavorless, and which must be combined with preparations having no other reason for existence than to lend flavor. The most perfect textural foods have no flavor, no fragrance, and, if possible, no color of their own. Shark's fin and bird's nest are perfect examples, of course, and other examples are fish maw, fish cheeks, and fish lips (p. 65).

At this point, you may be eager to leave the exotic realms of Oriental food tasting and return to the more familiar limits of Western foods. One important component of Western food technology is the development of new artificial sweeteners in a country that is increasingly weight conscious. Sometimes these sweeteners are discovered by accident.

For example, in 1965 a researcher named James Schlatter was working with proteins and happened to lick his fingers. They were surprisingly sweet, and thus the sweetener called aspartame ("NutraSweet") was discovered. Compadre, Pezzuto, Kinghorn, and Kamath (1985) discovered another sweetener, which hasn't yet been commercially developed. They were examining a book called *Natural History of New Spain*, written by a Spanish physician named Hernandez in about 1570, and noticed that the author mentioned a sweet plant known to the Aztecs. They tracked down the plant and isolated a sweet component from the leaves and flowers, naming it "Hernandulcin" in honor of the physician.

The most common application of taste research is in taste testing, which is described in a chapter by Moskowitz (1978c). Moskowitz describes the three principal classes of taste testing used today: discrimination tests, affective tests, and descriptive tests.

Discrimination tests involve determining whether two kinds of foods can be distinguished. Discrimination tests are particularly useful when a product developer wants to substitute one kind of food for another. For example, would the consumer notice a flavor change if imitation vanilla were substituted for pure vanilla extract? Discrimination tests might be relevant if consumers have become accustomed to one product and the product developers want to introduce a variant product. After all, if the familiar product is quite different from the new product, consumers might believe that the new product has an off-flavor.

Discrimination tests are also used when a company wants to make certain that all the batches of a product are similar. A company does not want one jar of applesauce to taste quite different from another. Typically, quality-control managers use panelists and discrimination tests to make sure that people cannot discriminate between the current batch being evaluated and a sample of the ideal product. For example, a panelist might sample two substances and report whether they taste similar or different.

Affective tests, or hedonic tests, are used when the product developer wants to measure how much people like a new product. When a food is being developed, there is a long sequence of tests, from the tests in the laboratory, to the taste testing in a supermarket, to trial testing in homes. Sometimes a simple "yes-no" affective scale is used. However, this scale produces less information than a scale with more categories, such as a commonly used nine-point scale.

Usually, panelists in the affective tests are provided with several varieties of a product, such as several different kinds of sausages. Sometimes the panelists also taste a reference sample, such as the best-selling product.

Descriptive tests require panelists to describe various qualities of a food product. Typically, the panelists have already been trained how to use a particular vocabulary, but they are encouraged to develop their own additional terms. For example, panelists might describe the texture in terms of its hardness, brittleness, or chewiness. Several standardized sets of descriptive terms have been developed. For example, in *Consumer Report's* evaluation of ice creams, taste testers could select from among the following terms to describe texture defects: icy, watery, gummy, soggy, and grainy ("Ice Cream," 1981). In summary, taste-test laboratories permit foods to be judged according to their similarity to other products, their pleasantness, and their descriptive characteristics.

Beverage Tasting

By now, you can probably guess that this section on beverage tasting involves much more than the stimulation of the taste buds. To show you how much we use our other senses to determine how something tastes, let's look more closely at wine tasting. If you have talked with a "wine pro," you know that sensory qualities in addition to taste are involved in evaluating wines. As Meltzer (1980) describes wine tasting, the first step involves judging a wine's appearance, so a visual judgment comes first. The two important as-

pects of a wine's appearance are its clarity and color, so a wine should be clear and clean looking. Any cloudiness or haze is a sign of a faulty fermentation process. Johnson (1971) describes 14 color terms that could be used to describe a wine's appearance, including brick red, ruby, and *pelure d'oignon* (or onion skin). Our everyday color terms—such as red, pink, and yellow—seem dull by comparison!

The second step in wine tasting involves judging the odor of the wine. Meltzer notes that experienced tasters believe that the odor of the wine tells the taster practically everything about a wine's character. To smell a wine, the taster swirls it around in a glass to make the wine even more volatile. Then the taster takes a couple of deep sniffs. Some descriptive terms used to characterize a wine's odor include "foxy," "heady," "lively," "sappy," and "musty" (Johnson, 1971). Older wines are described in terms of their complex "bouquets."

Notice that wine tasters may generate a long list of adjectives before a single taste bud has been stimulated. The third step involves the actual tasting of the wine. The tasting confirms the impressions already obtained by judging the wine's appearance and odor. Meltzer suggests that wine tasters should inhale a mouthful of air as they sip. They should next roll the wine around in their mouths. This step ensures that the wine comes into contact with all parts of the mouth and that the volatile odors reach the olfactory epithelium. This step also permits the taster to assess the viscosity of the wine (Amerine & Roessler, 1983). At this step the wine is actually "tasted."

Wine tasters note three aspects of a wine's taste: sweetness, sourness, and bitterness. As Johnson remarks, all other words describing a wine's taste are actually derived from another sense. In a balanced wine the sweet, sour, and bitter tastes are in harmony (Meltzer, 1980). For example, a wine that is too acid tastes tart, whereas a wine that has too little acidity tastes flat. Furthermore, a young red wine that has too much grape tannin will taste unpleasantly bitter.

Demonstration 13.9

Tea Tasting

This demonstration is an abridged version of the tea-tasting procedure used in tea research at the Tocklai Experimental Station, located in the Assam region of Northeast India (Das, 1981). (Courtesy of A. K. Das.)

Select three varieties or brands of tea. Place 1 teaspoon of each of the three kinds of dried tea leaves on a piece of white paper in front of you. Add another teaspoon of each kind of tea to three teapots or other containers. Heat fresh water to the boiling point and add 1 cup of water to each of the three containers. Allow the tea to brew for 5 minutes, then pour each tea liquid into a separate cup. Place a sample of each of the three moist (infused) tea leaves on a plate. You are now ready to judge the dried leaves, the infused leaves, and the tea itself.

First, look at the dried leaves. Are the colors black, gray-black, or brown-black? A tea that is old will look spotted. Is each leaf well-rolled and tightly twisted, or is it open and flaky? Now smell the leaves. Place your nose near the leaves and breathe in. (In Assam a tea taster would bury his or her nose in the dry leaves to appreciate the full aroma.) The tea should not smell burnt or smoky. Finally, feel these leaves; they should not be spongy or damp.

Now judge the infused leaves. The perfect color for infused leaves is bright copper or red. Bright green, dull, or dark leaves indicate inferior teas or damage during processing. All leaves should be approximately the same size. Smell the infused leaves while they are still fairly hot. There should be a delicate aroma; fruity, burnt, smoky, and sour odors indicate faulty treatment during manufacturing.

Finally, judge the tea liquid. Suck in a quantity of liquid and air. According to A. K. Das, Tea Taster, the liquid should be tasted with as much noise as will ensure the sucking of the tea well up onto the palate. Roll the liquid on your palate and allow the air you sucked in to pass out slowly through your nose. (Notice that this process ensures that the aroma reaches your olfactory epithelium.) Observe whether the tea is brisk, as opposed to flat. For example, fresh spring water is brisk, whereas cold boiled water is flat. Now notice the color of the liquid. Is it pale and light or strongly colored? Allow the liquid to cool and notice whether there is a precipitate at the bottom of the cup. The presence or absence of a precipitate is not related to the quality of the tea. However, if a precipitate *is* formed, it should be bright rather than dull or muddy.

As you can see, tea tasting—like wine tasting—involves far more than taste. Smell is critical in judging the dried leaf, the infused leaf, and the liquid. You also made

---

Demonstration 13.9

Continued

visual judgments about the shape and size of the leaves, as well as many assessments of color. Finally, you touched the dried leaves. In fact, judgments about taste itself involve only a relatively small portion of the tea-tasting procedure.

The final step in wine tasting involves considering the wine's aftertaste. After the wine has been swallowed (or spit out), the wine taster determines how long the flavors remain. If the flavor is gone in less than 6 seconds, it is said to have a "short finish." A wine with a "good finish" has a crisp, lingering taste that remains more than 6 seconds. Furthermore, new flavors may appear after the wine is no longer in the mouth. The wine taster notes whether these flavors are pleasant or unpleasant. One important aspect of judging wines is determining whether the taste and the aftertaste meet the expectations created by the initial judgments of the wine's odor.

We have seen that wine tasters consider visual and odor stimuli to be critical components in judging a wine. The actual taste of the wine is less important, as reflected by the short list of adjectives used to describe taste. Finally, judgments about aftertaste primarily concern the duration of the taste rather than involving new categories of adjectives.

As you can see, wine tasting is a complicated process, one that involves much more than the taste buds. This process requires an evaluation of complex visual qualities. Wine tasting also relies strongly upon odor, and wine tasters take special precautions to enhance a wine's odor. Wine tasting also involves judgments about the relative contribution of the sweet, sour, and bitter tastes.

Finally, it considers how the odor and taste components change with the passage of time.

Some groups of people emphasize the importance of wine tasting. In other areas, a whiskey taster would be held in higher esteem. Still other cultures award prestige to tea tasters. For example, in a region of India called Assam, the tea taster is highly revered. Demonstration 13.9 is a simplified version of some components of tea tasting in Assam.

Summary: Application of Taste Research

1. In other cultures visual and auditory components of food may be even more important than in the United States.
2. The search for artificial sweeteners has led to the discovery of aspartame and hernandulcin.
3. Discrimination tests involve determining whether two kinds of foods can be distinguished; they are important in determining whether ingredients can be substituted and whether different batches of a product are similar.
4. Affective tests measure food preferences; descriptive tests measure food qualities such as hardness and gumminess.
5. Beverage tasting involves judgments about the beverage's appearance, odor, viscosity, and taste.

Review

1. Distinguish between *taste* and *flavor*. What are some of the components of flavor, and how does odor contribute to flavor?
2. Describe the four basic taste qualities that humans perceive. Where is each of these

qualities most noticeable in the mouth? Why does the information on taste coding indicate a less-than-perfect relationship between taste receptors and these four basic taste qualities?
3. How does smoking influence taste sen-

sitivity and the hedonics of taste? What other characteristics of the taster were discussed in this chapter? Discuss their influence on both thresholds and hedonics.

4. Suppose that a friend is particularly enthusiastic about the kind of "four-alarm chili" that most people consider life threatening. Gather the information about the sensory and perceptual aspects of spiciness covered in this chapter to provide a synthesis for this person.

5. List three kinds of thresholds discussed in this chapter and provide information about taste in relation to these thresholds.

6. You have put too much sugar in a salad dressing. How would dinner guests' ability to detect the sugar be influenced by each of these factors:

    a. you serve the salad after the main course—a somewhat sweet chicken dish—rather than before the meal

    b. you add yellow food coloring to the dressing

    c. you chill the salad thoroughly.

7. Stimulus qualities were discussed in connection with thresholds and hedonics. Summarize each factor and indicate its effects on perception.

8. Describe adaptation in the laboratory and contrast it with adaptation in everyday life.

9. Discuss the three kinds of taste modifiers mentioned in this chapter and note whether each one causes cross-adaptation or cross-enhancement.

10. Suppose you are a food technologist associated with a company that manufactures a commercially prepared food. Choose a food you might wish to test and discuss how you might conduct discrimination tests, affective tests, and descriptive tests.

New Terms

taste	somatosensory cortex	water taste
flavor	detection threshold	taste modifiers
taste tetrahedron	recognition threshold	MSG
taste bud	difference threshold	gymnema sylvestre
papillae	nontasters	miracle fruit
microvilli	PTC	forced-choice method
taste pore	PROP	hedonics
trigeminal nerve	adaptation	discrimination tests
soft palate	cross-adaptation	affective tests
thalamus	cross-enhancement	descriptive tests

Recommended Readings

Carterette, E. C., & Friedman, M. P. (Eds.). (1978). *Handbook of perception.* (Volumes VIA and X). New York: Academic Press. *Volume VIA of this handbook covers topics such as the history of taste research, the neural coding of taste, and the hedonics of taste. Volume X has an excellent chapter on food technology.*

Keverne, E. B. (1982). Chemical senses: Taste. In H. B. Barlow & J. D. Mollon (Eds.), *The senses* (pp. 428–447). Cambridge: Cambridge University Press. *This chapter provides a concise overview of taste, with particular emphasis on the anatomical and physiological aspects.*

Logue, A. W. (1986). *The psychology of eating and drinking.* New York: Freeman. *Logue's book expands beyond the topics in this chapter to include topics such as anorexia, obesity, and alcohol abuse. Her style is clear and interesting, so the book can be read by those with little background in perception.*

chapter *14*
Attention

Outline

Vigilance
Dependent variable
Factors affecting vigilance

Search
Nature of the material
Are eye movements necessary for
   a shift in attention?
Practice
In-Depth: Two levels of processing in
   search tasks
Application: Reading X-rays

Selective Attention
Features of the unattended
   message
Divided attention
Theories of attention

Preview

Attention is the focusing or concentration of mental activity. This chapter contains three sections: (1) vigilance, (2) search, and (3) selective attention.

On a vigilance task, you try to detect signals that occur infrequently over a long period. Three dependent variables measured in vigilance studies are reaction time, detection rate, and false-alarm rate. People who work on a vigilance task for a long time usually show a decrease in performance, or a vigilance decrement. As you might imagine, a number of variables influence performance on vigilance tasks; these include instructions, practice, personality characteristics, temperature, and noise.

On a search task you try to find targets that occur infrequently and whose location is uncertain. Search performance is influenced by factors such as the target's physical characteristics and the context in which it appears. On some kinds of tasks, people who have practiced for a long time can search for ten targets as quickly as for one. The in-depth section in this portion of the chapter examines evidence for two kinds of stimulus processing, an automatic kind and one that requires focused attention. Finally, the section on search discusses an application of this area of research, how radiologists search for abnormalities in an X-ray.

In selective attention you pay attention to one activity and therefore notice little about others. For example, participants in selective-attention studies may fail to notice whether the unattended message is in English or a foreign language. When attention is divided between two tasks, performance may suffer; however, with practice people can perform remarkably well on divided-attention tasks. This part of the chapter also discusses theories of attention, which differ mainly in their views about whether there are limits to attention and where these limits might occur in stimulus processing.

Attention is a word with varied meanings. We will define **attention** as the focusing or concentration of mental activity. This chapter examines three components of attention particularly important in perception: vigilance, search, and selective attention. Let's consider an everyday example of each area. Suppose you volunteer to make the coffee at a party, and you must watch for the red light to light up on the coffeepot, indicating that the coffee is ready; this is an example of vigilance. Imagine you are looking through the yellow pages of a telephone directory to find the name of the radio repair shop on Jefferson Avenue; this is an example of search. Finally, suppose you are standing in the lobby of a theater before a play and you try to follow a conversation taking place four feet away, although the voices of the conversationalists are partly masked by other speakers; this is an example of selective attention.

In all these situations we perceive or notice certain stimuli but ignore others; consistent with the definition of attention, we focus our mental activity on selected stimuli from the multitude of competing stimuli. You'll note that the examples involved only vision and audition; this bias reflects the research on attention, which almost completely ignores the skin senses, odor, and taste. In everyday life we may search for an object in a dark room, using active touch, and we may focus our selective attention on an unusual fragrance or a food texture. Thus, many of the concepts of attention are potentially applicable to the "minor senses," although they have not been explored experimentally.

VIGILANCE

Vigilance involves the detection of signals presented infrequently over a long period. A comprehensive chapter on the topic of vigilance was written by Raja Parasuraman (1986) of Catholic University, who points out that an important component of vigilance is sustained attention. Vigilance tasks have fairly simple, specified stimuli that appear at a predictable location. The uncertainty in a vigilance task involves timing; stimuli appear at unpredictable intervals. For example, in an industrial setting one of a worker's duties may be to monitor a screen and respond whenever a dial exceeds a certain number. Vigilance can be contrasted with our next topic, search, which involves little or no uncertainty about timing; however, the location is unpredictable. For example, you are not certain *where* the name of the radio repair shop will appear in the telephone directory.

Research on vigilance began with a classic article by Mackworth (1948), reporting how Royal Air Force operators showed less accurate radar monitoring after about half an hour of continuous watch. Since that initial article, more than 1500 papers have appeared on the topic of vigilance (Parasuraman, 1986). An important research issue involves the choice of the dependent variable. We will also consider factors that influence vigilance.

Dependent Variable

As discussed in Chapter 6, the **dependent variable** describes the behavior of an experiment's participants. In a vigilance experiment, for example, the dependent variable assesses how well the participants perform the vigilance task. Think for a moment what you might select as a dependent variable if you were the experimenter in a study in which observers watched a screen and reported when they saw brief signal flashes. What kinds of measures would you obtain to adequately describe the observers' performance?

The three major dependent variables used in vigilance studies are reaction time, detection rate, and false-alarm rate. In measuring reaction time, for example, the experimenter measures the number of milliseconds between the presentation of the signal and the observer's response. Detection rate measures the proportion of "hits," or occasions when the signal is presented and the observer reports perceiving it. Finally, false-alarm rate measures the proportion of occasions when the signal is *not* presented and the observer nonetheless reports perceiving it. As Parasuraman (1986) stresses, all three measures are needed to obtain a complete picture of vigilance.

Let's see how each of these measures of vigilance might change as a function of the length of time the observer has been watching for the signal. In general, performance tends to decline, a phenomenon known as **vigilance decrement.** Figure 14.1 shows some representative graphs of these three performance measures. As you can see, reaction times lengthen (Figure 14.1a). Detection rates also decrease (Figure 14.1b). Finally, false-alarm rates decrease, indicating that people decrease the rate of reporting signals that did *not* occur, as well as signals that did occur (Figure 14.1c). In other words, people respond less often, as time passes.

Signal-detection methods can be used in vigilance studies. A signal-detection approach to vigilance decrements usually shows that the criterion (β) shifts as time passes; that is, the observer is less willing to say "I detect the stimulus." The *d'* measure of sensitivity also may decrease with the passage of time; observers can become less competent in distinguishing signal from noise (Davies, Jones, & Taylor, 1984).

Factors Affecting Vigilance

Naturally, detection rates and other vigilance measures vary widely. Some factors that influence these rates include instructions, practice, personal characteristics of the observer, and environmental conditions.

As you recall, an observer's criterion determines his or her hit rate and false-alarm rate. Therefore, we can expect these measures to be strongly influenced by the experimenter's instructions. People who are told, for example, to be cautious about reporting a signal will be likely to have a low detection rate as well as a low false-alarm rate.

Practice also has an important effect on the vigilance measures. Studies have shown that observers who practice a vigilance task for many hours show a shift in criterion so that it is stable and optimal after a total of about 10 hours of practice (Moray, Fitter, Ostry, Favreau, & Nagy, 1976; Williges, 1976).

The personal characteristic most thoroughly studied in vigilance tasks is introversion-extroversion; introverts tend to focus inward, on themselves rather than other people, whereas extroverts tend to focus outward on other people. Which kind of person do you think would perform better on vigilance tasks? According to a review of 13 stud-

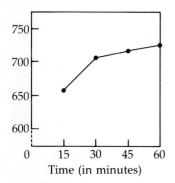 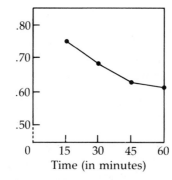 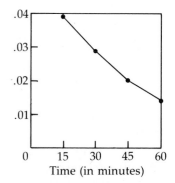

a. Average reaction time (in milliseconds)

b. Average probability of detection

c. Average probability of false alarm

Figure 14.1 Typical example of vigilance decrement as assessed by reaction times, detection rates, and false-alarm rates.

Demonstration 14.1

*Example of
Vigilance Task*

The next time you go to a movie in a commercial theater and the movie is somewhat dull, try this vigilance task. Each reel in a film is about 20 minutes long, and it is specially marked to warn the projectionist to change reels. At the end of all reels except the last, there is a small circle in the upper right-hand corner; a second circle will appear several seconds later as a second warning. See whether you can notice these "signals." Calculate the number of reels in the movie (if each reel is 20 minutes long) and determine whether you were able to locate all the signals.

---

ies, introverts tend to have higher detection rates and lower false-alarm rates (Davies, Jones, & Taylor, 1984). As a result of this combination of measures, they have higher sensitivities, or d's. In other words, if you want someone to watch the coffee pot and report when it's ready, choose an introvert!

Environmental factors influence vigilance, although the results are not entirely consistent. In general, however, vigilance performance is best in moderate temperatures (Hancock, 1984, 1986b). Another environmental factor that can affect vigilance performance is noise. Like temperature, noise often has inconsistent effects. For example, continuous noise degrades performance on complex vigilance tasks but not simple ones. When there is intermittent noise and more noise than silence, low-intensity noise can facilitate vigilance, whereas high-intensity noise tends to harm it (Hancock, 1984). These findings may seem puzzling initially, but they do make sense. A sporadic noise that isn't too loud may help people keep their attention on a boring task, but a loud sporadic noise would be distracting.

In summary, we have seen that instructions to observers can alter the signal-detection criteria they select, and practice encourages them to select optimal criteria. Furthermore, introverts perform better on vigilance tasks than extroverts. Although the results are not entirely consistent, vigilance tends to be best in moderate temperatures

and in quiet conditions. Now try Demonstration 14.1 as an illustration of a real-life vigilance task.

Summary: Vigilance

1. Attention involves focusing or concentration of mental activity. Three components of attention are vigilance, search, and selective attention.
2. Vigilance involves the sustained detection of infrequently presented signals.
3. Three major dependent variables in vigilance research are reaction time, detection rate, and false-alarm rate. Performance tends to change as a function of continuous vigilance; reaction times lengthen, and detection rates and false-alarm rates decrease, a phenomenon called vigilance decrement.
4. Factors that influence vigilance include instructions, practice, introversion-extroversion, temperature, and noise.

SEARCH

In the previous section, we saw that vigilance tasks involve infrequent stimuli and uncertainty about *when* these stimuli will occur. In contrast, **search** involves infrequent stimuli and uncertainty about *where* they will occur.

Search the earlier pages of this chapter to

find a reference to the following paper: Davies, Jones, and Taylor (1984). Now contemplate how you conducted that search. Did you reread the chapter, word for word, until you finally reached that study? It is more likely that your eyes skimmed the pages quickly. You probably ignored most of the other material in your single-minded search for this reference. In fact, Neisser (1964) demonstrated that irrelevant words in a search are not examined closely enough to be recalled later. When observers were tested after searching through a list of words, they usually did not distinguish the words that had appeared on the list from the words that had not.

Think about the numerous occasions in everyday life in which you conduct searches. You arrive at a party and your eyes rapidly inspect the scene for a friend who said he would be there. You look at a menu, searching for the chicken enchilada you know you want. You look at a list on a bulletin board to find your own name and the grade you received in a course. You inspect another list to see if a course for next semester is still being offered.

Psychologists interested in search have examined a number of topics we will consider in this section. The first topic is how performance is influenced by the nature of the material. Our next topic concerns covert attention; can attention be shifted in a search task without moving one's eyes? Practice is the third topic in this section, followed by an in-depth examination of the theory that there are two kinds of search patterns. The last section involves an application of search in the reading of X rays.

Nature of the Material

Try Demonstration 14.2, a variation of a classic study by Neisser (1964). First of all, did it seem to you as if you identified each letter to determine if it was an *N*? Neisser's subjects reported that the irrelevant letters often were only a blur or were simply not seen. The "blur" of irrelevant letters should have been especially true for you on list A, which contained letters with rounded shapes. Neisser found that search times were much faster for lists in which the irrelevant letters were very different in shape from the target. Thus similarity between the target and the background items is an important determinant of how quickly we can search.

Eriksen and Schultz (1979) examined some other physical characteristics that influence search speed. They found that a target could be located more easily if it had greater figure-ground contrast than the other items. It was also easier to locate if it was larger than the other items. Textbooks, such as the one you are now reading, take advantage of these two principles. Notice that new terms appear in boldfaced print, making them easier to find. On page 462, look for the word *dyslexia*, and notice how it is easy to locate. Then look for the word *remedial* which is in regular print. It is relatively hard to find. Also, the headings in the chapters are larger than the other words. Thus you can readily find the section on VIGILANCE. Boldness of print and print size should help you learn material, and they should also be useful when you search for a specific topic.

Which is a better cue for visual search, shape or color? Rayner (1978) and Bundesen and Pedersen (1983) summarize a number of studies that favor color as a cue. For example people searched for a target dial in an arrangement of 16 dials. Search speeds were faster if the dials differed in color than if they differed in shape. Rayner points out that these results make sense, given that visual acuity is relatively poor in our peripheral vision. Thus it is relatively difficult to identify a shape not registered on your fovea. However, peripheral vision can detect color somewhat more readily. We use the information from our peripheral vision to guide our next eye movements. If you are searching for a yellow target, a yellow blur in the periphery will alert your eye to move the fovea toward that area. If you are searching for a square, however, a square in the periphery may not be noticed. You may already have been aware of the importance of color in search. When

---

Demonstration 14.2

Search Times as Function of Type of Irrelevant Letters

A. Search the following strings of letters for the target letter *N*. Measure the number of seconds the task requires.

```
O S Q C O
Q S O C Q
S Q C S O
C Q S C O
S Q O Q C
O O S Q C
C S O C Q
Q S O N C
S Q Q S S
O C Q S Q
```

B. Search the following strings of letters for the target letter *N*. Again measure the number of seconds that the task requires.

```
M W Z K W
W M K W M
K W Z W M
M Z K M W
Z K W M K
M W Z K W
K M K Z W
Z K W K Z
M Z N M Z
Z K W Z M
```

---

you look for your car in a crowded parking lot, do you look for its color or its shape?

Try Demonstration 14.3 before you read the next sentence. These tasks both point out the importance of context in search. For example, Healy (1976) instructed subjects to circle instances of the letter *t* in a long passage. People were especially likely to overlook the *t*s in the word *the*. Exercise A in Demonstration 14.3 has 36 *t*s, of which 8 appear in the word *the*. Were most of your omissions on the word *the*? Healy suggests that high-frequency words such as *the* are searched in terms of units larger than individual letters.

How many *f*s did you find in Exercise B? In fact, there are 17 *f*s in this selection. Schin-

dler (1978) found that when people searched a prose passage, they were highly accurate in detecting letters in the content words—that is, the important nouns and verbs. However, they made many errors in detecting letters in the function words such as *of, on,* and *an*. Schindler considers several different explanations for these findings. One possibility is that when people learn to read sentences, they learn to direct little of their visual attention to function words. Consequently, they fail to notice the individual letters in the words. Did you notice all the *f*s in the *of*s? (There are 9.)

In summary, we have seen that performance on a search task can be influenced by

Demonstration 14.3

Context and Search

A. Read the passage below and count the number of *t*s in the entire paragraph. Perform the task visually, without marking in the book.

All in all, thought Cynthia Farnsworth, the evening had been an enormous success. Most of the guests seemed to be quite impressed by the hors d'oeuvres, which were made out of artichokes and crabmeat. The soup had been a particular hit, especially since it was served in a bowl made out of a hollowed-out pumpkin. For the main course, she had decided on one of Julia Child's cold buffet recipes, *foies de volaille en aspic*. The vegetable was one of John's favorites, cold *ratatouille*. All of them even took second helpings of the dessert, a *clafouti* made out of fresh blueberries that one of the neighborhood children had picked.

B. Now reread the passage and count the number of times you see the letter *f* in the entire paragraph. Again, do not mark in the book. Then read the text for the answers.

physical characteristics such as shape, size, and color. Finally, context is important; some letters seem nearly invisible in the context of certain words.

Are Eye Movements Necessary for a Shift in Attention?

A major portion of Chapter 4 concentrated on eye movements. In that chapter you learned that, since the fovea is the region of the retina in which vision is best, people use eye movements so that new or important material can be registered on the fovea. As you were trying Demonstrations 14.2 and 14.3, you probably also had the sense that your eyes had to move to shift your attention from one letter to the next. On tasks such as these, the visual system overcomes the limited resolving ability of the outer regions of the retina by shifting fixation (Jonides, 1983).

Michael Posner and his colleagues at University of Oregon have investigated whether people can shift their attention at a higher level of processing without actually moving their eyes (Posner, 1980, 1982; Posner, Snyder, & Davidson, 1980). This shifting atten-

tion without moving the head or eyes is called **covert attention;** in contrast, shifting attention that is accompanied by head or eye movement is called **overt attention.**

Posner's studies of covert attention used a task somewhat different from the customary search tasks. Basically, observers were asked to fixate the center of a screen and to watch for a warning signal. This warning signal was either a digit from 1 to 4 (to indicate the area of the screen in which the stimulus would probably appear) or a neutral signal that provided no hint about stimulus location. They were not permitted to move their eyes away from the center of the screen toward the anticipated location; in other words, they could not shift their overt attention. Their task was to respond as quickly as possible when the signal appeared.

The results showed that observers responded significantly faster when the position of the stimulus had been predicted by the warning signal than when there was just a neutral signal. Furthermore, Posner and his colleagues included another condition in which the warning signal occasionally provided incorrect information; for example, it might indicate Position 1, yet the stimulus actually appeared at Position 3. On these trials, observers responded significantly slower than in the condition with the neutral warning signal.

In other words, these studies demonstrated covert attention; we can pay attention to a location mentally, even if we do not look directly at it. When our "mind's eye" is in the anticipated location, we detect stimuli readily; when our "mind's eye" is elsewhere, we take longer to detect the stimuli. Furthermore, other studies show that our covert attention can be shifted in depth (that is, closer or further from the observer) as well as in the other two dimensions (Downing & Pinker, 1985). Eye movements are therefore not necessary to shift attention.

Practice

It is clear that practice improves performance on search tasks. Neisser (1964) reported that search time decreases drastically when the task is practiced constantly. For example, a beginning searcher might initially require more than one second to process one line of a display such as the one in Demonstration 14.2. After 2 weeks of practice, however, the same person might require less than one tenth of a second to process a line. Neisser suggests that as people practice scanning, they discover the perceptual operations that help them scan efficiently. For instance, some people might initially search one line at a time, fixating each item separately and successively. After extensive practice they may be able to examine several lines at the same time.

Even more impressive is Neisser's report that practiced subjects can search for up to ten targets in the same amount of time they require for a single target. Neisser asked subjects to scan mixed lists of letters and numbers, looking for the symbols *A, F, K, U, 9, H, M, P, Z,* and *4.* At first they required almost three times as long to search for ten targets as they required to search for one target. After 2 weeks of practice, search speeds were identical for the one-target and the ten-target

groups. Notice, then, that people with sufficient practice seem to be able to pay attention to ten targets as readily as they pay attention to one.

Neisser's results suggest that observers who practice a search task can shift from a serial process to a parallel process. A **serial process** requires the targets to be processed one at a time. For example, suppose your targets are *A, F, K,* and *U.* If you conduct a serial search on a line from the stimulus array—say *Q, Y, E,* and *U*—you first inspect this line to see if it contains an *A,* then inspect it for *F,* and then for *K,* and then for *U.* If people require much longer to search for four targets than to search for one, we suspect that the search process is serial.

On the other hand, a **parallel process** is one that allows all the targets to be processed at the same time. If you conduct a parallel search on a line from the stimulus array, you inspect that line only once, searching for all four targets at the same time. If people take about the same amount of time to search for four or more targets as to search for one, we suspect that the search process is parallel. Neisser's results suggest that the search process is primarily serial at the beginning of practice and primarily parallel after 2 weeks of practice, because at that time the search speeds for the one-target and the ten-target groups were equivalent. (Incidentally, you can remember the word "serial" because a serial on television is a series that runs one episode at a time. The word "parallel" can be remembered because parallel lines go in the same direction simultaneously.)

Surprising as Neisser's results are for the ten-target group, it is important to note that the ten-target condition may not exhaust the limits of human capacity for multiple searching. Neisser points out that some professions demand even more astounding searches. For example, consider the people who work in a newspaper-clipping agency. This agency may have hundreds of clients who want clippings of any newspaper articles in which they—or their company—are mentioned. Furthermore, many clients may want relevant articles on a number of topics. For example, a peace group might ask for every article about dis-armament, arms control, and nuclear weap-ons. Neisser remarks that it takes at least a year to train a reader to search newspapers at the rate of more than 1000 words a minute, simultaneously looking for dozens of differ-ent key words.

Neisser proposed that the search speed of practiced searchers does not depend upon the number of targets. However, as Rabbitt (1978) points out, people can scan for ten tar-gets as quickly as for one target only when the targets are relatively rare. When the tar-gets appear frequently in a display, then a ten-target search takes longer than a one-tar-get search.

Another problem with Neisser's proposal concerns the speed-accuracy tradeoff. Ac-cording to the **speed-accuracy trade-off**, faster speeds produce lower accuracy. You have probably noticed this in proofreading papers. The faster you proofread, the more misspellings and typographical errors you miss. At slower speeds, you are more accu-rate in your search. As Sperling and Dosher (1986) point out, participants in search tasks are traditionally asked to respond as quickly as possible while making as few mistakes as possible. These two goals are clearly incom-patible, so people must somehow compro-mise between speed and accuracy. In Neis-ser's studies, as Rabbitt (1978) notes, the participants decided in favor of speed, and their error rate was high, often more than 20%.

Rabbitt describes studies in which people were instructed either to search quickly (and presumably make many errors) or to search accurately (and presumably work slowly). These studies showed that Neisser's results held true when people searched *quickly*. In other words, when they were fast and sloppy, the number of targets did not influ-ence search speed. However, when people searched *accurately*, search time increased markedly as the number of targets increased. If people want to search accurately, they must look for all the items in the target set, and they must examine every item in the stimulus array. However, if they want to search

quickly, they can omit some of the target items from the search, and their examination of the stimulus array may be incomplete. Thus their search for ten items may be im-pressively rapid because it is really just a par-tial search. Other researchers share Rabbitt's skepticism about whether search can be a par-allel process (Kleiss & Lane, 1986); even with practice, they argue, there are clear limits to human search capacity.

In this section we have seen that practice improves search speed. Furthermore, in some conditions—when targets are rare and when error rates are high—practiced observ-ers can search for many targets as quickly as they search for a single one. When tasks are repeated so often that they can be performed automatically, our ability to do several things at once is impressive. A number of research-ers have explored a related topic, the idea that there are two levels of processing in search tasks. This issue will be explored in depth in the next section.

▶ **IN-DEPTH:**
TWO LEVELS OF PROCESSING IN
SEARCH TASKS

Current researchers in search and atten-tion generally support the view that there are two levels of processing in search tasks; each level has its own distinct characteristics. One of the first experiments to make a distinction between these two levels was conducted by Walter Schneider, now at University of Pitts-burgh and Richard Shiffrin of Indiana Uni-versity (Schneider & Shiffrin, 1977; Shiffrin & Schneider, 1977). The task they used involved a more complex procedure than Neisser's task because participants saw a rapid series of 20 pictures or frames on each trial. Each frame contained four locations, which could be occupied by a number, a letter, or a set of dots. The numbers and letters could occupy 1, 2, or all 4 of the locations. Figure 14.2 shows a typical frame. Before seeing the 20 pictures, each participant was instructed to remember and search for either 1 or 4 targets. Thus, both target-set size and frame size were varied.

There were two additional variables in this

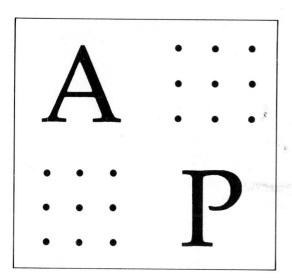

Figure 14.2 Typical frame in studies by Schneider and Shiffrin (1977).

study. The amount of time each frame was exposed varied between 40 and 800 milliseconds. In addition, these researchers examined both consistent and varied mapping. In the consistent mapping condition, the target-set items and the irrelevant items were from different categories. For example, a person might search for numbers, with the irrelevant items being letters. The varied-mapping condition was much more challenging. First of all, the target-set items and the irrelevant items were all from the same category. For example, a person might search for numbers, with the irrelevant items also being numbers. Furthermore, target-set items on one trial often became irrelevant items on the next trial. (On Trial 1, for example, you might search for an *E*, with irrelevant items being *A, C, N, S*, and so forth; on Trial 2, you might search for an *S*, with irrelevant items being *E, A, C, N*, and so forth.)

Now let's consider the results of this study. The factors affecting accuracy were different for the two mapping conditions. In the easier, consistent-mapping condition, the only variable that had an important effect on accuracy was the frame-exposure time; peo-

ple were more accurate when they saw each frame for a long time. However, neither target-set size nor frame size influenced accuracy; that is, people were just as accurate in searching for one item as for four. People were also just as accurate when there were four letters or numbers on each frame as when there was only one letter or number. The consistent-mapping condition was so easy that people performed it rather automatically, even with a large number of target-set items and irrelevant items. People in this condition apparently conducted a parallel search, looking for all four targets in all four positions simultaneously.

The varied-mapping condition produced a different pattern. Exposure time influenced accuracy; as in the consistent-mapping condition, people were more accurate with long exposure times. However, the two other variables also influenced accuracy. Performance was more accurate when searching for one target than for four, and people were more accurate when there was only one letter or number on each frame than when there were four. This task could not be performed automatically. People in this condition apparently conducted a serial search, looking for each target—one at a time—through all items in a frame.

Schneider and Shiffrin therefore proposed two levels of processing in search tasks. **Automatic search** can be used on easy search tasks involving highly familiar items; this search can be parallel. **Controlled search** must be used on difficult search tasks, where items must be searched one at a time.

The theory of two levels of processing has been developed further in the research of Anne Treisman, now at University of California at Berkeley. Treisman (1986) writes,

Some simple generalizations about visual information processing are beginning to emerge. One of them is a distinction between two levels of processing. Certain aspects of visual processing seem to be accomplished simultaneously (that is, for the entire visual field at once) and automatically (that is, without attention being focused on any one part of the visual field). Other aspects of visual processing seem to depend on focused attention and are done serially, or one at a time, as if a mental spotlight were being moved from one location to another (p. 114B).

Treisman and her colleagues have developed an approach to attention that they call **feature-integration theory** (Treisman & Gelade, 1980). Let's examine this model and then see how it can be applied to search. The first stage in this model, **preattentive processing,** involves the automatic registration of features, using parallel processing across the visual field. The second stage of this model, **focused attention,** involves the identification of objects by serial processing. Focused attention is described as the "glue" that binds the separate features into a unitary object. (You'll notice that preattentive processing is roughly equivalent to automatic search, and focused attention is roughly equivalent to controlled search.)

Treisman and Gelade (1980) examined these two kinds of processing approaches by studying two different kinds of stimulus situations, one that used isolated features and one that used combinations of features. These researchers proposed that if isolated features are processed automatically in preattentive processing, then a target different from its neighboring, irrelevant items should be located rapidly. It should seem to "pop out" of the display automatically. In a series of studies Treisman and Gelade discovered that if a target feature differed from the irrelevant items with respect to a simple feature such as orientation or color or curvature, observers could detect the target just as fast when it was presented in an array of 30 items as when it was presented in an array of three (Treisman, 1986; Treisman & Gelade, 1980). Try Demonstration 14.4a to illustrate how a blue letter seems to "pop out," whether there are 2 or 29 irrelevant items; this search involves preattentive processing.

The second part of Demonstration 14.4 demonstrates a search for a target that is an object—a conjunction (or combination) of properties. When you search for a blue *N* among red *N*s and blue *O*s, you must use focused attention because you are forced to focus attention on one item at a time; you are searching at the object level rather than the feature level. On this more complex task, the time taken to find the target increases dramatically as a function of the number of distractors. Furthermore, the time taken to determine that the target is *not* present increases even more dramatically as a function of the number of distractors.

Demonstration 14.4

Searching for Isolated Features versus Conjunctions

Locate two colored markers that have clear, bright colors, such as bright red and bright blue. Then follow the directions for A and B.

A. On a plain sheet of white paper, make one blue *N*, one red *O*, and one red *N*. On a second sheet, make 1 blue *N*, 14 red *O*s, and 15 red *N*s, placing these figures in random order on the sheet. Ask a friend to locate the blue figure on each sheet and notice whether the second task takes substantially longer.

B. Keep the first sheet of paper from Part A. Take a third sheet of paper. Make 1 blue *N*, 9 red *N*s, 10 blue *O*s, and 10 red *O*s. Ask a friend to locate the blue *N* on each sheet and notice whether the second task takes substantially longer.

In other research Treisman and Souther (1985) found that people use preattentive processing when a simple feature is *present* in a target, but they use focused processing when that same feature is *absent* from the target. Figure 14.3 shows displays similar to the ones people examined in Treisman and Souther's study. In Figure 14.3a people searched for a circle with a line; in Figure 14.3b they searched for a circle without a line. As you can see, the circle with a line "pops out" in the left-hand display, but you must inspect the display on the right more closely to determine that it contains the target.

Let's look at the results of Treisman and Souther's study. Figure 14.4 shows the search time when the target was included in the display (positive) as well as the search time when the target was not included (negative). As the figure shows, when the target is a circle with a line, the number of items in the display has little effect on search time (in either the positive or negative situations). However, when the target is a circle without a line, the number of items in the display has a strong effect on search time (particularly in the negative situation). When we are looking for a feature that is present, we can use preattentive processing; when we are looking for a feature that is absent, we must use focused attention.

Feature-integration theory suggests that when attention is either overloaded or distracted, features can be combined inappropriately in perception; an inappropriate combination is called an **illusory conjunction.** When the circumstances prevent us from looking at an object with focused attention, we jumble together the features in the attempt to perceive the object. Treisman and Schmidt (1982) conducted several experiments on illusory conjunctions. In a representative experiment, for example, these authors asked people to look at displays that consisted of two black numbers on either side of a row of three larger, colored letters. The observers were specifically told to attend to the black numbers and report them as well as anything they happened to notice about the colored letters.

The results of this experiment showed

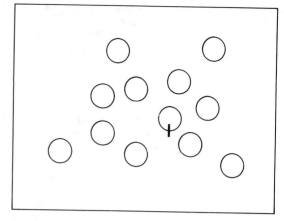

a.

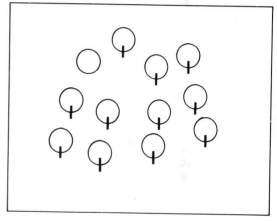

b.

Figure 14.3 Stimuli used in Treisman and Souther's (1985) study. (From A. Treisman & J. Souther, Search symmetry: A diagnostic for preattentive processing of separable figures, *Journal of Experimental Psychology: General, 114* (1985), 285–310. Copyright 1985 by the American Psychological Association. Reprinted with permission of the publisher and author.)

that the observers were highly accurate on the main task of reporting the black numbers; this high accuracy suggests that the task had indeed controlled their attention. Our concern, however, is with illusory conjunctions on the colored letters. On about one third of the trials, observers reported an illusory con-

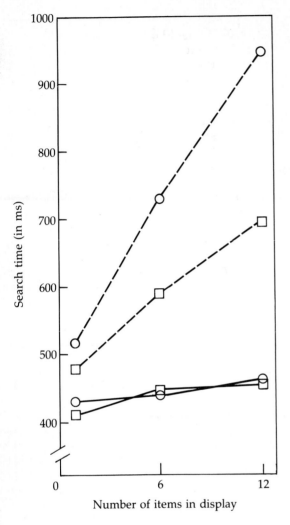

Search time (in ms)

Number of items in display

Target

O━ ━ ━O Without line, target not in display

□━ ━ ━□ Without line, target in display

O━━━━O With line, target not in display

□━━━━□ With line, target in display

Figure 14.4 Results of Treisman and Souther's (1985) study. (From A. Treisman & J. Souther, Search symmetry: A diagnostic for preattentive processing of separable figures, *Journal of Experimental Psychology: General, 114* (1985), 285–310. Copyright 1985 by the American Psychological Association. Reprinted with permission of the publisher and author.)

junction. For example, a person who saw a red *O* and a green *X* might report having seen a red *X*. Without focused attention, the features of an object become "unglued" from each other and are recombined arbitrarily. This arbitrary recombination frequently produces illusory conjunctions.

Why don't we experience illusory conjunctions more frequently? Treisman (1986) suggests that top-down processing helps to screen out inappropriate combinations. She discusses a study in which people saw a set of three colored objects, with two black numbers placed on either side. As in the Treisman and Schmidt study, the participants were instructed to report the numbers. The colored objects included items such as a narrow orange triangle, which was described beforehand as either "an orange carrot" or "an orange triangle." People who had anticipated seeing familiar objects in familiar colors were not likely to report illusory conjunctions; the "carrot" remained orange. However, when the combinations of shapes and colors was simply arbitrary, as in the case of the orange triangle, the features of an object often separated from each other; people were likely to report illusory conjunctions. As Treisman (1986) concludes, prior knowledge and expectations help people to use attention efficiently; even with minimal attention, the features of an object remain combined. Consistent with Theme 4 of this book, cognitive processes aid perception.

A final study on illusory conjunctions is related to the word-superiority effect discussed in Chapters 6, 10, and 11. Treisman and Souther (1986) quickly presented displays of several letter sequences to observers who were instructed to report what they saw. They often reported seeing a word such as *day* when the fragments had been *dax* and *kay*. When several letter strings are presented so quickly that the items do not receive focused attention, illusory conjunctions appear that are consistent with expectations.

This in-depth section on two levels of processing first examined the research of Schneider and Shiffrin, which concluded that automatic search (used on easy tasks with familiar items) is parallel, whereas controlled search (used on difficult tasks with unfamiliar items) is serial. The remainder of the section considered Treisman's research on feature-integration theory. According to this theory, preattentive processing is automatic and uses parallel processing. In contrast, focused attention involves the identification of objects and uses serial processing. Preattentive processing can be used to search for isolated features and features present in a display; focused attention must be used to search for combinations of features and features absent from a display. Finally, when people are prevented from using focused attention, the features of objects can become separated. As a result, people experience illusory conjunctions; they report combinations of shapes and colors that never existed. Top-down processes discourage unlikely combinations (such as a carrot in a color other than orange) and encourage highly likely combinations (such as common English words).

Application: Reading X-rays

It is likely that you have had an X-ray taken at some point in your life. A radiologist then looked at the X-ray to determine whether there were any abnormal structures in the film, a process called **film reading** (Kundel & Nodine, 1978). Film reading involves search and recognition. The radiologist must decide whether any usual structures differ from the accepted limits for size, shape, and position (for example, an enlarged heart) or whether any new structures are present that are not normally part of the film (for example, a lung tumor).

Kundel and Nodine decided to investigate how radiologists searched for a particular kind of lung abnormality, a faint, round structure called a nodule. This kind of nodule might be found in the early stages of lung cancer. Their study is particularly important because earlier research had shown that errors in film reading are surprisingly high for detecting small lung cancers. One estimate, for example, showed that radiologists missed about 30% of small lung cancers and mistakenly reported small lung cancers—when none existed—about 5% of the time (Guiss &

Kuenstler, 1960). Take a moment to try Demonstration 14.5 before you read further.

Kundel and Nodine recorded the eye movements of radiologists as they examined an X-ray. Sometimes the X-ray was normal. Other times, the researchers altered the X-ray so that it contained a small nodule. The results showed several tendencies in search techniques. First of all, radiologists typically either detected the nodule in the first 10 seconds of search or else missed it completely. Second, scanning patterns were neither systematic nor complete. Third, radiologists often began by giving the entire film a preliminary survey, moving their eyes in a wide circle.

In later work Kundel and Nodine (1983) discuss the importance of top-down processing in film reading. Rather than systematically taking in the stimuli and analyzing them in a bottom-up fashion, radiologists quickly focus attention on the radiological abnormality. Once they have a concept about the abnormality, they then use eye fixations to "flesh out" the details.

Thomas (1976) provides some additional information about reading X-rays. He points out that highly experienced radiologists really have little understanding of their own search techniques. They instruct their students to proceed in an orderly fashion through the X-ray, inspecting the film rib by rib. In fact the "masters" do not really search in this systematic fashion—they just *think* they do. (Incidentally, the nodule in Demonstration 14.5 is below the fifth rib on the left side of the X-ray.)

Summary: Search

1. Search involves infrequent stimuli and uncertainty about where these stimuli will occur.
2. Search performance is influenced by physical characteristics and context.
3. In covert attention, people shift their attention without moving their head or eyes; for example, people can shift their attention to a different part of a screen without moving their eyes.
4. With extensive practice on a task in which

Demonstration 14.5

Searching an X-ray

Search the X-ray below to see whether there is a nodule in one of the lungs. The answer appears at the end of this section.

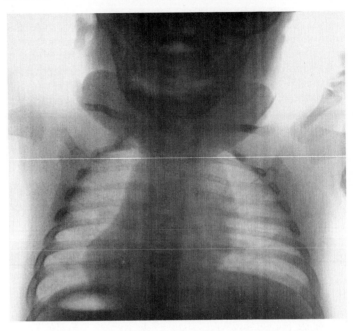

Photo by Ron Pretzer.

targets are rare or error rates are high, people can search for ten targets as quickly as for one; search can be parallel instead of serial.

5. On tasks in which targets are frequent or error rates are low, a search for many targets requires much more time than a search for a single target.

6. According to the research of Schneider and Shiffrin, automatic search is parallel, whereas controlled search is serial.

7. According to Treisman's feature-integration theory, preattentive processing is automatic and parallel, whereas focused attention—which involves the identification of objects—uses serial processing.

8. When people cannot use focused attention, they may experience illusory conjunctions.

9. When radiologists search for an abnor-

mality in an X-ray, they either locate it within 10 seconds or miss it completely. Furthermore, their search rapidly concentrates on the region of abnormality, and their search patterns are not systematic or complete.

SELECTIVE ATTENTION

Selective attention occurs when a person is confronted with two or more simultaneous messages and must focus on one while disregarding the other(s) (Hawkins & Presson, 1986). Selective attention has its advantages and disadvantages. An advantage is that we can concentrate on one kind of activity without interference from other activities. Imagine how complicated life would be if you lacked this ability to focus and you were simultaneously aware of everything that was registered by your senses—all the sights, sounds, tactile sensations, odors, and tastes.

On the other hand, there are disadvantages. You may wish at times that you could study for an exam, eat pizza, carry on a conversation, and listen to music—all at the same time. Unfortunately, however, if you are studying for an exam, you may be able to eat pizza or listen to music, but you probably cannot carry on a conversation. Thus the selectivity of attention can be frustrating; attention to one activity means neglecting another. Incidentally, we discussed a similar situation in Chapter 6 when we examined ambiguous figure-ground relationships. Remember the impossibility of attending to both the vase and the faces simultaneously in Figure 6.13.

Selective attention can sometimes be impressively powerful because people focus so intently on one message that they fail to notice other events happening simultaneously. For example, consider a study by Becklen and Cervone (1983). People watched a television screen that showed two independent superimposed basketball games. In one game the players wore black shirts, and in the other they wore white shirts. The watchers were instructed to attend to the game with the black shirts and to ignore the second game. A short time after the session began, an unexpected event occurred within the unattended game; a woman carrying a large white umbrella sauntered across the screen for a period of 5.5 seconds, during which time she took eight steps. When questioned afterwards, only 18 of the 85 watchers reported having noticed the umbrella woman! People focused their attention so thoroughly on the black-shirt basketball game that they failed to observe this highly unusual event.

Most of the research on selective attention involves selective listening rather than selective looking; people are instructed to follow only one auditory message when they hear two or more. Try noticing how often this occurs in everyday life. For example, you try to follow your professor's lecture despite the distraction of a similar voice in a neighboring classroom. In most cases the spatial origin of the sound provides a powerful tool in selective listening (Hawkins & Presson, 1986). As you'll recall from the in-depth discussion of sound localization in Chapter 9, humans have fairly impressive abilities to identify the direction from which a sound is coming. In the classroom you focus your attention on the message coming from the position directly in front of you; you ignore the message coming from behind.

Selective attention is a topic that has intrigued researchers in both perception and cognition. One of the most common issues in selective attention concerns the unattended stimulus. If two messages are presented simultaneously and a person pays attention to only one of them, what features of the unattended message will be noticed?

Features of the Unattended Message

Perhaps you have had this experience. You have been concentrating on the music from a radio while a friend has been talking to you. Suddenly, you realize that you haven't noticed much about the conversation. Your attention was focused on the music, and most of the features of the conversation were ignored.

One popular way to study selective attention is the shadowing technique. The **shadowing technique** requires a person to listen to a series of words and to repeat the words after the speaker. The name "shadow" is appropriate because the listener must follow the speaker as closely as a shadow. The shadowing task is particularly difficult if the words are presented quickly; this task effectively captures the listener's attention. In a **dichotic listening task** listeners must shadow a message presented to one ear while ignoring a different message presented to the other ear. If the listener is struggling to shadow the first message, how much of the second message will he or she notice? The answer, as we will see, is "very little."

Cherry (1953) performed a classic study using the shadowing technique. Cherry recorded the same speaker reading two different messages. People wore earphones that presented a different message to each ear, and they were instructed to shadow one of the messages. Cherry found that people recalled little of the unattended message. In fact, Cherry changed the message in the unattended ear to German words, and people reported that they assumed that the unattended message was in English. Their attention was so focused upon the material to be shadowed that they were not even aware of the switch to a different language!

In other studies Cherry found that people were usually able to detect when the voice reading the unattended message was switched from a male to a female. However when the unattended message was played backwards (so that a message like *He goes home* became *moh zoge eeh*), only a few people noticed anything unusual about the reversed speech. In summary, Cherry's study showed that the sex of the speaker (or more likely, the pitch of the speaker's voice) may be noticed in the unattended message, but people do not notice whether it is English, German, or gibberish.

One exception to the general rule about people noticing little about the unattended message occurs when this message includes their own name. Moray (1959) asked people to shadow a passage of light fiction. The unattended ear sometimes received messages such as "All right, you may stop now" and sometimes received messages in which the listener's name appeared, for example, "John Smith, you may stop now." People were more likely to obey the instructions in the un-

attended ear if these were preceded by their own names. They rarely stopped for the "All right, you may stop now" instructions, but they stopped about a third of the time for the "John Smith, you may stop now" instructions.

In everyday situations you probably notice your own name even more often than one third of the time. You may be talking with one person, successfully ignoring the many other conversations within your hearing range. If your name is mentioned, however, you suddenly attend to that previously unattended conversation. In everyday situations we can probably switch more readily. After all, we are not shadowing the words of the person with whom we are conversing, so it is easier to monitor other conversations.

So far, it seems that people notice little about the message in the unattended ear. However, there is evidence that people can occasionally acquire some semantic information—that is, information about meaning—from the unattended message (Johnston & Dark, 1986). Try Demonstration 14.6 to illustrate this point.

Did you switch your attention to the message you were supposed to ignore, in order to continue the meaningful sequence in the passage? Demonstration 14.6 is a visual variation on experiments in which subjects initially shadowed a meaningful passage (for example, Treisman, 1960). Suddenly, however, the message in that ear switched to a series of unrelated words. At that same time the meaningful passage continued in the other ear. Some people began to shadow the message

---

Demonstration 14.6

Acquiring Semantic Information from Unattended Messages

Read the following passage, paying attention only to the *italicized* words; ignore the words in normal print.

Once upon a general *time there lived a* principle *most noble* system *and intelligent princess* processes *who longed* resource *to travel* performance *around the entire* experiment *world and* paper *to climb the highest* mountains *and to swim* data *the* widest oceans *interactions.*

"They threw stones toward
the bank yesterday."

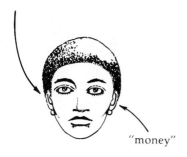

a.   This subject chooses as an equivalent
     sentence, "They threw stones toward the
     savings and loan association yesterday."

"They threw stones toward
the bank yesterday."

b.   This subject chooses as an equivalent
     sentence, "They threw stones toward the
     side of the river yesterday."

Figure 14.5   Setup for the Mackay (1973) study.

in the "wrong" ear. These people must have acquired some information about the meaning of the "wrong" message, or else they would not have known to switch their attention.

A study of Mackay (1973) further illustrates that people can acquire semantic information from the unattended message. As Figure 14.5 illustrates, people listened to ambiguous sentences. For example, "They threw stones toward the bank yesterday" could refer either to a river bank or a bank where money is kept. During each ambiguous sentence the unattended ear received an important message. For the stone-throwing sentence, Mackay presented either the word "river" or the word "money" at the same time as the word "bank" entered the attended ear. People were then asked whether the sentence meant "They threw stones toward the side of the river yesterday" or "They threw stones toward the savings and loan association yesterday." They showed some tendency to interpret the sentence so that it was consistent with the word presented in the "unattended" message.

However, Treisman, Squire, and Green (1974) emphasize that the effect of the unattended message was small in the Mackay study. In some conditions, for example, there was only a 4% shift in the interpretation of the unattended sentence. Thus, we should accept Johnston and Dark's (1986) conclusion that irrelevant stimuli *sometimes* undergo semantic analysis; however, semantic analysis clearly does not occur for all irrelevant stimuli.

Johnston and Dark (1986) point out that top-down processes can influence whether listeners attend to semantic aspects of irrelevant stimuli. Specifically, words that are particularly meaningful and important may be noticed; in fact, if these words are included in the unattended message, they may prevent listeners from attending to the primary message. Nielsen and Sarason (1981) included various kinds of words in the irrelevant message on a dichotic listening task. College-age students were instructed to shadow the primary message. This shadowing ability was not disrupted when the irrelevant message included words that were neutral or were related to topics such as hostility or university life. However, when the irrelevant message included sexually explicit words, students were less accurate in shadowing the primary message. This decrease in accuracy was particularly strong for the more anxious students.

Klatzky (1980) points out that we need to

consider the difficulty of the shadowing task in dichotic listening studies. People may be able to analyze the message in the unattended ear if the shadowing task is not challenging enough. If the message in the attended ear is spoken at a fairly leisurely pace, then listeners may be able to spare some attention for the unattended ear. As a result, they may sometimes notice features of the unattended message that are relatively subtle, such as meaning. However, if the shadowing task is difficult, there may be little or no semantic analysis of the unattended message.

In summary, we have seen that people do *not* notice the following characteristics of the unattended message: (1) whether it is English or a foreign language and (2) whether it is normal English or the same sounds played backwards. However, they *do* notice, at least some of the time, (1) the sex of the speaker, (2) whether their own name is mentioned, and—if the task is not too challenging—(3) semantic characteristics of the message.

Divided Attention

So far our discussion of attention has created a rather gloomy picture of human ability. When we pay attention to one event, we notice little about another event. We have seen that when we pay very close attention to one conversation, we will not learn much about another conversation. In many cases, then, it is difficult to divide our attention so that two activities are performed accurately. Sometimes it is difficult to divide our attention because of physical limitations. For example, you cannot play the piano and eat a taco simultaneously with your right hand. It is even difficult to play the piano with your right hand and hit a golf ball with your left hand.

Nonetheless, it is clear that you frequently divide your attention in everyday experiences. In **divided attention,** attention is distributed among more than one of the competing sources (Swets, 1984).

Right now, for example, you may be listening to music as you read this sentence. You can walk and talk at the same time. In fact, several years ago a popular insult was that someone was so stupid that he or she couldn't walk and chew gum at the same time. Easy tasks can be done while walking, but more difficult tasks cannot. When you are walking with a friend, ask your friend to multiply 5 times 9. The friend will probably keep walking at the same rate. Then ask your friend to multiply 23 times 17 and watch the walking slow to a halt!

Let's examine a study that demonstrates the difficulty of dividing attention between two activities. The study was conducted by Neisser and Becklen (1975) using a method similar to the television setup of Becklen and Cervone that was described at the beginning of this section. Participants in this study watched a television screen that simultaneously showed two different kinds of games. As Figure 14.6 shows, one game was a hand game that you probably played when you were younger. Observers were told to press a switch with their right hands whenever one of the players successfully slapped the other's hands. The other game was a ball game, in which three men moved around and threw the ball to one another. Observers were told to press a second switch with their left hands whenever the ball was bounced or thrown from one player to another.

Neisser and Becklen found that people had little difficulty following one game at a time, even though another game was superimposed. However, when they were required to monitor both games at the same time, their performance deteriorated drastically. In fact, when Neisser and Becklen recorded the number of times that subjects should have pressed the switch but failed to do so, this error rate was eight times as high when two games were monitored as when one game was monitored. Neisser and Becklen propose that it is difficult to follow two events at once for several reasons. Perhaps the most important is that event perception is so organized that when we follow one structured flow of information, we cannot follow a second, unrelated flow of information.

Can people learn to do two complicated activities at the same time? Spelke, Hirst, and

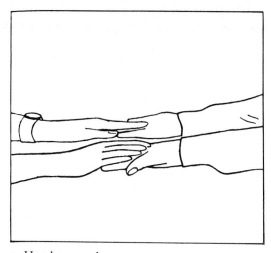

a. Hand game alone

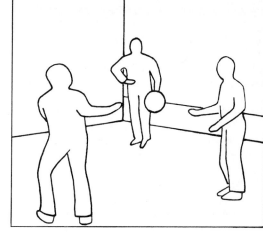

b. Ball game alone

Figure 14.6 Outline tracings of images in Neisser and Becklen's (1975) study. (From U. Neisser & R. Becklen, Selective looking: Attending to visually significant events, *Cognitive Psychology*, 1975, Figure 1, p. 485.)

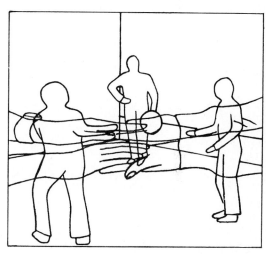

c. Hand game and ballgame combined

Neisser (1976) trained two college students for an hour a day for a whole semester. These students read stories to themselves while the experimenter dictated words to them to copy. At first, this task was very difficult. Imagine how slowly you would read this paragraph if you were simultaneously copying irrelevant words! However, after six weeks, reading speed and comprehension returned to normal. By the end of the semester the students were even able to categorize the dictated word (for example, write FURNITURE when they heard the word CHAIR) without any deterioration in their reading performance.

Additional research with a larger number of participants confirmed these findings (Hirst, Spelke, Reaves, Caharack, & Neisser, 1980). This research also explored and rejected two alternative hypotheses. Specifically, people who had extensively practiced the tasks did not seem to simply alternate, or switch back and forth, between reading and writing. Furthermore, the writing task did not seem to become "automatic" with practice.

If Hirst and his coauthors reject alternation and automaticity as explanations for the participants' ability to do two tasks at once, what do they propose instead? As they write,

> In our opinion, actions change qualitatively when they are practiced. A skilled individual has learned to detect new stimulus constellations and execute new patterns of action, not just to do old things intermittently or unconsciously. The experienced bird-watcher who scans treetops for a woodpecker is not automatically processing the same feature that she once examined in a conscious way; the commands that a skilled typist issues automatically to his fingers are not the same as those that governed his behavior as a novice (p. 116).

Other researchers have verified that practice enables people to divide their attention remarkably well. In Shaffer's (1975) study, a skilled typist was able to recite nursery rhymes while typing at a high speed from a visually presented text. With some kinds of tasks, well-practiced people seem to be able to pay attention to more than one task at a time.

In this section on selective attention, we have seen that people are able to notice some—but not all—features of the unattended message. We have also seen that it is difficult to divide attention between two simultaneous tasks, although people can sometimes perform both tasks at the same time if they have practiced extensively. In the next section we will examine theories of selective attention.

Theories of Attention

Some theories of attention propose that there are distinct limits to our attention capacities. These limits make it necessary for attention to be selective, although the theorists who support this approach disagree about whether the selectivity takes place early or late in the processing of stimuli. Other theories suggest, in contrast, that attention does not need to be limited.

Limited-Attention Theories

People who support a limited-attention theory often refer to a "bottleneck" in attention. Think about what happens whey you try to pour a large volume of water from a bottle that has a narrow neck. Some of the water escapes immediately through the opening, but the rest must wait. Some theorists have proposed that there is a similar bottleneck when humans process information. That is, we cannot process all the information simultaneously because we have a biologically based bottleneck. Some of the information flows readily through the bottleneck, but other information is left behind. Bottles of water are ultimately emptied, but for human information processors the information keeps on flowing. Consequently, the information left behind is forgotten before we can ever respond to it.

Bottleneck theories differ in terms of the location of the bottleneck. Broadbent (1958), one of the earliest researchers in the field of attention, proposed that the bottleneck occurs early in the processing of information, just after the information has been recorded by the sense organs. Figure 14.7 illustrates this early-bottleneck theory. Thus if a person hears the word "apple" in the attended ear, this word will pass through the bottleneck. The word "pencil," which was presented in the unattended ear, will be stopped at the bottleneck. This bottleneck occurs very early in the system, even before pattern recognition. However, there are problems with Broadbent's model. For example, it cannot account for people noticing their own name when it is spoken in the unattended ear.

Treisman (1964) presented a modification of Broadbent's early-bottleneck theory. According to her **attenuation model,** the message from the unattended ear is attenuated, or reduced, rather than being blocked completely. Still, enough of the message comes through for it to be partially analyzed. Con-

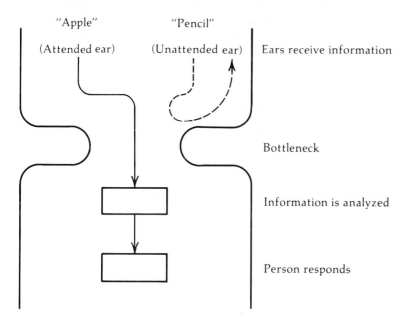

Figure 14.7 Example of early-bottleneck model (schematic).

sequently, some features of the unattended message will be noticed.

Other theorists propose that the bottleneck occurs much later in the processing of information. Deutsch and Deutsch (1963), for example, suggested that all the information is fully processed, and the bottleneck occurs just before the person responds. As Figure 14.8 shows, pattern recognition occurs for all stimuli. The bottleneck in fact reflects the notion that our memory is limited. We choose to remember some things and to forget others. Consequently, we choose to report the message of the attended ear and to forget the message of the unattended ear.

In summary, the bottleneck theories of attention propose a fixed limit on our ability to process stimuli. According to early-bottleneck theories, that fixed limit occurs prior to pattern recognition. According to late-bottleneck theories, that fixed limit occurs after pattern recognition but before the person responds. This late-bottleneck model would allow for the processing of semantic infor-

mation in the unattended ear, whereas the early-bottleneck model suggests that people notice little information about the unattended message.

Johnson and Dark's (1986) review of selective attention points out that there has been massive research during the last 30 years regarding the controversy between early- and late-bottleneck theories. Unfortunately, evidence seems to be available for *both* theories, so the location of the bottleneck cannot be established with certainty.

Unlimited-Attention Theories

The controversy between the early- and late-bottleneck theories continues, yet there are others who suggest that there is no evidence for a bottleneck—at *any* location. Ulric Neisser, whose work we have discussed throughout this chapter, is a major proponent of this viewpoint. You'll recall that he found that people who had practiced a search task extensively were able to search for multiple targets as quickly as for a single target. Fur-

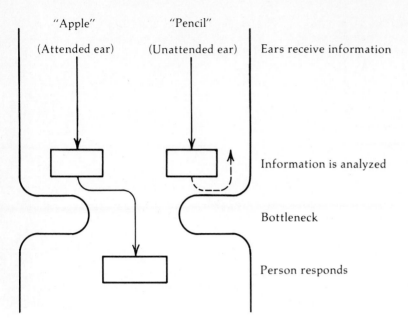

Figure 14.8 Example of late-bottleneck model (schematic).

thermore, Neisser and his coworkers discovered that people who practiced extensively could read and copy words simultaneously (Spelke, Hirst, & Neisser, 1976; Hirst et al., 1980).

Neisser and his colleagues believe that the "evidence for capacity limitations may only be the result of testing at low levels of practice" (Banks & Zender, 1984, p. 541). In contrast, when practice is adequate, there should be no real limitations. As Neisser (1976) wrote, "There is no physiologically or mathematically established limit on how much information we can pick up at once" (p. 99). According to this view, then, humans do not have clearly defined limits to their attention. Instead, they can change the way they perform tasks by practicing them extensively. As a result, humans can perform two tasks simultaneously; attention can be successfully divided.

Summary: Selective Attention

1. Selective attention involves the presentation of two or more simultaneous messages; one message must be attended to, while the others must be disregarded. In a selective-attention task people may fail to notice fairly major events in the unattended message, as demonstrated in the "umbrella woman" study.

2. When people shadow one message, they do not notice whether the unattended message is in English or a foreign language or whether it is in normal English or nonsense; however, they sometimes notice the sex of the speaker, whether their own name is mentioned, and some semantic features of the message. Words from the unattended message may hinder attention to the primary message if the words are particularly significant to the individual.

3. When attention is divided between two tasks, performance may suffer. However, with practice, people can divide attention remarkably well. Practice seems to influence the way people perform the tasks; they do not simply alternate rapidly between the two tasks or perform one of the tasks automatically.

4. Some theories of attention propose a bot-

tleneck, or biologically based restriction on the amount of information to which people can attend.

5. Broadbent proposes an early bottleneck, immediately after the information has been recorded by the sense organs. Other variations of bottleneck models include either a reduction—rather than a blocking—of the message from the unattended ear or a fixed limit later in the system, after pattern recognition.

6. Neisser and his colleagues suggest that limitations on attention occur only when there are low levels of practice. With sufficient practice, there are no necessary limits on human attention.

Review

1. Describe an example of vigilance that you might encounter in your everyday activities. Explain how a vigilance decrement might be revealed in three kinds of dependent variables that could be measured in connection with your vigilance performance on that task.

2. Review the factors that can influence vigilance. Taking all these factors together, describe a situation in which performance on vigilance tasks is likely to be excellent. Describe another situation in which performance is likely to be poor.

3. Describe a typical vigilance task, search task, and selective-attention task. What characteristics do these tasks share, and how do they differ?

4. A common-sense interpretation of visual attention suggests that we can only pay attention to a region that is registered on our foveas, and a shift in attention would have to be accompanied by eye movements. Explain how the research on covert attention, performed by Posner and his colleagues, suggests that eye movements are not necessary for a shift in attention.

5. Review the factors that influence performance on search tasks. Then think of an example from daily life to illustrate each of these factors.

6. The topic of practice was discussed at several points during this chapter. Bring to-

gether this information, relating it also to Neisser's views on whether attention is limited or unlimited.

7. Describe feature-integration theory, as developed by Treisman and her colleagues. Contrast preattentive processing with focused attention. What happens when people are prevented from using focused attention to view objects? What do these results suggest about the limits of attention?

8. Describe a typical selective-attention task and contrast it with a typical divided-attention task. Why are the two kinds of tasks somewhat similar? Imagine yourself at a crowded party; describe how you might find yourself sometimes performing a selective attention task and, at other times, a divided-attention task.

9. Imagine that you are trying to listen to the news on one radio station, yet there is constant interference from the next station on the dial. If you are paying close attention to the news, what features from the other station would you notice? Which features would you be unlikely to notice?

10. At the beginning of the chapter we noted that the research on attention explored only vision and hearing. Skim through the chapter and note how some of the topics could be expanded to apply to the skin senses, smell, and taste.

New Terms

attention

vigilance

dependent variable

vigilance decrement

search

covert attention

overt attention

serial process

parallel process

speed-accuracy trade-off

automatic search

controlled search

feature-integration theory

preattentive processing

focused attention

illusory conjunction

film reading

selective attention

shadowing technique

dichotic listening task

divided attention

attenuation model

Recommended Readings

Boff, K. R., Kaufman, L., & Thomas, J. P. (Eds.). (1986). *Handbook of perception and human performance.* New York: Wiley. *These two volumes of the handbook include three chapters relevant to attention, Chapter 2 on information processing, Chapter 26 on auditory information processing, and Chapter 43 on vigilance.*

Johnston, W. A., & Dark, V. J. (1986). Selective attention. *Annual Review of Psychology.* Palo Alto, CA: Annual Reviews. *This is a superb, well-organized review of the research and theory on selective attention.*

Parasuraman, R., & Davies, D. R. (Eds.). (1984). *Varieties of attention.* Orlando, FL: Academic Press. *This book includes chapters on topics such as the two levels of processing, search, vigilance, and applications in industrial settings.*

Posner, M. I., & Marin, O. S. M. (Eds.). (1985). *Attention and performance XI.* Hillsdale, NJ: Lawrence Erlbaum. *A collection of 35 chapters from a conference on attention, this book covers topics such as the biological aspects of attention, covert attention, and divided attention.*

Treisman, A. (1986). Features and objects in visual processing. *Scientific American, 225* (5), 114B–125. *Treisman's article provides a clear summary of feature-integration theory.*

chapter 15
The Development of Perception

Preview

Most of the research discussed in the previous 14 chapters involved college-age people. In this chapter we examine perception in three other age categories: infancy, childhood, and late adulthood and old age.

Research with infants is hampered because of their limited abilities in communicating their perceptual skills to researchers. However, several research techniques have been developed that reveal that infants are more perceptually skilled than we once thought. For example, at a young age babies can see colors, make sophisticated judgments about speech sounds, and imitate adult facial expressions. Also, they respond to sweet, bitter, and sour substances shortly after birth. However, infants differ from adults in acuity, eye coordination, and constancy, as well as the anatomical maturity of their sensory systems.

Research with children is difficult because they may not understand the task instructions, and they have limited motor skills. As children grow older, they change in their shape perception, their understanding of pictures, their responses to constancy tasks, and their ability to pay attention to important information and to ignore irrelevant information.

Research that compares older adults with college-age students frequently fails to equate the two groups on factors such as education level and health. Elderly people are more likely than younger people to have visual impairments or acuity problems as well as distortions in color perception. As they grow older, people experience a hearing loss for certain tones when the listening conditions are not ideal; speech perception may be impaired. However, elderly people may not differ from younger people in some measures of touch, smell, and taste. Furthermore, elderly people make good use of top-down processing to facilitate perception.

Imagine that a 6-month old infant, a 6-year old child, and a 60-year old grandparent are all gathered at the same family reunion. Would they perceive the environment in the same way? Would their perceptual responses to colors, shapes, and movements be similar? Would they share the same auditory experiences? Would they react the same way to touch, warmth, and other skin senses? Would the food smell and taste the same to all three people? These three people all encounter the same sights, sounds, touch sensations, smells, and tastes. However, are their perceptions equivalent? Alternatively, do perceptual processes change so substantially as people grow older that these three people would have entirely different perceptions of the world?

In the first 14 chapters of this book we concentrated almost exclusively upon perception in young adults. As you can imagine, most perception research uses college students, who typically take part in an experiment as part of their course in introductory psychology. In this chapter we will examine how perception changes as a function of development. What kinds of perceptual abilities does a young infant have? How does perception develop during childhood? Furthermore, how do the perceptual abilities of older adults differ from the abilities of young adults?

In this chapter you will see that our perceptual systems continue to develop from the moment of birth through late adulthood and old age. The infant comes into the world with remarkably good perceptual systems, which continue to develop and mature. Many aspects of perception remain strong throughout old age, but other aspects show some deterioration and loss as we grow older.

We will examine three age categories in this chapter: (1) infancy, (2) childhood, and (3) late adulthood and old age. As we will note, each age category presents methodological problems in research. Infants cannot supply verbal responses, so researchers must devise other methods of assessing their perceptual abilities. Children can provide verbal responses, but researchers must still be con-cerned that performance deficits might be due to motor inability or failure to understand the instructions. In the case of the elderly, any performance deficits might be due to poor health and other factors rather than to a decline in perceptual abilities.

INFANCY

William James, the 19th-century American psychologist, proclaimed that the world of a newborn is a "great blooming, buzzing confusion" (James, 1890, p. 488). According to this view, newborn infants opened their eyes and saw an unstructured, unpatterned chaos. In the last 100 years, psychologists have drastically revised their ideas about what infants perceive. We now have evidence that the newborn has remarkably good perceptual systems—much better than the early researchers had imagined.

It is difficult to assess infants' perceptual abilities because their motor and verbal skills are so limited that they cannot inform us about their perceptual capacities. After all, an infant cannot say, "The left-hand figure is farther away." In animal research, psychologists have had to devise special techniques to gather information from pigeons and rats. Similarly, psychologists have been forced to invent clever methods for discovering infants' perceptual capacities. The results obtained with these methods are a major reason for our altered assessment of infant perception in recent years.

Most of the methods are variations of one of three basic methods: preference, habituation, and conditioning. We will be examining each of these methods in this chapter. It seems, then, that infants are not severely handicapped with respect to their perceptual capacities, but they are handicapped in terms of informing us about what they can perceive.

Vision in Infancy

Our discussion of infant vision will include several topics: (1) visual abilities, (2) color perception, (3) shape perception, (4) distance and motion perception, and (5) constancy.

Visual Abilities

How does the visual equipment of a newborn compare with the visual equipment we have as adults? The optical quality of the young infant's eye appears to be remarkably good (Banks & Salapatek, 1983; Movshon & Van Sluyters, 1981); that is, the cornea and the lens have the capability to focus an image on the retina. However, the retina itself is still not fully developed. As it happens, the cones and rods in the periphery of the retina are nearly adultlike. However, the receptors in the fovea are relatively immature (Abramov et al., 1982; Banks & Salapatek, 1983). As we will see, this immaturity has important implications for acuity.

As we move to higher levels in the visual system, we see that the lateral geniculate nucleus (LGN) is already distinctly layered in the newborn infant. However, the cell bodies in each layer are smaller than in adults (Banks & Salapatek, 1983). It seems that the pathways between the LGN and the cortex—as well as the visual cortex itself—are not fully developed at birth (Maurer & Lewis, 1979). However, development progresses rapidly; these regions are reasonably mature by 2 months of age.

When ophthalmologists measure your acuity, they may ask you to name the letters in each row of the Snellen eye chart. Think for a moment how you might try to measure acuity for a newborn. As you can imagine, early researchers had difficulty devising a measurement technique.

Robert Fantz was responsible for a major breakthrough in measuring acuity in infancy, using the preference method. The **preference method** is based on the idea that if the infant spends consistently longer looking at one figure in preference to another figure, then the infant must be able to discriminate between the two figures. Researchers using the preference method try to discover the smallest width of a striped pattern that a baby will prefer to a uniform gray pattern that is equivalent in brightness.

Fantz (1961) placed the infants in a small crib inside a special "looking chamber." He attached pairs of test objects—slightly separated from each other—onto the ceiling of the chamber. The researcher could look through a peephole to see the infants' eyes. Mirrored in the center of the eye, just over the pupil, would be the tiny image of the test object that the infant was looking at, for example, a striped patch or a gray patch. The amount of time the infant spent looking at the striped patch and the amount of time spent looking at the gray patch were both recorded. For example, a particular infant might look at the striped patch 65% of the time and the gray patch 35% of the time. The testing sessions were carefully controlled, so that the striped patch would appear on the left half the time and on the right half the time to ensure that any effects of position preference did not confound the study.

What does the information about looking times tell us? Well, if the infants were *unable* to tell the difference between the two objects, then the two looking times should be roughly equivalent. For example, the baby might look at one figure 48% of the time and at the other figure 52% of the time. However, if the baby looks at one figure for a consistently longer time (such as 65% for a striped patch and 35% for a gray patch), then we can conclude that the baby can tell the difference between the two figures. That is, the baby's acuity is good enough that the narrow stripes are distinguishable from the gray patch.

Studies using Fantz's preference method show that 1-month-olds can distinguish between a gray patch and stripes $\frac{1}{16}$ inch (1.6 mm) wide when both patches are placed 10 inches (25 cm) from the infants' eyes (Atkinson & Braddick, 1981). This acuity, in Snellen notation, would be 20/400, or about 5% of adult acuity. Although this acuity isn't very impressive, it is still sufficient to provide the infant with some functional vision.

Acuity improves rapidly, particularly as the receptors in the fovea develop. Babies 6 months old can see stripes $\frac{1}{64}$ inch (0.4 mm) wide, which is equivalent to 20/100 vision (Bornstein, 1984c). By 1 year of age, acuity is approximately 20/60 (Gwiazda, Brill, Mohindra, & Helds, 1980). Now try Demonstration 15.1 to illustrate the preference method for measuring infant acuity.

Researchers have also discovered that infants' accommodation abilities are better than had been suspected, but they are still limited in comparison to adults' accommodation abilities (Atkinson & Braddick, 1981; Salapatek, Bechtold, & Bushnell, 1976; Ruff, 1982). Thus, infants have some difficulty focusing on objects close to their eyes or far away.

If you have had the opportunity to watch a newborn baby, you might have noticed something unusual about the baby's eye movements. In particular, the eyes occasionally move in different directions from each other (Bornstein, 1984c). The eye muscles are not well enough developed at birth to keep both eyes on the same target. Thus newborn babies must often receive information from only one eye and ignore information from the other eye. Like other visual abilities, however, eye coordination improves rapidly during the first few months of life.

Color Perception

Can babies see color? In general, the evidence suggests that 1-month-old infants have difficulty discriminating red or green stimuli from a yellow background. By 3 months of age, however, infants seem to be trichromats (Teller, 1981; Teller & Bornstein, 1986).

One of the primary researchers in infant color vision is Marc Bornstein of New York University, whose work on color categories we examined in Chapter 5. Bornstein has demonstrated that infants seem to sort colors into separate categories in much the same way that adults sort colors.

Demonstration 15.1

Preference Method for Measuring Acuity

Prop up your textbook and walk backward until the narrow-striped patch on the right is indistinguishable from the uniform gray patch in the middle. If 1-month-old babies saw these two patches at a distance of 10 inches, they would look at them equally; they would appear to be the same. However, if the striped patch on the left looked as different from the uniform gray patch as it does to you now, babies might look at the striped patch more than at the uniform gray patch; they would appear to be different. Incidentally, when all stimuli are presented at a distance of 10 inches from babies, 1-month-olds can distinguish the left-hand striped patch ($\frac{1}{16}$″ wide) from the uniform gray patch; 6-month-olds can distinguish the right-hand striped patch ($\frac{1}{64}$″ wide) from the uniform gray patch.

  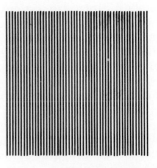

Adults typically divide the spectrum into a small number of basic color names. For example, consider the spectrum in Color Plate 1. If we asked English speakers to name the color represented by a light of 450 nm, almost everyone would reply "blue." If we asked them to name the color represented by a light of 480 nm, they would still respond "blue." However, a light of 510 nm would produce the answer "green." Notice that 480 nm is equally distant *physically* from 450 nm and 510 nm (that is, 30 nm). However, 480 nm is closer *psychologically* to 450 nm than to 510 nm; after all, people respond "blue" both to 450 nm and to 480 nm, but they have a different psychological response, "green," to 510 nm.

Bornstein, Kessen, and Weiskopf (1976) wondered whether infants divide the spectrum in the same fashion. Unfortunately, you cannot point to a light of 480 nm and expect an infant to produce a color label. Instead, Bornstein and his colleagues used the habituation method. The **habituation method** is based on a phenomenon known as habituation, which is a decrease in attention to repeated stimulation. We have discussed adaptation throughout this book, and initially, habituation may sound like adaptation. However, adaptation involves a decrease in responsiveness from the sensory receptors. In contrast, habituation is a cognitive process, which involves mental representations and memory (Bornstein, 1985b). When a baby pays less attention to an object that has been presented several times, the baby is demonstrating that he or she remembers seeing the object.

For example, suppose that we present a 480-nm light repeatedly to an infant. After a number of presentations, the infant will show habituation and pay less attention to the light. If we then present a 680-nm light, the baby will probably show **dishabituation,** or an increase in looking time. Apparently, the 680-nm light looks different from the previous 480-nm light, so the baby will pay attention to it.

As we said earlier, adults think that a 510-nm light looks different from a 480-nm light,

but a 450-nm light looks much the same as a 480-nm light. Using the habituation method, Bornstein and his colleagues showed that 4-month-olds agree with adults.

Specifically, they habituated infants to a 480-nm light. Then when they presented a 450-nm light, the infants ignored the light, indicating that they perceived that it was the same color as the earlier 480-nm light. However, when infants who had been habituated to a 480-nm light were shown a 510-nm light, they showed dishabituation; they looked at the new light. This dishabituation indicates that they perceived that it was a different color from the earlier 480-nm light. Combining this information with data from other wavelengths, Bornstein and his colleagues concluded that infants' and adults' color worlds are organized similarly. Infants, like adults, show categorical perception of colors, with colors in the same category treated similarly. More information on infant color vision can be found in a review article by Teller and Bornstein (1986).

Shape Perception

Studies on shape perception in infancy tend to fall into two categories: (1) studies on the characteristics of shapes that infants prefer to examine and (2) studies on the recognition of faces.

Using the preference method described earlier, Fantz (1961) demonstrated that infants are more interested in looking at patterns than at bright colors. Fantz presented 2- to 3-month-olds with six test objects—flat disks 6 inches in diameter. Three of these objects had patterns—a cartoonlike face, a patch of printed words, and a bull's-eye. The other three were plain—red, fluorescent yellow, and white. The disks were presented one at a time, and Fantz measured how long the infants looked at each object the first time it was presented. The cartoonlike face was the clear winner, followed by the newsprint and the bull's-eye. Try Demonstration 15.2 to see if your results are similar.

Many of you will experience difficulty in locating infants and children to test with the demonstrations in this chapter. Demonstra-

Demonstration 15.2
_____

Infants' Preferences
for Shape

This demonstration requires a 2- to 6-month-old infant. You will also need to make six test objects, each a circle 6" in diameter. Cut three circles out of plain white paper. Leave one of them white. On the other two, draw a cartoon-like face and a bull's eye, using a black marker; use the designs below. Cut a fourth circle out of newspaper. The fifth and sixth circles should be cut from bright yellow and red paper. Using a watch with a second hand, present one test object at a time. Measure the number of seconds the baby looks at each object before glancing away. Incidentally, if you cannot find an infant, try the demonstration on an older child or adult to see if the results are comparable to Fantz's results with young infants.

tions 15.2 and 15.4 may be tested with an adult, if necessary. If you do locate a child of the appropriate age, you must be sure to obtain permission from the child's parents before proceeding. Tell the parents that you will not be testing the child's abilities. Instead, you simply want to observe a normal child's perceptual reactions, as part of a course assignment. Be sure to show the material to the parents before you begin.

In later research Fantz and Yeh (1979) demonstrated that as newborns mature, their preferences change. Initially, they prefer simple patterns with highly contrasting elements; by 5 months of age, they like to look at objects with subtle variations in contrast. Other researchers have discovered that young infants generally display three preference patterns: (1) they prefer curvilinear patterns to straight-line patterns; (2) they prefer concentric patterns (as in a bull's-eye) to nonconcentric patterns; and (3) they prefer designs with multiple orientations to designs

with all lines in the same orientation (Banks & Salapatek, 1983; Ruff & Birch, 1974).

It is also clear that babies like to look at human faces. Psychologists used to think that babies were born with an unlearned preference for the human face. However, more recent research suggests that babies prefer to look at faces because faces have a high degree of contour and because they move. Other objects that have the same amount of contour and movement capture babies' attention just as much as faces (Flavell, 1977).

Other research on infants' perception of faces asks a different question: How old must an infant be to recognize a parent's face? Psychologists had previously been pessimistic about infants' ability to recognize faces. In fact, they argued that infants could not form emotional attachments to their parents until at least 6 months of age because they could not distinguish parents from strangers. However, more recent studies have demonstrated that we had underestimated infants' abilities;

they seem to be able to make these discriminations somewhere between 1 and 3 months of age (Bushnell, 1982; Barrera & Maurer, 1981; Ruff, 1982).

In the last few years psychologists have discovered that infants are even more amazing than we had expected because they can appreciate facial expressions. For example, Caron, Caron, and Myers (1982) observed that by 7 months of age, babies could distinguish between happy and surprised facial expressions. Caron and her colleagues used the habituation method, described earlier, and demonstrated that babies who had seen several faces wearing happy expressions were likely to pay more attention to a face that was surprised in contrast to yet another happy face. Also 3-month-olds prefer to look at faces that are smiling intensely rather than half-hearted smiles (Kuchuk, Vibbert, & Bornstein, 1986). Parents who want their baby's attention should therefore smile broadly but intersperse the smiles with a few astonished stares.

Perception of Distance and Motion

A 10-month-old infant crawls down the hallway and pauses at the top of the stairs, looking back and forth between the step and the next step down. Can infants see depth? Are they aware which surfaces are farther away from them? These questions were investigated by Gibson and Walk (1960), who measured depth perception with a visual cliff.

As Figure 15.1 shows, a **visual cliff** is a

kind of apparatus in which infants must choose between a side that looks shallow and a side that looks deep. Babies are placed on a central board with a sheet of strong glass extending outward on both sides. On one side a checkerboard pattern is placed directly under the glass. On the other the same checkerboard pattern is placed some distance beneath the glass. The apparatus is called a visual cliff because of the apparent drop-off on the "deep side" of the central board. To an adult the pattern on the upper side of Figure 15.1 looks farther away because the elements in the pattern are smaller. Gibson and Walk wondered whether infants' perceptions would be similar.

In one experiment Gibson and Walk tested 36 babies between 6 and 14 months of age. They placed a baby on the central board and asked the baby's mother to call to the baby from both the shallow and the deep side. Gibson and Walk found that 27 babies moved off the central board at some time during the experiment, and all 27 crawled at least once onto the shallow side. In contrast, only three babies crawled onto the deep side. Thus, babies old enough to crawl are able to discriminate between deep and shallow; their depth perception is well enough developed that they could avoid the potentially dangerous deep side. Later studies have also shown that experience with crawling is related to avoiding the deep side of a visual cliff (Rader, Bausano, & Richards, 1980; Richards & Rader, 1981).

The visual cliff was originally designed to test infants old enough to crawl. Later researchers measured depth perception in terms of a change in the infant's heart rate. Infants as young as 2 to 4 months showed a greater change in their heart rate when placed over the deep side of the visual cliff than when placed over the shallow side (Campos, Langer, & Krowitz, 1970).

In general, babies can use binocular depth information by the age of 4 or 5 months (Banks & Salapatek, 1983; Fox, 1981; Yonas & Granrud, 1985). This is also the age at which babies begin to appreciate depth information shown in pictures (Kaufmann, Maland, &

Figure 15.1 Visual cliff.

Yonas, 1981; Yonas, Cleaves, & Pettersen, 1978). By the time babies reach the ripe old age of 6 months, then, they are reasonably expert in knowing that their toes are farther away than their knees and the mobile above their crib is closer than the ceiling.

Babies respond to movement as soon as they are born. Goren, Sarty, and Wu (1975) presented a variety of facelike cartoons to babies who were an average of 9 minutes old. Babies consistently turned their heads to follow the moving stimulus. By 5 months they can make relatively subtle motion discriminations (Ruff, 1985). Babies also appreciate biological motion. As you'll recall from the indepth discussion in Chapter 7, biological motion is the pattern of movement of living things. At some time between the ages of 6 and 9 months, babies develop the ability to look at a display of moving lights and perceive the pattern as representing the motion of a person (Berthenthal et al., 1985; Fox & McDaniel, 1982). Thus, babies are born with the ability to appreciate primitive motion, and an understanding of more subtle kinds of movement is developed before they are 1 year old.

Constancy

In Chapter 8 we talked about the nightmare that would result if all our perceptual constancies were to disappear. Objects would grow and shrink, become alternately regular in shape and then irregular, and change from light to dark. Objects would also change their color, speed, location, and even their existence from moment to moment. Fortunately, we know from our own experience that adults have perceptual constancy. However, none of us can remember what objects looked like when we were infants. Are infants blessed with the constancies? Alternatively, do parents grow and then shrink as they approach and then move away? Does the shape of the baby food jar change as the infant inspects it from different angles? Unfortunately, the answers to these questions are still controversial.

Cognitive psychologists in the tradition of the Swiss psychologist Jean Piaget have ex-

tensively examined one aspect of constancy called **object permanence**, or the belief that an object still exists even though it is no longer visible. (For example, you know that a paperclip still exists, even if you completely cover it with your hand.) Of the more perceptual constancies, only size constancy and shape constancy have been examined systematically.

Size constancy seems to be present in 6-month-old infants, but it is not clear whether it is present in even younger infants. Let's look at a classic experiment by Bower that showed evidence of size constancy in babies as young as 6 weeks of age; then we will summarize some more recent evidence.

So far we have discussed two major methods for assessing infants' perceptual skills: preference and habituation. Bower (1966) employed the third major method: conditioning. In the **conditioning method** the experimenter selects a response that the baby can make and delivers a reward when the baby makes that particular response. Bower selected head turning as an appropriate response in his studies. Infants responded by turning their heads as little as one cm (0.4 inch), a response that was neither difficult nor tiring for even young infants. Bower chose an interesting reward for these head-turning responses: peekaboo. When the infant turned his or her head, the experimenter would pop up in front of the infant, smiling and nodding, patting the infant on the stomach, and speaking cheerfully. This multimedia peekaboo game proved to be such a delightful reward for young babies that they responded for a long time to earn a peekaboo.

How did Bower use the conditioning method to provide information about size constancy? Bower trained infants to perform the head-turning response only when a particular white cube was present. If they turned their heads when the cube was not present, they received no peekaboo reward.

Next Bower tested for **generalization**, or the tendency to make a learned response to stimuli that resemble the original stimulus. In the generalization phase of the experiment, Bower presented the original white cube and three other cubes, as illustrated in Figure 15.2. He measured the number of head-turning responses that each cube elicited. The number of responses can be interpreted as an index of an object's similarity to the original cube. For example, we would expect infants to turn their heads most frequently when the original cube is presented during the generalization phase. However, we would expect almost no head turns if a completely different object, such as an old tennis shoe, were presented. The white cubes numbered 1, 2, and 3 in Figure 15.2 should elicit an intermediate number of responses, depending upon the extent to which the infants perceive them as similar to the original cube.

Bower was particularly interested in the number of responses provided to Stimulus 1, which was a cube the same size as the original cube, except that it was far away. A large number of responses to this cube could be interpreted as a demonstration of size constancy, or the recognition that an object stays the same size despite changes in its distance.

Infants 6 to 8 weeks of age responded a total of 98 times to the original stimulus, 58 times to Stimulus 1, 54 times to Stimulus 2, and only 22 times to Stimulus 3. Because of

the relatively large number of responses to Stimulus 1, Bower concluded that infants have some size constancy. Further evidence for this conclusion came from the low response rate for Stimulus 3, an object that occupied the same amount of space on the retina as the original stimulus. Infants recognized that this stimulus was different from the original stimulus, so they responded less.

More recent studies, using both the conditioning method and the habituation method, have been more pessimistic about size constancy in very young infants (Day & McKenzie, 1977; McKenzie, Tootell, & Day, 1980). It seems safe to conclude that some aspects of size constancy can be found in 6-month-olds, but we can't draw conclusions about younger infants (Banks & Salapatek, 1983). As we saw, some form of depth perception is developed by 4 months of age, and information about depth may facilitate an appreciation for size constancy during the next 2-month period.

It is also unclear when infants develop shape constancy. Bower (1966) used the conditioning method to test infants for shape constancy in figures that were tilted. He con-

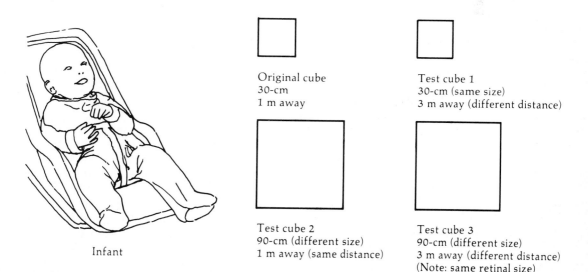

Figure 15.2 Setup for Bower's (1966) experiment.

cluded that 2-month-old infants responded as if objects kept the same shape, despite the angle from which they were viewed. However, more recent evidence suggests that shape constancy develops at about 3 or 4 months of age (Banks & Salapatek, 1983; Bornstein, Krinsky, and Benasich, 1986; Caron, Caron, & Carlson, 1979). Even if the age of size constancy is 4 months, rather than 2, think about this impressive accomplishment. A 4-month-old weighs about 15 pounds, won't crawl for 4 more months, and won't say a word for 8 more months. Nevertheless, this baby knows that an oval shape viewed from an angle is really a circle and a trapezoidal shape from an angle is really a square!

Hearing in Infancy

Perception of Nonspeech Sounds

Even before babies are born, they have many opportunities to hear. Life in the uterus may be dark, but it certainly isn't quiet. For example, the sound level in the vicinity of the head is about 80 dB, primarily due to the noise from the mother's pulse. This is approximately the intensity of loud music from the radio. Noises from the outside world also reach the fetus; low-frequency sounds may be only 20 dB less intense inside the uterus (Morse & Cowan, 1982). A pregnant woman should think twice before buying tickets for a heavy-metal rock concert because the fetus can't wear earplugs!

We discussed the difficulty of determining what a newborn can *see*. It's even trickier to determine what a newborn can *hear*. In visual research we can measure an infant's eye movements or fixation patterns; however, we can't directly measure the ear's "fixation patterns" (Aslin, Pisoni, & Jusczyk, 1983). Therefore, the methods we discussed in connection with infant vision must be modified to accommodate the additional challenges of measuring hearing in infancy.

The auditory system develops early in the prenatal period. For example, the eustachian tube is largely formed at 10 weeks after conception, and the ossicles (the bony structures

in the middle ear) have reached their adult size and general shape by about 15 weeks after conception (Bredberg, 1985). The middle and inner ear are therefore relatively well developed when the baby is born (Walk, 1978). Higher levels of auditory processing are not yet mature, however, and they continue to develop during the first 2 years of life (Morse & Cowan, 1982).

In general, hearing thresholds in newborns are about 10 to 20 dB higher than in adults (Aslin et al., 1983). Also, newborns seem to be more sensitive to complex noises—which are more similar to the sounds in their everyday environment—than to acoustically pure tones (Haith & Campos, 1977).

One of the most impressive findings about young infants is that they can recognize short tunes, even when the tunes are transposed into slightly higher or lower keys. Using the habituation-dishabituation method, Trehub (1985) showed that infants as young as 2 months of age paid more attention to a melody that was a rearrangement of a familiar six-note tune, in contrast to the same familiar tune at a slightly higher or lower pitch. The constancy in music discussed in Chapter 10 therefore begins to develop very early in infancy.

However, perhaps the most impressive talent of young infants is their ability to perceive human speech. We will examine infant speech perception in the next section.

▶ **IN-DEPTH:**
INFANT SPEECH PERCEPTION

Language is one of the most remarkable human accomplishments. By the age of 6, children have some mastery of about 14,000 words. If this feat doesn't seem particularly remarkable, consider how much effort an adult must make to learn perhaps 1000 words in a foreign language (Carey, 1978; Matlin, 1983). Furthermore, children learn to speak without the kind of formal training they receive in reading or arithmetic (Eimas, 1985). How can they master language so readily? Research in the last two decades has demonstrated that they have a "head start." Young infants have inborn knowledge and capacities for language; they can discriminate between speech sounds before they are able to produce any recognizable sounds of their own (Aslin et al., 1983; Eimas, 1985). Our first topic in this in-depth section is speech-sound discriminations. Our second topic is voice recognition, another impressive accomplishment of young infants.

Speech-Sound Discriminations

Young infants can discriminate between remarkably similar phonemes, the basic units of speech. For example, Peter Eimas of Brown University and his colleagues tested speech perception in infants between 1 and 4 months old (Eimas, Siqueland, Jusczyk, & Vigorito, 1971). Basically, they used the habituation method combined with the high-amplitude sucking procedure. In the **high-amplitude sucking procedure**, babies suck on a pacifier attached to a recording device; if they suck fast enough, a machine presents a speech sound. For example, babies might suck to produce the sound *bah*. At first, the babies would suck vigorously to produce the *bah* sound. However, after about 5 minutes, habituation occurred, and the number of sucking responses decreased. Then the researchers presented a new sound, such as *pah*.

Eimas and his colleagues found that babies showed dishabituation when the new speech sound was presented; sucking returned to the previous vigorous level. In other words, babies indicated by their dishabituation that *pah* sounded different from bah. Other research has shown that infants discriminate between *sah* and *vah*, between *rah* and *lah*, and between *fah* and *thah* (Eilers & Minifie, 1975; Eimas, 1975; Jusczyk, Murray, & Bayly, 1979). In fact, Aslin and his coauthors (1983) conclude that infants can discriminate nearly all the phonemic contrasts found in English. Speech sounds can even be discriminated when they appear in three-syllable nonsense words (Goodsitt, Morse, Ver Hoeve, & Cowan, 1984).

Infant speech perception is also similar to adult speech perception in that both are cat-

egorical. The issue of categorical perception was discussed in connection with color vision (Chapter 5), speech perception (Chapter 10), and infant color vision (present chapter). We say that categorical perception occurs when we have difficulty discriminating between members of the *same* category but we are readily able to discriminate between members of *different* categories (Jusczyk, 1986). There is evidence that infants, like adults, find it easy to discriminate between sounds from two different categories, such as /p/ and /b/, but they have difficulty discriminating between two different examples of /p/ (Eimas et al., 1971). In reviewing the literature on categorical perception in infancy, Eimas (1985) writes,

> It is difficult to see how learning could account for the mode of perception we have demonstrated in infants. What events during the first few weeks of life would train an infant to respond categorically to gradations of acoustic properties? A simpler view is that categorization occurs because a child is born with perceptual mechanisms that are tuned to the properties of speech. These mechanisms yield the forerunners of the phonemic categories that later will enable the child unthinkingly to convert the variable signal of speech into a series of phonemes and thence into words and meanings (p. 49).

Categorical perception allows infants to recognize phonemes consistently, even when they show acoustical variability. For example, a *pah* sound will be categorized with other *pah* sounds, even though it is acoustically near the borderline of the *bah* sounds. Furthermore, infants—like adults—have an additional ability that enhances phoneme recognition. Specifically, infants have what could be called *speech sound constancy*. As discussed in Chapter 10, a sound is *not* consistently pronounced in a consistent fashion by all speakers on all occasions. Some speakers have higher voices than others, and a speaker may pronounce a phoneme sometimes with a falling pitch and sometimes with a rising pitch. However, Patricia Kuhl of the University of

Washington has demonstrated that babies who have been reinforced for turning their heads when a male speaker produces an /a/ sound (but not an /i/ sound) will turn their heads when either a female speaker or a child speaker produces an /a/ sound (Kuhl, 1979, 1985). By 6 months of age, infants realize that an /a/ sound remains an /a/ sound, even though the specific sound waves vary tremendously from one speaker to another.

In summary, then, young infants have the ability to make discriminations between similar phonemes. Equally important, they have the ability to see the similarity between other speech sounds. They can place speech sounds in the same category despite acoustical differences and despite differences in speakers.

Now consider a related issue. Suppose that an infant growing up in an English-speaking home hears two speech sounds considered different from each other in another language but not in English. Will this baby be able to discriminate between these two sounds? In other words, is speech discrimination innate, so that it does not depend on the language environment in which the baby is raised? Alternately, will the baby fail to discriminate between these two sounds because infants need to *learn* to make discriminations, based on experience with a language?

The answer to this question is probably complex. In fact, it is likely that both alternatives are correct, depending upon the kind of phonemic distinction. For example, a large number of studies have examined phonemes that differ with respect to place of articulation. In Hindi, for instance, the /t/ sound is sometimes made by placing the tongue against the back of the teeth and sometimes by placing the tongue farther back along the roof of the mouth. English does not distinguish between these two /t/ sounds, but Hindi does. Janet Werker of Dalhousie University and Richard Tees of the University of British Columbia examined this specific phoneme contrast (Werker & Tees, 1984). They also included additional phonemic contrasts from Hindi and Salish, a North American Indian language; all phonemic contrasts were ones that are not important in English.

When Werker and Tees tested infants from English-speaking backgrounds, they found that the ability to distinguish between the Hindi phonemes and between the Salish phonemes was excellent in 6- to 8-month-old infants (Figure 15.3). However, the ability declined dramatically until it was negligible at 1 year of age. Notice, however, that 1-year-old infants from Hindi and Salish backgrounds have no difficulty making these distinctions. It seems from these results that infants about 6 months old have the ability to make discriminations in languages other than their own. However, this ability fades as children use their own language. In contrast, children for whom the contrast is important improve their ability to make these same discriminations.

This pattern of results has been found for phonemic distinctions from Czech (Trehub, 1976) as well as Hindi and Salish (Werker, Gilbert, Humphrey, & Tees, 1981; Werker & Tees, 1984). Furthermore, infants from English-speaking backgrounds, like English-speaking adults, can distinguish between the sounds *rah* and *lah*; however, Japanese-speaking adults cannot distinguish between these two sounds (Eimas, 1975; Miyawaki et al., 1975). Thus, some kinds of phonemic distinctions are present in infancy but are lost later, when the distinction is not used in one's language. However, the results of other studies suggest that some kinds of phonemic discriminations are *not* inborn; they need to be learned by exposure to a language in which the distinctions are important (Eilers, Gavin, & Wilson, 1979; Eilers, Gavin, & Oller, 1982; Morse & Cowan, 1982; Streeter, 1976).

Voice Recognition

Infant speech perception involves more than just the perception of phonemic distinctions. The speech that infants hear comes from people, and it is important to recognize who is speaking. It is also important to recognize that there must be a correspondence between how the speaker *looks* and how the speaker *sounds*.

At what age can babies recognize their mothers' voice? The research of Anthony DeCasper and William Fifer (1980) of the Uni-

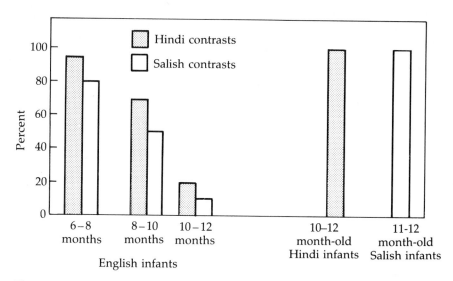

Figure 15.3 Ability to perform phonemic contrasts, as function of age and linguistic experience. (Based on Werker & Tees, 1984. Used with permission.)

versity of North Carolina suggests that 3-*day* old babies have this capability. In this study babies sucked on pacifiers at different rates to produce either the voice of their mother or the voice of a female stranger. Amazingly, these tiny babies produced their mother's voice more frequently than the stranger's voice. There seem to be two possible explanations for this early recognition ability: (1) The baby may form a strong bond with the mother and her voice shortly after birth, or (2) the mother's voice may be transmitted to the fetus prior to birth without substantial distortion in quality.

Infants also have the ability to categorize male and female voices. By the age of 7 months—or perhaps earlier—babies can reliably discriminate between males and females, and the discrimination does not seem to be based only on voice pitch (Morse & Cowan, 1982).

Babies also realize that there must be some correspondence between the voice they hear and the facial configuration they see. For example, in one study infants between the ages of 3 and 7 months faced their mother and father. One parent's tape-recorded voice was then presented from a location between the

two parents. Infants as young as 3 months tended to turn toward the appropriate parent. They realize, then, that Mother's voice should come from Mother's face and Father's voice should come from his face (Spelke, 1985). Similarly, 2-week-old babies prefer to watch Mother's voice presented together with her face; they tended to *avoid* looking at Mother's voice presented with a stranger's face or a stranger's voice presented with a mother's face (Carpenter, 1975).

In case you are not yet totally impressed with young infants, consider a study by Patricia Kuhl and Andrew Meltzoff (1982) of the University of Washington. Babies 4 to 5 months old listened to tape recordings of either the vowel sound from *pop* or the vowel sound from *peep*. While they listened to the vowel sound, they looked at two films placed side by side. One film showed a speaker making the *pop* vowel sound, and the other film showed the same speaker making the *peep* vowel sound. Infants looked consistently longer at the film with the lip configuration that matched the vowel. If babies hear the *ee* sound, they want to see the corners of the speaker's mouth drawn apart in a configuration appropriate to that vowel.

Finally, babies appreciate that when they hear a happy voice, the face of the speaker should be happy, and an angry voice should be accompanied by an angry face. Arlene Walker-Andrews (1986) of Rutgers University studied 7-month-old infants in a preference-method experiment similar to the one used by Kuhl and Meltzoff. Babies heard a recording of either a happy or an angry voice, while they saw a pair of films—of a happy speaker and an angry speaker—projected side by side. The lower one third of the face was covered so that infants could not rely on mouth movements to match the voice with the film. Walker-Andrews measured the amount of time the baby fixated each film.

The results are shown in Figure 15.4. As you can see, babies who heard the happy voice tended to watch the happy face, and babies who heard the angry voice tended to watch the angry face.

Let's review the kinds of speech-perception abilities young infants possess. They can make nearly all the phonetic distinctions important to the language in which they are raised. Their speech perception, like that of adults, is categorical, and they also have "speech sound constancy" across a variety of speakers. Young infants are superior to older infants and adults with respect to their ability to make some phonemic distinctions *not* found in their language environment. At 3 days of age, babies can recognize their mothers' voices. By 7 months they can categorize female and male voices; even earlier, they match mother's voice with her face. Infants also realize that a certain vowel sound should correspond with an appropriate lip arrangement and that a happy voice should come from a happy face.

The word *infant* originally meant "not speaking." It is true that infant's speech *production* is limited. However, it is equally true that their speech *perception* is remarkably sophisticated, even when they are only a few months old. ■

Other Senses in Infancy

About a decade ago Haith and Campos (1977) reviewed the research on human infancy and pleaded with perception researchers to adapt the clever methods used in vision research in order to examine the other senses. We now know much more about hearing, but we still know very little about touch, smell, and taste.

Touch is primarily studied in connection with reflexes. Newborn infants have many reflex responses to being touched at different spots. For example, if you touch a baby's cheek on one side of the mouth, the baby's head will turn in the direction of the touch. This particular reflex makes sense, because it allows babies to find a nipple that has slipped to the side of their mouths. Other reflexes are more puzzling, such as the reflex of curving the back in response to stroking alongside the spine. Other aspects of reflexes and touch sensitivity are discussed by Reese and Lipsitt (1970).

One-year-old infants are able to recognize the shapes of objects by touch alone, as was demonstrated by Gottfried and Rose (1980).

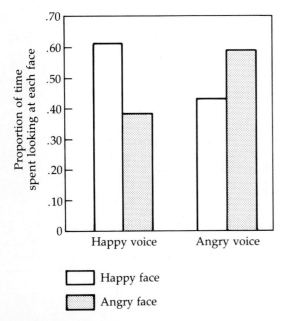

Figure 15.4 Proportion of time spent looking at happy and angry faces, as function of type of voice heard. (Based on Walker-Andrews, 1986.)

These researchers found that babies placed in a dark room played with new objects more than familiar objects. Perhaps future research will determine whether even younger infants have tactile recognition memory.

One of the most impressive demonstrations of infant ability is related to touch. Meltzoff and Moore (1977) found that 2- and 3-week-old infants can imitate an adult's gestures. An experimenter stuck out his tongue, opened his mouth, and puckered his lips. The infant's responses were surprisingly similar to the adult's, as Figure 15.5 shows. These same imitative abilities have recently been found in 3-day-olds and in newborns averaging 42 minutes of age (Field, Woodson, Greenberg, & Cohen, 1982; Meltzoff & Moore, 1983).

Notice what an impressive accomplishment is represented when babies show facial imitation. Their vision has to be precise enough to discriminate the facial gesture, they need to be able to make the motor movement (such as protrusion) that will match the movement they wish to imitate, and they need to be motivated to want to imitate (Meltzoff & Moore, 1985). In fact, imitation of facial movement involves a complex coordination of visual and kinesthetic skills.

Research on smell has demonstrated that

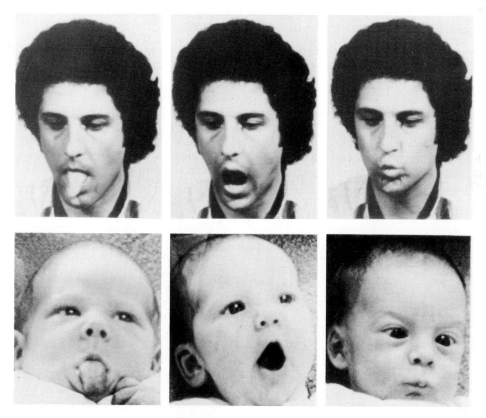

Figure 15.5 Sample photographs of 2- and 3-week-old infants imitating an adult. (From ''Imitation of Facial and Manual Gestures by Human Neonates'' by A. N. Meltzoff and M. K. Moore, *Science, 198* (7 Oct. 1977), Fig. 1, pp. 75–78. Copyright 1977 by the American Association for the Advancement of Science.)

young infants are sensitive to a wide variety of odors, such as the rotten egg smell of the oriental seasoning asafoetida and the pleasant smell of lavender (e.g., Self, Horowitz, & Paden, 1972). Furthermore, female infants who were exposed to an odor for 24 hours preferred that odor at a later time to an unfamiliar odor; male infants, however, showed no difference in preferences (Balogh & Porter, 1986).

Several studies have also tried to determine whether newborns can discriminate between the smell of their mothers and the smell of strangers. Macfarlane (1977) took two breastpads and placed one on each side of an infant's mouth. One of the pads had been worn for several hours by the infant's mother, and the other had been worn by another nursing mother. By the time the infants were 6 days old, they could discriminate between the two pads; that is, they turned to their own mother's pad more frequently than to the stranger's pad. Cernoch and Porter (1985) found that breast-feeding infants could recognize their mother's odor by 2 weeks of age, but bottle-feeding infants could not. However, Russell (1976) found no differences in sucking responses made to a mother's pad and to a stranger's pad until 6 weeks of age. Thus, babies can smell the difference between mother and a stranger at a young age, but it is unclear just how early this skill is acquired.

Taste buds appear early in prenatal development, and they seem to be functional at birth (Mistretta, 1981). Babies can make facial expressions in response to various taste stimuli when they are just a few hours old. For example, Steiner (1979) placed a sweet substance on newborns' tongues and documented that the infants relaxed their faces into an expression of enjoyment resembling a smile. A sour substance leads to a puckering of the lips, and a bitter substance causes an expression of disgust. Furthermore, Steiner even found the facial reaction to sour stimuli in premature babies and in severely retarded babies. It seems, then, that babies do not need to engage in higher mental processes to decide whether a taste is pleasant or unpleasant; the response is inborn and reflexlike.

Several chapters in a book called *Taste and Development* (Weiffenbach, 1977) are devoted to the preference for sweet substances. It is unfortunate that we are born loving sweet foods because of the relationship between sugar consumption and heart disease, diabetes, and obesity.

Desor, Maller, and Greene (1977) report that infants drank more water when it had been sweetened. For example, 1- to 3-day-old infants drank more than twice as much of a very sweet solution as they drank of plain water. Furthermore, newborns even preferred the sweet solution to regular infant formula. Finally, Desor, and his coauthors demonstrate that newborns' sweet preference is quite similar to the preference shown by older infants and by adults. Interestingly, newborns can distinguish among several different sugar solutions; they prefer fructose and sucrose to lactose and glucose (Bornstein, 1984c).

Throughout this discussion of infancy we have seen evidence for Theme 3 of this book. The human sensory systems perform remarkably well in gathering information about stimuli—even when an infant is only a few days old. Infants do not experience the "blooming, buzzing confusion" that James described because they are born with sensory equipment that provides information about the sights, sounds, tactile experiences, smells, and tastes of their world. Furthermore, perceptual development during infancy is rapid. By the time babies leave infancy (a period typically specified as ending at 12 to 18 months of age), their sensory capabilities are impressively mature. In the next section, then, we consider perception in childhood.

Summary: Infancy

1. Each of the age categories examined in this chapter—infancy, childhood, and late adulthood/old age—presents methodological problems in research.
2. Psychologists are more optimistic about infants' perceptual abilities than they used to be, primarily because of the de-

velopment of three research methods that can reveal infants' skills: preference, habituation, and conditioning.

3. The fovea of the newborn is not mature at birth; the lateral geniculate nucleus and the visual cortex are also not fully developed.

4. The preference method can be used to measure acuity by finding the narrowest stripes that will be looked at for a longer period of time than a uniform gray patch. Acuity develops rapidly during the first year of life.

5. Infants have some accommodation abilities, although they are not equivalent to adults' abilities; newborns' eyes occasionally move in separate directions.

6. Babies seem to be trichromats by the age of 3 months, and they also have categorical perception for colors, as assessed by the habituation method.

7. Young infants generally prefer curvilinear patterns, concentric patterns, and multiple-orientation designs; they also like to look at faces.

8. Babies can recognize faces at about 2 months of age, they can appreciate facial expressions, and they pay most attention to broad smiles.

9. Studies using the visual cliff show that infants as young as 2 months perceive depth; by about 4 months of age, babies begin to appreciate binocular depth information and depth in pictures.

10. Babies respond to movement as soon as they are born, and they begin to appreciate biological motion at about 6 months of life.

11. A study by Bower using the conditioning method showed evidence of size and shape constancy in 6-week-old infants, but other studies have suggested that the constancies develop between 4 and 6 months.

12. Prior to birth the fetus is exposed to many sounds; the auditory system develops early in the prenatal period, but higher levels of auditory processing are not mature at birth.

13. Newborns have somewhat higher audi-

tory thresholds than adults; infants as young as 2 months show constancy for musical tunes.

14. Young infants can discriminate between similar phonemes, and they have categorical perception for phonemes as well as constancy for phonemes spoken by different people. Young infants can make some phonemic distinctions that are not important in the language of their environment; other phonemic distinctions require language experience.

15. At 3 days of age babies can recognize their mothers' voices. At an early age they can categorize female and male voices and can match mother's voice with her face. Infants also appreciate that a certain vowel sound should correspond with a particular lip arrangement and that vocal tone should match facial expression.

16. When babies are touched on various parts of their bodies, different reflexes are elicited. Babies can imitate adult facial gestures when they are 1 hour old.

17. Babies are sensitive to a variety of odors; young babies can smell the difference between mother and a stranger at a young age, but it is not clear exactly how early this skill is acquired.

18. Babies can make facial expressions to various taste stimuli when they are just a few hours old; they drink more water if sweet substances have been added.

CHILDHOOD

Ironically, we seem to know less about children's perceptual abilities than about infants' perceptual abilities. The nonvisual senses have been particularly ignored, so we will confine our discussion of childhood perception to vision.

Fortunately, it is somewhat easier to perform research on children than on infants. A 5-year-old can point to show the direction that the letter *E* is facing, for example. However, a 3-year-old might not understand the task instructions. Furthermore, children's motor skills are still somewhat limited. For example, if we ask 5-year-olds to copy a figure and their figures are quite different from the original, the difference might very likely be due to their limited motor coordination in handling a pencil rather than to distorted perception.

Let's look at four topics concerning children's vision: (1) shape, (2) picture perception, (3) constancy and illusions, and (4) attention.

Shape Perception in Childhood

Try Demonstration 15.3, which illustrates children's ability to copy and match shapes. Several studies, summarized by Vernon (1976), have shown that young children are highly inaccurate in copying geometric figures. It might be tempting to conclude that young children have poor shape perception. However, as you probably discovered in doing Demonstration 15.3, children can discriminate between different shapes, even if they cannot copy them correctly. As Vernon points out, the motor skills of young children may be inadequate for drawing shape characteristics with precision. In contrast, children are reasonably accurate in arranging matchsticks into a series of shapes, a task that

presumably requires less motor skill than drawing.

Incidentally, these studies suggest that it may be unwise to teach children to print letters at an early age. There seems to be a rapid improvement in copying shapes when children are between 5 and 6 years of age. This is the approximate age at which our schools teach children to print, so educators have planned a curriculum appropriate to a developmental level.

As children grow older, there is a substantial change in their perception of the relationship between the parts and the whole in a shape. Try Demonstration 15.4 to determine how children respond to a whole figure made up of identifiable parts. In a classic experiment Elkind, Koegler, and Go (1964) asked children to describe figures similar to those in the demonstration. Children who were 4 and 5 years of age focused upon the parts in each figure. A typical description of the top right figure, for example, might be "a banana and some other fruit." In contrast, 7-year-olds often reported both the parts and the whole in each figure, for example, "fruits and a face." Still older children, 8 or 9 years of age, almost always responded in terms of both the parts and the whole, pointing out

---

Demonstration 15.3

―――――――――

Copying and Matching Shapes

For this demonstration you will need a child between 3 and 5 years of age. Draw neatly two identical circles, squares, triangles, and two identical more complex figures. Show the child one of each figure and ask him or her to copy it as carefully as possible.

Now present two identical figures plus one different figure, as illustrated below. Ask the child to point to the two figures that are the same of the three. Repeat this matching test with each of the other three kinds of figures.

Demonstration 15.4

Children's Whole-Part Perception

For this demonstration you will need a child between the ages of 3 and 11 years of age. Ask the child to describe each of the figures below.

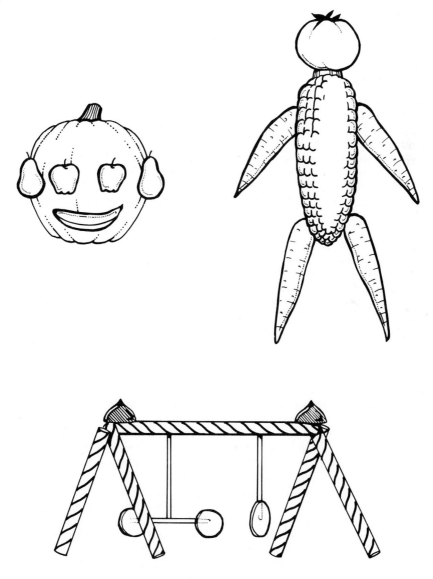

the relationship between the two, such as "a face made out of fruit."

Children are less sensitive than adults to the orientation of a figure. For example, children under the age of 10 can remember a picture of a face equally well upright and upside down, whereas adults have difficulty with upside-down faces (Carey & Diamond, 1977). Think about how children's printing is represented by adults. For example, an adult cartoonist might show a boy's clubhouse with a sloppily lettered sign, "GIRLƧ ⅄EEP OUT." In fact, children really do make many letter reversals in their printing. In other words, young children cannot discriminate letter orientation as accurately as adults. Very young children have difficulty discriminating an upright figure from the same figure turned upside down, but their accuracy on these tasks increases rapidly as they grow older. However, reversals from left to right are a much more frequent cause of difficulty (Heydorn & Cheek, 1982). Thus, even a 6-year-old will have difficulty telling a *b* from a *d*.

Most children outgrow their difficulties with letter orientation during the early school years. However, children with **dyslexia** read substantially more poorly than would be expected from their intelligence (Just & Carpenter, 1987). Dyslexic children, like younger children, continue to confuse letters of similar shapes but different orientations (Pavlidis & Miles, 1981). A dyslexic child typically has a good vocabulary, knows what the words mean, and can use the words in conversation (Smith, 1978). However, he or she is unable to read. Often the difficulty extends beyond merely confusing similar letters to confusing similar words, such as *bat* and *bit*. Other aspects of dyslexia and remedial training are discussed by Hynd and Hynd (1984), Just and Carpenter (1987), and Pavlidis and Miles (1981).

In this section on shape perception we have seen that young children have trouble copying shapes, a difficulty at least partially due to the motor aspects of the task. Furthermore, young children also have trouble determining the relationship between the parts and the whole in a picture, and they are also relatively insensitive to the orientation of a figure. Each of these perceptual skills improves as children mature.

Picture Perception in Childhood

Suppose that you show a color photograph to a group of toddlers. Will they be able to appreciate the fact that this photo may show familiar objects and that it also conveys depth information? According to Eleanor Gibson and Elizabeth Spelke (1983), children can transfer from objects to pictures and from pictures to objects by the time they are 24 to 28 months old.

We saw in the infancy section that babies develop some sensitivity to pictorial depth information before they are 1 year old. As they mature, they develop this sensitivity further, although they generally use this depth information less accurately than adults (Gibson & Spelke, 1983). Two-year-olds appreciate that interposition is a distance cue that signifies one object is in front of another, and 3-year-olds are sensitive to shading information.

As we saw in Chapter 7, adults can understand that a static picture is meant to convey motion. Children as young as 4 know that if a cartoon shows an unstable position, such as a running posture with one leg off the ground, the viewer should conclude that motion is intended. However, children under the age of 12 do not understand that movement lines and dust clouds are supposed to represent motion (Friedman & Stevenson, 1975; Gibson & Spelke, 1983). As children grow older, they appreciate many subtleties in pictures.

Furthermore, the way children scan pictures changes as they grow older. For example, Vurpillot (1968, 1976) showed children drawings of pairs of houses and instructed them to determine whether the two houses were the same or different. She analyzed eye-movement recordings and found that children under the age of 5 were incomplete and unsystematic in their scanning patterns. Often they would not compare all the pairs of windows; they would respond "same" prematurely. In fact, they typically searched only about half the windows before responding! Young children also had shorter search times than older children, and they differed in the efficiency of their scanning. Children over the age of 5 typically compared windows a pair at a time, but younger children seldom did.

In summary, then, an appreciation of the representational qualities of pictures involves the gradual development of object recognition, depth perception, and movement perception. In addition, as children mature, they change the way they inspect pictures.

Constancy in Childhood

We saw in the last section that infants probably have less size and shape constancy than adults. Children also typically perform differently from adults on tasks that require constancy judgments. In a typical experiment a stick is placed at different distances from the viewer. The observer is asked to adjust the height of a comparison stick until it matches the height of the distant stick. Adults are accurate on this task. For example, if a stick 1 m high is placed 30 m away, adults adjust the height of the comparison stick so that it is approximately 1 m high. In other words, adults acknowledge that the size of the stick remains the same, even though the distance changes.

In general, children show fairly good constancy up to a distance of about 3 m. When objects are moved farther away, however, children show less constancy. For example, at a distance of 30 m, children might adjust the comparison stick so that it is only 70 cm, rather than 100 cm (1 m). To children, a distant figure seems to look smaller.

Some psychologists argue that children might not understand the instructions. Perhaps they believe they are supposed to adjust the height of the comparison stick so that it is the same height as the distant figure *seems* to be (that is, apparent height), instead of the same height as the distant figure *really is*. As children grow older, they may be more likely to adopt the "really is," objective interpre-

tation that the adults typically adopt. As a consequence, it may be the interpretation of instructions, rather than constancy itself, that changes as children grow older.

Attention in Childhood

As children grow older, they have increasing control over their attention processes. Flavell (1977) states:

> One thing that seems to develop, then, is the capacity for controlled selective attention to wanted information coupled with controlled selective inattention to unwanted information (p. 169).

Consequently, older children can adjust their attention to meet the demands of the task (Lane & Pearson, 1982). For instance, in a study by Hale and Taweel (1974), 8-year-old children paid attention to two features of a stimulus, (e.g., color and shape) when this was a useful strategy. However, they paid attention to only one feature (e.g., color) when the other feature (e.g., shape) did not provide helpful information. In other words, 8-year-olds can be flexible about what they attend to. In contrast, 5-year-olds did not show this kind of flexible strategy of attention.

As Flavell wrote, older children also develop the ability to ignore unwanted information. This generalization is nicely illustrated in a study by Neisser (1979). You will recall the umbrella-woman study described in the previous chapter. Neisser tried a variant of this study with first- and fourth-grade students as well as adults. Observers were instructed to monitor a ball game by pressing a key whenever a critical event occurred in the ball game. At one point a young woman with an open umbrella sauntered across the playing area. When Neisser asked people afterwards whether they had noticed the umbrella woman, he received a positive response from only 21% of college students and 22% of fourth graders. In contrast, 75% of the first graders noticed her. Young children could not ignore the umbrella woman, even though she was irrelevant to the assigned task.

Notice that this chapter has provided two examples of a decrease in perceptual ability as people grow older. As infants approach childhood, they lose the ability to distinguish between certain speech sounds not found in their native language. As children grow older, they lose the ability to notice events that they are not supposed to notice. Perceptual development therefore involves learning some discriminations and objects to be noticed; it also involves selectively ignoring other information.

Summary: Childhood

1. Testing perceptual abilities in children is difficult because of their limited understanding of task instructions and limited motor skills.
2. Children show inaccuracy in copying geometric figures, which may be due to motor skill inadequacies rather than perceptual immaturity.
3. Young children describe a figure in terms of its parts; older children describe a figure in terms of the parts, the whole, and the relationship between parts and whole.
4. Children are less sensitive than adults to the orientation of a figure; children with dyslexia continue to have difficulty with letter orientation.
5. A 2-year-old can identify familiar objects in a photograph; 2-year-olds appreciate interposition as a distance due, and 3-year-olds are sensitive to shading information. The appreciation for the motion in a picture develops more slowly.
6. Children under the age of 5 are unsystematic and incomplete when they scan pictures.
7. Children typically show less constancy than adults, although children may misinterpret the task instructions.
8. As children grow older, they are increasingly able to pay attention to important information and increasingly able to ignore irrelevant information.

LATE ADULTHOOD AND OLD AGE

Before examining perceptual changes during aging, we need to discuss a potential methodological problem in studies using elderly people. It is often difficult to locate a group of young people identical to the elderly group in all important characteristics except age. Imagine, for example, that you want to know whether hearing sensitivity declines during aging. You test a group of college students whose average age is 19 and a group of residents of a nursing home whose average age is 78, and you find that the college students have more sensitive hearing.

The problem is that the two groups differ with respect to age, but they also differ with respect to a number of **confounding variables**, or factors—other than the factor being studied—present to different extents in the two groups. For example, the college students are probably much healthier than the nursing home residents. Furthermore, the college students almost certainly have had more education than a general population of people in a nursing home. Many studies fail to equate the education level or intelligence of the young and elderly people. For example, Basowitz and Korchin (1957) used young doctors and nurses for their young group and a general nursing home population for their elderly group in a study on figure-ground relationships. Storandt (1982) points out another confounding variable: Elderly people, particularly those living in nursing homes, are more likely than younger people to be taking medications that interfere with perceptual processes.

If you make no attempt to control for confounding variables such as health, education level, and medication intake, then any differences between the young and the elderly people could be due to these factors rather than the critical factor, the changes in the perceptual processes that occur with aging. In summary, we must often be cautious about the interpretation of studies comparing young and elderly people, particularly when other factors might be responsible for any differences in performance.

It is clear, however, that some sensory processes change during aging. As you read the rest of this chapter, it would be useful for you to contemplate what daily life would be like with these alterations in your perceptual experiences. How would you try to compensate for these changes?

Vision in Adulthood and Old Age

Let us examine some changes that occur in vision during aging. We will begin with the more basic visual abilities, then we will consider visual perception.

Visual Abilities

Some substantial changes occur in the structure and functioning of the visual system as humans grow older. For example, pupil size decreases (Whitbourne, 1985). There are also significant changes in the lens of the eye. The lens grows somewhat like an onion over the course of the life span, adding layer after layer (Bornstein, 1984c). As a result, the lens grows substantially thicker (Dalziel & Egan, 1982; Spector, 1982). This thickening of the lens, the decrease in pupil size, and other age-related changes in the eye decrease the amount of light that can reach the retina. In fact, the retina of a 60-year-old receives only about one third as much light as the retina of a 20-year-old (Ordy, Brizzee, & Johnson, 1982).

The thickening of the lens has an important influence on color vision. Specifically, the layers of the lens are pigmented; as these layers build up, the pigments absorb light primarily in the blue portion of the spectrum. As a result, the perception of blue colors systematically declines as people grow older (Bornstein, 1977, 1984c). Discriminations between yellow and white are also difficult. Everyday color experiences are therefore somewhat modified, and there are important implications for specific activities. For example, Weale (1982) notes that people in the diamond trade are supposed to be able to distinguish white from yellow diamonds, since yellow diamonds are lower in value. However, this distinction is difficult for older people. Research by Hurd and Blevins (1984) demonstrated that elderly people also had difficulty distinguishing between yellow and white pills and between blue and green pills. Obviously, special precautions need to be taken to make certain that elderly people do not take the wrong medication by mistake.

The thickening of the lens has yet another implication for vision; as the lens thickens, it also becomes less elastic (Carter, 1982; Elworth, Larry, & Malmstrom, 1986; Whitbourne, 1985). As a result, the eye muscles have difficulty changing the shape of the lens so that nearby objects can be seen. This difficulty is called **presbyopia**, a kind of farsightedness that occurs with aging. (The word stem *presby* means old, and *opia* refers to eyes, so presbyopia literally means "old eyes.") A person who previously was nearsighted—seeing nearby but not distant objects—may now require bifocals. **Bifocals** are special eyeglasses that have two types of lenses, an upper lens for improving eyesight for distant objects and a lower lens to be used for reading and other close work. Older people who have presbyopia and do not use glasses find that they can see an object more clearly if they hold it some distance from their eyes.

We have seen that changes in the lens of the eye can create problems in the amount of light that reaches the retina, in color vision, and in accommodation. In addition, changes in the lens are primarily responsible for the difficulty that older people have with glare (Bailey, 1986; Carter, 1982; Whitbourne, 1985). Since the lens becomes thicker, more opaque, and more pigmented, the lens scatters the light. Thus on a bright, sunny day elderly people may have trouble locating a friend on a beach or noticing a stop sign when they are driving. Inside the home, elderly people need more illumination than younger people, and a too-bright lamp might make it difficult to read the slick surface of some magazines. Facilities designed for elderly people should be carefully planned to reduce the problem of glare.

Acuity also tends to decrease as people grow older (Owsley, Sekuler, & Siemsen, 1983; Weale, 1982; Whitbourne, 1985). To some extent, this decrease can be traced to a loss of visual pigments in the photoreceptors for elderly people (Kilbride, Hutman, Fishman, & Read, 1986). However, elderly people sometimes receive poor scores on acuity tests like the Snellen test, which was shown in Figure 4.1, because they are less willing than young people to make guesses about letters on the eye chart (Sekuler, Kline, & Dismukes, 1982).

The decline in acuity is particularly noticeable for dynamic visual acuity. As Chapter 4 noted, dynamic visual acuity is the ability to perceive details on a moving object. Fozard, Wolf, Bell, McFarland, and Podolsky (1977) point out that tests of acuity for stationary objects are less accurate in predicting how older people can perceive details on a moving object, in contrast to their predictive value for younger people. Thus the standard types of static acuity tests given by motor vehicle departments may not be useful in predicting how well older people can see a moving object.

Furthermore, the standard kind of acuity tests may not predict how well an older driver can see at night. Sivak, Olson, and Pastalan (1981) conducted a study in an actual driving situation. People either drove or rode in an automobile at night while watching for a small reflecting sign that had been placed along the side of the road. The sign showed the letter E, which faced either to the right or to the left. Sivak and his colleagues measured the distance at which people could identify which direction the *E* was facing. The observers in this study were 12 people between 18 and 24 years of age and 12 people between 62 and 74. The groups were equivalent on measures of static acuity with a well-lit target. (However, the authors do not mention how the observers were selected or whether other kinds of potentially confounding variables were controlled.)

The results of the study showed that the older observers needed to be much closer to the sign to identify it, in comparison with the younger observers. Typically, a young observer identified the sign at a distance of 200 m (656 ft), and an elderly observer identified the same sign at a distance of 140 m (459 ft). An implication of this finding is that at night, older drivers—in contrast to younger drivers—have less time to act on the information in highway signs. In establishing standards for highway signs, data from older drivers in nighttime conditions should be considered.

Leon Pastalan (1982) of the University of Michigan designed a special pair of spectacles to simulate the visual experiences of elderly people. The lenses let in less light, reduce acuity, and are modified to mimic the thickened lenses of the eye. Figure 15.6a shows a typical scene without the lenses; Figure 15.6b shows how the same scene might look to an elderly person. Notice, for example, that contrasts are blurred and that some objects (such as the arrows on the glass doors) seem to disappear completely. The comparison between the two photos is indeed impressive. However, you'll notice that many important contours and details are still retained in the simulated elderly vision represented on the right. Many visual abilities decrease as people grow older, but for the majority, vision still remains adequate for most purposes.

Unfortunately, however, about 1 in 20 people over the age of 65 suffers from more severe visual disorders (Greenberg & Branch, 1982). You may recall the discussion of glaucoma in Chapter 3. In **glaucoma** extra fluid inside the eyeball causes too much pressure. The additional pressure may damage the optic nerve, and it may cause **cataracts** (clouded lenses). The type of glaucoma associated with old age develops gradually rather than suddenly. Also, it is not related to the kinds of problems for which people typically consult an eye specialist, such as needing a new pair of glasses. Regular physical examinations of older people should include an assessment of fluid pressure in the eyeball, just as physical exams include blood-

Figure 15.6 Scene as it would look to young adult and older adult. (Photos courtesy of L. A. Pastalan.)

Visual Perception

pressure assessment. With regular examinations for glaucoma, abnormal eyeball-pressure problems could be detected before they cause damage.

Visual Perception

We have discussed structural changes within the eye as people grow older, and these changes can influence basic visual abilities. Does aging also influence the higher levels of visual processing, the aspects of vision typically associated with perception rather than sensation? Unfortunately, there are far fewer studies on perception in the elderly than on perception in infancy, so our knowledge about visual perception in the elderly is often incomplete.

Some evidence suggests that depth perception is diminished in elderly people (Corso, 1981; Whitbourne, 1985). For example, binocular disparity seems to be less useful for people 50 or older. This topic deserves much more research; elderly people are likely to suffer from broken bones when they fall, and faulty depth perception (if it really is a

problem for elderly people) could contribute to accidental injuries.

In general, older adults are slower than younger adults in visual information processing (Walsh, 1982a, 1982b). This slowing may be at least partly traced to the loss of neurons in the visual cortex of elderly people (Devaney & Johnson, 1980).

Hoyer and Plude (1982) approach visual information processing from a different perspective. They agree that the visual stimulus that reaches the receptors may be somewhat limited because of age-related changes. People who emphasize data-driven or bottom-up approaches to perception might therefore stress the limitations of vision in the elderly. However, Hoyer and Plude point out that we must examine conceptually driven or top-down processes for elderly people. In particular, as Theme 4 of your textbook emphasizes, our knowledge and expectations can guide perception—even when the "data" are less than ideal.

A study by Cohen and Faulkner (1983), which provides support for Hoyer and

Plude's argument, examined how sentence context facilitated the recognition of individual words. In Chapter 6 we discussed the word-superiority effect; a letter can be recognized more readily within the context of a word. In Chapter 10 we saw that auditory perception is influenced by sentence context. Similarly, if people read the sentence "The dentist advised the children to brush their _____ " it should be easy to recognize the last word as "teeth."

Cohen and Faulkner tested both young (19- to 34-year-olds) and old (63- to 80-year-olds) people and found that both groups recognized words faster when sentence context was supplied. When the sentence context strongly predicted the final word (as in the dentist sentence), the young and old participants showed similar contextual facilitation. However, when the sentence context suggested several possibilities, the older participants showed significantly greater contextual facilitation than the younger participants. For example, consider the sentence "When they travelled abroad they visited lots of ruins"; many words other than "ruins" could have been used in the sentence. The older people benefitted more than the younger ones from these sentence contexts. It seems that older people have learned to take advantage of the hints provided by context, even when the hints are rather subtle. Cohen and Faulkner conclude that elderly people make increased use of context in order to compensate for decreased sensory processing.

Hearing in Adulthood and Old Age

In hearing, the most common problem associated with aging is presbycusis. (The word is derived from *presby*, meaning "old," and *cusis*, which is related to hearing, as in the word *acoustic*; literally, then, *presbycusis* means "old hearing.") Technically, **presbycusis** means a progressive loss of hearing in both ears for high-frequency tones, and the term encompasses a variety of specific auditory disorders. Somewhere between one-tenth and one-third of people over the age of 65 have hearing impairments due to pres-

bycusis (Whitbourne, 1985). Thus, a substantial number of elderly people—although far from a majority—suffer from presbycusis.

Interestingly, the incidence of presbycusis is different in cultures where there is less exposure to noise. Bornstein (1984c) summarizes evidence that elderly people in Africa are less likely than elderly Americans to experience presbycusis. Although there are many confounding variables in cross-cultural studies (Corso, 1981), the studies do suggest that presbycusis is largely caused by noise in the environment. Presbycusis is not inevitable as people grow old, and its incidence could be decreased by reducing or avoiding loud noises.

The most important consequence of presbycusis is that people have difficulty perceiving speech. Since presbycusis involves high-frequency tones, the phonemes in English most affected by presbycusis are those with high-frequency components. These include the sounds in italics in the following words: bu*s*, *z*ebra, *sh*oes, a*z*ure, ben*ch*, and fu*dg*e (Whitbourne, 1985). A listener with presbycusis is likely to confuse two acoustically similar words, such as *fifty* and *sixty* (Bergman, 1980). Contemplate for a moment how this kind of confusion could be socially important when discussing the cost of an item, someone's address, or someone's age. Also, since it is difficult to hear the /s/ and /z/ phonemes, English-speaking people with presbycusis will inevitably have trouble distinguishing plurals.

A large-scale study demonstrated age-related differences in speech perception and showed that these differences are magnified in certain settings (Bergman et al., 1976). The participants in this study were 282 adults in the New York City area between the ages of 20 and 89. Some test sentences were presented normally, without any distortions or other competing noises. As Figure 15.7 shows, people of all ages performed reasonably well on these normal sentences. For example, people in the oldest age group (80 to 89) made only about 15% more errors than people in the youngest age group (20 to 29).

However, the pattern was different when the speech was distorted in several different

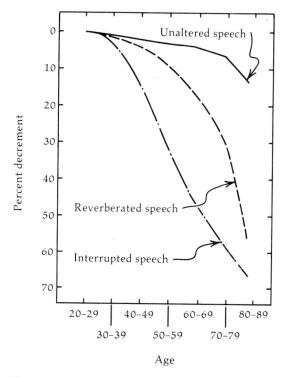

Figure 15.7 Age-related differences in intelligibility for speech in cross-sectional study. (From Bergman et al., Age-related decrement in hearing for speech: Sampling and longitudinal studies *Journal of Gerontology*, 1976, Figure 1, p. 534.)

ways. For example, when the sentences were presented in a reverberation pattern—which resembled listening to echoing speech in a hall with poor acoustics—the elderly group made close to 60% more errors than the youngest age group. In many of these speech-distorted conditions, even people in the 40 to 49 age group made substantially more errors than people in the youngest age group. In other research Bergman (1980) demonstrated that elderly people are especially likely to have difficulty hearing speech when there are loud noises or when they are trying to listen to the telephone while people around them are talking. In summary, most elderly people can understand speech well in an ideal, quiet environment. However, in a noisy environ-

ment or when speech is distorted, older people have more difficulty than young people in understanding speech.

It's important to consider the implications of this study. If you want to talk to an elderly person, do not leave the record player on at full volume in the background. An echo from a microphone system in a large auditorium will create more problems for an elderly person than for a young person. Also, an elderly person will have more difficulty listening to a telephone conversation if a faulty connection distorts the speaker's voice or if there is a loud conversation in progress. The most effective way to be heard by an elderly person is to speak at a lower pitch, to avoid the presbycusis problem, and to speak more quietly, to avoid producing the extraneous noise that interferes with speech perception (Whitbourne, 1987).

Some people have argued that hearing loss in later life causes emotional problems such as social isolation and depression. However, Whitbourne (1985) concludes from her examination of the literature that older people with hearing loss are not typically maladjusted or disturbed. Nonetheless, interpersonal relationships may be strained because people may fail to communicate appropriately with hearing-impaired people. Also, elderly people with hearing impairments are isolated from the cognitive stimulation of radio, television, and general conversation. They may, as a consequence, feel they have little to contribute to a discussion. It is clear that people with normal hearing need to help arrange the auditory environment so that people with hearing impairments can hear as well as possible, and they also need to include the hearing-impaired in conversations and other social interactions.

Other Senses in Adulthood and Old Age

Surprisingly little is known about how touch, smell, and taste change as we grow older. Often it is difficult to reach simple conclusions about these minor senses. For example, sensitivity to touch on the hairy-skin areas of the body does not decrease in later life (Whitbourne, 1985). However, sensitivity does change for the glabrous-skin areas. In a representative study, Thornbury and Mistretta (1981) found that touch thresholds for the pad of the index finger were significantly lower in older adults. However, these authors also found large individual differences; some 85-year-olds had lower thresholds (i.e., greater sensitivity) than some 30-year-olds.

In general, elderly people are less sensitive to cold environments than younger people (Corso, 1981; Whitbourne, 1985). Many elderly people suffer from **hypothermia**, or abnormally low body temperatures. Unfortunately, however, they may not experience cold so intensely as younger adults. Since hypothermia is life threatening, physicians and others who work with the elderly should realize that cold environments may be dangerous for people with temperature insensitivity (Corso, 1981).

Let's consider pain perception. In comparison with young adults, are elderly people more sensitive, less sensitive, or equally sensitive? The studies in this area permit all three conclusions (Kenshalo, 1977; Whitbourne, 1985). If the findings are this contradictory, we cannot draw clear-cut conclusions about changes in pain sensitivity as we grow older.

However, the vestibular system is often affected by old age. According to Whitbourne (1985), elderly people often experience **vertigo** (the sensation that either you or your surroundings are spinning) or **dizziness** (a vague feeling of unsteadiness, lightheadedness, or floating). As a consequence, older adults may have difficulty maintaining their posture while moving or standing still.

Let's shift, now, to the topic of smell. In general, studies show that elderly people are less sensitive to odor perception. For example, thresholds are higher for older adults (Whitbourne, 1985), and their magnitude estimations are lower for above-threshold odorants (Stevens & Crain, 1985). There are also age differences in magnitude estimations when odorants are placed in the mouth, so that the odor reaches the receptors through the "back door," as well as for odorants presented to the nose (Stevens & Cain, 1986).

Elderly people also seem to be less able to distinguish among odors associated with various foods, such as apples, corn, bacon, and chocolate (Schiffman & Pasternak, 1979). In a large-scale study Doty and his colleagues (1984) found that more than half of people between the ages of 65 and 80 had difficulty identifying "scratch-and-sniff" odors.

Initially, it seems easy to conclude that there are age-related changes in odor perception. However, Whitbourne (1985) points out that some studies do not show age differences. Furthermore, she notes that confounding variables may be partially responsible for some of the findings. Many of the elderly people in the study by Doty and his coauthors (1984) lived in nursing homes, and people in nursing homes are generally less sensitive to odors, regardless of their age. Still, we can conclude that many elderly people have reduced sensitivity to smell. Two important consequences are that elderly people often complain that food lacks flavor and that elderly people are less likely than younger people to detect gas leaks and smoke from fires (Doty et al., 1984).

Finally, let's consider taste. The number of taste buds decreases as we age (Bradley, 1977). Taste sensitivity may also decrease somewhat during the aging process; many, but not all, studies show that elderly people have higher taste thresholds than younger people (Corso, 1981; Moore, Nielsen, & Mistretta, 1982; Whitbourne, 1985). Furthermore, individual differences are large. In the study by Moore and her colleagues, for instance, the oldest participant, who was 90 years old, had a detection threshold for sucrose lower than that of almost all the 20-year-olds.

In the section on smell we saw that age tended to influence both threshold and above-threshold judgments. In contrast, age seems to have relatively little influence on above-threshold intensity judgments for tastes (Stevens, Bartoshuk, & Cain, 1984). This means that a salty taste clearly above threshold should taste equally salty to adults of all ages. In general, however, young people are more accurate than elderly people in identifying food flavors (Murphy, 1985; Schiffman, 1977).

Odor perception and taste perception are somewhat less sensitive in older people. When these two kinds of perception operate together, as they do in flavor perception, older people have more substantial problems. An important consequence may be that elderly people are less motivated to eat, so they may be less interested in preparing nutritious food. Furthermore, elderly people who are less sensitive to salty and sweet tastes may tend to oversalt or oversweeten their foods, a habit that can lead to health problems.

In this section on older adults we have seen that sensory and perceptual changes accompany aging. However, these changes are often small, and some areas are not substantially affected by age. Also, there are enormous individual differences; only a small proportion of elderly people experience disabling visual or hearing problems, and many retain their sensitivity to touch, smell, and taste. Finally, we should remember Hoyer and Plude's (1982) important point that elderly people may compensate for sensory deficits by taking advantage of top-down processes; their knowledge and prior learning can guide and clarify their perceptual experience.

Summary: Late Adulthood and Old Age

1. Frequently, studies compare elderly people with college students, who differ from them not only in age but probably also in education level, intelligence, health, and medication status.
2. The lens of the eye thickens during old age. This thickening has several implications: (a) reduced light to the retina, (b) changes in color perception, (c) presbyopia, and (d) glare.
3. Acuity also decreases with old age; the decline is a particular problem for dynamic visual acuity.
4. Approximately 1 older person in 20 suffers from glaucoma and cataracts.
5. Depth perception is diminished in elderly people.
6. Older adults are slower than younger adults in visual information processing. However, top-down processes can help compensate for perceptual deficits in old age; for example, older people are more likely than younger people to benefit from subtle contextual information.
7. Between one-tenth and one-third of elderly people suffer from presbycusis, although its incidence is different in other cultures.
8. An important consequence of presbycusis is difficulty in speech perception, which is magnified when speech is distorted or when there are other loud noises. Hearing loss may produce a strain in interpersonal relationships.
9. Sensitivity to touch decreases in later life for hairy-skin areas but not for glabrous-skin areas; elderly people are less sensitive to the cold, but there are no clear-cut age trends in sensitivity to pain. Older adults are more likely than younger adults to have vestibular problems.
10. Elderly people are generally less sensitive to odors, but there are exceptions.
11. Elderly people are generally less sensitive to tastes, but their above-threshold judgments are not substantially different from those of younger people. Elderly people are less accurate in identifying food flavors.
12. Although there are some sensory and perceptual changes as people grow older, these are seldom disabling. There are large individual differences, and top-down processing facilitates perception.

Review

1. To what extent does the infant's visual world resemble the "great blooming, buzzing confusion" that James described? In what respects is an infant's world orderly and somewhat similar to the visual world of the adult?
2. The section on vision introduced you to three experimental methods. Name them,

describe how each was used to test visual skills, and discuss how you might use each to discover something about infants' capacities for smell.

3. In two areas in this chapter we discussed how infants' perception involves categorical perception. Discuss these two areas and speculate about whether categorical perception might be found in other senses as well.

4. Imagine that you have been asked to design toys for infants that will attract their visual attention. What kinds of characteristics should these toys have?

5. A frequent issue in developmental psychology is the extent to which a particular skill is inborn versus learned. What would you conclude about the components of speech perception? What kinds of implications does your conclusion suggest for the development of language?

6. Consider touch, smell, and taste. How do infants and elderly people differ from young adults in these areas? How are they similar?

7. Imagine that your brother teaches elementary school. From the section on perception in childhood, what hints could you give him that might be useful in a teaching situation?

8. As Flavell (1977) said, older children develop the ability to pay attention to wanted information and to ignore unwanted information. Summarize the information that supports this statement. Also, recall any information from your experience with children that provides additional evidence for this statement.

9. Suppose that an elderly relative will be visiting you for the weekend. What kinds of information from the chapter would be helpful in making the visit as successful as possible? (Consider all the perceptual systems.)

10. Summarize what happens to the perceptual processes during aging. (In some cases you may not be able to draw a firm conclusion.) Be certain to mention individual differences.

New Terms

preference method

habituation method

dishabituation

visual cliff

object permanence

conditioning method

generalization

high-amplitude sucking procedure

dyslexia

confounding variables

presbyopia

bifocals

glaucoma

cataracts

presbycusis

hypothermia

vertigo

dizziness

Recommended Readings

Bornstein, M. H. (1984c). Perceptual development. In M. H. Bornstein & M. E. Lamp (Eds.), *Developmental psychology: An advanced textbook* (pp. 81–131). Hillsdale, NJ: Lawrence Erlbaum Associates. *This chapter provides an excellent overview of the development of perception, with primary emphasis on infancy. Other topics include philosophical questions concerning the development of* perception *and a clear explanation of experimental methodology.*

Corso, J. F. (1981). *Aging sensory systems and perception.* New York: Praeger. *Corso's book is a review of the literature on vision, hearing, and other senses in old age, with more emphasis on sensation than perception.*

Field, T. M., Huston, A., Quay, H. C. Troll, L., & Finley, G. E. (Eds.). (1982). *Review of human development*. New York: Wiley. *Two chapters from this book are particularly relevant, one on infant hearing and one on infant visual perception.*

Mussen, P. H. (Ed.). (1983). *Handbook of child psychology* (Vols. II and III). New York: Wiley. *These two volumes include three useful chapters, one on infant visual perception, one on infant hearing, and one on the development of perception (primarily in childhood).*

Sekuler, R., Kline, D., & Dismukes, K. (Eds.). (1982). *Aging and human visual function*. New York: Alan R. Liss. *This volume covers a wide variety of topics related to vision in the elderly, from chapters emphasizing anatomical changes to chapters summarizing visual information processing; a section on practical implications is particularly interesting.*

Whitbourne, S. K. (1985). *The aging body: Physiological changes and psychological consequences*. New York: Springer-Verlag. *Every public library and college library should own this clearly written and comprehensive book, which contains four chapters on aging perceptual systems.*

Bibliography

Abramov, I., & Gordon, J. (1973). Vision. In E. C. Carterette & M. P. Friedman (Eds.), *Handbook of perception* (Vol. 3). New York: Academic.

Abramov, I., Gordon, J., Hendrickson, A., Hainline, L., Dobson, V., & LaBessiere, E. (1982). The retina of the newborn infant. *Science, 217,* 265–267.

Akil, H., Watson, S. J., Young, E., Lewis, M. E., Khachaturian, H., & Walker, J. M. (1984). Endogenous opioids: Biology and function. *Annual Review of Neuroscience, 7,* 223–255.

Albright, T. D. (1984). Direction and orientation selectivity of neurons in visual area MT of the macaque. *Journal of Neurophysiology, 52,* 1106–1130.

Albright, T. D., Desimone, R., & Gross, C. G. (1984). Columnar organization of directionally selective cells in visual area MT of the macaque. *Journal of Neurophysiology, 51,* 16–31.

Algom, D., & Marks, L. E. (1984). Individual differences in loudness processing and loudness scales. *Journal of Experimental Psychology: General, 113,* 571–593.

Alpern, M. (1981). Color blind color vision. *Trends in NeuroSciences, 4,* 131–135.

American Psychological Association. (1981). *Ethical principles of psychologists.* Washington, DC: American Psychological Association.

Amerine, M. A., & Roessler, E. B. (1983). *Wines: Their sensory evaluation.* New York: Freeman.

Amoore, J. E. (1970). *Molecular basis of odor.* Springfield, IL: Thomas.

Amoore, J. E. (1977). Specific anosmia and the concept of primary odors. *Chemical Senses and Flavor, 2,* 267–281.

Andersen, G. J. (1986). Perception of self-motion: Psychophysical and computational approaches. *Psychological Bulletin, 99,* 52–65.

Andersen, G. J., & Braunstein, M. L. (1983). Dynamic occlusion in the perception of rotation in depth. *Perception & Psychophysics, 34,* 356–362.

Anderson, J. R. (1985). *Cognitive psychology and its implications* (2nd ed.). New York: Freeman.

Anstis, S. M. (1974). A chart demonstrating variations in acuity with retinal position. *Vision Research, 14,* 589–592.

Anstis, S. M. (1978). Apparent movement. In R. Held, H. W. Leibowitz, & H. L. Teuber (Eds.), *Handbook of sensory physiology: Vol. 8. Perception.* Berlin: Springer-Verlag.

Anstis, S. M. (1980). The perception of apparent movement. In the Royal Society (Ed.), *The psychology of vision* (pp. 153–168). Cambridge: Cambridge University Press.

Arnheim, R. (1974). *Art and visual perception: A psychology of the creative eye.* Berkeley: University of California.

Arnheim, R. (1986). The two faces of Gestalt psychology. *American Psychologist, 41,* 820–824.

Arvidson, K., & Friberg, U. (1980). Human taste response and taste bud number in fungiform papillae. *Science, 209,* 807–808.

Aslin, R. N., Pisoni, D. B., & Jusczyk, P. W. (1983). Auditory development and speech perception in infancy. In P. H. Mussen (Ed.), *Handbook of child psychology* (Vol. II, pp. 574–687). New York: Wiley.

Atkinson, J., & Braddick, O. (1981). Acuity, contrast sensitivity and accommodation in infancy. In R. N. Aslin, J. R. Alberts, & M. R. Petersen (Eds.), *Development of perception* (Vol. 2). New York: Academic.

Atkinson, R. C., & Schiffrin, R. M. (1968). Human memory: A proposed system and its control processes. In K. W. Spence & J. T. Spence (Eds.), *The psychology of learning and motivation: Advances in research and theory* (Vol. 2). New York: Academic.

Attneave, F. (1982). Prägnanz and soap bubble systems: A theoretical exploration. In J. Beck (Ed.), *Organization and representation in perception* (pp. 11–29). Hillsdale, NJ: Erlbaum.

Bahill, A. T., & La Ritz, T. (1984). Why can't batters keep their eyes on the ball? *American Scientist, 72,* 249–253.

Bahill, A. T., & McDonald, J. D. (1983). Smooth pursuit eye movements in response to predictable target motions. *Vision Research, 23,* 1573–1583.

Bahill, A. T., & Stark, L. (1979). The trajectories of saccadic eye movements. *Scientific American, 240,* 108–117.

Bailey, I. L. (1986). The optometric examination of the elderly patient. In A. A. Rosenbloom & M. W. Morgan (Eds.), *Vision and aging* (pp. 189–209). New York: Professional Press Books.

Baird, J. C. (1982). The moon illusion: II. A reference theory. *Journal of Experimental Psychology: General, 111,* 304–315.

Baird, J. C., & Noma, E. (1978). *Fundamentals of scaling and psychophysics.* New York: Wiley.

Baird, J. C., & Wagner, M. (1982). The moon illusion: I. How high is the sky? *Journal of Experimental Psychology: General, 111,* 296–303.

Baker, A. H., & Weisz, G. (1984). Misinterpretation of instructions in an aftereffect task. *Perceptual & Motor Skills, 59,* 159–162.

Ball, K., & Sekuler, R. (1980). Models of stimulus uncertainty in motion perception. *Psychological Review, 87,* 435–469.

Balogh, R. D., & Porter, R. H. (1986). Olfactory preferences resulting from mere exposure in human neonates. *Infant Behavior and Development.* In press.

Balota, D. A., Pollatsek, A., & Rayner, K. (1985). The interaction of contextual constraints and parafoveal visual information in reading. *Cognitive Psychology, 17,* 364–390.

Banks, M. S., & Salapatek, P. (1983). Infant visual perception. In P. H. Mussen (Ed.), *Handbook of child psychology* (Vol. II, pp. 435–571). New York: Wiley.

Banks, W. P. (1985). Eye movements as a handle on cognition in reading. *Contemporary Psychology, 30,* 684–685.

Banks, W. P., & Zender, J. P. (1984). A test of time sharing in auditory attention. *Bulletin of the Psychonomic Society, 22,* 541–544.

Barber, J. (1986). Hypnotic analgesia. In A. D. Holzman & D. C. Turk (Eds.), *Pain management: A handbook of psychological treatment approaches* (pp. 151–167). New York: Pergamon.

Barber, T. X. (1982). Hypnosuggestive procedures in the treatment of clinical pain. In T. Millon, C. Green, & R. Meagher (Eds.), *Handbook of clinical health psychology.* New York: Plenum.

Barclay, C. D., Cutting, J. E., & Kozlowski, L. T. (1978). Temporal and spatial factors in gait perception that influence gender recognition. *Perception & Psychophysics, 23,* 145–152.

Barrera, M., & Mauer, D. (1981). Recognition of mother's photographed face by the three-month-old infant. *Child Development, 52,* 714–716.

Barten, S., Birns, B., & Ronch, J. (1971). Individual differences in the visual pursuit behavior of neonates. *Child Development, 42,* 313–319.

Bartoshuk, L. M. (1971). The chemical senses: I. Taste. In J. W. Kling & L. A. Riggs (Eds.), *Woodworth & Schlosberg's experimental psychology* (3rd ed.). New York: Holt, Rinehart & Winston.

Bartoshuk, L. M. (1974). Taste illusions: Some demonstrations. *Annals of the New York Academy of Sciences, 237,* 279–285.

Bartoshuk, L. M. (1978). History of taste research. In E. C. Carterette & M. P. Friedman (Eds.), *Handbook of perception* (Vol. 6A). New York: Academic.

Bartoshuk, L. M. (1980, September). Separate worlds of taste. *Psychology Today, 14,* 48–56, 63.

Basowitz, H., & Korchin, S. J. (1957). Age differences in the perception of closure. *Journal of Abnormal & Social Psychology, 54,* 93–97.

Bassili, J. N. (1978). Facial motion in the perception of faces and of emotional expression. *Journal of Experimental Psychology: Human Perception and Performance, 4,* 373–379.

Batteau, D. W. (1967). The role of the pinna in human localization. *Proceedings of the Royal Society of London Series B, 168,* 158–180.

Beagley, W. K. (1985). Interaction of Müller-Lyer with filled-unfilled space illusion: An explanation of Müller-Lyer asymmetry. *Perception & Psychophysics, 37,* 45–49.

Beck, J. (1974). Dimensions of an achromatic surface color. In R. B. MacLeod & H. L. Pick (Eds.), *Perception: Essays in honor of James J. Gibson.* Ithaca, NY: Cornell University.

Beck, J. (Ed.). (1982). *Organization and representation in perception.* Hillsdale, NJ: Erlbaum.

Becklen, R., & Cervone, D. (1983). Selective looking and the noticing of unexpected events. *Memory & Cognition, 11,* 601–608.

Bedwell, C. H., Grant, R., & McKeown, J. R. (1980). Visual and ocular control anomalies in relation to reading difficulty. *British Journal of Educational Psychology, 50,* 61–70.

Beecher, H. K. (1959). *Measurement and subjective responses: Qualitative effects of drugs.* New York: Oxford University Press.

Beets, M. G. J. (1978). Odor and stimulant structure. In E. C. Carterette & M. P. Friedman (Eds.), *Handbook of perception* (Vol. 6A). New York: Academic.

Beidler, L. M., & Smallman, R. L. (1965). Renewal of cells within taste buds. *Journal of Cell Biology, 27*, 263–272.

Békésy, G. von (1960). *Experiments in hearing.* New York: McGraw-Hill.

Bell, P. A., Fisher, J. D., & Loomis, R. J. (1978). *Environmental psychology.* Philadelphia: Saunders.

Bellisimo, A., & Tunks, E. (1984). *Chronic pain.* New York: Praeger.

Bem, S. L. (1985). Androgyny and gender schema theory: A conceptual and empirical integration. In T. B. Sonderegger (Ed.), *Nebraska Symposium on Motivation, 1984: Psychology and gender* (pp. 179–226). Lincoln: University of Nebraska Press.

Benson, A. J. (1982). The vestibular sensory system. In H. B. Barlow & J. D. Mollon (Eds.), *The senses* (pp. 333–368). Cambridge: University Press.

Benzschawel, T., & Cohn, T. E. (1985). Detection and recognition of visual targets, *Journal of the Optical Society of America, Series A, 2*, 1543–1550.

Berbaum, K., Bever, T., & Chung, C. S. (1983). Light source position in the perception of object shape. *Perception, 12*, 411–416.

Berbaum, K., Bever, T., & Chung, C. S. (1984). Extending the perception of shape from known to unknown shading. *Perception, 13*, 479–488.

Berbaum, K., & Lenel, J. C. (1983). Objects in the path of apparent motion. *American Journal of Psychology, 96*, 491–501.

Berbaum, K., Lenel, J. C., & Rosenbaum, M. (1981). Dimensions of figural identity and apparent motion. *Journal of Experimental Psychology: Human Perception and Performance, 7*, 1312–1317.

Berbaum, K., Tharp, D., & Mroczek, K. (1983). Depth perception of surfaces in pictures: Looking for conventions of depiction in Pandora's box. *Perception, 12*, 5–20.

Bergman, M. (1980). *Aging and the perception of speech.* Baltimore: University Park Press.

Bergman, M., Blumenfeld, V. G., Cascardo, D., Dash, B., Levitt, H., & Margulies, M. K. (1976). Age-related decrement in hearing for speech: Sampling and longitudinal studies. *Journal of Gerontology, 31*, 533–538.

Berkeley, G. (1709/1957). *An essay towards a new theory of vision.* London: Dent.

Berkley, M. A. (1982). Neural substrates of the visual perception of movement. In A. H. Wertheim, W. A. Wagenaar, & H. W. Leibowitz (Eds.), *Tutorials on motion perception* (pp. 201–229). New York: Plenum.

Berlá, E. P. (1982). Haptic perception of tangible graphic displays. In W. Schiff & E. Foulke (Eds.), *Tactual perception: A sourcebook* (pp. 364–386). Cambridge: University Press.

Beroza, M., & Knipling, E. F. (1972). Gypsy moth control with the sex attractant pheromone. *Science, 177*, 19–27.

Bershader, D. (1981). I can't hear you when the water's running. *The Stanford Magazine, 9*(1), 14–21.

Berthenthal, B. I., Proffitt, D. R., Spetner, N. B., & Thomas, M. A. (1985). The development of infant sensitivity to biomechanical motions. *Child Development, 56*, 531–543.

Bertino, M., Beauchamp, G. K., & Engelman, K. (1982). Long-term reduction in dietary sodium alters the taste of salt. *American Journal of Clinical Nutrition, 36*, 1134–1144.

Best, C. T., Morrongiello, B., & Robson, R. (1981). Perceptual equivalence of acoustic cues in speech and nonspeech perception. *Perception & Psychophysics, 29*, 191–211.

Biederman, I. (1981). On the semantics of a glance at a scene. In M. Kubovy & J. R. Pomerantz (Eds.), *Perceptual organization.* Hillsdale, NJ: Erlbaum.

Biederman, I. (1985). Human image understanding: Recent research and a theory. *Computer Vision, Graphics, and Image Processing, 32*, 29–73.

Biederman, I. (1987). Scene perception. *Scientific American,* In press.

Biederman, I., Mezzanotte, R. J., & Rabinowitz, J. C. (1982). Scene perception: Detecting and judging objects undergoing relational violations. *Cognitive Psychology, 14*, 143–177.

Birren, F. (1976). *Color perception in art.* New York: Van Nostrand Reinhold.

Blakemore, C., & Campbell, F. W. (1969). On the existence of neurones in the human visual system selectively sensitive to the orientation and size of retinal images. *Journal of Physiology, 203*, 237–260.

Bliss, J. C., Katcher, M. H., Rogers, C. H., & Shepard, R. P. (1970). Optical to tactile image conversion for the blind. *IEEE Transactions, 11*, 58–65.

Bliss, J. C., & Moore, M. W. (1974). The Optacon reading system. *Education of the Visually Handicapped, 4*, 98–102.

Bohlander, R. W. (1984). Eye position and visual attention influence perceived auditory direction. *Perceptual and Motor Skills, 59*, 483–510.

Bolles, R. C., & Fanselow, M. S. (1982). Endorphins and behavior. *Annual Review of Psychology, 33*, 87–101.

Bond, Z. S., & Garnes, S. (1980). Misperception and

production of fluent speech. In R. A. Cole (Ed.), *Perception and production of fluent speech* (pp. 115–132). Hillsdale, NJ: Erlbaum.

Bonnet, C. (1982). Thresholds of motion perception. In A. H. Wertheim, W. A. Wagenaar, & H. W. Leibowitz (Eds.), *Tutorials on motion perception* (pp. 41–79). New York: Plenum.

Boring, E. G. (1942). *Sensation and perception in the history of experimental psychology*. New York: Appleton-Century-Crofts.

Bornstein, M. H. (1975). Qualities of color vision in infancy. *Journal of Experimental Child Psychology, 19,* 401–419.

Bornstein, M. H. (1977). Developmental pseudo-cyananopsia: Ontogenetic change in human color vision. *American Journal of Optometry & Physiological Optics, 54,* 464–469.

Bornstein, M. H. (1984a). A descriptive taxonomy of psychological categories used by infants. In C. Sophian (Ed.), *Origins of cognitive skills*. Hillsdale, NJ: Erlbaum.

Bornstein, M. H. (1984b). Psychology and art. In M. H. Bornstein (Ed.), *Psychology and its allied disciplines: Vol. 1. Psychology and the humanities* (pp. 1–73). Hillsdale, NJ: Erlbaum.

Bornstein, M. H. (1984c). Perceptual development. In M. H. Bornstein & M. E. Lamb (Eds.), *Developmental psychology: An advanced textbook* (pp. 81–131). Hillsdale, NJ: Erlbaum.

Bornstein, M. H. (1985a). Infant into adult: Unity to diversity in the development of visual categorization. In J. Mehler & R. Fox (Eds.), *Neonate cognition: Beyond the blooming buzzing confusion.* Hillsdale, NJ: Erlbaum.

Bornstein, M. H. (1985b). Habituation of attention as a measure of visual information processing in human infants: Summary, systematization and synthesis. In G. Gottlieb & N. A. Krasnegor (Eds.), *Measurement of audition and vision in the first year of postnatal life.* Norwood, NJ: Ablex.

Bornstein, M. H. (1987). Perceptual categories in vision and in audition. In S. Harnad (Ed.), *Categorical perception.* New York: Cambridge University Press.

Bornstein, M. H., Kessen, W., & Weiskopf, S. (1976). Color vision and hue categorization in young human infants. *Journal of Experimental Psychology: Human Perception and Performance, 2,* 115–129.

Bornstein, M. H., Krinsky, S. J., & Benasich, A. A. (1986). Fine orientation discrimination and shape constancy in young infants. *Journal of Experimental Child Psychology, 41,* 49–60.

Bornstein, M. H., & Monroe, M. D. (1980). Chro-

matic information processing: Rate depends on stimulus location in the category and psychological complexity. *Psychological Research, 42,* 213–225.

Bourne, L. E., Dominowski, R. L., Loftus, A. F., & Healy, A. F. (1986). *Cognitive processes* (2nd ed.). Englewood Cliffs, NJ: Prentice-Hall.

Bower, T. G. R. (1966). The visual world of infants. *Scientific American, 215*(6), 80–92.

Bowmaker, J. K., & Dartnall, H. M. A. (1980). Visual pigments of rods and cones in a human retina. *Journal of Physiology, 298,* 501–511.

Boyce, P. R. (1981). *Human factors in lighting.* New York: MacMillan.

Boynton, R. M. (1971). Color vision. In J. W. Kling & L. A. Riggs (Eds.), *Woodworth & Schlosberg's experimental psychology* (3rd ed.) (pp. 315–368). New York: Holt, Rinehart & Winston.

Boynton, R. M. (1979). *Human color vision.* New York: Holt, Rinehart & Winston.

Boynton, R. M. (1983). Mechanisms of chromatic discrimination. In J. D. Mollon & L. T. Sharpe (Eds.), *Colour vision* (pp. 409–423). London: Academic.

Brady, J. (1982, November). Perfume. *Signature,* 77–89.

Bradley, R. M. (1977). Effects of aging on the sense of taste: Anatomical considerations. In S. S. Han & D. H. Coons (Eds.), *Special senses in aging: A current biological assessment.* Ann Arbor: Institute of Gerontology, University of Michigan.

Braunstein, M. L. (1976). *Depth perception through motion.* New York: Academic.

Braunstein, M. L., & Anderson, G. J. (1981). Velocity gradients and relative depth perception. *Perception & Psychophysics, 29,* 145–155.

Braunstein, M. L., & Andersen, G. J. (1984). Shape and depth perception from parallel projections of three-dimensional motion. *Journal of Experimental Psychology: Human Perception and Performance, 10,* 749–760.

Bredberg, G. (1985). The anatomy of the developing ear. In S. E. Trehub & B. A. Schneider (Eds.), *The anatomy of the developing ear* (pp. 3–20). New York: Plenum.

Breitmeyer, B. G. (1980). Unmasking visual masking: A look at the "why" behind the veil of the "how." *Psychological Review, 87,* 52–69.

Breitmeyer, B. G. (1984). *Visual masking: An integrative approach.* New York: Oxford University Press.

Bridgeman, B., & Delgado, D. (1984). Sensory effects of eye press are due to efference. *Perception & Psychophysics, 36,* 482–484.

Broadbent, D. E. (1958). *Perception and communication*. London: Pergamon.

Brodie, E. E., & Ross, H. E. (1984). Sensorimotor mechanisms in weight discrimination. *Perception & Psychophysics, 36*, 477–481.

Brown, C. C. (1984). *The many facets of touch*. Skillman, NJ: Johnson & Johnson.

Bruce, V., & Green, P. (1985). *Visual perception: Physiology, psychology and ecology*. Hillsdale, NJ: Erlbaum.

Brugge, J. F., & Reale, R. A. (1985). Auditory cortex. In A. Peters & E. G. Jones (Eds.), *Cerebral cortex* (Vol. 4, pp. 229–271). New York: Plenum.

Buckalew, L. W., & Coffield, K. E. (1982). An investigation of drug expectancy as a function of capsule color and size and preparation form. *Journal of Clinical Psychopharmacology, 2*, 245–248.

Bundesen, C., & Pedersen, L. F. (1983). Color segregation and visual search. *Perception & Psychophysics, 33*, 487–493.

Burdach, K. J., Kroeze, J. H. A., & Koster, E. P. (1984). Nasal, retronasal, and gustatory perception: An experimental comparison. *Perception & Psychophysics, 36*, 205–208.

Burg, A. (1971). Vision and driving: A report on research. *Human Factors, 13*, 79–87.

Burgess, P. R., Wei, J. Y., Clark, F. J., & Simon, J. (1982). Signaling of kinesthetic information by peripheral sensory receptors. *Annual Review of Neuroscience, 5*, 171–187.

Burns, E. M. (1981). Circularity in relative pitch judgments for inharmonic complex tones: The Shepard demonstrations revisited, again. *Perception & Psychophysics, 30*, 467–472.

Burns, E. M., & Ward, W. D. (1982). Intervals, scales, and tuning. In D. Deutsch (Ed.), *The psychology of music* (pp. 241–269). New York: Academic.

Burt, P., & Sperling, G. (1981). Time, distance, and feature trade-offs in visual apparent motion. *Psychological Review, 88*, 171–195.

Bushnell, I. W. R. (1982). Discrimination of faces by young infants. *Journal of Experimental Psychology, 33*, 298–308.

Cahoon, D., & Edmonds, E. M. (1980). The watched pot still won't boil: Expectancy as a variable in estimating the passage of time. *Bulletin of the Psychonomic Society, 16*, 115–116.

Cain, W. S. (1978a). History of research on smell. In E. C. Carterette & M. P. Friedman (Eds.), *Handbook of perception* (Vol. 6A). New York: Academic.

Cain, W. S. (1978b). The odoriferous environment and the application of olfactory research. In E.

C. Carterette & M. P. Friedman (Eds.), *Handbook of perception* (Vol. 6A). New York: Academic.

Cain, W. S. (1979). To know with the nose: Keys to odor identification. *Science, 203*, 467–470.

Cain, W. S. (1980). Chemosensation and cognition. In H. van der Starre (Ed.), *Olfaction and taste VII* (pp. 347–358). London: IRL.

Cain, W. S. (1981). Olfaction and the common chemical sense: Similarities, differences, and interactions. In H. R. Moskowitz & C. Warren (Eds.), *Odor quality and intensity as a function of chemical structure* (pp. 109–121). Washington, DC: American Chemical Society.

Cain, W. S. (1982). Odor identification by males and females: Predictions vs. performance. *Chemical Senses, 7*, 129–142.

Campbell, F. W., & Robson, J. G. (1964). Application of Fourier analysis of the modulation response of the eye. *Journal of the Optical Society of America, 54*, 518A.

Campbell, F. W., & Robson, J. G. (1968). Application of Fourier analysis to the visibility of gratings. *Journal of Physiology, 197*, 551–566.

Campbell, J. N., & LaMotte, R. H. (1983). Latency to detection of first pain. *Brain Research, 266*, 203–208.

Campos, J. J., Langer, A., & Krowitz, A. (1970). Cardiac responses on the visual cliff in prelocomotor human infants. *Science, 170*, 196–197.

Cannon, J. T., Liebeskind, J. C., & Frenk, H. (1978). Neural and neurochemical mechanisms of pain inhibition. In R. A. Sternbach (Ed.), *The psychology of pain*. New York: Raven.

Carey, S. (1978). The child as word learner. In M. Halle, J. Bresnan, & G. A. Miller (Eds.), *Linguistic theory and psychological reality*. Cambridge, MA: MIT.

Carey, S., & Diamond, R. (1977). From piecemeal to configurational representation of faces. *Science, 195*, 312–314.

Carlson, N. R. (1986). *Physiology of behavior* (3rd ed.) Newton, MA: Allyn & Bacon.

Carlson, V. R. (1977). Instructions and perceptual constancy judgments. In W. Epstein (Ed.), *Stability and constancy in visual perception: Mechanisms and processes*. New York: Wiley.

Caron, A. J., Caron, R. F., & Carlson, V. R. (1979). Infant perception of the invariant shape of objects varying in slant. *Child Development, 50*, 716–721.

Caron, R. F., Caron, A. J., & Myers, R. S. (1982). Abstraction of invariant face expressions in infancy. *Child Development, 53*, 1008–1015.

Carpenter, E. (1980, February). If Wittgenstein had been an Eskimo. *Natural History, 89*, 72–79.

Carpenter, G. (1975). Mother's face and the newborn. In R. Lewis (Ed.), *Child alive*. London: Temple Smith.

Carroll, J. D. (1984). Multidimensional scaling. In R. J. Corsini (Ed.), *Encyclopedia of psychology* (Vol. 2, pp. 400–404). New York: Wiley.

Carter, J. H. (1982). The effects of aging upon selected visual functions: Color vision, glare sensitivity, field of vision, and accommodation. In R. Sekular, D. Kline, & K. Dismukes (Eds.), *Aging and human visual function* (pp. 121–130). New York: Alan R. Liss.

Carterette, E. C., & Friedman, M. P. (1978). Preface. In E. C. Carterette & M. P. Friedman (Eds.), *Handbook of perception* (Vol. 6B). New York: Academic.

Catlin, F. I. (1984). Studies of normal hearing. *Audiology, 23*, 241–252.

Cattell, J. M. (1986). The time it takes to see and name objects. *Mind, 11*, 63–65.

Cernoch, J. M., & Porter, R. H. (1985). Recognition of maternal axillary odors by infants. *Child Development, 56*, 1593–1598.

Chapman, C. R., Chen, A. C., & Bonica, J. J. (1977). Effects of intrasegmental electrical acupuncture on dental pain: Evaluation by threshold estimation and sensory decision theory. *Pain, 3*, 213–227.

Chastain, G. (1986). Word-to-letter inhibition: Word-inferiority and other interference effects. *Memory & Cognition, 14*, 361–368.

Cherry, E. C. (1953). Some experiments on the recognition of speech with one and with two ears. *Journal of Acoustical Society of America, 25*, 975–979.

Chung, C. S., & Berbaum, K. (1984). Form and depth in global stereopsis. *Journal of Experimental Psychology: Human Perception and Performance, 10*, 258–275.

Clark, F. J., & Horch, K. W. (1986). Kinesthesia. In K. R. Boff, L. Kaufman, & J. P. Thomas (Eds.), *Handbook of perception and human performance* (Vol. I, pp. 13-1–13-62). New York: Wiley.

Clark, W. C. (1969). Sensory-decision theory analysis of the placebo effect on the criterion pain and thermal sensitivity (d'). *Journal of Abnormal Psychology, 74*, 363–371.

Clulow, F. W. (1972). *Color: Its principles and their applications*. New York: Morgan and Morgan.

Cohen, G., & Faulkner, D. (1983). Word recognition: Age differences in contextual facilitation effects. *British Journal of Psychology, 74*, 231–251.

Cohen, M., & Grossberg, S. (1986). Neural dynamics of speech and language coding: Developmental programs, perceptual grouping, and competition for short-term memory. *Human Neurobiology, 5*, 1–22.

Cohen, S., Evans, G. W., Krantz, D. S., & Stokols, D. (1980). Physiological, motivational, and cognitive effects of aircraft noise on children. *American Psychologist, 35*, 231–243.

Cohen, S., Glass, D. C., & Phillips, S. (1977). Environment and health. In H. E. Freeman, S. Levine, & L. C. Reeder (Eds.), *Handbook of medical sociology*. Englewood Cliffs, NJ: Prentice-Hall.

Cohn, T. E., & Lasley, D. J. (1986). Visual sensitivity. *Annual Review of Psychology, 37*, 495–521.

Cole, R. A., & Jakimik, J. (1980). A model of speech perception. In R. A. Cole (Ed.), *Perception and production of fluent speech* (pp. 133–163). Hillsdale, NJ: Erlbaum.

Cole, R. A., & Scott, B. (1974). Toward a theory of speech perception. *Psychological Review, 81*, 348–374.

Collings, V. B. (1974). Human taste response as a function of locus of stimulation on the tongue and soft palate. *Perception & Psychophysics, 16*, 169–174.

Compadre, C. M., Pezzuto, J. M., Kinghorn, A. D., & Kamath, S. K. (1985). Hernandulcin: An intensely sweet compound discovered by a review of ancient literature. *Science, 227*, 417–419.

Cooper, W. E. (1983). The perception of fluent speech. *Annals of the New York Academy of Sciences, 405*, 48–63.

Coren, S. (1972). Subjective contours and apparent depth. *Psychological Review, 79*, 359–367.

Coren, S. (1981). The interaction between eye movements and visual illusions. In D. F. Fisher, R. A. Monty, & J. W. Senders (Eds.), *Eye movements: Cognition and visual perception*. Hillsdale, NJ: Erlbaum.

Coren, S., & Girgus, J. S. (1972). Illusion decrement in intersecting line figures. *Psychonomic Science, 26*, 108–110.

Coren, S., & Girgus, J. S. (1978). *Seeing is deceiving: The psychology of visual illusions*. Hillsdale, NJ: Erlbaum.

Coren, S., & Girgus, J. S. (1980). Principles of perceptual organization and spatial distortion: The Gestalt illusions. *Journal of Experimental Psychology: Human Perception and Performance, 6*, 404–412.

Coren, S., Girgus, J. S., Erlichman, H., & Hakstean, A. R. (1976). An empirical taxonomy of visual illusions. *Perception & Psychophysics, 20*, 129–137.

Coren, S., & Porac, C. (1983). Subjective contours and apparent depth: A direct test. *Perception & Psychophysics, 33,* 197–200.

Coren, S., Porac, C., & Ward, L. M. (1984). *Sensation and perception* (2nd ed.). New York: Academic.

Corso, J. F. (1981). *Aging sensory systems and perception.* New York: Praeger.

Craig, J. C., & Sherrick, C. E. (1982). Dynamic tactile displays. In W. Schiff & E. Foulke (Eds.), *Tactile perception: A sourcebook* (pp. 209–233). Cambridge: Cambridge University Press.

Craig, K. D. (1978). Social modeling influences on pain. In R. A. Sternbach (Ed.), *The psychology of pain.* New York: Raven.

Critelli, J. W., & Neumann, K. F. (1984). The placebo: Conceptual analysis of a construct in transition. *American Psychologist, 39,* 32–39.

Cross, I., Howell, P., & West, R. (1983). Preferences for scale structure in melodic sequences. *Journal of Experimental Psychology: Human Perception and Performance, 9,* 444–460.

Crozier, W. R.,, & Chapman, A. J. (Eds.). (1984). *Cognitive processes in the perception of art.* New York: Elsevier.

Cumming, G. D. (1978). Eye movements and visual perception. In E. C. Carterette & M. P. Friedman (Eds.), *Handbook of perception* (Vol. 9). New York: Academic.

Cutting, J. E. (1978). Generation of synthetic male and female walkers through manipulation of a biomechanical invariant. *Perception, 7,* 393–405.

Cutting, J. E. (1983). Perceiving and recovering structure from events. In SIGGRAPH/SIGART Interdisciplinary Workshop (Ed.), *Motion: Representation and perception.* New York: Association for Computing Machinery.

Cutting, J. E. (1986). *Perception with an eye for motion.* Cambridge, MA: MIT.

Cutting, J. E. (1987). Perception and information. *Annual Review of Psychology, 38,* 61–90.

Cutting, J. E., & Kozlowski, L. T. (1977). Recognizing friends by their walk: Gait perception without familiarity cues. *Bulletin of the Psychonomic Society, 9,* 353–356.

Cutting, J. E., Proffitt, D. R., & Kozlowski, L. T. (1978). A biomechanical invariant for gait perception. *Journal of Experimental Psychology: Human Perception and Performance, 4,* 357–372.

Dallenbach, K. M. (1927). The temperature spots and end organs. *American Journal of Psychology, 39,* 402–427.

Dallos, P. (1978). Cochlear electrophysiology. In R. F. Naunton & C. Fernandez (Eds.), *Evoked electrical activity in the auditory nervous system* (pp. 141–147). New York: Academic.

Dallos, P. (1981). Cochlear physiology. *Annual Review of Psychology, 32,* 153–190.

Dalziel, C. C., & Egan, D. J. (1982). Crystalline lens thickness changes as observed by psychometry. *American Journal of Optometry & Physiological Optics, 59,* 442–447.

Darian-Smith, I. (1982). Touch in primates. *Annual Review of Psychology, 33,* 155–194.

Dartnall, H. J. A., Bowmaker, J. J., & Mollon, J. D. (1983). Microspectrophotometry of human photoreceptors. In J. D. Mollon & L. T. Sharpe (Eds.), *Color vision* (pp. 69–80). London: Academic.

Das, A. K. (1981). Tea testing at the Tocklai Experimental Station, Assam, India. Personal communication.

Davidoff, J. B. (1975). *Differences in visual perception: The individual eye.* New York: Academic.

Davies, D. R., Jones, D. M., & Taylor, A. (1984). Selective and sustained attention tasks: Individual and group differences. In R. Parasuraman & D. R. Davies (Eds.), *Varieties of attention* (pp. 395–447). Orlando, FL: Academic.

Dawson, W. E. (1982). On the parallel between direct ratio scaling of social opinion and of sensory magnitude. In B. Wegener (Ed.), *Social attitudes and psychophysical measurement* (pp. 151–176). Hillsdale, NJ: Erlbaum.

Day, R. H., & McKenzie, B. E. (1977). Constancies in the perceptual world of the infant. In W. Epstein (Ed.), *Stability and constancy in visual perception.* New York: Wiley.

Dearborn, G. V. N. (1932). A case of congenital general pure analgesia. *Journal of Nervous and Mental Disorders, 75,* 612–615.

DeCasper, A. J., & Fifer, W. P. (1980). Of human bonding: Newborns prefer their mothers' voices. *Science, 208,* 1174–1176.

Delk, J. L., & Fillenbaum, S. (1965). Difference in perceived color as a function of characteristic color. *American Journal of Psychology, 78,* 290–293.

Deregowski, J. B. (1980). *Illusions, patterns and pictures. A cross-cultural perspective.* London: Academic.

Deregowski, J. B. (1984). *Distortion in art: The eye and the mind.* London: Routledge & Kegan Paul.

Desor, J. A., & Beauchamp, G. K. (1974). The human capacity to transmit olfactory information. *Perception & Psychophysics, 16,* 551–556.

Desor, J. A., Maller, O., & Greene, L. S. (1977). Preference for sweet in humans: Infants, children and adults. In J. M. Weiffenbach (Ed.), *Taste and development: The genesis of sweet preference.* Bethesda, MD: U. S. Department of Health, Education and Welfare.

Deutsch, D. (1973). Octave generalization of specific interference effects in memory for tonal pitch. *Perception & Psychophysics, 13,* 271–275.

Deutsch, D. (1982). Grouping mechanisms in music. In D. Deutsch (Ed.), *The psychology of music* (pp. 99–134). New York: Academic.

Deutsch, D. (1983). The octave illusion in relation to handedness and familial handedness background. *Neuropsychologia, 21,* 289–293.

Deutsch, D. (1984). Psychology and music. In M. H. Bornstein (Ed.), *Psychology and its allied disciplines* (Vol. I, pp. 155–194). Hillsdale, NJ: Erlbaum.

Deutsch, D. (1986). Auditory pattern recognition. In K. R. Boff, L. Kaufman, & M. P. Thomas (Eds.), *Handbook of perception and human performance* (Vol. II, pp. 32-1–32-49). New York: Wiley.

Deutsch, D., & Feroe, J. (1981). The internal representation of pitch sequences in tonal music. *Psychological Review, 88,* 503–522.

Deutsch, J. A., & Deutsch, D. (1963). Attention: Some theoretical considerations. *Psychological Review, 70,* 80–90.

DeValois, R. L., Abramov, I., & Jacobs, G. H. (1966). Analysis of response patterns of LGN cells. *Journal of the Optical Society of America, 56,* 966–977.

DeValois, R. L., & DeValois, K. K. (1975). Neural coding of color. In E. C. Carterette & M. P. Friedman (Eds.), *Handbook of perception* (Vol. 5). New York: Academic.

DeValois, R. L., & DeValois, K. K. (1980). Spatial vision. *Annual Review of Psychology, 31,* 309–341.

DeValois, R. L., Thorell, L. G., & Albrecht, D. G. (1985). Periodicity of striate-cortex-cell receptive fields. *Journal of the Optical Society of America (A), 2,* 1115–1123.

Devaney, K. O., & Johnson, H. A. (1980). Neuron loss in the aging visual cortex of man. *Journal of Gerontology, 35,* 836–841.

Dichgans, J., & Brandt, T. (1978). Visual-vestibular interaction: Effects on self-motion perception and postural control. In R. Held, H. W. Leibowitz, & H. L. Teuber (Eds.), *Handbook of sensory physiology: Vol. 8. Perception.* Berlin: Springer-Verlag.

Diem, G., & Rose, D. P. (1985). Has breast self-examination had a fair trial? *New York State Journal of Medicine, 85,* 479–480.

Ditchburn, R. W. (1973). *Eye-movements and perception.* Oxford: Clarendon.

Ditchburn, R. W. (1981). Small involuntary eye movements: Solved and unsolved problems. In D. Fisher, R. A. Monty, & J. W. Senders (Eds.) *Eye movements: Cognition and visual perception* (pp. 227–235). Hillsdale, NJ: Erlbaum.

Dobelle, W. H., Mladejovsky, M. G., & Girvin, J. P. (1974). Artificial vision for the blind: Electrical stimulation of visual cortex offers hope for a functional prosthesis. *Science, 183,* 440–444.

Dodd, B. (1977). The role of vision in the perception of speech. *Perception, 6,* 31–40.

Doty, R. L. (1981). Olfactory communication in humans. *Chemical Senses, 6,* 351–376.

Doty, R. L., Green, P. A., Ram, C., & Yankell, S. L. (1982). Communication of gender from human breath odors: Relationship to perceived intensity and pleasantness. *Hormones and Behavior, 16,* 13–32.

Doty, R. L., Orndorff, M. M., Leyden, J., & Kligman, A. (1978). Communication of gender from human axillary odors: Relationship to perceived intensity and hedonicity. *Behavioral Biology, 23,* 373–380.

Doty, R. L., Shaman, P., Applebaum, S. L., Giberson, R., Sikorski, L., & Rosenberg, L. (1984). Smell identification ability: Changes with age. *Science, 226,* 1441–1443.

Dougher, M. J. (1979). Sensory decision theory analysis of the effects of anxiety and experimental instructions on pain. *Journal of Abnormal Psychology, 88,* 137–144.

Dowling, J. E., & Boycott, B. B. (1966). Organization of the primate retina: Electron microscopy. *Proceedings of the Royal Society* (London), Series B, *166,* 80–111.

Dowling, W. J. (1973). The perception of interleaved melodies. *Cognitive Psychology, 5,* 372–377.

Downing, C. J., & Pinker, S. (1985). The spatial structure of visual attention. In M. I. Posner & O. S. M. Marin (Eds.), *Attention and performance XI* (pp. 171–187). Hillsdale, NJ; Erlbaum.

Drewnowski, A., & Greenwood, M. R. C. (1983). Cream and sugar: Human preferences for high-fat foods. *Physiology & Behavior, 30,* 629–633.

Drewnowski, A., Grinker, J. A., & Hirsch, J. (1982). Obesity and flavor perception: Multidimensional scaling of soft drinks. *Appetite: Journal for Intake Research, 3,* 361–368.

DuBose, C., Cardello, A. V., & Maller, O. (1980). Effects of colorants and flavorants on identification, perceived flavor intensity, and hedonic quality of fruit-flavored beverages and cake. *Journal of Food Science, 45,* 1393–1415.

Dykes, R. W. (1983). Parallel processing of somatosensory information: A theory. *Brain Research Reviews, 6,* 47–115.

Dyson, M. C., & Watkins, A. J. (1984). A figural approach to the role of melodic contour in melody recognition. *Perception & Psychophysics, 35,* 477–488.

Edington, B. (1979). Personal communication.

Edwards, P. W., Zeichner, A., Kuczmierczyk, A. R., & Boczkowski, J. (1985). Familial pain models: The relationship between family history of pain and current pain experience. *Pain, 21*, 379–384.

Edworthy, J. (1985). Melodic contour and musical structure. In P. Howell, I. Cross, & R. West (Eds.), *Musical structure and cognition* (pp. 169–188). London: Academic.

Eilers, R. E., Gavin, W. J., & Wilson, W. R. (1979). Linguistic experience and phonemic perception in infancy: A crosslinguistic study. *Child Development, 50*, 14–18.

Eilers, R. E., Gavin, W. J., & Oller, D. K. (1982). Cross-linguistic perception in infancy: Early effects of linguistic experience. *Journal of Child Language, 9*, 289–302.

Eilers, R. E., & Minifie, F. D. (1975). Fricative discrimination in early infancy. *Journal of Speech and Hearing Research, 18*, 158–167.

Eimas, P. D. (1975). Auditory and phonetic coding of the cues for speech: Discrimination of the [r-1] distinction by young adults. *Perception & Psychophysics, 18*, 341–347.

Eimas, P. D. (1985). The perception of speech in early infancy. *Scientific American, 252(1)*, 46–52.

Eimas, P. D., & Kavanagh, J. F. (1986). Otitis media, hearing loss, and child development: a NICHD conference summary. *Public Health Reports, 101*, 289–293.

Eimas, P. D., Siqueland, E. R., Jusczyk, R., & Vigorito, J. (1971). Speech perception in infants. *Science, 171*, 303–306.

Eisler, H., Linde, L., Troeng, G., Lazar, R., Eisler, B. M., et al. (1980). A complementary bibliography of the psychology of time. *American Psychological Association J.S.A.S. Catalog of Selected Documents in Psychology*, Number 2101.

Elkind, D., Koegler, R., & Go, E. (1964). Studies in perceptual development: 2. Part-whole perception. *Child Development, 35*, 81–90.

Elton, D., Stanley, G., & Burrows, G. (1983). *Psychological control of pain.* Sydney, Australia: Grune & Stratton.

Elworth, C. L., Larry, C., & Malmstrom, F. V. (1986). Age, degraded viewing environments, and the speed of accommodation. *Aviation, Space, and Environmental Medicine, 57*, 54–58.

Engen, T. (1963). Cross adaptation to aliphatic alcohols. *American Journal of Psychology, 76*, 96–102.

Engen, T. (1971). Psychophysics: I. Discrimination and detection. In J. W. Kling & L. A. Riggs (Eds.), *Woodworth & Schlosberg's experimental psychology* (3rd ed.) (pp. 11–46). New York: Holt, Rinehart & Winston.

Engen, T. (1982). *The perception of odors.* New York: Academic.

Engen, T., & Ross, B. M. (1973). Long-term memory of odors with and without verbal descriptions. *Journal of Experimental Psychology, 100*, 221–227.

Enns, M. P., & Hornung, D. E. (1985). Contributions of smell and taste to overall intensity. *Chemical Senses, 10*, 357–366.

Enroth-Cugell, C., & Robson, J. G. (1984). Functional characteristics and diversity of cat retinal ganglion cells. *Investigative Ophthalmology and Visual Science, 23*, 250–265.

Epstein, W. (1977). Historical introduction to the constancies. In W. Epstein (Ed.), *Stability and constancy in visual perception* (pp. 1–22). New York: Wiley-Interscience.

Epstein, W., & Franklin, S. (1965). Some conditions of the effect of relative size on perceived distance. *American Journal of Psychology, 78*, 466–470.

Epstein, W., Hatfield, G., & Muise, G. (1977). Perceived shape at a slant as a function of processing load. *Journal of Experimental Psychology: Human Perception and Performance, 3*, 473–483.

Erickson, R. P. (1982). Studies on the perception of taste: Do primaries exist? *Physiology & Behavior, 28*, 57–62.

Eriksen, C. W., & Schultz, D. W. (1979). Information processing in visual search: A continuous flow conception and experimental results. *Perception & Psychophysics, 25*, 249–263.

Escher, M. C. (1971). *The graphic work of M. C. Escher.* New York: Balantine.

Evans, E. F. (1982a). Basic physics and psychophysics of sound. In H. B. Barlow & J. D. Mollon (Eds.), *The senses* (pp. 239–250). Cambridge: Cambridge University Press.

Evans, E. F. (1982b). Functions of the auditory system. In H. S. Barlow & J. D. Mollon (Eds.), *The senses* (pp. 307–332). Cambridge: Cambridge University Press.

Evans, E. F. (1982c). Functional anatomy of the auditory system. In H. B. Barlow & J. D. Mollon (Eds.), *The senses* (pp. 251–306). Cambridge: Cambridge University Press.

Falmagne, J. C. (1985). *Elements of psychophysical theory.* Oxford: Oxford University Press.

Fantz, R. E. (1961). The origin of form perception. *Scientific American, 204(5)*, 66–72.

Fantz, R. L., & Yeh, J. (1979). Configural selectivities: Critical for development of visual perception and attention. *Canadian Journal of Psychology, 33*, 277–287.

Feather, B. W., Chapman, C. R., & Fisher, S. B. (1972). The effect of a placebo on the perception of painful radiant heat stimuli. *Psychosomatic Medicine, 34,* 290.

Festinger, L., Allyn, M. R., & White, C. W. (1971). The perception of color with achromatic stimulation. *Visual Research, 11,* 591–612.

Feuerstein, M., Labbé, E. E., & Kuczmierczyk, A. R. (1986). *Health psychology: A psychobiological perspective.* New York: Plenum.

Field, T. M., Woodson, R., Greenberg, R., & Cohen, D. (1982). Discrimination and imitation of facial expressions by neonates. *Science, 218,* 179–181.

Filsinger, E. E., & Fabes, R. A. (1985). Odor communication, pheromones, and human families. *Journal of Marriage and the Family, 47,* 349–359.

Fineman, M. (1981). *The inquisitive eye.* New York: Oxford University Press.

Finlay, D. (1982). Motion perception in the peripheral visual field. *Perception, 11,* 457–462.

Finlay, D., & Wilkinson, J. (1984). The effects of glare on the contrast sensitivity function. *Human Factors, 26,* 283–287.

Fisher, J. D., Rytting, M., & Heslin, R. (1976). Hands touching hands: Affective and evaluative effects of an interpersonal touch. *Sociometry, 39,* 416–421.

Fisk, A. D., & Schneider, W. (1981). Control and automatic processing during tasks requiring sustained attention: A new approach to vigilance. *Human Factors, 23,* 737–750.

Flavell, J. H. (1977). *Cognitive development.* Englewood Cliffs, NJ: Prentice-Hall.

Foley, J. M. (1977). Effect of distance information and range on two indices of visually perceived distance. *Perception, 6,* 449–460.

Foley, J. M. (1978). Primary distance perception. In R. Held, H. W. Leibowitz, & H. L. Teuber (Eds.), *Handbook of sensory physiology* (Vol. VIII, pp. 181–213). Berlin: Springer-Verlag.

Foley, J. M. (1980). Binocular distance perception. *Psychological Review, 87,* 411–434.

Foley, J. M. (1985). Binocular distance perception: Egocentric distance tasks. *Journal of Experimental Psychology: Human Perception and Performance, 11,* 132–149.

Forbes, T. W. (1972). Visibility and legibility of highway signs. In T. W. Forbes (Ed.), *Human factors in highway traffic safety research.* New York: Wiley.

Foster, R. S., Costanza, M. C., & Worden, J. K. (1985). The current status of research in breast self-examination. *New York State Journal of Medicine, 85,* 480–482.

Foulke, E. (1982). Reading braille. In W. Schiff & E. Foulke (Eds.), *Tactual perception: A sourcebook* (pp. 168–208). Cambridge: Cambridge University Press.

Fox, R. (1981). Stereopsis in animals and human infants: A review of behavioral investigations. In R. N. Aslin, J. R. Alberts, & M. R. Petersen (Eds.), *Development of perception* (Vol. 2, pp. 335–381). New York: Academic.

Fox, R., & McDaniel, C. (1982). The perception of biological motion by human infants. *Science, 218,* 486–487.

Fozard, J. L., Wolf, E., Bell, B., McFarland, R. A., & Podolsky, S. (1977). *Handbook of the psychology of aging.* New York: Van Nostrand Reinhold.

Fraisse, P. (1984). Perception and estimation of time. *Annual Review of Psychology, 35,* 1–36.

Franks, J. J., & Bransford, J. D. (1971). Abstraction of visual patterns. *Journal of Experimental Psychology, 90,* 65–74.

Fraser, A. B., & Mach, W. H. (1976). Mirages. *Scientific American. 234,* 102–111.

Friedman, S. L., & Stevenson, M. B. (1975). Developmental changes in the understanding of implied motion in two-dimensional pictures. *Child Development, 46,* 773–778.

Friedman, S. L., & Stevenson, M. B. (1980). Perception of movement in pictures. In M. A. Hagen (Ed.), *The perception of pictures* (Vol. 1). New York: Academic.

Fuchs, A., & Binder, M. D. (1983). Fatigue resistance of human extraocular muscles. *Journal of Neurophysiology, 49,* 28–34.

Galanter, E. (1962). Contemporary psychophysics. In R. Brown, E. Galanter, E. H. Hess, & G. Mandler (Eds.), *New directions in psychology.* New York: Holt, Rinehart & Winston.

Geisler, W. S. (1984). Physical limits of acuity and hyperacuity. *Journal of the Optical Society of America Series A, 1,* 775–782.

Gelb, A. (1929). Die "Farbenkonstanz" der Sehding. *Handbuch der normalen and pathologischen Physiologie, 12,* 594–678.

Gelfand, S. A. (1981). *Hearing.* New York: Marcel Dekker.

Gent, J. F., & Bartoshuk, L. M. (1983). Sweetness of sucrose, neohesperidin dihydrochalcone, and saccharin is related to genetic ability to taste the bitter substance 6-n-propylthiouracil. *Chemical Senses, 7,* 265–272.

Gescheider, G. A. (1976). *Psychophysics: Method and theory.* Hillsdale, NJ: Erlbaum.

Gescheider, G. A. (1985). *Psychophysics: Method, theory, and application* (2nd ed). Hillsdale, NJ: Erlbaum.

Gesteland, R. C. (1978). The neural code: Integrative neural mechanisms. In E. C. Carterette & M. P. Friedman (Eds.), *Handbook of perception* (Vol. 6A). New York: Academic.

Gesteland, R. C. (1982). The new physiology of odor. *Environmental Progress, 1,* 94–97.

Gibbons, B. (1986, September). The intimate sense of smell. *National Geographic, 170,* 324–361.

Gibson, E. J. (1969). *Principles of perceptual learning and development.* Englewood Cliffs, NJ: Prentice-Hall.

Gibson, E. J., Gibson, J. J., Smith, O. W., & Flock, H. R. (1959). Motion parallax as a determinant of perceived depth. *Journal of Experimental Psychology, 58,* 40–51.

Gibson, E. J., & Levin, H. (1975). *The psychology of reading.* Cambridge, MA: MIT.

Gibson, E. J., Schapiro, F., & Yonas, A. (1968). Confusion matrices for graphic patterns obtained with a latency measure. In *The analysis of reading skill: A program of basic and applied research* (pp. 76–96). Final Report, Project No. 5-1213, Cornell University and U.S. Office of Education.

Gibson, E. J., & Spelke, E. S. (1983). The development of perception. In P. H. Mussen (Ed.), *Handbook of child psychology* (Vol. III, pp. 1–76). New York: Wiley.

Gibson, E. J., & Walk, R. D. (1960). The "visual cliff." *Scientific American, 202* (4), 64–71.

Gibson, J. J. (1950). *The perception of the visual world.* Boston: Houghton Mifflin.

Gibson, J. J. (1959). Perception as a function of stimulation. In S. Koch (Ed.), *Psychology: A study of a science* (Vol. 1). New York: McGraw-Hill.

Gibson, J. J. (1962). Observations on active touch. *Psychological Review, 69,* 477–491.

Gibson, J. J. (1966). *The senses considered as perceptual systems.* Boston: Houghton Mifflin.

Gibson, J. J. (1979). *The ecological approach to visual perception.* Boston: Houghton Mifflin.

Gibson, J. J. (1982a). Notes on affordances. In E. Reed & R. Jones (Eds.), *Reasons for realism* (pp. 401–418). Hillsdale, NJ: Erlbaum.

Gibson, J. J. (1982b). Perception and judgment of aerial space and distance as potential factors in pilot selection and training. In E. Reed & R. Jones (Eds.), *Reasons for realism* (pp. 29–43). Hillsdale, NJ: Erlbaum.

Gilchrist, A. L. (1977). Perceived lightness depends on perceived spatial arrangement. *Science, 195,* 185–187.

Gilchrist, A. L. (1980). When does perceived lightness depend on perceived spatial arrangement? *Perception & Psychophysics, 28,* 527–538.

Gilinsky, A. S. (1980). The paradoxical moon illusions. *Perceptual and Motor Skills, 50,* 271–283.

Gillam, B. (1980). Geometrical illusions. *Scientific American, 242,* 102–111.

Gillam, B., Flagg, T., & Finlay, D. (1984). Evidence for disparity change as the primary stimulus for stereoscopic processing. *Perception & Psychophysics, 36,* 559–564.

Glass, P., Avery, G. B., Subramanian, K., Keys, M. P., Sostek, A. M., & Friendly, D. S. (1985). Effect of bright light in the hospital nursery on the incidence of retinopathy of prematurity. *The New England Journal of Medicine, 313,* 401–404.

Gogel, W. C. (1976). An indirect method of measuring perceived distance from familiar size. *Perception & Psychophysics, 20,* 419–429.

Gogel, W. C. (1977). The metric of visual space. In W. Epstein (Ed.), *Stability and constancy in visual perception: Mechanisms and processes.* New York: Wiley.

Goldstein, A. (1976). Opioid peptides endorphins in pituitary and brain. *Science, 193,* 1081–1086.

Goodsitt, J. V., Morse, P. A., Ver Hoeve, J. N., & Cowan, N. (1984). Infant speech recognition in multisyllabic contexts. *Child Development, 55,* 903–910.

Goodson, F. E., Snider, T. Q., & Swearingen, J. E. (1980). Motion parallax in the perception of movement by a moving subject. *Bulletin of the Psychonomic Society, 16,* 87–88.

Goren, C. C., Sarty, M., & Wu, P. Y. K. (1975). Visual following and pattern discrimination of face-like stimuli by newborn infants. *Pediatrics, 56,* 544–549.

Gottfried, A. W., & Rose, S. A. (1980). Tactile recognition memory in infants. *Child Development, 51,* 69–74.

Gottschaldt, K. M., & Vahle-Hinz, C. (1981). Merkle cell receptors: Structure and transducer function. *Science, 214,* 183–185.

Gouras, P., & Zrenner, E. (1981). Color coding in the primate retina. *Vision Research, 21,* 1591–1598.

Graham, C. H., & Hsia, Y. (1958). Color defect and color theory. *Science, 127,* 675–682.

Graham, N. (1981). Psychophysics of spatial-frequency channels. In M. Kuboby & J. Pomerantz (Eds.), *Perceptual organization* (pp. 1–25). Hillsdale, NJ: Erlbaum.

Green, D. G., & Powers, M. K. (1982). Mechanisms of light adaptation in rat retina. *Vision Research, 22,* 209–216.

Green, D. M. (1976). *An introduction to hearing.* Hillsdale, NJ: Erlbaum.

Green, D. M. (1983). Profile analysis: A different view of auditory intensity discrimination. *American Psychologist, 38,* 133–142.

Green, D. M., Kidd, G., & Picardi, M. C. (1983). Successive versus simultaneous comparison in auditory intensity discrimination. *Journal of the Acoustical Society of America, 73,* 639–643.

Green, D. M., & Swets, J. A. (1966). *Signal detection theory and psychophysics.* New York: Wiley.

Green, M. (1983). Inhibition and facilitation of apparent motion by real motion. *Vision Research, 23,* 861–865.

Greenberg, D. A., & Branch, L. G. (1982). A review of methodologic issues concerning incidence and prevalence data of visual deterioration in elders. In R. Sekuler, D. Kline, & K. Dismukes (Eds.), *Aging and human visual function* (pp. 279–296). New York: Alan R. Liss.

Gregory, R. L. (1973). *Eye and brain* (2nd ed.). New York: World University Library.

Gregory, R. L. (1974). Choosing a paradigm for perception. In E. C. Carterette & M. P. Friedman (Eds.), *Handbook of perception* (Vol. 1). New York: Academic.

Gregory, R. L., & Gombrich, E. H. (1973). *Illusion in nature and art.* New York: Scribner's.

Gregory, R. L., & Harris, J. P. (1984). Real and apparent movement nulled. *Nature, 307,* 729–730.

Gregson, R. A. (1984). Similarities between odor mixtures with known components. *Perception & Psychophysics, 35,* 33–40.

Groner, R., Menz, C., Fisher, D. F., & Monty, R. A. (Eds.). (1983). *Eye movements and psychological functions: International view.* Hillsdale, NJ: Erlbaum.

Grossberg, J. M., & Grant, B. F. (1978). Clinical psychophysics: Applications of ratio scaling and signal detection methods to research on pain, fear, drugs, and medical decision making. *Psychological Bulletin, 85,* 1154–1176.

Grossberg, S., & Mingolla, E. (1985). Neural dynamics of form perception: Boundary completion, illusory figures, and neon color spreading. *Psychological Review, 92,* 173–211.

Grosslight, J. H., Fletcher, H. J., Masterson, R. B., & Hagen, R. (1978). Monocular vision and landing performance in general aviation pilots: Cyclops revisited. *Human Factors, 20,* 27–33.

Guiss, L. W., & Kuenstler, P. (1960). A retrospective view of survey photofluorograms of persons with lung cancer. *Cancer, 13,* 91–95.

Guth, S. K. (1981). The science of seeing—a search for criteria. *American Journal of Optometry and Physiological Optics, 58,* 870–885.

Gwiazda, J., Brill, S., Mohindra, I., & Helds, R. (1980). Preferential looking acuity in infants from two to fifty-eight weeks of age. *American Journal of Optometry & Physiological Optics, 57,* 428–432.

Haber, R. N. (1974). Information processing. In E. C. Carterette & M. P. Friedman (Eds.), *Handbook of perception* (Vol. 1). New York: Academic.

Haber, R. N. (1985). Perception: A one-hundred-year perspective. In S. Koch & D. E. Leary (Eds.), *A century of psychology as science* (pp. 250–281). New York: McGraw-Hill.

Hagen, M. A. (1980). *The perception of pictures* (Vols. 1 and 2). New York: Academic.

Hagen, M. A. (1985). James J. Gibson's ecological approach to visual perception. In S. Koch & D. E. Leary (Eds.), *A century of psychology as science* (pp. 231–249). New York: McGraw-Hill.

Hagen, M. A. (1986). *Varieties of realism: Geometries of representational art.* Cambridge: Cambridge University Press.

Haith, M. M., & Campos, J. J. (1977). Human infancy. *Annual Review of Psychology, 28,* 251–293.

Hale, G. A., & Taweel, S. S. (1974). Age differences in children's performance on measures of component selection and incidental learning. *Journal of Experimental Child Psychology, 18,* 107–116.

Hall, M. J., Bartoshuk, L. M., Cain, W. S., & Stevens, J. C. (1975). PTC taste blindness and the taste of caffeine. *Nature* (London), *253,* 442–443.

Hallett, P. E. (1986). Eye movements. In K. R. Boff, L. Kaufman, & J. P. Thomas (Eds.), *Handbook of perception and human performance* (Vol. 1, pp. 10-1–10-112). New York: Wiley.

Halperin, Y., Nachson, I., & Carmon, A. (1973). Shift of ear superiority in dichotic listening to temporally patterned nonverbal stimuli. *Journal of the Acoustical Society of America, 53,* 46–50.

Halpern, B. P. (1982). Environmental factors affecting chemoreceptors: An overview. *Environmental Health Perspectives, 44,* 101–105.

Halpern, B. P., & Meiselman, H. L. (1980). Taste psychophysics based on a simulation of human driinking. *Chemical Senses, 5,* 279–294.

Halpern, D. F., & Salzman, B. (1983). The multiple determination of illusory contours: 1. A review. *Perception, 12,* 281–291.

Halpern, D. F., Salzman, B., Harrison, W., & Widaman, K. (1983). The multiple determination of illusory contours: 2. An empirical investigation. *Perception, 12,* 293–303.

Halpin, Z. T. (1986). Individual odors among mammals: Origins and functions. *Advances in the Study of Behavior, 16,* 39–70.

Hammerschmidt, D. E. (1984). Don't crowd your slides! *Journal of the Americal Medical Association, 252,* 775–776.

Han, J. S., & Terenius, L. (1982). Neurochemical basis of acupuncture analgesia. *Annual Review of Pharmacological Toxicology, 22*, 193–220.

Hancock, P. A. (1984). Environmental stressors. In J. S. Warm (Ed.), *Sustained attention in human performance* (pp. 103–142). New York: Wiley.

Hancock, P. A. (1986a). The effect of skill on performance under an environmental stressor. *Aviation, Space, and Environmental Medicine, 57*, 59–64.

Hancock, P. A. (1986b). Sustained attention under thermal stress. *Psychological Bulletin, 99*, 263–281.

Hanig, D. P. (1901). Zur Psychophysik des Geschmackssinnes. *Philosophische Studien, 17*, 576–623.

Hardy, J. D., Stolwijk, J. A. J., & Hoffman, D. (1968). Pain following step increase in skin temperature. In D. R. Kenshalo (Ed.), *The skin senses*. Springfield, IL: Thomas.

Harrington, T. L., Harrington, M. K., Wilkins, C. A., & Koh, Y. O. (1980). Visual orientation by motion-produced blur patterns: Detection of divergence. *Perception & Psychophysics, 28*, 293–305.

Hartline, H. K., Wagner, H. G., & Ratliff, F. (1956). Inhibition in the eye of Limulus. *Journal of General Physiology, 39*, 651–673.

Hartman, B. J. (1982). An exploratory study of the effects of disco music on the auditory and vestibular systems. *Journal of Auditory Research, 22*, 271–274.

Harvey, L. O., Roberts, J. O., & Gervais, M. J. (1983). The spatial frequency basis of internal representations. In H. G. Geissler, H. F. J. M. Buffart, E. L. J. Leeuwenberg, & V. Sarris (Eds.), *Modern issues in perception* (pp. 217–226). Amsterdam: North-Holland.

Hassett, J. (1980, December). Acupuncture is proving its points. *Psychology Today, 14*, 81–89.

Hatfield, G., & Epstein, W. (1985). The status of minimum principle in the theoretical analysis of visual perception. *Psychological Bulletin, 97*, 155–186.

Havener, W. H. (1979). *Synopsis of ophthalmology* (5th ed.). St. Louis: Mosby.

Hawkins, H. L., & Presson, J. C. (1986). Auditory information processing. In K. R. Boff, L. Kaufman, & J. P. Thomas (Eds.). *Handbook of perception and human performance* (Vol. II, pp. 26-1–26-44). New York: Wiley.

Healy, A. F. (1976). Detection errors on the word *The*: Evidence for reading units larger than letters. *Journal of Experimental Psychology: Human Perception and Performance, 2*, 235–242.

Heider, E. R., & Olivier, D. C. (1972). The stucture of the color space in naming and memory for two languages. *Cognitive Psychology, 3*, 337–354.

Heller, H. C., Crawshaw, L. I., & Hammel, H. T. (1978). The thermostat of vertebrate animals. *Scientific American, 239*, 102–113.

Heller, M. A. (1980). Tactile retention: Reading with the skin. *Perception & Psychophysics, 27*, 125–130.

Heller, M. A. (1982). Visual and tactual texture perception: Intersensory cooperation. *Perception & Psychophysics, 31*, 339–344.

Heller, M. A. (1983). Haptic dominance in form perception with blurred vision. *Perception, 12*, 607–613.

Heller, M. A. (1984a). Active and passive touch: The influence of exploration time on form recognition. *Journal of General Psychology, 110*, 243–249.

Heller, M. A. (1984b). Personal communication.

Hemholtz, H. von (1863). Die Lehre von den Tonempfindungen als physiologische Grundlege für die Theorie der Musik. [Translated by A. J. Ellis (1930). *The sensations of tone*. New York: Longmans, Green.]

Helmholtz, H. von (1866). *Handbuch der physiolgischen Optik*. Hamburg & Leipzig: Voss.

Henkind, P., Priest, R. S., & Schiller, G. (1983). *Compendium of ophthalmology*. Philadelphia: Lippincott.

Henning, G. J., Brouwer, J. N., Van der Wel, H., & Francke, A. (1969). Miraculin, the sweet-inducing principle from miracle fruit. In C. Pfaffman (Ed.), *Olfaction and taste*. New York: Rockefeller University Press.

Henning, H. (1916). Die Qualitätsreibe des Geschmacks. *Zeitschrift für Psychologie, 74*, 203–219.

Henning, H. (1927). Psychologische Studien am Geschmacksinn. In E. Abderhalden (Ed.), *Handbuch der biologischen Arbeitsmethoden*. Berlin: Urban & Schwarzenberg.

Hensel, H. (1981). *Thermoreception and temperature regulation*. London: Academic.

Hensel, H. (1982). *Thermal sensations and thermoreceptors in man*. Springfield, IL: Thomas.

Hershenson, M. (1982). Moon illusion and spiral aftereffect: Illusions due to the loom-zoom system? *Journal of Experimental Psychology: General, 111*, 423–440.

Heydorn, B., & Cheek, E. H. (1982). Reversals in reading and writing: Perceptual, developmental, diagnostic, and remedial aspects. *Reading Improvement, 19*, 123–128.

Hirst, W., Spelke, E., Reaves, C. C., Caharack, G.,

& Neisser, U. (1980). Dividing attention without alternation or automaticity. *Journal of Experimental Psychology: General, 109,* 98–117.

Hochberg, J. (1971a). Perception: I. Color and shape. In J. W. Kling & L. A. Riggs (Eds.), *Woodworth & Schlosberg's experimental psychology* (3rd ed.) (pp. 395–474). New York: Holt, Rinehart & Winston.

Hochberg, J. (1971b). Perception: II. Space and movement. In J. W. Kling & L. A. Riggs (Eds.), *Woodworth & Schlosberg's experimental psychology* (3rd ed.) (pp. 475–550). New York: Holt, Rinehart & Winston.

Hochberg, J. (1978a). *Perception.* Englewood Cliffs, NJ: Prentice-Hall.

Hochberg, J. (1978b). Art and perception. In E. C. Carterette & M. P. Friedman (Eds.), *Handbook of perception* (Vol. 10). New York: Academic.

Hochberg, J. (1979). Sensation and perception. In E. Hearst (Ed.), *The first century of experimental psychology* (pp. 89–142). Hillsdale, NJ: Erlbaum.

Hochberg, J. (1984). Form perception: Experience and explanations. In P. C. Dodwell & T. Caelli (Eds.), *Figural synthesis* (pp. 1–30). Hillsdale, NJ: Erlbaum.

Hochberg, J. (1986). Representation of motion and space in video and cinematic displays. In K. R. Boff, L. Kaufman, & J. P. Thomas (Eds.), *Handbook of perception and human performance* (Vol. 1, pp. 22-1–22-64). New York: Wiley.

Hochberg, J., & Brooks, V. (1960). The psychophysics of form. Reversible-perspective drawings of spatial objects. *American Journal of Psychology, 73,* 337–354.

Hochberg, J., & Brooks, V. (1978). The perception of motion pictures. In E. C. Carterette & M. P. Friedman (Eds.), *Handbook of perception* (Vol. 10). New York: Academic.

Hochberg, J., & McAlister, E. (1953). A quantitative approach to figural "goodness." *Journal of Experimental Psychology, 46,* 361–364.

Hockett, C. F. (1955). A manual of phonology, memoir 11. *International Journal of American Linguistics, 21* (pt. 1).

Hoffman, D. D. (1983, December). The interpretation of visual illusion. *Scientific American, 249* (6), 154–162.

Holway, A. F., & Boring, E. G. (1940a). The moon illusion and the angle of regard. *American Journal of Psychology, 52,* 509–516.

Holway, A. F., & Boring, E. G. (1940b). The moon illusion and the angle of regard: Further experiments. *American Journal of Psychology, 53,* 537–553.

Holway, A. F., & Boring, E. G. (1941). Determinants of apparent visual size with distance variant. *American Journal of Psychology, 54,* 21–37.

Hood, D. C., & Finkelstein, M. A. (1986). Sensitivity to light. In K. R. Boff, L. Kaufman, & M. P. Thomas (Eds.), *Handbook of perception and human performance* (pp. 5-1–5-66). New York: Wiley.

Horner, D. G. (1982). Can vision predict baseball players' hitting ability? *American Journal of Optometry and Physiological Optics, 59,* 69P.

Hornung, D. E., & Enns, M. P. (1987). The contribution of smell and taste to overall intensity: A model. *Perception & Psychophysics.* In press.

Hovde, G. (1978). Visual illusions. *Psychological Reports Aarhus, 3,* 1–152.

Howard, I. P. (1986). The perception of posture, self motion, and the visual vertical. In K. R. Boff, L. Kaufman, & J. P. Thomas (Eds.), *Handbook of perception and human performance* (Vol. I, pp. 18-1–18-62). New York: Wiley.

Howe, E. S., & Brandau, C. J. (1983). The temporal course of visual pattern encoding: Effects of pattern goodness. *Quarterly Journal of Experimental Psychology, 35A,* 607–633.

Howe, E. S., & Jung, K. (1986). Immediate memory span for two-dimensional spatial arrays: Effects of pattern symmetry and goodness. *Acta Psychologica, 61,* 37–51.

Hoyer, W. J., & Plude, D. J. (1982). Aging and the allocation of attentional resources in visual information-processing. In R. Sekuler, D. Kline, & K. Dismukes (Eds.), *Aging and human visual function* (pp. 245–263). New York: Alan R. Liss.

Hubel, D. H. (1982). Explorations of the primary visual cortex, 1955–1978. *Nature, 299,* 515–524.

Hubel, D. H., & Livingstone, M. S. (1983). The 11th J. A. F. Stevenson Memorial Lecture: Blobs and color vision. *Canadian Journal of Physiology and Pharmacology, 61,* 1433–1441.

Hubel, D. H., & Wiesel, T. N. (1965). Receptive fields of single neurons in two nonstriate visual areas (18 and 19) of the cat. *Journal of Neurophysiology, 28,* 229–289.

Hubel, D. H., & Wiesel, T. N. (1977). Functional architecture of macaque monkey visual cortex. *Proceedings of the Royal Society of London, 198,* 1–59.

Hubel, D. H., & Wiesel, T. N. (1979). Brain mechanisms and vision. *Scientific American, 241* (3), 150–162.

Hubel, D. H., Wiesel, T. N., & Stryker, M. P. (1978). Anatomical demonstration of orientation columns in macaque monkey. *Journal of Comparative Neurology, 177,* 361–380.

Huey, E. B. (1968). *The psychology and pedagogy of reading.* Cambridge, MA: MIT. (Original work published 1908.)

Huggins, A. W. F. (1981). Speech perception and auditory processing. In D. J. Getty & J. H. Howard (Eds.), *Auditory and visual pattern recognition* (pp. 79–91). Hillsdale, NJ: Erlbaum.

Humphrey, A. L., & Hendrickson, A. E. (1980). Radial zones of high metabolic activity in squirrel monkey striate cortex. *Society for Neuroscience Abstracts, 6,* 315.

Hung, D. L., & Tzeng, O. (1981). Orthographic variations and visual information processing. *Psychological Bulletin, 90,* 377–414.

Hurd, P. D., & Blevins, J. (1984). Aging and the color of pills. *New England Journal of Medicine, 310,* 202.

Hurvich, L. M. (1981). *Color vision.* Sunderland, MA: Sinauer.

Hurvich, L. M., & Jameson, D. (1957). An opponent-process theory of color vision. *Psychological Review, 64,* 384–404.

Hurvich, L. M., & Jameson, D. (1966). *The perception of brightness and darkness.* Boston: Allyn & Bacon.

Hyman, A. (1983). The influence of color on the taste perception of carbonated water preparations. *Bulletin of the Psychonomic Society, 21,* 145–148.

Hyman, A., Mentzer, T., & Calderone, L. (1979). The contribution of olfaction to taste discrimination. *Bulletin of the Psychonomic Society, 13,* 359–362.

Hynd, G. W., & Hynd, C. R. (1984). Dyslexia: Neuroanatomical/neurolinguistic perspectives. *Reading Research Quarterly, 4,* 482–495.

Iavecchia, J. H., Iavecchia, H. P., & Roscoe, S. N. (1983). The moon illusion revisited. *Aviation, Space, and Environmental Medicine, 54,* 39–46.

"Ice Cream." (1981, June). *Consumer Reports, 46,* 316–321.

Iggo, A. (1982). Cutaneous sensory mechanisms. In H. B. Barlow & J. D. Mollon (Eds.), *The senses* (pp. 369–408). Cambridge: Cambridge University Press.

Ittelson, W. H., & Kilpatrick, F. P. (1951). Experiments in perception. *Scientific American, 185* (2), 50–55.

Jaeger, W. (1972). Genetics of congenital colour deficiencies. In D. Jameson & L. M. Hurvich (Eds.), *Visual psychophysics* (Vol. VII/4). Berlin: Springer-Verlag.

James, G. A. (1982). Mobility maps. In W. Schiff & E. Foulke (Eds.), *Tactual perception: A source-book* (pp. 334–363). Cambridge: Cambridge University Press.

James, W. (1890). *The principles of psychology.* New York: Henry Holt.

Jameson, D. (1972). Theoretical issues of color vision. In D. Jameson & L. M. Hurvich (Eds.), *Visual psychophysics* (Vol. VII/4). Berlin: Springer-Verlag.

Jameson, D., & Hurvich, L. M. (1978). Dichromatic color language: "Reds" and "greens" don't look alike but their colors do. *Sensory Processes, 2,* 146–155.

Jaremko, M. E., Crusco, A. H., & Lau, G. (1983). Effects of public description on the detection and tolerance of laboratory pain. *Journal of Behavior Therapy & Experimental Psychiatry, 14,* 43–48.

Jenkins, W. M., & Merzenich, M. M. (1984). Role of cat primary auditory cortex for sound localization behavior. *Journal of Neurophysiology, 52,* 819–847.

Jesteadt, W., Bacon, S. P., & Lehman, J. R. (1982). Forward masking as a function of frequency, masker level, and signal delay. *Journal of the Acoustical Society of America, 71,* 950–962.

Johansson, G. (1973). Visual perception of biological motion and a model for its analysis. *Perception & Psychophysics, 14,* 201–211.

Johansson, G. (1974). Projective transformations as determining visual space perception. In R. B. MacLeod & H. L. Pick, Jr. (Eds.), *Perception: Essays in honor of James J. Gibson.* Ithaca, NY: Cornell University Press.

Johansson, G. (1975). Visual motion perception. *Scientific American, 232,* 76–88.

Johansson, G. (1982). Visual space perception through motion. In A. H. Wertheim, W. A. Wagenaar, & H. W. Leibowitz (Eds.), *Tutorials on motion perception* (pp. 19–39). New York: Plenum.

Johansson, G. (1985). About visual event perception. In W. H. Warren, Jr., & R. W. Shaw (Eds.), *Persistence and change: Proceedings of the First International Conference on Event Perception* (pp. 29–54). Hillsdale, NJ: Erlbaum.

Johansson, G., von Hofsten, C., & Jansson, G. (1980). Event perception. *Annual Review of Psychology, 31,* 27–63.

Johansson, R. S., & LaMotte, R. H. (1983). Tactile detection thresholds for a single asperity on an otherwise smooth surface. *Somatosensory Research, 1,* 21–31.

Johnson, H. (1971). *The world atlas of wine.* New York: Simon & Schuster.

Johnson, J., & Ketchum, W. C., Jr. (1983). *American

folk art of the twentieth century. New York: Cynthia Parzych.

Johnston, W. A., & Dark, V. J. (1986). Selective attention. *Annual Review of Psychology, 37,* 43–75.

Jones, B., & O'Neil, S. (1985). Combining vision and touch in texture perception. *Perception & Psychophysics, 37,* 66–72.

Jonides, J. (1983). Further toward a model of the mind's eye's movement. *Bulletin of the Psychonomic Society, 21,* 247–250.

Joubert, C. E. (1984). Structured time and subjective acceleration of time. *Perceptual and Motor Skills, 59,* 335–336.

Juola, J. F. (1979). Pattern recognition. In R. Lachman, J. L. Lachman, & E. C. Butterfield (Eds.), *Cognitive psychology and information processing: An introduction.* Hillsdale, NJ: Erlbaum.

Jusczyk, P. W. (1986). Speech perception. In K. R. Boff, L. Kaufman, & J. P. Thomas (Eds.), *Handbook of perception and human performance* (Vol. II, pp. 27-1–27-57). New York: Wiley.

Jusczyk, P. W., Murray, J., & Bayly, J. (1979). *Perception of place-of-articulation in fricatives and stops by infants.* Paper presented at Society for Research in Child Development, San Francisco.

Just, M. A., & Carpenter, P. A. (1987). *The psychology of reading and language comprehension.* Newton, MA: Allyn & Bacon.

Kahneman, D. (1968). Method, findings, and theory in studies of visual masking. *Psychological Bulletin, 70,* 404–425.

Kallman, H. J., & Massaro, D. W. (1979). Similarity effects in backward recognition masking. *Journal of Experimental Psychology: Human Perception & Performance, 5,* 110–128.

Kallman, H. J., & Morris, M. D. (1984). Backward recognition masking as a function of ear of mask presentation. *Perception & Psychophysics, 35,* 379–384.

Kanizsa, G. (1976). Subjective contours. *Scientific American, 234* (4), 48–52.

Kare, M. R., & Ficken, M. S. (1963). Comparative studies on the sense of taste. In Y. Zotterman (Ed.), *Olfaction and taste.* New York: Macmillan.

Kaufman, L., & Rock, I. (1962). The moon illusion. I. *Science, 136,* 953–961.

Kaufman, R., Maland, J., & Yonas, A. (1981). Sensitivity of 5- and 7-month-old infants to pictorial depth information. *Journal of Experimental Child Psychology, 32,* 162–168.

Kelling, S. T., & Halpern, B. P. (1983). Taste flashes: Reaction times, intensity, and quality. *Science, 219,* 412–414.

Kennedy, J. M. (1974). *The psychology of picture perception.* San Francisco: Jossey-Bass.

Kennedy, J. M. (1982). Haptic pictures. In W. Schiff & E. Foulke (Eds.), *Tactual perception: A sourcebook* (pp. 305–333). Cambridge: Cambridge University Press.

Kenshalo, D. R. (1971). The cutaneous senses. In J. W. Kling & L. A. Riggs (Eds.), *Woodworth & Schlosberg's experimental psychology* (3rd ed.). New York: Holt, Rinehart & Winston.

Kenshalo, D. R. (1977). Age changes in touch, vibration, temperature, kinesthesis, and pain sensitivity. In J. E. Birren & K. W. Schaie (Eds.), *Handbook of the psychology of aging.* New York: Van Nostrand Reinhold.

Kenshalo, D. R. (1978). Biophysics and psychophysics of feeling. In E. C. Carterette & M. P. Friedman (Eds.), *Handbook of perception* (Vol. 6B). New York: Academic.

Kenshalo, D. R., Holmes, C. E., & Wood, P. B. (1968). Warm and cool thresholds as a function of rate of stimulus temperature change. *Perception & Psychophysics, 3,* 81–84.

Keverne, E. B. (1982). Chemical senses: taste. In H. B. Barlow & J. D. Mollon (Eds.), *The senses* (pp. 428–447). Cambridge: Cambridge University Press.

Kilbride, P. E., Hutman, L. P., Fishman, M., & Read, J. S. (1986). Foveal cone pigment density difference in the aging human eye. *Vision Research, 26,* 321–325.

Kirman, J. H. (1982). Current developments in tactile communication of speech. In W. Schiff & E. Foulke (Eds.), *Tactual perception: A sourcebook* (pp. 234–262). Cambridge: Cambridge University Press.

Klatzky, R. L. (1980). *Human memory: Structures and processes* (2nd ed.). San Francisco: Freeman.

Kleiss, J. A., & Lane, D. M. (1986). Locus and persistence of capacity limitations in visual information processing. *Journal of Experimental Psychology: Human Perception and Performance, 12,* 200–210.

Koelega, H. S., & Koster, E. P. (1974). Some experiments on sex differences in odor perception. *Annals of the New York Academy of Sciences, 237,* 234–246.

Koffka, K. (1935). *Principles of Gestalt psychology.* New York: Harcourt Brace.

Köhler, W. (1947). *Gestalt psychology: An introduction to new concepts in modern psychology.* New York: Liveright.

Kolers, P. A. (1983). Perception and representation. *Annual Review of Psychology, 34,* 129–166.

Kovi, P. (1980, September). The sweet truth about wine. *Cuisine, 9,* 12–14.

Kroeze, J. H. A. (1979). Functional equivalence of the two sides of the human tongue. *Perception & Psychophysics, 25,* 115–118.

Krueger, L. E. (1982). A word-superiority effect with print and braille characters. *Perception & Psychophysics, 31,* 345–352.

Krumhansl, C. L. (1983). Perceptual structures for tonal music. *Music Perception, 1,* 28–62.

Krumhansl, C. L. (1985, July-August). Perceiving tonal structure in music. *American Scientist, 73,* 371–378.

Krumhansl, C. L., & Kessler, E. J. (1982). Tracing the dynamic changes in perceived tonal organization in a spatial representation of musical keys. *Psychological Review, 89,* 334–368.

Kryter, K. D. (1985). *The effects of noise on man* (2nd ed.). Orlando, FL: Academic.

Kubovy, M., & Pomerantz, J. R. (Eds.). (1981). *Perceptual organization.* Hillsdale, NJ: Erlbaum.

Kuchuk, A., Vibbert, M., & Bornstein, M. H. (1986). The perception of smiling and its experiential correlates in 3-month-old infants. *Child Development, 57,* 1054–1061.

Kuhl, P. K. (1979). Speech perception in early infancy: Perceptual constancy for spectrally dissimilar vowel categories. *Journal of the Acoustical Society of America, 66,* 1668–1679.

Kuhl, P. K. (1985). Methods in the study of infant speech perception. In G. Gottlieb & N. A. Krasnegor (Eds.), *Measurement of audition and vision in the first year of postnatal life* (pp. 223–251). Norwood, NJ: Ablex.

Kuhl, P. K., & Meltzoff, A. N. (1982). The bimodal perception of speech in infancy. *Science, 218,* 1138–1141.

Kundel, H. L., & Nodine, C. F. (1978). Studies of eye movements and visual search in radiology. In J. W. Senders, D. F. Fisher, & R. A. Monty (Eds.), *Eye movements and the higher psychological functions.* Hillsdale, NJ: Erlbaum.

Kundel, H. L., & Nodine, C. F. (1983). A visual concept shapes image perception. *Radiology, 146,* 363–368.

Kupchella, C. (1976). *Sights and sounds.* Indianapolis: Bobbs-Merrill.

Kuznicki, J. T., & McCutcheon, N. B. (1979). Cross-enhancement of the sour taste on a single human taste papilla. *Journal of Experimental Psychology: General, 108,* 68–89.

Laing, D. G. (1982). Characterisation of human behavior during odor perception. *Perception, 11,* 221–230.

Laing, D. G. (1983). Natural sniffing gives optimum odour perception for humans. *Perception, 12,* 99–118.

Laing, D. G. (1986). Identification of single dissimilar odors is achieved by humans with a single sniff. *Physiology & Behavior, 37,* 163–170.

Laing, D. G., Panhuber, H., Willcox, M. E., & Pittman, E. A. (1984). Quality and intensity of binary odor mixtures. *Physiology & Behavior, 33,* 309–319.

Laming, D. (1985). Some principles of sensory analysis. *Psychological Review, 92,* 462–485.

Lancet, D. (1984). Molecular view of olfactory reception. *Trends in NeuroSciences, 7,* 35–36.

Lane, D. M., & Pearson, D. A. (1982). The development of selective attention. *Merrill-Palmer Quarterly, 28,* 317–337.

Lang, G. (1979, July). The best seafood in the world (naturally, a report from Hong Kong). *Food & Wine, 2,* 59–67.

Lappin, J. S. (1985). Reflections on Gunnar Johansson's perspective on the visual measurement of space and time. In W. H. Warren, Jr., & R. E. Shaw (Eds.), *Persistence and change: Proceedings of the First International Conference on Event Perception* (pp. 67–86). Hillsdale, NJ: Erlbaum.

Lappin, J. S., & Preble, L. D. (1975). A demonstration of shape constancy. *Perception & Psychophysics, 25,* 180–184.

Lawless, H. T. (1984). Oral chemical irritation: Psychophysical properties. *Chemical Senses, 9,* 143–155.

Lawless, H. T., & Engen, T. (1977). Associations to odors: Interference, memories, and verbal labeling. *Journal of Experimental Psychology, 3,* 52–59.

Lawless, H. T., Rozin, P., & Shenker, J. (1985). Effects of oral capsaicin on gustatory, olfactory and irritant sensations and flavor identification in humans who regularly or rarely consume chili pepper. *Chemical Senses, 10,* 579–589.

Lawless, H. T., & Skinner, E. F. (1979). The duration and perceived intensity of sucrose taste. *Perception & Psychophysics, 25,* 180–184.

Lawless, H. T., & Stevens, D. A. (1983). Cross adaptation of sucrose and intensive sweeteners. *Chemical Senses, 7,* 309–315.

Layton, B. (1975). Differential effects of two nonspeech sounds on phonemic restoration. *Bulletin of the Psychonomic Society, 6,* 487–490.

Lee, D. N. (1980). The optic flow field: The foundation of vision. In The Royal Society (Ed.), *The psychology of vision* (pp. 169–179). Cambridge: University Press.

Leguire, L. E., Blake, R., & Sloane, M. E. (1981). A novel illusion of bars made from triangles. *Science, 212,* 1172–1175.

Leibowitz, H. W. (1971). Sensory, learned, and cognitive mechanisms of size perception. *Annals of the New York Academy of Sciences, 188,* 47–62.

Leibowitz, H. W., & Owens, D. A. (1986). We drive by night. *Psychology Today, 20*(1), 55–58.

Leibowitz, H. W., Post, R. B., Brandt, T., & Dichgans, J. (1982). Implications of recent developments in dynamic spatial orientation and visual resolution for vehicle guidance. In A. H. Wertheim, W. A. Wagenaar, & H. W. Leibowitz (Eds.), *Tutorials on motion perception* (pp. 231–260). New York: Plenum.

Leibowitz, H. W., Shiina, K., & Hennessy, R. T. (1972). Oculomotor adjustments and size constancy. *Perception & Psychophysics, 12,* 497–500.

Leibowitz, H. W., Shupert, C. L., Post, R. B., & Dichgans, J. (1983). Expectation and autokinesis. *Perception & Psychophysics, 34,* 131–134.

Lennie, P. (1980). Parallel visual pathways: A review. *Vision Research, 20,* 561–594.

Lennie, P. (1984). Recent developments in the physiology of color vision. *Trends in Neuro-Sciences, 7,* 243–248.

Leo, J. (1986, December 1). The hidden power of body odors. *Time Magazine, 128,* 67.

Levine, J. D., Gordon, N. C., & Fields, H. L. (1979). The role of endorphins in placebo analgesia. In J. J. Bonica, J. C. Liebesking, & D. Albe-Fessard (Eds.), *Advances in pain research and therapy* (Vol. 3). New York: Raven.

Levinson, S. E., & Liberman, M. Y. (1981, April). Speech recognition by computer. *Scientific American, 244,* 64–76.

Liberman, A. M. (1982). On finding that speech is special. *American Psychologist, 37,* 148–167.

Liberman, A. M., Harris, K. S., Hoffman, H. S., & Griffith, B. C. (1957). The discrimination of speech sounds within and across phoneme boundaries. *Journal of Experimental Psychology, 54,* 358–368.

Liberman, A. M., & Studdert-Kennedy, M. (1978). Phonetic perception. In R. Held, H. W. Leibowitz, & H. L. Teuber (Eds.), *Handbook of sensory physiology: Vol. 8. Perception.* New York: Springer-Verlag.

Liebeskind, J. C., & Paul, L. A. (1977). Psychological and physiological mechanisms of pain. *Annual Review of Psychology, 28,* 41–60.

Lim, D. J. (1980). Cochlear anatomy related to cochlear micromechanics: A review. *Journal of the Acoustical Society of America, 67,* 1686–1695.

Lindauer, M. S. (1984). Phenomenological method. In R. J. Corsini (Ed.), *Encyclopedia of psychology.* New York: Wiley.

Lindsay, P. H., & Norman, D. A. (1977). *Human information processing* (2nd ed.). New York, Academic Press.

Lippman, C. W. (1952). Certain hallucinations peculiar to migraine. *Journal of Nervous and Mental Diseases, 116,* 346–351.

Liss, P., & Reeves, A. (1983). Interruption of dot processing by a backward mask. *Perception, 12,* 513–529.

Livingstone, M. S., & Hubel, D. H. (1983). Specificity of cortico-cortical connections in monkey visual system. *Nature, 304,* 531–534.

Llewellyn-Thomas, E. (1981). Can eye movements save the earth? In D. F. Fisher, R. A. Monty, & J. W. Senders (Eds.), *Eye movements: Cognition and visual perception* (pp. 317–321). Hillsdale, NJ: Erlbaum.

Loeb, M. (1981). The present state of research on the effects of noise: Are we asking the right questions? *The Journal of Auditory Research, 21,* 93–104.

Loftus, E. F. (1977). Shifting human color memory. *Memory & Cognition, 5,* 696–699.

Loftus, G. R. (1985). Size illusion, distance illusion, and terrestrial passage. Comment on Reed. *Journal of Experimental Psychology: General, 114,* 119–121.

Logue, A. W. (1986). *The psychology of eating and drinking.* New York: Freeman.

Loomis, J. M., & Lederman, S. J. (1986). Tactual perception. In K. R. Boff, L. Kaufman, & J. P. Thomas (Eds.), *Handbook of perception and human performance* (Vol. II, pp. 31-1–31-41). New York: Wiley.

Loudon, D., & Della Bitta, A. J. (1979). *Consumer behavior: Concepts and applications.* New York: McGraw-Hill.

Luce, R. D. (1984). Time perception: Discussion paper. *Annals of the New York Academy of Sciences, 423,* 78–81.

Lundin, R. W. (1984). Structuralism. In R. J. Corsini (Ed.), *Encyclopedia of psychology* (Vol. 3, pp. 374–375). New York: Wiley.

MacDonald, W. A., & Hoffman, E. R. (1973). The recognition of road pavement messages. *Journal of Applied Psychology, 57,* 314–319.

Mace, W. M. (1977). James J. Gibson's strategy for perceiving: Ask not what's inside your head, but what your head's inside of. In R. Shaw & J. Bransford (Eds.), *Perceiving, acting and know-*

ing: Toward an ecological psychology. Hillsdale, NJ: Erlbaum.

Macfarlane, A. (1977). *The psychology of childbirth.* Cambridge, MA: Harvard University Press.

Mackay, D. G. (1973). Aspects of the theory of comprehension, memory and attention. *Quarterly Journal of Experimental Psychology, 25,* 22–40.

Mackworth, N. H. (1948). The breakdown of vigilance during prolonged visual search. *Quarterly Journal of Experimental Psychology, 1,* 6–21.

Madden, T. M., & Burt, G. S. (1981). Inappropriate constancy scaling theory and the Mueller-Lyer illusion. *Perceptual and Motor Skills, 52,* 211–218.

Maga, J. A. (1974). The influence of color on taste thresholds. *Chemical Senses and Flavor, 1,* 115–120.

Maloney, L. T., & Wandell, B. A. (1986). Color constancy: A method for recovering surface spectral reflectance. *Journal of the Optical Society of America A, 3,* 29–33.

Malow, R. M., Grimm, L., & Olson, R. E. (1980). Differences in pain perception between myofascial pain dysfunction patients and normal subjects: A signal detection analysis. *Journal of Psychosomatic Research, 24,* 303–309.

Marks, W. B., Dobelle, W. H., & MacNichol, E. F. (1964). Visual pigments of single primate cones. *Science, 143,* 1181–1183.

Marr, D. (1982). *Vision.* San Francisco: Freeman.

Masin, S. C., & Vidotto, G. (1983). A magnitude estimation study of the inverted-T illusion. *Perception & Psychophysics, 33,* 582–584.

Massaro, D. W. (1987). Categorical partition: A fuzzy logical model of categorization behavior. In S. Harnad (Ed.), *Categorical perception.* New York: Cambridge University Press.

Massaro, D. W., & Cohen, M. M. (1983a). Categorical or continuous speech perception: A new test. *Speech Communication, 2,* 15–35.

Massaro, D. W., & Cohen, M. M. (1983b). Evaluation and integration of visual and auditory information in speech perception. *Journal of Experimental Psychology: Human Perception and Performance, 9,* 753–771.

Mastai, M. I. d'O. (1975). *Illusion in art.* New York: Abaris.

Matin, L. (1982). Visual localization and eye movements. In A. H. Wertheim, W. A. Wagenaar, & H. W. Leibowitz (Eds.), *Tutorials on motion perception* (pp. 101–156). New York: Plenum.

Matlin, M. W. (1979). *Human experimental psychology.* Monterey, CA: Brooks/Cole.

Matlin, M. W. (1983). *Cognition.* New York: Holt, Rinehart & Winston.

Matlin, M. W. (1987). *The psychology of women.* New York: Holt, Rinehart & Winston.

Matlin, M. W., & Stang, D. (1978). *The Pollyanna principle: Selectivity in language, memory, and thought.* Cambridge, MA: Schenkman.

Maurer, D., & Lewis, T. L. (1979). A physiological explanation of infants' early visual development. *Canadian Journal of Psychology, 33,* 232–252.

Mayer, D. J., Price, D. D., Rafii, A., & Barber, J. (1976). Acupuncture hypalgesia: Evidence for activation of a central control system as a mechanism of action. In J. J. Bonica & D. Albe-Fessard (Eds.), *Advances in pain research and therapy* (Vol. 1). New York: Raven.

McBurney, D. H. (1978). Psychological dimensions and perceptual analysis of taste. In E. C. Carterette & M. P. Friedman (Eds.). *Handbook of perception* (Vol. 6A). New York: Academic.

McBurney, D. H., & Gent, J. F. (1979). On the nature of taste qualities. *Psychological Bulletin, 86,* 151–167.

McBurney, D. H., & Moskat, L. J. (1975). Taste thresholds in college-age smokers and nonsmokers. *Perception & Psychophysics, 10,* 249–252.

McBurney, D. H., & Shick, T. R. (1971). Taste and water taste of twenty-six compounds for man. *Perception & Psychophysics, 10,* 249–252.

McCaul, K. D., & Malott, J. M. (1984). Distraction and coping with pain. *Psychological Review, 95,* 516–533.

McClellan, P. G., Bernstein, I. H., & Garbin, C. P. (1984). What makes the Mueller a liar: A multiple-cue approach. *Perception & Psychophysics, 36,* 234–244.

McClelland, J. L., & Rumelhart, D. E. (1981). An interactive activation model of context effects in letter perception: Part I. An account of basic findings. *Psychological Review, 88,* 375–407.

McClintock, M. K. (1971). Menstrual synchrony and suppression. *Nature, 229,* 244–245.

McConkie, G. W. (1982). Some perceptual aspects of reading. *Volta Review, 84,* 35–42.

McConkie, G. W. (1983). Eye movements and perception during reading. In K. Rayner (Ed.), *Eye movements in reading: Perceptual and language processes* (pp. 65–96). New York: Academic.

McConkie, G. W., & Rayner, K. (1975). The span of the effective stimulus during a fixation in reading. *Perception & Psychophysics, 17,* 578–586.

McConkie, G. W., & Zola, D. (1984). Eye movement control during reading. The effect of word units. In W. Prinz & A. F. Sanders (Eds.), *Cognition and motor processes* (pp. 63–74). Berlin: Springer-Verlag.

McFadden, D. (1982). *Tinnitus: Facts, theories and treatments.* Washington, DC: National Academy Press.

McFadden, D., & Plattsmier, H. S. (1983). Aspirin can potentiate the temporary hearing loss induced by intense sounds. *Hearing Research, 9,* 295–316.

McKelvie, S. J. (1984). Effect of psychophysical method on measurement of the Müller-Lyer illusion. *Perceptual & Motor Skills, 58,* 822.

McKenzie, B. E., Tootell, H. E., & Day, R. H. (1980). Development of visual size constancy during the first year of human infancy. *Developmental Psychology, 16,* 163–174.

Meltzer, P. (1980, Summer). How to taste and remember wines like a pro. *Food & Wine, 3,* 14–17.

Meltzoff, A. N., & Moore, M. K. (1977). Imitation of facial and manual gestures by human neonates. *Science, 198,* 75–78.

Meltzoff, A. N., & Moore, M. K. (1983). Newborn infants imitate adult facial gestures. *Child Development, 54,* 702–709.

Meltzoff, A. N., & Moore, M. K. (1985). Cognitive foundations and social functions of imitation and intermodal representation in infancy. In J. Mehler & R. Fox (Eds.), *Neonate cognition: Beyond the blooming buzzing confusion* (pp. 139–156). Hillsdale, NJ: Erlbaum.

Melzack, R. (1973). *The puzzle of pain.* London: Penguin.

Melzack, R., & Dennis, S. G. (1978). Neurophysiological foundations of pain. In R. A. Sternbach (Ed.), *The psychology of pain.* New York: Raven.

Melzack, R., & Wall, P. D. (1965). Pain mechanisms: A new theory. *Science, 150,* 971–979.

Melzack, R., & Wall, P. D. (1982). *The challenge of pain.* New York: Basic.

Melzack, R., Wall, P. D., & Ty, T. C. (1982). Acute pain in an emergency clinic: Latency of onset and descriptor patterns related to different injuries. *Pain, 14,* 33–43.

Metelli, F. (1982). Some characteristics of Gestalt-oriented research in perception. In J. Beck (Ed.), *Organization and representation in perception* (pp. 219–234). Hillsdale, NJ: Erlbaum.

Michael, C. R. (1978). Color vision mechanisms in monkey striate cortex: Dual-opponent cells with concentric receptive fields. *Journal of Neurophysiology, 41,* 572–588.

Michaels, C. F., & Carello, C. (1981). *Direct perception.* Englewood Cliffs, NJ: Prentice-Hall.

Midkiff, E. E., & Bernstein, I. L. (1985). Targets of learned food aversions in humans. *Physiology & Behavior, 34,* 839–841.

Miller, J. D. (1978). Effects of noise on people. In E. C. Carterette & M. P. Friedman (Eds.), *Handbook of perception* (Vol. 4). New York: Academic.

Miller, J. L., Aibel, I. L., & Green, K. (1984). On the nature of rate-dependent processing during phonetic perception. *Perception & Psychophysics, 35,* 5–15.

Mistretta, C. M. (1981). Neurophysiological and anatomical aspects of taste development. In R. N. Aslin, J. R. Alberts, & M. P. Petersen (Eds.), *Development of perception* (Vol. 1, pp. 433–455). New York: Academic.

Mitchison, G. J., & McKee, S. P. (1985). Interpolation in stereoscopic matching. *Nature, 315,* 402–404.

Mitchison, G. J., & Westheimer, G. (1984). The perception of depth in simple figures. *Vision Research, 24 ,* 1063–1073.

Miyawaki, K., Strange, W., Verbrugge, R., Liberman, A., Jenkins, J., & Fijimura, A. (1975). An effect of linguistic experience: The discrimination of /r/ and /l/ by native speakers of Japanese and English. *Perception & Psychophysics, 18,* 331–340.

Mizusawa, K., Sweeting, R. L., & Knouse, S. B. (1983). Comparative studies of color fields, visual acuity fields, and movement perception limits among varsity athletes and non-varsity groups. *Perceptual & Motor Skills, 56,* 887–892.

Mo, S. S. (1975). Temporal reproduction of duration as a function of numerosity. *Bulletin of the Psychonomic Society, 5,* 165–167.

Moir, H. C. (1936). Some observations on the appreciation of flavour in foodstuffs. *Chemistry & Industry, 55,* 145–148.

Mollon, J. D. (1982a). Colour vision and colour blindness. In H. B. Barlow & J. D. Mollon (Eds.), *The senses* (pp. 165–191). Cambridge: Cambridge University Press.

Mollon, J. D. (1982b). Color vision. *Annual Review of Psychology, 33,* 41–85.

Moore, B. C. J. (1977). *Introduction to the psychology of hearing.* Baltimore: University Park Press.

Moore, B. C. J. (1982). *An introduction to the psychology of hearing* (2nd ed.). New York: Academic.

Moore, L. M., Nielsen, C. R., & Mistretta, C. M. (1982). Sucrose taste thresholds: Age-related differences. *Journal of Gerontology, 37,* 64–69.

Morais, J., Cary, L., Alegria, J., & Bertelson, P. (1979). Does awareness of speech as a sequence of phones arise spontaneously? *Cognition, 7,* 323–331.

Moray, N. (1959). Attention in dichotic listening: Affective cues and the influence of instructions. *Quarterly Journal of Experimental Psychology, 11,* 59–60.

Moray, N., Fitter, M., Ostry, D., Favreau, D., & Nagy, V. (1976). Attention to pure tones. *Quarterly Journal of Experimental Psychology, 28,* 271–283.

Morgan, M. J., Watt, R. J., & McKee, S. P. (1983). Exposure duration affects the sensitivity of vernier acuity to target motion. *Vision Research, 23,* 541–546.

Morrison, L. C. (1984). Visual localization with eye movements: A review. *Ophthalmic and Physiological Optics, 4,* 339–353.

Morrison, R. E., & Rayner, K. (1981). Saccade size in reading depends upon character spaces and not visual angle. *Perception & Psychophysics, 30,* 395–396.

Morse, P. A., & Cowan, N. (1982). Infant auditory and speech perception. In T. M. Field, A. Huston, H. C. Quay, L. Troll, & G. E. Finley (Eds.), *Review of human development* (pp. 32–61). New York: Wiley.

Morton, J., & Long, J. (1976). Effects of word transitional probability on phoneme identification. *Journal of Verbal Learning and Verbal Behavior, 15,* 43–51.

Moskowitz, H. R. (1978a). Odors in the environment: Hedonics, perfumery, and odor abatement. In E. C. Carterette & M. P. Friedman (Eds.), *Handbook of perception* (Vol. 10). New York: Academic.

Moskowitz, H. R. (1978b). Food and food technology: Food habits, gastronomy, flavors, and sensory evaluation. In E. C. Carterette & M. P. Friedman (Eds.), *Handbook of perception* (Vol. 10). New York: Academic.

Moskowitz, H. R. (1978c). Taste and food technology: Acceptability, aesthetics, and preference. In E. C. Carterette & M. P. Friedman (Eds.), *Handbook of perception* (Vol. 6A, pp. 157–194). New York: Academic.

Moskowitz, H. R. (1982). Utilitarian benefits of magnitude estimation scaling for testing product acceptability. In J. T. Kuznicki, A. F. Rutkiewic, & R. A. Johnson (Eds.), *Selected sensory methods: Problems and approaches to measuring hedonics* (pp. 11–33)). Philadelphia, PA: American Society for Testing and Materials.

Mountcastle, V. B. (1957). Modality and topographic properties of single neurons of cat's somatic sensory cortex. *Journal of Neurophysiology, 20,* 408–434.

Movshon, J. A., & Van Sluyters, R. C. (1981). Visual neural development. *Annual Review of Psychology, 32,* 477–522.

Moyer, R. S., Sklarew, P., & Whiting, J. (1982). Memory psychophysics. In H. C. Geissler & P. Petzold (Eds.), *Psychophysical judgment and the process of perception* (pp. 35–46). Amsterdam: North-Holland.

Mozell, M. M. (1971). Olfaction. In J. W. Kling & L. A. Riggs (Eds.), *Woodworth & Schlosberg's experimental psychology* (3rd ed.). New York: Holt, Rinehart & Winston.

Murphy, B. J. (1978). Pattern thresholds for moving and stationary gratings during smooth eye movement. *Vision Research, 18,* 521–530.

Murphy, C. (1985). Cognitive and chemosensory influences on age-related changes in the ability to identify blended foods. *Journal of Gerontology, 40,* 47–52.

Murphy, C., & Cain, W. S. (1980). Taste and olfaction: Independence vs interaction. *Physiology & Behavior, 24,* 601–605.

Murphy, C., Cain, W. S., & Bartoshuk, L. M. (1977). Mutual action of taste and olfaction. *Sensory Processes, 1,* 204–211.

Musicant, A. D., & Butler, R. A. (1984). The influence of pinnae-based spectral cues on sound localization. *Journal of the Acoustical Society of America, 75,* 1195–1200.

Myers, A. K. (1982). Psychophysical scaling and scales of physical stimulus measurement. *Psychological Bulletin, 92,* 203–214.

Nafe, M. P., & Wagoner, K. S. (1941). The nature of pressure adaptation. *Journal of General Psychology, 25,* 323–351.

Naj, A. K. (1986, November 25). Hot topic: Chilies cause pleasant pain, even mild euphoria. *The Wall Street Journal, 1,* 20.

Nathan, P. (1982). *The nervous system* (2nd ed.). Oxford: Oxford University Press.

Nathans, J., Thomas, D., & Hogness, D. S. (1986). Molecular genetics of human color vision: The genes encoding blue, green, and red pigments. *Science, 232,* 193–202.

Naus, M. J., & Shillman, R. J. (1976). Why a Y is not a V: A new look at the distinctive features of letters. *Journal of Experimental Psychology: Human Perception and Performance, 2,* 394–400.

Neisser, U. (1964). Visual search. *Scientific American, 210,* 94–102.

Neisser, U. (1976). *Cognition and reality*. San Francisco: Freeman.

Neisser, U. (1979). The control of information pickup in selective looking. In A. D. Pick (Ed.), *Perception and its development: A tribute to Eleanor J. Gibson*. Hillsdale, NJ: Erlbaum.

Neisser, U. (1981). Obituary: James J. Gibson (1904–1979). *American Psychologist, 36*, 214–215.

Neisser, U., & Becklen, R. (1975). Selective looking: Attending to visually specified events. *Cognitive Psychology, 7*, 480–494.

Neuweiler, G., Bruns, V., & Schuller, G. (1980). Ears adapted for the detection of motion, or how echolocating bats have exploited the capacities of the mammalian auditory system. *Journal of the Acoustical Society of America, 68*, 741–753.

Newman, C. G. (1970). The influence of texture density gradients on judgments of length. *Psychonomic Science, 20*, 333–334.

Newman, C. V., Whinham, E. A., & MacRae, A. W. (1973). The influence of texture on judgments of slant and relative distance in a picture with suggested depth. *Perception & Psychophysics, 14*, 280–284.

Nielsen, L. L., & Sarason, I. G. (1981). Emotion, personality, and selective attention. *Journal of Personality and Social Psychology, 41*, 945–960.

Noble, W. (1983). Hearing, hearing impairment, and the audible world: A theoretical essay. *Audiology, 22*, 325–338.

Nordmark, J. O. (1978). Frequency and periodicity analysis. In E. C. Carterette & M. P. Friedman (Eds.), *Handbook of perception* (Vol. 4). New York: Academic.

Norman, D. A., & Rumelhart, D. E. (1975). *Explorations in cognition*. New York. W. H. Freeman and Company.

Oakley, B. (1986). Basic taste physiology: Human perspectives. In H. L. Meiselman & R. S. Rivlin (Eds.), *Clinical measurement of taste and smell* (pp. 5–18). New York: Macmillan.

Obusek, C., & Warren, R. M. (1973). Relation of the verbal transformation and the phonemic restoration effects. *Cognitive Psychology, 5*, 97–107.

O'Day, W. T., & Young, R. W. (1978). Rhythmic daily shedding of outer segment membranes by visual cells in the goldfish. *Journal of Cell Biology, 76*, 593–604.

Oldfield, S. R., & Parker, S. P. A. (1984). Acuity of sound localisation: A topography of auditory space: I. Normal hearing conditions. *Perception, 13*, 581–600.

Oldfield, S. R., & Parker, S. P. A. (1986). Acuity of sound localisation: A topography of auditory space: III. Monaural hearing conditions. *Perception, 15*, 67–81.

Olson, H. F. (1967). *Music, physics, and engineering* (2nd ed.). New York: Dover.

Olzak, L. A., & Thomas, J. P. (1986). Seeing spatial patterns. In K. R. Boff, L. Kaufman, & J. P. Thomas (Eds.), *Handbook of perception and human performance* (pp. 7-1–7-56). New York: Wiley.

O'Mahony, M. (1978). Smell illusions and suggestion: Reports of smells contingent on tones played on television and radio. *Chemical Senses and Flavour, 3*, 183–187.

O'Mahony, M. (1984). Alternative explanations for procedural effects on magnitude-estimation exponents for taste, involving adaptation, context, and volume effects. *Perception, 13*, 67–73.

O'Mahony, M., & Ishii, R. (1986). A comparison of English and Japanese taste languages: Taste descriptive methodology, codability and the unami taste. *British Journal of Psychology, 77*, 161–174.

O'Mahony, M., & Thompson, B. (1977). Taste quality descriptions: Can the subject's response be affected by mentioning taste words in the instructions? *Chemical Senses and Flavor, 2*, 283–298.

Orchik, D. J., Schumaier, D. R., Shea, J. J., & Moretz, W. H. (1985). Intensity and frequency of sound levels from cordless telephones. *Clinical Pediatrics, 24*, 688–689.

Ordy, J. M., Brizzee, K. R., & Johnson, H. A. (1982). Cellular alterations in visual pathways and the limbic system: Implications for vision and short-term memory. In R. Sekuler, D. Kline, & K. Dismukes (Eds.), *Aging and human visual function* (pp. 79–114). New York: Alan R. Liss.

O'Regan, K. (1979). Saccade size control in reading: Evidence for the linguistic control hypothesis. *Perception & Psychophysics, 25*, 501–509.

O'Regan, K. (1980). The control of saccade size and fixation duration in reading: The limits of linguistic control. *Perception & Psychophysics, 28*, 112–117.

Ornstein, R. E. (1969). *On the experience of time*. Hammandsworth, England: Penguin.

Ornstein, R. E., & Thompson, R. F. (1984). *The amazing brain*. Boston: Houghton-Mifflin.

Owsley, C., Sekuler, R., & Siemsen, D. (1983), Contrast sensitivity throughout adulthood. *Vision Research, 23*, 689–699.

Paap, K. R., Newsome, S. L., McDonald, J. E., &

Schvaneveldt, R. W. (1982). An activation-verification model for letter and word recognition: The word-superiority effect. *Psychological Review, 89,* 573–594.

Palmer, S. E. (1975a). Visual perception and world knowledge: Notes on a model of sensory-cognitive interaction. In D. A. Norman & D. E. Rumelhart (Eds.), *Explorations in cognition.* San Francisco: Freeman.

Palmer, S. E. (1975b). The effects of contextual scenes on the identification of objects. *Memory & Cognition, 3,* 519–526.

Palmer, S. E. (1982). Symmetry, transformation, and the structure of perceptual systems. In J. Beck (Ed.), *Organization and representation in perception* (pp. 95–144). Hillsdale, NJ: Erlbaum.

Parasuraman, R. (1986). Vigilance, monitoring, and search. In K. R. Boff, L. Kaufman, & J. P. Thomas (Eds.), *Handbook of perception and human performance* (43-1–43-39). New York: Wiley.

Parkes, A. S., & Bruce, H. M. (1961). Olfactory stimuli in mammalian reproduction. *Science, 134,* 1049–1054.

Parks, T. E. (1984). Illusory figures: A (mostly) atheoretical review. *Psychological Bulletin, 95,* 282–300.

Parks, T. E. (1986). Illusory figures, illusory objects, and real objects. *Psychological Review, 93,* 207–215.

Pastalan, L. A. (1982). Environmental design and adaptation to the visual environment of the elderly. In R. Sekuler, D. Kline, & K. Dismukes (Eds.), *Aging and human visual function* (pp. 323–333). New York: Alan R. Liss.

Patterson, R. D., & Green, D. M. (1978). Auditory masking. In E. C. Carterette & M. P. Friedman (Eds.), *Handbook of perception* (Vol. 4). New York: Academic.

Paulus, K., & Reisch, A. M. (1980). The influence of temperature on the threshold values of primary tastes. *Chemical Senses, 5,* 11–21.

Pavlidis, G. T., & Miles, T. R. (1981). *Dyslexia research and its applications to education.* Chichester, England: Wiley.

Pedersen, D. M., & Wheeler, J. (1983). The Müller-Lyer illusion among Navajos. *Journal of Social Psychology, 121,* 3–6.

Penfield, W., & Rasmussen, T. (1950). *The cerebral cortex of man.* New York: Macmillan.

Pert, C. B., & Snyder, S. H. (1973). Opiate receptor: Demonstration in nervous tissue. *Science, 179,* 1011–1014.

Pfaffmann, C. (1978). The vertebrate phylogeny, neural code, and integrative processes of taste.

In E. C. Carterette & M. P. Friedman (Eds.), *Handbook of perception* (Vol. 6A). New York: Academic.

Phillips, D. P., & Brugge, J. F. (1985). Progress in neurophysiology of sound localization. *Annual Review of Psychology, 36,* 245–274.

Piaget, J. (1954). *The construction of reality in the child.* New York: Basic.

Pierce, J. R. (1983). *The science of musical sound.* New York: Freeman.

Pinker, S. (1984). Visual cognition: An introduction. *Cognition, 18,* 1–63.

Pirenne, M. H. (1975). Vision and art. In E. C. Carterette & M. P. Friedman (Eds.), *Handbook of perception* (Vol. 5). New York: Academic.

Pisoni, D. B., & Tash, J. B. (1974). Reaction times to comparisons within and across phonetic categories. *Perception & Psychophysics, 15,* 205–290.

Pittenger, J. B. (1986). What's happening out there? [Review of *Persistence and change: Proceedings of the First International Conference on Event Perception*]. *Contemporary Psychology, 31,* 100–101.

Poggio, T. (1984). Vision by man and machine. *Scientific American, 250,* (4), 106–116.

Poggio, G. F., & Poggio, T. (1984). The analysis of stereopsis. *Annual Review of Neuroscience, 7,* 379–412.

Pokorny, J., & Smith, V. C. (1986). Colorimetry and color discrimination. In K. R. Boff, L. Kaufman, & J. P. Thomas (Eds.), *Handbook of perception and human performance* (Vol. 1, pp. 8-1–8-51). New York: Wiley.

Pola, J., & Matin, L. (1977). Eye movements following autokinesis. *Bulletin of the Psychonomic Society, 10,* 397–398.

Pollack, I. (1978). Decoupling of auditory pitch and stimulus frequency: The Shepard demonstration revisited. *Journal of the Acoustical Society of America, 63,* 202–206.

Pollack, I., & Pickett, J. M. (1964). The intelligibility of excerpts from conversational speech. *Language & Speech, 6,* 165–171.

Pollatsek, A., Bolozky, S., Well, A. D., & Rayner, K. (1981). Asymmetries in the perceptual span for Israeli readers. *Brain and Language, 14,* 174–180.

Pomerantz, J. R. (1986). Visual form perception: An overview. In E. Schwab & H. Nusbaum (Eds.), *Pattern recognition by humans and machines: Visual perception* (Vol. 2, pp. 1–30). Orlando, FL: Academic.

Pomerantz, J. R., & Kubovy, M. (1981). Perceptual organization: An overview. In M. Kubovy, &

J. R. Pomerantz (Eds.), *Perceptual organization* (pp. 423–456). Hillsdale, NJ: Erlbaum.

Pomerantz, J. R., Sager, L. C., & Stoever, R. J. (1977). Perception of wholes and of their component parts: Some configural superiority effects. *Journal of Experimental Psychology: Human Perception & Performance, 3,* 422–435.

Porter, R. H., Cernoch, J. M., & McLaughlin, F. J. (1983). Maternal recognition of neonates through olfactory cues. *Physiology & Behavior, 30,* 151–154.

Porter, R. H., & Moore, J. D. (1981). Human kin recognition by olfactory cues. *Physiology & Behavior, 27,* 493–495.

Posner, M. I. (1980). Orienting of attention. *Quarterly Journal of Experimental Psychology, 32,* 3–25.

Posner, M. I. (1982). Cumulative development of attentional theory. *American Psychologist, 37,* 168–179.

Posner, M. I., Goldsmith, R., & Welton, K. E., Jr. (1967). Perceived distance and the classification of distorted patterns. *Journal of Experimental Psychology, 73,* 28–38.

Posner, M. I., Snyder, C. R. R., & Davidson, B. J. (1980). Attention and the detection of signals. *Journal of Experimental Psychology: General, 109,* 160–174.

Post, R. B., & Leibowitz, H. W. (1985). A revised analysis of the role of efference in motion perception. *Perception, 14,* 631–643.

Post, R. B., Leibowitz, H. W., & Shupert, C. L. (1982). Autokinesis and peripheral stimuli: Implications for fixational stability. *Perception, 11,* 477–482.

Poulton, E. C. (1969). Skimming lists of food ingredients printed in different sizes. *Journal of Applied Psychology, 53,* 55–58.

Poulton, E. C. (1970). *The environment at work.* Springfield, IL: Thomas.

Power, R. P. (1981). The dominance of touch by vision: Occurs with familiar objects. *Perception, 10,* 29–33.

Poynter, W. D. (1983). Duration judgment and the segmentation of experience. *Memory & Cognition, 11,* 77–82.

Poynter, W. D., & Homa, D. (1983). Duration judgment and the experience of change. *Perception & Psychophysics, 33,* 548–560.

Prak, N. L. (1977). *The visual perception of the built environment,* Delft: Delft University Press.

Priest, H. F., & Cutting, J. E. (1985). Visual flow and direction of locomotion. *Science, 227,* 1063–1064.

Probst, T., Krafczyk, S., Brandt, T., & Wist, E. R.

(1984). Interaction between perceived self-motion and object motion impairs vehicle guidance. *Science, 225,* 536–538.

Rabbitt, P. (1978). Sorting, categorization and visual search. In E. C. Carterette & M. P. Friedman (Eds.), *Handbook of perception* (Vol. 9). New York: Academic.

Rabin, M. D., & Cain, W. S. (1984). Odor recognition: Familiarity, identifiability, and encoding consistency. *Journal of Experimental Psychology: Learning, Memory, and Cognition, 10,* 316–325.

Rabin, M. D., & Cain, W. S. (1986). Determinants of measured olfactory sensitivity. *Perception & Psychophysics, 39,* 281–286.

Rachlin, H. (1985). Pain and behavior. *The Behavioral and Brain Sciences, 8,* 43–83.

Rader, N., Bausano, M., & Richards, J. E. (1980). On the nature of the visual-cliff-avoidance response in human infants. *Child Development, 51,* 61–68.

Ramachadran, V. S. (1986, August). *Utilitarian theory of perception.* Paper presented at American Psychological Association. Washington, D.C.

Rasch, R. A., & Plomp, R. (1982). The listener and the acoustic environment. In D. Deutsch (Ed.), *The psychology of music* (pp. 135–145). New York: Academic.

Raskin, L. A., Maital, S., & Bornstein, M. H. (1983). Perceptual categorization of color: A life-span study. *Psychological Research, 45,* 135–145.

Ratliff, F. (1984). Why Mach bands are not seen at the edges of a step. *Vision Research, 24,* 163–165.

Rayner, K. (1978). Eye movements in reading and information processing. *Psychological Bulletin, 85,* 618–660.

Rayner, K. (Ed.). (1983a). *Eye movements in reading: Perceptual and language processes.* New York: Academic.

Rayner, K. (1983b). The perceptual span and eye movement control during reading. In K. Rayner (Ed.), *Eye movements in reading: Perceptual and language processes* (pp. 97–120). New York: Academic.

Rechschaffen, A., & Mednick, S. A. (1955). The autokinetic word technique. *Journal of Abnormal and Social Psychology, 51,* 346.

Reddy, R. (1976). Speech recognition by machine: A review. *Proceedings of the IEEE, 64,* 501–531.

Redington, K. (1984). Taste differences between cigarette smokers and nonsmokers. *Pharmacology Biochemistry & Behavior, 21,* 203–208.

Reed, C. F. (1984). Terrestrial passage theory of

the moon illusion. *Journal of Experimental Psychology: General, 113,* 489–516.

Reed, C. F. (1985). More things in heaven and earth: A reply to Loftus. *Journal of Experimental Psychology: General, 114,* 122–144.

Reed, E., & Jones, R. (Eds.). (1982). *Reasons for realism: Selected essays of James J. Gibson.* Hillsdale, NJ: Erlbaum.

Reese, H. W., & Lipsitt, L. P. (1970). *Experimental child psychology.* New York: Academic.

Reeves, A. (1983). Distinguishing opponent and non-opponent detection pathways in early dark adaptation. *Vision Research, 23,* 647–654.

Regan, D. (1982). Visual information channeling in normal and disordered vision. *Psychological Review, 89,* 407–444.

Regan, D. (1985). "How do we avoid confounding the direction we are looking and the direction we are moving?" Response. *Science, 227,* 1064–1065.

Regan, D., & Beverley, K. I. (1982). How do we avoid confounding the direction we are looking and the direction we are moving? *Science, 215,* 194–196.

Regan, D., & Beverley, K. I. (1984). Figure-ground segregation by motion contrast and by luminance contrast. *Journal of the Optical Society of America A, 1,* 433–442.

Regan, D., Beverley, K., & Cynader, M. (1979). The visual perception of motion in depth. *Scientific American, 241* (1), 136–151.

Reicher, G. M. (1969). Perceptual recognition as a function of meaningfulness of stimulus materials. *Journal of Experimental Psychology, 81,* 275–280.

Remez, R. E., Rubin, P. E., Pisoni, D. B., & Carrell, T. D. (1981). Speech perception without traditional speech cues. *Science, 212,* 947–950.

Restle, F. (1970). Moon illusion explained on the basis of relative size. *Science, 167,* 1092–1096.

Richards, J. E., & Rader, N. (1981). Crawling-onset age predicts visual cliff avoidance in infants. *Journal of Experimental Psychology: Human Perception and Performance, 7,* 382–387.

Richards, W. (1975). Visual space perception. In E. C. Carterette & M. P. Friedman (Eds.), *Handbook of perception* (Vol. 5). New York: Academic.

Riggs, L. A. (1971). Vision. In J. W. Kling & L. A. Riggs (Eds.), *Woodworth & Schlosberg's experimental psychology* (3rd ed.). New York: Holt, Rinehart & Winston.

Riggs, L. (1983). Optics, the eye, and the brain. *Journal of the Optical Society of America, 73,* 736–741.

Risset, J. C. (1978). Musical acoustics. In E. C. Carterette & M. P. Friedman (Eds.), *Handbook of perception* (Vol. 4). New York: Academic.

Risset, J. C., & Wessel, D. L. (1982). Exploration of timbre by analysis and synthesis. In D. Deutsch (Ed.), *The psychology of music* (pp. 25–58). New York: Academic.

Rivlin, R., & Gravelle, K. (1984). *Deciphering the senses.* New York: Simon & Schuster.

Robinson, J. O. (1972). *The psychology of visual illusion.* London: Hutchinson.

Rock, I. (1983). *The logic of perception.* Cambridge, MA: MIT.

Rock, I., & Anson, R. (1979). Illusory contours as the solution to a problem. *Perception, 8,* 665–681.

Rock, I., & Ebenholtz, S. (1959). The relational determination of perceived size. *Psychological Review, 66,* 387–401.

Rock, I., & Kaufman, L. (1962). The moon illusion, II. *Science, 136,* 1023–1031.

Rogel, M. J. (1978). A critical evaluation of the possibility of higher primate reproductive and sexual pheromones. *Psychological Bulletin, 85,* 810–830.

Rogers, T. B., Kuiper, N. A., & Kirker, W. S. (1977). Self-reference and the encoding of personal information. *Journal of Personality and Social Psychology, 35,* 677–688.

Rosch, E. (1978). Human categorization. In N. Warren (Ed.), *Studies in cross-cultural psychology* (Vol. 1). London: Academic.

Rose, J. E., Brugge, J. F., Anderson, D. J., & Hind, J. E. (1967). Phase locked response to low-frequency tones in single auditory nerve fibers of the squirrel monkey. *Journal of Neurophysiology, 30,* 769–793.

Rose, J. E., Gross, N. B., Geisler, C. D., & Hind, J. E. (1966). Some neural mechanisms in the inferior colliculus of the cat which may be relevant to localization of a sound source. *Journal of Neurophysiology, 29,* 288–314.

Ross, H. E., & Ross, G. M. (1976). Did Ptolemy understand the moon illusion? *Perception, 5,* 377–385.

Ross, J. (1976). The resources of binocular perception. *Scientific American, 234* (3), 80–86.

Rubin, E. (1915/1958). Synoplevede Figurer. Copenhagen: Cyldendalske. Abridged translation by M. Wertheimer: Figure and ground. In D. C. Beardslee & M. Wertheimer (Eds.), *Readings in perception.* Princeton, NJ: Van Nostrand.

Rubin, P., Turvey, M. T., & Van Gelder, P. (1976). Initial phonemes are detected faster in spoken words than in nonspoken words. *Perception & Psychophysics, 19,* 394–398.

Ruff, H. A. (1982). The development of object perception in infancy. In T. M. Field, A. Huston, H. C. Quay, L. Troll, & G. E. Finley (Eds.), *Review of human development* (pp. 93–106). New York: Wiley.

Ruff, H. A. (1985). Detection of information specifying the motion of objects by 3- and 5-month-old infants. *Developmental Psychology, 21,* 295–305.

Ruff, H. A., & Birch, H. G. (1974). Visual fixation in 3-month-old infants: The effect of concentricity, curvilinearity and number of directions. *Journal of Experimental Child Psychology, 17,* 460–473.

Rumelhart, D. E., & McClelland, J. L. (1982). An interactive activation model of context effects in letter perception: Part 2. The contextual enhancement effect and some tests and extensions of the model. *Psychological Review, 89,* 60–94.

Runeson, S., & Frykholm, G. (1983). Kinematic specifications of dynamics as an informational basis for person-and-action perception: Expectation, gender-recognition, and deceptive intention. *Journal of Experimental Psychology: General, 112,* 585–615.

Rushton, W. A. H. (1958). Kinetics of cone pigments measured objectively in the living human fovea. *Annals of the New York Academy of Science, 74,* 291–304.

Rushton, W. A. H. (1975). Visual pigments and color blindness. *Scientific American, 232,* 64–74.

Russell, M. J. (1976). Human olfactory communication. *Nature, 260,* 520–522.

Russell, M. J., Switz, G. M., & Thompson, K. (1980). Olfactory influences on the human menstrual cycle. *Pharmacology, Biochemistry, & Behavior, 13,* 737–738.

Rutherford, W. (1886). A new theory of hearing. *Journal of Anatomy and Physiology, 21,* 166–168.

Ryan, A., Dallos, P., & McGee, T. (1979). Psychophysical tuning curves and auditory thresholds after hair cell damage in the chinchilla. *Journal of the Acoustical Society of America, 66,* 370–378.

Safire, W. (1979, May 27). "Mondegreens: I led the pigeons to the flag." *The New York Times Magazine,* 9–10.

Salapatek, P., Bechtold, A. G., & Bushnell, E. W. (1976). Infant visual acuity as a function of viewing distance. *Child Development, 47,* 860–863.

Samuel, A. G. (1981). Phonemic restoration: Insights from a new methodology. *Journal of Experimental Psychology: General, 110,* 474–494.

Samuel, A. G. (1987). Lexical uniqueness effects on phonemic restoration. *Journal of Memory and Language, 26,* 36–56.

Samuel, A. G., & Ressler, W. H. (1986). Attention within auditory word perception: Insights from the phonemic restoration illusion. *Journal of Experimental Psychology: Human Perception & Performance, 12,* 70–79.

Sanders, R. (1986). Eye to eye. *UCSF Magazine, 9,* 2–15.

Scharf, B. (1978). Loudness. In E. C. Carterette & M. P. Friedman (Eds.), *Handbook of perception* (Vol. 4). New York: Academic.

Scharf, B. (1983). Loudness adaptation. In J. V. Tobias & Earl D. Schubert (Eds.), *Hearing research and theory* (Vol. 2, pp. 1–56). New York: Academic.

Scharf, B., & Buus, S. (1986). Audition I. In K. R. Boff, L. Kaufman, & J. P. Thomas (Eds.), *Handbook of perception and human performance.* (Vol. 1, pp. 14-1–14-71). New York: Wiley.

Scharf, B., & Houtsma, A. J. M. (1986). Audition II. In K. R. Boff, L. Kaufman, & J. P. Thomas (Eds.), *Handbook of perception and human performance* (Vol. 1, pp. 15-1–15-60). New York: Wiley.

Scherer, K. R. (1986). Vocal affect expression: A review and a model for future research. *Psychological Bulletin, 99,* 143–165.

Schiffman, S. S. (1974). Physiochemical correlates of olfactory quality. *Science, 185,* 112–117.

Schiffman, S. S. (1977). Food recognition by the elderly. *Journal of Gerontology, 32,* 586–592.

Schiffman, S. S., & Dackis, C. (1975). Taste of nutrients: Amino acids, vitamins, and fatty acids. *Perception & Psychophysics, 17,* 140–146.

Schiffman, S. S., & Erikson, R. P. (1980). The issue of primary tastes versus a taste continuum. *Neuroscience and Behavioral Reviews, 4,* 109–117.

Schiffman, S. S., & Pasternak, M. (1979). Decreased discrimination of food odors in the elderly. *Journal of Gerontology, 34,* 73–79.

Schiffman, S. S., Reynolds, M. L., & Young, F. W. (1981). *Introduction to multidimensional scaling.* New York: Academic.

Schindler, R. M. (1978). The effect of prose context on visual search for letters. *Memory & Cognition, 6,* 124–130.

Schneider, W., & Shiffrin, R. M. (1977). Controlled and automatic information processing: I. Detection, search, and attention. *Psychological Review, 84,* 1–66.

Sekuler, R. (1975). Visual motion perception. In E. C. Carterette & M. P. Friedman (Eds.), *Handbook of perception* (Vol. 5). New York: Academic.

Sekuler, R., Ball, K., Tynan, P., & Machamer, J.

(1982). Psychophysics of motion perception. In A. H. Wertheim, W. A. Wagennar, & H. W. Leibowitz (Eds.), *Tutorials on motion perception* (pp. 81–100). New York: Plenum.

Sekuler, R., Kline, D., & Dismukes, K. (Eds.). (1982). *Aging and human visual function.* New York: Alan R. Liss.

Self, P. A., Horowitz, F. D., & Paden, L. Y. (1972). Olfaction in newborn infants. *Developmental Psychology, 7,* 349–363.

Semb, G. (1968). Detectability of the odor of butanol. *Perception & Psychophysics, 4,* 335–340.

Shaffer, L. H. (1975). Multiple attention in continuous verbal tasks. In P. M. Rabbitt & S. Dornic (Eds.), *Attention and performance* (Vol. 5). London: Academic.

Sharma, S., & Moskowitz, H. (1972). Effect of marihuana on the visual autokinetic phenomenon. *Perceptual & Motor Skills, 35,* 891.

Shelton, B. R., Rodger, J. C., & Searle, C. L. (1982). The relation between vision, head motion and accuracy of free-field auditory localization. *Journal of Auditory Research, 22,* 1–7.

Shepard, R. N. (1964). Circularity in judgments of relative pitch. *Journal of the Acoustical Society of America, 36,* 2346–2353.

Shepard, R. N. (1967). Recognition memory for words, sentences, and pictures. *Journal of Verbal Learning and Verbal Behavior, 6,* 156–163.

Shepard, R. N. (1982a). Structural representations of musical pitch. In D. Deutsch (Ed.), *The psychology of music* (pp. 343–390). New York: Academic.

Shepard, R. N. (1982b). Geometrical approximations to the structure of musical pitch. *Psychological Review, 89,* 305–333.

Sherrick, C. E., & Cholewiak, R. W. (1986). Cutaneous sensitivity. In K. R. Boff, L. Kaufman, & J. P. Thomas (Eds.), *Handbook of perception and human performance* (Vol. I, pp. 12-1–12-58). New York: Wiley.

Shiffrin, R. M., & Schneider, W. (1977). Controlled and automatic human information processing: II. Perceptual learning, automatic attending and a general theory. *Psychological Review, 84,* 127–190.

Silverman, W. P. (1985). Two types of word superiority effects in a speeded matching task. *Memory & Cognition, 13,* 50–56.

Sinclair, S. (1985). *How animals see.* New York: Facts on File Publications.

Sivak, M., Olson, P. L., & Pastalan, L. A. (1981). Effect of driver's age on nighttime legibility of highway signs. *Human Factors, 23,* 59–64.

Sivian, L. S., & White, S. D. (1933). On minimum audible sound fields. *Journal of the Acoustical Society of America, 4,* 288–321.

Sloan, L. L. (1980). Need for precise measures of acuity. *Archives of Ophthalmology, 98,* 286–290.

Sloboda, J. A. (1985). *The musical mind.* Oxford: Clarendon.

Smith, M., Smith, L. G., & Levinson, B. (1982). The use of smell in differential diagnosis. *Lancet, 2,* 1452.

Smith, M. D. (1978). *Educational psychology and its classroom applications.* (2nd ed.). Boston: Allyn & Bacon.

Smith, O. W., Smith, P. C., Geist, C. C., & Zimmerman, R. R. (1978). Apparent size contrasts of retinal images and size constancy as determinants of the moon illusion. *Perception & Motor Skills, 46,* 803–808.

Snyder, S. H. (1977). Opiate receptors and internal opiates. *Scientific American, 236,* 44–56.

Solman, R. T., May, J. G., & Schwartz, B. D. (1981). The word superiority effect: A study using parts of letters. *Journal of Experimental Psychology: Human Perception & Performance, 7,* 552–559.

Spector, A. (1982). Aging of the lens and cataract formation. In R. Sekuler, D. Kline, & K. Dismukes (Eds.), *Aging and human visual function* (pp. 27–43). New York: Alan R. Liss.

Spelke, E. S. (1985). Preferential-looking methods as tools for the study of cognition in infancy. In G. Gottlieb & N. A. Krasnegor (Eds.). *Measurement of audition and vision in the first year of postnatal life* (pp. 323–361). Norwood, NJ: Ablex.

Spelke, H. W., Hirst, W., & Neisser, U. (1976). Skills of divided attention. *Cognition, 4,* 215–230.

Sperling, G., & Dosher, B. A. (1986). Strategy and optimization in human information processing. In K. R. Boff, L. Kaufman, & J. P. Thomas (Eds.), *Handbook of perception and human performance* (Vol. I, pp. 2-1–2-65). New York: Wiley.

Spoehr, K. T., & Lehmkuhle, S. W. (1982). *Visual information processing.* San Francisco: Freeman.

Staller, J. D. (1982). Word superiority in word detection. *Perception & Psychophysics, 31,* 237–242.

Standing, L. (1973). Learning 10,000 pictures. *Quarterly Journal of Experimental Psychology, 25,* 207–222.

Standing, L., Conezio, J., & Haber, R. N. (1970). Perception and memory for pictures: Single-trial learning of 2560 visual stimuli. *Psychonomic Science, 19,* 73–74.

Stebbins, W. C. (1983). *The acoustic sense of animals.* Cambridge, MA: Harvard University Press.

Steinberg, R. (1969). *The cooking of Japan.* New York: Time-Life.

Steiner, J. E. (1979). Human facial expressions in response to taste and smell stimulation. In H. W. Reese & L. P. Lipsitt (Eds.), *Advances in child development and behavior* (Vol. 13). New York: Academic.

Sterling, P. (1983). Microcircuitry of the cat retina. *Annual Review of Neuroscience, 6,* 149–185.

Sternbach, R. A. (1968). *Pain: A psychophysiological analysis.* New York: Academic.

Sternbach, R. A. (1978). Psychological dimensions and perceptual analyses, including pathologies of pain. In E. C. Carterette & M. P. Friedman (Eds.), *Handbook of perception* (Vol. 6B). New York: Academic.

Sternbach, R. A. (1983). Ethical considerations in pain research in man. In R. Melzack (Ed.), *Pain measurement and assessment* (pp. 259–265). New York: Raven.

Sternbach, R. A., & Tursky, B. (1965). Ethnic differences among housewives in psychophysical and skin potential responses to electric shock. *Psychophysiology, 1,* 241–246.

Stevens, J. C. (1979). Variation of cold sensitivity over the body surface. *Sensory Processes, 3,* 317–326.

Stevens, J. C., Bartoshuk, L. M., & Cain, W. S. (1984). Chemical senses and aging: Taste *versus* smell. *Chemical Senses, 9,* 167–179.

Stevens, J. C., & Cain, W. S. (1985). Age-related deficiency in the perceived strength of six odorants. *Chemical Senses, 10,* 517–529.

Stevens, J. C., & Cain, W. S. (1986). Smelling via the mouth: Effect of aging. *Perception & Psychophysics, 40,* 142–146.

Stevens, J. C., & Green, B. G. (1978). History of research on feeling. In E. C. Carterette & M. P. Friedman (Eds.), *Handbook of perception* (Vol. 6B). New York: Academic.

Stevens, J. C., Marks, L. E., & Simonson, D. C. (1974). Regional sensitivity and spatial summation in the warmth sense. *Physiology & Behavior, 13,* 825–836.

Stevens, K. N. (1980). Acoustic correlates of some phonetic categories. *Journal of the Acoustical Society of America, 68,* 836–842.

Stevens, K. N. (1981). Constraints imposed by the auditory system on the properties used to classify speech sounds: Data from phonology, acoustics, and psychoacoustics. In T. Myers, J. Laver, & J. Anderson (Eds.), *The cognitive representation of speech.* Amsterdam: North-Holland.

Stevens, S. S. (1955). The measurement of loudness. *Journal of the Acoustical Society of America, 27,* 815–829.

Stevens, S. S. (1962). The surprising simplicity of sensory metrics. *American Psychologist, 17,* 29–39.

Stevens, S. S. (1975). Psychophysics: *Introduction to its perceptual, neural and social prospects.* New York: Wiley.

Stevens, S. S., Volkman, J., & Newman, E. C. (1937). A scale for the measurement of the psychological magnitude of pitch. *Journal of the Acoustical Society of America, 8,* 185–190.

Stokes, D. (1985, Summer). The owl and the ear. *The Stanford Magazine, 13,* 24–28.

Storandt, M. (1982). Concepts and methodological issues in the study of aging. In R. Sekuler, D. Kline, & K. Dismukes (Eds.), *Aging and human visual function* (pp. 269–278). New York: Alan R. Liss.

Streeter, L. (1976). Language perception of 2-month-old infants shows effects of both innate mechanisms and experiences. *Nature, 259,* 39–41.

Stromeyer, C. F. (1978). Form-color aftereffects in human vision. In R. Held, H. W. Leibowitz, & H. L. Teuber (Eds.), *Handbook of sensory physiology* (Vol. 8). Berlin: Springer-Verlag.

Svaetichin, G. (1956). Spectral response curves from single cones. *Acta Physiologica Scandinavica Supplementum, 134,* 17–46.

Svaetichin, G., & MacNichol, E. E., Jr. (1958). Retinal mechanisms for achromatic vision. *Annals of the New York Academy of Sciences, 74,* 385–404.

Swets, J. A. (1984). Mathematical models of attention. In R. Parasuraman & D. R. Davies (Eds.), *Varieties of attention* (pp. 395–447). Orlando, FL: Academic.

Taus, R. H., Stevens, J. C., & Marks, L. E. (1975). Spatial location of warmth. *Perception & Psychophysics, 17,* 194–196.

Taylor, I., & Taylor, M. M. (1983). *The psychology of reading.* New York: Academic.

Taylor, W., Pearson, J., Mair, A., & Burns, W. (1965). Study of noise and hearing in jute weaving. *Journal of the Acoustical Society of America, 38,* 113–120.

Teghtsoonian, M. (1983). Olfaction: Perception's Cinderella. *Contemporary Psychology, 28,* 763–764.

Teghtsoonian, R., Teghtsoonian, M., Berglund, B., & Berglund, U. (1978). Invariance of odor strength with sniff vigor: An olfactory analogue to size constancy. *Journal of Experimental Psychology: Human Perception and Performance, 4,* 144–152.

Teller, D. Y. (1981). Color vision in infants. In R. N. Aslin, J. R. Alberts, & M. R. Petersen (Eds.), *Development of perception* (Vol. 2, pp. 297–311). New York: Academic.

Teller, D. Y., & Bornstein, M. H. (1986). Infant color vision and color perception. In P. Salapatek & L. B. Cohen (Eds.), *Handbook of infant perception*. New York: Academic.

Thayer, S. (1982). Social touching. In W. Schiff & E. Foulke (Eds.), *Tactual perception: A sourcebook* (pp. 263–304). Cambridge: Cambridge University Press.

Thayer, S., & Schiff, W. (1975). Eye-contact, facial expression and the experience of time. *Journal of Social Psychology, 95,* 117–124.

Thomas, E. L. (1976). Advice to the searcher or what do we tell them? In R. A. Monty & J. W. Senders (Eds.), *Eye movements and psychological processes.* Hillsdale, NJ: Erlbaum.

Thomas, J. P. (1985). Detection and identification: How are they related? *Journal of the Optical Society of America, Series A, 2,* 1457–1467.

Thompson, R. F. (1985). *The brain: An introduction to neuroscience.* New York: Freeman.

Thornbury, J. M., & Mistretta, C. M. (1981). Tactile sensitivity as a function of age. *Journal of Gerontology, 36,* 34–39.

Thurlow, W. R. (1971). Audition. In J. W. Kling & L. A. Riggs (Eds.), *Woodworth and Schlosberg's experimental psychology* (3rd ed.). New York: Holt, Rinehart & Winston.

Tootell, R. B. H., Silverman, M. S., Switkes, E., & DeValois, R. L. (1982). Deoxyglucose analysis of retinotopic organization in primate striate cortex. *Science, 218,* 902–904.

Toufexis, A. (1983, July 18). The bluing of America. *Time Magazine, 122,* 62.

Tougas, Y., & Bregman, A. S. (1985). Crossing of auditory streams. *Journal of Experimental Psychology: Human Perception & Performance, 11,* 788–798.

Townsend, J., & Ashby, G. (1982). Experimental tests of contemporary mathematical models of visual letter recognition. *Journal of Experimental Psychology: Human Perception and Performance, 8,* 834–864.

Trehub, S. E. (1976). The discrimination of foreign speech contrasts by infants and adults. *Child Development, 47,* 466–472.

Trehub, S. E. (1985). Auditory pattern perception in infancy. In S. E. Trehub & B. A. Schneider (Eds.), *The anatomy of the developing ear* (pp. 183–195). New York: Plenum.

Treisman, A. M. (1960). Contextual cues in selective listening. *Quarterly Journal of Experimental Psychology, 12,* 242–248.

Treisman, A. M. (1964). Monitoring and storage of irrelevant messages and selective attention. *Journal of Verbal Learning and Verbal Behavior, 3,* 449–459.

Treisman, A. M. (1986, November). Features and objects in visual processing. *Scientific American, 255* (5), 114B–125.

Treisman, A. M., & Gelade, G. (1980). A feature-integration theory of attention. *Cognitive Psychology, 12,* 97–136.

Treisman, A. M., & Schmidt, H. (1982). Illusory conjunction in the perception of objects. *Cognitive Psychology, 14,* 107–141.

Treisman, A. M., & Souther, J. (1985). Search asymmetry: A diagnostic for preattentive processing of separable features. *Journal of Experimental Psychology: General, 114,* 285–310.

Treisman, A. M., & Souther, J. (1986). Illusory words: The roles of attention and of top-down constraints in conjoining letters to form words. *Journal of Experimental Psychology: Human Perception and Performance, 12,* 3–17.

Treisman, A. M., Squire, R., & Green, J. (1974). Semantic processing in dichotic listening: A replication. *Memory & Cognition, 2,* 641–646.

Tsal, Y. (1984). A Mueller-Lyer illusion induced by selective attention. *Quarterly Journal of Experimental Psychology, 36A,* 319–333.

Tsao, Y., Wittlieb, E., Miller, B., & Wang, T. (1983). Time estimation of a secondary event. *Perception & Motor Skills, 57,* 1051–1055.

Turk, D. C., Meichenbaum, D., & Genest, M. (1983). *Pain and behavioral medicine: A cognitive-behavioral perspective.* New York: Guilford.

Ullman, S. (1983). The measurement of visual motion. *Trends in NeuroSciences, 6,* 177–179.

Underwood, N. R., & McConkie, G. W. (1985). Perceptual span for letter distinctions during reading. *Reading Research Quarterly, 20,* 153–162.

Uttal, W. R. (1981). *A taxonomy of visual processes.* Hillsdale, NJ: Erlbaum.

Vallbo, Ä. B. (1981). Sensations evoked from the glabrous skin of the human hand by electrical stimulation of unitary mechanosensitive efferents. *Brain Research, 215,* 359–363.

van den Brink, G. (1982). On the relativity of pitch. *Perception, 11,* 721–731.

Van Dyke, D. (1980). Personal communication.

Van Heyningen, R. (1975). What happens to the human lens in cataract. *Scientific American, 233* (6). 70–81.

van Tuijl, H. (1980). Perceptual interpretation of complex line patterns. *Journal of Experimental Psychology: Human Perception and Performance, 6,* 197–221.

Vaughan, D., & Asbury, T. (1986). *General oph-thalmology* (11th ed.). Los Altos, CA: Lange.

Verillo, R. T. (1975). Cutaneous sensation. In B. Scharf (Ed.), *Experimental sensory psychology.* Glenview, IL: Scott, Foresman.

Vernon, M. D. (1976). Development of perception of form. In V. Hamilton & M. D. Vernon (Eds.), *The development of cognitive processes.* London: Academic.

Vierck, C. (1978). Somatosensory system. In R. B. Masterton (Ed.), *Handbook of behavioral neuro-biology* (Vol. I, pp. 249–309). New York: Plenum.

Vierling, J. S., & Rock, J. (1967). Variations of olfactory sensitivity to exaltolide during the menstrual cycle. *Journal of Applied Psychology, 22,* 311–315.

Virshup, A. (1985, November 18). Restaurant loudness. *New York Magazine, 18,* 32–37.

Vogel, J. M., & Teghtsoonian, M. (1972). The effects of perspective alterations on apparent size and distance scales. *Perception & Psychophysics, 11,* 294–298.

Von Ehrenfels, C. (1890). *Uber Gestaltqualitäten Vierteljahrschrift für Wissenschaftliche Philosophie, 14,* 249–292.

Von Holst, E. (1954). Relations between the central nervous system and the peripheral organs. *British Journal of Animal Behaviour, 2,* 89–94.

von Noorden, G. K. (1981). New clinical aspects of stimulus deprivation amblyopia. *American Journal of Ophthalmology, 92,* 416–421.

von Winterfeldt, D., & Edwards, E. (1982). Costs and payoffs in perceptual research. *Psychological Bulletin, 91,* 609–622.

Vurpillot, E. (1968). The development of scanning strategies and their relation to visual differentiation. *Journal of Experimental Child Psychology, 6,* 632–650.

Vurpillot, E. (1976). *The visual world of the child.* New York: International Universities.

Wade, N. (1982). *The art and science of visual illusions.* London: Routledge & Kegan Paul.

Walk, R. D. (1978). Perceptual learning. In E. C. Carterette & M. P. Friedman (Eds.), *Handbook of perception* (Vol. 9). New York: Academic.

Walker, J. (1982). The amateur scientist. *Scientific American, 246* (4), 150–160.

Walker-Andrews, A. S. (1986). Intermodal perception of expressive behaviors: Relation of eye and voice? *Developmental Psychology, 22,* 373–377.

Wall, P. D. (1979). On the relation of injury to pain. *Pain, 6,* 253–264.

Wallach, H. (1985). Learned stimulation in space and motion perception. *American Psychologist, 40,* 399–404.

Wallach, H., & O'Connell, D. N. (1953). The kinetic depth effect. *Journal of Experimental Psychology, 45,* 205–217.

Wallach, H., & O'Leary, A. (1979). Adaptation in distance perception with head-movement parallax serving as the veridical cue. *Perception & Psychophysics, 25,* 42–46.

Wallis, C. (1984, July 11). Unlocking pain's secrets. *Time Magazine, 124,* 58–66.

Walsh, D. A. (1982a). The development of visual information processing in adulthood and old age. In R. Sekuler, D. Kline, & K. Dismukes (Eds.), *Aging and human visual function* (pp. 203–230). New York: Alan R. Liss.

Walsh, D. A. (1982b). The development of visual information processes in adulthood and old age. In F. I. M. Craik & S. Trehub (Eds.), *Aging and cognitive processes* (pp. 99–125). New York: Plenum.

Ward, L. M., Porac, C., Coren, S., & Girgus, J. S. (1977). The case for misapplied constancy scaling: Depth association elicited by illlusion configurations. *American Journal of Psychology, 90,* 609–620.

Warren, R. M. (1982). *Auditory perception: A new synthesis.* Elmsford, NY: Pergamon.

Warren, R. M. (1983). Auditory illusions and their relation to mechanisms normally enhancing accuracy of perception. *Journal of Audio Engineering Society, 31,* 623–630.

Warren, R. M. (1984). Perceptual restoration of obliterated sounds. *Psychological Bulletin, 96,* 371–383.

Warren, R. M., & Sherman, G. (1974). Phonemic restorations based on subsequent context. *Perception & Psychophysics, 16,* 150–156.

Warren, R. M., & Warren, R. P. (1970, December). Auditory illusions and confusions. *Scientific American, 223,* 30–36.

Warren, W. H., & Shaw, R. E. (1985a). Preface. In W. H. Warren, Jr., & R. E. Shaw (Eds.), *Persistence and change: Proceedings of the First International Conference on Event Perception* (pp. xiii–xv). Hillsdale, NJ: Erlbaum.

Warren, W. H., & Shaw, R. E. (Eds.). (1985b). *Persistence and change: Proceedings of the First International Conference on Event Perception.* Hillsdale, NJ: Erlbaum.

Wasserman, G. S. (1978). *Color vision: An historical introduction.* New York: Wiley.

Watkins, L. R., & Mayer, D. J. (1982). Organization of endogenous opiate and nonopiate pain control systems. *Science, 216,* 1185–1192.

Watson, A. B. (1986). Temporal sensitivity. In K. R. Boff, L. Kaufman, & J. P. Thomas (Eds.), *Handbook of perception and human performance* (Vol. 1, pp. 6-1–6-43). New York: Wiley.

Weale, R. A. (1982). *A biography of the eye.* London: Lewis.

Wegener, B. (1982). Fitting category to magnitude scales for a dozen survey-assessed attitudes. In B. Wegener (Ed.), *Social attitudes and psychophysical measurement* (pp. 379–399). Hillsdale, NJ: Erlbaum.

Weiffenbach, J. M. (1977). (Ed.), *Taste and development: The genesis of sweet preference.* Bethesda, MD: U. S. Department of Health, Education and Welfare.

Weinstein, S. (1968). Intensive and extensive aspects of tactile sensitivity as a function of body part, sex, and laterality. In D. R. Kenshalo (Ed.), *The skin senses.* Springfield, IL: Thomas.

Weisenberg, M. (1977). Pain and pain control. *Psychological Bulletin, 84,* 1008–1044.

Weisenberg, M. (1984). Cognitive aspects of pain. In P. D. Wall & R. Melzack (Eds.), *Textbook of pain* (pp. 162–172). Edinburgh: Churchill Livingstone.

Weisstein, N., Maguire, W., & Williams, M. C. (1982). The effect of perceived depth on phantoms and the phantom motion aftereffect. In J. Beck (Ed.), *Organization and representation in perception.* Hillsdale, NJ: Erlbaum.

Welch, R. B. (1978). *Perceptual modification: Adapting to altered sensory environments.* New York: Academic.

Welch, R. B., & Warren, D. H. (1980). Immediate perceptual response to intersensory discrepancy. *Psychological Bulletin, 88,* 638–667.

Wenger, M. A., Jones, F. N., & Jones, M. H. (1956). *Physiological psychology.* New York: Holt, Rinehart & Winston.

Werker, J. F., Gilbert, J., Humphrey, K., & Tees, R. (1981). Developmental aspects of cross-language speech perception. *Child Development, 52,* 349–355.

Werker, J. F., & Tees, R. C. (1984). Cross-language speech perception: Evidence for perceptual reorganization during the first year of life. *Infant Behavior and Development, 7,* 49–63.

Werner, H. (1935). Studies on contour. *American Journal of Psychology, 37,* 40–64.

Wertheim, A. H., Wagenaar, W. A., & Leibowitz, H. W. (Eds.). (1982). *Tutorials on motion perception.* New York: Plenum.

Wertheimer, M. (1923). Untersuchungen zür Lehre von der Gestalt, II. *Psychologische Forschung, 4,* 301–350. Translated as Laws of organization in perceptual forms. In W. D. Ellis (Ed.). (1955), *A source book of Gestalt psychology.* London: Routledge & Kegan Paul.

Wertheimer, M. (1974). The problem of perceptual structure. In E. C. Carterette & M. P. Friedman (Eds.), *Handbook of perception* (Vol. 1). New York: Academic.

Westheimer, G. (1986). The eye as an optical instrument. In K. R. Boff, L. Kaufman, & J. P. Thomas (Eds.), *Handbook of perception and human performance* (Vol. I, pp. 4-1–4-20). New York: Wiley.

Wever, E. G. (1949). *Theory of hearing.* New York: Wiley.

Whitbourne, S. K. (1985). *The aging body: Physiological changes and psychological consequences.* New York: Springer-Verlag.

Whitbourne, S. K. (1987). Personal communication.

White, B. W., Saunders, F. A., Scadden, L., Bach-y-Rita, P., & Collins, C. C. (1970). Seeing with the skin. *Perception & Psychophysics, 7,* 23–27.

White, C. W., & Montgomery, D. A. (1976). Memory colors in afterimages: A bicentennial demonstration. *Perception & Psychophysics, 19,* 371–374.

Wideman, M. V., & Singer, J. E. (1984). The role of psychological mechanisms in preparation for childbirth. *American Psychologist, 39,* 1357–1371.

Wiest, W. M., & Bell, B. (1985). Stevens's exponent for psychophysical scaling of perceived, remembered, and inferred distance. *Psychological Bulletin, 98,* 457–470.

Wightman, F. L. (1981). Pitch perception: An example of auditory pattern recognition. In D. J. Getty & J. H. Howard, Jr. (Eds.), *Auditory and visual pattern recognition* (pp. 3–25). Hillsdale, NJ: Erlbaum.

Wilkins, P. A., & Acton, W. I. (1982). Noise and accidents—A review. *Annals of Occupational Hygiene, 25,* 249–260.

Willer, J. C., Dehen, H., & Cambier, J. (1981). Stress-induced analgesia in humans: Endogenous opioids and naloxone-reversible depression of pain reflexes. *Science, 212,* 689–690.

Williges, R. C. (1976). The vigilance increment: An ideal observer hypothesis. In T. B. Sheriday & G. Johannsen (Eds.), *Monitoring behavior and supervisory control.* New York: Plenum.

Wolfe, J. M. (Ed.). (1986). *The mind's eye.* New York: Freeman.

Wolfert, P. (1973). *Couscous and other good food from Morocco.* New York: Harper & Row.

Woodrow, K. M., Friedman, G. D., Siegelaub, A. B., & Collen, M. F. (1972). Pain tolerance: Differences according to age, sex, and race. *Psychosomatic Medicine, 34,* 548–556.

Worthey, J. A. (1985). Limitations of color constancy. *Journal of the Optical Society of America, 2,* 1014–1026.

Wright, R. W. (1982). *The sense of smell.* Boca Raton, FL: CRC Press.

Wright, W. D. (1972). Colour mixture. In D. Jameson & L. M. Hurvich (Eds.), *Visual psychophysics* (Vol. III/4). Berlin: Springer-Verlag.

Wyszecki, G. (1986). Color appearance. In K. R. Boff, L. Kaufman, & J. P. Thomas (Eds.), *Handbook of perception and human performance* (Vol. 1, pp. 9-1-9-57). New York: Wiley.

Yamamoto, T., Yuyama, N., & Kawamura, Y. (1981). Central processing of taste perception. In Y. Katsuki, R. Norgren, & Sato, M. (Eds.), *Brain mechanisms of sensation* (pp. 197–207). New York: Wiley.

Yellott, J. I. (1981). Binocular depth inversion. *Scientific American, 245* (1), 148–159.

Yellott, J. I., Wandell, B., & Cornsweet, T. (1984). The beginning of visual perception: The retinal image and its initial encoding. In J. Brookhard & V. Mountcastle (Eds.), *Handbook of physiology. The nervous system III* (pp. 257–316). Baltimore: Williams & Wilkins.

Yin, T. C. T., & Kuwada, S. (1983). Binaural interaction in low-frequency neurons in inferior colliculus of the cat. Effects of changing frequency. *Journal of Neurophysiology, 50,* 1020–1042.

Yonas, A., Cleaves, W., & Pettersen, L. (1978). Development of sensitivity to pictorial depth. *Science, 200,* 77–79.

Yonas, A., Goldsmith, L. T., & Hallstrom, J. L. (1978). Development of sensitivity to information provided by cast shadows in pictures. *Perception, 7,* 333–341.

Yonas, A., & Granrud, C. E. (1985). Reaching as a measure of infants' spatial perception. In G. Gottlieb & N. A. Krasnegor (Eds.), *Measurement of audition and vision in the first year of postnatal life: A methodological overview* (pp. 301–322). Norwood, NJ: Ablex.

Young, F. A. (1981). Primate myopia. *American Journal of Optometry & Physiological Optics, 58,* 560–566.

Young, F. A., Singer, R. M., & Foster, D. (1975). The psychological differentiation of male myopes and nonmyopes. *American Journal of Optometry & Physiological Optics, 52,* 679–686.

Zakia, R. (1975). *Perception and photography.* Englewood Cliffs, NJ: Prentice-Hall.

Zakia, R., & Todd, H. (1969). *101 experiments in photography.* Dobbs Ferry, NY: Morgan & Morgan.

Zeki, S. M. (1980). The representation of colors in the cerebral cortex. *Nature, 284,* 412–418.

Zeki, S. M. (1981). The mapping of visual functions in the cerebral cortex. In Y. Katsuki, R. Norgren, & M. Sato (Eds.), *Brain mechanisms of sensation* (pp. 105–128). New York: Wiley.

Zwislocki, J. J. (1978). Masking: Experimental and theoretical aspects of simultaneous, forward, backward, and central masking. In E. C. Carterette & M. P. Friedman (Eds.), *Handbook of perception* (Vol. 4). New York: Academic.

Glossary

A guide has been provided for words whose pronunciation may be ambiguous; the accented syllable is indicated by italics.

ABX paradigm Experimental design in which three stimuli are presented in a row, with A different from B and X identical to either A or B; observers must judge whether the X matches the A or the B stimulus.

Accommodation Change in the shape of the lens of the eye, necessary to keep an image in proper focus on the retina; it occurs as the observer focuses on objects at different distances.

Achromatic afterimage [ā-crow-*maa*-tick] Image that appears after the presentation of a stimulus; both the stimulus and the afterimage are uncolored, and one is the opposite of the other.

Achromatic vision Noncolored vision, involving the rods.

Action potentials Short bursts of electrical activity such as those generated by the ganglion cells.

Active touch Touch perception in which a person actively explores objects and touches them.

Acuity Degree of precision with which fine details can be seen.

Acupuncture Procedure that involves the insertion of thin needles into various locations on the body to relieve pain.

Adaptation Change in sensitivity (see also dark adaptation and light adaptation).

Adaptation stimulus In dark adaptation studies, the intense light to which observers are exposed prior to the darkness.

Additive mixture In color mixing, the addition of beams of light from different parts of the spectrum.

Affective tests In food-testing research, tests that measure how much people like a product; also known as hedonic tests.

Albedo Proportion of light reflected by an object; the albedo remains constant despite changes in the amount of light falling on the object.

Amacrine cells (*am*-ah-krihn) Cells in the retina that allow the ganglion cells to communicate with each other; they also allow the bipolar cells to communicate with each other.

Ambiguous figure-ground relationships Situations in which the figure and the ground reverse from time to time, with the figure becoming the ground and then becoming the figure again.

Amblyopia (am-blih-*owe*-phi-ah) Visual disorder, arising from strabismus, that involves blurry vision.

Amblyoscope Piece of equipment that tests the degree to which people can fuse images presented to both eyes.

Amplitude In vision, the height of the light wave; amplitude is related to the brightness of a visual stimulus. In audition, the change in pressure created by sound waves; amplitude is related to the loudness of an auditory stimulus.

Analgesic medication Class of drugs specifically designed to relieve pain.

Analytic sense Sense in which the observer can detect the separate parts; for example, in hearing, an observer can typically separate two notes played together.

Anomalous trichromat (uh-*nomm*-uh-luss try-krow-mat) Person who resembles a normal trichromat in requiring three colors to produce all other colors; however, this person uses different proportions of those three colors than the normal trichromat.

Apparent-distance theory Theory of the moon illusion in which the moon seems to be farther from the viewer when it is on the horizon than when it is at the zenith.

Aqueous humor (*a*-kwee-us) Watery liquid found between the cornea and the lens.

Area 17 Area of the visual cortex where the neurons from the lateral geniculate nucleus terminate.

Area 18 Part of the secondary visual cortex.

Area 19 Part of the secondary visual cortex.

Ascending method of limits Modification of the method of limits that uses only ascending series.

Ascending series Series of trials in the method of limits in which the stimulus is systematically increased.

Association cortex Part of the visual cortex that stores associations between visual qualities and past experience.

Astigmatism Visual disorder in which the cornea is not perfectly round; therefore, if the eye is focused for some parts of the cornea, it is out of focus for others.

Atmospheric perspective Distance cue provided by the fact that distant objects often look blurry and bluish in contrast to nearby objects.

Attack In music perception, the beginning buildup of a tone.

Attention Focusing or concentration of mental activity.

Attenuation model Model of attention suggested by Treisman in which the message from the unattended ear is reduced rather than blocked completely.

Audiometry Measurement of the sensitivity of audition, typically by measuring thresholds for tones of differing frequency.

Auditory adaptation Decrease in the perceived loudness of a tone after it has been presented continuously.

Auditory cortex Portion of the cortex located in a groove on the temporal lobe of the cortex; the auditory cortex is responsible for higher levels of auditory processing.

Auditory fatigue Change in thresholds for other tones that occurs after a loud tone is presented and then turned off.

Auditory nerve Bundle of nerve fibers that carries information from the inner ear to higher levels of auditory processing.

Autokinesis (ah-toe-kin-*nee*-siss) Illusion of movement in which a stationary object, with no clear background, appears to move.

Automatic search Kind of search that can be used on easy search tasks involving highly familiar items.

Autoradiography Technique in which radioactive substances, absorbed by portions of the brain, are converted into photographs.

β *(beta)* (*bay*-tuh) Symbol for criterion, which is the measure in signal-detection theory that assesses the observer's willingness to say "I detect the stimulus."

Backward masking Phenomenon in which accuracy is reduced for reporting a visual stimulus because it was followed by a stimulus presented to the same region of the eye.

Ballistic movements Movements that have predetermined destinations.

Basilar membrane Membrane on the base of the organ of Corti, in the inner ear.

Beats Changes in loudness produced by certain tone combinations.

Behaviorism Approach to psychology that stresses the objective description of an organism's behavior.

Bifocals Special eyeglasses that have two types of lenses, one for distant objects and one for close objects.

Binaural (buy-*nohr*-ul) Pertaining to both ears.

Binocular disparity Source of distant information provided by the fact that the two eyes have slightly different views of the world.

Biological motion Pattern of movement of living things.

Bipolar cells (*buy*-pole-ur) Cells in the retina that receive information from the rods and cones and pass it on to ganglion cells.

Blend In odor perception, a mixture that resembles both components; it is nearly impossible to separate the two parts.

Blind spot Region of the eye in which there is no vision because the optic disk contains no light receptor.

Blobs "Blob"-shaped cells distributed throughout the column structure in the primary cortex that respond to color.

Border contrast Phenomenon in which the contrast at a contour seems to be much stronger than it really is.

Bottom-up processing Approach that emphasizes how the sensory receptors register the stimuli, with information flowing from this low level upward to the higher, more cognitive levels.

Braille Representation of letters in the alphabet by a system of raised dots, used in books for the blind.

Brightness Psychological reaction corresponding to the intensity of light waves; the apparent intensity of a visual stimulus.

Brightness constancy Phenomenon in which an object seems to stay the same brightness despite changes in the amount of light falling on it.

Candelas per meter square (cd/m²) Measure of the

amplitude of light, based on how much light is reflected from the surface of the stimulus.

Case of the missing fundamental A phenomenon in which listeners report the pitch of certain complex stimuli as being the pitch of a tone never presented.

Cataracts Clouding of the lens of the eye, caused by injury or disease.

Categorical perception Grouping perceptions into categories, which occurs when people have difficulty discriminating between members of the same category, although discriminations can be readily made between members of different categories.

Categorization Process of treating objects as similar or equivalent, as in categorical perception.

Center of movement Point on the human body where the stress lines cross each other, important in the perception of biological motion.

Cerebral cortex (suh-*ree*-brul) Outer part of the brain.

Chemical senses Smell and taste.

Choroid (*kore*-oid) Layer on the back of the eye just inside the sclera; choroid provides nutrients for the retina and absorbs extra light.

Chromatic adaptation Decrease in response to a color after it is viewed continuously for a long time.

Cilia (*sill*-ee-uh) Tiny hairlike protrusions from the receptor cells in the auditory and olfactory systems.

Ciliary muscles (*sill*-ee-air-ee) Muscles that are attached to the lens and control its shape.

Cochlea (*cock*-lee-ah) Bony, fluid-filled structure containing the receptors for auditory stimuli.

Cochlear duct (*cock*-lee-er) One of the canals in the cochlea.

Cochlear nucleus A structure in auditory processing to which the auditory nerve travels after leaving the inner ear.

Cognition Acquisition, storage, retrieval, and use of knowledge.

Cognitive-behavioral approaches In the treatment of pain, methods that help the patient develop more adaptive cognitive and behavioral reactions to a physical problem.

Color constancy Tendency to see the hue of an object as staying the same despite changes in the color of the light falling on it.

Color solid Three-dimensional figure, resembling two cones joined together, that represents the hue, saturation, and brightness of all colors; also called a color spindle.

Color vision deficiencies Disorders or difficulties

in discriminating different colors, commonly called "color blindness."

Color wheel Circle with the different wavelengths arranged around the edge, used to represent the colors of the spectrum.

Column In the visual cortex, a vertical series of cells that have the highest response rate to a line of one particular orientation.

Comparison stimulus The stimulus in discrimination studies that varies throughout the experiment.

Complementary hues Hues whose additive mixture makes gray, such as blue and yellow.

Complex cells Cells in Area 17 of the visual cortex that respond most vigorously to moving stimuli.

Complex tones Tones that cannot be represented by a simple sound wave and are more likely to be encountered in everyday life.

Conceptually driven processing Approach that emphasizes the importance of the observers' concepts and cognitive processes in shaping perception.

Conditioning method In testing infant perception, a method in which the experimenter selects a response that the baby can make and delivers a reward when the baby makes that particular response; later, the experimenter tests for generalization to new stimuli.

Conduction deafness Type of deafness that involves problems in conducting the sound stimulus, occurring in either the external ear or the middle ear.

Cone of confusion Cone-shaped area around each ear in which the auditory system receives the same set of information about the source of the sound.

Cones Photoreceptors used for color vision under well-lit conditions.

Confounding variables Factors in an experiment—other than the factor being studied—that are present to different extents in the groups being studied.

Conjunctiva (con-junk-*tie*-vah) Pink mucous membrane that lines the eyelid and attaches the eye to the eyelid.

Conjunctivitis (con-junk-tih-*vie*-tis) Inflammation of the conjunctiva.

Consonance Combination of two or more tones, played at the same time, that is judged pleasant.

Constancy Tendency for qualities of objects to seem to stay the same, despite changes in the way people view the objects.

Constriction   Closing of the iris, making the pupil smaller.

Constructivist theory   Theory that proposes that the perceiver has an internal constructive (or problem-solving) process that transforms the incoming stimulus into the perception.

Contour   Location at which there is a sudden change in brightness.

Contrast sensitivity function   Diagram that shows the relationship between spatial frequency and sensitivity.

Contrast theory   Theory of brightness constancy in which an object's intensity is perceived in comparison to the intensity of other objects in the scene.

Controlled search   Type of search that must be used on difficult search tasks, where items must be searched one at a time.

Convergence   Type of vergence movement of the eyes in which the eyes move toward each other to look at nearby objects.

Cornea   (*kore*-nee-uh) Clear membrane just in front of the iris.

Corneal abrasion   Scratched cornea.

Corollary discharge theory   Theory of motion perception in which the visual system compares the movement registered on the retina with signals that the brain sends regarding eye movements.

Correct rejection   In signal-detection theory, a correct rejection occurs when a signal is not presented and the observer does not report it.

Cortical magnification   Overrepresentation of information from the fovea with respect to the cortex.

Counterirritants   Methods of pain control that stimulate or irritate one area so that pain is diminished in another.

Covert attention   Shifting attention without moving the head or eyes.

Criterion   The measure in signal-detection theory that assesses the observer's willingness to say "I detect the stimulus."

Cross-adaptation   In odor perception, the change in theshold for one odor that occurs after exposure to another.

Cross-enhancement   Lowering a threshold for one substance after adaptation to another.

Cross-modality comparisons   Technique in which observers are asked to judge stimuli in one mode of perception (such as hearing) by providing responses from another mode (such as sight).

Cue   Any factor that lets an observer make a decision automatically, such as a distance cue; cues do not require elaborate thought.

d'   (dee prime) In signal-detection theory, an index of sensitivity; *d'* depends upon the intensity of the stimulus and the sensitivity of the observer.

Dark adaptation   Increase in sensitivity that occurs as the eyes remain in the dark.

Dark adaptation curve   Graph showing the relationship between the time in the dark and the threshold for the test stimulus.

Data-driven processing   Approach that emphasizes how the sensory receptors register the stimuli, with information flowing from this low level upward to the higher, more cognitive levels.

Decay   In music perception, the decrease in amplitude at the end of a tone.

Decibels   One measure of the amount of pressure created by a stimulus such as a sound wave; abbreviated dB.

Dependent variable   The measure in an experiment that describes the participant's behavior.

Depth perception   Perception of objects as three dimensional, having depth in addition to height and width.

Dermis   Middle layer of skin, which makes new skin cells.

Descending series   Series of trials in the method of limit in which the stimulis is systematically decreased.

Descriptive tests   In food-tasting research, tests that require participants to describe various qualities of a food product.

Detached retina   Disorder of the retina in which a hole in the retina permits fluid to flow through, separating the retina from the choroid layer.

Detection   In acuity measures, a task that requires the observer to judge whether a target is present or absent.

Detection threshold   Smallest amount of energy required for the stimulus to be reported 50% of the time.

Deuteranopes   (*doo*-tur-uh-nopes) People who are dichromats and are insensitive to green.

Diabetic retinopathy   (reht-n-*ah*-puh-thee) Kind of blindness caused by diabetes, which involves thickened blood vessels.

Dichotic listening task   (die-*kott*-ick) Task in which listeners must shadow a message presented in one ear while ignoring a different message presented to the other ear.

Dichromat (*die*-krow-mat) Person who requires only two primary colors to match his or her perception of all other colors.

Difference threshold The smallest change in a stimulus that is required to produce a difference noticeable 50% of the time.

Dilation Opening the iris, making the pupil larger.

Direct perception explanation In constancy, a theory proposed by J. J. Gibson in which people notice the size of an object by comparing it to the texture of the surrounding area.

Direct perception theory Theory proposed by J. J. Gibson stating that the environment can be directly perceived from the rich information in the stimulus.

Discrimination In psychophysics, the smallest amount that a stimulus must be changed to be perceived as just noticeably different.

Discrimination tests In food-tasting research, tests that involve determining whether two kinds of foods can be distinguished.

Disc-shedding Process of shedding old discs in the photoreceptors.

Dishabituation Increase in looking time that occurs when a new stimulus is presented following repeated presentations of another stimulus.

Disocclusion (dis-uh-*clue*-zyun) Process in which a moving object systematically uncovers the background.

Disparity-selective cells Cells in area 18 of the visual cortex that produce a high rate of electrical discharge when stimuli are registered on different areas of the two retinas.

Dissonance Combination of two or more tones, played at the same time, that is judged unpleasant.

Distal stimulus Stimulus or object as it exists in the world, as opposed to the proximal stimulus.

Distinctive features Characteristics of letters, such as straight versus curved lines.

Distraction In the treatment of pain, a method that refocuses attention toward something other than the pain.

Divergence Type of vergence movement of the eyes in which the eyes move apart from each other.

Divided attention Situation in which attention is distributed among more than one of the competing sources.

Dizziness Vague feeling of unsteadiness, light-headedness, or a floating sensation.

Doctrine of specific nerve energies Theory proposed by Müller that each different sensory nerve has its own characteristic type of activity and therefore produces different sensations.

Double-opponent process cell Cell whose center increases its response rate to one color and decreases its response rate to the "opposite" color; the cell's surrounding area has the opposite response pattern.

Double pain Experience of sharp pain followed by dull pain.

Duplicity theory Approach to vision that proposes two separate kinds of photoreceptors, rods and cones.

Dynamic visual acuity In acuity measures, a task in which acuity is measured when there is relative motion between the observer and the object.

Dynes One type of measurement of air pressure.

Dyslexia (diss-*leck*-see-uh) Disorder in which people read substantially more poorly than would be expected from their intelligence.

Ear infection Condition in which the eustachian tube becomes swollen, cutting off the middle ear from the respiratory tract.

Eardrum Thin piece of membrane that vibrates in response to sound waves.

Ecological validity The principle that the results obtained in the laboratory should also hold true in real life.

Egocentric distance Distance between the observer and an object, as used in depth perception.

Electrical response audiometry Technique used to assess deafness, in which electrical activity is recorded at locations in the auditory pathway, in response to auditory stimulation.

Electromagnetic radiation All forms of waves produced by electrically charged particles.

Emmert's law Principle that an afterimage appears larger if it is projected on a more distant surface.

Emmetropic Referring to people with normal accommodation of the eyes.

Empiricism Approach to perception that states that basic sensory experiences are combined, through learning, to produce perception.

Encapsulated endings Small capsules or bulbs on the end of some kinds of skin receptors.

End note In perfume development, the fragrance that remains for a long time, after the top note and middle note have evaporated.

Endorphins   Morphine-like substances that occur naturally within the body.

Epidermis   Outer layer of skin, which has many layers of dead skin cells.

Epistemology   Branch of philosophy that concerns how we acquire knowledge.

Equal loudness contour   Graph showing the relationship between tone frequency and the number of decibels required to produce a tone of equal loudness.

Errors of anticipation   Errors in psychophysics testing in which observers provide a different answer from the one they provided on the last trial; they "jump the gun."

Errors of habituation   Errors in psychophysics testing in which observers keep giving the same answer as on the last trial.

Eustachian tube   (you-*stay*-she-un) Structure in the middle ear that connects the ear to the throat.

Event perception   Approach to perception that examines the change over time in the environment (such as changes in an object's shape) and the perception of meaning (such as changes in a person's movement because of a limp).

Events   Changes in structure over time, as applied to the Gibsonian emphasis on event perception.

Existence constancy   Object permanence, or the knowledge that objects still seem to exist, even though they are no longer visible.

External auditory canal   Tube that runs inward from the pinna to the eardrum.

Extraocular muscles   Muscles that allow the eyes to move.

Extrastriate cortex   (*ex*-tra-*strie*-ate) Region of the visual cortex that receives information already processed by Area 17, as well as from the superior colliculus.

Eye-movement theory   Explanation of illusions in terms of eye-movement patterns.

False alarm   In signal-detection theory, a false alarm occurs when the signal is not presented and the observer reports it nevertheless.

Familiar size   An object's customary or standardized size, used as a source of information in distance perception.

Farsighted   Referring to people who cannot see nearby objects.

Feature-integration theory   Theory proposed by Treisman that involves preattentive processing in the first stage and focused attention in the second stage.

Fechner's law   ($R = k \log I$) Fechner's law says that the magnitude of the psychological reaction (R) is equal to a constant (k) multiplied by the logarithm of the intensity (I) of the physical stimulus.

Field dependence   Reliance on the orientation of the room to determine an upright position.

Field independence   Reliance on the orientation of one's own body to determine an upright position.

Figure   In shape perception, a distinct shape with clearly defined edges.

Filled space–open space illusion   Illusion in which a distance that is filled seems longer than a distance that is unfilled (see Demonstration 8.8).

Film-reading   Process of looking at an X ray to determine whether the film shows any abnormal structures.

Fixation pause   The pause between two saccadic eye movements.

Flavor   Experience of taste, smell, touch, pressure, and pain associated with substances in the mouth.

Floaters   Groups or strings of material formed from the red blood cells, found in the vitreous humor.

Focused attention   In Treisman's feature-integration theory, the identification of objects in the second stage of processing.

Forced-choice method   Psychophysical method in which observers must choose which of several presentations actually contained the stimulus.

Foreign body   Object that does not belong in a particular location, such as a chip of metal in the cornea.

Formants   Horizontal bands of concentrated sound in a speech spectrogram.

Forward masking   Phenomenon in which accuracy is reduced for reporting a visual stimulus because it was preceded by a stimulus presented to the same region of the eye.

Fourier analysis   (foo-*ryay*) Process in which a stimulus is analyzed into its component sine waves.

Fourier synthesis   Process of adding together a series of sine waves; reverse of Fourier analysis.

Fovea   (*foe*-vee-ah) Region of the retina in which vision is sharpest.

Fragrance library   In perfume manufacturing, a collection of different fragrances at high concentrations.

Free nerve endings   Skin receptors that do not have bulbs or capsules on the end nearest the epidermis.

Frequency   Number of cycles a sound wave completes in 1 second.

Frequency theory   Theory of auditory processing that proposes that the entire basilar membrane vibrates at a frequency that matches the frequency of a tone.

Frequency tuning curve   Graph showing the relationship between the frequency of an auditory stimulus and an auditory nerve fiber's response rate.

Fundamental frequency   The component of a complex sound wave that has the lowest frequency.

Ganglion cells   (*gang*-glee-un) Cells that run from the bipolar cells of the retina toward the brain.

Ganzfeld   (*gahntz*-feldt) A visual field that has no contours, based on the German word for "whole field."

Gate-control theory   Theory that proposes that pain perception is a complex process in which the neural fibers interact and the brain also has an influence.

Gaze-contingent paradigm   Research method used in studying saccadic eye movements, in which the readers' eye movements are tracked and the text display is changed as the readers progress through the text.

Generalization   Tendency to make a learned response to stimuli that resemble the original stimulus; used in examining infant perception.

Gestalt   (geh-*shtahlt*) Configuration or pattern.

Gestalt approach   Approach to perception that emphasizes that we perceive objects as well-organized, whole structures rather than as separated, isolated parts.

Gibsonian approach   (gibb-*sone*-ee-un) Approach to perception that emphasizes that perceptions are rich and elaborate because the stimuli in the environment are rich with information, rather than because thought processes provide that richness; the Gibsonian approach is named after psychologist James J. Gibson.

Glabrous skin   Kind of skin on the soles of the feet and the palms of the hands; does not contain hairs.

Glaucoma   (glaw-*koe*-mah) Visual disorder in which excessive fluid inside the eye causes too much pressure, ultimately producing damage to the ganglion cells in the retina and to the optic nerve.

Golgi tendon organs   (*goal*-jee) Receptors in tendons that respond when the muscle exerts tension on the tendon.

Ground   In shape perception, the background that appears to be behind the figure.

Ground theory   Theory proposed by J. J. Gibson in which distance perception depends upon information provided by surfaces in the environment.

Gymnema sylvestre   A taste modifier that reduces the intensity of sweet substances.

Habituation method   In testing infant perception, a method based on a decrease in attention to repeated stimulation.

Hair cells   Receptors for auditory stimuli, located in the organ of Corti.

Hairy skin   Type of skin that covers most of the human body and contains hairs.

Haptic perception   Perception of objects by touch.

Harmonics   Other components of a complex tone, excluding the fundamental frequency.

Hedonics   (hih-*donn*-icks) Area of perception that involves judgments of pleasantness and unpleasantness.

Height cues   Distance information provided by the fact that objects near the horizon are farther away than those far from the horizon.

Helicotrema   (hell-ih-koe-*treh*-ma) Tiny opening at the end of the vestibular canal in the inner ear.

High-amplitude sucking procedure   Technique used to assess infant perception, in which babies suck on a pacifier attached to a recording device; a sufficiently fast sucking rate produces a stimulus such as a speech sound.

Hit   In signal-detection theory, a hit occurs when the signal is presented and the observer reports it.

Horizontal cells   Cells in the retina that allow the photoreceptors to communicate with each other.

Horizontal-vertical illusion   An illusion shaped like an inverted T in which the vertical line looks longer than the horizontal line (see Demonstration 8.7).

Hue   Psychological reaction of color that corresponds to the length of light waves.

Hypercolumn   A sequence of 18 to 20 adjacent columns in the visual cortex; a hypercolumn includes enough columns to complete a full cycle of stimulus-orientation preferences.

Hypercomplex cells   Cells found in Areas 18 and 19 of the visual cortex that respond most vigorously to moving lines and corners of a specific size.

Hypermetropic   Referring to people who are far-sighted and cannot see nearby objects.

Hypnosis   Altered state of consciousness in which a person is susceptible to suggestions from the hypnotist; hypnosis is used to help people suffering from chronic pain.

Hypothermia   Abnormally low body temperature.

Hz   (hurtz) Abbreviation for the name of Heinrich Hertz; Hz represents the number of cycles a sound wave completes in 1 second.

Identification   Modification of the method of limits in which observers are required to classify or identify the stimulus as well as detect it; in acuity, a measure that requires observers to identify a figure.

Illusion   An incorrect perception.

Illusory conjunction   In Treisman's feature-integration theory, an inappropriate combination of features from two stimuli.

Illusory contour   Phenomenon in which contours are seen, even though they are not physically present.

Illusory movement   Perception that an object is moving, even though it is really stationary.

Impedance   Resistance to the passage of sound waves.

Impedance mismatch   Condition in which the impedances for two media differ; sound waves cannot be readily transmitted when there is an impedance mismatch.

Incorrect comparison theory   Theory of illusions that states that observers base their judgments on the incorrect parts of the figure.

Incus   Anvil-shaped bones in the middle ear.

Independent variable   The variable in an experiment that experimenters manipulate.

Indirect perception theories   Theories that assume that the senses receive an impoverished description of the world.

Induced movement   Illusion of movement that occurs when a visual frame of reference moves in one direction and produces the illusion that a stationary target is moving in the opposite direction.

Inducing areas   Regions of an illusory contour figure in which true contours exist.

Inducing lines   Lines in an illusory contour figure that encourage the perception of illusory contours.

Inferior colliculus   Structure in auditory processing between the superior olivary nucleus and the medial geniculate nucleus.

Information-processing approach   Approach that identifies psychological processes and connects them by specific patterns of information flow.

Inner hair cells   Auditory receptors on the inner side of the organ of Corti, most likely sensitive to a tone's frequency.

Interaural intensity difference   Situation in which a sound reaches the two ears at different intensities; used as a source of information in sound localization.

Interaural time difference   Source of information in sound localization, consisting of the onset difference and the phase difference.

Interposition   Distance cue in which one object partly covers another.

Intraocular lens   Substitute lens inserted into the eye after removing a defective lens.

Invariant features   Features of a phoneme that remain constant and do not vary from one word to the next, such as the hissing sound of the phoneme /s/.

Invariants   In the theory of J. J. Gibson, the aspects of perception that persist over time and space and are left unchanged by certain kinds of transformations.

Involuntary eye movements   Unavoidable small eye movements that occur during fixation.

Iris   Ring of muscles in the eye surrounding the pupil; the colored part of the visible eye.

Iritis   (eye-*rye*-tis) Inflamation of the iris.

Ishihara test   (ih-she-*hah*-rah) Test for color deficiencies in which the observer tries to detect a number hidden in a pattern of different-colored circles.

Just noticeable difference (jnd)   Smallest difference in sensation that can be noticed.

Kinesthesia   Sensation of movement or static limb position.

Kinesthetic information   Nonvisual information (such as muscular information) that can be used to judge distance.

Kinetic depth effect   Phenomenon in which a figure looks flat when it is stable but appears to have depth once it moves.

Lamaze method   (luh-*mahz*) Method of prepared childbirth that educates women about the anatomy of childbirth, controlled muscular relaxation, and focusing attention on something other than pain.

Latency   Time taken to respond to a stimulus.

Lateral geniculate nucleus (LGN)   (jen-*ick*-you-late) Part of the thalamus where most of the ganglion cells transfer their information to new neurons.

Lateral inhibition Inhibition of neural activity for points near the part of the retina that is stimulated by light.

Lateral superior olivary nucleus (LSO) Part of the superior olivary nucleus that is specialized for processing high-frequency auditory information.

Law of closure Gestalt law that says that a figure is perceived as closed and complete rather than containing a blank portion.

Law of common fate Gestalt law that says that items perceived as moving in the same direction are seen as belonging together.

Law of good continuation Gestalt law that says that a line is perceived as continuing in the same direction it was going prior to intersection.

Law of nearness Gestalt law that says that items are grouped together that are near each other.

Law of Prägnanz (*prayg*-nahntz) Gestalt law that says that, when faced with several alternate perceptions, the one that will actually occur is the one with the best, simplest, and most stable shape.

Law of similarity Gestalt law that says that items are grouped together that are similar.

Left visual field Portion of the visual world on the left-hand side.

Lemniscal system (lemm-*niss*-kull) One of the two neuronal systems responsible for the skin senses; it has larger nerve fibers and faster transmission.

Lens Structure inside the eye whose shape changes to bring objects into focus.

Light Portion of the electromagnetic radiation spectrum made up of waves that range in length from about 400 nm to about 700 nm.

Light adaptation Decline in sensitivity that occurs as the eyes remain in the light.

Linear perspective Distance cue provided by the fact that parallel lines appear to meet in the distance.

Logarithm Type of numerical transformation; the logarithm of a number equals the exponent to which 10 must be raised to equal that number.

Loudness Psychological reaction that corresponds roughly to a tone's amplitude.

Luminance Amount of light that enters the eye.

Mach bands (mock) Phenomenon in which bright and dark regions are perceived within a single stripe, although there is no corresponding variation in the physical distribution of light.

Macula lutea (*mack*-yool-uh *loo*-tea-uh) Region of the retina, slightly larger than the fovea, in which vision is particularly sharp.

Magnitude estimation Technique in which the observer is told that one particular stimulus is to be assigned a certain value, and this value is used as a "yardstick" to estimate the magnitude of all future stimuli.

Malleus (*mal*-lee-uss) Hammer-shaped bone in the middle ear.

Manner of articulation One of the three dimensions in pronouncing consonants; it specifies how completely the air is blocked and where it passes.

Masking In audition, a phenomenon in tone combinations in which one tone masks another.

Medial geniculate nucleus (jen-*ick*-you-late) Structure in auditory processing between the inferior colliculus and the auditory cortex.

Medial superior olivary nucleus (MSO) Part of the superior olivary nucleus specialized for processing low-frequency auditory information.

Mel scale In audition, a scale produced by magnitude estimation, in which a 1000-Hz tone, with an intensity of 60 dB, is assigned a pitch of 1000 mels, and comparison tones are assigned other, relative mel values.

Memory color Phenomenon in which an object's typical color influences the observer's perception of the object's actual color.

Metamers Pairs of lights that look exactly the same but are composed of physically different stimuli.

Method of adjustment Psychophysical technique in which observers adjust the intensity of the stimulus until it is barely detectable.

Method of adjustment for measuring discrimination Psychophysical technique in which observers adjust the comparison stimulus by themselves until the comparison stimulus seems to match the standard stimulus.

Method of constant stimuli Psychophysical technique in which the stimuli are presented in random order.

Method of constant stimuli for measuring discrimination Psychophysical technique in which the experimenter presents the comparison stimuli in random order and asks observers to judge whether each comparison stimulus is greater than or less than the standard stimulus.

Method of limits Psychophysical technique in which the researcher begins with a stimulus that is clearly noticeable and then presents increasingly weaker stimuli until observers are unable to detect the stimulus; these trials alternate with trials in which increasingly stronger stimuli are presented.

Method of limits for measuring discrimination Psychophysical technique in which the standard stimulus remains the same, and the comparison stimulus varies from low to high on some series and from high to low on other series.

Microelectrodes Very small electrodes used in single cell recording.

Microspectrophotometry Procedure in which an extremely small beam of light, from one part of the color spectrum, is passed through individual receptors in dissected retinal tissue; the amount of light absorbed at each wavelength is then measured.

Microvilli (*my*-crow-*vill*-lie) Tips of the taste receptors.

Middle note In perfume development, the fragrance that arrives after the top note has disappeared.

Miracle fruit A taste modifier that sweetens the taste of sour substances.

Mirage Illusion due to physical processes, specifically, the optical properties of the atmosphere.

Miss In signal-detection theory, a miss occurs when a signal is presented and the observer does not report it.

Modeling approach In the treatment of pain, an approach that stresses that people can learn by watching another person in a situation.

Modulus In magnitude estimation, the value assigned to the standard stimulus; other stimuli are assigned numbers based on the modulus.

Molecular weight Sum of the atomic weights of all the atoms in the molecule.

Monaural (monn-*ahr*-ul) Pertaining to only one ear.

Monochromat (*mah*-noe-crow-mat) Person who requires only one color to match his or her perception of all other colors; every hue looks the same to this person.

Monochromatic colors Colors produced by a single wavelength.

Monocular factors Factors seen with one eye that can provide information about distance.

Moon illusion Illusion in which the moon at the horizon looks bigger than the moon at its highest position.

Motion constancy Phenomenon in which an object seems to maintain the same speed despite changes in its distance from the viewer.

Motion parallax Distance cue provided by the fact that as the observer moves the head sideways, objects at different distances appear to move in different directions and at different speeds.

Motion perspective Continuous change in the way objects look as the observer moves about in the world.

Motor theory of speech perception Theory in which humans possess a specialized device that allows them to decode speech stimuli and permits them to connect the stimuli they hear with the way these sounds are produced by the speaker.

Movement aftereffects Illusion of movement that occurs after looking at continuous movement; when looking at another surface, it will seem to move in the opposite direction.

MSG Monosodium glutamate, a substance used in cooking that reduces the thresholds for sour and bitter tastes.

Mucus Thick secretions on the olfactory epithelium.

Müller-Lyer illusion (*mew*-lur *lie*-ur) Famous illusion in which two lines of the same length appear to be different in length because of "wings" pointing outward on one line and inward on the other line (see Figure 8.6).

Multidimensional scaling Mathematical procedure by which observers' judgments about the similarities and dissimilarities of objects can be represented spatially, as in a map.

Myopic Referring to people who are nearsighted and cannot see faraway objects.

Nalaxone Antagonist for opiate drugs, used in studies of endorphins.

Nanometer (nm) One billionth of a meter; measure used for wavelength.

Nasal cavity Hollow space behind each nostril.

Nearsighted Referring to people who cannot see faraway objects.

Negative afterimage Image that appears after the presentation of a stimulus; the afterimage is the opposite of the original stimulus; successive color contrast is one kind of negative afterimage.

Nerve deafness Type of deafness that involves problems either in the cochlea or in the auditory nerve.

Neurons (*new*-rons) Nerve cells.

Noise In signal-detection theory, the situation in which no signal occurs. In audition, irrelevant, excessive, or unwanted sound.

Nonspectral hues Hues that cannot be described in terms of a single wavelength from a part of the spectrum.

Nontasters In taste perception, people who are insensitive to some particular tastes.

Normal trichromat (*try*-krow-mat) Person who requires three primary colors to match all other colors.

Object permanence The belief that an object still exists even though it is no longer visible.

Occlusion (uh-*clue*-zyun) Process in which a moving object systematically covers up the background.

Octave Term used by musicians to represent the distance between two notes that have the same name, such as two adjacent C notes on the piano.

Octave generalization Phenomenon in which the auditory system regards two tones with the same name as identical, although they differ in tone height.

Octave illusion Musical illusion in which one tone is presented to one ear and another tone an octave away is simultaneously presented to the other ear. The tones shift from ear to ear, yet the listener reports one ear hearing only high notes and the other hearing only low notes.

Ocular dominance Tendency for cells in the visual cortex to have a higher response rate for one of the two eyes.

Odor constancy Tendency for the perceived strength of an odor to remain the same despite variations in the vigor of the sniff.

Odor mixture The simultaneous presentation of two odors that do not cause a chemical reaction.

Odor pollution Situation in which unpleasant odors escape from a source and linger in the atmosphere.

Odorant Smell stimulus.

Olfaction Smell.

Olfactometer (ol-fack-*tom*-uh-ter) Piece of equipment that presents smells during the measurement of thresholds.

Olfactory bulb Structure that receives the signals from the smell receptors.

Olfactory epithelium Region at the top of the nasal cavity that contains the smell receptor cells.

Onset difference Arrival of a sound at one ear prior to the other ear, used as a source of information in sound localization.

Op Art Artistic movement that developed in the 1960s that attempted to produce a strictly optical art.

Ophthalmologists Doctors specializing in eye diseases.

Ophthalmology Branch of medicine concerned with visual problems.

Ophthalmoscope Special tool used to look inside the eye.

Opiate receptors Specific locations on the surface of brain cells that respond to opiate drugs in a lock-and-key fashion.

Opponent-process theory Theory of color vision that states that there are cells in the visual system that respond to stimulation by an increase in activity when one color is present and by a decrease in activity when another color is present.

Opsin (*opp*-sin) Large protein component of photopigments.

Optacon Electronic device that converts materials on a printed page into electrical impulses that produce a vibration pattern on the tip of the index finger, used by blind people.

Optic chiasm (*kie*-as-em) Area in which the two optic nerves come together and cross over.

Optic disk Region of the retina in which the optic nerve leaves the eye.

Optic nerve Bundle of ends from the ganglion cells that passes out of the eye toward the optic chiasm.

Optic tract Bundle of nerve fibers in the visual system that runs between the optic chiasm and the superior colliculus or the lateral geniculate nucleus.

Organ of Corti (*court*-eye) Part of the cochlea that contains the auditory receptors.

Orientation tuning curve Graph illustrating the relationship between the angular orientation of a line and a cell's response rate.

Ossicles Three bones in the middle ear: malleus, incus, and stapes.

Outer hair cells Auditory receptors on the outer side of the organ of Corti, most likely responsible for detecting sounds near threshold.

Oval window Membrane that covers an opening in the cochlea.

Overconstancy Phenomenon in which the observer overcorrects for distance and makes overly large estimates for the size of distant objects.

Overt attention Shifting of attention, accompanied by head or eye movements.

Overtones Harmonics, or the other components of a complex tone, excluding the fundamental frequency, that are multiples of that fundamental frequency.

Pacinian corpuscles One variety of skin receptors with encapsulated endings; they are very sensitive to the indentation of the skin.

Pain Perception of actual or threatened tissue damage and the private experience of unpleasantness.

Pain threshold Intensity of stimulation in which pain is reported on half the trials.

Pain tolerance Maximum pain level at which people voluntarily accept pain.

Papillae (paa-*pill*-ee) Small bumps on the tongue that contain the taste buds.

Paradoxical cold Phenomenon in which a very hot stimulus produces the sensation of cold by stimulating a cold spot.

Parallel process Processing information that requires the targets or tasks to be handled one at a time.

Parallel transmission Tendency for some sounds in a syllable to be transmitted at about the same time rather than one at a time.

Passive touch Touch perception in which an object is placed on the skin of a passive person.

Pattern recognition Perceptual process in which an observer identifies a complex arrangement of sensory stimuli.

Pattern theory Theory about the skin senses that proposes that the pattern of nerve impulses determines sensation.

Payoff In signal-detection theory, the rewards and punishments associated with a particular response.

Perception Interpretation of sensations, involving meaning and organization.

Perceptual span Region seen during the fixation pause.

Peripheral vision Vision in which the image is registered on the side of the retina rather than at the fovea.

Permanent threshold shift Permanent increase in a hearing threshold as a result of exposure to noise.

Phantom limb pain Perceived pain in an amputated arm or leg.

Phase difference Situation in which soundwaves are at different phases within a cycle when they arrive at the two ears; used as a source of information in sound localization.

Phenomenological observation Approach in which observers look at their immediate experience and attempt to describe it completely.

Pheromones (*fear*-uh-moans) Substances that act like chemical signals in communicating with other members of the same species.

Phi movement Illusion of movement in which observers report that they see movement, yet they cannot perceive an actual object moving across a gap; phi movement can be produced by two light flashes about 100 milliseconds apart.

Phoneme Basic unit of speech, such as an /h/ or an /r/ sound.

Phonemic restoration Phenomenon that occurs when a speech sound is replaced or masked by an irrelevant sound and the perceptual system restores or fills in the gap appropriately.

Phons Unit of measurement such that all sounds equal in phons have the same perceived loudness, even though they may be different in terms of decibels.

Photopic vision (foe-*top*-ick) Vision that uses cones.

Photopigments Chemical substances that accomplish the transduction of light.

Photoreceptors Light receptors; the rods and cones.

Pictorial cues Cues used to convey distance in a picture.

Pinna Flap of external tissue, typically referred to as "*the* ear."

Pitch Psychological reaction that corresponds to the frequency of a tone.

Place of articulation One of the three dimensions for consonants; specifies where the airstream is blocked when the consonant is spoken.

Place theory Theory of auditory processing that proposes that each frequency of vibration causes a particular place on the basilar membrane to vibrate.

Placebo (pluh-*see*-bow) Inactive substance such as a sugar pill that the patient believes is a medication.

Poggendorf illusion Line-direction illusion in which a line disappears at an angle behind a solid figure and appears on the other side at a position that seems incorrect.

Point of subjective equality Value of the comparison stimulus that the observer considers to be equal to the value of the standard stimulus.

Pointillism Artistic technique in which discrete dots of pigment are applied to a canvas; the dots blend into solid colors when viewed from a distance.

Position constancy Phenomenon in which an object seems to stay in the same place despite the body's movement relative to that object.

Preattentive processing In Treisman's feature-integration theory, the automatic registration of stimulus features.

Preference method In testing infant perception, a method based on the idea that if the infant spends consistently longer looking at one figure in preference to another figure, the infant must be able to discriminate between the two figures.

Presbycusis (prez-bee-*koo*-siss) Progressive loss of hearing in both ears for high-frequency tones, occurring with aging.

Presbyopia (prez-bee-*owe*-pee-ah) Type of farsightedness that occurs with aging.

Primary visual cortex Area of the visual cortex where the neurons from the lateral geniculate nucleus terminate.

Probability distribution In signal-detection theory, a curve showing the probability of various stimulus intensities.

Probe-tone technique Technique in which the listener hears either a musical chord or a scale in order to establish a key; then a probe tone is presented and the listener is asked to rate how well that tone fits within the octave of the key being examined.

PROP Bitter substance, 6-n-propylthiouracil, which some people cannot taste.

Proprioception Sensation of movement or the sensation of static limb position; synonym for kinesthesia.

Protanopes (*proe*-tuh-nopes) People who are dichromats and insensitive to deep red.

Prototype Ideal figure, proposed to serve as a basis of comparison in the prototype-matching approach to pattern recognition.

Prototype-matching theory Theory of pattern recognition in which a particular object is compared with an abstract, idealized pattern stored in memory.

Proximal stimulus Representation of objects in contact with a sense organ, such as the representation on the retina, as opposed to the distal stimulus.

Psychophysics Study of the relationship between physical stimuli and psychological reactions to those stimuli.

PTC Bitter substance, phenylthiocarbamide, which some people cannot taste.

Pupil Opening in the center of the iris.

Pure tones Tones that can be represented by a simple sine wave.

Purity In the description of color, the lack of white light; colors low in purity have large amounts of white light added to the monochromatic light.

Purkinje shift (purr-*kin*-gee) Phenomenon in which an observer's sensitivity to various wavelengths shifts toward the shorter wavelengths as he or she shifts from cone to rod conditions.

Pursuit movements Slow, smooth eye movements used in tracking an object moving against a stationary background.

Receiver operating characteristic (ROC) curve In signal-detection theory, a curve showing the relationship between the probability of a hit and the probability of a false alarm.

Receptive field For a given cell, the portion of the retina that, when stimulated, produces a change in the activity of that cell.

Recognition threshold In taste perception, the concentration of a solution that can be recognized by quality.

Recruitment Condition in which a deaf person perceives very loud sounds normally but does not hear weak sounds at all.

Reference theory Theory of the moon illusion in which both the sky and the ground are important referents when observers judge the size of the moon.

Refractory period Time immediately following a neuronal response in which the neuron cannot produce another response.

Relative distance Distance between two objects, as used in depth perception.

Relative size Object's size relative to other objects, used as a cue in distance perception.

Relative-size explanation Theory of size constancy in which people notice the size of an object compared to other objects, thereby retaining constancy.

Resolution In acuity measures, a task that requires the observer to discriminate a separation between the parts of a target.

Resolve To detect a separation in a pattern.

Retina (*reh*-tin-nuh) Portion of the eye that absorbs light rays; contains the photoreceptors.

Retinal (*reh*-ti-nal) Component of photopigments, related to vitamin A.

Retinal size Amount of space an object occupies on the retina.

Retinopathy of prematurity (reht-n-*ah*-puh-thee) Visual disorder experienced by some premature infants in which the undeveloped retina is damaged by bright lights.

Retinotopic   Arrangement in which the spatial distribution is similar to that found on the retina; for example, in the lateral geniculate nucleus (LGN) ganglion cells that originated on neighboring parts of the retina also terminate on neighboring parts of the LGN.

Rhodopsin   (roe-*dopp*-sin) Photopigment found in rods.

Right visual field   Portion of the visual world on the right-hand side.

Rods   Photoreceptors used for black-and-white vision under poorly lit conditions.

Round window   Membrane that covers an opening in the tympanic canal.

Saccade   (suh-*kaad*) A single rapid eye movement in which the eye is moved from one location to the next.

Saccadic movement   (suh-*kaad*-dick) Very rapid eye movements in which the eye is moved from one fixation point to the next.

Sander parallelogram   Line-length illusion involving the diagonal lines in a parallelogram (see Figure 8.10).

Saturation   Psychological reaction to the purity of a light; a highly saturated light appears to have little white light added to it.

Sclera   Shiny white part of the external eye.

Scotoma   (skuh-*toe*-muh) Blind area caused by damage to the visual cortex; plural is scotomata (skuh-*toe*-muh-tuh).

Scotopic vision   (skoe-*top*-ick) Vision that uses rods.

Search   Task that involves looking for infrequent stimuli whose location is uncertain.

Secondary visual cortex   Region of the visual cortex that receives information that has already been processed by Area 17 as well as from the superior colliculus.

Selective adaptation procedure   Technique in which a particular stimulus is continuously exposed, in order to produce "fatigue" in neurons sensitive to certain spatial frequencies.

Selective attention   Focusing attention on one of several simultaneous messages, disregarding the others.

Self-motion illusion   Perception that one is moving, although he or she is really stationary.

Sensation   Immediate and basic experiences generated by isolated, simple stimuli.

Sensitivity measure   The measure in signal-detection theory that depends upon the intensity

of the stimulus and the sensitivity of the observer.

Serial process   Processing information that requires the targets or tasks to be handled one at a time.

Shading   Distance cue provided by the pattern of light and shadows.

Shadowing technique   Method that requires a person to listen to a series of words and to repeat the words after the speaker.

Shape   Area set off from the rest of a visual stimulus because it has a contour.

Shape constancy   Phenomenon in which an object seems to stay the same shape despite changes in its orientation.

Shape-slant invariance hypothesis   Theory of shape constancy in which the viewer calculates objective shape by combining information about an object's retinal shape and its slant.

Signal   Stimulus used in psychophysics studies, most often in signal-detection theory.

Signal-detection theory (SDT)   Psychophysical approach that assesses both the observer's sensitivity and his or her decision-making strategy (or criterion).

Signal + noise   In signal-detection theory, the situations in which the appropriate signal occurs, in addition to the irrelevant "noise."

Simple cells   Cells in layer IVb of Area 17 of the visual cortex that respond most vigorously to lines.

Simultaneous brightness contrast   Phenomenon in which the apparent brightness of part of a figure can be changed because another part of the figure is present at the same time.

Simultaneous color contrast   Situation in which the appearance of a color is changed because of another color present at the same time.

Sine wave   Smooth wave pattern resembling the pattern of light waves.

Single cell recording   Research technique in which small electrodes are placed in a precise location to record action potentials, such as those generated by a single ganglion cell.

Sinusoidal grating   (sine-you-*soid*-ul) Set of blurry stripes that alternate between dark and light.

Size constancy   Phenomenon in which an object seems to stay the same size despite changes in its distance.

Size cues   Distance information conveyed by relative size.

Size-distance invariance hypothesis   Theory of constancy in which the viewer calculates an object's perceived size by combining the object's retinal size and its perceived distance.

Soft palate   Region in the upper part of the mouth above the back of the tongue.

Somatosensory cortex   Region of the cortex that processes information about touch and taste.

Sone scale   Scale of loudness obtained by the magnitude-estimation technique, in which a 40-dB tone at 1000 Hz is assigned a loudness of 1 sone.

Sound shadow   Barrier that reduces the intensity of the sound; for example, with respect to the left ear, the head produces a sound shadow, for sounds produced on the right side of the head.

Sound spectrogram   Diagram that shows the frequency components of speech.

Sounds   Successive changes in atmospheric pressure.

Spatial frequency channels   Channels in the visual system that are sensitive to a narrow range of spatial frequencies.

Specificity theory   Theory based on the doctrine of specific nerve energies stating that each kind of skin receptors responds exclusively to only one kind of physical stimulus, and each kind of receptor is responsible for only one kind of sensation.

Specificity theory of pain perception   Theory stating that pain is produced by the stimulation of specific pain receptors.

Spectral sensitivity   Region of the spectrum in which light is absorbed, such as the region in which a particular kind of cone absorbs light.

Speech spectrogram   Diagram that shows the frequency components of speech.

Speed-accuracy trade-off   Relationship between speed and accuracy such that an increase in one factor produces a decrease in the other.

Spinothalamic system   (spy-know-thuh-*laa*-mick) One of the two neuronal systems responsible for the skin senses; it has smaller nerve fibers and slower transmission.

Square wave   One kind of product of a Fourier synthesis, a series of regularly repeating dark and light stripes with crisp edges.

Stabilized retinal image techniques   Procedures in which the image projected onto the retina is stabilized so that a constant image is projected.

Standard   In magnitude estimation, the stimulus that is assigned a certain value; other stimuli are judged in terms of this standard.

Standard stimulus   The stimulus in discrimina-

tion studies that remains constant throughout the experiment.

Stapes   (*stay*-peas) Stirrup-shaped bone in the middle ear.

Static visual acuity   Ability of the observer to perceive details of an object that is not moving.

Steady state   In music perception, the middle portion of a tone.

Stereoblindness   Inability to use depth from binocular vision, often resulting from strabismus.

Stereochemical theory   Theory proposed by Amoore that odorous molecules have definite shapes that determine the kind of odor we smell.

Stereopsis   Ability to judge depth with two eyes, as provided by binocular disparity.

Stereoscope   Piece of equipment that presents two photographs of a scene taken from slightly different viewpoints; one picture is presented to each eye, creating the impression of depth.

Stereoscopic picture   Two pictures, one presented to the right eye and one presented to the left eye, creating the impression of depth.

Stevens's power law   ($R = kI^n$) Stevens's power law says that the magnitude of the psychological reaction (R) is equal to a constant (k) multiplied by the intensity (I) of the stimulus, which has been raised to the nth power.

Stimulation-produced analgesia   Procedure in which certain regions of the brain are electrically stimulated, leading to a loss of sensitivity to pain.

Strabismus   (struh-*biz*-muss) Visual disorder that occurs when the muscles for the two eyes do not work together and an object's image falls on different regions of the two retinas; sometimes called "cross-eye."

Striate cortex   (*strie*-ate) Area of the visual cortex where the neurons from the lateral geniculate nucleus terminate, called striate because of its microscopically visible stripes.

Stroboscopic movement   (stroe-buh-*skope*-ick) Illusion of movement produced by a rapid pattern of stimulation on different parts of the retina.

Structuralism   Approach to psychology that proposed that all experiences can be analyzed and broken down into their most basic sensations.

Subcutaneous tissue   Inner layer of skin, which contains connective tissue and fat globules.

Subjective contour   Phenomenon in which contours are seen, even though they are not physically present; known also as illusory contour.

Substantia gelatinosa   Proposed part of the gate-control theory, which receives stimulation from the large fibers and inhibition from the small fibers.

Subtractive mixture   In color mixing, combining dyes or pigments or else placing two or more colored filters together.

Successive color contrast   Situation in which the appearance of a color is changed because of another color presented beforehand.

Superior colliculus   (kole-*lick*-you-luss) Portion of the brain important for locating objects and their movement.

Superior olivary nucleus   A structure in auditory processing between the cochlear nucleus and the inferior colliculus.

Synthetic sense   One of the senses in which an observer cannot detect the separate parts; for example, in vision, an observer cannot detect the components of a color mixture.

Tactile Vision Substitution System (TVSS)   Electronic device that uses a television camera to record a scene and then converts the image into vibrations applied to a person's back, used by blind people.

Tadoma method   Method of communication in which a deaf person places his or her hands on the lips and jaw of the speaker to pick up tactile information about speech.

Taste   Perceptions that result from the contact of substances with special receptors in the mouth.

Taste bud   Receptor for taste stimuli.

Taste modifiers   Special substances that change the flavor of other food by modifying the receptors on the tongue.

Taste pore   The opening in the taste bud.

Taste tetrahedron   Four-sided figure representing one of the four basic tastes (sweet, salty, bitter, and sour) at each of the four corners.

Tectorial membrane   Membrane that rests at the top of the organ of Corti in the inner ear.

Template-matching theory   Theory of pattern recognition in which a letter or other object is compared with a specific pattern stored in memory.

Temporary threshold shift   Temporary increase in a hearing threshold as a result of exposure to noise.

Terrestrial passage theory   Theory of the moon illusion in which observers mistakenly treat the moon as if it were an object moving through the earth's atmosphere.

Test stimulus   In dark adaptation studies, the small spot of light for which the threshold is measured after the lights have been turned off.

Texture gradient   Distance cue provided by the fact that the texture of surfaces becomes denser as the distance increases.

Thalamus   (*thaal*-uh-muss) Region in the base of the brain, intermediate between the taste cells and the somatosensory cortex.

Theory of misapplied constancy   Theory of illusions in which observers interpret certain cues in an illusion as cues for maintaining size constancy.

Theory of spatial frequency   Theory of perception in which the visual system breaks the stimulus down into a series of narrow light and dark stripes.

Thermal adaptation   Decrease in the perceived intensity of a hot or cold temperature as time passes.

Timbre   (*tam*-burr) Tone's sound quality.

Tinnitus   High-pitched ringing in the ears, caused by a high fever, ear infection, or large doses of aspirin.

"Tip-of-the-nose" phenomenon   Ability to recognize an odorant as familiar, although its name cannot be recovered.

Tonality   Organization of pitches around one particular tone.

Tone chroma   (*crow*-mah) Similarity shared by all musical tones that have the same name.

Tone height   Increase in pitch of a tone that accompanies an increase in frequency.

Tonic   One of the 12 pitches within an octave; serves as the tone around which all others in the octave are organized.

Tonometry   Technique in which a special instrument is used to measure the pressure inside the eye.

Tonotopic organization   Type of organization found on the basilar membrane, in which there is a systematic relationship between the frequency of tones and their location on the basilar membrane.

Top-down processing   Approach that emphasizes the importance of the observers' concepts and cognitive processes in shaping perception.

Top note   In perfume development, the first impact of a fragrance.

Touch adaptation   Decrease in the perceived intensity of a repeated tactile stimulus.

Tracking shot   Film technique in which the camera moves along a track at right angles to the direction of the camera.

Transduction   Process of converting light into a form that can be transmitted through the visual system.

Transmission cells   Cells proposed by gate-control theory that are in the spinal cord and receive input from two kinds of neural fibers.

Traveling wave Pressure wave in auditory processing that travels from the base to the apex of the cochlea.

Trichromatic theory Theory of color vision stating that there are three kinds of color receptors, each sensitive to light from a different part of the spectrum.

Trigeminal nerve A nerve important in olfaction and taste; it has free nerve endings extending into the olfactory epithelium and also registers the spiciness of food such as chili peppers.

Tritanopes (*try*-tuh-nopes) People who are dichromats and have difficulty with blue shades.

Trompe l'oeil (tromp *leh*-yeh) Technique in painting that "fools the eye" by creating an impression of depth when the surface is really just two-dimensional.

Turbinate bones Three bones located in the nasal cavity.

2-Deoxyglucose technique Technique that uses a radioactive chemical to record cell activity; used to verify the column structure of the cortex.

Two-point detection threshold Method of measuring the ability to notice that two different points, rather than a single point, are being touched on the skin.

Tympanic canal Canals in the cochlea.

Tympanic membrane Thin piece of membrane that vibrates in response to sound waves.

Unconscious inference Proposed explanation for constancy in which the observer arrives at a perception via a reasoning-like process without conscious awareness.

Underconstancy Phenomenon in which the observer undercorrects for distance and makes judgments that underestimate the true size of distant objects.

Velocity detection threshold The minimum velocity that can be detected in motion perception.

Vergence movement Eye movements in which the angle between the lines of sight changes and the eyes move toward or away from each other.

Vernier acuity In acuity measures, a task that requires the observer to report whether an upper vertical line is displaced to the right or the left of the lower line.

Version movements Eye movements in which the angle between the lines of sight remains constant and the eyes move in the same direction.

Vertigo Sensation that either the observer or the surroundings are spinning.

Vestibular canal (ves-*tih*-bue-lur) Canal in the cochlea on which the stapes rests.

Vestibular sense (ves-*tih*-bue-lur) System that provides information about orientation, movement, and acceleration.

Vigilance Task that involves the detection of signals presented infrequently over a long period.

Vigilance decrement Decline in performance after an observer has been performing for an extended period.

Visual acuity Ability to see fine details in a scene.

Visual angle Size of the angle formed by extending two lines from the observer's eye to the outside edges of the target.

Visual cliff Kind of apparatus in which infants must choose between a side that looks shallow and a side that looks deep.

Visual cortex Portion of the cerebral cortex that is concerned with vision.

Vitreous humor (*vit*-ree-us) Thick, jellylike substance found within the eye, behind the lens.

Vocal tract Anatomical structures involved in speaking, located above the vocal cords.

Voiced consonant Consonant that is spoken with vibration of the vocal cords.

Voiceless consonant Consonant that is spoken without vibration of the vocal cords.

Voicing One of the three dimensions for consonants; voicing specifies whether the vocal cords vibrate.

Volatile (*voll*-uh-tull) Having the ability to evaporate.

Volley principle Proposal that was added to the frequency theory of auditory processing, which stated that clusters of neurons could "share" in producing a required firing rate.

W cells Rare type of ganglion cells, also called "sluggish cells," that respond slowly to stimulation and respond best to moving stimuli.

Water taste Distinct taste for water following adaptation to another taste; for example, water tastes sweet after adaptation to a sour substance.

Wavelength The distance light travels during one cycle.

Weber's fraction (k) Number obtained in discrimination studies that represents the change in stimulus intensity divided by the original intensity.

Weber's law ($\Delta I/I = k$) Weber's law says that if we take the change in intensity and divide it by the original intensity, we obtain a constant number (k).

Word apprehension effect Word-superiority effect.

Word-letter phenomenon Phenomenon in which a single letter can be identified faster when it is part of a word than when it appears alone.

Word-superiority effect (WSE) Phenomenon in which letters are perceived better when they appear in words than in strings of unrelated letters.

X cells Most common type of ganglion cells, which respond in a sustained fashion and pick up precise details about the stimulus.

Y cells Type of ganglion cells that respond quickly and are especially sensitive to movement.

Author Index

Subject Index

Note: This index includes all boldfaced terms